Sponsor's Message

It is inevitable that any sponsorship will at some stage come to a close, and as we waved goodbye to the last ever Benson and Hedges Cup final it was a time to remember so many golden moments. Sadly, it is also the last time I will put pen to paper in this, our last *Benson and Hedges Cricket Year*.

It all started 31 years ago when cricket was in financial crisis. We took our idea of a second one-day competition to the Test and County Cricket Board and the Benson and Hedges Cup was born. However, in recent years, I have been rather disappointed that the qualifying rounds were scheduled in the largely wet April weeks and that the Benson and Hedges Cup has been viewed by some as a second-class citizen within domestic cricket.

The Benson and Hedges Cup gave cricketers an immediate focus and the counties a chance to tempt its members from a winter's slumber back to the grounds for 50-over cricket in the early-season sunshine. And I believe our final in June produced more even encounters, as it was less affected by the vagaries of a toss of the coin on a damp September morning.

Over the past three decades, the greatest players in world cricket have graced the Benson and Hedges Cup and the competition has staged many of cricket's historical moments, in both qualifying matches and our finals at Lord's. Who can forget Eddie Hemmings swatting four off the last ball to clinch victory for Nottinghamshire in 1989? An ecstatic Mike Gatting collecting the trophy in the pouring rain in '86? Or John Abrahams winning the Gold Award after scoring nought and not bowling a ball in the 1984 final? And Mike Procter's memorable hat-trick in the 1977 semi-final against Hampshire. These moments will live forever in cricket history.

It is worth remembering that the Benson and Hedges Cup was the competition that launched Ian Botham towards stardom when, as an 18-year-old in 1974, he lost his front teeth after being struck in the mouth by a ball from Andy Roberts, took guard and went on to win the game. If records are your fancy, Graham Gooch ended his career with 22 Gold Awards and a helmet full of batting honours. I could write for pages about Procter's hat-trick, De Silva's hundred in the 1999 final and two virtuoso performances from the late Ben Hollioake.

This year's final, though not a classic, saw two young cricketers play with style and confidence – one would imagine that Ian Bell and Jim Troughton will feature in English cricket for many years to come.

We were promised an Indian summer, with tourists from the sub-continent providing wristy entertainment and above all a chance to watch arguably the greatest living batsman – that little master, Sachin Tendulkar. However, the summer will be remembered for two batsmen, England's Michael Vaughan and India's Rahul Dravid. Dravid scoring three back-to-back centuries while Vaughan agonizingly missing out on a double hundred twice. Rain on the last day of the Oval Test confirmed the series was drawn and both sides took positives from a hard-fought summer.

Without a match-fit Muralitharan, Sri Lanka were beaten by an increasingly confident England with the summer split by a tantalizing three-way NatWest Series – although football did its best to blight the cricket season. The final between India and England was full of passion and packed with drama with an Indian victory snatched from England's grasp.

Nasser Hussain's England now face their sternest test – the Ashes series in Australia this winter. We wish them well.

As ever, the 21st edition of the *Benson and Hedges Cricket Year* reviews the highlights and low points of the international and domestic year from around the world. And editor Jonathan Agnew delves into the issues of the cricket world in his typically forthright and witty style.

And so this is our last *Benson and Hedges Cricket Year*. Our appreciation goes to publishers Bloomsbury, to Aggers and his army of writers who once again have produced a wonderful read. But more importantly to you – thank you for your support.

We have enjoyed our time in cricket. I hope you enjoy this edition of the *Benson and Hedges Cricket Year* and may domestic cricket, and the fortunes of England in particular, continue to prosper.

Barry Jenner
Managing Director, UK
Gallaher Limited

Benson and Hedges

Cricket Year

Benson and Hedges

Cricket Year

Twenty-First Edition

September 2001 to September 2002

Edited by **Jonathan Agnew**

with additional contributions by
Qamar Ahmed
Charlie Austin
Mark Baldwin
Tony Cozier
Ralph Dellor
Sunil Gavaskar
Jim Maxwell
Marcus Prior
Craig Ray
Telford Vice
Bryan Waddle

BLOOMSBURY

Edited by Jonathan Agnew
with additional contributions by
Qamar Ahmed
Charlie Austin
Mark Baldwin
Tony Cozier
Ralph Dellor
Sunil Gavaskar
Jim Maxwell
Marcus Prior
Craig Ray
Telford Vice
Bryan Waddle
with special thanks to R. Mohan and Utpal Shuvro

First published in 2002 by
Bloomsbury Publishing Plc
38 Soho Square
London W1D 3HB

www.bloomsburymagazine.com

A copy of the CIP entry for this book is available from the
British Library.

ISBN 0 7475 5948 1

10 9 8 7 6 5 4 3 2 1

Project editor: Chris Hawkes
Design: Kathie Wilson at designsection
Statistics: Wendy Wimbush
Pictures researched and supplied by David Munden at
Sportsline Photographic
www.sportsline.org.uk

Printed and bound in Great Britain
by Butler and Tanner, Frome

Contents

INTRODUCTION

By Jonathan Agnew

INTRODUCTION
By Jonathan Agnew

After 31 years, this is the final summer of cricket sponsorship by Benson and Hedges. The new laws introduced by the government preventing advertising in sport by tobacco companies has brought the curtain down on both the Benson and Hedges Cup – which has been running since 1972 – and the *Benson and Hedges Cricket Year*, now in its 21st edition. I do not intend entering the debate about the merit, or otherwise, of the legislation but, instead, I will seize the opportunity to pay tribute to the generous sponsor that gave me the unforgettable experience of playing – with mixed fortunes – in a Lord's final. (We won, but I bowled rather feebly.) Benson and Hedges have also given me my first attempt at editing a seriously intimidating and demanding book, which I have enjoyed greatly.

The Benson and Hedges Cup, which was introduced in 1972, recently became the target for criticism from ill-informed pundits who found themselves sucked in by the view – offered by the players – that county cricketers play too much cricket! With the top English cricketers now centrally contracted and, therefore, protected (too much in my view) from the day-to-day rigours of the county circuit, the notion that our up-and-coming professionals play too much is absurd. The Benson and Hedges Cup always guaranteed crucial early-season competition at a time when the county championship was barely waking up. It offered the chance for the best amateurs in the Minor Counties to compete, as a unit, with the top flight and, indeed, on one occasion they defeated a Leicestershire team that consisted, amongst others, of David Gower, Andy Roberts and Peter Willey! Every summer the Benson and Hedges Cup also offered each and every county professional a glimpse of the 'big time' by appearing in front of a packed Lord's. Believe me, that is an experience you savour forever.

So, instead of a highly competitive tournament that, with its 50-over format, was also serious preparation for international cricket, we are now bracing ourselves for the introduction of a 20-overs-per-side competition. This comes complete with 'golden overs' – the equivalent of playing your joker – and, indeed, only the absence of Stuart Hall and dear old Eddie Waring will convince one that this is not some nightmarish re-hash

of *It's a Knockout*. In purely cricketing terms, this tournament offers absolutely nothing and it will be foolish of the England and Wales Cricket Board to market it as anything that suggests it is. However – and this might startle one or two – I believe this does offer the counties a real opportunity to make welcome and genuine contact with the public and, hopefully, cricket followers of the future. Forget the cricket: that must be purely a sideshow to the main event. Instead, throw open the county grounds for a summer party – a barbeque, a disco, steel bands: the works! And make it a three-line whip for the players from both teams to be present and to mingle with the members and supporters when they have finished their exertions (they are, after all, unlikely to be terribly tired). This is a chance to remove barriers and for county cricket to make new friends because, let us face it, without drastic action county cricket runs the serious risk of withering on the vine. Such has been the emphasis on developing the national team, and its considerable needs, that our county game has been largely ignored. Lord MacLaurin was quite correct in targeting the top of the pyramid during his time as chairman of ECB, and the counties have a financial lifeline as a result, but although Mike Soper narrowly lost the election to succeed him, the Surrey man's anguished plea on behalf of county cricket was a reminder to everyone that there is a real danger of our domestic system being dismissed as an irrelevance and, possibly, even an irritation.

Again central contracts only give further weight to that view, not merely because of the withdrawal of the best players, but the new system has now encouraged Test matches to become eight-day 'media opportunities'. Meticulously stage-managed interviews with members of the Test squad three days before the match is actually starting to devour what little newspaper space might otherwise have been devoted to coverage of county cricket, and I will be the first to admit that it is not always easy to be sure when the county scores will be broadcast on the radio. It is now time to alter the focus and to make county cricket important once again.

With the enormous sums of money made available through television rights – although possibly not for much longer in this part of the world – it is little wonder that international cricket is mushrooming in order to satisfy the voracious appetites of the world's Cricket Boards. There is already evidence of the players' well-being and interests being overlooked as they are dispatched from one continent to another in a global merry-go-round that is in danger of spinning out of control. The International Cricket Council has been transformed under the presidency of Malcolm Gray,

---

Previous page: Graham Thorpe's bitter divorce, and his worries about maintaining contact with his children, led to his withdrawal from the tour of Australia. Thorpe's unhappy situation highlighted the problems faced by several players.

with the chief executive, Malcolm Speed, offering strong leadership and, above all, far greater transparency and accessibility, but these two charismatic Australians found themselves unwittingly involved in the extraordinary contracts row that preceded the ICC Champions Trophy, and which threatens to overshadow the build-up to the 2003 World Cup. Quite how the signing away of the players' commercial rights was achieved by the previous administration, we will probably never know. The implications for the Indian cricketers, in particular, were so severe that they refused to sign their contracts, resisting overwhelming pressure from the former president of the ICC, now the president of the Indian Board, Jagmohan Dalmiya, until their demands for compensation were finally met. With no regular income from the BCCI, apart from appearance money and touring fees, India's cricketers had managed to cash in on their unique marketability to create a situation that suited both themselves and the Board. Then, with no warning, they were expected to break their personal contracts, accept a meagre appearance fee for the short trip to Sri Lanka and, in so doing, allow their names to be associated with any company or product the ICC wished, even if this happened to be the main competitor of their own sponsors. It does not require one to be a fully paid-up member of Militant to realize how unrealistic and unfair these demands were, and to gauge quite how low a priority the players themselves had become in the minds of some administrators.

Then there is the question of the players' families. This was highlighted by Graham Thorpe's unhappy situation during the past year, but there have been other cases of divorce involving England cricketers very recently including Darren Gough and Mark Butcher. With the national divorce rate running at close to 50 per cent of marriages, it would be unrealistic to expect the England cricket team to be entirely immune, but with the players spending more and more time away from home, it is welcome to note that the ECB now pays for the players' wives and children to join their fathers on tour. And to think that only six years ago, David Lloyd and Mike Atherton, then the coach and captain, took the cruellest of decisions and banned wives and girlfriends for the entire winter in Zimbabwe and New Zealand. It is, I know, only if one has experienced the pain and trauma of divorce – coupled with a life that takes one away from home so much – that Thorpe's situation can be appreciated. Having been there myself, I admire him enormously for having the resolve and courage to put his children first. This winter's tour would probably have been Thorpe's last crack at the Ashes – the ultimate cricketing contest which, in five attempts, he has never won. After initially making himself available, he finally changed his mind and declined his final chance. As young Henry and Amelia Thorpe pick up the pieces of their shattered lives, they will not be feeling that they are the luckiest kids in the world. In time, though, I am sure they will come to appreciate the sacrifice that their father has made.

On a happier and final note, the summer spent broadcasting Test Match Special over the Internet was quite an eye-opener. I had no idea that cricket was followed so intently all over the world. While it was amusing to send regular greetings to our listener who was working in the dark in a research station in Antarctica, it was the scale of feedback we were constantly receiving from Indian cricket fans in America that really made an impact. With Pakistan, sadly, appearing to be off limits to touring teams, and while India refuses to play its neighbour on the subcontinent, at least, is this not the perfect opportunity for cricket to spread its wings and attract new audiences? Morocco has emerged as the newest venue, and we welcome the Tangier Stadium to the fold. So why not America, with its vast ex-pat population already playing the game in local leagues? And for that matter, why can England not stage a Test series between India and Pakistan? Technically, it is perfectly feasible with there being more than enough grounds to choose from, and the time difference with Asia makes it perfect for television. Large, excitable crowds would be guaranteed and this, in itself, would do more to encourage the next generation of British Asians to take up the sport they follow with a passion than any number of plastic Kwik Cricket sets ever could.

Thirty-one years ago, at the time of the first Benson and Hedges final, England won the Ashes under Ray Illingworth and cricket was, truly, the summer sport. That is no longer the case, and as we reluctantly close this particular chapter of English county cricket, we do so with the game facing an uncertain future here. If ever there was a time for bold, innovative and imaginative decisions to be taken by the administrators – coupled with an acknowledgement by our young professionals that only hard work will make them capable of beating the best – it is now. Even Australians recognize that world cricket needs England to be strong, but the England team will only ever be as good as the domestic system allows it to be.

Jonathan Agnew
Leicestershire, September 2002

THE YEAR IN PICTURES

Below: The Ahmedabad groundsman prepares the pitch during an interval in the second Test between India and England.

Above: On their winter tour of India, England were more than aware of the threat of Sachin Tendulkar, but tackling the beturbaned off spinner, Harbhajan Singh, would be a new experience.

Right: A tour of the subcontinent is always full of surprises. The first Test at Mohali provided England with their first taste of Test cricket under floodlights.

Above: The sun
starts to set at
Ahmedabad, where
play was extended
due to the use of
lights.

Right: Michael
Vaughan will still be
kicking himself for
this moment of
thoughtlessness at
Bangalore which
cost him his wicket,
handled the ball.

Left: Two of the many heroes of Christchurch, Graham Thorpe and Nathan Astle reflect on an extraordinary match. Thorpe made 200 not out, but was embarrassed to have won the Man of the Match award ahead of Astle, whose whirlwind 222 threatened to win the match for New Zealand.

Above: Mark Butcher and Graham Thorpe fight back tears as England remember Ben Hollioake who was killed in a car crash in Perth shortly after leaving the tour of New Zealand.

Left: The young wicketkeeper, James Foster, had first-hand experience of the gulf that exists between county and Test cricket when he deputized for Alec Stewart.

Above: Nasser Hussain makes his point after scoring his first century for England in his 72nd one-day innings. Critics had been suggesting that he should relinquish his place at No. 3 in the batting order.

Right: Mohammad Kaif celebrates the end of the remarkable NatWest series final at Lord's. The 21-year-old scored 87 and made the winning hit as India overhauled England's target of 326.

Above: For Sri Lanka's Ruchira Perera, a Lord's Test was not a happy occasion. His clearly suspect action was reported by the umpires and the fast bowler took no further part in the series.

Above left: The only surprise about Muttiah Muralitharan's painful encounter with Andrew Flintoff at Old Trafford was that the master spinner – and reluctant No. 11 – was anywhere near the stumps.

Above right: Alistair Dobson, an Australian, took the Lord's security by surprise and escorted a bemused Sachin Tendulkar to the Long Room during the first Test between England and India.

Right: A break for rain during the Indian summer at Trent Bridge.

These spectators had clearly heard the forecast of a
washout for the final day of the series at The Oval,
and came prepared for the worst!

Michael Vaughan, undisputedly England's
player of the summer, celebrates another
century at The Oval.

Above: Angus Fraser, the Middlesex and England seam bowler, hung up his boots in the early season to join the Independent. The old warhorse took 177 wickets in 46 Tests.

Left: Michael Powell, the captain of Warwickshire, ends an era by holding the Benson and Hedges Cup aloft for the last time.

ENGLAND

Sri Lanka in England
NatWest Trophy Triangular Series
India in England

SRI LANKA IN ENGLAND
By Jonathan Agnew

26-28 April 2002 at Canterbury
Sri Lankans 375 (DPMD Jayawardene 119,
RP Arnold 81, PA de Silva 63, TT Samaraweera 57)
Kent 419 for 6 dec. (DP Fulton 116, MV Fleming 102,
GO Jones 76*)
Match drawn – no play was possible on the first day

After a first-day washout the strengths and weaknesses of the touring Sri Lankans were neatly summed up on the two weather-shortened days which followed. When the match eventually started, on a Saturday of free admission granted by the Kent club, it was Sri Lanka's batting power which became apparent – even after the loss of three cheapish top-order wickets. Mahela Jayawardene, surely now the most accomplished of the Sri Lankan strokemakers, eased his way to 119 with 18 fours, Russel Arnold hit an aggressive 109-ball 81, and Thilan Samaraweera helped himself to 57 from No. 7. But it was Aravinda de Silva's 63 off 81 balls which brought the Kent faithful most pleasure. De Silva, back in the squad for this England tour despite a long time spent out of favour and his veteran status, responded by underlining his class. Kent supporters, of course, witnessed it from close quarters in 1995, when he scored 1,781 first-class runs for the county at an average of 59.37. Martin Saggers and James Golding each emerged from all the run-making with four wickets, however, as Sri Lanka totalled 375, and then on the final day it was the turn of Kent's batsmen to highlight the glaring weakness of the touring team – the lack of depth in their bowling attack. With Muttiah Muralitharan injured, and Chaminda Vaas being rested for the bigger matches ahead, Sri Lanka saw their second stringers taken apart by David Fulton and Matthew Fleming. Fulton scored a speedy 116 from 117 balls, with 17 fours and two sixes, but Fleming's 102 was simply violent – it took him just 66 balls at the end of a day in which both Matthew Walker, with 40, and Geraint Jones, with a career-best 76 not out, also took advantage of the batting practice on offer. Kent finally brought the match to a premature end by declaring on 419 for 6.

7-9 May 2002 at Chester-le-Street
Durham 469 (PD Collingwood 190, P Mustard 75,

Previous page: Michael Vaughan celebrates England's dramatic victory over Sri Lanka in the third Test.

GJ Muchall 69)
Sri Lankans 167 (PA de Silva 53) and (following on)
282 for 4 (RP Arnold 112, PA de Silva 63*)
Match drawn

Sri Lanka felt the full chill of late Spring in the North East as they struggled to draw a three-day encounter with Durham at Chester-le-Street. Paul Collingwood gave them the runaround in the field on the first two days, hitting 190 to expose the flaws in an attack without Muttiah Muralitharan. Gordon Muchall (69) scored a maiden first-class 50, as did another of Durham's rich crop of youthful cricketers, 19-year-old wicketkeeper Phil Mustard, who reached 75. In reply to Durham's first-innings score of 469, the Sri Lankans folded dismally to 167 all out, Marc Symington picking up 4 for 27, before pulling themselves together with a second-innings total of 282 for 4. Russel Arnold did his Test chances no harm with 112, while the veteran Aravinda de Silva added a determined unbeaten 63 to his first-innings score of 53.

11-13 May 2002 at Shenley
Sri Lankans 186 (ST Jayasuriya 52) and 281 for 4
(DPMD Jayawardene 125*, HP Tillekeratne 71*)
Middlesex 274 (EC Joyce 93, OA Shah 65)
Match drawn – no play was possible on the third day

The Sri Lankans, from 81 without loss, fell away alarmingly to 186 all out on the first day of their three-day fixture against Middlesex at Shenley. Sanath Jayasuriya (52) and Marvan Atapattu (46) offered an initial mini-feast of strokeplay, but then Ben Hutton (4 for 37) led a Middlesex fightback which continued with fine innings from Owais Shah (65) and Ed Joyce (93). Aaron Laraman finished on 39 not out as Middlesex totalled 274, but by the close of the second day Sri Lanka had regained the upper hand by reaching 281 for 4. Mahela Jayawardene flicked two sixes and caressed 17 fours in a lovely unbeaten 125, while Hashan Tillekeratne, who had come in at 102 for 4, finished up on 71 not out. The final day was, sadly, washed out by rain.

npower FIRST TEST
16-20 May 2002 at Lord's

Now that the ICC world championship of cricket is upon us, Test series are being crammed in at every opportunity. The reality in England is that one unfortunate team has to come and play in mid-May – a time when a dry and only fairly warm day is a bonus.

Last year it was Pakistan who caught a cold. This year it was Sri Lanka's turn. Is it merely a coincidence that it should be Asian teams, used to broiling heat, that are subjected to this, I wonder? The answer is 'probably not', since next summer will see Zimbabwe draw the short straw and, besides, Sri Lanka have been so desperate to prove themselves in a full, three-match series, that they would probably have come here at Christmas, if necessary.

Despite their keenness – and their impressive nine-match winning run – there will have been serious concerns in the Sri Lankan 'think-tank' before the players left Colombo. Each ground would have been carefully scrutinized with the view being formed that Old Trafford – the venue for the last Test – represented their best chance of winning and Lord's – the opener – the most likely place for England to dominate. At least, that's how it seemed, because if ever a team appeared relieved to leave HQ with a draw, despite having dominated the match, it was Sanath Jayasuriya's Sri Lankans.

Even his tactics on the final day suggested that a draw would be enough. This, when England led by

only 41 runs with eight wickets left. Astonishingly, Sri Lankan fielders were dispatched to man the boundary rope rather than form a slip cordon, and while England must be credited for their determined fightback that rescued them from what seemed to be certain defeat at the end of the third day, Jayasuriya's failure to go for the kill remains a mystery.

It might be that he was merely relieved to emerge unscathed from a match that was missing Muttiah Muralitharan. Recovering from a shoulder operation, the controversial off spinner was likely to feature in the final match and one felt that Sri Lanka were happy to wait for his return. England, on the other hand, were without their main spearhead, Darren Gough, and had sprung a surprise in recalling Dominic Cork and, in particular, John Crawley, when surely this was a golden opportunity to introduce Ian Bell, the highly talented 20-year-old batsman from Warwickshire.

The damp and miserable build-up to the match which, incidentally, was the earliest start ever to a Test in England, suggested that an insertion was on the cards. When Nasser Hussain lost his 19th toss out of 22, however, England found themselves in the field, and looked horribly rusty. Cork apart, the bowlers had scarcely played since returning from New Zealand in early April and, despite the denials from the England dressing room, it looked like it, too. Andy Caddick and Matthew Hoggard were especially disappointing and, in the 65th over, Sri Lanka were 261 for 2 – Jayasuriya having run himself out and Sangakkara edging a ball so wide he must have put his back out. Jayawardene and Atapattu, the class acts in the visitors' line-up, added 206 for the third wicket and although Jayawardene lazily flicked Flintoff to midwicket for 107, the Sri Lankans were not finished yet.

Aravinda de Silva made his Test debut at Lord's in 1984 and now that he was saying goodbye he clearly had a major score in mind. With the relentless Atapattu, he piled on 146 before the opener, who has a remarkable appetite for converting centuries into doubles, surprised everyone by falling for the hook trap only 15 runs away from a sixth Test score in excess of 200. Cork celebrated in typically belligerent style but, with Sri Lanka now on 407 for 4, England were already on a match-salvaging exercise. De Silva was snared down the legside for 88 (just as he was on his debut for rather less), but Arnold made an

Marvan Atapattu, a man with a penchant for scoring double centuries, on his way to 185 in the first Test of the summer at Lord's.

FIRST TEST – ENGLAND v. SRI LANKA
16-20 May 2002 at Lord's

SRI LANKA

	First innings		Second innings	
MS Atapattu	c Trescothick b Cork	185	c Butcher b Caddick	17
ST Jayasuriya (capt)	run out (Vaughan/Stewart)	18		
*K Sangakkara	c Flintoff b Hoggard	10	(2) not out	6
M Jayawardene	c Trescothick b Flintoff	107	(3) not out	14
PA de Silva	c Stewart b Cork	88		
RP Arnold	c Trescothick b Hoggard	50		
HP Tillekeratne	not out	17		
WPUJC Vaas	c Trescothick b Cork	6		
DNT Zoysa	c Stewart b Flintoff	28		
TCB Fernando	not out	6		
PDRL Perera	did not bat			
Extras	b 1, lb 13, w 1, nb 25	40	b 5, lb 2, nb 8	15
	(8 wickets dec.)	555	(1 wicket)	42

	First innings				Second innings			
	O	M	R	W	O	M	R	W
Caddick	38.3	6	135	0	7	2	10	1
Hoggard	39	4	160	2	1	0	7	0
Cork	35.3	11	93	3				
Flintoff	39	8	101	2	5	0	18	0
Butcher	3	0	17	0				
Vaughan	14	2	35	0				

Fall of Wickets
1-38, 2-55, 3-261, 4-407, 5-492, 6-492, 7-505, 8-540
1-16

ENGLAND

	First innings		Second innings	
ME Trescothick	c Jayasuriya b Zoysa	13	lbw b Zoysa	76
MP Vaughan	c Zoysa b Perera	64	c Sangakkara b Perera	115
MA Butcher	c Jayawardene b Fernando	17	run out (Vaas/Sangakkara)	105
N Hussain (capt)	c Sangakkara b Zoysa	57	lbw b Perera	68
GP Thorpe	lbw b Perera	27	c Fernando b de Silva	65
JP Crawley	c Sangakkara b Vaas	31	not out	41
*AJ Stewart	run out (sub: UDU Chandana)	7	not out	26
A Flintoff	c Sangakkara b Fernando	12		
DG Cork	c Sangakkara b Fernando	0		
AR Caddick	c Sangakkara b Perera	13		
MJ Hoggard	not out	0		
Extras	b 4, lb 7, w 9, nb 14	34	b 1, lb 9, w 1, nb 22	33
		275	(5 wickets dec.)	529

	First innings				Second innings			
	O	M	R	W	O	M	R	W
Vaas	21.1	4	51	1	44	8	113	0
Zoysa	19	3	82	2	34	6	84	1
Fernando	22	5	83	3	26	1	86	0
Perera	11	0	48	3	30	4	90	2
de Silva					27	7	63	1
Jayasuriya					25	6	66	0
Arnold					4	1	7	0
Tillekeratne					1	1	0	0

Fall of Wickets
1-17, 2-43, 3-149, 4-203, 5-203, 6-214, 7-237, 8-237, 9-267
1-168, 2-213, 3-372, 4-432, 5-483

Umpires: DJ Harper & S Venkataraghavan
Toss: Sri Lanka
Man of the Match: MS Atapattu

Match drawn

attractive half-century before Jayasuriya declared on 555 for 8 with nine overs remaining on the second day. England lost Trescothick before the close.

The third day was nothing short of calamitous for England as they were bowled out for 275 and made to follow on, 280 runs behind. When Vaughan and Hussain were together, adding 106 for the third wicket, there was little sign of what was to follow. They were parted at 149 for 3 when Hussain edged the towering left-armer, Zoysa, to the keeper for 57, but it was the aggressive spell by the Sri Lankan's fastest bowler, Ruchira Perera, that caught the eye.

There seemed no doubt to me whatsoever that he was throwing virtually every delivery – and this was without any need for confirmation from television replays. Frankly, if coaches, referees and umpires are unable to detect an action as flawed as this, they have no business being in the game. It is not Perera's fault – far from it – but his fault should have been detected, and helped, long before this Test match. It is true that throwing is a controversial subject and, because of the saga involving Muralitharan, the Sri Lankans are particularly – and unnecessarily – touchy about it, but the laws of the game are in place for a reason, and Perera's action, which was reported by the umpires after the game, was as clear an example of a throw as you could wish to see.

He tempted Vaughan to hook to long leg for 64, and when he trapped Thorpe lbw on the back foot for 27, England's slide had begun. The last five wickets fell for 61, despite a fighting 31 from Crawley, and England's openers were back in the middle again long before the end of the day.

Far from collapsing this time, England rattled up their highest score for 60 Tests as Vaughan and Trescothick put on 168 for the first wicket, Butcher and Vaughan made centuries and the first five batsmen all passed 50 for the first time since the timeless Test in Durban of 1939. As the runs piled up, Jayasuriya became increasingly defensive, as if he simply could not face the possibility of England, somehow, turning the tables. He need not have worried, but in 13 hostile, short-pitched overs before the end of the match, England's chastened pace bowlers spelled out an altogether different approach for the two Tests that lay ahead.

24–27 May 2002 at Cardiff
Sri Lankans 337 for 7 (K Sangakkara 113, HP Tillekeratne 81, ST Jayasuriya 57)
Glamorgan did not bat
Match drawn – no play was possible on the second, third and fourth days

Only the first day was possible at Sophia Gardens, Cardiff, with total washouts on scheduled days two, three and four consigning this match to a watery grave. Sri Lanka, put in by Steve James, reached 337 for 7 with Sanath Jayasuriya blazing the trail with a typically gung-ho innings of 57 from 44 balls. One shot off Simon Jones went for six over cover. Russel Arnold made 46, but the best batting of the day came from Kumar Sangakkara, with 113 off 152 balls, and the ever-dependable Hashan Tillekeratne with 81. Alex Wharf, who took 4 for 71, was the pick of the Glamorgan bowlers.

npower SECOND TEST
30 May–2 June 2002 at Edgbaston

The possible return to the Sri Lankan team of Muttiah Muralitharan dominated the build-up to the

second Test of the series that was, by now, beginning to be utterly swamped by the football World Cup. Eventually the Sri Lankan management could deny Murali, an irrepressible character, no longer and, in fact, he bowled 63 overs in England's only innings!

After their below-par efforts at Lord's, there was much interest in how England's bowlers, in particular, would perform on a ground that has been to their liking in recent years. Hoggard's confidence appeared to be especially fragile, but when Hussain won the toss he had no hesitation in asking Sri Lanka to bat first on a ground that had been under water only a few days before. By tea, the decision had already been vindicated as the visitors had subsided to 108 for 6, and were already struggling to compete in the match.

Those wickets had all been shared by Hoggard and Caddick, but it was Alex Tudor, who had replaced Cork, who broke the one stubborn partnership of the innings. He trapped Tillekeratne lbw for 23 after the little left-hander had put on 33 with Vaas, who promptly played Flintoff onto his stumps. Murali then emerged to flail his bat one-handed and the innings ended with a chaotic run out, which rather summed up Sri Lanka's feeble effort.

England's batsmen soon put that total of 162 into perspective – they passed it with only one wicket down – and quickly built a substantial lead. Murali toiled away. At first, he was keen to maintain a low profile in the field, then he dived on his shoulder, survived the experience and pushed himself to such an extent that in the end he pulled a groin muscle!

There was little in this damp, slow pitch for him, but having removed Vaughan, sweeping, for 46, his next victim – Butcher – received an early nomination for 'ball of the century'. The left-hander was quietly building on his confident century at Lord's and looked for all the world as if he would saunter to another when, out of the blue, he received a ball from Murali that pitched 18 inches outside his leg stump, spun sharply and hit the off bail. Butcher might have had 94 runs to his name, but that ball was unplayable under the circumstances and Butcher's rueful smile to the bowler said it all: 'respect!'

Hussain was bowled in Murali's next over for 22, and there was a danger that England

Muttiah Muralitharan marked his return to fitness by bowling 64 overs at Edgbaston.

SECOND TEST – ENGLAND v. SRI LANKA
30 May–2 June 2002 at Edgbaston

SRI LANKA

	First innings		Second innings	
MS Atapattu	c Stewart b Hoggard	13	b Hoggard	56
ST Jayasuriya (capt)	c Stewart b Caddick	8	b Hoggard	12
*K Sangakkara	c Stewart b Flintoff	16	lbw b Hoggard	1
M Jayawardene	c Flintoff b Caddick	47	c Thorpe b Caddick	59
PA de Silva	c Trescothick b Hoggard	10	c Thorpe b Caddick	47
HP Tillekeratne	lbw b Tudor	20	b Caddick	39
RP Arnold	c Flintoff b Caddick	1	c Giles b Hoggard	4
WPUJC Vaas	b Flintoff	23	st Stewart b Giles	28
DNT Zoysa	c Hoggard b Tudor	0	(10) not out	1
TCB Fernando	run out (Caddick/Tudor)	13	(9) b Hoggard	0
M Muralitharan	not out	0	absent injured	
Extras	b 1, nb 10	11	b 4, lb 4, nb 17	25
		162		**272**

	First innings				Second innings			
	O	M	R	W	O	M	R	W
Caddick	17	4	47	3	25	4	67	3
Hoggard	17	4	55	2	23	2	92	5
Giles	4	1	7	0	26.1	3	57	1
Tudor	9.5	3	25	2	9	1	25	0
Flintoff	5	0	27	2	6	0	23	0

Fall of Wickets
1-23, 2-23, 3-76, 4-96, 5-100, 6-108, 7-141, 8-141, 9-159
1-28, 2-30, 3-135, 4-156, 5-233, 6-238, 7-247, 8-247, 9-272

ENGLAND

	First innings	
ME Trescothick	c Tillekeratne b Vaas	161
MP Vaughan	c Jayasuriya b Muralitharan	46
MA Butcher	b Muralitharan	94
N Hussain (capt)	b Muralitharan	22
GP Thorpe	c Vaas b Fernando	123
*AJ Stewart	c Tillekeratne b Muralitharan	7
A Flintoff	c Tillekeratne b Muralitharan	29
AJ Tudor	c Tillekeratne b Zoysa	3
AF Giles	c Sangakkara b Zoysa	0
AR Caddick	c Sangakkara b Zoysa	3
MJ Hoggard	not out	17
Extras	lb 19, w 6, nb 15	40
		545

	First innings			
	O	M	R	W
Vaas	41	3	141	1
Zoysa	24	3	93	3
Muralitharan	64	12	143	5
Fernando	21.5	2	92	1
Jayasuriya	6	2	27	0
de Silva	7	0	30	0

Fall of Wickets
1-92, 2-294, 3-338, 4-341, 5-368, 6-426, 7-436, 8-444, 9-454

Umpires: DJ Harper & S Venkataraghavan
Toss: England
Man of the Match: MJ Hoggard

England won by an innings & 111 runs

might not reach the 500 or so they would have wanted. Graham Thorpe, who has happy memories of Edgbaston, quickly settled in, but his partners fell like ninepins. Four wickets fell for 28 and, on 61, Thorpe was joined by the No. 11, Hoggard. Not even a supreme optimist would have given Thorpe a cat in hell's chance of reaching his century, but reach it he did in a remarkable, record-breaking partnership of 91, of which Hoggard's contribution was 17 in two hours of priceless defence. The innings ended when Thorpe was caught at third man for 123, giving England an unassailable lead of 383.

Although Jayasuriya and Sangakkara were both dismissed cheaply by Hoggard, Sri Lanka closed the third day on 132 for 2, with Atapattu and Jayawardene apparently determined to deny England

Graham Thorpe, who was to take a break from all cricket later in the summer, celebrates his century as England piled on the runs at Edgbaston.

for as long as possible. In the third over of the following morning, however, Hoggard struck again when Atapattu edged him onto his stumps for 56. Caddick took the key wickets of Jayawardene for 59 and de Silva for 47 – which earned him special praise after the game from his captain – and although Vaas flung the bat for 28, his stumping sealed Sri Lanka's fate and gave England a 1–0 lead in the series.

During the course of this match the news broke of the death in South Africa of Hansie Cronje in a plane crash. That such a young man, aged 32, should lose his life in such a way is a tragedy, and it was time for those of us who had been severe in our criticism of him to reflect. It is true that he, and his match-fixing cohorts, did more to damage the game of cricket than possibly anyone else in the sport's history. It is also absolutely true that Cronje was a personable man, a gifted and wholehearted cricketer and, because of his work in underprivileged areas, a hero to many black African children. All of us who worked with Hansie also got to know members of his family, for whom the last two years have been especially difficult. This was a tragic final chapter to a desperately sad story.

npower THIRD TEST
13–17 June 2002 at Old Trafford

As the nation ground to a halt with football fever, few optimists believed that the Old Trafford Test would manage to grab the limelight. Such was the recognition that cricket was on a hiding to nothing, that a giant screen was erected in the car park at the Stretford End, allowing the Saturday spectators to abandon the Test and watch, instead, England's World Cup footballers take on Denmark in Japan. Sure enough, the ground emptied at the appointed hour and the cheers of the assembled thousands

Alec Stewart buried any further speculation about his future with a century at Old Trafford.

echoed around the abandoned seats. Ninety minutes later, they were all back in excellent spirits and the controversial decision to bow to football had undoubtedly been a complete success.

And yet despite this obvious distraction – and others, such as a day's worth of bad weather, the absence of Darren Gough, an injury to Andy Caddick and a belting, flat pitch – England's cricketers completed a breathtaking win late on the final day. This gave them an overwhelming 2–0 victory in the series and ensured that the summer game featured on at least one or two back pages that week.

England's rich run of form with the bat continued the moment Nasser Hussain chose to have first use of the bone-hard pitch. Sri Lanka had made a couple of changes to their bowling attack to the surprise of many – not least Eric Upashantha, one of the bowling replacements himself, who was drafted into the Test on the back of the 18-0-126-0 he bagged against the MCC the previous week. Poor chap, he proceeded to have a complete nightmare.

At lunch on the first day, England had already scored 105 for the loss of Michael Vaughan who was deceived by Dilhara Fernando's magnificent slower ball and was caught at mid-off for 36. As Trescothick and Butcher tucked into some mediocre fare during the afternoon, Upashantha – who had already generously served up scores of half volleys – allowed the most straightforward catch it is possible to imagine to slip through his fingers at square leg. It was Trescothick who prospered on 66, but on 81 he was brilliantly caught by Jayawardene low down at slip off Muralitharan and England were 192 for 2.

Hussain fell in exactly the same manner as Vaughan for 16, and Upashantha's day took a noticeable upturn before the close when he had Thorpe caught behind off the inside edge for 32. England were 273 for 4, and there was more than just the merest possibility of Muralitharan running through the lower order to restore the balance the following morning.

We had not reckoned, though, on the subdued mood of the Sri Lankans. The captain, Jayasuriya, had been relegated to No. 6 in the batting order. Word had it that it was not a move to his liking, and his disappointment showed. His team quickly picked it up. Meanwhile Alec Stewart was playing an innings that was, literally, to ensure his survival at Test level. James Foster was recovering fast from the broken wrist that had sidelined him at the start of the summer and, clearly, he would be back in the selectors' minds for the series against India. Stewart is nothing if not a survivor and, after being dropped in the gully on 0, made Sri Lanka pay for their error by scoring his 15th Test century. It was a crucial innings both personally and for his team which, with some help from Giles who scored 45, passed 500 for the third consecutive time. England have never managed that before.

THIRD TEST – ENGLAND v. SRI LANKA
13-17 June 2002 at Old Trafford

ENGLAND

	First innings		Second innings	
ME Trescothick	c Jayawardene b Muralitharan	81	not out	23
MP Vaughan	c Vaas b Fernando	36	not out	24
MA Butcher	lbw b Vaas	123		
N Hussain (capt)	c Muralitharan b Fernando	16		
GP Thorpe	c Sangakkara b Upashantha	32		
*AJ Stewart	c Tillekeratne b Muralitharan	123		
A Flintoff	run out (Vaas)	1		
AJ Tudor	c Arnold b Vaas	19		
AF Giles	c Sangakkara b Muralitharan	45		
AR Caddick	not out	2		
MJ Hoggard	lbw b Fernando	7		
Extras	b 5, lb 10, nb 12	27	lb 2, nb 1	3
		512	(0 wickets)	50

	First innings				Second innings			
	O	M	R	W	O	M	R	W
Vaas	38	8	121	2	1	0	8	0
Upashantha	8	0	65	1				
Fernando	29.2	2	154	3	2	0	23	0
Muralitharan	60	20	137	3	2	0	17	0
de Silva	2	0	5	0				
Jayasuriya	8	2	15	0				

Fall of Wickets
1-66, 2-192, 3-219, 4-262, 5-354, 6-361, 7-400, 8-502, 9-503

ENGLAND

	First innings		Second innings	
MS Atapattu	retired hurt	10	(10) lbw b Giles	6
RP Arnold	c Vaughan b Tudor	62	(1) c Stewart b Tudor	109
*KC Sangakkara	c Thorpe b Hoggard	40	lbw b Tudor	32
DPM Jayawardene	c & b Tudor	17	c Hussain b Giles	28
PA de Silva	c Hussain b Flintoff	18	c Vaughan b Tudor	40
ST Jayasuriya (capt)	lbw b Hoggard	35	(2) b Hoggard	26
HP Tillekeratne	c Flintoff b Giles	20	(6) not out	32
WPUJC Vaas	lbw b Hoggard	14	(7) lbw b Hoggard	1
KEA Upashantha	c Stewart b Tudor	1	(8) c Stewart b Flintoff	3
CRD Fernando	not out	6	(9) lbw b Giles	4
M Muralitharan	c Stewart b Tudor	6	c sub (MJ Powell) b Giles	0
Extras	b 1, lb 3, nb 20	24	b 9, lb 9, w 2, nb 7	27
		253		308

	First innings				Second innings			
	O	M	R	W	O	M	R	W
Caddick	5.3	2	17	0				
Hoggard	16	4	38	3	37	8	97	2
Flintoff	23	5	65	1	29	7	78	1
Tudor	25	8	65	4	21	6	44	3
Giles	23	3	64	1	24.2	4	62	4
Vaughan					2	0	9	0

Fall of Wickets
1-107, 2-143, 3-149, 4-171, 5-219, 6-227, 7-228, 8-240, 9-253
1-44, 2-110, 3-170, 4-233, 5-263, 6-264, 7-270, 8-285, 9-308

Umpires: SA Bucknor & DL Orchard
Toss: England
Man of the Match: AJ Tudor

England won by ten wickets

TEST MATCH AVERAGES
England v. Sri Lanka

ENGLAND

Batting	M	Inns	NO	HS	Runs	Av	100	50	c/st
ME Trescothick	3	5	1	161	354	88.50	1	2	5
MA Butcher	3	4	0	123	339	84.75	2	1	1
MP Vaughan	3	5	1	115	285	71.25	1	1	2
GP Thorpe	3	4	0	123	247	61.75	1	1	3
AJ Stewart	3	4	1	123	163	54.33	1	–	9/1
N Hussain	3	4	0	68	163	40.75	–	2	2
MJ Hoggard	3	3	2	17*	24	24.00	–	–	1
AF Giles	2	2	0	45	45	22.50	–	–	1
A Flintoff	3	3	0	29	42	14.00	–	–	4
AJ Tudor	2	2	0	19	22	11.00	–	–	1
AR Caddick	3	3	1	13	18	9.00	–	–	–

Also batted in one Test: DG Cork 0; JP Crawley 31, 41*

Bowling	Overs	Mds	Runs	Wkts	Av	Best	10m	5/inn
AJ Tudor	64.5	18	159	9	17.66	4-65	–	–
AF Giles	77.3	11	190	6	31.66	4-62	–	–
MJ Hoggard	133	22	449	14	32.07	5-92	–	1
AR Caddick	93	18	276	7	39.42	3-47	–	–
A Flintoff	107	20	312	6	52.00	2-27	–	–

Also bowled: MA Butcher 3-0-17-0; DG Cork 35.3-11-93-3; MP Vaughan 16-2-44-0

SRI LANKA

Batting	M	Inns	NO	HS	Runs	Av	100	50	c/st
MS Atapattu	3	6	1	185	277	55.40	1	1	2
DPMD Jayawardene	3	6	1	107	272	54.40	1	1	2
RP Arnold	3	5	0	109	226	45.20	1	2	1
HP Tillekeratne	3	5	2	39	128	42.66	–	–	5
PA de Silva	3	5	0	88	203	40.60	–	1	4
K Sangakkara	3	6	1	40	105	21.00	–	–	10/-
ST Jayasuriya	3	5	0	35	99	19.80	–	–	2
DNT Zoysa	2	3	1	28	29	14.50	–	–	1
WPUJC Vaas	3	5	0	28	72	14.40	–	–	2
TCB Fernando	2	3	1	13	19	9.50	–	–	1
M Muralitharan	2	3	1	6	6	3.00	–	–	1

Also batted in one Test: CRD Fernando 6*, 4; KEA Upashantha 1, 3
PDRL Perera played in one Test but did not bat

Bowling	Overs	Mds	Runs	Wkts	Av	Best	10m	5/inn
PDRL Perera	41	4	138	5	27.60	3-48	–	–
M Muralitharan	126	32	297	8	37.12	5-143	–	1
DNT Zoysa	77	12	259	6	43.16	3-93	–	–
TCB Fernando	69.5	8	271	4	67.75	3-83	–	–
WPUJC Vaas	145.1	23	434	4	108.50	2-121	–	–

Also bowled: RP Arnold 4-1-7-0; PA de Silva 36-7-98-1; CRD Fernando 31.2-2-177-3; ST Jayasuriya 39-10-108-0; HP Tillekeratne 1-1-0-0; KEA Upashantha 8-0-65-1

Opposite: England knew they had an outside chance of winning the Test when Michael Powell, the substitute, caught Muralitharan off the bowling of Ashley Giles.

Sri Lanka's reply began on the third afternoon and, when they closed on 130 for 1, it seemed that they would be able to avoid the follow-on and save the game. By tea on the fourth day, they had been rolled over for 253, losing eight wickets for 123 runs and conceding a lead of 259. England's young seam bowlers had performed heroically.

Caddick managed to bowl 5.3 overs before leaving the field with a badly torn side muscle, but Hoggard, Tudor and Flintoff stepped into the breach admirably. Flintoff was the bully, constantly banging the ball in at ribcage height – and while he forced Atapattu to retire hurt with a nasty hand injury, Hoggard and Tudor picked up the rewards. Seven Sri Lankans reached double figures, but only one progressed beyond 40.

England now faced a race against time, and began the final day needing to take nine Sri Lankan wickets – although there was also a doubt as to whether or not Atapattu would be able to bat again. Sri Lanka put up a much more disciplined display as they followed on and, led by Arnold who made his third Test century, in six hours, seemed well set to earn the draw. At tea, they had lost only four wickets and were just six runs behind with Arnold still at the crease. He fell in the third over afterwards, caught behind off Tudor for 109, and the floodgates suddenly opened as Giles nabbed three quick wickets, including the last two with consecutive balls.

This left England needing to chase a target of 50 off only six overs and, as the players dashed into the dressing room, as many as seven batsmen put their pads on! Three warning lights glowed on the 'bad light meter' but, in fact, Trescothick and Vaughan needed only five overs to seal England's second victory at Old Trafford for 21 years.

NatWest Series Warm-Up Games

21 June 2002 at Taunton
Somerset 241 (48 overs) (M Burns 63, KA Parsons 50, DNT Zoysa 4 for 49)
Sri Lankans 178 (42 overs) (MN Nawaz 61, KP Dutch 4 for 30, MPL Bulbeck 4 for 36)
Somerset won by 63 runs

A below-par Sri Lanka were beaten by 63 runs at Taunton, bowled out for 178 in reply to the county side's 241. It was the end of a bad week for the Sri Lankans, who also confirmed that their match-winning bowler, Muttiah Muralitharan, would not be playing in the NatWest Series and was to return home to rest his barely healed shoulder injury. In

his absence, Somerset were able to rally from 75 for 4 thanks to a stand of 84 between acting captain Mike Burns (63) and Keith Parsons (50). Matt Bulbeck then picked up an encouraging 4 for 36, with Keith Dutch adding a late haul of 4 for 30 with his cleverly varied off breaks to an earlier, spirited knock of 32.

23 June 2002 at Bristol
Sri Lankans 275 for 8 (50 overs) (RP Arnold 80, MN Nawaz 64, ST Jayasuriya 53, IJ Harvey 4 for 35)
Gloucestershire 182 (36.1 overs) (CM Spearman 76)
Sri Lankans won by 93 runs

Sanath Jayasuriya, following the trials and tribulations of the 2–0 Test series defeat against England, looked back to his rampant one-day best as the Sri Lankans brushed aside Gloucestershire by 93 runs at Bristol. Jayasuriya, out for a duck in the previous warm-up match for the NatWest Series against Somerset, raced to 53 from 44 balls at the head of the order – and thrashed two sixes over cover point. Mahela Jayawardene (42), Russel Arnold (80) and Naveed Nawaz (64) then each took up the baton to ensure a fine Sri Lankan total of 275 for 8, despite Ian Harvey's 4 for 35. In reply, Craig Spearman struck a six and ten fours in his 66-ball 76, but had little support as Gloucestershire slipped to 182 all out.

24 June 2002 at Northampton (floodlit)
Northamptonshire 246 for 5 (50 overs) (MB Loye 123, DJG Sales 65)
Sri Lankans 249 for 2 (43.1 overs) (RS Kaluwitharana 140*, DPMD Jayawardene 67*)
Sri Lankans won by eight wickets

Sri Lanka eased to victory in their final game before the start of the NatWest series, brushing aside Northamptonshire by eight wickets in a floodlit encounter at Wantage Road. Northants made a useful 246 for 5 from their 50 overs, with Mal Loye (123) and David Sales (65) putting on 150 for the second wicket, but, with Romesh Kaluwitharana at his destructive best at the top of the order, it proved nowhere near enough. The diminutive Kalu, the wicketkeeper-batsman who was one of the stars of the 1996 World Cup, thrashed two sixes and 18 fours in an unbeaten 140 from 135 balls. Mahela Jayawardene, with a stylish 67 not out, helped Kalu to add an unbroken 180 as Sri Lanka rushed to victory with almost seven overs unbowled.

NATWEST TROPHY TRIANGULAR SERIES
(England, India and Sri Lanka)

By Jonathan Agnew

As one of the most outspoken critics of the ECB's one-day tournaments of late, it comes as a great pleasure to report that the NatWest series, involving England, India and Sri Lanka, was an outstanding success. For a change, cricket came first and the players responded magnificently to put on a competition that will be remembered for many years.

It proved beyond all measure that dumbing-down tactics are not required to make international cricket an attractive proposition – popular opera singing replaced the moronic interval entertainment of last year, and the blasts of music were kept to a sane minimum.

Marcus Trescothick scored a century in the final of the NatWest series. Unfortunately it was, again, in a losing cause.

There were complaints before the final at Lord's that the MCC had banned those irritating, green horns that were blown from morning to night at other venues. 'How typically old fashioned,' we were told by those who believe it is essential to blast a horn while watching cricket. And yet the standard of the cricket on offer that day proved beyond doubt that horns add precisely nothing to the atmosphere of a match and, far from being fuddy-duddy, the MCC proved again that – on special occasions – there is no substitute for tradition. It was a magnificent day that could so easily have been spoiled by those who are blind to the fact that cricket is quite capable of generating its own excitement and atmosphere.

It was unfortunate that Sri Lanka were so awful that the finalists were settled well before the end of the qualifying round. Jayasuriya's men managed only one win when they beat England on a spinner's pitch at Old Trafford, otherwise they were roundly outplayed.

England's most convincing victory came at Headingley where, despite a superb 112 from

India's march to victory over Sri Lanka at The Oval was halted, temporarily, by the antics of a streaker. Sachin Tendulkar, at least, saw the funny side of the situation.

Jayasuriya that came from only 87 balls, they overcame their target of 241 in 32 overs with four balls to spare. Trescothick underlined his importance to England's one-day plans, and Ronnie Irani – who was recalled to the fold on the back of some outstanding performances for Essex – featured heavily in England's win over India at The Oval. Irani scored 53 batting at No. 3, and took 5 for 26 as India succumbed by 64 runs. Time will tell whether or not Ronnie has it in him to be selected for the World Cup, but he could not have done any more.

The position of No. 3 in England's batting order continued to cause great debate. Hussain has occupied that slot since being moved away from opening after the previous World Cup, and scores his runs at a rate of 68 per 100 balls. He is regularly tied down, some say, and resorts to desperate means to loosen the shackles. Others wonder where else he can possibly bat other than at three because the innings can always be bolstered by big hitters later on.

The issue rumbled on into the final where Hussain scored his first century in 72 one-day innings. It was a typical effort – dropped on 26 and the start was tortuous – yet Hussain chose to mark his celebration with an extraordinary display towards the media centre. Repeatedly he turned and pointed to the No. 3 on his back, as well as mouthing well-chosen expletives, as if to suggest that this innings answered his critics. Unfortunately, it merely clouded the debate still further as it now seems inevitable that Hussain will bat in that position in the World Cup.

His innings of 115 helped England to their fourth-highest one-day score of 325 for 5. Trescothick made a punchy 109 from 100 balls and Flintoff added some much-needed impetus at the end by scoring 40 from 32 balls. It was a stiff target, but the weather was beautiful, and India boasted one of the strongest batting line-ups in the world.

However, it was not long before India had slumped to 146 for 5 and Sachin Tendulkar was trudging back towards the Long Room. The little master had been bowled by Giles for 14 and India had lost five wickets for 40 runs. The game was rushing away from them.

Youvraj Singh and Mohammad Kaif came together in what was presumed to be a fruitless exercise. The two youngsters – both only 21 – moved along smoothly at a run a ball with Youvraj, it transpired later, batting with a broken finger. This was soon forgotten as the left-hander opened his shoulders and lofted the ball into the Tavern Stand, with the hundred partnership arriving from only 90 balls.

Whatever the arguments about Hussain's position might be, there is no disputing that he is a fine leader and, having been forced from the field for a while, England began to look lost without him. When the captain returned, it began to look too late as India needed 69 from the last ten overs.

Finally, Youvraj was caught at short fine leg for 69 off 63 balls. Harbhajan added 57 with Kaif in just six overs and with England starting to crumble under the pressure, Kaif made the winning hit to finish unbeaten on 87 from only 75 balls, as India won a truly memorable final with three balls to spare. The tournament deserved a thrilling finale, and it got one – this was the finest one-day international I have ever seen.

Match One

27 June 2002 at Trent Bridge (floodlit)
England 293 for 6 (50 overs) (AJ Stewart 83, A Flintoff 50*)
Sri Lanka 249 for 9 (50 overs) (RS Kaluwitharana 52)
England (4 pts) won by 44 runs
Man of the Match: A Flintoff

Match Two

29 June 2002 at Lord's
England 271 for 7 (50 overs) (ME Trescothick 86, N Hussain 54)
India 272 for 4 (48.5 overs) (V Sehwag 71, Yuvraj Singh 64*)
India (4 pts) won by 6 wickets
Man of the Match: Yuvraj Singh

Mohammad Kaif, India's batting hero at Lord's, dives in for the winning run as the visitors rallied from 146 for 5 to beat England with three balls to spare and take the NatWest Series trophy.

NATWEST TROPHY FINAL – ENGLAND v. INDIA
13 July 2002 at Lord's

ENGLAND

ME Trescothick	b Kumble	109
NV Knight	b Zaheer Khan	14
N Hussain (capt)	b Nehra	115
A Flintoff	b Zaheer Khan	40
MP Vaughan	c Mongia b Zaheer Khan	3
PD Collingwood	not out	3
RC Irani	not out	10
*AJ Stewart		
AF Giles		
AJ Tudor		
D Gough		
Extras	b 2, lb 16, w 7, nb 6	31
	(for 5 wickets) 50 overs	**325**

	M	O	R	W
Nehra	10	0	66	1
Zaheer Khan	10	1	62	3
Kumble	10	0	54	1
Harbhajan Singh	10	0	53	-
Ganguly	3	0	28	-
Sehwag	4	0	26	-
Yuvraj Singh	3	0	18	-

Fall of Wickets
1-42, 2-227, 3-307, 4-312, 5-312

INDIA

V Sehwag	b Giles	45
SC Ganguly (capt)	b Tudor	60
D Mongia	c Stewart b Irani	9
SR Tendulkar	b Giles	14
*R Dravid	c Knight b Irani	5
Yuvraj Singh	c Tudor b Collingwood	69
Mohammad Kaif	not out	87
Harbhajan Singh	b Flintoff	15
A Kumble	c Stewart b Flintoff	0
Zaheer Khan	not out	4
A Nehra		
Extras	b 3, lb 8, w 6, nb 1	18
	(for 8 wickets) 49.3 overs	**326**

	O	M	R	W
Gough	10	1	63	-
Tudor	9	0	62	1
Flintoff	7.3	0	55	2
Irani	10	0	64	2
Giles	10	0	47	2
Collingwood	3	0	24	1

Fall of Wickets
1-106, 2-114, 3-126, 4-132, 5-146, 6-267, 7-314, 8-314

Umpires: DA Bucknor & DR Shepherd
Toss: England
Man of the Match: Mohammad Kaif
Player of the Series: ME Trescothick

India won by two wickets

Match Three
30 June 2002 at The Oval
Sri Lanka 202 for 8 (50 overs)
(DPMD Jayawardene 62)
India 203 for 6 (45.2 overs)
India (4 pts) won by four wickets
Man of the Match: AB Agarkar

Match Four
2 July 2002 at Headingley
Sri Lanka 240 for 7 (32 overs)
(ST Jayasuriya 112)
England 241 for 7 (31.2 overs)
(ME Trescothick 82)
England (4 pts) won by three wickets
Man of the Match: ST Jayasuriya

Match Five
5 July 2002 at Chester-le-Street (floodlit)
India 285 for 4 (50 overs) (SR Tendulkar 105*,
R Dravid 82)
England 53 for 1 (12.3 overs)
Match abandoned - 2 pts each

Match Six
6 July 2002 at Edgbaston
Sri Lanka 187 (48.2 overs) (MS Atapattu 50)
India 188 for 6 (48.1 overs) (R Dravid 64)
India (4 pts) won by four wickets
Man of the Match: R Dravid

Match Seven
7 July 2002 at Old Trafford
Sri Lanka 229 (49.4 overs) (K Sangakkara 70,
MP Vaughan 4 for 22)
England 206 (47.4 overs)
Sri Lanka (4 pts) won by 23 runs
Man of the Match: K Sangakkara

Match Eight
9 July 2002 at The Oval
England 229 for 8 (32 overs) (RC Irani 53)
India 165 (29.1 overs) (RC Irani 5 for 26)
England (5 pts) won by 64 runs
Man of the Match: RC Irani

Match Nine
11 July 2002 at Bristol (floodlit)
India 304 (50 overs) (SR Tendulkar 113)
Sri Lanka 241 (44.1 overs) (K Sangakkara 66,
MS Atapattu 53, Harbhajan Singh 4 for 46)
India (5 pts) won by 63 runs
Man of the Match: SR Tendulkar

INDIA IN ENGLAND
By Jonathan Agnew (with Sunil Gavaskar)

22 June 2002 at Hove (floodlit)
Sussex 203 for 8 (50 overs) (A Nehra 4 for 27)
Indians 205 for 7 (48.5 overs) (SR Tendulkar 75*,
D Mongia 56)
Indians won by three wickets

Sachin Tendulkar prepared himself for the upcoming NatWest Series by hitting an unbeaten 75 to guide the Indians to a hard-fought, three-wicket win over Sussex at Hove. Sussex, who totalled 203 for 8 with Murray Goodwin top scoring with 49, looked to be heading for a comfortable defeat as Tendulkar helped Dinesh Mongia (56) take the Indians to 126 for 2. But then Mongia was caught off Will House, and the steady fall of wickets at the other end meant that Tendulkar had to give the situation his full attention.

24 June 2002 at Canterbury
Kent 284 (50 overs) (RWT Key 76, A Symonds 75,
MA Ealham 74*, Zaheer Khan 4 for 38)
Indians 263 (48.5 overs) (SC Ganguly 64, JM Golding
4 for 42, MA Ealham 4 for 45)
Kent won by 21 runs

Kent put in an equally fine display at Canterbury to beat a full-strength India side by 21 runs. First, the county side ran up 284 with Rob Key and Andrew Symonds featuring in a second-wicket stand worth 128. Mark Ealham then hit five sixes in his 74 not out to keep the momentum going, but it was the unsung James Golding who really kept Kent on top. Virender Sehwag (45) and Saurav Ganguly (64) looked initially as if they were capable of deciding the match by themselves, plundering 85 from the first 13 overs, but then Golding removed Sehwag, and Ganguly was needlessly run out. Dinesh Mongia (37) threatened, as did Rahul Dravid, with 34 against his former county team-mates, but Golding removed both Mongia and Yuvraj Singh either side of claiming the most valuable scalp of all – Sachin Tendulkar. The 'Little Master', on 15, bottom-edged an attempted pull onto his stumps and, after that, Ealham settled matters by taking four wickets in 11 balls as the Indians grew more and more desperate.

26 June 2002 at Leicester
Indians 315 for 7 (50 overs) (V Sehwag 98,
SC Ganguly 68, Mohammad Kaif 52)

Leicestershire 261 for 7 (50 overs) (TR Ward 95,
IJ Sutcliffe 50)
Indians won by 54 runs

Virender Sehwag and Saurav Ganguly put on a highly entertaining 132 for the first wicket as the Indians totalled 315 for 7 from their 50 overs and proceeded to beat Leicestershire by 54 runs at Grace Road. Mohammad Kaif also struck 52 and, although Trevor Ward (95) and Iain Sutcliffe (50) replied by adding 136 themselves in an opening stand for the county side, Leicestershire could only reach 261 for 7. Yuvraj Singh took 3 for 48 from his ten overs of left-arm spin.

16–18 July 2002 at Arundel
Indians 253 for 7 dec. (D Mongia 87, VVS Laxman 85)
and 255 (Mohammad Kaif 77, Wasim Jaffer 52,
JJC Lawson 6 for 76)
West Indies A 266 (DS Smith 69, RO Hinds 62,
DJJ Bravo 55) and 81 for 4
Match drawn

VVS Laxman, the acting captain, made the most of a chance of match practice in the genteel surroundings of Arundel by hitting 85 on the opening day of the Indians' fixture against West Indies A. Dinesh Mongia, too, impressed with 87, before a first-innings declaration came at 253 for 7. There were half-centuries from Devon Smith, Ryan Hinds and Dwayne Bravo in the West Indies A reply of 266, and Harbhajan Singh conceded 50 runs in one five-over spell as Hinds and Bravo added 101 in just 17 overs for the fifth wicket. Harbhajan, however, recovered his poise after having Bravo lbw, and ended with 4 for 79. Most impressive was Ajit Agarkar, who struck twice with the new ball and finished with 4 for 55. The Indians reached 87 for 3 by the close of the second day, and Wasim Jaffer went on from his overnight 43 not out to score 52. There was 77, too, from Mohammad Kaif, but the third-day honours went to Jermaine Lawson, a 20-year old fast bowler from Jamaica, who took 6 for 76 as India were bowled out for 255. Technically, the young West Indians needed 243 in 40 remaining overs for victory, but instead they batted out time for the draw finishing on 81 for 4.

20–22 July 2002 at Southampton Rose Bowl
Indians 236 (R Dravid 78, SD Udal 5 for 59) and
139 for 4 dec. (SB Bangar 52*)
Hampshire 123 and 186
Indians won by 66 runs

Sanjay Bangar illustrated his all-round qualities as India beat Hampshire by 66 runs in a low-scoring contest on another moderate Rose Bowl pitch. Rahul Dravid's 78 was the mainstay of the Indians' first-innings score of 236, with Shaun Udal including the scalp of Sachin Tendulkar for just three in his haul of 5 for 59. Hampshire, however, folded for 123 in reply, with Bangar's medium pace bringing him 4 for 40 and Saurav Ganguly chipping in with 3 for 10. Bangar then scored an unbeaten 52 before an Indian second-innings declaration came at 139 for 4, and by the close he had also removed two Hampshire batsmen. It was soon over on the last day, Bangar finishing with 3 for 27 and Anil Kumble 4 for 58 as Hampshire were dismissed for 186.

npower FIRST TEST
25–29 July 2002 at Lord's

There was a particular anticipation ahead of the opening Test of the series because of the overwhelming feeling of unfinished business. Rain had washed out the final Test between these two teams before Christmas just as the contest was hotting up and things were becoming interesting. This was especially true of the manner in which England were trying to deal with Sachin Tendulkar.

In Bangalore, they became so desperate to contain the master batsman, that England's bowlers simply fired the ball out of his reach. It was a ghastly tactic that Nasser Hussain tried to vindicate when he pointed out that Tendulkar, in frustration, was finally stumped for the first time in his Test career. What Hussain conveniently glossed over was the fact that Tendulkar had made 92!

So the question of how England's experimental attack – which included the young Welsh tearaway, Simon Jones – would deal with the maestro dominated the build-up in conditions that resembled the dry heat of Lucknow rather than Lord's.

Crucially, Hussain won the toss and the captain then played one of his finest innings as his team took control from the outset. Vaughan recorded one of

No gestures this time – just an outstanding innings of 155 by Nasser Hussain at Lord's.

his rare failures of the summer, lbw for a duck in the second over, and although England were 78 for 3 when Graham Thorpe missed a straight ball from Zaheer to be out for four, Hussain teamed up, first with John Crawley, who scored a fine 64, and then, spectacularly, with Andrew Flintoff who added vital urgency to the innings. The burly all-rounder smashed 59 from only 62 balls, and then Craig White joined in the fun, making 53. After seven-and-a-half hours at the crease, Hussain was seventh out for 155 as he edged Agarkar to Ratra, and the feeling was that, at 357 for 7, England's innings would quickly draw to a close.

Jones was chosen to add some pace to an attack that was missing both Darren Gough and Andy Caddick. It is fair to assume that no one expected a great deal when he emerged from the pavilion to play his first Test innings batting at No. 10. It was a different matter when his second scoring stroke was a magnificently launched six into the pavilion off his

SUNIL GAVASKAR'S VIEW

India's confidence was high after their spectacular victory in the NatWest Series final a few days earlier and, considering it was at the same venue where the first Test was to be played, one could understand their optimism. However, they forgot to make the mental adjustment between one-day cricket and Test cricket and paid the price.

Hussain did the right thing by his team by winning the toss and then batting with confidence and authority to score a century. India compounded their own problems by omitting the off spinner Harbhajan Singh from its XI to play an extra seamer. It didn't work, as both Nehra and Agarkar were unable to exploit the conditions and instead gave away runs easily. Kumble is not the same bowler overseas as he is in India where the pitches help him, and although he appealed quite spectacularly, they fell on deaf ears most times. Alec Stewart, who became the most capped played for England in this game, missed out on a big score but the tail wagged, with debutant Simon Jones playing exactly like a tail-ender should, not only added valuable runs for his team, but also provided plenty of entertainment for the spectators.

One thought that Hussain would have given Jones the new ball straightaway for he was high on confidence and nicely warmed up after his batting efforts, but the England skipper stuck to the tried-and-tested bowlers, Hoggard and Flintoff. The Yorkshireman got a wicket in his first over with Jaffer playing all over a straight delivery. Virender Sehwag, who was promoted to open the batting, did a marvellous job playing shots all around the ground, and it was only his haste in trying to get to the three-figure mark before the day's play ended that lost him his wicket. The biggest blow was the loss of Dravid and Tendulkar, and with the innings folding up for 221, England were in a good position to apply the pressure.

They did that splendidly, with Vaughan and Crawley getting centuries and ensuring that India had a huge mountain to climb to get to a victory. India has a pretty good record of chasing targets and that is perhaps the reason why Hussain presented India with a 500-plus total to chase. His cautiousness was justified to some extent because India did get close to 400, in spite of not having a major contribution from Sachin Tendulkar.

Setting off in chase of a score like that means a good start is a must and India got that through Sehwag and Jaffer before Simon Jones, who worked up a good speed, came to knock Sehwag's off stump out of its socket. Vaughan, who is developing into a pretty useful off spinner, got rid of Jaffer after his half-century and Tendulkar was nicely set up by Hoggard who, after a succession of out-swingers, bowled an in-swinger which the little champion missed and lost his middle stump. The discipline showed by Laxman and Agarkar was a lesson to the seniors in the team and the much-criticized Agarkar played splendidly to notch up his first Test century. It was not enough to prevent India losing the game, but it gave them the belief that, with a bit more application and self-control, this English attack could be collared.

Frustrated, then defeated: Sachin Tendulkar is comprehensively bowled by Matthew Hoggard.

opposite number, Zaheer Khan. Jones' contribution in a partnership of 62 with White was a thoroughly entertaining 44 from 43 balls and after edging to slip of Kumble, the rousing cheers that escorted him from the ground must have done wonders for his confidence.

The last three wickets added 130 with great gusto, and England's total of 487 at tea on the second day represented a fine recovery from 263 for 5. There was little in the pitch to concern the batsmen and, in Tendulkar, Dravid, Laxman and Ganguly, the Indian line-up was on a par with the best in the world. Now Hussain's master plan would be thoroughly put to the test.

By the close of the second day, India were already in trouble. Frustrated by England's extremely disciplined, but negative, line of attack, their star-studded batsmen simply could not bear to be tied down and dictated to in such a way. Sehwag made a dashing 84 but, in trying to dominate Giles, who was bowling over the wicket, he edged onto his pads and the ball trickled onto his wicket. Not a pretty end to a typically violent and entertaining innings from only 96 balls, and India were 128 for 2. Two runs later, the nightwatchman, Nehra, was lbw to Flintoff and India found themselves starting the third morning on 130 for 3, with Dravid and Tendulkar at the crease.

Now Hussain turned the screw and, with barely a ball bowled that would have hit the stumps, England merely sat back and waited for India's leading batsmen to run out of patience. Dravid and Tendulkar added 32 in 17 painstaking overs before Dravid was taken in the gully off Hoggard. His 46 had taken four hours. After 61 deliveries in which he made just 16 – which included two fours – Tendulkar snapped. Another ball well wide of the off stump from White was needlessly pursued and Stewart grabbed the edge. India were 176 for 5 at lunch, having scored only 46 runs in the session and whatever one thought of the plan (I hate it!) it was working.

Only one run later, Ganguly sliced a catch to his most vulnerable area – backward point – for five, and although the unassuming Laxman crafted 43 not out, India were dispatched for 221. Jones captured a couple of late wickets but, generally, the speed of his bowling did not live up to expectation. Wisely, Hussain decided not to enforce the follow-on but to make use of the pitch while it was still at its best.

Crawley will thank his captain for that. He scored exactly 100 not out to establish his place in the team, but the innings of real quality came from Vaughan, who notched up his second Test century

of the summer at Lord's. There was a questionable moment when, on 86, he was given the benefit of the doubt by the third umpire for a catch behind, but his innings of 100 was full of glorious drives and pulls and included 11 fours. Importantly, both Vaughan and Crawley scored their runs at a rate that enabled Hussain to declare half an hour before lunch on the fourth day with an unassailable lead of 567.

By the close, India had subsided at 232 for 6 and the match was all but over. Jaffer made a patient 53 and Dravid 63, but the middle order was blown away by Giles and Hoggard, who dismissed Tendulkar, bowled for 12 off his pad, Ganguly, a duck and Ratra for one. India lost four wickets for 30 runs and defeat was a formality.

On the final day, however, we caught the first glimpse of Indian resistance. Principally this came from Agarkar, who surprised everyone by scoring his first Test century – 109 not out from 190 balls. Laxman, again, was the only top-order batsman to do himself justice with 74, but White wrapped up the innings in the early afternoon to give England victory by 170 runs.

Fast bowler, Simon Jones, made an impact with the bat in his first Test innings at Lord's.

FIRST TEST – ENGLAND v. INDIA
25–29 July 2002 at Lord's

ENGLAND

	First innings		Second innings	
MA Butcher	c Wasim Jaffer b Kumble	29	lbw b Kumble	18
MP Vaughan	lbw b Zaheer Khan	0	c Wasim Jaffer b Nehra	100
N Hussain (capt)	c Ratra b Agarkar	155	c Ratra b Agarkar	12
GP Thorpe	b Zaheer Khan	4	c Ganguly b Kumble	1
JP Crawley	c Dravid b Sehwag	64	not out	100
*AJ Stewart	lbw b Zaheer Khan	19	(7) st Ratra b Kumble	33
A Flintoff	c Ratra b Agarkar	59	(6) c Tendulkar b Nehra	7
C White	st Ratra b Kumble	53	not out	6
AF Giles	b Nehra	19		
SP Jones	c Dravid b Kumble	44		
MJ Hoggard	not out	10		
Extras	b 11, lb 11, w 2, nb 7	31	b 5, lb 14, nb 5	24
		487	(6 wickets)	301

	First innings				Second innings			
	O	M	R	W	O	M	R	W
Nehra	30	4	101	1	14	1	80	2
Zaheer Khan	36	13	90	3	11	1	41	-
Agarkar	21	3	98	2	11.4	1	53	1
Kumble	42.2	9	128	3	24	1	84	3
Ganguly	3	1	16	-				
Sehwag	10	0	32	1	2	0	10	-
Tendulkar					2	0	14	-

Fall of Wickets
1-0, 2-71, 3-78, 4-223, 5-263, 6-356, 7-357, 8-390, 9-452
1-32, 2-65, 3-76, 4-213, 5-228, 6-287

INDIA

	First innings		Second innings	
Wasim Jaffer	b Hoggard	1	c Hussain b Vaughan	53
V Sehwag	b Giles	84	b Jones	27
R Dravid	c Vaughan b Hoggard	46	b Giles	63
A Nehra	lbw b Flintoff	0	(11) c Thorpe b White	19
SR Tendulkar	c Stewart b White	16	(4) b Hoggard	12
SC Ganguly (capt)	c Vaughan b Flintoff	5	(5) lbw b Hoggard	0
VVS Laxman	not out	43	(6) c Vaughan b Jones	74
*A Ratra	c Stewart b Jones	1	(7) c Butcher b Hoggard	1
AB Agarkar	c Flintoff b Jones	2	(8) not out	109
A Kumble	b White	0	(9) c & b Hoggard	15
Zaheer Khan	c Thorpe b Hoggard	3	(10) c Stewart b White	7
Extras	b 4, lb 8, nb 8	20	b 4, lb 3, w 2, nb 8	17
		221		397

	First innings				Second innings			
	O	M	R	W	O	M	R	W
Hoggard	16.5	4	33	3	24	7	87	4
Flintoff	19	9	22	2	17	2	87	-
Giles	9	1	47	1	9	7	75	1
Jones	21	2	61	2	17	1	68	2
White	16	3	46	2	16.4	2	61	2
Vaughan					6	2	12	1

Fall of Wickets
1-2, 2-128, 3-130, 4-162, 5-168, 6-177, 7-191, 8-196, 9-209
1-61, 2-110, 3-140, 4-140, 5-165, 6-170, 7-296, 8-320, 9-334

Umpires: RE Koertzen & RB Tiffin
Toss: England
Test Debut: SP Jones (England)
Man of the Match: N Hussain

England won by 170 runs

31 July–3 August 2002 at Worcester
Indians 417 for 8 dec. (SR Tendulkar 169, R Dravid 53*)
Worcestershire 200 for 6 (SD Peters 50)
*Match drawn – no play was possible on the
first and second days*

After the loss of the first two days to rain, the Indians were grateful both to a break in the weather at Worcester and to a return to top form by Sachin Tendulkar when the match finally got under way. Coming in to face a hat-trick ball from Gareth Batty, following the off spinner's removal of Virender Sehwag and Wasim Jaffer for bright 40s, Tendulkar was a whisker away from touching a well-disguised arm ball. Thereafter, he looked in no trouble at all as he added a brilliant 169 to his previous three first-class tour scores of three, 16 and 12. He hit 30 fours and his last 69 runs took just 52 balls. Rahul Dravid, not appearing until No. 7, finished up on 53 not out as India reached the close of the scheduled third day on 417 for 8. After an overnight declaration, though, there was more rain and only 54 overs were available to the Indian bowlers as Worcestershire replied with 200 for 6 and the match meandered to a draw.

npower SECOND TEST
8–12 August 2002 at Trent Bridge

Flushed with their success at Lord's, England arrived at Trent Bridge on the crest of a wave. Hussain was being hailed as the greatest captain since Mike Brearley by a section of the media that had yet to understand the full implications of the tactics employed by England ever since the series in India the previous winter. That it requires great discipline and patience on behalf of the bowlers is not disputed, but if this is to be the manner in which every team plays Test cricket in the future, the game is doomed.

It was also an indictment on the theory that England's bowlers were presented with ideal conditions at Trent Bridge where, after India chose to bat, the ball swung prodigiously. Whether it was because Hoggard, in particular, was still 'grooved' (Duncan Fletcher's word, not mine) to propelling the ball well out of the batsman's reach, or if it was merely an off day, we will never know. The fact is that instead of dismissing India for less than 200, the visitors were allowed to reach 357. The highlight was a patient century from Virender Sehwag, his highest Test score. He and Ganguly, who made 68, added 71 after Tendulkar suffered the ignominy of dragging a long hop from Cork onto his stumps for

It was Michael Vaughan's summer. Here he is on his way to 197 at Trent Bridge.

Opposite: Not to be outdone, Rahul Dravid was equally graceful and averaged over 100 in the series.

34. Agarkar maintained his promise with 34 before Harbhajan Singh appeared to play a riotous cameo of 54 from just 37 balls. Steve Harmison, who replaced the injured Jones, picked up three late wickets, while Hoggard, if he is honest, will reflect that his 4 for 105 was not the best performance of his career.

Bad weather was never far away, so England needed to score quickly if they were to put the Indians under pressure. That was the theory: the reality was a remarkable display of positive batting, led by Vaughan, whose Test-best score of 197 came from only 258 balls. In awesome form, Vaughan simply could not be contained and virtually his only blemish – a firm-footed drive – led to his downfall. He was not alone in caning the inadequate Indian attack: Stewart made 87 from just 92 balls, Flintoff's 33 came from 46 and White, who made an explosive 94, was denied a century when Harmison sliced a drive to point for three. England's total of 617 was their highest since July 1990 and gave them a lead of 260 with a day and a quarter left to play. By the close, India had made 99 for 2 with Tendulkar and Dravid at the crease.

The offer of free admission for the final day paid off when virtually a full house gathered in the hope of seeing a Tendulkar century. A narrow majority would have preferred this to have been made in a losing cause, but his innings of 92 was anything but a disappointment. It was the under-used Vaughan who dismissed him – tempting a drive at an off break that turned deliciously and bowled

SUNIL GAVASKAR'S VIEW

Having lost the first Test of the series India were on the back foot and when they arrived at the Trent Bridge ground for the Test they would have been dismayed by the conditions that greeted them. It was a typical English summer day with grey clouds and the threat of rain and the kind of temperature which makes a player want to be more in the dressing room than on the field. Batting first was not going to be easy and so it turned out.

Virender Sehwag, who had narrowly missed a century at Lord's in the first Test, played with admirable discipline in the first two hours before lunch and then let fly a volley of shots that got him to a superb century. The Indian total, however, was not one that would have made the match safe for them and they had to bowl exceptionally well to stay in the game. They were criticized for leaving Harbhajan Singh out of their XI for the first Test, so they brought him in to replace Kumble and persisted with the three-man seam attack. Harbhajan had already played his part with the bat, scoring a breezy 54, but it was his wicket-taking ability that India were looking for. He had to contend with Michael Vaughan, who with superb use of his feet, nullified the turn that Harbhajan was getting. The seam bowlers were what Vaughan faces day in and day out in the county championship so he was not too bothered by them. His range of shots was all round the dial and his positive footwork had to be seen to be believed. He was unlucky to miss his double century by only three runs, but he had given England exactly what they wanted.

Stewart batted well again and England's balance is great simply because they have in him a batsman of such good quality coming in at a position where the second new ball can be tackled and scored from. The England declaration may have been delayed because of the strong Indian batting line-up and England did not want to have a situation similar to the one Australia faced in Calcutta in 2001. There, Laxman played a superb innings and his partnership with the unsung Dravid ensured a turnaround that will forever be a golden chapter in Indian cricket history.

It was Dravid who set the tone for the second innings here. He was back to the No. 3 position which he had vacated temporarily to accommodate the then in-form Laxman, but with the opening position shaky, India wanted a player with a solid technique and a cool temperament to protect its strokeplayers. Dravid was just the man they wanted and he did everything that was asked of him. He played the moving ball with certainty and confidence and blunted the English

attack for Tendulkar and Ganguly to come out and play their shots. He reached a century while Tendulkar and Ganguly narrowly missed theirs, but the match was saved by the determination shown by the young debutant Parthiv Patel. He hung in there, and ensured that England did not sneak in just as they had done earlier in the summer against Sri Lanka at Old Trafford.

England have themselves to blame for not going 2–0 up in the series. Their attitude was a bit too cautious and Hussain's field placings were more for effect than a result. The Indians were able to pick boundaries regularly and keep the score ticking at a healthy rate. It was clear that, by now, India had shrugged off the one-day mentality while batting which had cost them the first Test and were now prepared to wait for the scoring opportunity. Though their batting had come good, their bowlers were still struggling to dismiss England, and that would have been their prime area for concern as they approached the remaining two Tests.

SECOND TEST – ENGLAND v. INDIA
8–12 August 2002 at Trent Bridge

INDIA

	First innings		Second innings	
Wasim Jaffer	b Hoggard	0	(2) lbw b Flintoff	5
V Sehwag	b White	106	(1) lbw b Hoggard	0
R Dravid	c Key b Hoggard	13	lbw b Cork	115
SR Tendulkar	b Cork	34	b Vaughan	92
SC Ganguly (capt)	c Stewart b Hoggard	68	b Harmison	99
VVS Laxman	c Key b Flintoff	22	c White b Cork	14
AB Agarkar	c Butcher b Harmison	34	lbw b Vaughan	32
*PA Patel	c Flintoff b Harmison	0	not out	19
Harbhajan Singh	c Hussain b Harmison	54	b Harmison	1
Zaheer Khan	not out	14	not out	14
A Nehra	c Stewart b Hoggard	0		
Extras	b 1, lb 8, w 2, nb 1	12	b 5, lb 12, w 4, nb 12	33
		357	**(8 wickets dec.)**	**424**

	First innings				Second innings			
	O	M	R	W	O	M	R	W
Hoggard	35.1	10	105	4	23	0	109	1
Cork	11	3	45	1	12	1	54	2
Harmison	20	7	57	3	29	5	63	2
Flintoff	27	6	85	1	22	2	95	1
White	8	0	56	1	8	2	15	-
Vaughan					21	5	71	2

Fall of Wickets
1-6, 2-34, 3-108, 4-179, 5-218, 6-285, 7-287, 8-295, 9-356
1-0, 2-11, 3-174, 4-309, 5-339, 6-378, 7-395, 8-396

ENGLAND

	First innings	
RWT Key	b Nehra	17
MP Vaughan	c Patel b Agarkar	197
MA Butcher	c Dravid b Harbhajan Singh	53
N Hussain (capt)	c Patel b Harbhajan Singh	3
JP Crawley	c Wasim Jaffer b Zaheer Khan	22
*AJ Stewart	b Zaheer Khan	87
A Flintoff	b Zaheer Khan	33
C White	not out	94
DG Cork	c Wasim Jaffer b Harbhajan Singh	31
MJ Hoggard	c Dravid b Nehra	32
SJ Harmison	c Wasim Jaffer b Agarkar	3
Extras	b 9, lb 17, w 4, nb 15	45
		617

	First innings			
	O	M	R	W
Nehra	32	3	138	2
Zaheer Khan	26	4	110	3
Agarkar	24.5	3	93	2
Harbhajan Singh	45	3	175	3
Ganguly	5	0	42	-
Tendulkar	6	0	15	-
Sehwag	6	1	18	-

Fall of Wickets
1-56, 2-221, 3-228, 4-272, 5-335, 6-432, 7-433, 8-493, 9-596

Umpires: RE Koertzen & RB Tiffin
Toss: India
Test Debut: SJ Harmison, RWT Key (England) and PA Patel (India)
Man of the Match: MP Vaughan

Match drawn

Opposite: Andrew Flintoff reached 33 at Trent Bridge, but Zaheer Khan was deceptively fast.

him through the gate. Dravid, at least, completed his century before falling lbw to Cork for 115, and although it was possible to portray the final day as being a race against time, the truth was that India always seemed likely to save the match. Ganguly played a heroic innings before falling to Harmison for 99 and the final resistance was provided by the diminutive wicketkeeper, Parthiv Patel, who battled away for 82 minutes. The manner in which he bravely withstood everything England could throw at him spectacularly belied his tender age of 17, and as India left the field having deserved their draw, there was a widespread belief that the momentum in the series had swung back to the visitors, despite England's 1–0 advantage.

14–17 August 2002 at Chelmsford
Indians 516 (SS Das 250, SC Ganguly 74) and 327 for 6 dec. (V Sehwag 142, SB Bangar 74)
Essex 279 (DDJ Robinson 59, A Flower 59, Harbhajan Singh 7 for 83) and 186 for 3 (RS Clinton 53)
Match drawn

Opener Shiv Sunder Das made as determined a bid for a Test match call-up as there has ever been in a tourist fixture – he scored 250 from 380 balls in eight-and-three-quarter hours during the Indians' draw with Essex at Chelmsford. Das struck four sixes and 32 fours and was last out in an Indian first-innings total of 516. Essex, in reply, were bowled out for 279, with Darren Robinson and Andy Flower both contributing 59 and Harbhajan Singh announcing he had signed for Lancashire for the 2003 season after picking up 7 for 83. There then followed an explosive 142 off just 156 balls by Virender Sehwag, including five sixes and 18 fours, before the Indians declared their second innings on 327 for 6. In the 56 overs that remained Essex scored 186 for 3, with Richard Clinton reaching 53 and the promising 17-year-old Ravinder Bopara finishing on 47 not out.

npower THIRD TEST
22–26 August 2002 at Headingley

It is not often that visiting teams from the subcontinent, traditionally armed with weak seam attacks, take on England at their own game at Headingley and come out on top. Yet Saurav Ganguly's team managed to level the series by utterly dominating England who, once again, squandered ideal bowling conditions.

During the first hour of the opening morning, it

seemed likely that we would have a three- or four-day Test match on our hands. The ball not only swung and seamed, but bounced noticeably more than is usual on this ground. Alec Stewart was regularly collecting the ball above his head but, far too often, he was also diving about to both his left and right. England's bowling was as wayward and impotent as it can ever have been and rather than being dispatched for 170, India managed to score an unbelievable 628 for 8 declared!

Andy Caddick, restored after injury, had a few arrogant comments to make about the efforts of the youngsters who had replaced him in the interim, but his performance bordered on the pathetic. Labouring in to bowl, he barely made the second new ball carry to the wicketkeeper. It seems that we can no longer trust county cricket to give us a fair indication either of a bowler's fitness or his form. Caddick had 'taken wickets for Somerset' recently to justify his recall to the Test team, but on this evidence, that is simply not enough. The same could also be said of Dominic Cork, who was selected this summer because he was county cricket's leading

Sachin Tendulkar was in rampant form at Headingley: the ground he calls his second home.

SUNIL GAVASKAR'S VIEW

It was extremely courageous on Saurav Ganguly's part to have opted to bat first in conditions that so suited the English bowlers. There was grass on the pitch, it was overcast and cold and the ball did everything. The problem for England was that their bowlers did not bowl at the stumps, so India were able to survive and then score enough runs to put England under pressure. England's tactics in the first Test were to bowl wide of the stumps, deny India scoring opportunities and frustrate them into playing reckless shots. It worked then because India were still in the one-day mindset, but by the end of the second Test they had shown that they were now prepared to wait for the scoring chance.

India also included both the spinners and brought in Sanjay Bangar who is a hard-working cricketer who values the India cap and would not give his wicket away. It was this stubborn approach – and plenty of courage and application – that saw Bangar and Dravid take some nasty blows on the body and on the gloves but still get right behind the line of the ball to thwart England's attempts to break through. It may not have been exciting stuff for those brought up on a diet of one-day cricket, but it was just what the connoisseurs wanted. The one-day followers got their wish the next day as Tendulkar and Ganguly played some exhilarating cricket to take India to a 600-plus total. Their path was made easy by the determination and application of the Bangar-Dravid partnership and they fully capitalized on the easier conditions and tired bowling with an assault, in some pretty poor light, that was electrifying.

India's bowlers used the conditions well and, with Bangar chipping in with the ball, England were in trouble. Vaughan batted well again, but he was unable to capitalize on a missed catch and was out on the very next ball he played.

Nasser Hussain's fighting second innings of 110 is ended by Sehwag's catch at short leg.

Stewart once again showed how useful he was down the order, but Flintoff disappointed. Playing him when he was not fully fit was a risk that did not work. Not only was he not able to bowl at full speed, his body language showed he was a bit nervous, too. No wonder he got a pair.

The England captain did his best to take the fight to India with some belligerent batting after the openers had been sent back early and he got help from his most experienced player, Stewart. Curiously, Anil Kumble – who has won many matches for India in India – has never been part of an India team to win a Test overseas. Here, it was his bowling that got both Hussain and Stewart out, and there was little resistance after that. Before lunch on the final day, India had wrapped up the match and levelled the series. It was truly a team effort with just about everybody contributing something with the bat or the ball or with a special effort on the field – like Sehwag's catch to get rid of Hussain. It was just the kind of performance to give hopes to the Indian cricket followers that the drought of an overseas Test series win was about to end at The Oval.

wicket-taker. The gulf between county cricket and Test cricket widens alarmingly every year.

The foundation for India's colossal score was a brave partnership on the first day of 170 between Sanjay Bangar – who had been promoted to open the innings – and Rahul Dravid. Together, they took the bruises phlegmatically and, in showing excellent judgement outside the off stump, hardly played at a ball that was not perfectly directed. And there were not many of those! Bangar was eventually caught down the legside for a hard-fought 68 from 236 balls: it was a study of patience and determination, but any hopes England might have harboured of clawing their way back into the game were snuffed out by Dravid and Tendulkar.

Dravid's resistance lasted into the second afternoon, after more than seven hours at the crease. He and Tendulkar had added 150 when, uncharacteristically, Dravid advanced down the pitch to Giles and was stumped by Stewart. India

were already in a commanding position at 335 for 3, but this set the scene for some remarkable hitting between tea and the close of play by Tendulkar and Ganguly, in particular. In 32 overs, 163 runs were added. The third new ball disappeared for 96 off 11 overs, and sailed out of the ground on six occasions! It was brilliant batting which completely battered England's hapless attack into submission and the fireworks only ended when Ganguly was bowled by Tudor for 128 from 167 balls. At the close of the second day, India were 584 for 4 – a scoreline that barely seemed credible, and Tendulkar was only 15 runs away from a double century.

The following morning was a further comedy of errors as England compounded their woes by dropping everything in sight. Key put down two, Hoggard and Crawley one apiece. In 40 minutes, 44

A rare defensive stroke by Saurav Ganguly during his entertaining innings of 128.

THIRD TEST – ENGLAND v. INDIA
22–26 August 2002 at Headingley

INDIA

	First innings	
SB Bangar	c Stewart b Flintoff	68
V Sehwag	c Flintoff b Hoggard	8
R Dravid	st Stewart b Giles	148
SR Tendulkar	lbw b Caddick	193
SC Ganguly (capt)	b Tudor	128
VVS Laxman	c Hussain b Tudor	6
AB Agarkar	b Caddick	2
*PA Patel	not out	7
Harbhajan Singh	c Hoggard b Caddick	18
A Kumble		
Zaheer Khan		
Extras	b 14, lb 13, w 5, nb 18	50
	(8 wickets dec.)	**628**

	O	M	R	W
Hoggard	36	12	102	1
Caddick	40.1	5	150	3
Tudor	36	10	146	2
Flintoff	27	6	68	1
Giles	39	3	134	1
Butcher	1	1	-	-
Vaughan	1	0	1	-

Fall of Wickets
1-15, 2-185, 3-335, 4-584, 5-596, 6-602, 7-604, 8-628

ENGLAND

	First innings		Second innings	
RWT Key	c Laxman b Zaheer Khan	30	lbw b Kumble	34
MP Vaughan	c Sehwag b Agarkar	61	lbw b Agarkar	15
MA Butcher	lbw b Kumble	16	c Dravid b Bangar	42
N Hussain (capt)	lbw b Zaheer Khan	25	c Sehwag b Kumble	110
JP Crawley	c Laxman b Harbhajan Singh	13	c Sehwag b Bangar	12
*AJ Stewart	not out	78	c Dravid b Kumble	47
A Flintoff	lbw b Harbhajan Singh	0	c Dravid b Zaheer Khan	0
AJ Tudor	c Sehwag b Agarkar	1	c Sehwag b Harbhajan Singh	21
AF Giles	lbw b Kumble	25	run out (Ganguly/Harbhajan Singh)	10
AR Caddick	b Harbhajan Singh	1	c Ganguly b Kumble	3
MJ Hoggard	c Sehwag b Kumble	0	not out	1
Extras	b 1, lb 12, nb 10	23	b 3, lb 5, nb 6	14
		273		**309**

	First innings				Second innings			
	O	M	R	W	O	M	R	W
Zaheer Khan	19	3	59	2	22	7	63	1
Agarkar	15	4	59	2	18	5	59	1
Bangar	4	1	9	-	13	2	54	2
Kumble	33	8	93	3	29.5	12	66	4
Harbhajan Singh	18	6	40	3	27	7	56	1
Sehwag					1	0	3	-

Fall of Wickets
1-67, 2-109, 3-130, 4-140, 5-164, 6-164, 7-185, 8-255, 9-258
1-28, 2-76, 3-116, 4-148, 5-265, 6-267, 7-267, 8-299, 9-307

Umpires: EAR de Silva & DL Orchard
Toss: India
Man of the Match: R Dravid

India won by an innings & 46 runs

runs were added for the loss of four wickets, including Tendulkar's for 193 as he fell lbw to Caddick who picked up three of the four wickets to give him 3 for 150 – figures that flattered him.

England needed the small matter of 429 to avoid the follow-on and it was no surprise they fell 156 runs short in the fourth over of the fourth day. Stewart, dropped first ball, made a fighting 78 not out, but having reached 130 for 2, England lost five wickets for 55 runs as Harbhajan and Kumble found some spin. Almost exactly a day later, the game was over amid joyous scenes. A large contingent of Indian supporters packed the Western Stand in the certain knowledge of seeing their team win, and they did not have to wait long. Hussain reached a courageous century after being dropped on 47. His 110 contained 18 fours and a six, but it really was only delaying the inevitable. Stewart, again, reminded his critics that he still has the stamina to take on the Australians in the winter by making 47, but Kumble wrapped it up, taking his fourth wicket and India's players – led by Ganguly – ran from the field clutching the stumps for a well-deserved celebration. One felt after Trent Bridge that the force was with India. With the deciding Test to play at The Oval the following week, there was absolutely no doubting it now.

28–30 August 2002 at Derby
Indians 445 for 8 dec. (A Ratra 101*, VVS Laxman 75) and 182 for 3 dec. (V Sehwag 104, SS Das 52)
Derbyshire 358 (RM Khan 91, SD Stubbings 66, DR Hewson 66)
Match drawn

Rawait Khan, a 20-year-old batsman in only his second first-class game, scored 91 for Derbyshire in their drawn three-day match against the Indian tourists. Steve Stubbings and Dominic Hewson both hit 66s as Derbyshire replied with 358 to an Indian first-innings total of 445 for 8 declared. Ajay Ratra had reached 101 not out for the touring team, and VVS Laxman stroked 75, and both sides seemed to regard the match simply in terms of practice. The final afternoon, however, was enlivened by Virender Sehwag's 97-ball 104 as the Indians made 182 for 3 declared in their second innings.

npower FOURTH TEST
5–9 September 2002 at The Oval

With too much apparently at stake, the final Test of the series – and the summer – was a huge

disappointment. Neither team seemed prepared to take the risk that might have earned victory, and this was particularly so of England, who restricted India to 283 for 4 in their first innings – still 232 runs behind England's 515. A new ball was available, but not taken, and rather than at least giving the impression of chasing a win, the bowling attack was modelled on the defensive approach of 'hiding the ball' that was employed in the first Test at Lord's.

In defence of the players, the pitch was extremely flat. Orders had been issued from the England management instructing Paul Brind, the groundsman at The Oval, not to do anything to encourage India's spinners. Brind, therefore, ensured the pitch was damp and held together and the batsmen prospered as a result.

The toss always seemed more important for England to win than India, in that Hussain did not

Opposite: Another century for Michael Vaughan but, again, he narrowly failed to reach 200.

In a summer packed full of runs, Dravid's 217 at The Oval was probably the highlight.

want to be subjected to batting last on the wearing strip. Ganguly called incorrectly, Hussain chose to bat first, and by the close of the first day, England – on 336 for 2 – had already done much to ensure that they could not lose the game. Once again, it was Michael Vaughan who dominated the proceedings, scoring his fourth century of the summer, and his third in this series. He has gone from strength to strength this season, feeding on his rapidly growing confidence, and his opening partnership with Trescothick, who scored 57, is now the most solid and trustworthy feature of England's cricket.

Mark Butcher put on 174 with Vaughan before falling in rather curious circumstances – caught at slip off the back of the bat as he aimed a sweep at Harbhajan. Vaughan had reached 182 by the end of the day and although he infuriated the media and the sponsors by declining to appear at a press conference that evening, he must have been

Sachin Tendulkar on his way to another half-century as India's first innings fell only seven runs short of England's.

with seven fingers to the press box when he reached his half-century. But it was his bowling for which he had been criticized, and Cork was one of only two players in this team – Tudor being the other – who was not chosen for the Ashes tour.

England started well in the field. Sehwag was promptly caught at slip off Caddick for 12 and, with the score on 87, Bangar nicked Hoggard to Butcher for 21. India were still 229 runs away from saving the follow-on, and English hopes were high. Yet again, however, they were dashed by Dravid. He added 91 with Tendulkar before Caddick surprised Tendulkar with a low full toss and trapped him lbw for 54, and Ganguly scored 51, despite England's monotonous short-pitched barrage. This was the moment that England might have struck, but the new ball was ignored for 20 overs while Cork, in particular, did little more than hurl the ball half way down the pitch and Giles aimed wide of the leg stump. The crowd was so disappointed at the end of the third day that a chorus of boos and wolf-whistles rang out across The Oval and many vowed never to return.

Dravid's resistance, and patience, lasted long into the fourth afternoon. He reached his second double century in Test cricket and broke the record for the number of runs scored by an Indian batsman in a Test series against England. Then, with his average neatly standing at exactly 100, and having batted for ten-and-a-half hours, he was horribly run out by Ratra for 217.

Laxman's 40 took India to within seven runs of England, but by the time Trescothick and Vaughan had rattled up a further 114 before the close of the fourth day, the match was going nowhere. Heavy rain washed out the final day altogether, and neither team seemed sorry to end the series all square.

anticipating reaching the double century that had eluded him at Trent Bridge. Cruelly, however, he fell just five runs short when he edged a fine delivery from Zaheer Khan to Ratra. An innings of 197 at Trent Bridge, 195 here – one day he is certain to reach his milestone.

England lost their way on the second day and failed to reach the total that the contributions from Vaughan, Butcher and Trescothick deserved. They added only 179 runs for the loss of eight wickets, and there seemed to be a worrying lack of direction. Cork, batting at No. 7 in place of the injured Flintoff, scored 52 and 'did a Hussain' in gesturing

FOURTH TEST – ENGLAND v. INDIA
5–9 September 2002 at The Oval

ENGLAND

	First innings		Second innings	
ME Trescothick	c Bangar b Zaheer Khan	57	not out	58
MP Vaughan	c Ratra b Zaheer Khan	195	not out	47
MA Butcher	c Dravid b Harbhajan Singh	54		
JP Crawley	lbw b Bangar	26		
N Hussain (capt)	c Laxman b Bangar	10		
*AJ Stewart	c Ratra b Harbhajan Singh	23		
DG Cork	lbw b Harbhajan Singh	52		
AJ Tudor	c Dravid b Harbhajan Singh	2		
AF Giles	b Dravid b Kumble	31		
AR Caddick	not out	14		
MJ Hoggard	lbw b Harbhajan Singh	0		
Extras	b 12, lb 31, w 1, nb 7	51	b 4, nb 5	9
		515	**(0 wickets)**	**114**

	First innings				Second innings			
	O	M	R	W	O	M	R	W
Zaheer Khan	28	4	83	2	5	0	37	–
Agarkar	24	4	111	–	4	0	15	–
Bangar	24	8	48	2	2	0	6	–
Harbhajan Singh	38.4	6	115	5	7	1	24	–
Kumble	35	11	105	1	10	2	28	–
Ganguly	4	1	6	–				
Tendulkar	2	0	4	–				

Fall of Wickets
1-98, 2-272, 3-349, 4-367, 5-372, 6-434, 7-446, 8-477, 9-514

INDIA

	First innings	
SB Bangar	c Butcher b Hoggard	21
V Sehwag	c Cork b Caddick	12
R Dravid	run out (Giles/Stewart)	217
SR Tendulkar	lbw b Caddick	54
SC Ganguly (capt)	c Stewart b Cork	51
VVS Laxman	c Giles b Caddick	40
AB Agarkar	b Vaughan	31
*A Ratra	c Butcher b Caddick	8
A Kumble	c Hussain b Giles	7
Harbhajan Singh	b Giles	17
Zaheer Khan	not out	6
Extras	b 10, lb 6, nb 28	44
		508

	First innings			
	O	M	R	W
Hoggard	25	2	97	1
Caddick	43	11	114	4
Giles	49	12	98	2
Tudor	19	2	80	–
Cork	22	5	67	1
Vaughan	12	1	36	1

Fall of Wickets
1-18, 2-87, 3-178, 4-283, 5-396, 6-465, 7-473, 8-477, 9-493

Umpires: DL Orchard & EAR de Silva
Toss: England
Man of the Match: R Dravid
Men of the Series: MP Vaughan and R Dravid

Match drawn

TEST MATCH AVERAGES
England v. India

ENGLAND

Batting	M	Inns	NO	HS	Runs	Av	100	50	c/st
C White	2	3	2	94*	153	153.00	–	2	1
MP Vaughan	4	7	1	197	615	102.50	3	1	3
AJ Stewart	4	6	1	87	287	57.40	–	2	7/1
N Hussain	4	6	0	155	315	52.50	2	–	4
JP Crawley	4	6	1	100*	237	47.40	1	1	–
MA Butcher	4	6	0	54	212	35.33	–	2	4
RWT Key	2	3	0	34	81	27.00	–	–	2
AF Giles	3	4	0	31	85	21.25	–	–	1
A Flintoff	3	5	0	59	99	19.80	–	1	3
MJ Hoggard	4	5	2	32	43	14.33	–	–	2
AR Caddick	2	3	1	14*	18	9.00	–	–	–
AJ Tudor	2	3	0	21	24	8.00	–	–	–

Also batted in two Tests: DG Cork 31, 52 (1 ct)
Also batted in one Test: SJ Harmison 3; SP Jones 44; GP Thorpe 4, 1 (2 ct)
ME Trescothick 57, 58*

Bowling	Overs	Mds	Runs	Wkts	Av	Best	10m	5/inn
SJ Harmison	49	12	120	5	24.00	3-57	–	–
C White	48.4	7	178	5	35.60	2-46	–	–
AR Caddick	83.1	16	264	7	37.71	4-114	–	–
MJ Hoggard	160	35	533	14	38.07	4-87	–	–
AF Giles	126	23	354	5	70.80	2-98	–	–
A Flintoff	112	25	357	5	71.40	2-22	–	–

Also bowled: MA Butcher 1-1-0-0; DG Cork 45-9-166-4; SP Jones 38-3-129-4;
AJ Tudor 55-12-226-2; MP Vaughan 40-8-120-4

INDIA

Batting	M	Inns	NO	HS	Runs	Av	100	50	c/st
R Dravid	4	6	0	217	602	100.33	3	1	10
SR Tendulkar	4	6	0	193	401	66.83	1	2	1
SC Ganguly	4	6	0	128	351	58.50	1	3	2
AB Agarkar	4	6	1	109*	210	42.00	1	–	–
VVS Laxman	4	6	1	74	199	39.80	–	1	3
V Sehwag	4	6	0	106	237	39.50	1	1	6
PA Patel	2	3	2	19*	26	26.00	–	–	2/-
Harbhajan Singh	3	4	0	54	90	22.50	–	1	–
Zaheer Khan	4	5	3	14*	44	22.00	–	–	–
Wasim Jaffer	2	4	0	53	59	14.75	–	1	5
A Kumble	3	3	0	15	22	7.33	–	–	–
A Nehra	2	3	0	19	19	6.33	–	–	–
A Ratra	2	3	0	8	10	3.33	–	–	5/2

Also batted in two Tests: SB Bangar 68, 21 (1 ct)

Bowling	Overs	Mds	Runs	Wkts	Av	Best	10m	5/inn
Harbhajan Singh	135.4	23	410	12	34.16	5-115	–	1
A Kumble	174.1	42	504	14	36.00	4-66	–	–
Zaheer Khan	147	32	483	11	43.90	3-90	–	–
AB Agarkar	118.3	20	488	8	61.00	2-59	–	–
A Nehra	76	8	319	5	63.80	2-80	–	–

Also bowled: SB Bangar 43-11-117-4; SC Ganguly 12-2-64-0; V Sehwag 19-1-63-1;
SR Tendulkar 10-0-33-0

Next page: Rahul Dravid enjoys the ovation from the packed Oval crowd as he reaches his third century of the series.

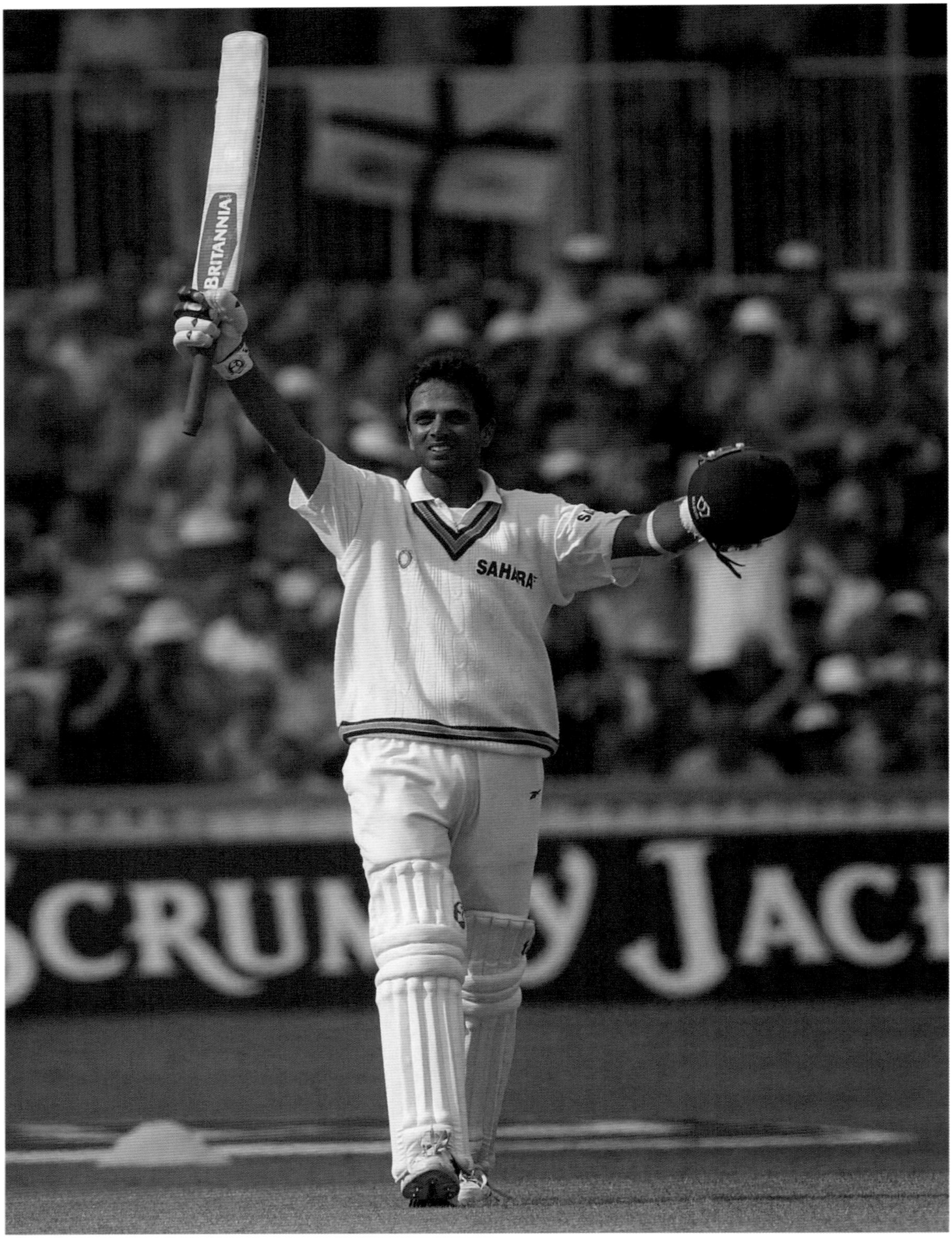
BRITANNIA
SAHARA
SCRUM
JAC

SUNIL GAVASKAR'S VIEW

All talk before the last Test began was about the contracts that the ICC had asked the Indian players to sign through their parent body, the BCCI. The rumblings regarding this issue had been there even before and during the previous Test match at Headingley, but the Indians had admirably kept cool and never lost their focus on the game. Now, though, it had become a bigger row because the ICC Champions Trophy was due to start within a couple of days of the end of The Oval Test. The Indian players were still not prepared to put their signatures on the dotted line. It was not the kind of 'off-the-field' tension or pressure that a side wanting to win a series would have asked for. India also needed to win the toss so its two spinners could make use of a wearing wicket on the last two days. But it was Hussain who got the choice after Ganguly guessed wrongly and, to rub salt in their wounds, Trescothick and Vaughan gave the home side a rousing start. Vaughan carried on to get close to a double century and, at the end of the day's play, England were in the driver's seat with the score on 336 for 2.

India pulled back the game somewhat the next morning with Bangar picking up two crucial wickets after Zaheer Khan had produced a peach of a delivery to deny Vaughan his double hundred. Not often is a batsman said to be nervous in the 190s, but having got out twice in the series in that region, Vaughan was jocularly referred to in that manner. Once again his sparkling batting had given England a great chance to put pressure on India, but it was wasted by some careless batting by the others. Still, 515 is a good score to try and win a game.

Hussain, however, was negative in his thinking and, instead of having fielders in catching positions, he had them saving runs which did not give his bowlers any confidence. Dravid, who like Vaughan was having a dream summer, kept going on and on. Tendulkar looked set to celebrate his 100th Test with a hundred, but was trapped leg before by a good yorker from Caddick – who made up for his disappointing showing at Leeds by bowling better and looking much more threatening. Dravid was out in the only manner possible, run out when Ratra called him for a non-existent run after a misfield, and India made the mistake of dragging on its innings when they should have declared in the hot sun. The flatness of the pitch became evident when Trescothick and Vaughan got off to a good start again. Both openers used the sweep shot especially well against the spinners, and Harbhajan Singh and Anil Kumble were thrown completely off track. Once they had got off to that start, a draw was the only possible result and a boring last day was in store for all concerned. Fortunately the rain came and we were spared!

So, the series was drawn and India returned home with a Test series win outside the subcontinent still an unattained goal. They had done enough, though, to show that they were combining well and if they could get a couple of wicket-taking bowlers they would win more matches. I must say that England were far too defensive, and seemed merely content not to be beaten. Perhaps injuries, which had robbed them of key players, were the reason behind this defensiveness. Like the Indians, their batting looks stronger than their bowling, which explains why this series was dominated by the batsmen and flat pitches.

Michael Vaughan displays his technique against spin that so impressed the Indian tourists.

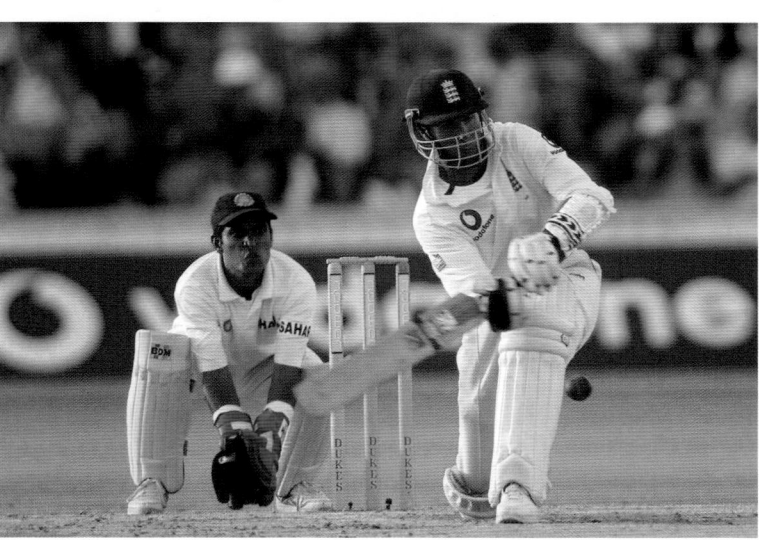

ENGLISH DOMESTIC SEASON INTRODUCTION
By Mark Baldwin

After three seasons of a two-division county championship, it is possible to start to make a judgment about it. Has it raised the standard of first-class domestic play, and has it made for a better breeding ground for the development of the England Test match cricketer?

Interestingly, one person who has already made up his mind about those questions is David Morgan, the new chairman of the England and Wales Cricket Board in succession to Lord MacLaurin.

Morgan, previously deputy chairman to MacLaurin and also a former chairman of Glamorgan, starts his initial two-year stint as head of the ECB believing that a return to a one-division championship is in the best interests of English cricket.

One of his first initiatives as ECB chairman, after taking over officially from MacLaurin on 1 January 2003, will be to launch a full and frank review of all the considerable changes to the structure of the domestic game during the past ten years. It promises to spark a lively debate.

Morgan says he is 'not convinced that two divisions are best for the development of England cricketers', nor that it has significantly raised the playing standards. He does not like the yo-yo effect of a three-up, three-down situation in two divisions of nine teams, and also feels that commercial interests are not best served by denying counties the opportunity to play all 17 other counties during the summer.

Local derbies (for instance Yorkshire v. Lancashire next season, Warwickshire v. Worcestershire last year and next, and Somerset v. Gloucestershire last summer) have been one of the main casualties of the switch to two divisions. Morgan also wants, as the result of the review, a better-organized and better-structured domestic fixture list.

More damaging, however, to the credibility of the two-division system is that a county as strong as Yorkshire (the 2001 champions) can suddenly find themselves relegated and outside of the so-called elite. Yorkshire, after a season which started badly but in which they were also heavily punished for ill-timed injuries and the mass unavailability of their England players, can in no way be ranked among the bottom nine teams in the land in terms of playing strength, but, in this current crazy set-up, the Cheltenham and Gloucester Trophy winners will have to play as 'second-class' citizens next summer.

Actually, and bizarrely, the cricket in Division Two next summer might just be of a higher standard when you look at the calibre of cricketers who will not get the chance to play for the championship title itself. Overseas stars like Shane Warne, Darren Lehmann, Mike Hussey and Andy Bichel, England squad men like Darren Gough, Michael Vaughan, Craig White, Matthew Hoggard, Richard Dawson, Marcus Trescothick, Andy Caddick, John Crawley, Dominic Cork, Simon Jones and Steve Harmison, and other international-class players such as Graeme Hick, Robert Croft and Chris Silverwood will all – officially, at least – be second-raters next year.

Can you imagine it if half the England soccer team, and a high number of the best overseas internationals, played not in the Premiership but in the Nationwide League? Or, more to the point, if English soccer administrators decided to split the Premiership in two so that there was a good chance that, say, Everton did not play Liverpool, Manchester City did not play United, Newcastle did not play Sunderland, and Arsenal might not even play Spurs?

The ECB, however, is still intent on marketing its 18 first-class counties as '18 centres of excellence', with each county being scheduled to have an operational academy (feeding the best of the talent from around the country into the National Academy) by next September. Logically, then, there has to be an equal, 18-county league – with each county knowing that, every April, it can become champions.

What Morgan, for one, recognizes is the destructive side of two divisions, in terms of what happens both on and off the field. Players, of course, like the cut and thrust of promotion and relegation (and coaches like the bonus of being able to claim that coming tenth, 11th or 12th in the pecking order represents a stunning success). But administrators are paid to see the wider picture and to realize that stimulating competition can also be achieved in an alternative structure – whether it be a single division with vastly increased prize-money impacting all the way down the table, or with a conference system which concludes with a series of play-off matches to determine the top positions.

If, for instance, every county were required to leave 'on deposit' a percentage (say £200,000) of the £1.2 million each receives from the ECB annually, as its share of the central income from international revenues, then the county championship could feature a prize fund (with sponsorship) of more than £4 million. You could have £1 million on offer to the champions, with a sliding scale down to £10,000 for the wooden spoonists. The top nine finishers would, in effect, make money – but the bottom nine would lose differing amounts of their original 'entrance fee'. Would that not give the championship 'cut and thrust'? Would not that help to generate 'tougher' cricket?

It is worth remembering, moreover, in the current climate, that the 2002 champions Surrey – the worthiest of winners, too, by a margin of more than 40 points – almost got stuck in the relegation mire themselves in 2001, only escaping when they beat a well below-strength Yorkshire (who had already been crowned champions) in a controversial penultimate match.

The fortunes of Essex and Derbyshire last summer also illustrate that one bad season does not necessarily, in cricket, mean that a county should be judged as down-and-outs. Essex, relegated from Division One of the championship in 2001 amid much dressing room acrimony, bounced back under Graham Gooch to enjoy a double promotion season and become one of only three counties (Surrey and Warwickshire being the others) to win more than £100,000 in prize money.

Derbyshire, bottom of both the Division Two championship and one-day league in 2001, and cruelly rubbished by commentators who should know better, mounted a serious promotion challenge in both competitions to cock a considerable snook at those critics.

The biggest disappointment of 2002 were Somerset, relegated from the top flights of the championship and one-day league, while Durham deserve encouragement (and not Derbyshire-style writing off) for sticking to a youth policy in the wake of a series of defeats that were much more a result of a debilitating catalogue of injuries to senior players like Martin Love, Paul Collingwood and Simon Brown.

Outside the ranks of the high-profile performers, there were memorable summers for players such as Ian Ward, Darren Robinson, Darren Maddy, Kevin Dean, Martin Saggers, Andy Harris, Amjad Khan and Kabir Ali. Exciting young players to emerge this past season include James Anderson, Jim Troughton, Ed Joyce and Rikki Clarke. Good independent judges like Steve Waugh, who played the final five weeks of the season with Kent, concluded (as did Warne and Glenn McGrath in their Division Two 2000 seasons) that the standard of English domestic cricket is very similar to that of Australia.

For man of the summer, though, there is no need to look any further than Adam Hollioake, the Surrey captain. After delaying his return to county cricket following the tragic death of his younger brother Ben, he threw himself into leading a campaign which resulted in the championship title and promotion from the Norwich Union League's Division Two. Not only that, he scored 738 runs from his nine championship appearances at an average of 67 and at almost a run a ball, besides making a sizeable all-round contribution to Surrey's one-day success. In terms of talent, performance and character, Surrey and Hollioake really have set a benchmark for others to follow.

Mark Baldwin, a former cricket correspondent of the Press Association, has written on cricket for The Times *and* The Cricketer *for the past four years.*

Surrey may have been deserving winners of this year's county championship, but does a two-tier system best serve the interests of the English game?

FRIZZELL COUNTY CHAMPIONSHIP
By Mark Baldwin

ROUND ONE: 19–22 APRIL 2002

Division One

at The Oval
Surrey 575 for 8 dec. (126 overs) (AD Brown 177,
N Shahid 150, AJ Stewart 99, MR Ramprakash 56) and
116 for 0 (MA Butcher 68*)
Sussex 308 (80.2 overs) (MH Yardy 93) and (following
on) 379 (CJ Adams 114, PA Cottey 114)
Surrey won by ten wickets
Surrey 19.75 pts, Sussex 5 pts (Surrey had 0.25 pt
deducted for a slow over rate)

at Old Trafford
Leicestershire 385 (99.5 overs) (VJ Wells 74,
DI Stevens 74, MG Bevan 66, ND Burns 51,
PAF DeFreitas 51) and 277 (DL Maddy 66, ND Burns 62,
KW Hogg 5 for 48)
Lancashire 275 (66.3 overs) (AJ Swann 80, GD Lloyd
51, PAJ DeFreitas 6 for 101) and
388 for 9 (GD Lloyd 73, SG Law 69, MJ Chilton 53)
Lancashire won by one wicket
Lancashire 17 pts, Leicestershire 6 pts (Leicestershire
had 1 pt deducted for a slow over rate)

at Canterbury
Kent 577 for 7 dec. (144 overs) (RWT Key 160,
DP Fulton 98, A Symonds 89, ET Smith 52,
PA Nixon 52, MM Patel 50*) and 163 for 4 dec.
Hampshire 671 (195 overs)
(JP Crawley 272, NC Johnson 117)
Match drawn
Kent 10 pts, Hampshire 11 pts

With champions Yorkshire not involved in the first
round of matches, chief rivals Surrey took advantage
of lovely early-season weather to get off to a flier
with a ten-wicket trouncing of newly-promoted
Sussex at The Oval.

The first day of the match saw Surrey announce
their intentions to repeat their championship
successes of 1999 and 2000: they piled up 461 for 4
from 104 overs with confident innings of 56 from
Mark Ramprakash and 99 from Alec Stewart
offsetting the early loss of both openers, and then an
explosive partnership between Alistair Brown and
Nadeem Shahid taking the game away from the
visitors. The match began with both teams, plus
umpires and ECB representatives, lining up on the

outfield to observe a poignant two minutes of
silence in memory of Ben Hollioake and Umer
Rashid, who had both died in tragic accidents
during the previous month. Surrey's batsmen, as if
charged by the responsibility of achieving something
worthwhile in the memory of their lost colleague,
smote 58 boundaries alone on this opening day.
Brown and Shahid, both unbeaten on 132 overnight,
took their own scores to 177 and a career-best 150
respectively the following morning, and their fifth-
wicket stand to 262. Sussex battled hard in reply to
Surrey's mammoth 575 for 8 declared, with Michael
Yardy impressing with a career-best 93, but – after a
wayward opening over which cost 20 runs – Alex
Tudor (4 for 84) and temporary overseas star Azhar
Mahmood proved potent enough to enforce the
follow-on early on the third day. Sussex, bowled out
for 308, then bravely reached 379 second time
around with Chris Adams and Tony Cottey both
hitting 114. Tudor and Ian Salisbury took three
wickets apiece and, after hitting an unbeaten 68 as
Surrey knocked off the 113 they required for victory,
acting captain Mark Butcher said that the bowling
of Tudor and Mahmood, in particular, had been Test
class on a belter of a pitch.

The other Division One winners were Lancashire,
who won a magnificent contest against
Leicestershire at Old Trafford by just one wicket in
a truly thrilling finish. It was enough to give the
much-, and often unfairly, maligned championship a
good name as tail-ender Gary Keedy whipped a ball
from Devon Malcolm off his pads for two to take
Lancashire to their fourth-innings target of 388. And
what a chase it had been as a clutch of Lancashire
players responded to the challenge of making the
highest total of the match to win. Mark Chilton
made 53, new signing Stuart Law 69 and Graham
Lloyd a typically buccaneering 73, but, even then, it
took a fighting stand between new skipper Warren
Hegg and fast bowler Glen Chapple – and then the
steady nerve of Keedy after he had been joined by
last man Mike Smethurst – to guide Lancashire to a
famous triumph. Leicestershire, meanwhile, having
controlled the first three days, were left to chastise
themselves for some shoddy bowling on the final
day. Skipper Vince Wells might have bowled himself
more, too, after taking the wickets of both Law and
Lloyd for a return of 2 for 30 from just eight overs.
It was Lancashire's highest fourth-innings winning
score for 67 years – but two days earlier they were
facing up to a disappointing start to the
championship season after being bowled out for 275
in reply to Leicestershire's first-innings total of 385.

DERBYSHIRE CCC

Home Ground:
Derby
Address:
County Ground, Nottingham Road,
Derby DE21 6DA
Tel: 01332 383211
Fax: 01332 290521
Email: derby@ecb.co.uk
Directions:
By road: From the south, exit M1 at junction 25,
follow A52 into Derby, take the fourth exit off
Pentagon Island. From the north, exit M1 at
junction 28, join A38 into Derby and then follow
directional signs.
Capacity: 4,000
Other grounds used: Chesterfield
Year formed: 1870

Chief Executive: John Smedley
Other posts: Commercial Manager: Keith
Stevenson; County Development Officer: Howard
Dytham; Head Groundsman: Neil Godrich;
Second XI coach: Adrian Pierson
Captain: Dominic Cork
County colours: Blue, brown and gold

HONOURS

COUNTY CHAMPIONSHIP
1936
SUNDAY LEAGUE/NUL
1990
BENSON & HEDGES CUP
1993
GILLETTE CUP/C&G TROPHY
1981

**National Cricket League
nickname:**
DERBYSHIRE SCORPIONS

Website:
www.dccc.org.uk

Robert Key whose good form for Kent was rewarded by an England call-up.

Phil DeFreitas, playing against one of his former counties, had followed up a 22-ball 51 – one of five Leicestershire half-centuries – by taking 6 for 101 as only Alec Swann (80) and Lloyd (51) made any headway. Leicestershire then totalled 277 in their second innings, with 66 from Darren Maddy and a second half-century of the match for new overseas player Michael Bevan, but Kyle Hogg – a six-foot-four-inch 18-year-old – impressed with 5 for 48 on his championship debut and, by the close of that third day, Lancashire were poised for their memorable push for victory at 132 for 1.

Kent and Hampshire settled for a high-scoring draw at Canterbury, on a pitch that was far too good for the toothless attacks on show. Kent, in their defence, were missing an entire first-choice seam attack in the injured trio Martin Saggers, Ben Trott and Mark Ealham, but promoted Hampshire's bowlers looked well below Division One standard as Robert Key and David Fulton took a heavy toll of them in an opening partnership of 266. Fulton, Kent's newly-appointed championship captain (club captain Matthew Fleming was to continue leading the one-day side), scored 98 to add to his nine hundreds in 2001, but it was the fluency and confidence of Key which most caught the eye on day one. Following a successful winter with the National Academy in Australia, the 22-year-old Key looked ready for a senior England call-up as he stroked 160 from just 179 balls – a career best. Andrew Symonds enjoyed himself with 89 as Kent converted their

overnight 340 for 2 to 577 for 7 declared on the second day, but the rest of the match belonged to John Crawley. Hampshire's new signing, who had arrived at Southampton with a five-year contract after an acrimonious winter split with Lancashire, wasted little time in showing his former employers what they were going to miss. He batted throughout the third day, moving from 56 to 223 not out, and when he was eventually out for an epic 272 on the final morning he had batted for nine-and-a-half hours in a masterful exhibition of controlled strokemaking and unwavering concentration. Crawley was joined in a stand of 232 in 70 overs by Neil Johnson (117), and Hampshire totalled 671 in all. In the time that was left, Kent skipped to 163 for 4 in their largely meaningless second innings.

Division Two

at Cardiff
Derbyshire 217 (57.3 overs) (JID Kerr 58, SP Jones 6 for 45) and 462 for 6 dec.
(SD Stubbings 128, DR Hewson 102*, AI Gait 80, MJ Di Venuto 62)
Glamorgan 175 (48.4 overs) (A Dale 56, DG Cork 6 for 51) and 341 (MA Wallace 106*, SP James 78, LJ Wharton 6 for 103)
Derbyshire won by 163 runs
Derbyshire 16 pts, Glamorgan 3 pts

at Chester-le-Street
Middlesex 347 (110.4 overs) (SG Koenig 100, AJ Strauss 70, DC Nash 66*) and 27 for 0
Durham 160 (54.3 overs) and 213 (ML Love 101*)
Middlesex won by ten wickets
Middlesex 18 pts, Durham 3 pts

at Worcester
Worcestershire 333 (118.4 overs) (BF Smith 129, DA Leatherdale 55, J Lewis 6 for 77)
and 295 (GA Hick 92, J Lewis 6 for 54)
Gloucestershire 268 (73.1 overs) (CM Spearman 111, MGN Windows 60, AJ Bichel 9 for 93) and 154
Worcestershire won by 206 runs
Worcestershire 18 pts, Gloucestershire 5 pts

Derbyshire provided the story of the week from Division Two, although there were impressive wins too for both Middlesex and Worcestershire.

Derided during 2001 and in the following winter months, after finishing bottom of both the championship and National League, Derbyshire cocked an almighty snook at their legions of critics by completing a stunning 163-run victory against Glamorgan in Cardiff. Derbyshire were a disgrace to first-class cricket, according to the trendy supporters of a pruned first-class structure, after their troubles of the previous season. But, buoyant after a tough winter of rehabilitation following prolonged injury problems, Derbyshire captain Dominic Cork had predicted a revival at the Racecourse Ground – which itself had undergone something of a winter transformation with the demolition of the decrepit old Grandstand. Cork was as good as his word, taking 6 for 51 as Glamorgan were bowled out for 175 in reply to Derbyshire's first-innings total of 217 and then taking

vital second-innings wickets after Derbyshire had put themselves in total control with a second innings of 462 for 6 declared. Jason Kerr's gutsy 58 had kept them afloat in the first innings, as the blinding pace of Simon Jones (6 for 45) threatened to rip them apart, but now Derbyshire's top order blossomed with Steve Stubbings hitting 128, Michael Di Venuto 62 from 63 balls and new signing Andrew Gait 80. Gait, a British passport holder, was born in Zimbabwe but had played for Free State in South Africa since 1998. Dominic Hewson, a winter signing from Gloucestershire, also made an unbeaten 102 on his debut for his new county, and by the close of the third day rejuvenated Derbyshire were sniffing the sweet scent of victory. Glamorgan, on 281 for 7 overnight thanks to the resistance of Mark Wallace and Mike Kasprowicz, who had already added 75, were finally all out for 341. Wallace, the highly-promising 20-year-old wicketkeeper, fully deserved his maiden first-class hundred but, while he remained 106 not out, Derbyshire were able to celebrate in style as Lian Wharton, the young left-arm spinner, finished with 6 for 103 from 29 overs.

Middlesex, another team to be written off by most pundits before the start of hostilities, and soon to lose their captain Angus Fraser to the sudden offer of the *Independent* newspaper's cricket correspondent job, also began the new season well with a ten-wicket win over Durham at Chester-le-Street. Sven Koenig, their new opener from South Africa (courtesy of a Greek passport), kicked off his county career with a determined 100, while Andy Strauss contributed a lively 70 to an opening stand of 103. David Nash's unbeaten 66 boosted Middlesex to a first-innings score of 347, and Durham were soon in trouble in reply. Youthful duo Nicky Peng and Gordon Muchall added 88 for the fifth wicket, but Durham were still bowled out for just 160 and, by the close of day two, were already 140 for 5 in their second innings after Fraser had enforced the follow-on. Martin Love's unbeaten 101, and a sixth-wicket stand of 87 with Andy Pratt (49), merely delayed the inevitable – Ashley Noffke again impressing with his second three-wicket bag of the match.

It was Andy Bichel who was the undoubted star of the show at New Road, but not before Ben Smith, the winter signing from Leicestershire, had immediately won over the Worcestershire faithful by hitting 129 on his championship and first-class debut for his new county. Smith's hundred, and a

Dominic Cork started the county season in tremendous form and was recalled by England.

dedicated 55 from David Leatherdale in a fifth-wicket partnership of 142, allowed Worcestershire to take early control of the match with a first-innings total of 333. Then came Bichel. Three days after arriving back from Australia to begin his second season as overseas player at Worcester, the bustling fast bowler was boasting the unsurprisingly career-best figures of 23.1-4-93-9 as Gloucestershire were dismissed for 268 in reply. Craig Spearman, Gloucestershire's new opener, hit 111 at just under a run a ball and completed his century with a six – but even the New Zealander with 19 Test caps and a Welsh mother had to bow to Bichel's mastery of seam and swing. Graeme Hick then stroked 92 from 111 balls on a pitch which Tim Packwood, the new Worcestershire groundsman, had managed to inject with more pace and bounce than is usually the case at early-season New Road. Leatherdale again chipped in with a useful unbeaten 49, and Worcestershire's second-innings score of 295 asked Gloucestershire to score 361 for victory on the final day. They fell way short of it, bowled out for just 154 after Bichel – who else? – had started the rot by nipping out makeshift opener Jack Russell the previous evening.

Round Two: 24–27 April 2002

Division One

at Headingley
Yorkshire 140 (75.5 overs) and 202 (CR Taylor 52*)
Surrey 510 (127.5 overs) (AJ Stewart 96, MA Butcher 83, IJ Ward 70, MR Ramprakash 65, Azhar Mahmood 64*, SP Kirby 5 for 129)
Surrey won by an innings & 168 runs
Surrey 20 pts, Yorkshire 3 pts

at Edgbaston
Warwickshire 297 (78.2 overs) (NMK Smith 96, MM Betts 56) and 150
Lancashire 251 (78.2 overs) (GD Lloyd 80, A Richardson 5 for 59) and 197 for 4 (D Byas 83*)
Lancashire won by six wickets
Lancashire 17 pts, Warwickshire 5 pts

at Southampton Rose Bowl
Leicestershire 428 (120 overs) (VJ Wells 150, DI Stevens 82, PAJ DeFreitas 51)
Hampshire 273 (97.4 overs) (JP Crawley 80) and (following on) 146 (WS Kendall 53* – carried his bat, DL Maddy 5 for 37)
Leicestershire won by an innings & 9 runs
Leicestershire 20 pts, Hampshire 5 pts

at Hove
Sussex 337 (90.2 overs) (MW Goodwin 162) and 396 for 7 dec. (CJ Adams 101, RSC Martin-Jenkins 86, MH Yardy 73)
Somerset 401 (111.5 overs) (PD Bowler 94, J Cox 65, MJ Wood 54, RJ Kirtley 5 for 90) and 94 for 2
Match drawn
Sussex 10 pts, Somerset 12 pts

Surrey's demolition of Yorkshire was the main talking point from the top division in this round of matches. Bowling out the champions for just 140 on the opening day, Surrey then replied with a mammoth 510 before dismissing Yorkshire again for 202 to complete victory by an innings and 168 runs comfortably inside three days. It could not have been a clearer expression of intent as Surrey's second successive championship win took them straight to the front in the long race for the domestic game's most highly-prized title. The end of April is mighty early to be handing out championship pennants, but Surrey's pace out of the blocks, and the massive strength in depth of their squad, made them even more overwhelming favourites – after this result – than they were at the start of the campaign. Alex Tudor (4 for 31) and Azhar Mahmood (3 for 33) were chiefly responsible for Yorkshire's demise on day one, and by the close Surrey openers Mark Butcher and Ian Ward had already posted 115 from 28 overs in reply. On the second day, Butcher went on to 83 and Ward 70, taking their first-wicket stand to 161, before Mark Ramprakash (65) and Alec Stewart (96) added a further 137 for the third wicket. Nadeem Shahid weighed in with 45 and Mahmood an unbeaten 64, and Surrey's eventual first-innings total was their highest at Headingley. In eight balls before the close Martin Bicknell and Tudor had sent back both Yorkshire openers without a run on the board and only a determined and patient 52 not out from 21-year-old Chris Taylor, and some tail-end defiance from Chris Silverwood, delayed Surrey on the third day. It was the sixth heaviest defeat in Yorkshire's history, and all the champions could plead in their own defence was to point to the absence of five senior players – Darren Gough, Michael Vaughan, Craig White, Anthony McGrath and Matthew Hoggard. Surrey, however, were not actually at full strength themselves!

Yorkshiremen everywhere were also hurt by the result from Edgbaston, where Lancashire beat Warwickshire by six wickets to register their own second win out of two matches. It was not so much the Lancashire victory, though, that caused their pain

DURHAM CCC

Home Ground:
Chester-le-Street
Address:
County Ground, Riverside,
Chester-le-Street,
Co. Durham DH3 3QR
Tel: 0191 387 1717
Fax: 0191 387 1616
Email: marketing@durham-ccc.org.uk
Directions:
By rail: Chester-le-Street (approx. 5 minutes by taxi or a 10-minute walk).
By road: Easily accessible from junction 63 of the A1(M). Nearby car parking is available on match days.
Disabled access:
Viewing points for spectators in wheelchairs; Members' Lounge has induction loop system for members who are hard of hearing; guide dogs allowed into ground.
Capacity: 10,000
Other grounds used:
Darlington CC (Feethams); Hartlepool CC; Stockton CC 01642 672835.
Year formed: 1882

Chief Executive: David Harker
Director of Cricket: Geoff Cook
Director of Operations: Lesley Williamson
First Team Coach: Martyn Moxon
Captain: Jonathan Lewis
Second XI coach: Alan Walker
County colours:
Yellow, blue, burgundy

HONOURS

NONE YET

National Cricket League nickname:
DURHAM DYNAMOS

Website:
www.durham-ccc.org.uk

as the brilliant unbeaten 83 by David Byas which saw them home on a tense third afternoon. Byas, who retired from first-class cricket after leading Yorkshire to the 2001 championship title, but then accepted Roses rivals Lancashire's offer of a one-year contract in a controversial return to the game, was joined by his new captain Warren Hegg (34 not out) in an unbeaten fifth-wicket stand of 70 in just ten overs. It was a thrilling response after Lancashire had stuttered to 127 for 4, on a still-unpredictable pitch, as Lancashire chased 197 for victory after bowling Warwickshire out for 150 in their second innings. Kyle Hogg impressed again with a spell of 8-5-16-3 as Warwickshire struggled to 124 for 7 on the second evening, and Peter Martin (4 for 41) made sure there was no late rally early on day three. Earlier, it had seemed that Warwickshire were in control of the match when a ninth-wicket stand of 101 between Neil Smith (96) and Mel Betts (56) had hauled their first innings up from the depths of 136 for 7 to 297 all out. It was Smith's highest score for four years in this the year where he is the county beneficiary. Lancashire's first innings ended at 251, despite Graham Lloyd's punchy 80, and Warwickshire seamer Alan Richardson (5 for 59) was presented with his county cap after a spell of 4 for 15 in 29 balls.

Leicestershire were Division One's other winners, trouncing newly promoted Hampshire by an innings and nine runs at Southampton to collect a maximum 20 points. Skipper Vince Wells led the way for Leicestershire with a first-innings score of 150, his 17th first-class century, and it was his fifth-wicket partnership of 149 with Darren Stevens (82), plus Phil DeFreitas' typically aggressive 51, which boosted the visitors to a first-innings 428. Darren Maddy then emerged as the unlikely bowling hero, picking up match figures of 9 for 74 – and a career-best 5 for 37 in Hampshire's second innings – as the home team succumbed on a seaming pitch. John Crawley's 80 and James Hamblin's robust 46 were the only scores of consequence in the first innings of 273, which ended with last man Alan Mullally running himself out attempting a sharp single with just six needed to avoid the follow-on. Opener Will Kendall could, at least, hold his head high after carrying his bat for 53. It was Hampshire's first championship defeat at their splendid new Rose Bowl home.

Bad weather on the third day, which prevented any cricket until 3.15pm, condemned the match between Sussex and Somerset at Hove to a draw. At the halfway stage it was Somerset, in fact, who held the slight advantage, having replied with 380 for 8 to Sussex's first-innings score of 337. But, on the eventual third-day resumption, and a successful Somerset bid for a fifth batting point as they totalled 401, only a Sussex second-innings collapse could have produced a positive result. As it was they batted solidly again, reaching 178 for 3 by the close, and on the final day Chris Adams took his overnight 68 to 101 before Michael Yardy (73) was joined by Robin Martin-Jenkins (86 with a six and 14 fours) in a stand of 93 in 16 overs for the sixth wicket that made the draw a certainty. Sussex eventually declared their second innings at 396 for 7, and then picked up just two Somerset second-innings wickets in the 32 overs they left themselves to bowl. The highlight of the match, however, was a majestic 162 off 168 balls by Murray Goodwin, the former Zimbabwe Test batsman. Goodwin, the Sussex opener, completed his hundred ten minutes before lunch on the first day, and his third 50 then occupied just 34 deliveries before he finally fell with the total on 259. In all he struck 26 boundaries and hardly seemed to miss any opportunity to pull or

Murray Goodwin, the former Zimbabwe Test batsman, scored 162 from 168 balls for Sussex against Somerset.

cut. In Somerset's first innings Peter Bowler top scored with 94 and there were half-centuries too for Jamie Cox and Matthew Wood.

Division Two

at Derby
Derbyshire 263 (75.4 overs) (MJ Di Venuto 56, DG Cork 56, SMA Bukhari 53) and 229 (KJ Dean 50)
Durham 258 (80.1 overs) (N Peng 108, DG Cork 5 for 72) and 232 (PD Collingwood 76, JA Daley 59*, DG Cork 5 for 54)
Derbyshire won by 2 runs – no play was possible on the third day
Derbyshire 17 pts, Durham 5 pts

at Lord's
Middlesex 462 (114.2 overs) (EC Joyce 119, OA Shah 63, AJ Strauss 62, PN Weekes 50)
Nottinghamshire 159 (60.4 overs) (ARC Fraser 5 for 61) and 272 (GE Welton 51, AA Noffke 7 for 100)
Middlesex won by an innings & 31 runs
Middlesex 20 pts, Nottinghamshire 2.5 pts
(Nottinghamshire had 0.5 pt deducted for a slow over rate)

at Northampton
Worcestershire 524 for 8 dec. (128.1 overs) (DA Leatherdale 154, SD Peters 146, Kabir Ali 51*)
Northamptonshire 614 for 5 dec. (174 overs) (MEK Hussey 170, RJ Warren 150*, MB Loye 139, AL Penberthy 63)
Match drawn
Northamptonshire 11 pts, Worcestershire 10 pts

at Chelmsford
Gloucestershire 379 (110.3 overs) (MW Alleyne 142*, CM Spearman 80, ID Fisher 65) and 195 for 4 dec. (KJ Barnett 100*)
Essex 379 (126.2 overs) (DDJ Robinson 131, A Flower 91, IJ Harvey 6 for 68)
Match drawn – no play was possible on the third day
Essex 11 pts, Gloucestershire 11 pts

The outstanding performance in this round of Division One games again came from unsung Derbyshire, who staged a never-say-die fightback in the field against Durham at Derby to claim a breathless two-run victory. Dominic Cork, their inspirational captain, took four wickets for six runs in a thrilling spell of 3.3 overs to deny Durham the win that had seemed to be theirs for the taking. Needing 235, Durham were cruising at 187 for 2

after fine batting from Jimmy Daley and Paul Collingwood (76). But then Daley had to retire hurt on 59, after being hit on the hand by the fiery Mohammad Ali, and wickets suddenly started to tumble. Ali played his part taking 3 for 69 but, as Daley returned later to finish unbeaten, it was the irrepressible Cork who seized the moment to finish with figures of 5 for 54 – and ten wickets in the match. 'This is probably the most exciting victory I have played in for Derbyshire,' said Cork. 'People say county cricket is dying, but this was just a fantastic game.' It began with Derbyshire totalling 263 in their first innings, with both Michael Di Venuto and Cork himself scoring 56, and then a No. 9 batsman, announced on the public address as Syed Bukhari, amazed the home supporters by blazing 53 off just 38 balls with 12 fours. It later emerged that Bukhari, a wiry Pakistan-born seamer with an English wife who had been signed from the Glamorgan Second XI, wished to be known as Mohammad Ali – and so scorecards and newspaper scoreboards were duly amended! Durham, however, soon showed that they, too, had a champion – by the name of Nicky Peng. Hit on the helmet by Ali when on 40, the 20-year-old Peng remained unperturbed and simply went on playing a high-quality innings in the seamer-friendly conditions. Cork, who else, took 5 for 72, but Peng's 108 enabled Durham to reach 258 and virtual parity at the midway stage of the match. By the close of the second day, Derbyshire were a nervy 190 for 9, with only Di Venuto (46) and Andrew Gait (35) having shown signs of permanence, and the tension grew throughout a third day that was washed away by rain. On the resumption, Derbyshire were boosted by a remarkable innings from tail-ender Kevin Dean. The fast bowler, whose previous career best was 27, completed a maiden first-class 50 to drag the home side up to 229 all out. Collingwood, who had picked up 4 for 31 with his seamers, then continued to do his best to win the match for Durham, but, in the end, an astonishing contest was settled by Cork.

On top of Division Two, however, after the first two rounds of games, sat Middlesex following their victory by an innings and 31 runs over Nottinghamshire at Lord's. The match provided a fitting farewell to championship cricket for Angus Fraser, who had decided to take up the offer of a post in the media. Fraser, the former England warhorse, delighted both himself and his many admirers by picking up 5 for 61 – his best first-class figures since August 1999 – as Notts were tumbled out for just 159 in their first innings. Fraser, though, could not make any impression when Notts followed on, finishing with 0 for 32 from 16 overs and thus failing to add to his career tally of 886 first-class wickets, taken at an average of just over 27 and including 177 in Tests. 'Not taking a wicket in their second innings didn't matter to me,' said Fraser, 'the bigger thing was winning the game.' Ashley Noffke, the Australian pace bowler standing in for Abdur Razzaq as Middlesex's overseas player, ended with a career-best haul of 7 for 100 as Notts were bowled out a second time for 272. Earlier, Middlesex had established their position of mastery by totalling 462 in their first innings. Andrew Strauss, the new captain in succession to Fraser, hit 62 while adding 103 for the first wicket with Sven Koenig (47), and that solid base was built upon by Ed Joyce's career-best 119 and half-centuries from Owais Shah and Paul Weekes.

Stephen Peters, a winter mover from Essex to Worcestershire, reached a maiden championship century in a high-scoring, weather-affected draw at Wantage Road. Peters made 146, completing his century with a pulled six, David Leatherdale a fine 154, and Kabir Ali a career-best 51 not out as Worcestershire piled up 524 for 8 declared. But, by the end of the second day, Northamptonshire were already 254 without loss in reply, with both Mike Hussey and Mal Loye unbeaten on 120! At that stage the match had produced 127 fours and seven sixes, a statistic which clearly illustrated the friendliness of the surface. Any remaining hopes of a positive result, even if it were a manufactured one, were ruled out by the rain which did not allow play on day three until 4.30pm, and which also interrupted the final day. In the time left, Northants merely continued to plunder the runs – eventually calling a halt at 614 for 5 declared with Hussey making 170, Loye 139, Russell Warren an unbeaten 150 and Tony Penberthy 63. Hussey and Loye's opening stand of 290 was the third highest in Northants' championship history.

There was a weather-ruined draw, too, at Chelmsford, where the third day was completely washed away by heavy showers. Until then Essex had replied determinedly with 305 for 4 to Gloucestershire's first-innings total of 379, with new overseas star Andy Flower making a high-class 91

Gloucestershire's captain, Mark Alleyne, rescued his team as they struggled against Essex in Division Two.

and helping Darren Robinson to add 164 for the fourth wicket. Robinson went on to 131, but Ian Harvey swept away the Essex lower order to take 6 for 68, on what was a fairly meaningless final day, to deny them a lead. Kim Barnett then helped himself to 100 not out as Gloucestershire played out time on 195 for 4. Mark Alleyne (33 not out) batted well for the second time in the match after earlier rallying his county's first innings with a brilliant unbeaten 142. Despite Craig Spearman's 80, Gloucestershire were struggling at 145 for 7 before Alleyne – dropped at slip by Jon Dakin when he was on 49 – was joined by Ian Fisher (65) in an eighth-wicket partnership worth 164.

ESSEX CCC

Home Ground:
The County Ground, Chelmsford
Address:
County Cricket Ground, New Writtle Street, Chelmsford, Essex CM2 0PD
Tel: 01245 252420
Fax: 01245 491607
Prospects of play: 01245 287921
Email: administration.essex@ecb.co.uk
Directions:
By rail: Chelmsford Station (8 minutes' walk away).
By road: M25 then A12 to Chelmsford. Exit Chelmsford and follow AA signs to 'Essex Cricket Club'.
Capacity: 6,000
Other grounds used: Castle Park, Colchester; Valentine's Park, Ilford; Southchurch Park, Southend-on-Sea.
Year formed: 1876

Chief Executive: DE East
Commercial Manager: Dave Comley
Other posts: Manager/Coach Cricket School: Alan Lilley; Head Groundsman: SG Kerrison
Club Coach: Graham Gooch
Club Captain: Nasser Hussain
Team Captain: Ronnie Irani
County colours: Blue, gold and red

HONOURS

COUNTY CHAMPIONSHIP
1979, 1983, 1984, 1986, 1991, 1992
SUNDAY LEAGUE/NUL
1981, 1984, 1985
REFUGE ASSURANCE CUP
1989
BENSON & HEDGES CUP
1979, 1998
GILLETTE CUP/C&G TROPHY
1985, 1997

National Cricket League nickname:
ESSEX EAGLES

Website:
www.essexcricket.org.uk

ROUND THREE: 8–11 MAY 2002

Division One

at The Oval
Lancashire 320 (70.1 overs) (A Flintoff 137) and 200
(Azhar Mahmood 8 for 61)
Surrey 216 (64.3 overs) (AJ Tudor 61, G Chapple 5 for
65) and 309 for 7 (MR Ramprakash 119*)
Surrey won by three wickets
Surrey 16 pts, Lancashire 6 pts

at Taunton
Yorkshire 213 (56.3 overs) (MJ Lumb 66, AR Caddick
5 for 72) and 280 (C White 69, MJ Lumb 62)
Somerset 232 (61.1 overs) (ID Blackwell 114) and 263
for 3 (64.2 overs) (ME Trescothick 134, PD Bowler 79*)
Somerset won by seven wickets
Somerset 16 pts, Yorkshire 4 pts

at Southampton Rose Bowl
Hampshire 345 (112.1 overs) (RA Smith 104, SD Udal
88, JRC Hamblin 50, MJ Saggers 5 for 74) and 111 for
2 (JP Crawley 50*)
Kent 118 (39 overs) and (following on) 337 (PA Nixon
77*, ET Smith 77, MM Patel 58)
Hampshire won by eight wickets
Hampshire 18 pts, Kent 3 pts

at Leicester
Leicestershire 523 (162.5 overs) (MG Bevan 146,
DI Stevens 125, IJ Sutcliffe 71, AF Giles 5 for 126) and
94 for 3
Warwickshire 177 (56 overs) (SM Pollock 59) and
(following on) 439 (NV Knight 130,
MJ Powell 67, JO Troughton 66, SM Pollock 66)
Leicestershire won by seven wickets
Leicestershire 19 pts, Warwickshire 1 pt

Surrey showed massive resilience at The Oval to
fight their way out of the tightest of corners against
Lancashire and emerge with a tremendous three-
wicket victory. At the end of the first day, however,
Surrey were seemingly without hope at 106 for 7 in
reply to a Lancashire first-innings total of 320 that
had been dominated by the awesome talent of
Andrew Flintoff. The England all-rounder, with
batting described in one national newspaper as
'restrained yet merciless', struck two sixes and 20
fours in a wonderful 106-ball 137. Flintoff then took
2 for 14 from six overs as only Ian Ward (48)
displayed any initial resistance. On the second
morning, however, Alex Tudor (61) was joined by

last man Jimmy Ormond (35 not out) in a precious
last-wicket stand of 52 that hauled Surrey's total up
to 216 all out. By the close, too, Lancashire were a
rather shaky 124 for 5 in their second innings, with
Azhar Mahmood snapping up all five wickets in a
12-over spell costing just 24 runs. More was to
follow from Mahmood, too, as the Pakistani seamer
went on to remove the first eight Lancashire
batsmen to finish with career-best figures of 8 for
61. Warren Hegg scored a battling 43, but
Lancashire's all-out total of 200 at least gave Surrey
a chance – and, like true champions in waiting, they
snatched it. Mark Ramprakash made a magnificent
unbeaten 119, finishing the game with a flourish by
hitting a ball from Gary Keedy for six, and Alec
Stewart also contributed 46 in a stand of 108 with
Ramprakash.

Champions Yorkshire, meanwhile, continued their
decline by being humbled by seven wickets by
Somerset at Taunton. Andy Caddick took 5 for 72 as
Yorkshire were dismissed for 213 on the first day,
and eight wickets in the match (giving him 48 in his
last ten innings of bowling for Somerset), but he also
became the first player to be penalized under the
new ECB directive on misbehaviour. Umpire David
Constant reported comments made by Caddick, and
the England fast bowler was later issued with an
official reprimand. Somerset, having been a sickly 26
for 4 and then 75 for 6 in their own first innings,
recovered to total 232 thanks to a superb 114 from
Ian Blackwell and a seventh-wicket partnership of
131 between him and Keith Dutch (46). Chris
Silverwood added 4 for 28 to his unbeaten 44 of the
opening day and, when Yorkshire batted again,
Craig White hit 69 and Michael Lumb followed up
his 66 in the first innings with another capable 62.
The champions, however, were bowled out for 280 –
losing their final wicket to the fourth ball of the
third day – and Marcus Trescothick then hammered
134 to rush Somerset to victory. Trescothick
thumped three sixes and 18 fours and put on 167
for the third wicket with Peter Bowler, who finished
on 79 not out.

Another Saturday crowd was lost to English
cricket at the Rose Bowl, where Hampshire also
wrapped up an eight-wicket win against Kent on the
Friday afternoon. Hampshire's first-innings total of
345 was based on a 48th first-class hundred for the
county by Robin Smith – just about justifying his
own decision to bat first after an initial collapse to
34 for 4. Indeed, from 160 for 7, Smith was joined
in an eighth-wicket stand of 109 by Shaun Udal,
who went on to score 88. James Hamblin further

Pakistan's all-rounder, Azhar Mahmood returned his career-best figures of 8 for 61 for Surrey against Lancashire.

boosted the total with a hard-hit 50, and soon Dimitri Mascarenhas (4 for 49) was undermining the Kent first innings. Bowled out for just 118, the visitors followed on and by the close of the second day were 148 for 4 with Ed Smith carrying hopes of salvation with an unbeaten 61. Smith, however, went for 77 early on the third day, leaving Paul Nixon (77 not out) and Min Patel (58) to force Hampshire to bat again with a seventh-wicket partnership worth 89. Mascarenhas again impressed with 4 for 73 as Kent were bowled out for 337, and John Crawley's unbeaten 50 guided Hampshire to their straightforward target.

Leicestershire stepped up their fine start to the championship season by defeating Warwickshire by seven wickets at Grace Road. They nearly made a mess of things, though, after forcing Warwickshire to follow on, by spilling a host of catches. In the end, by finally bowling out their visitors for 439 in their second innings, Leicestershire were left a victory target of 94 in 16 overs. Michael Bevan's unbeaten 38 saw them home, completing quite a match for the Australian left-hander. On the opening day, his 32nd birthday, Bevan had reached 99 not out as Leicestershire closed on 292 for 4. Iain Sutcliffe had made 71, but the stage was Bevan's, and he duly completed his hundred the next morning – going on to share a fifth-wicket stand of 163 with Darren Stevens. Bevan was eventually out for 146, while the 26-year-old Stevens

hit 125, only his second first-class ton. By the close, Warwickshire were 36 for 3 in reply to Leicestershire's imposing 523, and by the third afternoon they were following on after being dismissed for 177 in spite of Shaun Pollock's 59. Bevan, by the way, removed three of Warwickshire's top five with his chinamen! Helped by Leicestershire's profligacy in the field, Warwickshire's second innings was a far sturdier affair, with Michael Powell leading the way with 67 and Nick Knight turning his overnight 75 not out into a determined seven-hour 130. Jim Troughton scored 66 as did Pollock, but the loss of five wickets for 44 runs finally undid Warwickshire and re-opened the door for a Leicestershire win.

Division Two

at Derby
Derbyshire 538 (119.2 overs) (MJ Di Venuto 230, DG Cork 60, Al Gait 53) and 33 for 2
Northamptonshire 131 (45.5 overs) and (following on) 439 (MEK Hussey 150, MB Loye 109, GP Swann 62)
Derbyshire won by eight wickets
Derbyshire 19.75 pts, Northamptonshire 8 pts
(Derbyshire had 0.25 pt deducted for a slow over rate)

at Trent Bridge
Essex 130 (47.4 overs) and 270 (AP Grayson 83, GJ Smith 8 for 53)
Nottinghamshire 213 (67.5 overs) (JER Gallian 52, RC Irani 6 for 71) and 188 for 3 (Usman Afzaal 85*)
Nottinghamshire won by seven wickets
Nottinghamshire 16 pts, Essex 2.5 pts (Essex had 0.5 pt deducted for a slow over rate)

at Worcester
Glamorgan 286 (91.4 overs) (J Hughes 74, RDB Croft 59, MJ Powell 53, Kabir Ali 5 for 80) and 348 (DL Hemp 64, MJ Powell 59, A Sheriyar 5 for 86)
Worcestershire 298 (96.1 overs) (A Singh 81, SD Peters 71, SD Thomas 5 for 77) and 226 (BF Smith 61, MS Kasprowicz 5 for 77)
Glamorgan won by 110 runs
Glamorgan 17 pts, Worcestershire 5 pts

Buoyant Derbyshire won themselves a third successive victory (the first time since 1954 that they had begun a championship campaign with three wins) by beating Northamptonshire by eight wickets at the Racecourse Ground. They also had good news off the field, with the confirmation that the club would be receiving a lottery grant of £1.6 million towards the building of a new indoor cricket school at their Derby headquarters. As if in celebration of this financial boost, Derbyshire ran up a commanding 487 for 7 from the 104 overs delivered to them on the opening day – Michael Di Venuto leading the rampage with a magnificent 230 from 254 balls. The Tasmanian struck 32 boundaries and was well supported by Andrew Gait (53), Chris Bassano (41) and Dominic Cork (60). Then, on the second day, after Derbyshire had finally been

bowled out for 538, the effervescent Cork found disconcerting movement off the seam with the new ball to take four wickets for just one run off 21 balls to wreck the Northants first innings. Cork finished with 4 for 29 and Kevin Dean took 3 for 28 as Northants scraped up to 131 all out thanks to a last-wicket stand of 34 between Carl Greenidge and Darren Cousins. The visitors made a much better fist of things in their second innings, an opening stand of 231 between Mike Hussey (150) and Mal Loye (109), and a punchy 62 from Graeme Swann, taking them to an eventual 439.

A testing pitch of inconsistent bounce at Trent Bridge, plus extravagant swing when clouds rolled over the ground, made batting difficult in a match won by Nottinghamshire by seven wickets over Essex. The pitch, indeed, was marked 'below average' by Phil Sharpe and David Hughes, the pitch inspectors, after a three-hour consultative meeting, but Notts escaped the eight-point censure that a mark of 'poor' would have brought. Essex, on the first morning, had no answer to the seam and swing of Andy Harris (4 for 41), Greg Smith (3 for 21) and Nadeem Malik (3 for 45) as they were dismissed for 130, and by the close a battling 52 by Jason Gallian had given Notts an immediate advantage at 152 for 5. They could only reach 213 all out on the following day, with Essex captain Ronnie Irani (6 for 71) condemning the pitch as 'downright dangerous'. Left-arm paceman Smith, who had struck an important unbeaten 35 at the end of the Notts first innings, then took 8 for 53 as Essex fought their way to 270 all out in their second innings. Paul Grayson batted with outstanding technique and character to score 83 off 109 balls, while Ashley Cowan provided some late-order resistance with 42. The game, however, was all over midway through the third day with Usman Afzaal's unbeaten 85 off 119 deliveries guiding Notts to their target with few alarms.

Glamorgan's 110-run victory against Worcestershire at New Road was a triumph for the persistence of Mike Kasprowicz, their Australian opening bowler. When he captured the eighth wicket to fall in Worcestershire's first innings, it was his first success of the championship season, with his 382nd delivery. But, by the end of the match, Kasprowicz was celebrating a second-innings haul of 5 for 77 as Worcestershire were bowled out for 226. Darren Thomas, with 3 for 54 to add to his 5 for 77

Michael Di Venuto drives another four in his innings of 230 for Derbyshire against Northamptonshire.

GLAMORGAN CCC

Home Ground:
Cardiff
Address:
Sophia Gardens, Cardiff CF1 9XR
Tel: 029 2040 9380
Fax: 029 2040 9390
Email: glam@ecb.co.uk
Directions:
By rail: Cardiff Central Train Station.
By road: From north, A470 and follow signs to Cardiff until junction with Cardiff by-pass then A48 Port Talbot and City Centre. Cathedral Road is situated off A48 for Sophia Gardens. From east, M4 Junction 29 then A48.
Capacity: 4,000
Other grounds used: Pontypridd, Mid Glamorgan; St Helens, Swansea; Rhos-on-Sea, Colwyn Bay; Pen-y-Pound Ground, Abergavenny.
Year formed: 1888

Chief Executive: Mike Fatkin
Head Groundsman: Len Smith
Captain: Steve James
Vice-captain: Robert Croft
County colours: Navy blue and yellow/gold

HONOURS

COUNTY CHAMPIONSHIP
1948, 1969, 1997
SUNDAY LEAGUE/NUL
1993, 2002

National Cricket League nickname:
GLAMORGAN DRAGONS

Website:
www.glamorgancricket.com

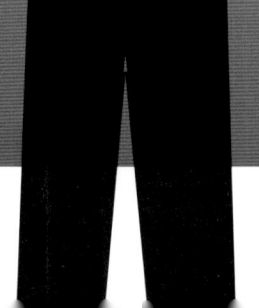

in the first innings, was the other bowling hero –
while Michael Powell led the way with the bat for
Glamorgan with innings of 53 and 59. The 20-year-
old Jonathan Hughes, however, top scored in
Glamorgan's first innings of 286 by striking 14 fours
in an aggressive 74, in just his second championship
appearance, while Robert Croft hit 59.
Worcestershire's first-innings total of 298 was a
disappointment after Stephen Peters (71) and
Anurag Singh (81) had added 156 for the first
wicket, and Alamgir Sheriyar's 5 for 86 could then
not prevent Glamorgan from running up 348 in
their second innings. Apart from Powell's second
half-century of the match, there was a good 64 from
David Hemp and a rumbustious last-wicket stand of
47 in 39 balls between Croft (39) and Simon Jones.
Ben Smith, with 61, offered the only real home
resistance as Kasprowicz and Thomas cleaned up.

ROUND FOUR: 15–18 MAY 2002

Division One

at Canterbury
Yorkshire 239 (87.2 overs) (C White 104, Amjad Khan
6 for 52) and 346 (RJ Blakey 90, RKJ Dawson 87,
DS Lehmann 72, MJ Saggers 5 for 82)
Kent 418 (105.3 overs) (RWT Key 114, DP Fulton 71)
and 169 for 6
Kent won by four wickets
Kent 20 pts, Yorkshire 4 pts

at Old Trafford
Sussex 423 (135.3 overs) (CJ Adams 217) and 221
for 7 (RR Montgomerie 80)
Lancashire 366 (110.5 overs) (SG Law 218, AJ Swann
51, JD Lewry 5 for 88)
Match drawn
Lancashire 11 pts, Sussex 12 pts

at Taunton
Somerset 565 (146.2 overs) (J Cox 176, MJ Wood 79,
KP Dutch 70, PD Bowler 60, M Burns 52)
Leicestershire 288 for 8 (65.2 overs) (IJ Sutcliffe 73,
DI Stevens 73)
Match drawn – no play was possible on the fourth day
Somerset 7 pts, Leicestershire 4 pts

at Edgbaston
Warwickshire 472 (163.1 overs) (NV Knight 255* –
carried his bat, A Richardson 91)
Hampshire 302 (105.5 overs) (NC Johnson 79,
N Pothas 59) and (following on) 306 for 5 dec.

(NC Johnson 74*, N Pothas 71*, DA Kenway 54)
Match drawn
Warwickshire 10 pts, Hampshire 10 pts

Kent added to the early-season woes of Yorkshire as
they beat the champions by four wickets at
Canterbury. A splendid four-day contest, however,
could have gone either way when Kent, chasing 168
on the last afternoon, slid to 95 for 6. Matthew
Fleming proved just the man for the situation,
though, marching in to hit an unbeaten 42 and with
help from Matthew Walker (31 not out) guided his
county to an important victory. The match began
with Kent bowling out Yorkshire for 239 in their
first innings, despite a fine 104 from Craig White.
Amjad Khan, however, Kent's fast bowling discovery
from Denmark, took 6 for 52 with a performance of
pace and heart, while Min Patel's crafty slow left-
arm spin earned him figures of 3 for 11 from 14
overs. Kent were then given the perfect start to their
reply by Rob Key (114) and David Fulton, the
championship captain, who scored 71. The Kent
openers put on 198, and Andy Symonds' 48 helped
Kent reach 418. By the close of the second day
Yorkshire were struggling on 22 for 2, after Martin
Saggers had struck twice with the new ball, and,
despite Darren Lehmann's 72, the champions looked
out of things at 151 for 6. Richard Blakey and
Richard Dawson, however, were having none of it,
putting on a courageous 162 for the seventh wicket.
Dawson, eventually, was out for 87 just before the
close, giving a catch off Patel, but Chris Silverwood
launched the last ball of the day, from Patel, for six
and – with Blakey 88 not out – Yorkshire had a lead
of 144 at 323 for 7. Blakey fell early the next
morning for a superb 90 and, with Saggers grabbing
the last two wickets for figures of 5 for 82, Yorkshire
were all out for 346. It was a great effort but, in the
end, not quite enough as Fleming had the final say.

Bad weather at Old Trafford put pay to any
possibility of an intriguing finish to a hard-fought
affair between Lancashire and Sussex. Sussex got in
the first blow, totalling 423 in their first innings with
Chris Adams, their in-form captain, scoring a
brilliant 217, despite needing treatment for a calf
muscle strain. Stuart Law, however, hit back with a
scintillating 218 of his own as Lancashire replied
with 366. But, without a last-wicket stand of 145
between Law and Gary Keedy, who contributed a
determined 25 not out, Sussex would have been
totally on top. As it was, they led by 243 going into
the final day, but only had time to convert their
overnight 186 for 6, in which Richard Montgomerie

A brilliant double century by Chris Adams, the captain of Sussex, was thwarted by bad weather at Old Trafford.

scored 80, into 221 for 7 as the rain arrived to produce a deflating draw.

Rain also cost Somerset the prospect of victory at Taunton, where, at the halfway stage of the match, they had reduced Leicestershire to 241 for 7 in reply to their mammoth first-innings total of 565. Less than ten overs were then possible, however, on the third day, in which Leicestershire progressed to 288 for 8 with Darren Stevens out for an aggressive 73, and the fourth day was washed out completely. Iain Sutcliffe also made 73 for Leicestershire, with 12 boundaries, but the best batting of the match came from Jamie Cox, the Somerset captain. Cox compiled a high-class 176, his 11th first-class century for the county, from 296 balls and with 29 fours, and was joined in a first-wicket stand of 184 by Matthew Wood (79). Thereafter, Mike Burns (52), Peter Bowler (60) and Keith Dutch (70) all made valuable contributions.

Perhaps the most remarkable achievement in championship cricket for many years, however, came at Edgbaston in a match eventually drawn after a gutsy fightback by Hampshire. But the plaudits still went to Nick Knight and, specifically, Alan Richardson of Warwickshire. They put on 214 for the tenth wicket, the fifth highest last-wicket stand in championship history, after Warwickshire had struggled somewhat to reach 258 for 9. The pair had time just to add 16 on the first evening, but then blossomed in the morning to take Warwickshire to a scarcely believable 472 all out. Knight carried his bat for a career-best knock of 255, but it was last man

Richardson who emerged as the most heroic figure – his 91 was not just the highest individual score made by a Warwickshire No. 11, it dwarfed his previous highest of 17 not out! The 27-year-old fast bowler's career average was less than six when he strode out to join Knight, and the partnership was only 21 runs short of the championship record for the tenth wicket when he was stumped sweeping. 'They will not believe this at home!' said Richardson, from Newcastle-under-Lyme, who before this game had been asking the county to release him from his contract. Richardson then took two wickets as Hampshire were dismissed for 302 in reply – Neil Johnson (79) and Nic Pothas (59) adding 87 for the sixth wicket – and 2 for 17 from eight further overs as, following on, Hampshire stuttered to 120 for 3 by the close of the third day. Robin Smith completed 25,000 first-class runs when reaching 19 in his first-innings score of 44. Derek Kenway then made 54 and Smith another gritty 43, but the Hampshire rearguard action was boosted on the final day by Johnson (74 not out) and Pothas (71 not out), who this time put on an unbroken 137 for the sixth wicket to save the game and take the second-innings total to 306 for 5 declared.

Division Two

at Northampton
Middlesex 541 (158.3 overs) (PN Weekes 107, SG Koenig 101, RMS Weston 72, DC Nash 55)
Northamptonshire 286 (70.1 overs) (AS Rollins 107, MEK Hussey 84, SJ Cook 8 for 63)
and (following on) 253 (JW Cook 84)
Middlesex won by an innings & 2 runs
Middlesex 20 pts, Northamptonshire 4 pts

at Worcester
Worcestershire 367 (99.5 overs) (AJ Bichel 65, BF Smith 61, A Singh 60) and 140 (JP Stephenson 7 for 44)
Essex 373 (135.5 overs) (Aftab Habib 117, DDJ Robinson 71, A Sheriyar 5 for 111) and 135 for 5
Essex won by five wickets
Essex 19 pts, Worcestershire 6 pts

at Bristol
Nottinghamshire 197 (57 overs) (JMM Averis 5 for 51) and 182 (GE Welton 68)
Gloucestershire 347 (109 overs) (CM Spearman 118, MGN Windows 53) and 33 for 3
Gloucestershire won by seven wickets
Gloucestershire 18 pts, Nottinghamshire 3 pts

GLOUCESTERSHIRE CCC

Home Ground:
Bristol
Address:
The Sun Alliance Ground, Nevil Road,
Bristol BS7 9EJ
Tel: 0117 910 8000
Directions:
By road: M5, M4, M32 into Bristol: exit at second
exit (Fishponds/Horfield), then third exit – Muller
Road. Almost at end of Muller Road (bus station on right),
turn left at Ralph Road. Go to the top, turn left and then
right almost immediately into Kennington Avenue. Follow
the signs for County Cricket.
Capacity: 8,000
Other grounds used: College Ground, Cheltenham;
Kings School, Gloucester
Year formed: 1870

Chairman: Alan Haines
Director of Cricket: Andy Stovold
Other posts: Chief Executive: Tom Richardson;
Youth Development Officer: Richard Holdsworth
Coach: John Bracewell
Captain: Mark Alleyne
Coaching contact: Andy Stovold, Director of Coaching
0117 910 8004
County colours: Blue, brown, gold, green and red,
sky blue

HONOURS

BENSON & HEDGES CUP
1977, 1999, 2000
GILLETTE CUP/C&G TROPHY
1973, 1999, 2000

National Cricket League nickname:
GLOUCESTERSHIRE GLADIATORS

Website:
www.glosccc.co.uk

HAMPSHIRE CCC

Home Ground:
Southampton
Address:
The Hampshire Rose Bowl, Botley Road,
West End, Southampton SO30 3XH
Tel: 02380 472002
Fax: 02380 472122
Indoor school: 02380 472468
Email: enquiries.hants@ecb.co.uk
Directions:
By rail: Southampton Parkway – 4 miles.
By road: From M27, exit junction 7 and take the
A334 then the B3035 (Botley Road, West End).
Capacity: 9,950
Year formed: 1863

Chief Executive: Graham Walker
Marketing Manager: Samantha White
Director of Cricket: Tim Tremlett
Other posts: Head Groundsman: Nigel Gray
Youth Development Officer: Alan Rowe
Cricket Development Coach: Raj Maru; Women's
Cricket Development Officer: Clair Slaney
Captain: Shane Warne
County colours: Navy blue, old gold

HONOURS

COUNTY CHAMPIONSHIP
1961, 1973
SUNDAY LEAGUE/NUL
1975, 1978, 1986
BENSON & HEDGES CUP 1988,
1992
GILLETTE CUP/C&G TROPHY
1991

National Cricket League nickname:
HAMPSHIRE HAWKS

Website:
www.hampshire.cricket.org

at Cardiff
Durham 162 (51.2 overs) (ML Love 71, SD Thomas 7 for 33) and 243 (PD Collingwood 99, GJ Muchall 77)
Glamorgan 205 (89 overs) (MJ Powell 62*) and 204 for 5 (SP James 121)
Glamorgan won by five wickets
Glamorgan 16 pts, Durham 3 pts

Middlesex went to the top of the Division Two table with victory by an innings and two runs over Northamptonshire at Wantage Road. Batting first, Middlesex amassed 541 with Sven Koenig (101) and Paul Weekes (107) playing the major innings. Robin Weston (72), David Nash (55) and Aaron Laraman

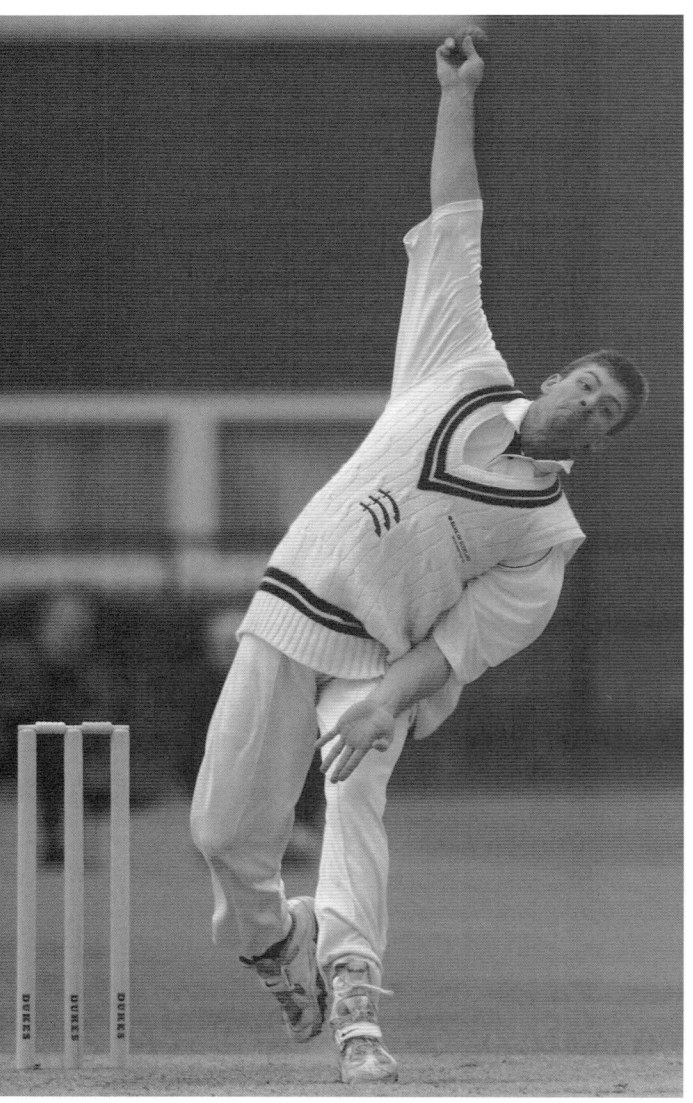

(43) all chipped in, while Ashley Noffke and Tim Bloomfield took further advantage of some ragged bowling to add 53 for the final wicket. Initially, through Mike Hussey (84) and Adrian Rollins (107), Northants put up a good fight, but once their first-wicket stand of 167 had been broken, the home side were in trouble. Rollins tried hard to battle on, with wickets falling around him, but an overnight 202 for 4 (Rollins 69 not out) soon became 286 all out and, by the end of the third day, Northants had been bowled out again for 253 with only Jeff Cook (84) resisting for long. Simon Cook was the Middlesex bowler who did virtually all of the damage to the Northants first innings, picking up a career-best 8 for 63 with an outstanding display, while Laraman (4 for 55) and Noffke (3 for 77) were most successful bowlers second time around.

A career-best haul of 7 for 44 by John Stephenson, the 37-year-old former England opener, earned Essex a five-wicket win over Worcestershire at New Road. A match that looked as though it was meandering to a stalemate suddenly exploded into life on the third evening when Stephenson reduced Worcestershire to 98 for 6 in their second innings with a spell of 5 for 22 in 9.5 overs. When he helped finish off the innings for 140 the next morning, Stephenson not only boasted a career-best analysis, but also ten wickets in a match for the very first time in his 17 years as a county cricketer. Essex, who had earlier in the game replied with 373 to Worcestershire's own first innings of 367, were now left with a fairly straightforward victory target, and Andy Flower's 47 and Ronnie Irani's unbeaten 32 saw the visitors past the winning post. Flower and Irani had also both contributed 40s to Essex's first innings, which was built around 71 from opener Darren Robinson and a fine 117 from Aftab Habib. Anurag Singh (60), Ben Smith (61) and Andy Bichel (65) were the main run getters in the Worcestershire first innings.

Gloucestershire moved themselves up into fourth place in the division by defeating Nottinghamshire by seven wickets at Bristol. James Averis enjoyed a career-best haul of 5 for 51 as Notts batted carelessly to be bowled out for 197 on day one, and by the close Gloucestershire were already in the driving seat at 165 for 2 in reply. Craig Spearman, on 99 not out overnight, went on to 118 in the morning and an important three-and-a-quarter hour 53 from Matt Windows provided the base for Ian Fisher (41) and

Simon Cook, the Middlesex seamer, propelled his team to the top of Division Two with eight wickets against Northamptonshire at Wantage Road.

Averis (43) to thrash 71 in 13 overs for the eighth wicket against a tiring attack. Gloucestershire's total of 347 clearly became a match-winning one as Notts folded again to 108 for 5 by the close of the second day. Guy Welton's 68 and Kevin Pietersen's powerful 46 not out the next morning were the only two innings of substance as Notts' second innings expired at 182. Averis and Jon Lewis picked up three wickets apiece, and Gloucestershire were only mildly irritated at losing three wickets themselves as they successfully achieved their small target of 33.

Durham's struggles continued at Cardiff where, despite a gutsy second-innings rally by Paul Collingwood and Gordon Muchall, they went down by five wickets to Glamorgan. Only Martin Love (71) made any impression in Durham's first innings of 162 as Darren Thomas produced both pace and swing to take championship-best figures of 7 for 33. Glamorgan found batting difficult themselves, with Michael Powell's unbeaten 62 chiefly responsible for getting them up to 205 all out in reply. Then came Collingwood (99) and 19-year-old Muchall, who hit a career-best 77 in his third championship game to help his senior partner add 140 for the fifth wicket. Sadly for Durham, however, they could only reach 243, as Thomas completed his first ten-wicket match haul, and a 44th first-class hundred from Steve James, who was only out for 121, two runs short of the victory target, guided Glamorgan home.

ROUND FIVE: 24–27 MAY 2002

Division One

at The Oval
Surrey 220 (69.1 overs) (IJ Ward 62, AR Caddick 5 for 66) and 332 (IJ Ward 67, AJ Stewart 53)
Somerset 253 (80.2 overs) (ID Blackwell 98) and 45 for 1
Match drawn – no play was possible on the third day
Surrey 8 pts, Somerset 9 pts

at Horsham
Leicestershire 264 (70.4 overs) (VJ Wells 86*, DI Stevens 50, RSC Martin–Jenkins 7 for 51) and 94 for 2
Sussex 247 (69.5 overs) (RR Montgomerie 122* – carried his bat, DE Malcolm 7 for 76)
Match drawn – no play was possible on the third and fourth days
Sussex 8 pts, Leicestershire 9 pts

at Headingley
Hampshire 354 (109.3 overs) (JP Crawley 79,

WS Kendall 67) and 62 for 1
Yorkshire 423 (134.5 overs) (RJ Blakey 83, C White 67, SP Kirby 57, MP Vaughan 54, DA Mascarenhas 5 for 87)
Match drawn
Yorkshire 12 pts, Hampshire 11 pts

A blank third day, due to rain, spoiled a potentially classic finish in the match between Surrey and Somerset at The Oval. Surrey, fielding 11 internationals, were bowled out for 220 in their first innings on the opening day, with a superb Andy Caddick taking 5 for 66 and Matt Bulbeck 4 for 60 – his best figures for three years. Martin Bicknell (4 for 72) and Alex Tudor (3 for 64) fought back on day two, but Somerset still won themselves a useful lead by reaching 253 as Ian Blackwell thumped 98 off just 112 balls, with 17 fours, and featured in a sixth-wicket stand worth 106 with Rob Turner. At 87 for 3 at the close of the second day, Surrey were in some bother, but rain then played its hand and, when the game resumed on the fourth morning, Ian Ward led some stubborn Surrey resistance with a determined 67. Ally Brown, Alec Stewart (53), Tudor and Bicknell all played their parts, too, and in the end the home side reached the safety of 332 all out. There was time only for Somerset to score 45 for 1 from ten overs in their second innings.

The bowling of Robin Martin-Jenkins and Devon Malcolm, and the batting of Richard Montgomerie and Vince Wells, provided rich entertainment in another match which promised much, but ultimately fell victim to the weather. Leicestershire, with eight second-innings wickets remaining, led Sussex by 111 runs when the last two days were lost to rain. Wells had remained 86 not out as Leicestershire were bowled out in their first innings for 264, Martin-Jenkins claiming a career-best 7 for 51. And only opener Montgomerie, carrying his bat valiantly for 122 not out, could resist the fire and brimstone of the remarkable 39-year-old Malcolm who, with the wind at his back, roared in to take 7 for 76 as Sussex were dismissed for 247.

Batsmen held sway at Headingley, though, even on a pitch of some uneven bounce, and the loss of all but ten overs of the third day's play meant an honourable draw between Yorkshire and Hampshire. John Crawley (79) and Will Kendall (67) put on 145 for the second wicket as Hampshire totalled 354 in their first innings, while Robin Smith (41) square cut Matthew Hoggard (4 for 93) for one memorable six. Half-centuries from Craig White and Michael Vaughan formed the basis of

Sussex were indebted to Richard Montgomerie's unbeaten 122 against Leicestershire, which was almost half of his team's total.

Yorkshire's first innings, while 83 from Richard Blakey and a last-wicket stand of 57 between Steve Kirby (57) and Hoggard boosted the total to an eventual 423. Dimitri Mascarenhas plugged away to finish with 5 for 87, and in the 18 remaining overs Hampshire reached 62 for 1 in their second innings before the draw was confirmed.

Division Two

at Chester-le-Street
Durham 470-8 dec. (140 overs) (A Pratt 93, ML Love 78, GJ Pratt 66, PD Collingwood 65, GJ Muchall 52)
Gloucestershire 132 (53.2 overs) and (following on) 261 for 8 (RC Russell 78*, MGN Windows 73)
Match drawn
Durham 12 pts,
Gloucestershire 6 pts

at Trent Bridge
Northamptonshire 277 (71.4 overs) (AL Penberthy 106*) and 159 (AS Rollins 60, AJ Harris 7 for 54)
Nottinghamshire 207 for 8 dec. (62 overs) (CG Greenidge 5 for 66) and 231 for 3 (JER Gallian 111*, Usman Afzaal 88)
Nottinghamshire won by seven wickets
Nottinghamshire 16 pts,
Northamptonshire 3.5 pts
(Northamptonshire had 0.5 pt deducted for a slow over rate)

at Chelmsford
Derbyshire 158 (49.4 overs) and 199
Essex 168 (52.3 overs) and 193 for 4 (RC Irani 101, A Flower 55*)
Essex won by six wickets – no play was possible on the first day
Essex 15 pts, Derbyshire 3 pts

Weather interruptions, and the doggedness of Jack Russell, prevented Durham from completing a morale-boosting victory over Gloucestershire at Chester-le-Street. As it was, the north-east county had to settle for the satisfaction of a fine performance and try to see beyond the frustration of failing to remove Russell, and James Averis, on the final afternoon. With a minimum of 42 overs of the match remaining, Gloucestershire were seemingly down and out at 177 for 7 in their second innings – still way behind on run aggregate after being bowled out for 132 in their first innings. But then Russell, with

KENT CCC

Home Ground:
Canterbury
Address:
St Lawrence Ground,
Old Dover Road,
Canterbury,
Kent CT1 3NZ
Tel: 01227 456886
Fax: 01227 762168
Indoor school: 01227 473605
Email: kent@ecb.co.uk
Directions:
By rail: Canterbury East/West.
By road: AA roadsigns
Capacity: 10,000
Other grounds used: The Mote, Maidstone;
The Nevill, Tunbridge Wells
Year formed: 1870

Chief Executive: Paul Millman
First Team Coach: Ian Brayshaw
Other posts: Head Groundsman: Mike Grantham;
Second Team Coach: Chris Stone; Marketing Manager:
Jon Fordham
Captain: David Fulton
County colours: Blue and white

HONOURS

COUNTY CHAMPIONSHIP
1906, 1909, 1910, 1913, 1970,
1977, 1978
SUNDAY LEAGUE/NUL
1972, 1973, 1976, 1995, 2001
BENSON & HEDGES CUP
1973, 1976, 1978
GILLETTE CUP/C&G TROPHY
1967, 1974

National Cricket League nickname:
KENT SPITFIRES

Website:
www.kentcountycricket.co.uk

78 not out, and Averis, who lasted 39 overs for his 14, dug in. In the end, Gloucestershire reached 261 for 8, but Graeme Bridge, who took 4 for 50 from 35 overs, and Ian Hunter, with 3 for 68 to add to his first-innings haul of three wickets, also finished with honour. Five Durham players also topped 50 in their own first innings of 470 for 8 declared, with Andrew Pratt top scoring with 93.

Nottinghamshire seemed to ease the pressure on

Clive Rice, their high-profile director of cricket, with a seven-wicket win at Trent Bridge which piled on the early-season agony for Northamptonshire. Rice went into the match with just ten wins from his previous 52 championship matches in charge, and the lack of progress made since his appointment in 1999 had been the subject of a club committee meeting two nights previously. Northants, though, seemed to be in control of the game until the start of the final day. The visitors had totalled 277 in their first innings, thanks in the main to Tony Penberthy's unbeaten 106, and Carl Greenidge had then taken 5 for 66, his first five-wicket haul for his new county, as Notts struggled through rain-affected second and third days to reach 207 for 8. But then they declared, and Andrew Harris produced career-best figures of 7 for 54 as Northants were tumbled out for 159. Adrian Rollins (60) and Mike Hussey had actually put on 57 for the first wicket inside nine overs before the collapse, which showed that there was nothing too wrong with the pitch, and Notts captain Jason Gallian confirmed that fact by cruising to an unbeaten 111. Despite an early stutter at 5 for 2, Gallian and Usman Afzaal (88) were untroubled as they added a match-winning 183 for the third wicket.

The loss of the opening day, to rain, did not prevent a result on a lively surface at Chelmsford, where Essex beat Derbyshire by six wickets to go third in the Division Two table. Richard Clinton, the Essex left-hander, suffered a broken wrist when he was hit by a ball from Mohammad Ali, and the match looked in the balance when the home side only gained a slender first-innings lead of ten because of Ashley Cowan's late hitting in a 47-ball 40 not out. Derbyshire, bowled out for 158 first time around, then recovered from 83 for 6 to reach 199, with Kevin Dean (48) joining Karl Krikken (48) in a seventh-wicket stand of 67. A testing target on paper, however, especially when Essex slid to

Jason Gallian steered Nottinghamshire to a rare championship victory over Northamptonshire.

26 for 3, was dismissed by the majestic Ronnie Irani, who struck 101 from just 70 balls and dominated a match-clinching partnership of 155 with Andy Flower. The Zimbabwean remained 55 not out when victory arrived.

ROUND SIX: 31 MAY–3 JUNE 2002

Division One

at Tunbridge Wells
Sussex 180 (68 overs) (MJ Saggers 6 for 39) and 354 (RR Montgomerie 79, MW Goodwin 76, MJ Prior 67, A Symonds 6 for 105)
Kent 343 (106.4 overs) (A Symonds 89, MA Ealham 83*) and 195 for 6 (ET Smith 82)
Kent won by four wickets
Kent 18 pts, Sussex 3 pts

at Leicester
Yorkshire 310 (105.4 overs) (C White 62, DS Lehmann 51, DE Malcolm 6 for 72) and 239 (DS Lehmann 119*, PAJ DeFreitas 5 for 38)
Leicestershire 346 (95.4 overs) (MG Bevan 142, DL Maddy 61) and 207 for 5 (MG Bevan 76*, DL Maddy 58)
Leicestershire won by five wickets
Leicestershire 18 pts, Yorkshire 5.5 pts (Yorkshire had 0.5 pt deducted for a slow over rate)

at Old Trafford
Surrey 382 (147 overs) (JN Batty 104, MR Ramprakash 71, IJ Ward 61, G Keedy 5 for 122) and 246 for 6 dec. (IJ Ward 106)
Lancashire 194 (76.1 overs) (G Chapple 51) and 112 for 3
Match drawn
Lancashire 6 pts, Surrey 10 pts

at Southampton Rose Bowl
Warwickshire 250 (111.2 overs) (MJ Powell 92, JO Troughton 73, AD Mullally 6 for 56) and 329 for 8 dec. (JO Troughton 131*)
Hampshire 277 (104 overs) (JP Crawley 60) and 142 for 7
Match drawn
Hampshire 9 pts, Warwickshire 9 pts

A magnificent spell of 5 for 16 in ten overs by Martin Saggers, immediately after lunch on the first day, set up an eventual four-wicket win for Kent against Sussex at Tunbridge Wells. The match had begun with Kent members in a near panic as the pavilion bar at the Nevill Ground found itself without beer, but the pumps were soon working as well as ever and, by tea-time, the Kent faithful had something to raise a glass to as Saggers' 6 for 39 left Sussex 180 all out. By the close Kent were 156 for 3 in reply and already in complete command. Andrew Symonds took his overnight 53 to 89 on the Saturday morning, and in the afternoon an unlikely 77-run stand for the final wicket, between Mark Ealham and Ben Trott, prevented a gutsy Sussex fightback from claiming full reward. Ealham ended on 83 not out but, on the third day, Kent's bowlers had to work hard to dismiss their opponents for 354 after Richard Montgomerie (79) and Murray Goodwin (76) had added 146 for the first wicket. Matt Prior then came up with a career-best 67, but Symonds' 6 for 105 meant that Kent needed 192 for victory. At the start of the final day they had already made it to 134 for 3, with Ed Smith unbeaten on 74. Smith fell early for 82, but there were no further alarms.

Free-falling champions Yorkshire had the additional indignity of being docked half a point for a slow over rate after losing by five wickets to Leicestershire at Grace Road. The match had begun promisingly enough for Yorkshire, who totalled 310 in their first innings with Craig White and Darren Lehmann both posting half-centuries. Devon Malcolm, however, raised spirits in the Leicestershire dressing room by taking 6 for 72 and, in the process, to become only the fifth bowler still playing to complete 1,000 first-class wickets (the others being Phil DeFreitas, Wasim Akram, Allan Donald and Phil Tufnell). Vic Craven, clean bowled, was his 1,000th victim – Surrey's England wicketkeeper-batsman Jack Richards had been his first, at Chesterfield in 1984. Michael Bevan's superb 142, supported by Darren Maddy's 61, then took Leicestershire to 348 in reply and only Lehmann, with a brave, unbeaten 119, could withstand the force of the two 1,000-wicket men, Malcolm and DeFreitas, as Yorkshire's second innings stumbled to 239 all out. Malcolm took 4 for 76 to complete a memorable ten-wicket match haul while DeFreitas picked up an impressive 5 for 38 from 22.4 overs. Despite being 63 for 3 early on the final day, Leicestershire were guided safely to their 202-run target by Maddy (58) and Bevan (76 not out).

Rain at the end of the third day, and for much of the fourth, saved Lancashire from a probable beating by Surrey at Old Trafford. Surrey's first-innings total of 382 was based on half-centuries from Ian Ward, captaining in the championship for the first time, and Mark Ramprakash, plus a second

Surrey's Jon Batty scored his second first-class hundred as Surrey piled on the runs against Lancashire.

first-class hundred by Jon Batty. Rikki Clarke hit 41 on his championship debut, and then Saqlain Mushtaq (4 for 43) and Ian Salisbury (2 for 16) spun Lancashire out for 194. Ward's 106 was the feature of Surrey's second innings of 246 for 6 declared but, in the end, he must have wished he had enforced the follow-on as the weather allowed Lancashire to escape at 112 for 3 from the mere 26 overs they had to face.

Poor weather on the final day at Southampton also helped Hampshire to hold out for a draw against Warwickshire. Hampshire were left hanging on at 142 for 7, but 33 overs were lost. Earlier, the match had been a showcase for the burgeoning talents of Jim Troughton. The young left-hander added 131 not out, his maiden championship century, to a first-innings knock of 63 – with his fine hundred enabling Warwickshire to declare second time around at 329 for 8. Hampshire, for whom Alan Mullally took 6 for 56 in Warwickshire's first innings 250, had then replied with 277.

Division Two

at Northampton
Northamptonshire 632 (146.2 overs) (MEK Hussey 140, JW Cook 90, AS Rollins 89, RJ Warren 87, TMB

Bailey 64, RSG Anderson 51, AL Penberthy 50) and 155
Essex 497 for 7 dec. (150.5 overs) (A Flower 103*, Aftab Habib 93, DDJ Robinson 68, JD Middlebrook 67, RC Irani 54) and 291 for 6 (A Flower 92*, JM Dakin 57)
Essex won by four wickets
Essex 19 pts, Northamptonshire 7 pts

at Derby
Derbyshire 354 (92.3 overs) (MJ Di Venuto 98, G Welch 63*) and 5 for 1
Glamorgan 157 (55.4 overs) (KJ Dean 7 for 42) and 200
Derbyshire won by nine wickets
Derbyshire 18.25 pts, Glamorgan 3 pts (Derbyshire had 0.75 pt deducted for a slow over rate)

at Bristol
Worcestershire 287 (102.2 overs) (WPC Weston 82, GA Hick 79) and 324 for 3 dec. (A Singh 187, GA Hick 72, WPC Weston 54)
Gloucestershire 130 (55.5 overs) (Kabir Ali 5 for 32) and 177 (CM Spearman 55, Kabir Ali 5 for 34)
Worcestershire won by 304 runs
Worcestershire 17 pts, Gloucestershire 3 pts

at Lord's
Durham 645 for 6 dec. (153 overs) (ML Love 251, GJ Muchall 127, JJB Lewis 71)
Middlesex 465 (167 overs) (OA Shah 112, AJ Strauss 96) and 194 for 5 (EC Joyce 71)
Match drawn
Middlesex 9 pts, Durham 11 pts

There were remarkable events at Wantage Road where Essex somehow conjured up a four-wicket win after seeing Northamptonshire pile up a mammoth 632 on the first two days! A club record seven players passed 50 in the Northants first innings, headed by Mike Hussey (140), although 19-year-old leg spinner Zoheb Sharif emerged from the carnage with a creditable 4 for 98 on his first-class debut. By the close of day two, Essex were a steady 186 for 2 from 63 overs, but then Aftab Habib, with 16 fours in his 93, and Andy Flower, with his first century of the season, built quickly on earlier innings of 68 and 67 from Darren Robinson and James Middlebrook respectively. Ronnie Irani's belligerent 54 enabled Essex to declare at 497 for 7 and, just before lunch on the final day, Northants were dismissed for 155 in their second innings, having begun the day on 58 for 2. Mark Ilott removed the dangerous Hussey for 41 and then John Stephenson (4 for 25) helped to rout the rest. Essex now had a minimum of 52 overs to reach their target of 291 – and they needed just 49.5 of them. Robinson

LANCASHIRE CCC

Home Ground:
Old Trafford
Address:
Old Trafford, Manchester M16 0PX
Tel: 0161 282 4000 (switchboard)
       0161 282 4040 (ticket/membership office)
Fax: 0161 873 8353 (ticket office)
Indoor cricket centre: 0161 282 4039
Email: enquiries@lccc.co.uk
Directions:
By rail: Manchester Piccadilly or Victoria then Metro link to Old Trafford (station alongside ground).
By road: M63, Stretford slip road (junction 7) on to A56; follow signs.
Capacity: 21,500
Other grounds used: Blackpool (Stanley Park); Liverpool (Aigburth); Southport (Trafalgar Road); Lytham (Church Road).
Year formed: 1864

Chairman: Jack Simmons MBE
Chief Executive: Jim Cumbes
Other posts: Head Groundsman: Peter Marron; Sales & Marketing Manager: Geoff Durbin
County coach: Mike Watkinson
Captain: Warren Hegg
County colours: Red, blue, green

HONOURS

COUNTY CHAMPIONSHIP
1881, 1897, 1927, 1928, 1930, 1934
JOINT CHAMPIONS
1878, 1882, 1889, 1950
SUNDAY LEAGUE/NUL
1999
BENSON & HEDGES CUP
1984, 1990, 1995, 1996
GILLETTE CUP/C&G TROPHY
1970, 1971, 1972, 1975, 1990, 1996, 1998

National Cricket League nickname:
LANCASHIRE LIGHTNING

Website:
www.lccc.co.uk

and Will Jefferson put on 85 for the first wicket, before Flower (92 not out from 91 balls) and Jon Dakin (57) added a match-winning 111 for the fifth wicket. Stephenson then kept the in-form Flower company until the finishing line was crossed. While Essex rejoiced, the Northants players were in shock.

Derbyshire, meanwhile, maintained their impressive start to the championship season with a two-day thrashing of Glamorgan at Derby. Michael Di Venuto (98 off 107 balls, with 17 fours) and Graeme Welch (63 not out) were the major contributors to Derbyshire's first-innings score of 354, and the opening day ended with Dominic Cork reducing Glamorgan to 22 for 2 in reply. That became 157 all out the following day, Kevin Dean almost single-handedly destroying the rest of the Glamorgan batting taking 7 for 42. Following on, the Welshmen were dismissed again for 200 with Dean adding a further 3 for 67 and Cork mopping up with 4 for 50. Derbyshire needed just four to win, but lost opener Steve Stubbings before clinching a nine-wicket victory.

Worcestershire seemed to enjoy rubbing in their complete dominance over Gloucestershire at Bristol before comfortably wrapping up an emphatic 304-run win inside three days. Mike Smith, whose last championship appearance was the first match of the 2001 season, made a welcome return with 4 for 61, but Worcestershire's first-innings 287, in which Philip Weston (82) and Graeme Hick (79) added 122 for the second wicket, still earned them a halfway lead of 157 as Gloucestershire slid to 130 all out in reply. Then, after Weston had again batted well for 54, Anurag Singh (187) and Hick (72) gorged themselves on the home bowling before the second-innings declaration came at 324 for 3. Singh's first hundred runs took him just 90 balls, but Kabir Ali tussled with him for the headlines by producing figures of 5 for 34 to go with his first innings 5 for 32 as Gloucestershire subsided weakly again for 177.

From an English perspective, the batting of 19-year-old Gordon Muchall was just as eye-catching as the career-best and majestic 251 compiled by Durham's Australian Martin Love at Lord's. Muchall's 127 against Middlesex was his maiden first-class century and, at times, the youngster and the accomplished Aussie were indistinguishable in terms of class. Phil Tufnell was far from amused as Love and Muchall put on 251 for the second wicket, and then Jon Lewis chipped in with 71 as Durham reached 645 for 6 declared, their highest total as a first-class county. Tufnell was reprimanded by the

umpires for using abusive language, but at least the former England spinner was then able to put his feet up as Middlesex batted from just before tea on the second day to almost an hour into the fourth day to total 465. Andy Strauss hit 96 and Owais Shah 112, but Middlesex still had to follow on and – at 29 for 3 in their second innings – the weary Durham bowlers were suddenly feeling rejuvenated. Ed Joyce, however, then joined Shah in a stand worth 101 and, perhaps more importantly, using up almost three hours. In the end, with Joyce scoring 71, Middlesex survived for the draw at 194 for 5.

ROUND SEVEN: 12–15 JUNE 2002

Division One

at Headingley
Sussex 435 (129.1 overs) (TR Ambrose 149, MJ Prior 83)
Yorkshire 216 (92.5 overs) (A McGrath 71, RJ Blakey 52, RJ Kirtley 5 for 49) and 125 (RJ Kirtley 5 for 41)
Sussex won by an innings & 94 runs
Sussex 20 pts, Yorkshire 4 pts

at The Oval
Kent 153 (43 overs) (PA Nixon 54, MP Bicknell 6 for 42) and 268
Surrey 361 (87.1 overs) (AD Brown 188, J Ormond 73) and 61 for 1
Surrey won by nine wickets
Surrey 19 pts, Kent 3 pts

at Edgbaston
Warwickshire 462 (142.4 overs) (JO Troughton 130, DP Ostler 81, IR Bell 72) and 206 for 7 dec. (SM Pollock 65)
Leicestershire 370 (115.2 overs) (TR Ward 89, GW Flower 75, ND Burns 64) and 154 (NMK Smith 5 for 42)
Warwickshire won by 144 runs
Warwickshire 20 pts, Leicestershire 6 pts

at Bath
Hampshire 252 (76.3 overs) (WS Kendall 88) and 98 (RL Johnson 7 for 43)
Somerset 161 for 9 dec. (74 overs) and 173 for 8
Match drawn
Somerset 7 pts, Hampshire 9 pts

James Kirtley took 5 for 49 and 5 for 41 as Sussex confirmed the remarkable decline of champions Yorkshire by beating them by an innings and 94 runs at Headingley. First, Sussex ran up 435, with

Tim Ambrose, the precocious 19-year-old Anglo-Aussie, compiling a highly mature 149 in just his seventh championship innings. Joining Ambrose in a sixth-wicket stand of 191 was another youngster, the 20-year-old wicketkeeper Matt Prior, who scored 83. Poor Gavin Hamilton, suffering the bowling 'yips', included 14 runs in wides in a 12-ball over that cost 17 runs. He was then taken off. Anthony McGrath (71) and Richard Blakey (52) then produced the only resistance of note as Yorkshire were tumbled out for 216 and just 125, largely by the pace and movement of Kirtley, and remained rooted to the bottom of the Division One table.

A superlative 188 by Alistair Brown proved the difference for Surrey against Kent at The Oval – a match which will also be remembered for the fact that play on the second morning was delayed for an hour and a half due to most of the Kent team being stuck in a London gridlock! Only two Kent players were at the ground at the scheduled 11am start – and that was because they were not staying at the team hotel just across the Thames. It took some of the other players three hours, even by various routes, to drive the six miles from the hotel to Kennington – while Min Patel, the left-arm spinner, did not arrive until 1.33pm because his car had overheated! Brown's hundred took him just 99 balls, and then he just kept on going at a similar rate until being the last man out. James Ormond, with 73, also played an important role as Surrey rallied from being 111 for 5 overnight, in reply to Kent's first-innings total of 153, to reach 361 all out. Kent, up against it, lost David Fulton for 48 to a brilliant catch in the gully by Ian Salisbury and were eventually all out for 268. Surrey, who knocked off the 61 runs they then required for the loss of only one wicket, were also left saluting Martin Bicknell. His 6 for 42 on the opening day had given him a five-wicket haul against all 17 other first-class counties.

Jim Troughton was awarded his county cap at Edgbaston after hitting 130 from 201 balls, with 23 fours, in just his sixth first-class match. It was an innings which helped Warwickshire to total 462 in the first four sessions of a match against Leicestershire which they eventually won by 144 runs. Ian Bell (72) and Dominic Ostler (81) also added 96 for the third wicket and Leicestershire, despite reaching 370 themselves with Trevor Ward making 89, Grant Flower 75 and Neil Burns 64, were soon facing an awkward last afternoon when Warwickshire declared their second innings on 206 for 7. Shaun Pollock then followed up his 65 by taking his second three-wicket haul of the game and,

with off spinner Neil Smith picking up 5 for 42, Leicestershire were bowled out for 154.

At Bath there was almost an astonishing victory for Somerset, despite the poor weather which caused interruptions to each of the first three days. Will Kendall's excellent 88 enabled Hampshire to reach 252 in their first innings and Somerset were struggling in their reply until, frustrated by the weather delays, they declared at 161 for 9 towards the end of the third day. Suddenly, in 3.3 overs, Hampshire lost their first four second-innings wickets for just three runs, with Nic Pothas averting a Matt Bulbeck hat-trick. Richard Johnson, who had taken the other two overnight wickets, then went on the next morning to take 7 for 43. Hampshire, at one stage 16 for 6, did however fight their way to 98 all out with Robin Smith (41 not out) adding a vital 36 for the ninth wicket with Chris Tremlett. Somerset, now needing 190 to win, slumped to 117 for 7 in the tricky conditions before recovering and eventually finishing up at 173 for 8. The last ball of the permitted 61 overs remained unbowled as both teams shook hands on what was, in the end, an exciting draw.

Division Two

at Ilford
Essex 498 for 9 dec. (162 overs) (RC Irani 207*, A Flower 85, WI Jefferson 59) and 68 for 1
Northamptonshire 204 (65 overs) (MEK Hussey 67) and 361 (MEK Hussey 71, TMB Bailey 68)
Essex won by nine wickets
Essex 20 pts, Northamptonshire 3 pts

at Trent Bridge
Nottinghamshire 393 (99 overs) (P Johnson 96, N Boje 84, JER Gallian 69) and 175 (DG Cork 6 for 78)
Derbyshire 392 (112.4 overs) (MJ Di Venuto 79, CWG Bassano 64, AI Gait 52) and 181 for 6 (CWG Bassano 79)
Derbyshire won by four wickets
Derbyshire 19 pts, Nottinghamshire 7 pts

at Chester-le-Street
Worcestershire 250 (77.5 overs) (DA Leatherdale 63, GJ Batty 56) and 60 for 5
Durham 243 (82.3 overs) (DRC Law 68, A Pratt 67, AA Donald 5 for 77)
Match drawn
Durham 8 pts, Worcestershire 9 pts

at Lord's
Glamorgan 369 (101.2 overs) (MJ Powell 122,

MP Maynard 90)
Middlesex 403 for 9 dec. (116.5 overs) (SG Koenig 86, EC Joyce 73)
Match drawn – no play was possible on the first day
Middlesex 12 pts, Glamorgan 11 pts

The contrasting fortunes of Essex and Northamptonshire were brought into sharp relief when the two counties met at Ilford. Essex, having totalled 498 for 9 declared in their first innings, then enforced the follow-on before condemning Northants to five successive championship defeats for the first time since 1961. At least Northants managed to avoid an innings defeat, reaching 361 second time around after initially being bowled out for 204. Will Jefferson added an unbeaten 33 to his first-innings 59 as Essex completed their own fourth championship win in a row, by nine wickets. The match was another triumph for Ronnie Irani, the in-form Essex captain, who lifted his season's first-class batting average to 72 by hitting three sixes and 20 fours in a superb unbeaten 207 during the first two days. Andy Flower hit 85 and then Ashley Cowan's 4 for 62 undermined the Northants first innings, with only Mike Hussey (67) resisting for long. Hussey again, with 71, did most to hold up Essex after Northants followed on – taking his summer first-class run tally to 872. Toby Bailey later made 68, but John Stephenson and James Middlebrook each took four wickets as the Northants second innings ended just over an hour into the final day.

Derbyshire, inspired once more by their captain Dominic Cork, won a hard-fought four-wicket victory at Trent Bridge – thus maintaining their 2002 renaissance, staying top of Division Two and putting one over their neighbours and rivals Nottinghamshire. For the first three days the contest was keen and even – Nottinghamshire running up 393 and Derbyshire replying with 392. Paul Johnson's 96 had seen the Nottinghamshire stalwart go past 20,000 first-class career runs in some style, while Jason Gallian and Nicky Boje also made good half-centuries. Michael Di Venuto launched the Derbyshire first innings with an 84-ball 79, while Andrew Gait included 11 boundaries in his 52, Chris Bassano stroked 64

and Mohammad Ali smashed 43 from 55 balls at the end. At the close of play on day three Nottinghamshire were 75 for 3, with Cork having snapped up two wickets in a fierce new-ball spell. Could Cork work his magic in the morning, too? He could indeed, taking his championship wicket tally to 41 by snapping up 6 for 78 as Nottinghamshire were hustled out for 175 in just a further 28.2 overs. Bassano's mature 79 then guided Derbyshire, not without some nervy moments, to their victory target.

Severe rain interruptions throughout the match,

Ronnie Irani on his way to 207 not out against Northants: an innings that prompted his recall to England's one-day team.

LEICESTERSHIRE CCC

Home Ground:
Grace Road, Leicester
Address:
County Ground,
Grace Road,
Leicester LE2 8AD
Tel: 0116 283 2128
Fax: 0116 244 0363
Email: leicestershirecc@ukonline.co.uk
Directions:
By road: Follow signs from city centre, or from southern ring road from M1 or A6.
Capacity: 5,500
Other grounds used: None
Year formed: 1879

Manager: Jack Birkenshaw
General Manager/Secretary: James Whitaker
Other posts: County coaches: Russell Cobb, John Smith, Phil Whiticase, Lloyd Tennant; Administrative Secretary: Kevin Hill
Captain: Vince Wells
Vice-captain: Ben Smith
County colours: Dark green and scarlet

HONOURS

COUNTY CHAMPIONSHIP
1975, 1996, 1998
SUNDAY LEAGUE
1974, 1977
BENSON & HEDGES CUP
1972, 1975, 1985

National Cricket League nickname:
LEICESTERSHIRE FOXES

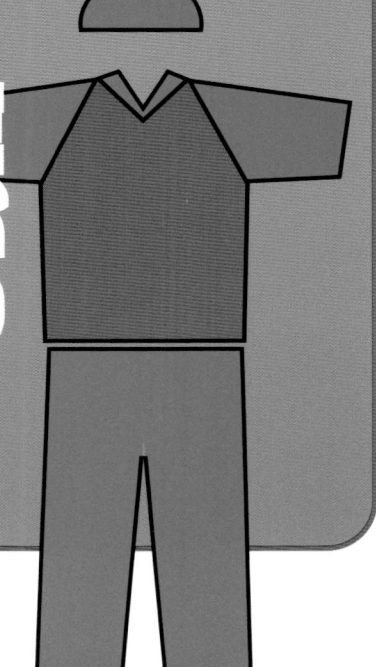

Website:
www.leicestershireccc.com

but especially on the last two days, left time enough only for the match between Durham and Worcestershire at Chester-le-Street to end in a draw. The fixture had significant consequences, however, for Durham, with Martin Love, their overseas player, breaking a finger and facing weeks out of the game. Worcestershire had a sixth-wicket partnership of 105 between David Leatherdale (63) and Gareth Batty (56) to thank for their progress to 250 all out, Nicky Hatch taking 4 for 61, while Durham replied solidly enough – despite the absence of Love – before Allan Donald wrapped up the innings at 243 to finish with 5 for 77 on his Worcestershire debut. For Durham, there was another promising knock of 46 by Gordon Muchall, 19, while Andrew Pratt scored 67 – taking 48 balls to get off the mark, but then just another 48 to reach 50 – and Danny Law made 68. In the time left, Neil Killeen picked up 4 for 26 as Worcestershire limped badly to 60 for 5.

Both teams were unhappy with covering arrangements at Lord's, where heavy overnight rain resulted in water getting underneath the covers and the abandonment of the first day's play between Middlesex and Glamorgan. In the 59 overs possible on the second day, Glamorgan reached 228 for 3 – stretching that to 369 all out with Michael Powell (122) and Matthew Maynard (90) adding 188 in 44 overs for the fourth wicket. Maynard, however, just missed out on becoming only the second Glamorgan batsman after Gilbert Parkhouse to score hundreds against all other first-class counties. Another 30 overs were lost to poor weather on the third day, too, leaving Middlesex to pile up 403 for 9 declared on the final day to make sure of maximum bonus points. Sven Koenig (86) and Ed Joyce (73) were the main suppliers of those runs.

ROUND EIGHT: 26–29 JUNE 2002

Division One

at Edgbaston
Warwickshire 230 (68.3 overs) and 423 (DP Ostler 175, JO Troughton 52, GG Wagg 51, PS Jones 6 for 110)
Somerset 208 (57 overs) (PD Bowler 57, M Burns 54) and 357 (RJ Turner 83*, ID Blackwell 64, M Burns 54)
Warwickshire won by 88 runs
Warwickshire 16 pts, Somerset 4 pts

at Liverpool
Lancashire 226 (61.1 overs) (SG Law 75, RC Driver 56, Amjad Khan 5 for 74) and 347 (AJ Swann 85, PJ Martin 80*, MJ Chilton 60, G Chapple 55)

Kent 214 (71 overs) (PJ Martin 5 for 54) and 360 for 4 (A Symonds 116*, DP Fulton 116, RWT Key 78)
Kent won by six wickets
Kent 15.5 pts, Lancashire 6 pts (Kent had 0.5 pt deducted for a slow over rate)

at Arundel
Yorkshire 255 (93.5 overs) (DS Lehmann 71) and 458 for 8 dec. (DS Lehmann 216, MJ Lumb 92)
Sussex 392 (111.2 overs) (MJ Prior 85, RR Montgomerie 78, MJG Davis 70*) and 216 for 9 (MJ Prior 70*)
Match drawn
Sussex 11 pts, Yorkshire 9 pts

Warwickshire earned themselves a second successive championship win by overcoming Somerset by 88 runs in a hard-fought affair at Edgbaston. On a pitch that got better as the game wore on, Somerset were bowled out for 357 in their second innings just before lunch on the final day. They made a fight of it, though, with Rob Turner (83 not out) and last man Richard Johnson, whose 38 contained three sixes, adding 60 for the tenth wicket. On the previous day, Michael Burns had scored 54 and Ian Blackwell a run-a-ball 64, but Jamie Spires, a 23-year-old slow left-arm spinner in only his third championship appearance, removed both Burns and Peter Bowler to put Warwickshire in control. Another young player, 19-year-old Graham Wagg, also impressed on his championship debut. First, he hit a six and six fours in an unbeaten 42 as Warwickshire totalled 230 on the opening day, and then he finished off the Somerset reply at 208 by taking the last four wickets for figures of 4 for 43. Wagg scored 51, too, with three sixes and six fours this time, as Warwickshire built a second-innings total of 423 on the second and third days. Steffan Jones battled away bravely, following the first-morning hamstring pull suffered by Johnson, to add 6 for 110 to his first-innings figures of 4 for 46, but Warwickshire were put in complete command by Dominic Ostler, who went past 10,000 career runs in the course of scoring a wonderful 175. It was his first hundred of the summer, and underlined his full recovery from a broken finger.

In another game where second-innings scoring was heavier than on the opening days, Kent defeated Lancashire by six wickets at Liverpool. Amjad Khan, Kent's 21-year-old fast bowler from Denmark, made a big contribution to the win – first taking 5 for 74 on day one as Lancashire were dismissed for 226, despite Stuart Law's 75, and then picking up three more wickets (as did Mark Ealham) as the home side were pegged back to 197 for 7 in their second innings by the end of day two after Alec Swann (85) and Mark Chilton (60) had put on 118 for the first wicket. In between, Kent had been bowled out for 214, with only Matthew Walker and Paul Nixon resisting for long, and Peter Martin (5 for 54) heading up a decent Lancashire seam bowling display. But, from the start of day three, batting seemed to get more straightforward with Martin clumping an unbeaten 80, Glen Chapple scoring 55, and Lancashire hauling themselves up to 347 all out. Now asked to make 360 for victory in the fourth innings, Kent responded with an opening stand worth 140 between David Fulton and Rob Key. By the close of the third day Kent were 174 for 2, despite Key falling for 78, and the next morning saw Fulton translate his overnight 82 into a five-hour 116. Andrew Symonds then produced some

Dominic Ostler passed 10,000 career runs on his way to 175 for Warwicks against Somerset.

scintillating strokeplay to reach 116 not out from 155 balls to see Kent home.

Yorkshire were denied a much-needed victory at Arundel by the unlikely resistance of Sussex No. 11 Mark Robinson. Having retired the previous September, to coach the second team, Robinson found himself pressed into emergency service for this match because of injury, poor form and unavailability. Indeed, it was the first time since 1997 that Sussex had gone into a championship fixture without either James Kirtley (on England one-day duty) or Jason Lewry (dropped). Robinson, then, who had taken two wickets in his first six overs when Yorkshire were bowled out for 255 on the opening day, became the home hero when he survived 11 balls on the final evening, and a last, desperate over by Craig White. Sussex had seemed to be in control when they totalled 392 in their first innings, Richard Montgomerie making 78, the 20-year-old Matt Prior a mature 85 and Mark Davis an unbeaten 70 from 81 balls. But Yorkshire hit back through Darren Lehmann who, having been bowled by a Robinson no-ball when he was on 17, went on to plunder 216 to add to his first-innings score of 71 and put on 238 for the fourth wicket with Michael Lumb (92). In the end, Yorkshire could even afford the luxury of declaring, at 458 for 8, but how they must have wished they had done so earlier when Robinson strode out to deny them as Sussex, for whom Prior again impressed with a battling 70 not out, clung on for a draw at 216 for 9.

Division Two

at Gloucester
Gloucestershire 383 (96.2 overs) (KJ Barnett 106, MW Alleyne 87, MCJ Ball 63, IJ Harvey 56, AP Cowan 5 for 68) and 322 for 7 dec. (RC Russell 107, ID Fisher 103*)
Essex 325 (127.1 overs) (Aftab Habib 66, AP Cowan 60*, JP Stephenson 57, IJ Harvey 5 for 64) and 381 for 7 (DDJ Robinson 175, Aftab Habib 82, IJ Harvey 6 for 90)
Essex won by three wickets
Essex 18 pts, Gloucestershire 7 pts

at Cardiff
Middlesex 633 for 7 dec. (163.1 overs) (Abdur Razzaq 203*, AJ Strauss 141, EC Joyce 129, OA Shah 62) and 85 for 2
Glamorgan 235 (56 overs) (MP Maynard 66, PCR Tufnell 6 for 96) and (following on) 481 (SP James 118, RDB Croft 75, MA Wallace 59)
Middlesex won by eight wickets
Middlesex 20 pts, Glamorgan 2 pts

at Northampton
Nottinghamshire 489 (147.1 overs) (CMW Read 127, JER Gallian 100, PJ Franks 67) and 172 (P Johnson 70)
Northamptonshire 420 (104.1 overs) (DJG Sales 179, MB Loye 105) and 242 for 4 (MB Loye 104*, JW Cook 68)
Northamptonshire won by six wickets
Northamptonshire 20 pts, Nottinghamshire 8 pts

at Worcester
Durham 120 (39.5 overs) and 215 (DRC Law 72*)
Worcestershire 643 for 7 dec. (148 overs) (GA Hick 315*, A Singh 88, BF Smith 83, AJ Bichel 78*)
Worcestershire won by an innings & 308 runs
Worcestershire 20 pts, Durham 2 pts

Essex went to the top of the Division Two table by pulling off a remarkable three-wicket win over Gloucestershire at the King's School, Gloucester. The home side set Essex 381 to win in 80 overs, and were shocked as Darren Robinson, with a breathtaking 175, and Aftab Habib (82) put on 180 for the second wicket to set up a successful chase. Ian Harvey did his best to hold back the tide of runs, with 6 for 90, but in the end Essex reached their target with eight balls to spare. Harvey had also taken 5 for 64 in the Essex first innings of 325, which had earned Gloucestershire a 58-run lead following their own 383 on the opening day. Kim Barnett hit a flamboyant 106, the irrepressible Harvey 56 and 158 was added in 35 overs by Mark Alleyne (87) and Martyn Ball (63). Ashley Cowan took 5 for 68 and scored an unbeaten 60 in the Essex first innings, but it was Mark Ilott and John Stephenson who had Gloucestershire in trouble at 90 for 6 on the third day before Jack Russell (107) and Ian Fisher (103 not out) rallied their side magnificently to an eventual 322 for 7 declared.

Middlesex maintained their good form by beating Glamorgan by eight wickets at Cardiff with Abdul Razzaq and Ed Joyce both reaching career bests as they added 320 for the fifth wicket in a massive first-innings total of 633 for 7 declared. Andy Strauss had opened up with 141, his first championship ton of the summer, and Owais Shah had scored 62, but it was Razzaq (203 not out) and Joyce (129) who turned on the power in a partnership that was only 18 runs short of a Middlesex record that has stood since 1895. Phil Tufnell then took 6 for 96 as Glamorgan crumbled to 235 all out in reply, but the Welsh county fought back to reach 481 in their second innings, with Steve James (118) hitting his 45th first-class century and both Robert Croft (75) and Mark Wallace (59) also resisting sternly. Middlesex, however, worked their way patiently through the order, with Razzaq and Tufnell both picking up three wickets, and Strauss joyfully thumped 48 as a small victory target was reached without much trouble.

Nottinghamshire, regrouping after the departure of Clive Rice their cricket manager, were beaten by Northamptonshire at Wantage Road despite recovering from 125 for 5 on the opening morning to reach 489 in their first innings. Jason Gallian, the captain, led the way with 100 and Notts were further boosted by 127 from Chris Read, the second hundred of his career, 67 from Paul Franks and a career-best, unbeaten 41 from Andy Harris. David Sales and Mal Loye, however, scored 179 and 105 respectively (Sales hitting two sixes and 24 boundaries) to take Northants to 420 in reply, and the match then turned as Jason Brown and Graeme Swann, the home spinners, began at last to take advantage of a dry pitch used twice in the previous

Graeme Hick recorded the highest score by a Worcestershire batsman at New Road: 315 not out against Durham.

MIDDLESEX CCC

Home Ground:
Lord's Cricket Ground
Address:
Lord's Cricket Ground,
St John's Wood, London NW8 8QN
Tel: 020 7289 1300
Fax: 020 7289 5831
Email: enquiries.middx@ecb.co.uk
Directions:
By underground: St John's Wood on Jubilee Line
(five minutes' walk).
By bus: 13, 82, 113 stop along east side of
ground; 139 at south-west corner; 274 at top
of Regent's Park
Capacity: 28,000
Other grounds used: Southgate; Richmond
Year formed: 1864

Chairman: Phil Edmonds
Secretary: Vinny Codrington
Head Coach: John Emburey
Assistant Coach: Jason Pooley
Captain: Andrew Strauss
County colours: Navy

HONOURS

COUNTY CHAMPIONSHIP
1903, 1920, 1921, 1947,
1949 (JOINT), 1976, 1977 (JOINT),
1980, 1982, 1985, 1990, 1993
SUNDAY LEAGUE/NUL
1992
BENSON & HEDGES CUP
1983, 1986
GILLETTE CUP/C&G TROPHY
1977, 1980, 1984, 1988

**National Cricket League
nickname:**
MIDDLESEX CRUSADERS

crusaders

Website:
www.middlesexccc.co.uk

week and reported to Lord's by the umpires, John Holder and Nigel Cowley, on the opening day. Paul Johnson (70) played the only innings of note second time around as Brown and Swann took three wickets apiece as Notts slid to 169 for 8 by the close of day three. The next morning saw Carl Greenidge clean up the tail, for the addition of just three more runs, and soon Loye was posting his second century of the match to lead Northants to their target of 242 for the loss of just four wickets. Loye ended up a triumphant 104 not out, and Jeff Cook weighed in with a valuable 68.

Durham's woes continued at New Road where Worcestershire overpowered them by an innings and 308 runs. The writing was on the wall when Durham were skittled out for only 120 on the opening day – Kabir Ali and Andy Bichel sharing eight wickets – and by the close the visitors were facing a nightmare with Worcestershire already on 264 for 2 and Graeme Hick on 119. Hick had been joined in a second-wicket stand of 190 by Anurag Singh (88), but the second day became a showcase for his mastery of all but the most excellent of attacks. Ben Smith made 83 and Bichel an explosive unbeaten 78, with three sixes and nine fours, but Hick was the focus of an adoring home crowd as he moved relentlessly to 315 not out – the highest individual score by a Worcestershire batsman at New Road, beating the 311 of Glenn Turner in 1982. In all, Hick hit two sixes and 49 fours and, after Worcestershire had finally declared at 643 for 7, Durham did well not to lose a wicket in the 16 overs that remained of what, for them, was a truly deflating second day. The next day, however, saw their overnight 50 for 0 become a sad 215 all out, with only Danny Law (72 not out) showing any fight and Kabir taking his season's wicket haul to 41 with 4 for 77.

ROUND NINE: 3–6 JULY 2002

Division One

at Taunton
Surrey 608 for 6 dec. (130.5 overs) (MR Ramprakash 218, R Clarke 153*, AJ Hollioake 87, N Shahid 51) and 324 for 5 dec. (JN Batty 151, IJ Ward 75, MR Ramprakash 53)
Somerset 554 (134.2 overs) (MJ Wood 106, M Burns 99, PCL Holloway 77, RJ Turner 56*) and 329 for 7 (MJ Wood 131, M Burns 68)
Match drawn
Somerset 7 pts, Surrey 8 pts

at Southampton Rose Bowl
Sussex 246 (85.4 overs) (RSC Martin-Jenkins 80*, SD Udal 5 for 56) and 111 for 4 dec.
Hampshire 163 (53.3 overs) (RSC Martin-Jenkins 5 for 37) and 56 for 0
Match drawn – no play was possible on the third day
Hampshire 7 pts, Sussex 8 pts

at Maidstone
Kent 306 (94.4 overs) (DP Fulton 101, RWT Key 62) and 118 for 5 dec.
Warwickshire 172 (60.3 overs) (MM Patel 5 for 56)
Match drawn – no play was possible on the first and third days
Kent 10 pts, Warwickshire 7 pts

at Leicester
Leicestershire 219 (67 overs) (DL Maddy 59) and 206 for 4 dec. (DL Maddy 79*, VJ Wells 50)
Lancashire 180 (55.4 overs) (MJ Chilton 57, DE Malcolm 5 for 52)
Match drawn – no play was possible on the first and third days
Leicestershire 8 pts, Lancashire 7 pts

Somerset made a courageous effort to chase 379 in what proved to be just 57 overs against Surrey at Taunton – finishing on 329 for 7 and taking the match run aggregate to 1,808, a record for a first-class match in England. Matthew Wood (131) and Mike Burns (68) put on 141 for the second wicket and Somerset began the final ten overs needing 104. Wickets began to fall, however, and soon the home side were content to hold on for the draw. Surrey's second-innings declaration at 324 for 5 had been set up by a career-best 151 by Jon Batty, their underrated reserve wicketkeeper, who hit 22 fours and two sixes and put on 153 for the first wicket with Ian Ward (75). Mark Ramprakash also made 53, to add to his first-innings 218, while another player to take a liking to Taunton's batsman-friendly surface was Rikki Clarke, the 20-year-old all-rounder, who struck four sixes and 20 boundaries in his career-best 153 not out. With Adam Hollioake hitting 87 from 83 balls in his first championship appearance of the campaign, Surrey were able to declare early on day two at a mammoth 608 for 6 declared. In reply, however, Somerset ran up 554 with Wood (106) scoring the first of his two hundreds in the match, Piran Holloway 77, Burns 99 and Rob Turner an unbeaten 56.

The other three matches in Division One were all badly affected by poor weather, and were also drawn.

Mark Ramprakash pressed his claim for a Test recall with a double century for Surrey against Somerset.

Robin Martin-Jenkins scored a chanceless 80 not out, from 96 balls, and then picked up 5 for 37 as Sussex had the better of things against Hampshire at Southampton, while David Fulton hit 101 and Min Patel took 5 for 56 as Kent earned themselves a first-innings lead against Warwickshire at Maidstone. As at The Mote, the scheduled first and third days were washed away at Leicester. Devon Malcolm's 5 for 52 on the fourth morning, taking his championship tally for the season to 36, tumbled out Lancashire for 180 in reply to Leicestershire's first-innings 219. Darren Maddy then made 79 not out, his second half-century of the game, as time ran out.

Division Two

at Swansea
Essex 283 (123 overs) (DDJ Robinson 72, Aftab Habib 61, RDB Croft 5 for 71) and 139 (SP Jones 5 for 28)
Glamorgan 311 (84.3 overs) (MJ Powell 90, AJ Clarke 5 for 54) and 112 for 2 (SP James 56)
Glamorgan won by eight wickets
Glamorgan 18 pts, Essex 5 pts

at Northampton
Durham 352 (109.4 overs) (GJ Pratt 78, ID Hunter 65) and forfeited their second innings
Northamptonshire forfeited their first innings and 353 for 9 (GP Swann 109, DJG Sales 74)
Northamptonshire won by one wicket – no play was possible on the third day
Northamptonshire 15 pts, Durham 4 pts

at Lord's
Worcestershire 502 for 4 dec. (123 overs) (VS Solanki 153*, BF Smith 124, GA Hick 88, DA Leatherdale 59*, WPC Weston 52) and 99 for 5
Middlesex 417 for 8 dec. (117.2 overs) (PN Weekes 127*, EC Joyce 70, SG Koenig 63)
Match drawn
Middlesex 10 pts, Worcestershire 11 pts

at Derby
Gloucestershire 179 (58.2 overs) (APR Gidman 67, DG Cork 5 for 67) and 225 for 7 (CM Spearman 95)
Derbyshire 398 (104.2 overs) (AI Gait 88, CWG Bassano 78, DG Cork 67)
Match drawn – no play was possible on the third day
Derbyshire 11 pts, Gloucestershire 6.25 pts
(Gloucestershire had 0.75 pt deducted for a slow over rate)

Simon Jones followed up a new-ball burst of 3 for 19 from Mike Kasprowicz the previous evening to polish off Essex and set up a comfortable eight-wicket win for Glamorgan at Swansea. Jones, bowling with considerable hostility, took 5 for 28 as Essex, 60 for 5 overnight, were dismissed for 139. That left Glamorgan needing a modest target and 56 from the dependable Steve James made sure there were no alarms. Essex had actually started the match well, reaching 208 for 3 by the close of a rain-shortened opening day, thanks in the main to an opening partnership of 95 between Darren Robinson (72) and Will Jefferson (43), but despite a further 61 from Aftab Habib they slipped to 283 all out. Robert Croft claimed five wickets, and Mike Powell's 90 hauled Glamorgan up to 311 in reply. Kasprowicz's wickets towards the end of the third day, and Jones' blitz the morning after, then proved decisive.

Rain allowed just 12 overs on the opening day at Northampton, and no play at all on the third, but two declarations on the final morning turned the game between Northamptonshire and Durham into a one-innings contest – and provided a thrilling finale. Durham had made 352 on the second day, with Gary Pratt impressing with 78 and Ian Hunter thumping three sixes and seven fours in his 68-ball 65. At 181 for 5, Northants looked out of it, despite a fine 74 from David Sales, but Graeme Swann took on the Durham spinners to turn the game on its head. Hitting six sixes in an 82-ball 109, Swann took Northants to within four runs of victory before being out. With just one wicket left, Northants managed to scramble across the finishing line – the victory also meaning that they swapped places in the table with Durham, who were now bottom.

Ben Smith, Vikram Solanki and Paul Weekes all made centuries in a high-scoring draw between Worcestershire and Middlesex at Lord's. Smith (124) and Solanki (153 not out) put on 201 in Worcestershire's 502 for 4 declared, with Graeme Hick hitting 88 and both Philip Weston and David Leatherdale chipping in with other half-centuries. Middlesex then replied by totalling 417 for 8 declared, with Weekes (127 not out) and Ed Joyce (70) adding 123 for the sixth wicket. Much time was lost to the weather on the first and third days – which was possibly a good thing for Worcestershire after Abdul Razzaq and Phil Tufnell had reduced them to 99 for 5 in the final session.

Rain cost Derbyshire victory against Gloucestershire at Derby, especially with the loss of the entire third day. Gloucestershire were reduced to 79 for 5 in the 26 overs possible on the opening day – Dominic Cork and Kevin Dean once again doing the damage – and that became 179 all out on day two, despite 67 on his first-class debut by 21-year-old Alex Gidman. Cork then added 67 to his first-innings haul of 5 for 67 after Andrew Gait (88) and Chris Bassano (78) had provided the solid base of Derbyshire's reply. But not even Cork could engineer a win as the clock ticked down on the final afternoon. Derbyshire, 226 for 4 at the end of the second day, needed a further 36 overs to boost their total to 398 and build up a big enough first-innings lead to put the pressure on their visitors. Craig Spearman (95) and Kim Barnett (49) then held them up with an opening stand of 115, but Cork (3 for 44) never gave up hope and Gloucestershire were only four runs in front when they lost their seventh wicket. Gidman and Jon Lewis, however, held out to bring Gloucestershire to barely deserved safety at 225 for 7.

ROUND TEN: 10–13 JULY 2002

Division One

at The Oval
Surrey 475 (115.5 overs) (MR Ramprakash 210*,

Dominic Cork found Test wickets rather more elusive than they were at the Racecourse Ground.

R Clarke 79, AJ Hollioake 56, DR Brown 7 for 110) and 137 (AJ Hollioake 52)
Warwickshire 293 (71.5 overs) (NMK Smith 74, SM Pollock 50, J Ormond 5 for 116) and (following on) 350 (MJ Powell 95, JO Troughton 94, J Ormond 5 for 62)
Warwickshire won by 31 runs
Warwickshire 17 pts, Surrey 8 pts

at Hove
Sussex 145 (50 overs) (Amjad Khan 6 for 56) and 450 (MW Goodwin 135, TR Ambrose 124, KJ Innes 56, MJ Prior 53)
Kent 349 (119.4 overs) (ET Smith 141*, Amjad Khan 58) and 85 for 5
Match drawn
Sussex 7 pts, Kent 10 pts

NORTHAMPTONSHIRE CCC

Home Ground:
Northampton
Address:
The County Ground, Wantage Road,
Northampton NN1 4TJ
Tel: 01604 514455
Fax: 01604 514488
Email: post@nccc.co.uk (general enquiries) or
commercial@nccc.co.uk (commercial enquiries)
Directions:
By rail: Castle Station, three miles.
By road: M1 to J15, A508 and follow RAC signs.
RAC signs from all other areas. Parking on ground when
space permits otherwise ample local street parking.
By coach: regular service from Greyfriars coach station.
Capacity: 4,250
Other grounds used: Campbell Park, Milton Keynes.
Year formed: 1878

Chairman: Lynn Wilson
Chief Executive: Stephen Coverdale
Director of Excellence: David Capel
Director of Cricket: Bob Carter
Captain: Mike Hussey
Coaching contact: Ian Lucas 01604 632917
County colours: Claret and gold

HONOURS

BENSON & HEDGES CUP
1980
GILLETTE CUP/C&G TROPHY
1976, 1992

National Cricket League nickname:
STEELBACKS

Website:
www.nccc.co.uk

STEELBACKS

at Leicester
Hampshire 311 (96.3 overs) (N Pothas 63, JP Crawley 60) and 283 (RA Smith 104, JD Francis 82)
Leicestershire 300 for 9 dec. (121.2 overs) (ND Burns 101, MG Bevan 62) and 72 for 4
Match drawn
Leicestershire 10 pts, Hampshire 10 pts

at Scarborough
Somerset 498 for 9 dec. (165.1 overs) (PD Bowler 84, KP Dutch 74, PCL Holloway 65, RJ Turner 63, KA Parsons 59)
Yorkshire 323 (131.2 overs) (DS Lehmann 64, MJ Lumb 57, VJ Craven 51) and (following on) 213 for 5 (DS Lehmann 75)
Match drawn
Yorkshire 9 pts, Somerset 11 pts

Warwickshire interrupted the march of Surrey to the championship title by winning a remarkable match at The Oval by 31 runs – after following on. It was Surrey's first defeat of the season, but it was really the result of time being lost to the weather during the previous three days that did for Adam Hollioake's all-conquering team. Surrey began the match by running up 475, and Mark Ramprakash hit a brilliant 210 not out to take his run tally for the past three innings to 481. Rikki Clarke added to his burgeoning reputation with 79, and then James Ormond (5 for 116) and Saqlain Mushtaq (4 for 97) combined to bowl out Warwickshire for 293. Michael Powell, the captain, led some stout second-innings resistance with 95, aided by Jim Troughton's 94, and although Ormond took another five-wicket haul, Surrey were beginning to run out of time. Warwickshire's eventual dismissal for 350 left the home side requiring 164 from 34 overs … a challenge that they could not resist. Hollioake, typically, produced a hard-hit 52, but the fall of Alistair Brown, when 66 more were needed from 13 overs, was a grievous blow. In the end, as wickets were frittered away, Neil Smith removed last man Ormond with 11 balls still remaining. Shaun Pollock took 4 for 44 and did much to frustrate the Surrey run chase.

Kent had the vision of an easy win over Sussex at Hove ripped from in front of their eyes by a tremendous fightback from the home side. Sadly for Martyn Sigley, the Kent physiotherapist and a former first-class player in New Zealand, he also felt by the end of the game that he had let the match itself slip through his fingers when he missed a catch at backward point on the second evening with Murray Goodwin on 29. Sigley was only fielding as a substitute because both Mark Ealham and Min Patel were off injured, but at the time it seemed as if Kent must win. Sussex, tumbled out for 145 on the first morning by Amjad Khan (6 for 56), had faced a 204-run deficit when they began their second innings. In between, Ed Smith had produced a seven-and-a-half hour 141 not out to guide Kent to 349, with Khan also coming up with an aggressive 58. Goodwin, reprieved, reached the close on 47 as Sussex limped to 114 for 3 with the fiery Khan snapping up two more wickets. But, during a rain-hit third day, Goodwin and Tim Ambrose gradually began to believe that they could engineer an escape. In the 52.2 overs possible, Sussex moved to 256 for 3 with Goodwin on 108 and Ambrose 101. The next morning saw them take their individual scores to 135 and 124 respectively, and their partnership to 236, before Kent were held up further by Matt Prior (53) and Kevin Innes (56). By now, Sussex were safe – and in the final session they rubbed salt into Kentish wounds by reducing them to 85 for 5 in their own second innings.

The 61st first-class hundred of Robin Smith's career enabled Hampshire to emerge with a draw against Leicestershire at Grace Road. Smith had provided the most effective resistance as Leicestershire, led by Phil DeFreitas, pressed for victory on the third evening. On the final morning, he turned his overnight 40 into 104, and Smith was helped by John Francis' 82 as he guided Hampshire from 102 for 4 to the safety of 283 all out. The earlier, rain-affected part of the match had seen Hampshire total 311 in their first innings, with John Crawley and Nic Pothas hitting half-centuries, and Leicestershire replying with 300 for 9 declared in

Kent's Danish-born fast bowler, Amjad Khan, hustled Sussex out for 145 at Hove.

which Neil Burns (101) and Michael Bevan (62) put on 107 for the sixth wicket.

Another draw was the result at Scarborough, where Somerset forced Yorkshire to follow on, but then ran out of time in a match which also lost significant time to bad weather. Five Somerset batsman got past 50, with Peter Bowler top scoring with 84, as the visitors ground their way to 498 for 9 declared. Darren Lehmann, Michael Lumb and Vic Craven also scored half-centuries in reply, but Matthew Bulbeck took 4 for 94 and Ian Blackwell an impressive 4 for 49 from 37 overs to reduce Yorkshire to 323. They had 70 overs to bat in their second innings, but Yorkshire reached 213 for 5, and safety, with few alarms.

Division Two

at Chester-le-Street
Durham 191 (56 overs) and 203 (N Peng 57)
Derbyshire 96 (26.5 overs) (MJ Di Venuto 57) and 209
Durham won by 89 runs
Durham 15 pts, Derbyshire 3 pts

at Southend
Essex 197 (87.2 overs) (GJ Batty 6 for 71) and 257 (ML Pettini 58, AP Cowan 53)
Worcestershire 373 (116.5 overs) (A Singh 124, VS Solanki 56, SJ Rhodes 56) and 82 for 2
Worcestershire won by eight wickets
Worcestershire 19 pts, Essex 3 pts

at Southgate
Gloucestershire 388 (141.3 overs) (KJ Barnett 182*) and 152 for 2 dec. (THC Hancock 63*)
Middlesex 301 for 9 dec. (123.2 overs) (AJ Strauss 82, SG Koenig 59, ID Fisher 5 for 87) and 241 for 5 (AW Laraman 82*, OA Shah 63)
Middlesex won by five wickets
Middlesex 18 pts, Gloucestershire 7 pts

at Trent Bridge
Glamorgan 213 (56.5 overs) (IJ Thomas 76) and 211 (MP Maynard 55, PJ Franks 5 for 51, CMW Read 5 catches)
Nottinghamshire 328 (100.4 overs) (GE Welton 115, Usman Afzaal 88, MS Kasprowicz 5 for 104) and 100 for 3 (JER Gallian 55*)
Nottinghamshire won by seven wickets
Nottinghamshire 18 pts, Glamorgan 4 pts

Durham achieved their first championship victory of the summer when they overcame Derbyshire by 89

runs at Darlington in a low-scoring affair. The ball swung prodigiously for Kevin Dean as he took 4 for 65 and 4 for 67 in Durham's innings of 191 and 203 but, in between, Derbyshire were themselves bowled out for 96. Michael Di Venuto showed that batting was possible with 57, but there were three silly run outs as well as some steady seam bowling from Neil Killeen (3 for 27) as Derbyshire saw their hopes dive. Yet, even chasing 299 for victory, they seemed to have an outside chance at 150 for 4, as Di Venuto, Chris Bassano and Graeme Welch all got into the 40s. Nicky Phillips, though, then came into the attack to take three wickets for no runs in four overs with his off breaks and, suddenly, it was all over with Derbyshire dismissed for 209.

Worcestershire thoroughly outplayed Essex at Southend to boost their own promotion ambitions with an eight-wicket win. Gareth Batty's controlled off spin was the architect of their success, with the former Surrey all-rounder taking 6 for 71 on the opening day as Essex were bowled out for 197. The second day was all about Worcestershire underlining their superiority by building a big lead – and Anurag Singh played his part to perfection with a classy 124. Vikram Solanki and Steve Rhodes both contributed 56 while, for Essex, left-arm paceman Justin Bishop took 3 for 59 in an eventual total of 373 after, mysteriously, being ignored until the 72nd over of the innings. By the close of the third day, Essex were 115 for 5, but 19-year-old Mark Pettini played well for 58 against the turning ball, Ashley Cowan thumped 53 and a last-wicket stand of 65 between Bishop and Andy Clarke boosted the second-innings total to 257 and made Worcestershire work harder than they might have expected to have done the night before.

Middlesex benefited from a generous declaration by Gloucestershire captain Mark Alleyne at Southgate to romp home by five wickets. Declaration cricket has become a rarity in the cut-throat world of two divisions, but Alleyne obviously thought his spinners Ian Fisher and Martyn Ball, who had shared eight Middlesex first-innings wickets, would be able to work their magic on the final afternoon. He thus closed Gloucestershire's second innings on 152 for 2, after Middlesex had replied with 301 for 9 declared to the visitors' own first innings of 388, and saw the home side cruise to their target of 240. Aaron Laraman led the way with a fine unbeaten 82, while Owais Shah hit 63. Kim Barnett illuminated the opening day with his 61st first-class hundred, and he also clocked up the 21st different venue at which he has scored a century.

NOTTINGHAMSHIRE CCC

Home Ground:
Trent Bridge
Address:
Trent Bridge,
Nottingham NG2 6AG
Tel: 0115 982 3000
Fax: 0115 945 5730
Ticket line: 0870 168 88 88
Email: administration.notts@ecb.co.uk
Alternative website: www.nottsccc.co.uk
Directions:
By road: Follow signs from Ring Road, towards
city centre.
Capacity: 14,500 (16,000 during Test Matches/ODIs)
Other grounds used: Worksop
Year formed: 1841

Chief Executive: David Collier
Director of Cricket: Mike Newell
Other posts: Head Groundsman: Steve Birks Sales;
Marketing Manager: Lisa Pursehouse; Academy
Director: Chris Tolley
Club Coach: Paul Johnson
Captain: Jason Gallian
County colours: Green and gold

HONOURS

COUNTY CHAMPIONSHIP
1907, 1929, 1981, 1987
SUNDAY LEAGUE/NUL
1991
BENSON & HEDGES CUP
1989
GILLETTE CUP/C&G TROPHY
1987

National Cricket League
nickname:
NOTTS OUTLAWS

Website:
www.trentbridge.co.uk

SOMERSET CCC

Home Ground:
Taunton
Address:
The Clerical Medical County Ground,
Taunton,
Somerset TA1 1JT
Tel: 01823 272 946
Fax: 01823 332 395
Centre of Cricketing Excellence: 01823 352266
Email: somerset@ecb.co.uk
Directions:
By road: M5 junction 25. Follow A358 to town centre.
Signposted from there.
Other grounds used: Bath
Year formed: 1875

Chief Executive: Peter Anderson
First XI Coach: Kevin Shine
Captain: Jamie Cox
Other posts: Head Groundsman: Phil Frost;
Second XI Coach: Mark Garaway
County colours: Black, white and maroon

HONOURS

SUNDAY LEAGUE/NUL
1979
BENSON & HEDGES CUP
1981, 1982
GILLETTE CUP/C&G TROPHY
1979, 1983, 2001

National Cricket League nickname:
SOMERSET SABRES

unofficial **Website:**
www.somersetcountycricket.co.uk

The oldest man in county cricket, Kim Barnett, notched up another century against Middlesex.

Nottinghamshire continued to show signs of a recovery of form by beating Glamorgan at Trent Bridge. Andy Harris and Paul Franks shared eight wickets as Glamorgan were bowled out for 213 on the first day, with Ian Thomas' 76 the only innings of note. Guy Welton, the 24-year-old opener with a career average of just over 20, then boosted his own confidence by scoring 115 and, with Usman Afzaal hitting 88, Nottinghamshire gained a decent first-innings lead at 328 all out. Franks, his rehabilitation from a long-term knee injury now seemingly complete, then took 5 for 51 as Glamorgan lost their last five second-innings wickets for 15 runs inside six overs to slump to 211. Jason Gallian, with 55 not out, guided his side home to a seven-wicket win.

ROUND 11: 18–22 JULY 2002

Division One

at Canterbury
Kent 374 (91.5 overs) (A Symonds 118, DP Fulton 62, RWT Key 57, Saqlain Mushtaq 5 for 122) and 260 (RWT Key 68, A Symonds 51)
Surrey 225 (50.5 overs) (AJ Hollioake 122*, MJ Saggers 5 for 66) and 410 for 8 (IJ Ward 168*, R Clarke 66, Saqlain Mushtaq 60)
Surrey won by two wickets
Surrey 16 pts, Kent 7 pts

at Taunton
Somerset 270 (68.2 overs) (MPL Bulbeck 53*) and 373 (ID Blackwell 114, M Burns 98)
Sussex 644 (151.3 overs) (RSC Martin-Jenkins 205*, PA Cottey 120, MJG Davis 111, TR Ambrose 68)
Sussex won by an innings & 1 run
Sussex 20 pts, Somerset 4 pts

at Headingley
Yorkshire 515 for 5 dec. (123.3 overs) (DS Lehmann 187, A McGrath 165) and 124 for 7
Lancashire 478 (145.3 overs) (AJ Swann 128, J Wood 64, G Chapple 60, G Keedy 57, SG Law 51)
Match drawn
Yorkshire 11 pts, Lancashire 10 pts

The destiny of the championship was surely settled at Canterbury, where Kent failed to prevent Surrey from scoring 410 in the fourth innings to win a remarkable match – even after the champions-elect had struggled initially to 208 for 7. Surrey's eventual two-wicket victory was a personal triumph for opener Ian Ward, who batted heroically for just four minutes short of eight hours to anchor the epic run chase with 168 not out from 367 balls. Saqlain Mushtaq, chancing his arm, first hit 60 to help Ward add 105 for the eighth wicket, but at 313 for 8 the odds were still very much on Kent. Yet James Ormond, the No. 10, defied his tail-end reputation to hit some memorable strokes in an unbeaten 43 and keep Ward company to the end. Kent, understandably shattered, would have been just 8.25 points behind the leaders if they had won the game themselves. 'I think this victory has sent a pretty strong message to the other counties,' said Ward, with classic understatement. Only a thunderous 122 not out from Adam Hollioake had kept Surrey in the match on day two as they were bowled out for 225 in reply to Kent's first-innings total of 374. David Fulton and Rob Key put on 121 for Kent's first wicket, scoring 62 and 57 respectively, and by the close Ward had gone to Amjad Khan with the new ball. It was Khan (4 for 91) and Martin Saggers

(5 for 66) who bowled Kent into their midway mastery, but only a solid anchor role by Key prevented the home side from throwing away a lot of that advantage with a sloppy batting performance in their second innings. Min Patel, however, hit a determined 43 not out on the third morning to push the Surrey target up above 400. Incredibly, it didn't prove enough – summing up neatly, and cruelly, the harsh truth about Surrey's strength in comparison to the chasing pack, mentally as much as in terms of playing ability.

A majestic 205 not out by Robin Martin-Jenkins – by some distance his career best – provided the cornerstone of Sussex's victory by an innings and one run against a sorry Somerset side at Taunton. Somerset had signed their own death warrant by batting poorly on the opening day – despite an unbeaten 53 from Matt Bulbeck they were bowled out for just 270 on another Taunton shirtfront, with Jason Lewry and Kevin Innes picking up three wickets apiece. Then the Sussex batsmen tucked in, with Tony Cottey reaching 120 and Tim Ambrose

An aggressive century by Adam Hollioake helped Surrey to an unlikely two-wicket win over Kent.

68, before Martin-Jenkins began to dominate proceedings. By the close of the second day, the tall all-rounder had reached 171 and his eighth-wicket stand with Mark Davis had already eclipsed the 100-year-old county record. Eventually, on the third morning, Davis was out for 111 after the pair had raised their partnership to 291, but Martin-Jenkins reached his deserved double hundred just before Sussex were at last bowled out for 644. Ian Blackwell struck 114 and Mike Burns made 98, but Somerset were dismissed for 373 before the third day was out with Lewry grabbing another four wickets and Billy Taylor picking up 4 for 68.

A Roses match, which lost more than half its first day to rain, ended up as a draw with Yorkshire on an uncomfortable 124 for 7 in their second innings. It did not matter too much because they had piled up 515 for 5 declared first time around, with Darren Lehmann (187) and Anthony McGrath (a career-best 165) putting together a Roses record third-wicket partnership of 317. Lehmann, however, had been dropped on 22 by David Byas of all people at slip, off 19-year-old debutant James Anderson. Darren Gough sent back Mark Chilton and Byas in his new-ball spell towards the end of the second day, but any hopes Yorkshire might have had of engineering a Lancashire follow-on were dashed by Alec Swann's 128, his first hundred for the county. There were half-centuries too for Stuart Law, Glen Chapple, John Wood and Gary Keedy as Lancashire totalled 478.

Division Two

at Southgate
Middlesex 538 (141.2 overs) (SG Koenig 113, DC Nash 81*, PN Weekes 71, BL Hutton 65, OA Shah 60) and 426 for 4 dec. (OA Shah 148*, EC Joyce 81, AJ Strauss 59, BL Hutton 57)
Essex 441 (129.4 overs) (RC Irani 182*, DDJ Robinson 73, Abdur Razzaq 7 for 133) and 53 for 1
Match drawn
Middlesex 12 pts, Essex 11 pts

at Worcester
Northamptonshire 387 (109 overs) (MEK Hussey 174, ME Cassar 55) and 77
Worcestershire 383 (95 overs) (VS Solanki 116, BF Smith 108, A Singh 51) and 82 for 2
Worcestershire won by eight wickets
Worcestershire 19 pts, Northamptonshire 7 pts

at Cheltenham
Gloucestershire 438 (128.5 overs) (CG Taylor 126,

RC Russell 84, ID Fisher 79*) and 293 (CM Spearman 180* – carried his bat)
Glamorgan 415 (104.4 overs) (MP Maynard 140, MA Wallace 69) and 320 for 8 (MP Maynard 118*, SP James 74)
Glamorgan won by two wickets
Glamorgan 20 pts, Gloucestershire 8 pts

at Derby
Derbyshire 353 (105.3 overs) (MJ Di Venuto 91, CWG Bassano 83, AI Gait 76) and 209 (AI Gait 53, N Boje 5 for 66)
Nottinghamshire 240 (78.1 overs) (KP Pietersen 103*, Usman Afzaal 58) and 323 for 9 (JER Gallian 111* – carried his bat)
Nottinghamshire won by one wicket
Nottinghamshire 16 pts, Derbyshire 7 pts

In the only match of the round to start on 18 July, Middlesex and Essex fought out a stormy draw at Southgate. The first day was uneventful enough as Middlesex moved smoothly to 376 for 6 on the back of a fine 113 from opener Sven Koenig, who hit a six and 17 fours in his 220-ball stay. Ben Hutton made 65, Owais Shah 60 and Paul Weekes 71, while David Nash (81 not out) was joined at the last by a sprightly Phil Tufnell, whose 45 from 37 balls with two sixes and four fours provoked much merriment among the crowd at his home club. In reply to Middlesex's 538, however, the second-day tranquillity at the picturesque Walker Ground was shattered when Tufnell began to get embroiled in a war of words with Essex captain Ronnie Irani. Irani was batting at the time, rallying Essex from 174 for 4 to an eventual 441 as he went on to finish with a gutsy unbeaten 182. The umpires, John Holder and Mark Benson, were forced to report the incident to Lord's, but what irked Irani and Essex more than the second-day spat was the way that Middlesex then declined to open up the game with a fourth-morning declaration. They had begun the last day on 116 for 1, a lead of 213, but Middlesex decided to bat on to 426 for 4 before a token declaration left Essex just 23 overs to bat out. Owais Shah scored an unbeaten 148 and Ed Joyce a fluent 81 amid all the sarcastic, and angry, comments. Afterwards, however, Middlesex attributed their hard-nosed attitude to the harsh reality of two-division competition.

Worcestershire's progress up the Division Two table continued with an eight-wicket win over Northants at Worcester. The visitors looked to be in control early on with Mike Hussey's 174 taking his side to 387 and his own run aggregate past 1,000 for the summer – the first player to do so. But, from 85 for 3 in reply, Worcestershire reached 383 thanks to attractive centuries from Ben Smith (108) and Vikram Solanki (116). Then, suddenly, the match was over as Northants slid perplexingly to 77 all out inside 36 overs. David Leatherdale (4 for 23) and Matt Mason (3 for 15) did most of the damage and Graeme Hick's unbeaten 36 swept Worcestershire unceremoniously to their target of 82.

Matthew Maynard was the star of Glamorgan's fine two-wicket victory over Gloucestershire at Cheltenham – although Craig Spearman ran him close. The first day hero, though, was Chris Taylor, whose 126 boosted Gloucestershire to 363 for 5 by the close. Jack Russell (84) then took his sixth-wicket stand with Ian Fisher to 94, and Fisher remained 79 not out as Gloucestershire's first-innings total reached 438. Back came Glamorgan, with Maynard hitting 140 and Mark Wallace 69 in a score of 415. Spearman then took centre stage with a marvellous hundred, but no home batsman could

New Zealand's Craig Spearman's highest first-class score could not prevent Gloucestershire losing to Glamorgan.

SURREY CCC

Home Ground:
The Fosters' Oval
Address:
The AMP Oval, Kennington,
London SE11 5SS
Tel: 020 7582 6660
Fax: 020 7735 7769
Email: enquiries@surreyccc.co.uk
Directions:
By rail: Vauxhall, SouthWest lines, five
minutes' walk away.
By underground: Northern Line, Oval Tube 100
yds away; Victoria Line, Vauxhall is five minutes
away.
By road: Situated on A202 near junction of A24 and A3
south of Vauxhall Bridge.
By bus: 36 and 185 from Victoria
Capacity: 16,500
Other grounds used: Guildford Cricket Club,
Woodbridge Road, Guildford.
Year formed: 1845

Chief Executive: Paul Sheldon
Chairman: Michael Soper
Captain: Adam Hollioake
County colours: Brown and silver

HONOURS

COUNTY CHAMPIONSHIP
1890, 1891, 1892, 1894, 1895,
1899, 1914, 1952–1958, 1971,
1999, 2000, 2002
SUNDAY LEAGUE/NUL
1996
BENSON & HEDGES CUP
1974, 1997, 2001
GILLETTE CUP/C&G TROPHY
1982

**National Cricket League
nickname:**
SURREY LIONS

Website:
www.surreyccc.co.uk

stay with him for long and, despite the former New Zealand Test opener's career-best, unbeaten knock of 180, Gloucestershire allowed themselves to be bowled out for 293. Simon Jones took 4 for 67, but the Welsh county were more indebted to Maynard, whose brilliant 118 not out neutered a wearing pitch and was his fourth successive century at the College Ground. Steve James played a worthy supporting role with 74, and Glamorgan romped to 320 for 8 to claim the dozen win points.

Derbyshire were shocked by the steely resolve of Nottinghamshire captain Jason Gallian at Derby, and the heroics of No. 11 Greg Smith during a nerve-tingling final session. The home county had looked in control of the match right from the opening day when, put in, they had responded with a first-innings 353 – of which Michael Di Venuto made 91, Chris Bassano 83 and Andrew Gait 76. Dominic Cork, the first bowler to 50 first-class wickets, then combined with Mathew Dowman to send Notts tumbling to 240 in reply, and another half-century from Gait helped Derbyshire to 209 in their second innings. There was a chink of light, though, for Notts at this stage after Nicky Boje had grabbed 5 for 66 to give himself nine wickets in the match and check the home side's total dominance. Gallian then anchored the run chase through 104.4 overs to steer his side to their distant target of 323. A sixth-wicket stand of 86 with Chris Read (47) made Derbyshire fear for the worst, but at 277 for 9 they still looked favourites. Smith, however, had other ideas and – while Gallian ended up 111 not out – the South African-born paceman finished on 16 when he pulled Cork for two to settle a thrilling encounter.

ROUND 12: 24–27 JULY 2002

Division One

at Southampton Rose Bowl
Lancashire 183 (76.2 overs) (A Swann 66, CT Tremlett 5 for 68) and 187 (SD Udal 5 for 59)
Hampshire 132 (53 overs) (WS Kendall 54, JM Anderson 6 for 23) and 127
Lancashire won by 111 runs
Lancashire 15 pts, Hampshire 3 pts

at Guildford
Yorkshire 172 (46 overs) and 446 (MJ Lumb 124, DS Lehmann 61, VJ Craven 56, RJ Blakey 50)
Surrey 382 (94.4 overs) (JN Batty 99, R Clarke 56, AD Brown 50) and 237 for 4 (IJ Ward 124*,

IDK Salisbury 59)
Surrey won by six wickets
Surrey 19 pts, Yorkshire 3 pts

at Edgbaston
Warwickshire 493 (127.3 overs) (NV Knight 245* – carried his bat, MJ Powell 57) and 284 for 6 dec. (NV Knight 97)
Sussex 377 (110.2 overs) (PA Cottey 137, RR Montgomerie 51) and 192 (PA Cottey 64, A Richardson 8 for 46)
Warwickshire won by 208 runs
Warwickshire 20 pts, Sussex 7 pts

at Leicester
Leicestershire 131 (52.2 overs) (MJ Saggers 5 for 44) and 400 (PAJ DeFreitas 114, IJ Sutcliffe 103, TR Ward 70, MG Bevan 61)
Kent 339 (95 overs) (RWT Key 127) and 193 for 4
Kent won by six wickets
Kent 18 pts, Leicestershire 3 pts

Hampshire were plunged into relegation trouble when they were not only beaten by Lancashire by 111 runs at the Rose Bowl, but had an eight-point penalty imposed for a poor pitch. Alec Swann's 66 had kept Lancashire afloat on day one, when Chris Tremlett had taken 5 for 68 as they were bowled out for 183, but the visitors' tyro fast bowler James Anderson replied with 6 for 23 on the second morning as Hampshire were tumbled out for 132 despite a gutsy 54 from Will Kendall. As the pitch continued to offer often spitefully inconsistent bounce, Lancashire made it to 187 in their second innings – Shaun Udal, the off spinner, taking 5 for 59. By the end of the second day, Hampshire were already 54 for 4 in their own second innings, and ECB pitch liaison officer, Tony Brown, had decided to convene a panel to ascertain whether the surface should be marked poor or unfit, the latter carrying a 20-point penalty. On the third day, Hampshire were bowled out for 127, with John Wood picking up 4 for 17 and Anderson claiming another three wickets.

Surrey won a six-wicket victory over previous champions Yorkshire at Guildford that was as symbolic as it was convincing. Yorkshire were bowled out for 172 on the opening day and never recovered the ground despite a much better second-innings showing of 446, of which Michael Lumb scored 124. A solid Surrey batting performance saw them run up 382 in their first innings, with Jon Batty making 99, and both Rikki Clarke and Alistair Brown half-centuries. The contributions of Nadeem

James Anderson, Lancashire's young fast bowler, took six wickets on a pitch that cost Hampshire eight penalty points.

Shahid and, down the order, Saqlain Mushtaq and James Ormond, were also invaluable and, in the end, nightwatchman Ian Salisbury (59) kept Ian Ward company on the final morning as the Surrey opener hit 124 not out to guide his side to their victory target of 237. The result maintained Surrey's remarkable record at their Guildford fortress – they have not lost there since Warwickshire beat them in 1994.

The prolific form of opener Nick Knight set up Warwickshire's 208-run victory over Sussex at Edgbaston. Mike Powell scored 57, Jim Troughton 45 and last man Alan Richardson 28 in a tenth-wicket stand worth 68, but all other contributions paled into insignificance alongside Knight's magnificent 245 not out. Carrying his bat, England's one-day specialist took Warwickshire's first-innings total up to 493, to which Sussex replied with 377 as Tony Cottey hit 137. Enter Knight again, his 97

taking his season's first-class run tally to 930 from six matches at an average of 103 as Warwickshire reached 284 for 6 declared in their second innings. Richardson then seized the important wicket of Murray Goodwin in the three overs to be bowled before the close of the third day, and the following day the tall seamer went on to take career-best figures of 8 for 46 as Sussex were bowled out for 192. Again, Cottey offered the stiffest resistance with 64.

Kent were made to work harder than they would have expected for a six-wicket victory at Leicester, the match stretching into the fourth day when Leicestershire scored 400 in their second innings. On the opening day, the home side had been skittled for 131, with Martin Saggers and David Masters picking up 5 for 44 and 4 for 36 apiece. Rob Key's 127 then made sure Kent cashed in on this early advantage by reaching 339 in their first innings, but, by the close of the second day, Leicestershire were already 151 without loss second time around with Iain Sutcliffe and Trevor Ward, against his former county, batting with authority. Ward was soon out for 70 on the resumption the next morning, but Sutcliffe went on to 103 and, after Michael Bevan hit 61, there was a classic counter-attacking 114, with three sixes and 17 fours, from Phil DeFreitas. Once again, however, Kent were indebted to the steadiness under pressure of Saggers (4 for 68), while Ed Smith's unbeaten 48, plus a good 46 from Matthew Walker, guided Kent to their victory target of 193 in reasonable comfort.

Division Two

at Chester-le-Street
Nottinghamshire 362 (101.1 overs) (Usman Afzaal 103, JER Gallian 75, PJ Franks 60) and 83 for 2
Durham 116 (36.5 overs) and (following on) 328 (JJB Lewis 70)
Nottinghamshire won by eight wickets
Nottinghamshire 19 pts, Durham 3 pts

at Northampton
Derbyshire 388 (102.1 overs) (AI Gait 175, CWG Bassano 57, GP Swann 6 for 126) and 282 (DG Cork 80, CWG Bassano 69)
Northamptonshire 210 (53 overs) (JW Cook 88) and 283 (AL Penberthy 62, TMB Bailey 50*)

Derbyshire won by 177 runs
Derbyshire 19 pts, Northamptonshire 4 pts

at Cheltenham
Gloucestershire 494 (139.2 overs) (THC Hancock 112,
APR Gidman 94, CG Taylor 67, MW Alleyne 62,
MGN Windows 55, Abdur Razzaq 5 for 125) and 230
(PCR Tufnell 8 for 66)
Middlesex 363 (108 overs) (PN Weekes 102, OA Shah
65) and 265 for 5 (BL Hutton 88, SG Koenig 53)
Match drawn
Gloucestershire 12 pts, Middlesex 10 pts

at Chelmsford
Essex 231 (103 overs) and 514 for 4 dec.
(A Flower 172*, DDJ Robinson 119, WI Jefferson 109)
Glamorgan 575 (125.3 overs) (SP James 249,
MP Maynard 76, RDB Croft 62)
Match drawn
Essex 8 pts, Glamorgan 12 pts

Nottinghamshire brushed aside Durham at Chester-
le-Street, winning by eight wickets at tea-time on the
third day. Usman Afzaal's 103 was the highlight of
the opening day, with Jason Gallian scoring 75 and
Paul Franks 60 in a first-innings total of 362.
Durham were then dismissed for just 116, with Greg
Smith picking up 4 for 24, and although the home
side did better second time around with 328 after
being asked to follow on, Jon Lewis leading the way
with 70, Notts were left needing only a
straightforward 83 for victory.

A superb innings of 175 by Andrew Gait, the 23-
year-old former South African Under 19 batsman,
provided the considerable base from which Derbyshire
built a 177-run victory over Northamptonshire at
Wantage Road. Graeme Swann's six wickets came at
some cost as Gait and Chris Bassano, with 57,
propelled Derbyshire to a first-innings total of 388. In
reply, Northants made just 210 despite 88 from Jeff
Cook, and Bassano added a second-innings 69 to his
first-innings effort as Derbyshire assumed total control
of the match with 282. Dominic Cork, coming in on a
king pair, also survived a Swann hat-trick ball – and hit
the second ball he faced for six! Overall, Cork lofted
four sixes in his 80 and then struck the killer blow by
having Mike Hussey taken at leg gully from the first
ball of the Northants second innings. Shorn of their
prolific opener, and captain, Northants lost wickets
steadily and were eventually bowled out for 283
despite fighting half-centuries from Tony Penberthy
and Toby Bailey.

Even a second-innings haul of 8 for 66 by Phil

Tufnell could not force a Middlesex victory against
Gloucestershire at Cheltenham. Needing 362 from
what turned out to be 80 overs, after dismissing
Gloucestershire for 230 in their second innings
thanks to Tufnell's flight and control, Middlesex
finished on 265 for 5 and happy with the draw that
maintained their unbeaten record in the division.
Ben Hutton top scored with 88 and, in the
Middlesex first innings, there had been a fine 102
from Paul Weekes. The match had begun with
Gloucestershire reaching 494, with Tim Hancock
hitting 112 and Alex Gidman an excellent 94 before
he was undone by an Abdul Razzaq yorker. Chris
Taylor, Matt Windows and Mark Alleyne also scored
half-centuries.

Glamorgan thought victory was a near-certainty
when they bowled out Essex for 231 on the opening
day at Chelmsford, and then totalled a mammoth
575 in reply. Steve James was the inspiration with a
brilliant 249, though both Matthew Maynard (76)
and Robert Croft (62) gave him hard-hitting support.
But then came a wonderful Essex rearguard action,
led by openers Darren Robinson (119) and Will
Jefferson (109) in an opening stand of 185. By the
close of the third day, Essex were 281 for 2,
Robinson falling to the last ball of the day and Andy
Flower on 36 not out. The final day was all about
Flower, who hit a six and 24 fours as he compiled
his highest score for the county and finished up on
172 not out. Essex, who ended on 514 for 4
declared, had by that stage seen off 171 overs.

ROUND 13: 7–11 AUGUST 2002

Division One

at Canterbury
Kent 271 (78 overs) (DP Fulton 89, A Symonds 69,
AR Caddick 5 for 65) and 286 for 7 dec. (MM Patel 71*,
MA Ealham 60, ET Smith 55)
Somerset 227 (70.5 overs) (MJ Wood 55, PD Bowler
50, Amjad Khan 5 for 76) and 177 (KA Parsons 52,
MJ Saggers 5 for 42)
Kent won by 153 runs
Kent 17 pts, Somerset 4 pts

at Hove
Surrey 193 (58.4 overs) and 296 (IJ Ward 76,
MR Ramprakash 64, MJG Davis 6 for 97)
Sussex 203 (66.1 overs) (AJ Tudor 5 for 66) and 288
for 6 (MW Goodwin 100, CJ Adams 62)
Sussex won by four wickets
Sussex 16 pts, Surrey 3 pts

SUSSEX CCC

Home Ground:
Hove
Address:
County Ground, Eaton Road, Hove,
East Sussex BN3 3AN
Tel: 01273 827100
Fax: 01273 771549
Membership: 01273 827133
Scoreline (home games only): 01273 827145
Email: fwatson@btconnect.com
Directions:
By rail: Hove station is a ten-minute walk.
By road: Follow AA signs. Street parking at no cost.
Capacity: 5,500
Other grounds used: Eastbourne, Horsham, Arundel
Year formed: 1839

Chief Executive: Nigel Russell
Captain: Chris Adams
Vice-captain: James Kirtley
Head Groundsman: Derek Traill
County colours: Dark blue, light blue and gold

HONOURS

SUNDAY LEAGUE/NUL
1982
GILLETTE CUP/C&G TROPHY
1963, 1964, 1978, 1986

National Cricket League nickname:
SUSSEX SHARKS

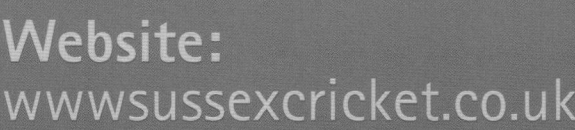

Website:
www.sussexcricket.co.uk

at Headingley
Warwickshire 233 (73.5 overs) (NV Knight 79) and 216 for 4 (NV Knight 109, IR Bell 55*)
Yorkshire 313 (98.4 overs) (DS Lehmann 75, CR Taylor 50)
Match drawn – no play was possible on the third day
Yorkshire 10 pts, Warwickshire 8 pts

at Old Trafford
Lancashire 163 (63 overs) (AJ Swann 84* – carried his bat, TM Tremlett 5 for 57) and 52 for 0
Hampshire 122 for 8 dec. (41.1 overs)
Match drawn – no play was possible on the second and third days
Lancashire 6 pts, Hampshire 7 pts

Kent, the only county with a realistic chance of catching leaders Surrey, kept their outside championship hopes alive with a 153-run win over Somerset at Canterbury. Andy Caddick, playing his first cricket since 17 June, boosted Somerset's morale by taking 5 for 65 on the opening day. Kent, however, with David Fulton making 89 and Andrew Symonds 69 in a first-innings total of 271, fought back to dismiss their visitors for 227 – with Amjad Khan again impressing with 5 for 76. Three more wickets for Caddick left the match evenly balanced for a time, but at the halfway stage Ed Smith was 54 not out as Kent reached 176 for 5 in their second innings. Bad weather allowed just 22 overs on day three, in which Kent lost Smith for 55, but saw Mark Ealham go to his half-century, and on the final morning Ealham (60) and Min Patel, with a 77-ball 71 not out, hit out to set up a declaration at 286 for 7. Martin Saggers then undermined the Somerset second innings with three wickets for 15 runs before lunch, and he went on to take 5 for 42 as the visitors, from 67 for 5, were eventually bowled out for 177.

Surrey themselves were on the receiving end of only their second championship defeat of the season, going down by four wickets to Sussex at Hove after what Chris Adams, the home captain, described as a contest 'close to Test cricket' in its intensity. Early moisture in the pitch was exploited by Kevin Innes (4 for 41) and James Kirtley (3 for 49) as Surrey were dismissed for 193 inside 59 overs, but by the close of day one Sussex themselves were struggling on 139 for 7. It took an unbeaten 41 by Innes to drag Sussex up to 203 and a meagre lead, with Alex Tudor taking 5 for 66, but an opening stand of 121 by Ian Ward (76) and Jon Batty (46) then seemed to have swung the match back Surrey's way

again. Mark Ramprakash also hit 64, but Surrey still fell away from 142 for 1 to 296 all out as Mark Davis, the off spinner, finished with 6 for 97. Surrey, indeed, only got as many as they did thanks to a fine piece of hitting from Mushtaq Ahmed, the former Pakistan leg spinner signed as a temporary replacement for his countryman Saqlain Mushtaq, who was away with the Pakistanis in Morocco. Mushtaq struck a six and eight fours in his 31-ball 47, but with ball rather than bat in hand he proved less effective. Try as he might through 29 overs, Mushtaq could not get a wicket – and Adams (62) even managed at one stage to hit him out of the attack. Sussex, who had been 85 for 2 overnight after setting out in search of 287 for victory, were boosted by a fourth-wicket stand of 106 on the final afternoon between Adams and Murray Goodwin, whose 100 eventually proved to be the decisive individual innings.

Nick Knight's glorious summer form continued at Headingley, where his first-innings 79 took the Warwickshire opener past 1,000 first-class runs in only his tenth innings – and his 109 on the final day kept his championship average in three figures. In between, Yorkshire replied with 313 to Warwickshire's first-innings score of 233 – and the third day was a complete washout. Ian Bell also made 55 not out as the visitors reached 216 for 4 as the match petered out into a draw.

Bad weather wiped away two full days at Old Trafford (the scheduled second and third) – a factor which undoubtedly prevented a decisive result. In the play that was possible, with the other two remaining days also suffering interruptions, Alec Swann achieved the distinction of carrying his bat for Lancashire. Swann's unbeaten 84 enabled his team to scrape together a first-innings total of 163, Chris Tremlett took 5 for 57, but Hampshire then struggled, too, against the pace and seam movement of Glen Chapple and James Anderson. On the fourth day, following the two lost days, Hampshire declared at 122 for 8 to deny their opponents a third bowling bonus point.

Division Two

at Derby
Essex 268 (75.1 overs) (DDJ Robinson 69, WI Jefferson 59, LD Sutton five catches) and 324 (DDJ Robinson 115, A Flower 75, G Welch 5 for 66)
Derbyshire 301 (90.1 overs) (CWG Bassano 152, LD Sutton 58) and 151
Essex won by 140 runs
Essex 17 pts, Derbyshire 6 pts

at Kidderminster
Worcestershire 201 (53.4 overs)
(A Singh 57, SCG MacGill 5 for 63)
and 336 for 5 dec. (GA Hick 126, GJ
Batty 66*, BF Smith 65)
Nottinghamshire 161 (42.4 overs)
(P Johnson 52*, MS Mason 5 for 50,
A Sheriyar 5 for 59) and 292 for 5
(Usman Afzaal 91, GE Welton 76,
P Johnson 56*)
Match drawn
Worcestershire 8 pts, Nottinghamshire
6.25 pts (Nottinghamshire had 0.75 pt
deducted for a slow over rate)

at Cardiff
Gloucestershire 396 (98.4 overs)
(IJ Harvey 123, CG Taylor 74 retired
hurt, RC Russell 52) and 7 for 0
Glamorgan 407 (100 overs)
(MJ Powell 135, RDB Croft 101*)
Match drawn – no play was possible
on the third day
Glamorgan 12 pts,
Gloucestershire 11 pts

at Lord's
Middlesex 400 for 4 dec. (111.5 overs)
(OA Shah 172*, BL Hutton 116)
Northamptonshire 231 (76.2 overs)
(ME Cassar 58)
Match drawn – no play was possible
on the third day
Middlesex 12 pts,
Northamptonshire 6 pts

Darren Robinson played two important innings for Essex as they defeated promotion-rivals Derbyshire.

At the age of 29, Essex opener Darren Robinson passed 1,000 championship runs in a season for the first time as Derbyshire were beaten by 140 runs in an important clash of promotion rivals at Derby. Robinson played two valuable innings for his county here, too, reaching 69 while adding a first-wicket 118 with Will Jefferson (59) in Essex's 268 on the opening day – and then hitting a fine 115 in the second innings. Chris Bassano's magnificent 152 out of 301 had given Derbyshire the mid-match advantage, but Robinson led the Essex counter-attack in a 157-run, third-wicket partnership with Andy Flower (75). Graeme Welch took 5 for 66, but Essex's 324 asked the home side to reach 292 for victory. It proved beyond them – Steve Selwood's 24 was the highest score in an all-out total of 151, as Joe Grant (4 for

45) and James Middlebrook, with 3 for 28 to add to his four first-innings wickets, wrapped up the Essex win.

There was a hard-fought draw at Kidderminster where Nottinghamshire, set 377 from 84 overs to beat Worcestershire, finished on 292 for 5 after good innings from Usman Afzaal (91) and Guy Welton (76) and a second unbeaten half-century in the match by Paul Johnson. Stuart MacGill, the 31-year-old Australian leg spinner making his county debut, took 5 for 63 as Worcestershire were bowled out for just 201 on the opening day. Johnson's resistance enabled Notts to reply with 161, Alamgir

WARWICKSHIRE CCC

Home Ground:
Edgbaston
Address:
County Ground,
Edgbaston,
Birmingham, B5 7QU
Tel: 0121 446 4422
Fax: 0121 446 4949
Ticket Hotline: 0121 446 5506
Indoor cricket centre: 0121 446 3633
Email: info@thebears.co.uk
Alternative website: www.warwickccc.org.uk
Directions:
By rail: New Street station, Birmingham
By road: M6 to A38M, to city centre, then follow signs to
County Ground.
Capacity: 20,000
Other grounds used: None
Year formed: 1882

Chairman: MJK Smith OBE
Chief Executive: Dennis Amiss MBE
Director of Coaching: Bob Woolmer
Other posts: 2nd XI Coach: Steve Perryman; Marketing
Manager: Peter Thompson; Indoor cricket centre coach:
RN Abberley
Captain: Michael Powell
County colours: Blue and white

HONOURS

COUNTY CHAMPIONSHIP
1911, 1951, 1972, 1994, 1995
SUNDAY LEAGUE/NUL
1980, 1994, 1997
BENSON & HEDGES CUP
1994, 2002
GILLETTE CUP/C&G TROPHY
1989, 1993, 1995

National Cricket League
nickname:
THE BEARS

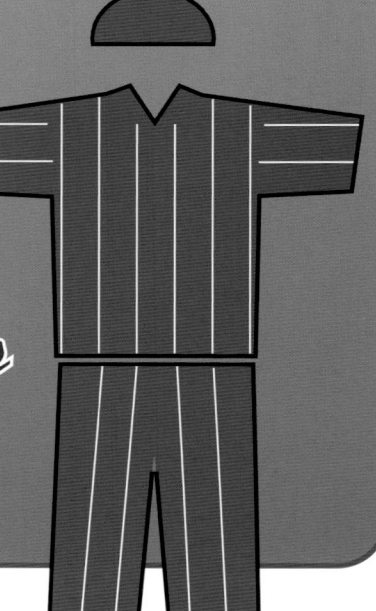

Website:
www.thebears.co.uk

WORCESTERSHIRE CCC

Home Ground:
Worcester
Address:
New Road, Worcester WR2 4QQ
Tel: 01905 748474
Fax: 01905 748005
Ticket office: 01905 422694
Cricket Development Admin Officer (Allan
Scrafton): 01905 429147
Directions:
By rail: Worcester Foregate Street Station (city
centre), half a mile from ground. Worcester
Shrub Hill Station, one mile from ground.
By road: From the north, M5 junction 6 then follow
signposted route to Worcester and city centre, then take
A44 for New Road.
By bus: Midland Red West Nos 23–6.
Disabled access: designated viewing area for
disabled visitors; free admission for carers;
disabled toilet facilities.
Capacity: 4,500
Other grounds used: Kidderminster CC, Chester
Road North, Kidderminster
Year formed: 1865

Chairman: John Elliott
Chief Executive: Mark Newton
Director of Cricket: Tom Moody
2nd XI Coach: Damian D'Oliveira
Captain: Graeme Hick
Vice-captain: Steve Rhodes
County colours: Green, black and white

Website:
www.wccc.co.uk

HONOURS

COUNTY CHAMPIONSHIP
1964, 1965, 1974, 1988, 1989
SUNDAY LEAGUE/NUL
1971, 1987, 1988, 1991
BENSON & HEDGES CUP
1991
GILLETTE CUP/C&G TROPHY
1994

**National Cricket League
nickname:**
WORCESTERSHIRE ROYALS

Sheriyar grabbing the first five wickets and Matt Mason the final five. Then, as batting conditions improved, Graeme Hick scored 126 – his 119th first-class hundred – Ben Smith 65 and Gareth Batty an unbeaten 66 as Worcestershire ran up 336 for 5 declared in their second innings.

Poor weather ruled out a meaningful contest at Cardiff, with the third day being washed out completely and both the second and fourth days also being badly affected. At least both Glamorgan and Gloucestershire were able to pick up all but the maximum number of bonus points, and play some attractive cricket when the rain relented. Gloucestershire's first-innings score of 396 was the result of a remarkable 123 from Ian Harvey, after the Australian had come in with the total 146 for 5 and proceeded to reach three figures in just 72 balls. Overall, he faced 103 deliveries, hitting four sixes and 14 fours. In reply, Glamorgan scored 407, with Mike Powell impressing with 135 and Robert Croft reaching the third first-class hundred of his career with a six and 16 fours.

A similar watery tale provided the news from Lord's where, again, the scheduled third day of the match between Middlesex and Northamptonshire was lost to the weather. Other lengthy interruptions blighted the game, too, although Middlesex had much the better of what play there was as they totalled 400 for 4 declared and then bowled out Northants for 231. Owais Shah (172 not out) and Ben Hutton (116) added 198 for the third wicket in the Middlesex first innings.

ROUND 14: 14–18 AUGUST 2002

Division One

at Leicester
Surrey 540 (128.4 overs) (MA Butcher 116, AD Brown 104, R Clarke 95, AJ Hollioake 80, DL Maddy 5 for 104) and 42 for 3
Leicestershire 290 (87.3 overs) (DL Maddy 81, Mushtaq Ahmed 5 for 71) and (following on) 289 (DL Maddy 94, IJ Sutcliffe 64)
Surrey won by seven wickets
Surrey 20 pts, Leicestershire 5 pts

at Edgbaston
Warwickshire 565 (145 overs) (JO Troughton 115, MA Wagh 109, DP Ostler 80, NV Knight 69, AF Giles 68, PA Nixon 3ct,2st) and 8 for 0
Kent 252 (85.5 overs) (PA Nixon 103, AF Giles 5 for 74) and (following on) 317 (MA Ealham 83, DD Masters 68,

AF Giles 7 for 142)
Warwickshire won by ten wickets
Warwickshire 20 pts, Kent 3 pts

at Old Trafford
Yorkshire 294 (115 overs) (MTG Elliott 83, RJ Blakey 77, JM Anderson 5 for 61) and 305 (GM Fellows 109, A McGrath 86)
Lancashire 301 for 9 dec. (87.4 overs) (AJ Swann 112) and 148 (RKJ Dawson 5 for 42)
Yorkshire won by 150 runs
Yorkshire 17 pts, Lancashire 6 pts

at Southampton Rose Bowl
Somerset 278 (96.5 overs) (RL Johnson 61, RJ Turner 57, KA Parsons 51) and 190
Hampshire 236 (96 overs) (JD Francis 53, RA Smith 52, ID Blackwell 5 for 49) and 233 for 6 (NC Johnson 57)
Hampshire won by four wickets
Hampshire 16 pts, Somerset 5 pts

Surrey played like champions as they overwhelmed Leicestershire at Grace Road by seven wickets. For a start, there were 60 fours and six sixes plundered on the opening day as Surrey ran up 454 for 6. Alistair Brown propelled one of the sixes over the pavilion as he struck 104 and put on 211 for the fourth wicket with Mark Butcher (116). Adam Hollioake's 80 took him just 74 balls and Rikki Clarke, 52 not out at the close, went on to reach 95 as Surrey totalled 540. Darren Maddy, who stuck at it bravely with his medium pacers to take 5 for 104, then hit 81 as Leicestershire at first put up a fight with the bat. But, from 167 for 1, they had declined to 265 for 6 by the close and to 290 all out early the following morning. Mushtaq Ahmed, having enjoyed dismissing Mohammad Kaif lbw for 13 when the Indian batsman padded up to a googly, finished with 5 for 71. The Pakistani leg spinner claimed another three wickets when Leicestershire, following on, were dismissed for 289. Alex Tudor took 4 for 54 and the home side's only resistance came in a second-wicket stand of 156 between Maddy, impressive again with 94, and Iain Sutcliffe (64). Leicestershire's defeat also coincided with the announcement by James Whitaker, their former championship-winning captain, that he was to resign as the club's chief executive.

Kent's flickering championship challenge finally faded away at Edgbaston where Warwickshire beat them by ten wickets to underline their own designs on a runners-up cheque worth £50,000. Mark Wagh, who missed the first three months of the

season after damaging knee ligaments playing football on the outfield, scored 109 in a second-wicket stand of 144 with the prolific Nick Knight (69). Dominic Ostler powered to 80 from 94 balls, with 17 boundaries, and Jim Troughton's 115 was his third century of the summer. To cap it all, Ashley Giles struck 68 as Warwickshire's first innings reached intimidating proportions at 565. More intimidating, however, was the blistering pace of New Zealand fast bowler Shane Bond (4 for 70) as Kent subsided to 252 all out in reply. Paul Nixon, once hooking Bond for three successive fours, tried hard to swim against the tide of the match with 103, but Giles followed up his first-innings figures of 5 for 74 by taking 7 for 142 as Kent were bowled out again for 317. Warwickshire were only held up by a ninth-wicket stand of 108 in 36 overs between Mark Ealham (83) and David Masters (68), which took the game into its fourth day.

A season's best 5 for 42 by Richard Dawson, the England off spinner, swept Yorkshire to a highly satisfying – and much-needed – 150-run victory against their Roses rivals Lancashire at Old Trafford. Dawson's haul left Lancashire all out for 148 in their second innings – a disappointing capitulation after the previous three days had been so hard-fought. Matthew Elliott scored an attractive 83 and Richard Blakey a determined 77 in the Yorkshire first innings of 294, while James Anderson impressed further with 5 for 61. Alec Swann (112) then played himself into Roses history as Lancashire replied with 301 for 9 declared, becoming the first batsman from the county to score hundreds in each of his first two Roses matches. Geoff Boycott achieved the feat for Yorkshire in his debut season of 1963. The match swung, though, on day three when, from 85 for 5, Yorkshire were rallied to 305 by batting of the highest resolve from Anthony McGrath (86) and

What's he conjuring up this time? Mushtaq Ahmed took five wickets for Surrey against Leicestershire.

Gary Fellows (109). They added a vital 95 for the sixth wicket, and Fellows then stayed on to inspire the tail to further resistance. By the close Lancashire were 36 for 2 in their second innings, with Swann one of the two men out, and the scene was set for Dawson.

Hampshire achieved their first championship win since 11 May by beating struggling Somerset by four wickets at Southampton. It also took them out of the bottom three. Somerset, from 102 for 5, reached a first-innings 278 thanks to half-centuries from Keith Parsons and Rob Turner and then a 37-ball 61 by Richard Johnson. Ian Blackwell seemed to be maintaining Somerset's control by taking 5 for 49 as Hampshire were bowled out for 236 in reply, despite 50s from Robin Smith and John Francis. But Somerset's second innings then fell away for 190, giving Hampshire the chance to turn the tables on their opponents. An opening partnership of 97 between Neil Johnson (57) and Jason Laney (46) set them on their way.

Division Two

at Trent Bridge
Nottinghamshire 470 (118.4 overs)
(KP Pietersen 254*, DJ Bicknell 108)
Middlesex 138 (38.4 overs) (SCG MacGill 6 for 54) and (following on) 259 (AJ Strauss 110, SG Koenig 52, SCG MacGill 8 for 111)
Nottinghamshire won by an innings & 73 runs
Nottinghamshire 20 pts, Middlesex 3 pts

at Derby
Derbyshire 190 (46.5 overs) (CWG Bassano 85, G Welch 64, A Sheriyar 6 for 71) and 243 (SA Selwood 99, KJ Dean 54*, GJ Batty 5 for 74)
Worcestershire 320 (89.5 overs) (SJ Rhodes 83) and 115 for 1 (VS Solanki 81*)
Worcestershire won by nine wickets
Worcestershire 18 pts, Derbyshire 3 pts

at Chester-le-Street
Durham 124 (42.1 overs) (MS Kasprowicz 6 for 47) and 114 (MS Kasprowicz 5 for 58)
Glamorgan 233 (70.5 overs) (AM Davies 5 for 61) and 9 for 0
Glamorgan won by ten wickets
Glamorgan 16 pts, Durham 3 pts

at Bristol
Gloucestershire 422 (97.3 overs) (MGN Windows 83, IJ Harvey 79, CM Spearman 71, JA Pearson 51,

ME Cassar 6 for 34) and 446 for 7 (APR Gidman 117, RC Russell 104*, ID Fisher 69)
Northamptonshire 746 for 9 dec. (167 overs) (MEK Hussey 310* – carried his bat, GP Swann 183, DJG Sales 70, AL Penberthy 61)
Match drawn
Gloucestershire 10 pts, Northamptonshire 12 pts

Nottinghamshire, the form team of Division Two, made it four wins out of five by crushing Middlesex by an innings and 73 runs at Trent Bridge. Stuart MacGill, their Australian leg spinner, was at the heart of the success as he added a second-innings bag of 8 for 111 to his 6 for 54 of the previous day. Middlesex, totally perplexed by MacGill's trickery, slid to 138 and 259, with only a second-innings century from Andy Strauss holding up Notts for long. All this came after the home side had racked up 470, largely on the back of a superlative and

Kevin Pietersen helped Notts to their fourth win out of five with 254 not out against Middlesex.

YORKSHIRE CCC

Home Ground:
Headingley
Address:
Headingley Cricket Ground,
Leeds LS6 3BU
Tel: 0113 278 7394
Fax: 0113 278 4099
Email: cricket@yorkshireccc.org.uk
Other grounds used: Scarborough
Year formed: 1863

Chairman: Geoff Cope
Chief Executive: Colin Graves
Secretary: David Ryder
Coach: Wayne Clarke
Captain: Darren Lehmann
Youth Development: Arnie Sidebottom
and Steve Oldham
County colours: Oxford blue, Cambridge blue and
gold

HONOURS

COUNTY CHAMPIONSHIP
1893, 1896, 1898, 1900, 1901,
1902, 1905, 1908, 1912, 1919,
1922, 1923, 1924, 1925, 1931,
1963, 1966, 1967, 1968, 2001
BENSON & HEDGES CUP
1987
SUNDAY LEAGUE/NUL
1983
GILLETTE CUP/C&G TROPHY
1965, 1969, 2002

**National Cricket League
nickname:**
YORKSHIRE PHOENIX

Website:
www.yorkshireccc.org.uk

chanceless 254 not out by Kevin Pietersen. His first hundred only took 88 balls, and there were three sixes and 28 fours in his double ton. It was the highest individual score by a Notts batsman for 65 years and, unsurprisingly, it earned him his county cap. Pietersen was joined in a fourth-wicket stand of 316 by Darren Bicknell (108).

Promotion dreams were also in the heads of Worcestershire's players and supporters after Graeme Hick's team had disposed of close rivals Derbyshire by nine wickets at Derby. Alamgir Sheriyar benefited to the tune of 6 for 71 as Derbyshire totalled just 190 after a slapdash first innings in which only Chris Bassano (14 fours in his score of 85) and Graeme Welch (64) stayed for long. A typically gutsy 83 from Steve Rhodes then made sure of a sizeable lead as Worcestershire replied with 320, and Derbyshire's fate was sealed when they subsided to 101 for 8 in their second innings. Steve Selwood and Kevin Dean did then mount a fighting rearguard action, but it was too late. Selwood, agonizingly, was caught behind for 99 after spending the night on the score, while Dean ended up 54 not out as Derbyshire were bowled out for 243. Vikram Solanki's uninhibited 81 not out, from 56 balls and with four sixes and 12 fours, then ensured that Worcestershire did not fret over reaching their modest victory target.

Mike Kasprowicz had figures of 6 for 47 (his best for the county) and 5 for 58 as Glamorgan brushed past Durham by ten wickets at Chester-le-Street. Michael Gough (30) and Andrew Pratt (40) were the only batsmen in double figures as Kasprowicz and Darren Thomas (4 for 23) bowled them out for 124 in their first innings. Then, after Glamorgan had totalled 223, Mark Davies picking up 5 for 61, Durham crashed again to 114 all out – after an opening stand of 77 between Gough and Gary Pratt. There were no less than six ducks in the Durham ranks, and this time Robert Croft (4 for 20) supplied the support role for Kasprowicz.

Jack Russell set a world record at Bristol as Gloucestershire held on for a draw in a high-scoring affair with Northamptonshire. Russell, the former England wicketkeeper, did not let through a single bye as Northants piled up 746 for 9 declared in their first innings, but there was little else to cheer up the home side as Mike Hussey led the run-feast. Gloucestershire had scored 422 themselves on day one, with Matt Cassar earning himself a remarkable career-best bowling analysis of 6 for 34 as Craig Spearman, John Pearson, Matt Windows and Ian Harvey all hit half-centuries. But this total soon

began to look inadequate as opener Hussey got to work. By the end of the second day he was on 203, while David Sales thumped four sixes in his 70 and Tony Penberthy weighed in with 61. Eventually, when the declaration came, Hussey ended up with an unbeaten 310 – taking his season's first-class run tally to 1,442. Moreover, Graeme Swann had scored a career-best 183 while adding 318 for the sixth wicket with Hussey. Gloucestershire were soon in trouble at 99 for 4 in their second innings, but Alex Gidman and Ian Harvey put on 85 for the fifth wicket and 21-year-old Gidman went on to reach 117, his maiden first-class century. When he was out there was also the little matter of Russell's tenth first-class hundred, an unbeaten 104, to hold off the frustrated Northants attack. Cassar added 4 for 100 to his first-innings haul, but Ian Fisher also hit 69 and, in the end, Gloucestershire survived quite comfortably at 446 for 7. Hussey, meanwhile, was on the field for the duration of the match – 25 hours and 45 minutes.

ROUND 15: 21–25 AUGUST 2002

Division One

at Hove
Sussex 240 (74.2 overs) (MW Goodwin 87, TR Ambrose 60) and 277 (CJ Adams 61, RSC Martin-Jenkins 55, G Chapple 6 for 66)
Lancashire 425 (123.5 overs) (SG Law 147, D Byas 71) and 93 for 3
Lancashire won by seven wickets
Lancashire 20 pts, Sussex 4 pts

at The Oval
Hampshire 190 (85.2 overs) (N Pothas 58, Saqlain Mushtaq 5 for 59) and 326 (AD Mascarenhas 94, Saqlain Mushtaq 6 for 121)
Surrey 576 (135.3 overs) (AD Brown 135, SA Newman 99, JN Batty 89, IJ Ward 87)
Surrey won by an innings & 60 runs
Surrey 20 pts, Hampshire 2 pts

at Taunton
Somerset 408 (106.2 overs) (ID Blackwell 110, M Burns 95) and 394 (ID Blackwell 81, M Burns 80, MJ Wood 68, SE Bond 5 for 64)
Warwickshire 304 (82.1 overs) (NV Knight 98, SRG Francis 5 for 73) and 310 for 9 (IR Bell 77, DP Ostler 55)
Match drawn
Somerset 12 pts, Warwickshire 10 pts

at Canterbury
Leicestershire 259 (91 overs) (IJ Sutcliffe 125* – carried his bat) and 530 (DL Maddy 156, PAJ DeFreitas 94, TR Ward 66)
Kent 379 (109.2 overs) (ET Smith 87, PA Nixon 86, MM Patel 82) and 58 for 0
Match drawn
Kent 11 pts, Leicestershire 9 pts

Lancashire stepped up their fight for Division One survival with an impressive seven-wicket win against Sussex at Hove. Glen Chapple, enjoying a fine season, returned match figures of 10 for 127 as Sussex were bowled out for 240 on the opening day, and then 277 on the third. In between, Lancashire ran up 425 in their own first innings, with Stuart Law dominating the home attack with 147 and David Byas contributing a useful 71. An important moment of the match came right at the end of the second day when Chapple removed Murray Goodwin to leave Sussex on 12 for 1 overnight. Goodwin had made 87 in the Sussex first innings, putting on 98 with Tim Ambrose (60), but now only Chris Adams (61) and Robin Martin-Jenkins (55) stood firm for long as Chapple added 6 for 66 to his earlier haul of 4 for 61. Law then stroked 45 not out to guide Lancashire to their small victory target of 93.

Surrey, meanwhile, continued to do what they were accustomed to doing to lesser teams – they annihilated Hampshire by an innings and 60 runs at The Oval. Spinners Saqlain Mushtaq and Ian Salisbury did most of the damage to the Hampshire batting, sharing 17 wickets in the match. Only Nic Pothas, with 58, put up a struggle as Saqlain (5 for 59) and Salisbury (3 for 44) routed Hampshire for 190 on the opening day. Surrey then scored 576, with Alistair Brown hitting four sixes in his run-a-ball 135, Ian Ward making 87 and Jon Batty 89. There was also an innings of 99, on his championship debut, from 22-year-old Scott Newman – which ended when he offered no stroke to a ball from James Tomlinson and was lbw. Dimitri Mascarenhas' gutsy 94 took the game into a fourth day – just – but honours in Hampshire's second-innings total of 326 again went to Saqlain (6 for 121) and Salisbury (3 for 104).

Somerset's hopes of protecting their Division One status took a grievous blow when Warwickshire's last-wicket pair of Shane Bond and Neil Carter batted through the final 12 overs of the match at Taunton to earn their side a draw. At 268 for 9, and despite half-centuries from Ian Bell and Dominic Ostler, Warwickshire looked to be heading for

Darren Maddy pitched in with a second-innings 156 for Leics against Kent.

defeat, but Bond and Carter put on 42 to deny Somerset the extra eight points. Perhaps Somerset had erred too much on the side of caution by opting not to declare their second innings and give themselves that little bit longer to bowl out the opposition. In the end, batting on until they were dismissed for 394 just over an hour before the close of play on the third day, Somerset left Warwickshire to score 499 in what turned out to be 117 overs.

Mike Burns made 95 and 80 in the match against his old club, but Somerset's most explosive batting came once again from Ian Blackwell. His first-innings 110 took just 86 balls, including two sixes and 16 fours, while he was ninth out for 81 second time around. Nick Knight scored 98 as Warwickshire replied with 304 to Somerset's first-innings score of 408, and fast bowler Bond demonstrated his wicket-taking abilities even on good pitches by including a spell of 4 for 29 in 11 overs, with three wickets taken by yorkers, in his overall 5 for 64 during the Somerset second innings.

Defiant hundreds by Iain Sutcliffe, on day one, and then Darren Maddy towards the end of the match, denied Kent the victory they so desired at Canterbury. Subsequently, as Maddy's six-and-a-half hour 156 inspired Leicestershire to a second-innings total of 530, Kent lost more vital ground to championship leaders Surrey. Opener Sutcliffe carried his bat for 125 not out to guide his side to 259 in their first innings, and Kent could only gain a lead of 120 as Ed Smith (87), Paul Nixon (86) and Min Patel (82 from 89 balls) all failed to convert fine innings into potentially match-winning big hundreds. There was also an injury scare for Steve Waugh, who had the tip of his right index finger split open after being struck on the glove by a lifter from Devon Malcolm. Waugh retired hurt on 12, but returned later in the day before falling for 16. Kent still had victory hopes, though, as Leicestershire ended the third day on 169 for 3. Trevor Ward had made 66 and Maddy was already 41 not out and, on the final morning, he resisted all that the tiring Kent bowlers could throw at him. Phil DeFreitas, having helped Maddy see off the threat of defeat, then enjoyed himself by thrashing his way to 94 – while even last man Malcolm later emerged to have some fun, hitting four sixes in his agricultural 44.

Division Two

at Lord's
Derbyshire 414 (116.5 overs) (MJ Di Venuto 192* – carried his bat, G Welch 50, AA Noffke 6 for 138) and 301 for 7 dec. (MJ Di Venuto 113, PCR Tufnell 5 for 80)
Middlesex 304 (104.4 overs) (EC Joyce 129, DC Nash 55) and 207 (EC Joyce 51, LJ Wharton 6 for 62)
Derbyshire won by 204 runs
Derbyshire 20 pts, Middlesex 6 pts

at Trent Bridge
Gloucestershire 173 (63.5 overs) (ID Fisher 57, RC Russell 54) and 219 (SCG MacGill 5 for 92)
Nottinghamshire 476 (105.4 overs) (KP Pietersen 116, P Johnson 83, CMW Read 80, Usman Afzaal 61)
Nottinghamshire won by an innings & 84 runs
Nottinghamshire 20 pts, Gloucestershire 2.25 pts
(Gloucestershire had 0.75 pt deducted for slow over rate)

at Colchester
Durham 259 (86.1 overs) (MA Gough 103) and 332 (GJ Pratt 65, AM Thorpe 61, NC Phillips 58*, A Pratt 51)
Essex 271 (92 overs) (GR Napier 54*) and 322 for 6 (JP Stephenson 100*, ML Pettini 64)
Essex won by four wickets
Essex 17 pts, Durham 5 pts

at Northampton
Glamorgan 144 (40.4 overs) (CG Greenidge 5 for 44) and 312 (MS Kasprowicz 72*, A Dale 52)
Northamptonshire 375 (97.4 overs) (AL Penberthy 99, RA White 80, ME Cassar 68) and 84 for 2 (RA White 60*)
Northamptonshire won by eight wickets
Northamptonshire 19 pts, Glamorgan 3 pts

Graeme Welch was mobbed by his team-mates at Lord's when, with just 11 balls remaining, he had a hobbling Phil Tufnell adjudged lbw to clinch a 204-run victory for Derbyshire against Middlesex.

Tufnell, despite an ankle injury, had survived for 90 minutes alongside Ashley Noffke, facing 58 balls for his seven runs in a courageous bid to claim a draw. The win boosted Derbyshire's own promotion hopes, but had worrying connotations for long-term Division Two leaders Middlesex who, in 2001, had also led the table for much of the summer before falling away alarmingly to finish fifth. Derbyshire's triumph was based on the magnificent batting of Michael Di Venuto, their Tasmanian left-hander, who not only carried his bat for 192 not out in the visitor's first-innings score of 414, but then added a determined 113 as Tufnell, with 5 for 80, tried to

Carl Greenidge swung the ball with great effect for Northants against Glamorgan.

bowl Middlesex back into the match. Ed Joyce was awarded his county cap after scoring 129 to rescue Middlesex from 37 for 4 and take them to 304, but Di Venuto's efforts, plus a second valuable lower-order innings of the match from Welch, enabled Derbyshire to declare at 301 for 7. Joyce again batted well for 51, but slow left-arm spinner Lian Wharton produced impressive career-best figures of 6 for 62 from 31 overs to undermine the Middlesex second innings. Noffke, with 31 not out, and Tufnell almost hung on – but Derbyshire were not to be denied.

Kevin Pietersen's parents, Jannie and Penny, returned to their South Africa home almost punch-drunk at the sight of their son tearing apart county bowling attacks. Just before their holiday came to an end, they watched Pietersen smash Gloucestershire for 116 off 137 balls at Trent Bridge to help Nottinghamshire to victory by an innings and 84 runs. The 22-year-old's latest boundary blitz – there were 19 fours and a six – took his run tally to 639 from four innings in nine days, at an average of 213! His parents' holiday had taken in all four knocks – and so their presence should be arranged by the ECB if, or as seems likely when, Pietersen is granted an England debut when he qualifies in 2005! Half-centuries from Jack Russell and Ian Fisher had been the sum of Gloucestershire's resistance when they were dismissed for 173 on the opening day, and soon Pietersen was giving Notts control of the match in a fourth-wicket stand of 154 with Usman Afzaal (61). A further partnership of 141 between Paul Johnson (83) and Chris Read (80) boosted Notts to 476, and victory came quickly on the third afternoon when Stuart MacGill (5 for 92) spun out Gloucestershire for 219 with, again, only Russell offering any meaningful resistance with 45 not out.

Essex, set 321 from 91 overs to beat Durham at Colchester, got home with four overs to spare as the remarkable John Stephenson completed an unbeaten 100. Stephenson, the 37-year-old who returned to the club at the start of the season to captain the second team and perhaps play the odd one-day league match, now added a match-winning century to his already earned status as Essex's leading first-class wicket-taker. He was joined in a fourth-wicket stand of 97 by 19-year-old Mark Pettini, who made 64, and Durham were left devastated to have lost a game in which they had seemed to be in control. Michael Gough's five-hour 103, his maiden championship hundred, had sustained a Durham first innings of 259, and Essex only got to 271 in reply, due to an unbeaten 54 from 49 balls, with three sixes, by Graham Napier batting

at No. 10. Four dropped catches, however, and a third day shortened by 36 overs due to rain, looked like denting Essex's hopes as Durham reached 323 for 8 by the close. Nicky Phillips, the acting captain, had become the fourth Durham batsman (after Gary Pratt, Ashley Thorpe and Andrew Pratt) to reach a half-century, but, on the final morning, he was left stranded on 58 not out by the fall of the last two wickets inside three overs – and Durham's worst fears were about to be realized.

The swing of Carl Greenidge, which earned him career-best figures of 5 for 44, inspired Northamptonshire to an eventual eight-wicket win over Glamorgan at Northampton. Greenidge's effort condemned Glamorgan to 144 all out on the first day and, by the close, they were already in deep trouble as Northants had replied with 205 for 3. Rob White, a 22-year-old Loughborough University student in his third championship game, hooked Simon Jones for six twice in three balls as he went quickly to 80 and, on the following day, Tony Penberthy played an acting captain's innings as he put on 150 for the fifth wicket with Matt Cassar (68). Unfortunately for him, Penberthy was then lbw to a Mike Kasprowicz in-swinger for 99, but Northants' 375 had put them in command. Adrian Dale's 52 could not prevent Glamorgan from sliding to 164 for 6 by the end of the second day, and only a spirited ninth-wicket stand of 58 by Kasprowicz (72) and Dean Cosker (36) made Northants bat again. White was glad they did, hooking Jones for two more sixes over fine leg as he powered his way to an unbeaten 60.

ROUND 16: 27–30 AUGUST 2002

Division One

at Edgbaston
Warwickshire 345 (118.2 overs) (NV Knight 74, JO Troughton 61) and 404 for 9 dec. (NV Knight 133, JO Troughton 63)
Surrey 544 (136.1 overs) (N Shahid 116, IJ Ward 114, MR Ramprakash 99, AJ Hollioake 82*, AD Brown 57)
Match drawn
Warwickshire 9 pts, Surrey 12 pts

at Leicester
Sussex 215 (80.2 overs) (RSC Martin-Jenkins 62, CJ Adams 60, DE Malcolm 5 for 38) and 142
Leicestershire 247 (101 overs) (IJ Sutcliffe 75) and 111 for 2
Leicestershire won by eight wickets
Leicestershire 16 pts, Sussex 4 pts

at Southampton Rose Bowl
Hampshire 269 (83.2 overs) (RA Smith 58) and 161
(RKJ Dawson 5 for 49)
Yorkshire 280 (88 overs) (MTG Elliott 92, SD Udal
5 for 69) and 152 for 3 (VJ Craven 72, MTG Elliott 52*)
Yorkshire won by seven wickets
Yorkshire 17 pts, Hampshire 5 pts

at Blackpool
Lancashire 251 (67.1 overs) (SG Law 77, RL Johnson 6
for 47) and 296 (D Byas 81, CP Schofield 77,
AR Caddick 6 for 84)
Somerset 140 (51.5 overs) (JM Anderson 6 for 41) and
71 (G Chapple 6 for 30)
Lancashire won by 336 runs
Lancashire 17 pts, Somerset 3 pts

Nick Knight batted with great skill, and no little
courage, to deny Surrey victory against
Warwickshire at Edgbaston. Knight, hobbling and
with a runner because of an aggravated groin injury,
battled through six-and-a-half hours to score 133
from 302 balls in a Warwickshire second innings of
404 for 9 declared. He was finally out just three
overs before the end of the match, giving Ian Ward
a distinguished maiden first-class wicket. Knight's
hundred was his fifth of the season, and he also
made 74 on the opening day during a Warwickshire
first innings of 345. Jim Troughton did his
burgeoning reputation no harm at all, either, by
hitting 61 and 63 off the champions-elect, going
past his 1,000 runs for the season in the process and
seeming to relish duelling with the likes of Saqlain
Mushtaq, who took 8 for 168 in the match. Ward's
114 was his fourth century of the summer and
Surrey's first innings also included 116 from
Nadeem Shahid, 57 from Alistair Brown and an
unbeaten 82 from Adam Hollioake, while Mark
Ramprakash hit three sixes before becoming the
fourth Surrey batsman to be dismissed for 99
during the season. Warwickshire set out again 199
runs behind, but thanks to Knight they survived.

Leicestershire's first win in seven championship
matches, an eight-wicket success against Sussex at
Grace Road, ensured the retention of their Division
One status. Sussex, by contrast, slipped into sixth
place after being bowled out for just 142 in their
second innings. Phil DeFreitas (4 for 42) and
Javagal Srinath (3 for 48) did the damage, while in
the Sussex first innings it was the oldest member of
Leicestershire's venerable pace attack, 39-year-old
Devon Malcolm, who took 5 for 38 to provoke a
collapse from 172 for 4 to 215 all out. Malcolm also

swung three sixes in his unbeaten 24 as he helped
Carl Crowe to boost the Leicestershire first innings
from 202 for 9 to 247 all out. Iain Sutcliffe had
earlier continued his fine form by hitting 75, and
there were no alarms in the Leicestershire top order
as they knocked off the 111 runs required for victory.

A second-innings collapse cost Hampshire dear at
Southampton, where Yorkshire kept alive their slim
hopes of avoiding the dreaded drop with a seven-
wicket win. Robin Smith's gutsy 58, and 40 from
Shaun Udal, had taken Hampshire to 269 in their
first innings. Udal then grabbed 5 for 69 to restrict
Yorkshire to 280 in reply. But then another off
spinner, Richard Dawson, got amongst the Hampshire
batting to finish with 5 for 49 as the home side slid
to 161 all out. Vic Craven, with 72, and Matthew
Elliott, who added an unbeaten 52 to his superb
first-innings 92, then hurried Yorkshire to victory.

Somerset coach Kevin Shine pulled no punches
after seeing his side crumble to a humbling 336-run
defeat against Lancashire at Blackpool. 'It was one
of the poorest performances I have seen from us,'
said Shine. 'We just laid down and let them roll over
us. We need to recover that willingness to fight.'
Somerset's first-innings score of 140 was bad enough,
but their capitulation for just 71 second time
around, the lowest total in the championship this
season, meant that the game was over half-an-hour
before lunch on the third day. Shine, however, did
reserve some praise for James Anderson, the fast
bowler who turned 20 a month earlier. Anderson
included a spell of 4 for 3 in nine balls in his first-
innings haul of 6 for 41, and then collected 3 for 16
as he helped Glen Chapple, with a career-best 6 for
30, to destroy the Somerset second innings. 'He
looks like he's going to be gold dust,' added Shine,
after Anderson had taken his short career's wicket
tally to 38. Richard Johnson did take 6 for 47 for
Somerset during Lancashire's first innings, and Andy
Caddick a season's best 6 for 84 in the Lancashire
second innings of 296, but Peter Bowler dropped
Stuart Law (77 in a Lancashire first innings of 251)
on nought to set the tone of the match. David Byas
scored 81 in Lancashire's second innings, while
Chris Schofield added 77 to his first-innings 40.

Division Two

at Worcester
Middlesex 531 (145.3 overs) (EC Joyce 125, DC Nash
100, SG Koenig 81, AA Noffke 76, Kabir Ali 5 for 100)
and 193 for 4
Worcestershire 319 (90.1 overs) (GA Hick 101,

A Singh 50, BF Smith 50) and (following on) 401 (GA Hick 69, BF Smith 60)
Middlesex won by six wickets
Middlesex 19.75 pts, Worcestershire 6 pts (Middlesex had 0.25 pt deducted for a slow over rate)

at Chester-le-Street
Durham 240 (84.3 overs) and 136 (MA Gough 67, CG Greenidge 6 for 40)
Northamptonshire 236 (68.5 overs) (GL Brophy 61*) and 141 for 3
Northamptonshire won by seven wickets
Northamptonshire 16 pts, Durham 4 pts

at Colwyn Bay
Nottinghamshire 464 (142.4 overs) (JER Gallian 171, GE Welton 92) and 274 for 5 (Usman Afzaal 104*, N Boje 70)
Glamorgan 495 (131 overs) (SP James 184, A Dale 109, MP Maynard 56, N Boje 6 for 128)
Match drawn
Glamorgan 10 pts, Nottinghamshire 12 pts

Middlesex rejuvenated their faltering promotion campaign by pulling off a six-wicket victory against fellow challengers Worcestershire at New Road. The win, however, came at a price, with captain Andy Strauss suffering a broken jaw after being struck a blow by a short ball from Kabir Ali during the successful run chase on the final afternoon. Kabir had taken five wickets, too, in a Middlesex first innings of 531 – including three in four balls in his third over to leave the visitors struggling at 25 for 3. Sven Koenig dug in with 81, however, and Ed Joyce passed 1,000 runs for the season during an enchanting innings of 125. Middlesex were also boosted by an eighth-wicket partnership of 139 between David Nash (100) and Ashley Noffke (76), but no moment was more important for them than the dismissal of Graeme Hick early on the third morning, without addition to his overnight 101. That proved to be the catalyst for a Worcestershire first-innings collapse from 231 for 2 to 319 all out, with Noffke and Chad Keegan taking four wickets apiece. Following on, Worcestershire reached the close of the third day on 251 for 5, Hick (69) and Ben Smith (60) having added 117 for the third wicket, and more lower-order resistance on the final day began to prompt some anxious Middlesex glances at the pavilion clock. But Noffke and

Keegan again shared eight wickets and, when Worcestershire were finally dismissed for 401, it left Middlesex needing 190 off 56 overs for victory. At 114 for 4, with Strauss out for 27 soon after being hit, there was more anxiety, but then Paul Weekes (40 not out) joined the impressive Joyce (46 not out) to make sure of 20 precious points.

A career-best 6 for 40 by Carl Greenidge, which destroyed the Durham second innings for 136, led to a straightforward seven-wicket win for Northamptonshire at Chester-le-Street. Until Greenidge's burst, however, the match was evenly poised with Northants bowled out for 236 in reply to Durham's first-innings score of 240. Gerard Brophy, a South African with Irish grandparents, scored an unbeaten 61 in the Northants first innings, while Rob White hooked three sixes off Steve Harmison during his innings of 45 when he and Mark Powell put on 96 for the Northants first wicket as they chased just 141 for victory.

Steve James, the Glamorgan captain, continued

Glamorgan's Steve James on his way to another hundred at his happy hunting ground: Colwyn Bay.

his remarkable run of success at Colwyn Bay by hitting the Nottinghamshire attack for 184 in a drawn encounter dominated by a flat pitch and weather interruptions on the final two days. James' latest North Walian epic took his Colwyn Bay run tally to 1,221 in 12 innings, at an average of 135.66, and he added 217 for the fourth wicket with Adrian Dale (109) as Glamorgan replied with 495 to Notts' first-innings 464. There was then time only for Notts to reach 274 for 5 in their second innings with Usman Afzaal finishing unbeaten on 104. Simon Jones, Glamorgan's England fast bowler, broke down in his first over on the opening morning, and Jason Gallian (171) put on 172 for the Notts first wicket with Guy Welton (92).

ROUND 17: 4–7 SEPTEMBER 2002

Division One

at Old Trafford
Lancashire 598 (152.5 overs) (PJ Martin 117*, D Byas 101, CP Schofield 91, G Chapple 65, AJ Swann 62)

Ryan Sidebottom took five wickets, but Yorkshire were penalised against Leicestershire.

Warwickshire 328 (89.2 overs) (NM Carter 70, DR Brown 68*, DP Ostler 63)
Match drawn
Lancashire 12 pts, Warwickshire 9 pts

at Scarborough
Yorkshire 276 (82 overs) (C White 161) and 347 for 8 dec. (AKD Gray 74*, RJ Blakey 63*, VJ Wells 5 for 39)
Leicestershire 279 (79.2 overs) (ND Burns 59, J Srinath 52, RJ Sidebottom 5 for 60) and 231 for 5 (DL Maddy 86, DI Stevens 80)
Match drawn
Yorkshire 9 pts, Leicestershire 9 pts (Yorkshire had 1 pt deducted for a slow over rate)

at Hove
Sussex 631 for 6 dec. (156 overs) (RR Montgomerie 196, MW Goodwin 119, MJ Prior 102*, RSC Martin-Jenkins 64)
Hampshire 401 (121.2 overs) (JS Laney 89, RA Smith 60, NC Johnson 51, RJ Kirtley 6 for 107) and (following on) 67 for 1 (NC Johnson 51*)
Match drawn
Sussex 12 pts, Hampshire 10 pts

at Taunton
Somerset 460 (111.5 overs) (MJ Wood 196, KA Parsons 68, J Cox 62) and 316 for 9 dec. (PD Bowler 81, J Cox 79)
Kent 400 for 6 dec. (120 overs) (ET Smith 154, PA Nixon 88, JC Tredwell 58) and 171 for 4 (PA Nixon 51*)
Match drawn
Somerset 11 pts, Kent 12 pts

Surrey were crowned champions without playing in this round of games – their triumph confirmed when Warwickshire failed to reach 400 in the first innings of their own rain-hit draw against Lancashire at Old Trafford. All Warwickshire's last remaining hopes of catching the leaders vanished when Lancashire ran up 598 in their first innings – David Byas (101) reaching his first hundred for the club, Peter Martin (117 not out) completing a remarkable best score by a Lancashire No. 10, and Chris Schofield fidgeting and flashing his way to a career-best innings of 91. Martin, who struck six sixes and 12 fours off a demoralized attack in a run-a-ball knock, put on 109 for the ninth wicket with Schofield and then 87 for the last wicket with James Anderson, who scored just 16. Earlier there had been solid innings of 62 from Alec Swann and 65 by Glen Chapple. All Surrey eyes then turned on Warwickshire's batsmen after more rain washed away most of the third day.

Dominic Ostler made 63, Dougie Brown an unbeaten 68 and Neil Carter a swashbuckling 70 off 61 balls, with two sixes and ten fours – but it was not enough as Warwickshire were bowled out for 328.

By contrast to Surrey's joy, there was more misery for Yorkshire at Scarborough – the scene of their own championship title-clinching performance of 12 months earlier. Despite a brilliant first-innings 161 from Craig White, and a wholehearted bowling display by Ryan Sidebottom, Leicestershire held on for a draw over a weather-interrupted last two days thanks, in the main, to a calm fourth-wicket stand of 128 between Darren Maddy (86) and Darren Stevens (80). From 54 for 3, Leicestershire finished on 231 for 5 to leave Yorkshire frustrated with just a draw from a game they simply had to win. White's great innings on day one was made out of 276 all out, and came off only 216 balls, with 26 fours. Sidebottom's 5 for 60, his first five-wicket return for two seasons, then pegged Leicestershire to 279 in reply, despite half-centuries from both Neil Burns and Javagal Srinath. Yorkshire, in some discomfort at 198 for 8 in their second innings, rallied to a declaration at 347 for 8 as Richard Blakey (63 not out) added an unbroken 149 with Andrew Gray (74 not out). It was gutsy stuff, but all too late in the season for Yorkshire.

Sussex were happy enough with their 12-point draw against Hampshire at Hove. Maintaining Division One status, in their first season back in the top flight, was the only aim of Chris Adams' men back in April – and this result all but made sure that ambition was achieved. An opening stand of 193, between Murray Goodwin and Richard Montgomerie, set Sussex on their way to an eventual 631 for 6 declared – and Montgomerie to an eventual 196. Goodwin made 119 and, later, Matthew Prior reached a maiden championship hundred and added 120 in 25 overs with Robin Martin-Jenkins (64) before ending up unbeaten on 102. Rain interruptions then helped Hampshire force the draw as they reached 401 and, following on, 67 for 1. Neil Johnson, overall a disappointment in his second season as Hampshire's overseas player, hit a pair of 51s – the second of them undefeated – while there were other half-centuries for Jason Laney (89) and Robin Smith (60), and a worthy 6 for 107 from Sussex fast bowler James Kirtley to underline the home side's dominance.

David Fulton, the Kent captain, put Somerset in at Taunton – and then saw them rattle up 433 for 5 by the close of the first day! In fairness to Fulton, he was probably hedging his bets in a match Kent

wanted to win to maintain their challenge for the £50,000 runners-up cheque: either bowl out Somerset cheaply and take early control, or leave his side with a second chance of a fourth-innings run chase against a side desperate themselves for a win as they tried to extricate themselves from the relegation mire. As it was, Kent's bowling was off-key and Matthew Wood took advantage of another blissful Taunton pitch to compile a magnificent 196. There were half-centuries, too, for Jamie Cox and Keith Parsons, but Kent fought back strongly on day two as Martin Saggers (4 for 87) and Amjad Khan (4 for 88) combined to close the Somerset first innings at 460, before Ed Smith's century led a confident reply. Not even a sixth-ball duck for Steve Waugh could prevent Kent from reaching 400 for 6 declared, with Smith scoring 154 and adding 196 for the fourth wicket with Paul Nixon (88). Somerset then did declare their second innings on 316 for 9 after Peter Bowler had made 81 and Cox 79, but weather delays on the final day prevented Kent from mounting any

Stephen Peters kept Worcestershire in the match against Glamorgan with a fine innings of 130.

sort of chase. The match petered out into a draw with Kent on 171 for 4 and Nixon unbeaten on 51.

Division Two

at Chelmsford
Middlesex 295 (109 overs) (BL Hutton 85) and 93
Essex 278 (88 overs) (Aftab Habib 65) and 111 for 4
Essex won by six wickets
Essex 17 pts, Middlesex 5 pts

at Bristol
Gloucestershire 192 (57.2 overs) (THC Hancock 54, G Welch 6 for 60) and 577 for 9 dec.
(MGN Windows 144, RC Russell 119*, RJ Sillence 101, J Lewis 57)
Derbyshire 187 (53.4 overs) (AM Smith 5 for 69) and 319 for 5 (MJ Di Venuto 175*, CWG Bassano 51)
Match drawn
Gloucestershire 7 pts, Derbyshire 7 pts

at Cardiff
Glamorgan 447 (130.5 overs) (A Dale 127*, MJ Powell 84, IJ Thomas 56) and 181 for 2
(DL Hemp 69*, MJ Powell 60*)
Worcestershire 381 (105.4 overs) (SD Peters 130, VS Solanki 94, GA Hick 58, AP Davies 5 for 79)
Match drawn
Glamorgan 12 pts, Worcestershire 11 pts

at Trent Bridge
Nottinghamshire 400 for 6 dec. (105.1 overs) (Usman Afzaal 103, GE Welton 77, DJ Bicknell 54)
Durham 132 (46.3 overs) and (following on) 153 for 5 (GJ Pratt 65)
Match drawn - no play was possible on the fourth day
Nottinghamshire 12 pts, Durham 5.75 pts (Durham had 0.25 pt deducted for a slow over rate)

Middlesex, 24 points clear at the top of Division Two before this game, found their nerves jangling after a six-wicket defeat against promotion rivals Essex at Chelmsford. Having played a game more than the other counties chasing three promotion places, and with only a visit to Derbyshire to come, Middlesex were suddenly under threat after being bowled out for a humbling 93 on the third morning. There was no blame in the pitch, only a fragility of mind caused, most probably, by the pressure of their position and the fact that they had been reduced to 21 for 3 in a tense eight overs the previous evening. Until then, the match had been both evenly and hard-fought, with Essex reaching 278 in reply to

Middlesex's first-innings 295 only because Graham Napier strode in at No. 10 to strike a determined 38 not out following a good middle-order partnership between Ronnie Irani (43) and Aftab Habib (65). Middlesex's first innings had featured strong performances by Ben Hutton (85) and Owais Shah (47), but now they fell apart as Jon Dakin (4 for 17) and Irani made early breakthroughs with the new ball and Joe Grant (3 for 19) helped prevent any sort of recovery. Essex were themselves a nervy 28 for 3 at the start of their own second innings, but Irani's 42 and Andy Flower's unbeaten 43 took them unflustered to a victory target of 111.

Both Derbyshire and Worcestershire had their promotion drives stalled by draws, while poor Nottinghamshire saw a certain victory against bottom club Durham snatched from their grasp by rain.

At Bristol, a superb innings of 175 not out by Michael Di Venuto enabled Derbyshire to emerge with honour from a match against Gloucestershire that looked to be taking a considerable turn for the worst when the home side rattled up a huge 577 for 9 declared in their second innings. Graeme Welch had taken 6 for 60 on the opening day when Gloucestershire had been bowled out for 192, but Derbyshire failed to take advantage by batting shoddily in return, and being dismissed themselves for 187 as Mike Smith bagged 5 for 69. At 178 for 5, Gloucestershire were only just ahead on points, but then came a stand of 114 between Matt Windows (144) and Jack Russell. The former England wicketkeeper was in classic, obdurate form with the bat, eventually grinding his way to an unbeaten 119 – his third hundred of the season – and featuring in further stands of 161 with Roger Sillence and 90 with Jon Lewis. There were 17 fours and a six in Sillence's hard-hit maiden century, while Lewis (57) completed his 50 from just 34 balls. Derbyshire were therefore set an intimidating 583 to win, but by the close they were 155 for 1, with Di Venuto already on 92, and the loss of 40 overs on the final day helped Di Venuto, with some assistance from Chris Bassano (51), to bat out time as Derbyshire closed the match on 319 for 5.

An unbeaten 127 off 186 balls from Adrian Dale, including 12 fours, guided Glamorgan to a first-innings score of 447 at Cardiff after Mike Powell (84) and Ian Thomas (56) had also frustrated the Worcestershire attack. Stephen Peters then hit back with 130, while Vikram Solanki (94) helped him to add 167 for the fourth wicket, but by now too much time had been lost to weather interruptions and, in the end, after Worcestershire had been bowled out for 381, there was time only for Glamorgan to go to

181 for 2 with unbeaten half-centuries from both David Hemp and Powell.

Rain meant that it took Nottinghamshire until early on the third day to reach 400 for 6 declared in their first innings, and maximum batting points. Guy Welton made 77 and Usman Afzaal 103, and by the close of that third day Durham were already following on at 153 for 5 having been dismissed for just 132 in their first innings. But no play at all was possible on the scheduled last day at Trent Bridge – leaving Notts to bewail the damage that the extra eight lost points might do to their promotion ambitions.

ROUND 18: 11–15 SEPTEMBER 2002

Division One

at Southampton Rose Bowl
Surrey 418 (127.2 overs) (IJ Ward 112, N Shahid 82, AD Brown 60, Saqlain Mushtaq 55) and 422 for 8 dec. (IJ Ward 156, GP Thorpe 143)
Hampshire 327 (76 overs) (JP Crawley 82, JD Francis 59) and 390 (N Pothas 99, NC Johnson 86, AD Mascarenhas 67, MP Bicknell 5 for 56)
Surrey won by 123 runs
Surrey 20 pts, Hampshire 6 pts

at Canterbury
Kent 405 (133.4 overs) (DP Fulton 177, RWT Key 75, ET Smith 68) and 144 for 4 (ET Smith 68)
Lancashire 197 (71.2 overs) (PA Nixon 5 catches) and (following on) 351 (MJ Chilton 90, SG Law 90)
Kent won by six wickets
Kent 19 pts, Lancashire 2 pts

at Leicester
Somerset 191 (42.3 overs) (M Burns 97*) and 101 (J Srinath 5 for 25)
Leicestershire 310 (81.4 overs) (TR Ward 84)
Leicestershire won by an innings & 18 runs
Leicestershire 18 pts, Somerset 2.75 pts (Somerset had 0.25 pt deducted for a slow over rate)

at Edgbaston
Warwickshire 601 for 9 dec. (145 overs) (DP Ostler 225, T Frost 103, KJ Piper 64*, MJ Powell 58) and 232 for 4 (MJ Powell 92*, MA Wagh 90)
Yorkshire 351 (86.1 overs) (MTG Elliott 74, RJ Blakey 70, C White 53, RKJ Dawson 50, MA Wagh 5 for 137) and (following on) 481 (MTG Elliott 127, RJ Blakey 103, GM Fellows 88, A McGrath 66, JAS Spires 5 for 165)
Warwickshire won by six wickets
Warwickshire 20 pts, Yorkshire 6 pts

Graham Thorpe returned to county cricket, following a seven-week break from the game due to his personal problems, and hit a second-innings 143 as new champions Surrey beat relegated Hampshire by 123 runs at Southampton. Opener Ian Ward, meanwhile, scored two hundreds in the match – making it three in successive championship innings – as Surrey totalled 418 and 422 for 8 declared. Hampshire, bowled out for 327 on the second day, fought hard to get to 390 second time around before succumbing to Martin Bicknell (5 for 56) and Ian Salisbury (4 for 116). Thorpe made only 19 in Surrey's first innings, as Ward (112), Nadeem Shahid (82), Alistair Brown (60) and Saqlain Mushtaq (55) all flourished, but on day three England's best batsman struck 21 fours from 222 balls as he helped the prolific Ward (156) to add 239 for the third wicket. John Crawley (82) top scored in the Hampshire first innings, while a seventh-wicket stand of 98 from Nic Pothas (99) and Dimitri Mascarenhas (67) held up Surrey on the final afternoon following a flowing 86 from Neil Johnson.

A fine 177 from David Fulton, and more effective seam and swing bowling by Martin Saggers, spearheaded Kent's six-wicket win over Lancashire at Canterbury. Fulton batted through a slightly shortened opening day for 137 not out, his fourth hundred of the season, and was well supported by both Rob Key (75) and Ed Smith (68). An overnight 286 for 2 ultimately became 405 all out, and by the close of the second day Lancashire were in trouble at 164 for 8. Saggers, backed up by Amjad Khan and Mark Ealham, took 4 for 34 as Lancashire were dismissed for 197 but, after Fulton had enforced the follow-on, Kent's bowlers were mastered for some time by Mark Chilton (90) and Stuart Law (90) in a third-wicket partnership of 164. At 224 for 3 going into the final day, Lancashire felt they could still save the game – but Saggers (4 for 64) and Khan (3 for 63) made sure they were bowled out for 351 to leave Kent's batsmen with a simple win target.

Somerset tumbled to their fifth defeat in seven games when Leicestershire mauled them by an innings and 18 runs inside two days at Grace Road. Only Michael Burns, adding an unbeaten 97 to previous summer scores of 99, 98 and 95, put up any sort of resistance as Somerset were dismissed for 191 on the opening day, and Javagal Srinath added 5 for 25 to his first-innings haul of 4 for 60 as the visitors subsided to 101 all out in 130 minutes following a Leicestershire first-innings score of 310. Trevor Ward, in search of a new contract, hit 84.

see Warwickshire reach a target of 232 from 51 overs with 18 balls to spare. Mike Powell (92 not out) and Mark Wagh (90 from 119 balls) made the eventual result a formality, in fact, by putting on 175 for the first wicket.

Division Two

at Derby
Middlesex 292 (107.3 overs) (PN Weekes 88, SG Koenig 72, KJ Dean 6 for 59) and 150
Derbyshire 137 (42 overs) (AA Noffke 8 for 24) and 232 (MJ Di Venuto 71, PCR Tufnell 5 for 35)
Middlesex won by 73 runs
Middlesex 17 pts, Derbyshire 3 pts

at Chester-le-Street
Essex 463 (130.3 overs) (Aftab Habib 123, ME Waugh 117) and 42 for 0
Durham 187 (66.4 overs) (MA Gough 75* – carried his bat) and (following on) 314 (AM Thorpe 95, BJ Hodge 56)
Essex won by ten wickets
Essex 20 pts, Durham 3 pts

Ian Ward's innings of 112 helped Surrey to another championship victory over Hampshire.

Warwickshire beat Yorkshire by six wickets in a fine game of cricket at Edgbaston that went almost to the last over. Warwickshire began the match by running up a massive 601 for 9 declared, the highlight of which was a brilliant 225 from 240 balls by Dominic Ostler. Reserve wicketkeeper Tony Frost, playing as a specialist batsman and slotted in at No. 3, responded with a stylish 103 and there were also half-centuries from Mike Powell and Keith Piper. Yorkshire, bowled out for 351 despite 74 from 66 balls by Matthew Elliott, 70 by Richard Blakey and half-centuries from both Craig White and Richard Dawson, put up a courageous fight of it after being asked to follow on. In truth, it gave them their only chance of winning the match, but it was still a fine effort to reach 481. Matthew Elliott's 127 and a fluent 66 from Anthony McGrath, at last beginning to show signs of reaching the cricketing maturity promised by his youthful successes, was followed by a sixth-wicket stand of 175 between Gary Fellows (88) and the splendidly in-form Blakey, who scored 103. Jamie Spires, the young left-arm spinner, battled hard too to add 5 for 165 to a first-innings haul of 4 for 99 – and his reward was to

at Trent Bridge
Nottinghamshire 404 (118.4 overs) (DJ Bicknell 112, JER Gallian 62, PJ Franks 57*, CMW Read 50) and 241 (BM Shafayat 104)
Worcestershire 397 (98.5 overs) (SJ Rhodes 124, DA Leatherdale 120, AJ Harris 5 for 115) and 134 (AJ Harris 5 for 56)
Nottinghamshire won by 114 runs
Nottinghamshire 20 pts, Worcestershire 7 pts

at Northampton
Northamptonshire 592 for 8 dec. (165.1 overs) (RA White 277, MJ Powell 107, ME Cassar 101*)
Gloucestershire 299 (89.3 overs) (CM Spearman 107, MGN Windows 89) and (following on) 234 (APR Gidman 66, CM Spearman 64, MGN Windows 52)
Northamptonshire won by an innings & 59 runs
Northamptonshire 20 pts, Gloucestershire 4 pts

The meeting of Derbyshire and Middlesex at Derby was always likely to provide an outcome central to the equation of who was going to win promotion to Division One of the championship. What actually happened, however, was both highly dramatic and – in Derbyshire's case – ruinous to their own chances. For some reason best known to themselves, Derbyshire produced a pitch for one of the most important games in their recent history that was below par to the degree that 23 wickets fell on an extraordinary second day. All four innings of the match featured on that day – a remarkable and rare occurrence – and despite a late rally, Derbyshire emerged from the wreckage with defeat by 73 runs and an eight-point penalty for a surface rated 'poor' for its chronically uneven bounce. Middlesex had reached 291 for 8 on the opening day, thanks to Paul Weekes' 88 and a gutsy 72 by Sven Koenig – but also to some ill-directed home bowling. Kevin Dean quickly polished off the tail the following morning to end up with 6 for 59 – and then the real carnage began. Derbyshire were skittled for 137, with Ashley Noffke returning the unsurprising career-best figures of 8 for 24 from 15 overs, but then hit back themselves to bowl out Middlesex for 150 in their second innings. A sensibly aggressive 49 not out by David Alleyne prevented a rout as Dean and Jason Kerr shared eight wickets, and by the

close Derbyshire had already lost Andrew Gait – who recorded a pair on the same day. A stand of 124 by Michael Di Venuto (71) and Chris Bassano, who added 44 to his first-innings score of 49, briefly raised hopes of a home victory against the odds, but soon Noffke (4 for 84) and Phil Tufnell (5 for 35) had wrapped up the Derbyshire second innings for 232 – and confirmed promotion for the division leaders. Derbyshire, licking their still-open and self-inflicted wounds, decided not to appeal against the pitch penalty which had scuppered their own prospects of reaching the top division.

Essex strengthened their own position in second place by overwhelming Durham by ten wickets at Chester-le-Street. Mark Waugh (117) and Aftab Habib (123) put on 218 for the fourth wicket as Essex totalled 463 in their first innings. Then, despite Michael Gough becoming just the third Durham opener to carry his bat, with an undefeated 75, the home side were rolled over for 187 with James Middlebrook taking 4 for 38. Durham did put up stiffer resistance in their second innings, scoring 314 with Ashley Thorpe top scoring with 95, but that left Essex with the simple matter of making 42 for victory. Durham, meanwhile, were confirmed as wooden spoonists by this result.

Nottinghamshire's promotion ambitions were also raised by a 114-run win against close rivals Worcestershire at Trent Bridge. A fine 112 by Darren Bicknell, plus half-centuries from Jason Gallian, Chris Read and Paul Franks, took Nottinghamshire to an important maximum five batting bonus points as well as putting them in early command with a first-innings score of 404. Worcestershire, however, bounced back with 397 – which represented a considerable achievement after they had declined to 120 for 6. The players who produced this stirring fightback, under pressure, were seasoned campaigners David Leatherdale and Steve Rhodes. Leatherdale, in his 15th summer with Worcestershire, scored 120 while wicketkeeper Rhodes, in his 18th season, contributed 124 to a county seventh-wicket record stand of 256. Andy Harris, though, blew away the tail to finish with 5 for 115 and a maiden first-class hundred by Bilal Shafayat, just two months beyond his 18th birthday, took Nottinghamshire to 241 in their second innings. With batting conditions getting more difficult, Worcestershire fell away to 40 for 4 by the close of the third day – and then 134 all out on the

Just like old times: Mark Waugh was at his languid best for Essex.

final morning. Harris again did most of the damage, with 5 for 56, while Stuart MacGill's leg breaks and googlies brought him 3 for 29.

Perhaps the most remarkable innings of the entire season, though, was played at Northampton – by 24-year-old Loughborough University student Rob White. In just his fifth first-class match, and opening the Northants innings with fellow Loughborough student Mark Powell, the unheralded White took the attack to the Gloucestershire bowlers with such devastating strokeplay that, on a flat pitch, he reached a hundred before lunch and then thundered on to a mammoth 277 with 41 fours and two sixes. Everything he tried came off, but the range and power of his strokes took the breath away. Powell, too, in only his third first-class appearance, also reached a maiden hundred – although his 107 was positively pedestrian as the two friends shared a memorable opening stand of 375. Matt Cassar, with 101 not out, then cashed in by hitting the dispirited bowlers for his first century since 1998 as Northants went on to total 592 for 8 declared. Gloucestershire were bowled out for 299 in reply, despite a third-wicket stand of 185 between Craig Spearman (107) and Matt Windows (89) that took them to 231 for 2, and spinners Monty Panesar (4 for 42) and Jason Brown (4 for 106) relished the chance to continue to press for victory when the follow-on was enforced. Spearman, with 64 out of the first 76, Windows (52) and Alex Gidman (66) all put up some resistance – but, in the end, Panesar and Brown shared another six wickets as Gloucestershire were dismissed for 234. Oh, and who took two late wickets with leg spin as the victory, by an innings and 59 runs, was completed? None other than White, of course, to set the seal on his astonishing match.

ROUND 19: 18–21 SEPTEMBER 2002

Division One

at The Oval
Surrey 494 (111.2 overs) (SA Newman 183, IJ Ward 118, JN Batty 74, J Srinath 5 for 114 including a hat-trick) and 492 for 9 dec. (AJ Hollioake 208, AD Brown 107)
Leicestershire 361 (93.5 overs) (DL Maddy 127*, IJ Sutcliffe 72, DI Stevens 53, JN Batty 5 catches) and 142 (ND Burns 68, TJ Murtagh 5 for 39)
Surrey won by 483 runs
Surrey 20 pts, Leicestershire 7 pts

at Hove
Sussex 352 (95.1 overs) (MW Goodwin 93, KJ Innes 60*, DR Brown 5 for 103) and 341 (MW Goodwin 111, MJG Davis 66)
Warwickshire 293 (66.4 overs) (NM Carter 103, T Frost 73, BV Taylor 5 for 90) and 405 for 7 (MJ Powell 103, DP Ostler 90, DR Brown 79*)
Warwickshire won by three wickets
Warwickshire 17 pts, Sussex 7 pts

at Headingley
Kent 399 (116.2 overs) (SR Waugh 146, ET Smith 67, JC Tredwell 61, MM Patel 52) and 103 for 2
Yorkshire 218 (60.1 overs) (C White 62) and (following on) 283 (RJ Blakey 94)
Kent won by eight wickets
Kent 19 pts, Yorkshire 2.25 pts (Yorkshire had 1.75 pts deducted for a slow over rate)

at Taunton
Somerset 221 (61.4 overs) and 129
Lancashire 228 (55.3 overs) (KW Hogg 50, MPL Bulbeck 6 for 93) and 124 for 2 (D Byas 63*, SG Law 57*)
Lancashire won by eight wickets
Lancashire 16 pts, Somerset 4 pts

Champions Surrey signed off from the 2002 season in some style at The Oval as they thumped Leicestershire by the remarkable margin of 483 runs. It was their tenth win of the campaign (a record for the two-division championship) but, more significantly, the biggest margin of victory in their county history – beating the 470-run triumph over Gloucestershire way back in 1913. The match also brought a memorable personal milestone for Ian Ward, the Surrey opener, whose first-innings 118 made him the first Surrey batsman since Jack Hobbs, in 1925, to score four hundreds in successive championship innings. It was also Ward's seventh century of a prolific season – although, on the opening day, even he had to concede second best to Scott Newman, his opening partner. The 22-year-old, dismissed for 99 a month earlier, spent 45 minutes in the 90s before completing a well-deserved maiden hundred. He then scored another 83 runs from just 89 balls to go on to a brilliant 183 after he and Ward had added 227 for the first wicket. Newman also put on 125 for the second wicket with Jon Batty (74) and Surrey went on to total 494 despite a late hat-trick from Javagal Srinath, whose victims were James Ormond (at the end of one over) and then Adam Hollioake and Paul

Sampson at the beginning of his next over. Leicestershire's reply of 361 was based around half-centuries from Iain Sutcliffe and Darren Stevens – and especially a gutsy unbeaten 127 from Darren Maddy who, with almost 1,200 runs and more than 40 wickets could claim to be the all-rounder of the championship season. At 89 for 4 in their second innings Surrey were still on top, but perhaps in need of some more inspiration. They got it, and how, as Hollioake joined Alistair Brown to add a rollicking 282 for the fifth wicket. Hollioake, who hit a hundred between lunch and tea on the third day, twice hooked Devon Malcolm for six and, remarkably, outscored the rapid Brown by almost two to one. On 146 not out overnight, with Surrey suddenly 335 for 4, Hollioake went on to score 208 – his maiden double hundred – on the final morning. Brown made 107 and Surrey batted on to a total of 492 for 9 declared, as Hollioake sought to demoralize his opponents. It seemed to work, too, as Leicestershire collapsed to 142 all out inside 39 overs, with Tim Murtagh snatching a career-best 5 for 39 and only Neil Burns, with 68, managing to hold back the irresistible Surrey tide for long.

Warwickshire grabbed second place, and the £50,000 runners-up cheque, with an astonishing three-wicket win over Sussex at Hove. Needing 401 for victory, after Sussex had dominated the first three days of the match, Warwickshire were inspired by an innings of 103 from Mike Powell, their captain, and by a powerful 90 off 102 balls from Dominic Ostler. Starting the final day on a distinctly unpromising 103 for 3, Warwickshire were later guided to their target by Dougie Brown (79 not out) and Mo Sheikh (43) who added a vital 75. Perhaps the innings which made the win possible, however, was played on day two by Neil Carter. The tail-ender smashed six sixes as he sped to 103 from just 67 balls. Moreover, Carter and last man Jamie Spires (37 not out) put on 119 in a mere 12 overs for the tenth wicket – which boosted Warwickshire from a sickly 174 for 9 to 293 all out in reply to Sussex's first innings of 352. Murray Goodwin, however, then added a classy 111 to his first-innings 93 and, when Mark Davis hit 66 and Kevin Innes batted well for the second time in the match to take Sussex to 341, it looked all over.

Sadly for Kent, pipped for second place, it wasn't. Kent had temporarily leapfrogged above Warwickshire when they disposed of Yorkshire by eight wickets inside three days at Headingley. On a pitch which always had something in it for the bowlers, Steve Waugh played the decisive innings of 146 for Kent, who reached a commanding 399 by the second morning. Ed Smith (67), Min Patel (52) and James Tredwell, with a career-best 61, all made invaluable contributions, but it was Australian Test captain Waugh who stole the show. Kent's seamers, led again by Martin Saggers (4 for 44) then dismissed Yorkshire for 218 and, following on, the home side were in deep trouble at 74 for 5. Fighting knocks from Craig White, Richard Blakey (94) and Richard Dawson at least made Kent bat again as Yorkshire scrambled up to 283 all out.

At Taunton, meanwhile, Lancashire set the seal on Somerset's miserable season by easing to an eight-wicket win which saw them clinch fourth place. At first, through their new-ball attack of Richard Johnson and Matt Bulbeck, the home side made a fight of it as Lancashire finished the opening day at 88 for 6 in reply to Somerset's 221. But lower-order aggression from Kyle Hogg (50) and Peter Martin (34 not out) hauled Lancashire up to 228, in spite of Bulbeck ending with career-best figures of 6 for 93 and Johnson picking up 4 for 68. Martin, moreover, took 4 for 29 with the ball as he and Chris Schofield (4 for 35) undermined the Somerset second innings. Their 129 left Lancashire with a modest win target and, despite an early wobble at 8 for 2, David Byas (63 not out) and Stuart Law (57 not out) made short work of it with a stand of 116 in just 15 overs.

Division Two

at Chelmsford
Nottinghamshire 341 (86.5 overs) (Usman Afzaal 134, CMW Read 73, DJ Bicknell 53) and 280 (BM Shafayat 70)
Essex 282 (88.4 overs) (JP Stephenson 65, Aftab Habib 50) and 343 for 3 (WI Jefferson 165*, ME Waugh 76, Aftab Habib 57*)
Essex won by seven wickets
Essex 16.5 pts, Nottinghamshire 6 pts (Essex had 0.5 pt deducted for a slow over rate)

at Worcester
Derbyshire 246 (88 overs) (AI Gait 58, JID Kerr 54, LD Sutton 51, GJ Batty 5 for 60, DJ Pipe 4 catches, 1 stumping) and 391 (SA Selwood 77, JID Kerr 68, AI Gait 67, NRC Dumelow 56)
Worcestershire 265 (68.3 overs) (VS Solanki 81, SD Peters 72) and 373 for 9 (DA Leatherdale 89*, GJ Batty 74, MS Mason 50, KJ Dean 5 for 143)
Worcestershire won by one wicket
Worcestershire 17 pts, Derbyshire 3.75 pts (Derbyshire had 0.25 pt deducted for a slow over rate)

at Bristol
Durham 216 (68.3 overs) (BJ Hodge 73, RJ Sillence
5 for 63, RC Russell 6 catches) and 312 (MA Gough 78)
Gloucestershire 359 (98.5 overs) (APR Gidman 96,
CM Spearman 89, SJ Harmison 5 for 65, A Pratt 5
catches) and 171 for 0 (CM Spearman 114*)
Gloucestershire won by ten wickets
Gloucestershire 19 pts, Durham 4 pts

at Cardiff
Glamorgan 348 (100 overs) (MJ Powell 113, RDB Croft
59*, MP Maynard 50, MWH Inness 7 for 90) and 528
for 7 dec. (MP Maynard 151, DL Hemp 108, MJ Powell
92, RDB Croft 71*, A Dale 50)
Northamptonshire 430 (109.3 overs) (AL Penberthy
130*, GL Brophy 110, RA White 69, SD Thomas 5 for
104) and 242 for 6 (MJ Powell 108*)
Match drawn
Glamorgan 10 pts, Northamptonshire 12 pts

Essex earned themselves the Division Two title, and
with it a cheque for £40,000, by beating
Nottinghamshire by seven wickets at Chelmsford.
Nottinghamshire, however, were not too displeased,
because they also made sure of the bonus points
they needed to gain promotion. Indeed, the visitors

seemed to have the best of the first half of the
match, totalling 341 with a brilliant 134 from Usman
Afzaal when asked to bat first, and bowling out
Essex for 282 in reply. Bilal Shafayat's mature 70
then boosted the Notts second innings to 280,
leaving the home side requiring 340 for victory. It
seemed a tall order, but enter Will Jefferson (all six
foot ten inches of him) to strike a superb, career-
best 165 not out, from just 214 balls, and master the
leg spin of Stuart MacGill. The Australian took only
1 for 121 from his 25 overs, and Essex strolled home
as Mark Waugh (76) and Aftab Habib (57 not out)
both gave the fast-improving opener solid support.

Worcestershire were left frustrated in an agonising
fourth place despite a marvellous one-wicket victory
against Derbyshire at New Road. Graeme Hick,
coming in at No. 11 because of a thumb broken in
the field, hit two fours in a dramatic little innings of
ten not out as Worcestershire, requiring 373 in the
fourth innings, got home thanks to a fifth-wicket
stand of 122 between David Leatherdale (89 not
out) and Gareth Batty, plus a remarkable maiden 50
off just 27 balls by Matt Mason. Fellow tail-ender

**Surrey are crowned county champions again after beating
Leicestershire by a record margin.**

Alamgir Sheriyar also played a part with a cavalier 18 as Derbyshire tasted ultimate despair after a season which saw them bounce back impressively from their double wooden spoon season of 2001 but which ended messily with their pitch penalty. An opening stand of 103 between Andrew Gait (58) and Luke Sutton (51) launched Derbyshire towards their first-innings score of 246, while Batty took 5 for 60 to become only the third slow bowler (after Saqlain and Shaun Udal) to go past 50 championship wickets for the season. Worcestershire's hopes of promotion were dashed when they were bowled out for 265 in reply, and thus failed to get the minimum of four batting points they required to have a chance of catching Nottinghamshire. Then came a Derbyshire second-innings rally to 391, with Gait, Steve Selwood (77), Jason Kerr and Nathan Dumelow all hitting half-centuries, and Worcestershire's brave finish. However, the home side's director of cricket, Tom Moody, said: 'We missed our chance of gaining promotion weeks ago.'

Durham's sad season was completed by yet another defeat – this time by Gloucestershire at Bristol, and the bottom club's sixth inside three days. A career-best 5 for 63 by Roger Sillence put Gloucestershire in control on day one, with Durham being bowled out for 216 despite Brad Hodge's 73. Craig Spearman had already made 80 not out, out of 144 for 4, by the close and although he went on only to 89 on the second day, there was also a fine 96 from Alex Gidman to propel Gloucestershire to 359 and a sizeable lead. Michael Gough (78) and Gary Pratt (41) produced a fighting first-wicket stand when Durham began their second innings, but a total of 312 left the home side needing only 170 for victory. Once again, Spearman was in spectacular form as he reached his fifth hundred of the season from 94 balls, with no fewer than 20 boundaries. With

Adam Hollioake, the Surrey captain, joined Surrey's championship-winning campaign midway through the season, but his impact was immense.

Spearman ending on 114 not out, Gloucestershire won by ten wickets.

Gerry Brophy, yet another of the South Africans coming into county cricket on an European passport (in his case, a British one) hit a maiden championship hundred as Northamptonshire drew with Glamorgan at Cardiff. A former South African Under 17 captain, Brophy scored 110 while putting on 174 for the sixth wicket with fellow century-maker Tony Penberthy. Their efforts allowed

Northants to total 430 in response to Glamorgan's first-innings total of 348, in which Mike Powell hit 113 to go past 1,000 championship runs for the season and Mathew Innes took 7 for 90. Glamorgan, however, regained control of the match by reaching 528 for 7 declared in their second innings with Matthew Maynard (151) adding 252 for the second wicket with David Hemp (108). Powell also enjoyed himself with 92, and Robert Croft likewise with an unbeaten 71, but perhaps the Welsh county delayed their declaration too long as Northants, having slid initially to 74 for 4 and then 152 for 6, managed to see it out for a draw at 242 for 6 with Mark Powell leading the rearguard action with a career-best unbeaten 108, and Toby Bailey staying with him at the end.

DIVISION ONE FINAL RESULTS

	P	W	L	D	Bat	Bowl	Pts
Surrey	**16**	**10**	**2**	**4**	**59**	**48**	**242.75**
Warwickshire	16	7	2	7	42	44	198.00
Kent	16	7	4	5	48	44	195.50
Lancashire	16	6	4	6	33	43	172.00
Leicestershire	16	5	5	6	42	46	171.00
Sussex	16	3	6	7	43	47	154.00
Hampshire *	16	2	5	9	35	44	131.00
Somerset	16	1	7	8	39	44	126.75
Yorkshire	16	2	8	6	35	45	124.75

Slow Over Rate Fines

Surrey	0.25 pt	v. Sussex (Oval) 19–22 April
Kent	0.50 pt	v. Lancashire (Liverpool) 26–29 June
Leicestershire	1.00 pt	v. Lancashire (Old Trafford) 19–22 April
Somerset	0.25 pt	v. Leicestershire (Leicester) 12–14 September
Yorkshire	0.50 pt	v. Leicestershire (Leicester) 31 May–3 June
	1.00 pt	v. Leicestershire (Scarborough) 4–7 September
	1.75 pt	v. Kent (Headingley) 18–20 September

* Eight points deducted for a substandard pitch v. Lancashire (Southampton) 25–27 July

DIVISION TWO FINAL RESULTS

	P	W	L	D	Bat	Bowl	Pts
Essex	**16**	**10**	**3**	**3**	**42**	**46**	**219.00**
Middlesex	16	7	3	6	61	43	211.75
Nottinghamshire	16	8	5	3	47	48	201.75
Worcestershire	16	7	4	5	53	43	200.00
Glamorgan	16	5	5	6	41	44	169.00
Derbyshire	16	7	7	2	37	48	167.75
Northamptonshire	16	5	7	4	46	41	162.50
Gloucestershire	16	2	7	7	42	44	136.50
Durham	16	1	11	4	21	42	90.75

Slow Over Rate Fines

Essex	0.50 pt	v. Nottinghamshire (Trent Bridge) 8–10 May
	0.50 pt	v. Nottinghamshire (Chelmsford) 18–21 September
Middlesex	0.25 pt	v. Worcestershire (Worcester) 27–30 August
Nottinghamshire	0.50 pt	v. Middlesex (Lord's) 24–27 April
	0.75 pt	v. Worcestershire (Kidderminster) 8–11 August
Derbyshire *	0.25 pt	v. Northamptonshire (Derby) 8–10 May
	0.75 pt	v. Glamorgan (Derby) 31 May–3 June
	0.25 pt	v. Worcestershire (Worcester) 18–21 September
Northamptonshire	0.50 pt	v. Nottinghamshire (Trent Bridge) 24–27 May
Gloucestershire	0.75 pt	v. Derbyshire (Derby) 3–6 July
	0.75 pt	v. Nottinghamshire (Trent Bridge) 21–23 August
Durham	0.25 pt	v. Nottinghamshire (Trent Bridge) 6–8 September

* Eight points deducted for a substandard pitch v. Middlesex (Derby) 11–13 September

COUNTY CHAMPIONSHIP FEATURES 2002

+ denotes 2nd innings

TOTALS OVER 600

746-9 dec.	Northamptonshire v. Gloucestershire	at Bristol
671	Hampshire v. Kent	at Canterbury
645-6 dec.	Durham v. Middlesex	at Lord's
644	Sussex v Somerset	at Taunton
643-7 dec.	Worcestershire v. Durham	at Worcester
633-7 dec.	Middlesex v. Glamorgan	at Cardiff
632	Northamptonshire v. Essex	at Northampton
631-6 dec.	Sussex v. Hampshire	at Hove
628-8 dec	INDIA V. ENGLAND	AT HEADINGLEY
617	ENGLAND v. INDIA	AT TRENT BRIDGE
614-5 dec.	Northamptonshire v. Worcestershire	at Northampton
608-6 dec.	Surrey v. Somerset	at Taunton
604	Cambridge Univ. CCE v. Oxford Univ. CCE	at Lord's
601-9 dec.	Warwickshire v. Yorkshire	at Edgbaston

TOTALS UNDER 100

71+	Somerset v. Lancashire	at Blackpool
77+	Northamptonshire v. Worcestershire	at Worcester
93+	Middlesex v. Essex	at Chelmsford
96	Derbyshire v. Durham	at Darlington
98+	Hampshire v. Somerset	at Bath

INDIVIDUAL SCORES OVER 200

315*	GA Hick	Worcestershire v. Durham	at Worcester
310*	MEK Hussey	Northamptonshire v. Gloucestershire	at Bristol
277	RA White	Northamptonshire v. Gloucestershire	at Northampton
272	JP Crawley	Hampshire v. Kent	at Canterbury
255*	NV Knight	Warwickshire v. Hampshire	at Edgbaston
254*	KP Pietersen	Nottinghamshire v.Middlesex	at Trent Bridge
251	ML Love	Durham v. Middlesex	at Lord's
250	SS Das	Indians v. Essex	at Chelmsford
249	SP James	Glamorgan v. Essex	at Chelmsford
230	MJ Di Venuto	Derbyshire v. Northamptonshire	at Northampton
225	DP Ostler	Warwickshire v. Yorkshire	at Edgbaston
218	SG Law	Lancashire v. Sussex	at Old Trafford
218	MR Ramprakash	Surrey v. Somerset	at Taunton
217	CJ Adams	Sussex v. Lancashire	at Old Trafford
217	R Dravid	INDIA v. ENGLAND	AT THE OVAL
216+	DS Lehmann	Yorkshire v. Sussex	at Arundel
210*	MR Ramprakash	Surrey v. Warwickshire	at The Oval
208+	AJ Hollioake	Surrey v. Leicestershire	at The Oval
207*	RC Irani	Essex v. Northamptonshire	at Ilford
205*	RSC Martin-Jenkins	Sussex v. Somerset	at Taunton
203*	Abdur Razzaq	Middlesex v. Glamorgan	at Cardiff

HUNDRED & 0 IN THE SAME MATCH

0 & 101*	ML Love	Durham v. Middlesex	at Chester-le-Street
0 & 102*	DR Hewson	Derbyshire v. Glamorgan	at Cardiff
0 & 106*	MA Wallace	Glamorgan v. Derbyshire	at Cardiff

COUNTY CHAMPIONSHIP FEATURES 2002

HUNDRED & 0 IN THE SAME MATCH cont.

0 & 109	MB Loye	Northamptonshire v. Derbyshire	at Derby
0 & 134	ME Trescothick	Somerset v. Yorkshire	at Taunton
118 & 0	CM Spearman	Gloucestershire v. Nottinghamshire	at Bristol
0 & 107	RC Russell	Gloucestershire v. Essex	at Gloucester
0 & 151	JN Batty	Surrey v. Somerset	at Taunton
141* & 0	ET Smith	Kent v. Sussex	at Hove
210* & 0	MR Ramprakash	Surrey v. Warwickshire	at The Oval
124 & 0	A Singh	Worcestershire v. Essex	at Chelmsford
152 & 0	CWG Bassano	Derbyshire v. Essex	at Derby
106 & 0	V Sehwag	INDIA v. ENGLAND	AT TRENT BRIDGE
0 & 109	GM Fellows	Yorkshire v. Lancashire	at Old Trafford
154 & 0	ET Smith	Kent v. Somerset	at Taunton
0 & 101	RJ Sillence	Gloucestershire v. Derbyshire	at Bristol
103 & 0*	NM Carter	Warwickshire v. Sussex	at Hove
134 & 0	Usman Afzaal	Nottinghamshire v. Essex	at Chelmsford
0 & 165*	WI Jefferson	Essex v. Nottinghamshire	at Chelmsford

TWO HUNDREDS IN THE SAME MATCH

105 & 104*	MB Loye	Northamptonshire v. Nottinghamshire	at Northampton
106 & 131	MJ Wood	Somerset v. Surrey	at Taunton
140 & 118*	MP Maynard	Glamorgan v. Gloucestershire	at Cheltenham
192* & 113	MJ Di Venuto	Derbyshire v. Middlesex	at Lord's
112 & 156	IJ Ward	Surrey v. Hampshire	at Southampton

PLAYERS WHO CARRIED THEIR BAT

+53* (146)	WS Kendall	Hampshire v. Leicestershire	at Southampton
+59* (232)	JA Daley	Durham v. Derbyshire	at Derby
255* (472)	NV Knight	Warwickshire v. Hampshire	at Edgbaston
122* (247)	RR Montgomerie	Sussex v. Leicestershire	at Horsham
+180* (293)	CM Spearman	Gloucestershire v. Glamorgan	at Cheltenham
245* (493)	NV Knight	Warwickshire v. Sussex	at Edgbaston
84* (163)	AJ Swann	Lancashire v. Hampshire	at Old Trafford
310* (746)	MEK Hussey	Northamptonshire v. Gloucestershire	at Bristol
192* (414)	MJ Di Venuto	Derbyshire v. Middlesex	at Lord's
125* (259)	IJ Sutcliffe	Leicestershire v. Kent	at Canterbury
75* (187)	MA Gough	Durham v. Essex	at Chester-le-Street

MOST FIRST-CLASS RUNS

1,759	IJ Ward	(Surrey)

FIRST PLAYER TO 1,000 FIRST-CLASS RUNS

MEK Hussey (Northamptonshire) 19 July

FASTEST FIRST-CLASS HUNDRED

MV Fleming	66 balls	Kent v. Sri Lankans	at Canterbury

EIGHT WICKETS IN AN INNINGS

9-93	AJ Bichel	Worcestershire v. Gloucestershire	at Worcester
8-24	AA Noffke	Middlesex v. Derbyshire	at Derby
8-46+	A Richardson	Warwickshire v. Sussex	at Edgbaston
8-53+	GJ Smith	Nottinghamshire v. Essex	at Trent Bridge
8-61+	Azhar Mahmood	Surrey v. Lancashire	at The Oval
8-63	SJ Cook	Middlesex v. Northamptonshire	at Northampton
8-66+	PCR Tufnell	Middlesex v. Gloucestershire	at Cheltenham

COUNTY CHAMPIONSHIP FEATURES 2002

EIGHT WICKETS IN AN INNINGS cont.

8-111+	SCG MacGill	Nottinghamshire v. Middlesex	at Trent Bridge

TEN WICKETS IN A MATCH

14-165	SCG MacGill	Nottinghamshire v. Middlesex	at Trent Bridge
12-108	AA Noffke	Middlesex v. Derbyshire	at Derby
12-131	J Lewis	Gloucestershire v. Worcestershire	at Worcester
12-216	AF Giles	Warwickshire v. Kent	at Edgbaston
11-74	GJ Smith	Nottinghamshire v. Essex	at Trent Bridge
11-105	MS Kasprowicz	Glamorgan v. Durham	at Chester-le-Street
11-122	AJ Harris	Nottinghamshire v. Northamptonshire	at Trent Bridge
11-154	IJ Harvey	Gloucestershire v. Essex	at Gloucester
11-180	Saqlain Mushtaq	Surrey v. Hampshire	at The Oval
10-66	Kabir Ali	Worcestershire v. Gloucestershire	at Bristol
10-75	RL Johnson	Somerset v. Hampshire	at Bath
10-83	SD Thomas	Glamorgan v. Durham	at Cardiff
10-88	Kabir Ali	Worcestershire v. Oxford Univ. CCE	at Oxford
10-90	RJ Kirtley	Sussex v. Yorkshire	at Headingley
10-104	JP Stephenson	Essex v. Worcestershire	at Worcester
10-109	KJ Dean	Derbyshire v. Glamorgan	at Derby
10-125	KJ Dean	Derbyshire v. Middlesex	at Derby
10-126	DG Cork	Derbyshire v. Durham	at Derby
10-127	G Chapple	Lancashire v. Sussex	at Hove
10-131	AJ Bichel	Worcestershire v. Gloucestershire	at Worcester
10-134	ME Cassar	Northamptonshire v. Gloucestershire	at Bristol
10-148	DE Malcolm	Leicestershire v. Yorkshire	at Leicester
10-156	PS Jones	Somerset v. Warwickshire	at Edgbaston
10-171	AJ Harris	Nottinghamshire v. Worcestershire	at Trent Bridge
10-178	J Ormond	Surrey v. Warwickshire	at The Oval
10-238	GP Swann	Northamptonshire v. Derbyshire	at Northampton

HAT-TRICK

J Srinath	Leicestershire v. Surrey	at The Oval

MOST FIRST-CLASS WICKETS

83	KJ Dean (Derbyshire)
83	MJ Saggers (Kent)

SIX DISMISSALS IN AN INNINGS

6ct	RC Russell	Gloucestershire v. Durham	at Bristol

EIGHT DISMISSALS IN A MATCH

9ct, 1st	AJ Stewart	Surrey v. Lancashire	at The Oval
9ct	RC Russell	Gloucestershire v. Durham	at Bristol
8ct	CMW Read	Nottinghamshire v. Essex	at Trent Bridge
8ct	MA Wallace	Glamorgan v. Essex	at Swansea
8ct	LD Sutton	Derbyshire v. Essex	at Derby

MOST DISMISSALS

68	(65ct, 3st)	CMW Read (Nottinghamshire)

MOST FIELD CATCHES

33	DP Fulton (Kent)

FIRST-CLASS AVERAGES
England

BATTING

	M	Inns	NO	HS	Runs	Av	100	50
R Dravid	7	9	1	217	773	96.62	3	3
NV Knight	10	19	3	255*	1520	95.00	5	5
ML Love	6	8	1	251	576	82.28	2	2
MP Vaughan	9	15	2	197	976	75.07	4	3
SR Tendulkar	6	8	0	193	573	71.62	2	2
ME Trescothick	6	11	2	161	622	69.11	2	4
MEK Hussey	13	23	2	310*	1442	68.66	5	4
AJ Hollioake	9	13	2	208	738	67.09	2	5
DS Lehmann	10	18	1	216	1136	66.82	3	7
MG Bevan	9	14	3	146	697	63.36	2	4
DPMD Jayawardene	6	11	2	125*	567	63.00	3	1
IJ Ward	17	31	3	168*	1759	62.82	7	7
KP Pietersen	12	17	3	254*	871	62.21	4	-
MJ Di Venuto	15	28	3	230	1538	61.52	4	7
RC Irani	12	19	3	207*	977	61.06	3	1
Abdur Razzaq	6	9	3	203*	364	60.66	1	-
MR Ramprakash	15	25	4	218	1194	56.85	4	6
GA Hick	18	30	4	315*	1453	55.88	4	6
MP Maynard	13	20	1	151	1058	55.68	3	6
D Ganga	5	8	2	139*	325	54.16	2	-
MTG Elliott	5	10	1	127	487	54.11	1	4
JP Crawley	15	25	4	272	1130	53.80	2	7
AJ Stewart	11	16	2	123	751	53.64	1	5
KJ Barnett	8	15	3	182*	641	53.41	3	1
PD Collingwood	7	12	0	190	636	53.00	1	4
SP James	14	22	1	249	1111	52.90	4	3
SG Law	15	26	3	218	1216	52.86	2	6
EC Joyce	18	27	3	129	1267	52.79	4	6
PN Weekes	18	25	6	127*	990	52.10	4	3
MA Gough	8	14	2	103	616	51.33	1	3
JO Troughton	14	24	3	131*	1067	50.80	3	6
R Clarke	10	16	2	153*	711	50.78	2	4
AD Brown	16	26	2	188	1211	50.45	5	3
MJ Powell (Gm)	16	26	3	135	1152	50.08	3	7
A Flower	16	29	6	172*	1151	50.04	2	6
PA de Silva	8	12	2	88	500	50.00	-	6
V Sehwag	8	13	0	142	640	49.23	1	3
GL Brophy	4	8	3	110	246	49.20	1	1
CM Spearman	17	34	4	180*	1444	48.13	5	7
AJ Strauss	17	27	2	141	1202	48.08	3	5
SC Ganguly	7	11	1	128	477	47.70	1	4
DL Maddy	16	29	4	156	1187	47.48	2	8
MS Atapattu	7	12	1	185	522	47.45	2	1
RJ Blakey	16	29	7	103	1041	47.31	1	8
OA Shah	17	26	3	172*	1084	47.13	3	6
MA Butcher	13	21	1	123	936	46.80	3	5
DS Smith	6	10	0	181	465	46.50	1	2
SG Koenig	18	29	2	141*	1251	46.33	4	7
DC Nash	15	19	5	100	646	46.14	1	4
DDJ Robinson	18	34	2	175	1474	46.06	5	6
HP Tillekeratne	8	13	5	81	366	45.75	-	2
Usman Afzaal	18	32	4	134	1275	45.53	5	6
RC Russell	17	28	6	119*	991	45.04	3	5
CJ Adams	10	19	0	217	848	44.63	3	3
BF Smith	18	30	3	137	1202	44.51	4	6
Aftab Habib	15	25	3	123	964	43.81	2	8
DP Fulton	17	33	2	171	1358	43.80	4	4
DJJ Bravo	6	11	3	77*	350	43.75	-	3
NM Carter	9	12	5	103	305	43.57	1	1
IJ Harvey	6	10	1	123	390	43.33	1	2
DA Leatherdale	14	23	4	154	823	43.31	2	4
DP Ostler	14	25	1	225	1039	43.29	2	5
RP Arnold	9	12	0	112	518	43.16	2	3
C White	13	24	2	161	947	43.04	2	7
VS Solanki	16	26	4	153*	944	42.90	2	5
ME Cassar	7	9	1	101*	343	42.87	1	3
CWG Bassano	14	26	1	152	1063	42.52	1	8
MW Goodwin	16	28	0	162	1179	42.10	5	3
RSC Martin-Jenkins	16	28	4	205*	1008	42.00	1	5
IJ Sutcliffe	16	29	3	125*	1088	41.84	2	5
RWT Key	17	31	1	160	1255	41.83	3	6
VVS Laxman	8	13	1	85	502	41.83	-	3

FIRST-CLASS AVERAGES
England

BATTING

	M	Inns	NO	HS	Runs	Av	100	50
AS Rollins	6	12	1	107	460	41.81	1	2
JER Gallian	16	29	3	171	1087	41.80	4	6
SD Peters	10	16	0	146	667	41.68	2	3
AL Penberthy	16	25	3	130*	909	41.31	2	5
ET Smith	17	32	2	154	1239	41.30	2	8
RO Hinds	5	9	2	75	289	41.28	-	3
JWM Dalrymple	8	14	1	148	535	41.15	2	1
N Hussain	8	12	0	155	483	40.25	2	2
MM Patel	16	20	6	82	561	40.07	-	5
SJ Rhodes	15	22	6	124	636	39.75	1	2
A Symonds	12	24	2	118	858	39.00	2	4
PD Trego	4	8	1	140	270	38.57	1	-
PJ Martin	12	16	5	117*	422	38.36	1	1
ID Blackwell	14	23	0	114	879	38.21	3	3
TR Ambrose	13	22	1	149	798	38.00	2	2
RR Montgomerie	16	28	1	196	1026	38.00	2	4
PA Nixon	16	30	7	103	865	37.60	1	6
GP Thorpe	8	14	0	143	526	37.57	2	1
BM Shafayat	7	13	1	104	450	37.50	1	2
N Shahid	13	20	1	150	712	37.47	2	3
GD Lloyd	7	13	1	80	449	37.41	-	5
M Burns	16	30	2	99	1047	37.39	-	9
A Dale	16	24	1	127*	859	37.34	2	3
VJ Wells	11	17	2	150	558	37.20	1	3
AJ Swann	18	31	2	118	1073	37.00	2	6
RJ Warren	6	11	1	150*	369	36.90	1	1
GE Welton	16	28	2	115	954	36.69	1	6
MGN Windows	17	31	2	145	1062	36.62	2	7
MB Loye	13	22	1	139	768	36.57	4	1
A Singh	18	32	0	187	1167	36.46	2	6
RDB Croft	17	24	3	101*	747	35.57	1	5
JW Cook	15	24	3	90	746	35.52	-	4
BJ Hodge	4	8	0	73	284	35.50	-	2
JN Batty	13	23	2	151	742	35.33	2	3
JP Stephenson	13	24	8	100*	562	35.12	1	2
MA Ealham	14	24	7	83*	594	34.94	-	3
APR Gidman	10	17	1	117	558	34.87	1	4
MJ Wood (Sm)	15	28	0	196	971	34.67	3	5
RA Smith	15	25	1	104	832	34.66	2	3
CMW Read	18	28	5	127	797	34.65	1	4
RS Clinton	5	8	1	107	242	34.57	1	1
AP Grayson	7	9	0	105	309	34.33	1	1
GP Swann	11	16	0	183	539	33.68	2	1
PD Bowler	14	25	2	94	766	33.30	-	7
AW Laraman	11	13	3	82*	330	33.00	-	1
PCL Holloway	7	13	0	88	428	32.92	-	3
CP Schofield	7	9	1	91	262	32.75	-	2
ND Burns	16	24	2	101	720	32.72	1	5
DI Stevens	17	29	3	125	850	32.69	1	6
WI Jefferson	15	29	4	165*	815	32.60	2	2
A McGrath	14	26	1	165	803	32.12	1	3
DJ Bicknell	13	23	0	114	734	31.91	2	2
KJ Innes	13	22	7	60*	478	31.86	-	2
PA Cottey	13	22	0	137	699	31.77	3	1
NC Johnson	17	29	2	117	857	31.74	1	6
J Cox	13	25	2	176	724	31.47	1	3
MJ Prior	16	27	3	102*	741	30.87	1	5
T Frost	7	11	1	103	308	30.80	1	1
AI Gait	17	31	1	175	983	30.71	1	8
AB Agarkar	7	9	1	109*	244	30.50	1	-
AJ Bichel	9	11	2	78*	274	30.44	-	2
DG Cork	11	16	0	80	487	30.43	-	5
MV Fleming	5	8	1	102	211	30.14	1	-
P Johnson	14	25	3	96	662	30.09	-	5
MJ Powell (Wa)	17	31	2	103	872	30.06	1	6
RJ Turner	16	27	4	83*	691	30.04	-	4
JID Kerr	7	12	2	68	299	29.90	-	3
D Byas	15	25	2	101	684	29.73	1	4
MA Sheikh	5	8	2	43	178	29.66	-	-
MS Kasprowicz	12	19	7	72*	352	29.33	-	1
N Boje	9	16	2	84	409	29.21	-	2
SB Bangar	7	11	1	74	291	29.10	-	3

FIRST-CLASS AVERAGES
England

BATTING

	M	Inns	NO	HS	Runs	Av	100	50
THC Hancock	9	17	3	112	406	29.00	1	2
PAJ DeFreitas	16	23	2	114	609	29.00	1	3
MH Yardy	10	17	0	93	492	28.94	-	2
BL Hutton	11	19	1	116	518	28.77	1	4
MP Bicknell	10	14	5	35*	258	28.66	-	-
A Flintoff	7	10	0	137	284	28.40	1	1
DR Law	6	10	1	72*	253	28.11	-	2
TJ Phillips	8	13	3	75	281	28.10	-	1
DL Hemp	12	20	2	108	505	28.05	1	2
DR Brown	16	28	4	79*	671	27.95	-	3
MA Wagh	10	18	0	109	503	27.94	1	2
GJ Pratt	16	27	0	78	746	27.62	-	4
GM Fellows	10	18	0	109	493	27.38	1	1
RS Morton	5	8	0	79	218	27.25	-	2
Harbhajan Singh	8	10	2	54	218	27.25	-	1
MJ Chilton	17	29	1	107	761	27.17	1	4
GG Wagg	5	8	2	51	161	26.83	-	1
ST Jayasuriya	8	12	0	57	322	26.83	-	3
MJ Lumb	16	30	1	124	777	26.79	1	4
K Sangakkara	9	15	2	113	345	26.53	1	1
RMS Weston	9	11	2	72	237	26.33	-	2
MJG Davis	15	22	4	111	474	26.33	1	2
MA Wallace	17	25	4	106*	553	26.33	1	2
SD Udal	17	26	6	88	516	25.80	-	1
GD Welch	14	23	5	64	460	25.55	-	3
Saqlain Mushtaq	10	13	2	60	278	25.27	-	2
MW Alleyne	14	25	3	142*	555	25.22	1	2
LP Simmons	5	8	1	81	176	25.14	-	1
PJ Franks	10	14	2	67	301	25.08	-	3
DJG Sales	14	22	0	179	551	25.04	1	3
SM Pollock	10	18	1	66	425	25.00	-	4
J Hughes	7	10	1	74	225	25.00	-	1
ID Fisher	16	26	3	103*	568	24.69	1	4
CG Taylor	15	29	2	126	664	24.59	1	2
GJ Muchall	15	25	0	127	613	24.52	1	3
IR Bell	16	28	1	77	658	24.37	-	4
WS Kendall	17	31	2	88	705	24.31	-	4
WPC Weston	8	15	2	82	315	24.23	-	3
KA Parsons	15	26	2	68	581	24.20	-	4
N Peng	12	21	0	108	508	24.19	1	2
Wasim Jaffer	7	13	1	53	290	24.16	-	2
SA Selwood	10	19	0	99	457	24.05	-	2
AD Mascarenhas	16	26	2	94	574	23.91	-	2
N Pothas	16	26	1	99	597	23.88	-	5
JJB Lewis	11	18	1	102	402	23.64	1	2
MM Betts	9	16	5	56	259	23.54	-	1
AP Cowan	10	15	2	60*	305	23.46	-	2
VJ Craven	11	21	2	72	439	23.10	-	3
TR Ward	14	24	0	89	554	23.08	-	4
JD Francis	10	17	0	82	391	23.00	-	3
NC Phillips	10	16	6	58*	226	22.60	-	1
AA Noffke	8	10	1	76	203	22.55	-	1
NH Fairbrother	12	19	1	101	406	22.55	1	1
SD Stubbings	11	20	1	128	428	22.52	1	1
CT Tremlett	11	14	6	40*	180	22.50	-	-
NMK Smith	8	15	0	96	337	22.46	-	2
G Chapple	16	23	1	65	493	22.40	-	4
RL Johnson	9	17	4	61	290	22.30	-	1
JS Laney	7	13	0	89	289	22.23	-	1
LD Sutton	10	19	1	80	400	22.22	-	3
RKJ Dawson	15	24	1	87	511	22.21	-	2
AF Giles	9	12	0	68	264	22.00	-	1
TMB Bailey	17	25	4	68	457	21.76	-	4
GJ Batty	18	27	4	74	491	21.34	-	3
MP Dowman	8	14	0	71	298	21.28	-	1
JM Dakin	14	20	3	57	359	21.11	-	1
GR Napier	9	13	2	54*	230	20.90	-	1
AM Thorpe	7	13	0	95	271	20.84	-	2
DR Hewson	11	20	1	102*	393	20.68	1	1
A Pratt	17	30	3	93	556	20.59	-	3
KJ Dean	17	26	9	54*	347	20.41	-	2
A Ratra	7	11	2	101*	183	20.33	1	-

FIRST-CLASS AVERAGES
England

BATTING

	M	Inns	NO	HS	Runs	Av	100	50
WK Hegg	16	23	2	62	416	19.80	-	1
GW White	8	14	2	36	234	19.50	-	-
IJ Thomas	9	15	1	76	273	19.50	-	2
MJ Walker	12	23	3	46	382	19.10	-	-
JJ Sayers	4	8	0	55	152	19.00	-	1
IDK Salisbury	14	20	2	59	340	18.88	-	1
RC Driver	5	8	2	56	113	18.83	-	1
CR Taylor	5	9	1	52*	150	18.75	-	2
GJ Smith	15	20	7	39*	243	18.69	-	-
ID Hunter	8	12	1	65	204	18.54	-	1
DA Kenway	8	15	2	54	238	18.30	-	1
SP Jones	13	18	6	44	218	18.16	-	-
JRC Hamblin	5	9	0	50	162	18.00	-	1
KP Dutch	16	27	3	74	432	18.00	-	2
MPL Bulbeck	16	27	7	53*	359	17.95	-	1
MS Mason	7	8	2	50	107	17.83	-	1
JD Middlebrook	18	28	4	67	417	17.37	-	1
MCJ Ball	7	10	3	63	119	17.00	-	1
J Wood	8	11	0	64	185	16.81	-	1
SJ Cook	15	18	2	43*	267	16.68	-	-
CEW Silverwood	12	19	2	44*	283	16.64	-	-
RSG Anderson	5	10	0	51	166	16.60	-	1
A Richardson	10	12	4	91	132	16.50	-	1
KJ Piper	8	12	2	64*	163	16.30	-	1
PA Patel	5	8	2	32	97	16.16	-	-
DD Cherry	5	8	0	47	129	16.12	-	-
MJ Symington	10	16	2	42	224	16.00	-	-
J Ormond	15	17	4	43*	208	16.00	-	-
Kabir Ali	17	21	4	51*	271	15.94	-	1
AJ Tudor	10	14	0	61	222	15.85	-	1
MJ Hoggard	9	11	5	32	95	15.83	-	-
G Keedy	16	22	8	57	219	15.64	-	1
Amjad Khan	16	19	5	58	213	15.21	-	1
PS Jones	7	8	3	37*	76	15.20	-	-
SMA Bukhari	15	24	2	53	333	15.13	-	1
JN Snape	5	8	0	28	117	14.62	-	-
J Lewis	16	25	6	57	273	14.36	-	1
CD Crowe	12	16	4	34	172	14.33	-	-
GD Bridge	10	15	2	49	184	14.15	-	-
RJ Cunliffe	5	10	1	30	121	13.44	-	-
AS Wright	5	8	1	28	94	13.42	-	-
SD Thomas	16	22	1	47	274	13.04	-	-
T Lungley	7	13	0	44	168	12.92	-	-
AM Smith	9	13	6	21	90	12.85	-	-
PCR Tufnell	14	15	8	45	89	12.71	-	-
RJ Kirtley	11	15	3	36*	146	12.16	-	-
KW Hogg	7	9	0	50	109	12.11	-	1
MJ Wood (Y)	9	17	0	43	201	11.82	-	-
AJ Harris	14	20	7	41*	151	11.61	-	-
DM Cousins	11	16	7	23*	103	11.44	-	-
KM Krikken	9	16	1	48	169	11.26	-	-
AM Davies	14	24	7	33	184	10.82	-	-
JF Brown	8	11	5	19	64	10.66	-	-
N Killeen	15	22	5	27*	178	10.47	-	-
DA Cosker	10	13	2	37	115	10.45	-	-
JMM Averis	5	8	0	43	83	10.37	-	-
JB Hockley	5	9	1	46	82	10.25	-	-
SP Kirby	10	17	3	57	141	10.07	-	1

Qualification: 8 completed innings, average 10.00

FIRST-CLASS AVERAGES
England

BOWLING

	Overs	Mds	Runs	Wkts	Av	Best	10m	5/inn
CP Schofield	122.2	27	331	18	18.38	4-35	-	-
J Srinath	179.2	29	561	30	18.70	5-25	-	2
DG Cork	403.4	101	1210	64	18.90	6-51	1	5
RC Irani	227.5	72	591	29	20.37	6-71	-	1
PJ Martin	452	143	1126	53	21.24	5-54	-	1
RL Johnson	307.1	66	914	43	21.25	7-43	1	2
MJ Saggers	571	111	1786	83	21.51	6-39	-	6
AJ Harris	413.4	93	1475	67	22.01	7-54	2	3
VJ Wells	155	41	421	19	22.15	5-39	-	1
JM Anderson	326.4	61	1114	50	22.28	6-23	-	3
MP Dowman	72	24	223	10	22.30	4-28	-	-
JP Stephenson	295.4	59	1082	48	22.54	7-44	1	1
RJ Kirtley	379	94	1199	53	22.62	6-107	1	4
SCG MacGill	227.4	37	930	40	23.25	8-111	1	4
KJ Dean	590	148	1951	83	23.50	7-42	2	3
DL Maddy	334.3	78	1025	43	23.83	5-37	-	2
T Lungley	117.4	32	416	17	24.47	3-43	-	-
MI Black	113.1	32	344	14	24.57	4-32	-	-
N Boje	238	58	671	27	24.85	6-128	-	2
TJ Murtagh	122.1	23	424	17	24.94	5-39	-	1
A Richardson	300.2	64	951	38	25.02	8-46	-	2
AJ Bichel	297	77	902	36	25.05	9-93	1	1
AA Noffke	305.1	57	1128	45	25.06	8-24	1	3
Kabir Ali	547.1	129	1781	71	25.08	7-43	2	5
AD Mullally	463.2	145	1156	46	25.13	6-56	-	1
PJ Franks	234.5	53	813	32	25.40	5-51	-	1
MN Malik	146.4	29	562	22	25.54	5-67	1	-
G Welch	486.1	157	1409	55	25.61	6-60	-	2
Saqlain Mushtaq	488.4	112	1359	53	25.64	6-121	1	3
PD Collingwood	96.4	24	258	10	25.80	4-31	-	-
AM Davies	357.5	106	942	36	26.16	5-61	-	1
SM Pollock	301.3	101	733	28	26.17	4-37	-	-
GJ Smith	400	85	1275	48	26.56	8-53	1	1
MS Kasprowicz	418.4	78	1413	53	26.66	6-47	1	4
AJ Tudor	322	74	1124	42	26.76	5-66	-	1
JJC Lawson	123.4	19	484	18	26.88	6-76	-	1
SJ Cook	367.2	71	1305	48	27.18	8-63	-	2
AP Cowan	276.1	70	843	31	27.19	5-68	-	1
AR Caddick	423.3	87	1313	48	27.35	6-84	-	4
SP Jones	323.5	53	1101	40	27.52	6-45	-	2
RC Driver	105	28	331	12	27.58	5-70	-	1
A Kumble	212	51	607	22	27.59	4-58	-	-
Harbhajan Singh	243.2	43	773	28	27.60	7-83	-	2
A McGrath	174.3	38	498	18	27.66	4-49	-	-
LJ Wharton	208.5	45	695	25	27.80	6-62	-	2
MS Mason	224.4	55	613	22	27.86	5-50	-	1
RD King	151	31	451	16	28.18	4-48	-	-
SB Bangar	132.5	25	395	14	28.21	4-40	-	-
GP Swann	270.5	60	884	31	28.51	6-126	1	1
GG Wagg	82.5	13	343	12	28.58	4-43	-	-
MWH Inness	116.4	25	429	15	28.60	7-90	-	1
KJ Innes	268.3	65	834	29	28.75	4-41	-	-
A Sheriyar	616.2	160	1905	66	28.86	6-71	-	5
ME Cassar	113.3	18	464	16	29.00	5-71	-	1
RJ Sidebottom	380.5	85	1190	41	29.02	5-60	-	1
Abdur Razzaq	206.3	25	757	26	29.11	7-133	-	2
CT Tremlett	336	83	1061	36	29.47	5-57	-	2
G Chapple	539.3	128	1594	54	29.51	6-30	1	3
AM Smith	270	55	916	31	29.54	5-69	-	1
SJ Harmison	324.2	75	1001	33	30.33	5-65	-	1
DE Malcolm	477.5	79	1826	60	30.43	7-76	1	4
JM Dakin	360.2	75	1233	40	30.82	4-17	-	-
AD Mascarenhas	420.5	144	1141	37	30.83	5-87	-	1
PCR Tufnell	514.5	104	1390	45	30.88	8-66	-	4
GJ Batty	613.1	162	1733	56	30.94	7-33	-	3
PAJ DeFreitas	566.4	150	1594	51	31.25	6-101	-	2
MP Bicknell	326	78	1067	34	31.38	6-42	-	2
SD Thomas	467.1	66	1637	52	31.48	7-33	1	1
N Killeen	391.1	108	1165	37	31.48	4-26	-	-
CG Greenidge	431	67	1681	53	31.71	6-40	-	3
Amjad Khan	485	75	2004	63	31.80	6-52	-	4
NC Phillips	210	47	671	21	31.95	4-103	-	-

FIRST-CLASS AVERAGES
England

BOWLING

	Overs	Mds	Runs	Wkts	Av	Best	10m	5/inn
GR Napier	172	33	639	20	31.95	3-47	-	-
IDK Salisbury	341.3	50	1192	37	32.21	4-59	-	-
BV Taylor	318.5	73	1041	32	32.53	5-90	-	1
MS Panesar	190.5	55	554	17	32.58	4-42	-	-
KW Hogg	175	41	621	19	32.68	5-48	-	1
CEW Silverwood	306.1	68	985	30	32.83	4-28	-	-
JB Grant	267.5	50	1086	33	32.90	5-38	-	1
DR Brown	493.4	75	1716	52	33.00	7-110	-	2
SD Udal	627.1	146	1858	56	33.17	5-56	-	4
DA Leatherdale	140.3	22	535	16	33.43	4-23	-	-
MPL Bulbeck	534	93	1940	58	33.44	6-93	-	1
ESH Giddins	232.5	49	736	22	33.45	4-113	-	-
MM Patel	525.3	152	1206	36	33.50	5-56	-	1
RO Hinds	105.1	18	338	10	33.80	3-54	-	-
SRG Francis	222.3	26	947	28	33.82	5-73	-	1
AF Giles	419.1	67	1222	36	33.94	7-142	1	3
RJ Logan	319.3	71	1191	35	34.02	4-64	-	-
JAS Spires	171.4	25	613	18	34.05	5-165	-	1
MA Ealham	351	107	954	28	34.07	3-22	-	-
AW Laraman	262.4	47	920	27	34.07	4-55	-	-
SP Kirby	331.1	68	1262	37	34.10	5-129	-	1
NMK Smith	126	27	411	12	34.25	5-42	-	1
RJ Sillence	100	11	449	13	34.53	5-63	-	1
MJ Symington	147	29	590	17	34.70	4-27	-	-
MJ Hoggard	364	71	1250	36	34.72	5-92	-	1
J Ormond	485.1	87	1780	51	34.90	5-62	1	2
J Wood	180.5	34	631	18	35.05	4-17	-	-
GD Bridge	247.5	61	753	21	35.85	4-50	-	-
RSC Martin-Jenkins	470.2	100	1477	41	36.02	7-51	-	2
SMA Bukhari	405	63	1708	47	36.34	3-48	-	-
NC Johnson	242.2	52	814	22	37.00	3-22	-	-
CD Crowe	193.2	51	593	16	37.06	4-63	-	-
JD Lewry	304.3	45	1227	33	37.18	5-88	-	1
DD Masters	243.1	47	864	23	37.56	4-36	-	-
ID Blackwell	312.5	83	830	22	37.72	5-49	-	1
J Lewis	536.1	137	1662	44	37.77	6-54	1	2
MCJ Ball	287	66	876	23	38.08	6-54	-	1
MJG Davis	347.2	71	1081	28	38.60	6-97	-	1
ID Hunter	206	42	775	20	38.75	3-44	-	-
RKJ Dawson	488.5	104	1551	40	38.77	5-42	-	2
KA Parsons	216.3	30	830	21	39.52	3-44	-	-
G Keedy	437.4	102	1313	33	39.78	5-122	-	1
MC Ilott	193.5	45	639	16	39.93	4-67	-	-
MA Wagh	203	43	604	15	40.26	5-137	-	1
M Burns	101.4	15	444	11	40.36	3-54	-	-
JF Brown	352.5	76	1138	28	40.64	4-88	-	-
JID Kerr	147.2	29	652	16	40.75	4-32	-	-
R Clarke	94.3	15	451	11	41.00	3-41	-	-
BW Gannon	162	36	626	15	41.73	3-41	-	-
C White	193.5	33	634	15	42.26	4-49	-	-
RDB Croft	619	138	1701	40	42.52	5-71	-	1
JE Bishop	120	17	470	11	42.72	3-59	-	-
APR Gidman	99	16	442	10	44.20	3-33	-	-
PS Jones	239.2	45	845	19	44.47	6-110	1	1
CB Keegan	211.5	32	855	19	45.00	4-47	-	-
JD Middlebrook	555.2	121	1736	38	45.68	4-38	-	-
AB Agarkar	162.3	32	640	14	45.71	4-55	-	-
A Symonds	187.2	34	602	13	46.30	6-105	-	1
DM Cousins	311.2	67	1024	22	46.54	4-75	-	-
TJ Phillips	209.5	32	844	18	46.88	4-102	-	-
NM Carter	228.1	35	957	20	47.85	4-46	-	-
AL Penberthy	292	76	833	17	49.00	3-21	-	-
MJA Whiley	175.4	28	803	16	50.18	3-60	-	-
DA Cosker	317.5	60	1012	20	50.60	4-135	-	-
MM Betts	248.4	34	1023	20	51.15	3-75	-	-
MW Alleyne	266	59	876	17	51.52	3-76	-	-
ID Fisher	514	103	1725	32	53.90	5-87	-	1
A Flintoff	251	53	768	14	54.85	2-22	-	-
KP Dutch	268.3	59	852	15	56.80	3-104	-	-
JAR Blain	192.4	21	909	16	56.81	4-144	-	-
PN Weekes	397	61	1198	21	57.04	3-27	-	-
JA Tomlinson	168.3	14	748	12	62.33	2-55	-	-

FIRST-CLASS AVERAGES
England

BOWLING

	Overs	Mds	Runs	Wkts	Av	Best	10m	5/inn
SJ Marshall	215.2	42	657	10	65.70	6-128	-	1

Qualification: 10 wickets in 8 innings

The following bowlers took 10 wickets in fewer than 8 innings:

	Overs	Mds	Runs	Wkts	Av	Best	10m	5/inn
Azhar Mahmood	109.2	27	345	20	17.25	8-61	-	1
IJ Harvey	152.2	29	533	28	19.03	6-68	1	3
PDRL Perera	115	13	433	17	25.47	4-66	-	-
SE Bond	95.4	23	330	12	27.50	5-64	-	1
AP Davies	116.2	14	420	15	28.00	5-79	-	1
DB Powell	81	19	303	10	30.30	3-55	-	-
JMM Averis	128	33	432	13	33.23	5-51	-	1
JC Tredwell	124.2	29	358	10	35.80	4-103	-	-
Mushtaq Ahmed	105	23	305	8	38.12	5-71	-	1
DNT Zoysa	110.2	15	421	10	42.10	3-93	-	-
A Nehra	114	14	473	11	43.00	4-85	-	-
Zaheer Khan	147	32	483	11	43.90	3-90	-	-
TCB Fernando	113.5	14	524	10	52.40	4-72	-	-

FIELDING

68 - CMW Read (66ct, 2st); 63 - ND Burns (61ct, 2st); 61 - MA Wallace (58ct, 3st);
53 - PA Nixon (49ct, 4st); 51 - RJ Turner (50ct, 1st); 49 - TMB Bailey (43ct, 6st);
46 - JN Batty (41ct, 5st), WK Hegg (44ct, 2st); 45 - A Pratt (42ct, 3st);
41 - MJ Prior (39ct, 2st), SJ Rhodes (37ct, 4st), RC Russell (39ct, 2st); 38 - AJ Stewart (34ct, 4ct);
37 - DC Nash (36ct, 1st); 36 - A Flower (35ct, 1st); 34 - N Pothas (30ct, 4st); 33 - DP Fulton;
31 - LD Sutton (30ct, 1st); 30 - RJ Blakey (29ct, 1st), GA Hick; 29 - MJ Di Venuto;
27 - NC Johnson; 26 - KM Krikken; 24 - DP Ostler, N Shahid; 23 - PN Weekes;
22 - PD Bowler, DL Maddy; 21 - MEK Hussey, SG Law; 20 - KP Dutch; 19 - BL Hutton;
18 - AD Brown, VS Solanki; 17 - AN Aymes (16ct, 1st), WI Jefferson, EC Joyce, DDJ Robinson;
16 - IJ Clifford (15ct, 1st), JER Gallian, RR Montgomerie, KA Parsons, A Ratra (14ct, 2st),
CM Spearman, DI Stevens, AJ Strauss, A Symonds, GE Welton 15 - D Byas, MJ Chilton,
DA Kenway, KJ Piper (14ct, 1st), CG Taylor; 14 - M Burns, R Dravid, MA Ealham, AI Gait,
MP Maynard, GJ Muchall; 13 - CWG Bassano, MW Goodwin, SM Pollock, DJ Pipe (12ct, 1st),
MJ Powell (Wa), K Sangakkara (12ct, 1st), V Sehwag; 12 - Aftab Habib, MW Alleyne, DG Cork,
WS Kendall, KP Pietersen, RWT Key, GJ Pratt, AJ Swann, Usman Afzaal, MJ Wood (Y);
11 - DJG Sales, IDK Salisbury, A Singh, MH Yardy; 10 - N Boje, PAJ DeFreitas, NH Fairbrother,
JS Foster (9ct, 1st), AJ Hollioake, NV Knight, IJ Ward;

Qualification: 10 or more catches

NORWICH UNION NATIONAL LEAGUE
By Mark Baldwin

12 May 2002: Division One
at Chester-le-Street
Warwickshire 207 for 7 (45 overs) (IR Bell 72)
Durham 163 for 9 (45 overs)
Warwickshire (4 pts) won by 44 runs

at Taunton
Yorkshire 307 for 4 (45 overs) (MJ Wood 105*,
DS Lehmann 104)
Somerset 306 for 8 (45 overs) (J Cox 99, ID Blackwell
79, PD Bowler 53)
Yorkshire (4 pts) won by 1 run

at Leicester
Leicestershire 283 for 5 (45 overs) (TR Ward 91,
DI Stevens 91)
Nottinghamshire 251 for 8 (45 overs) (Usman Afzaal 63)
Leicestershire (4 pts) won by 32 runs

Shaun Pollock, with more than a little help from the
likes of Nick Knight and Ian Bell, brought a large
measure of reality to Durham's first match in the
upper tier of the Norwich Union League. First the
South African captain hit two sixes and two fours in
a breezy 25 from No. 3, before watching Knight (40)
and Bell (72) employ more conventional methods on
a slow, seaming pitch as Warwickshire totalled 207
for 7 from their 45 overs. Then, armed with the new
ball, he soon had Durham reeling at 22 for 3 in reply
– a state from which they never really recovered,
despite a fourth-wicket stand of 58 between Martin
Love and Jon Lewis. Neil Smith, the off spinner,
removed both and Durham eventually slid to defeat
by 44 runs as they finished on 163 for 9.

Runs, however, were in more plentiful supply in
the other two Division One matches. At Taunton,
for instance, Somerset failed by just one run to
match Yorkshire's massive 307 for 4 – a total built
around centuries from Matthew Wood (105 not out)
and Darren Lehmann (104). When Marcus
Trescothick was trapped lbw for a duck by Matthew
Hoggard just five balls into their reply, Somerset
fans were in despair, but Jamie Cox (99) and Peter
Bowler (53) put on 112 for the second wicket and
then Ian Blackwell emerged to bludgeon 79 in a
third-wicket partnership worth 103 with his captain.
In the end, though, amid great excitement, Somerset
could not hit the four they required from the last ball
of the match – the two runs bringing the home side's
total to a glorious, but tantalizingly short, 306 for 8.

At Grace Road, too, there were runs galore with
Leicestershire totalling 283 for 5 and beating
Nottinghamshire by 32 runs after the visitors replied
bravely with 251 for 8. Trevor Ward and Darren
Stevens both contributed hard-hit 91s for
Leicestershire, while Michael Bevan and Phil
DeFreitas struck telling blows at the end of the
innings. Usman Afzaal top scored with 63 for Notts,
and Chris Read made a jaunty 34, but Leicestershire
held their discipline in the field.

Division Two
at Derby
Sussex 166 for 8 (45 overs)
Derbyshire 168 for 4 (42 overs) (MJ Di Venuto 84)
Derbyshire (4 pts) won by six wickets

at Southampton Rose Bowl
Hampshire 219 for 5 (45 overs) (N Pothas 53*,
DA Kenway 50)
Gloucestershire 173 (38.3 overs) (CM Spearman 82,
DA Mascarenhas 5 for 27)
Hampshire (4 pts) won by 46 runs

at The Oval
Lancashire 68 (20.4 overs) (MP Bicknell 5 for 26,
AJ Stewart 5 catches)
Surrey 69 for 4 (11.5 overs)
Surrey (4 pts) won by six wickets

Derbyshire added to their exhilarating start to the
championship season by winning their opening game
in the Norwich Union League by six wickets. To the
delight of the home fans at Derby, they first contained
Sussex to 166 for 8 and then knocked off the runs
with a comfortable three overs to spare. Michael Di
Venuto led the way with a composed 84 from 113
balls, and the Tasmanian found solid support from
both Andrew Gait and Chris Bassano (38).

There was a notable scalp for Hampshire at the
Rose Bowl, with promotion favourites Gloucestershire
going down by 46 runs. Dimitri Mascarenhas first
thumped an unbeaten 39 in six overs as he and Nic
Pothas (53 not out) added a quick-fire 62 for the
sixth wicket to boost the Hampshire total to 219 for
5. Then Mascarenhas claimed the wickets of both
Kim Barnett and Chris Taylor in his first over with
the new ball, going on to finish with 5 for 27 as
Gloucestershire were dismissed for 173, despite
Craig Spearman's excellent 82 from 76 balls,
containing a six and 13 fours.

Surrey crushed Lancashire at The Oval, bowling
out their visitors for just 68 in 20.4 overs and then

completing a six-wicket win after only 11.5 overs of frantic batting themselves. Martin Bicknell took 5 for 26, exploiting helpful conditions masterfully as Lancashire equalled their lowest total in one-day league cricket. Ed Giddins was also a handful, picking up two cheap wickets, and the match was all over by 4.18pm.

19 May 2002: Division One
at Canterbury
Kent 180 (44.2 overs) (MJ Walker 54)
Yorkshire 181 for 5 (41.2 overs) (DS Lehmann 69*)
Yorkshire (4 pts) won by five wickets

at Trent Bridge
Warwickshire 236 for 8 (45 overs) (SM Pollock 70)
Nottinghamshire 151 (41.1 overs) (Usman Afzaal 51)
Warwickshire (4 pts) won by 85 runs

at Worcester
Worcestershire 254 for 7 (45 overs) (BF Smith 66, A Singh 65, SRG Francis 4 for 60)
Somerset 127 (32.4 overs) (Kabir Ali 4 for 15)
Worcestershire (4 pts) won by 127 runs

at Cardiff
Glamorgan 161 for 8 (45 overs)
Durham 141-9 (45 overs) (MS Kasprowicz 4 for 28)
Glamorgan (4 pts) won by 20 runs

Kent, the champions, opened the defence of their one-day league trophy by slumping to a five-wicket defeat to Yorkshire – on home soil at Canterbury. The day started badly for Kent, with skipper Matthew Fleming edging the very first ball of the match to slip, and it did not get much better, despite a responsible fifth-wicket stand of 57 between David Fulton and Matthew Walker (54). Seventeen-year-old Tim Bresnan impressed with the ball and a Kent total of 180 never looked as though it would be enough. Craig White, however, played on to Martin Saggers from the first ball of the Yorkshire reply, and at 64 for 4 the visitors were in much need of a substantial innings from their captain, Darren Lehmann. They got it, with Lehmann finishing unbeaten on 69, with Gary Fellows also playing sensibly and well for his 35 not out as victory came with 20 balls to spare.

Joining Yorkshire at the head of the fledgling Division One table, also with two wins out of two, were Warwickshire, who beat Nottinghamshire by 85 runs at Trent Bridge. Shaun Pollock's 70 off 76 balls, with two big sixes, was the highlight of Warwickshire's 45-over total of 236 for 8, and soon Notts had no

hope as they slumped to 30 for 4 with Pollock striking two blows with the new ball. Usman Afzaal did hit 51 as Notts made it to 151 all out, but by then the match had long ceased to be any sort of contest.

Kabir Ali took 4 for 15, the best one-day figures of his young career, as Worcestershire overpowered Somerset by 127 runs at Worcester. Somerset, reeling on 40 for 6 after Kabir had done his work, limped to 127 all out in reply to Worcestershire's challenging 254 for 7 – a total built on innings of 65 from Anurag Singh, 66 from Ben Smith and useful late contributions from both David Leatherdale (39) and the evergreen Steve Rhodes (42).

At Cardiff it was another fierce new-ball spell, this time by Mike Kasprowicz, which settled the match between Glamorgan and Durham in the Welsh county's favour. On a slow, seaming pitch, Glamorgan had needed to work hard for their total of 161 for 8, with Michael Powell remaining unbeaten on 47, but it was Kasprowicz's opening burst which undermined the Durham reply and ensured that victory was achieved by 20 runs. Kasprowicz clean bowled both Nicky Peng and Martin Love, and also had Gary Pratt lbw as Durham slid to 27 for 3. Robert Croft soon made it 65 for 5 with the wickets of Paul Collingwood and Jon Lewis and, despite Andrew Pratt's 42, Durham were slipping behind the clock well before Kasprowicz returned to claim another wicket and finish with figures of 4 for 28.

Division Two
at Bristol
Surrey 163 for 9 (45 overs) (AD Brown 54, J Lewis 4 for 22)
Gloucestershire 164 for 9 (43.3 overs)
Gloucestershire (4 pts) won by one wicket

at Old Trafford
Sussex 160 (41.4 overs)
Lancashire 161 for 6 (40.5 overs) (SG Law 71*)
Lancashire (4 pts) won by four wickets

at Chelmsford
Derbyshire 155 (44.3 overs)
Essex 159 for 3 (37 overs)
Essex (4 pts) won by seven wickets

at Northampton
Middlesex 146 (40.2 overs) (DM Cousins 4 for 13, TMB Bailey 5 catches)
Northamptonshire 149 for 4 (31.3 overs) (DJG Sales 66, MEK Hussey 56)
Northamptonshire (4 pts) won by six wickets

Gloucestershire shocked Surrey at Bristol by pulling off a thrilling one-wicket win with nine balls to spare. Replying to Surrey's 163 for 9 on a sluggish pitch, Gloucestershire seemed out of the hunt at 115 for 8. But then Martyn Ball (45) was joined by Jon Lewis (27 not out) in a match-winning partnership of 31 and, when Ball was bowled by Rikki Clarke, last man Mike Smith helped Lewis to inch over the winning line. Surrey's innings was launched by a stand of 86 between openers Ian Ward and Alistair Brown (54), but Lewis (4 for 22) cut through the middle order to restrict the visitors to a total only boosted at the end by an unbroken tenth-wicket stand of 32 between Jon Batty and Ed Giddins.

An unbeaten 71 from Stuart Law provided the only real quality of an untidy match at Old Trafford, won comfortably by Lancashire by four wickets over Sussex, despite rain and bad light further blighting proceedings towards the end. John Wood was the best bowler on view, taking 3 for 21 as Sussex struggled to reach 160 all out, while Mike Yardy took 3 for 36 in the Lancashire reply.

Essex remained unbeaten in one-day cricket by easing past Derbyshire to win by seven wickets at Chelmsford. Ashley Cowan took 3 for 21 as Derbyshire limped to 155 all out, and an unbroken partnership of 71 between Andy Flower (43 not out) and Ronnie Irani (29 not out) completed the formalities.

Toby Bailey, the Northamptonshire wicketkeeper, impressed with five fine catches as the home side bowled out Middlesex for just 146 at Wantage Road, and then knocked off the runs in 31.3 overs to earn themselves a six-wicket win. Mike Hussey (56) and David Sales (66) added further polish to the home side's performance with a third-wicket stand of 109 after Darren Cousins (4 for 13) had led the way with the ball.

26 May 2002: Division One
at Old Trafford
Lancashire v. **Middlesex**
No play possible – 2 pts each

No play was possible in the match between Lancashire and Middlesex so the sides shared the points.

4 June 2002: Division One
at Edgbaston
Durham 72 (21.2 overs) (NM Carter 5 for 31)
Warwickshire 73 for 3 (11.1 overs)
Warwickshire (4 pts) won by seven wickets

at Tunbridge Wells
Nottinghamshire 191 for 9 (45 overs)
Kent 181 for 5 (34.1 overs) (RWT Key 68*, MV Fleming 64)
Kent (4 pts) won by five wickets (DL Method: Kent target 179 from 39 overs)

at Leicester
Glamorgan 194 for 6 (45 overs) (SP James 86)
Leicestershire 149 (39.2 overs) (IJ Sutcliffe 57)
Glamorgan (4 pts) won by 45 runs

at Headingley
Yorkshire 128 (33.4 overs) (Kabir Ali 5 for 36)
Worcestershire 129 for 4 (37.1 overs)
Worcestershire (4 pts) won by six wickets

A dream day for Neil Carter ended with Warwickshire staying top of the table as they trounced Durham by seven wickets in a match that lasted just 32.3 overs at Edgbaston. Durham, who were understandably tired after playing on ten of the previous 11 days, were skittled for 72 in 21.2 overs as Carter, with 5 for 31, and Shaun Pollock (3 for 10) ran riot on a blameless pitch. Carter, a South African with a British passport, then thrashed 24 off just nine balls after opening the Warwickshire innings. Pollock finished with 29 not out off 20 balls, and he and Bob Woolmer, the director of cricket and former South Africa coach, had ample time (thanks to the 3.51pm finish) to catch their overnight flight to attend the funeral of Hansie Cronje.

Contrasting innings of excellence by Matthew Fleming and Rob Key swept Kent to victory by five wickets over Nottinghamshire at Tunbridge Wells. James Golding (3 for 25) bowled well as Notts were restricted to 191 for 9 from their 45 overs, and then a short shower during the tea interval left Kent needing 179 from 39 overs, according to the Duckworth-Lewis regulations. Fleming responded with 64 off only 44 balls, with a six and nine fours, and his fellow opener Key stayed throughout to anchor the run chase with a mature 68 and keep order through a clatter of middle-order wickets.

Glamorgan defeated Leicestershire by 45 runs at Grace Road, a fine 86 from Steve James enabling the Welsh county to total 194 for 6 and then accurate seam bowling from Adrian Dale (3 for 28) being chiefly responsible for Leicestershire's demise to 149 all out.

Worcestershire, like Glamorgan, made it two wins out of two as they beat Yorkshire by six wickets at Headingley. Kabir Ali, initially thumped for 16 runs from his first three deliveries by Craig White, whose

45 took 42 balls, bounced back to finish with 5 for 36. With Allan Donald picking up 2 for 27 on his Worcestershire debut, Yorkshire were bundled out for 128. Ben Smith's unbeaten 38, however, ensured there would be no further surprises.

Division Two
at Northampton
Northamptonshire 229 for 6 (45 overs) (MB Loye 86, MEK Hussey 69)
Surrey 224 (44.2 overs) (AD Brown 55, R Clarke 52)
Northamptonshire (4 pts) won by 5 runs

at Horsham
Sussex 240 (45 overs) (MJ Prior 73)
Essex 208 (40.2 overs) (RC Irani 51, GR Napier 50)
Sussex (4 pts) won by 32 runs

at Lord's
Hampshire 183 for 8 (45 overs)
Middlesex 181 for 9 (45 overs)
Hampshire (4 pts) won by 2 runs

at Old Trafford
Gloucestershire 269 for 8 (45 overs) (KJ Barnett 66, J Wood 5 for 49)
Lancashire 190 (41 overs)
Gloucestershire (4 pts) won by 79 runs

An opening partnership of 127 between Mike Hussey (69) and Mal Loye (86) set Northamptonshire on their way to a narrow five-run win against Surrey at Northampton. A total of 229 for 6, however, did not seem near enough as Alistair Brown blazed his way to a 29-ball 55 and then Rikki Clarke (52) joined Mark Ramprakash (44) in a fifth-wicket stand of 63 that was ended at 180. Suddenly, Northants sensed their chance and further wickets began to fall. Eventually, 11 runs were required from the last two overs – Carl Greenidge returned to mop up the Surrey tail and put the finishing touches to a fine match.

A mature innings of 73 from the highly promising 20-year-old wicketkeeper, Matt Prior, plus an unbeaten 41 from Kevin Innes, boosted Sussex's total to 240 and proved match-winning knocks as Essex were bowled out for 208 in reply. Not even innings of 50 from Graham Napier, off 58 balls with three sixes, 49 from Andy Flower and a 41-ball 51 by their captain, Ronnie Irani, could prevent an Essex defeat as the last 15 overs were played out in pouring rain.

David Nash almost pulled an unlikely victory out of the hat at Lord's, but in the end he managed to hit the last two balls of the game for just four and two

as Middlesex went down by two runs to Hampshire. Nash's brave, unbeaten 30 apart, though, Middlesex were outplayed by their visitors, who earlier reached 183 for 8 with Nic Pothas finishing on 39 not out.

Gloucestershire put rumours of internal dissent to one side as they overpowered Lancashire by 79 runs at Old Trafford. Kim Barnett hit 66 and Ian Harvey 47 from just 25 balls as Gloucestershire ran up 269 for 8 from their 45 overs. On a fine pitch, however, Lancashire batted disappointingly with only Stuart Law (39) and Graham Lloyd (41) looking capable of mounting a challenging reply and Andrew Flintoff out for a single when he hoicked a long hop straight to midwicket.

9 June 2002: Division One
at Cardiff
Glamorgan 155 for 7 (23 overs)
Kent 155 for 9 (23 overs) (RWT Key 51)
Match tied – 2 pts each

at Oakham School
Leicestershire 11 for 0 (3 overs)
Worcestershire did not bat
Match abandoned – 2 pts each

at Edgbaston
Warwickshire v. **Somerset**
No play possible – 2 pts each

at Trent Bridge
Nottinghamshire v. **Yorkshire**
No play possible – 2 pts each

The only match, during this round of fixtures, to escape the weather was at Cardiff – and what a match it was as Glamorgan and Kent fought out a thrilling tie. Rain early in the day had, however, caused the match to be reduced to 23 overs per side and Kent did well to keep Glamorgan to 155 for 7, after the first four overs, bowled by James Golding and Jamie Hewitt, had cost 42 runs as Robert Croft and David Hemp (39) hit the ground running. Canny bowling by Mark Ealham, Matthew Fleming and James Tredwell pegged back the Welsh county and Kent seemed to be cruising to victory when Rob Key (51) was joined in stands of 50 and 26 by Andy Symonds and Ealham. But then Key missed a reverse sweep off the bowling of Croft and, in the end, it came down to Kent needing six runs for victory from the final over with four wickets in hand. Adrian Dale, thrown the ball, responded by taking the wickets of Ealham and Geraint Jones –

and not conceding a run – from his first four deliveries. Golding then struck a searing straight drive for four, but the last ball was right up in the blockhole and the all-rounder could only squeeze it to short midwicket for the single which tied the scores.

Leicestershire made 11 without loss in the three overs possible before the rain came at Oakham School, where they were entertaining Worcestershire, while the two other scheduled Division One games (Nottinghamshire v. Yorkshire at Trent Bridge, and Warwickshire v. Somerset at Edgbaston) were washed out without a ball being bowled.

Division Two
at Southampton Rose Bowl
Hampshire v. **Derbyshire**
No play possible – 2 pts each

at Northampton
Northamptonshire v. **Gloucestershire**
No play possible – 2 pts each

at Lord's
Sussex 25 for 1 (5.2 overs)
Middlesex did not bat
Match abandoned – 2 pts each

In Division Two there were also two total washouts, at Southampton (Hampshire v. Derbyshire) and Northampton (Northants v. Gloucestershire). At Lord's, Sussex lost opener Mike Yardy to Chad Keegan for nought, but had rallied to 25 for 1 from 5.2 overs against Middlesex when the weather closed in on what was Paul Weekes' benefit match.

16 June 2002: Division One
at Headingley
Warwickshire 187 (44.5 overs)
Yorkshire 162 for 9 (40 overs)
Warwickshire (4 pts) won by 14 runs (DL Method: Yorkshire target 177 from 40 overs)

at Trent Bridge
Kent 317 for 8 (45 overs) (RWT Key 114)
Nottinghamshire 185 (37 overs) (PJ Franks 60)
Kent (4 pts) won by 132 runs

at Bath
Leicestershire 147 (37.5 overs) (TR Ward 62)
Somerset 148 for 3 (32.2 overs) (KA Parsons 59*, M Burns 54*)
Somerset (4 pts) won by seven wickets

at Chester-le-Street
Worcestershire 265 (44.4 overs) (BF Smith 83, N Killeen 4 for 48)
Durham 99 for 8 (29.3 overs) (DA Leatherdale 5 for 9)
Worcestershire (4 pts) won by 121 runs (DL Method: Durham needed to have 221 from 29.3 overs when rain stopped play)

Warwickshire, unbeaten in limited-overs cricket since 3 May, stayed four points clear at the top of Division One by producing a clinical, if unspectacular, performance to dispose of Yorkshire at Headingley. Dougie Brown, with 37 batting at No. 7, was the only Warwickshire batsman to reach 20, but their total of 187 was still too much for a Yorkshire side who had their victory target reduced to 177 from 40 overs following a weather interruption. Matthew Wood scored 42, and Simon Katich an unbeaten 39, but Shaun Pollock took 3 for 20 from his eight overs to lead a disciplined Warwickshire display in the field as Yorkshire were held to 162 for 9.

Kent thrashed Nottinghamshire by 132 runs at Trent Bridge, hitting a collective eight sixes and 33 fours in their 45-over total of 317 for 8 and then dismissing the home side for 185. Matthew Fleming led the Kent assault with 49 from 37 balls, and Rob Key provided the longer-term substance with a high-class innings of 114 from 98 deliveries. Key himself provided four of Kent's sixes and seven of the other boundaries. A bright 36 off 26 balls by Paul Johnson, at the head of the Nottinghamshire order, was the only challenge of note, until Paul Franks – making his first appearance at Trent Bridge for more than a year because of a serious knee injury – smote a spirited 67-ball 60.

Unbeaten half-centuries from Mike Burns and Keith Parsons guided Somerset to a comfortable, seven-wicket win against Leicestershire to provide at least one sunny memory for the home county following a soggy festival week at Bath. Parsons had earlier taken 3 for 29 with the ball, too, as Leicestershire were bowled out for 147, despite an excellent 62 from opener Trevor Ward.

A gloomy Chester-le-Street day ending in drizzle was grimmer still for Durham when they finished a hopeless 121 runs short of their Duckworth-Lewis target, at 99 for 8, in reply to Worcestershire's commanding 265. Ben Smith's 83 was the highlight of an entertaining Worcestershire innings, but Durham's reply was woefully inadequate and David Leatherdale enjoyed himself by taking 5 for 9 in just 3.3 overs of medium pace.

Division Two
at Bristol
Middlesex 142 (37.3 overs) (AJ Strauss 65)
Gloucestershire 144 for 5 (24.2 overs) (IJ Harvey 60)
Gloucestershire (4 pts) won by five wickets

at Derby
Northamptonshire 180 for 8 (45 overs) (AL Penberthy 55*)
Derbyshire 182 for 7 (43.4 overs) (JID Kerr 65*)
Derbyshire (4 pts) won by three wickets

at Ilford
Lancashire 203 (44.2 overs) (MJ Chilton 84)
Essex 204 for 3 (39 overs) (DDJ Robinson 76, A Flower 56*, RC Irani 51*)
Essex (4 pts) won by seven wickets

at Southampton Rose Bowl
Hampshire 178 for 8 (45 overs)
Surrey 180 for 7 (44.1 overs) (IJ Ward 51)
Surrey (4 pts) won by three wickets

Ian Harvey's 60 from just 41 balls enabled leaders Gloucestershire to make short work of Middlesex's total of 142, even on a tricky pitch at Bristol, and romp home by five wickets with 20.4 overs in hand. Only Andy Strauss, with 65 from 84 balls, held up the Gloucestershire bowlers for long and Mark Alleyne, the home captain, followed up his earlier return of 3 for 30 with an unbeaten 32.

A remarkable, swashbuckling 65 not out by Jason Kerr – his highest limited-overs innings – swept Derbyshire to an unlikely three-wicket victory over Northamptonshire at Derby. Kerr, coming in with his side 88 for 7 in reply to the visitors' 180 for 8, in which Tony Penberthy top scored with an unbeaten 55, dominated a match-winning stand of 94 in 22 overs with Luke Sutton. Victory came, in the end, with eight balls to spare and Sutton was 27 not out.

Not even the returning favourite, Stuart Law, could derail the 'Essex Express' at Ilford. Lancashire were brushed aside by seven wickets as Essex set a ninth one-day win out of ten matches alongside a run of four consecutive championship victories. Law, in fact, cheered to the crease, could only manage one boundary in his 45-ball 28 as Lancashire totalled 203, mainly due to Mark Chilton's 84. Then, despite the early losses of Graham Napier and Will Jefferson to Peter Martin, Essex cruised home with Darren Robinson hitting 76 and both Andy Flower and Ronnie Irani finished with unbeaten half-centuries.

Surrey's three-wicket win against Hampshire at the Rose Bowl provided a fitting return to cricket for Adam Hollioake, who also took a wicket with his third ball. Hollioake, the Surrey captain, had been given all the time off he needed by his county following the tragic death of his younger brother, Ben, in a car crash in Australia three months earlier. After playing in a second team match, though, on his late return to England following the birth of his first child – named Benaya – Hollioake felt ready to resume his own cricket career. Warm applause greeted him in Southampton, and his third-ball wicket of John Crawley, for 34, plus two more besides, did much to restrict the home side to 178 for 8. Surrey's reply was based on Ian Ward's 51, but Chris Tremlett bowled especially well for his 3 for 25 and, after Hollioake was out for a useful 15, it was left to Martin Bicknell and Ian Salisbury – in an unbroken eighth-wicket stand of 25 – to guide Surrey home with five balls remaining.

Yorkshire's Richard Dawson spun out four Durham batsmen for 37 runs.

23 June 2002: Division One
at Chester-le-Street
Yorkshire 269 for 5 (45 overs) (DS Lehmann 70,
CEW Silverwood 58)
Durham 239 for 9 (45 overs) (GJ Pratt 61, RKJ Dawson
4 for 37)
Yorkshire (4 pts) won by 30 runs

A savage 58 from 32 balls by Chris Silverwood, sent
in at No. 3 to cause just that sort of havoc, gave
Yorkshire the early momentum they needed to run
up a total large enough to withstand a spirited
Durham reply at Chester-le-Street. Darren Lehmann
thumped 70, Anthony McGrath and Michael Lumb
chimed in with 40 and 42 not out respectively, and
Yorkshire soon had 269 for 5 on the board from
their 45 overs. Gary Pratt pushed Durham up above
the asking rate early on with 61, his side's first half-
century in the competition this year, but wickets
then began to tumble, chiefly to Richard Dawson (4
for 37) and only 20 runs plundered off an irrelevant
final over, from Gary Fellows, boosted the final
Durham total to 239 for 9.

Division Two
at Derby
Lancashire 174 for 7 (45 overs)
Derbyshire 179 for 3 (41.1 overs) (SD Stubbings 98*)
Derbyshire (4 pts) won by seven wickets

at The Oval
Sussex 150 (43.1 overs) (RSC Martin-Jenkins 50,
ESH Giddins 5 for 20)
Surrey 152 for 4 (38.5 overs) (N Shahid 50*)
Surrey (4 pts) won by six wickets

Derbyshire moved into second place in the table by
bowling well to restrict Lancashire to 174 for 7 and
then romping home by seven wickets with Steve
Stubbings (98 not out) being joined in an unbroken
stand of 83 in ten overs by Dominic Cork, who
ended unbeaten on 28.
    There was a straightforward win, too, for Surrey
against Sussex at The Oval. Ed Giddins took 5 for
20 against his former county as Sussex were bowled
out for 150 with only Robin Martin-Jenkins (50)
making any headway. Surrey, too, initially struggled
for fluency, but then Adam Hollioake joined Nadeem
Shahid in an unbroken partnership of 75 that took

**Shaun Pollock, who scored 111 not out, rescued Warwickshire
from 75 for 6 to within five runs of the 233 they needed to
beat Worcestershire.**

them flying past their target with almost six overs in
hand. Shahid finished on 50 not out and Hollioake's
unbeaten 42 from 34 balls included two sixes off
Mark Robinson, whose last two overs cost 33 runs.
Victory came at a cost for Surrey, however, with
Martin Bicknell suffering a broken wrist in a freak
accident. Losing his footing after bowling the first
ball of his sixth over, Bicknell fell heavily on his wrist
and would be out of action for more than a month.

24 June 2002: Division One
at Worcester
Worcestershire 232 for 7 (45 overs) (VS Solanki 119,
GA Hick 50)
Warwickshire 228 for 7 (45 overs) (SM Pollock 111*,
TL Penney 50)
Worcestershire (4 pts) won by 4 runs

An heroic, late partnership of 134 in 20 overs
between Shaun Pollock and Trevor Penney, who
made 50 despite batting with a runner because of a
strained hamstring, took Warwickshire from the

depths of 75 for 6 to defeat by just four runs in reply to Worcestershire's 232 for 7 at New Road. The win took Worcestershire above their West Midlands rivals at the top of Division One, on run rate, but it was a mighty close thing as Pollock finished on 111 not out. The South African captain took the match right to the last ball, from which he could manage only a single, even after the final over had begun with 20 still required. Earlier Pollock had taken two cheap wickets as Worcestershire built their total on the back of an attractive second-wicket stand of 86 between Vikram Solanki and Graeme Hick. When Hick fell for 50, Solanki made it his business to anchor the whole innings with a stylish, but responsible, 119 not out.

30 June 2002: Division One

at Edgbaston
Kent 266 for 9 (45 overs) (MA Ealham 53, GG Wagg 4 for 50)
Warwickshire 126 for 3 (20.1 overs)
Warwickshire won by 19 runs (DL Method: Warwickshire needed to have 107 from 20.1 overs when rain stopped play)

at Worcester
Worcestershire 144 (43.1 overs) (BF Smith 54)
Durham 65 for 1 (10.4 overs)
Durham (4 pts) won by nine wickets (DL Method: Durham needed to have 62 from 10.1 overs when rain stopped play)

at Taunton
Somerset 220 for 9 (45 overs) (MJ Wood 58, M Burns 51, AP Davies 4 for 33)
Glamorgan 209 for 9 (38.5 overs) (A Dale 63)
Glamorgan (4 pts) won by one wicket (DL Method: Glamorgan target 209 from 39 overs)

at Trent Bridge
Leicestershire 259 for 7 (45 overs) (VJ Wells 68, DI Stevens 54)
Nottinghamshire 263 for 5 (44.3 overs) (JER Gallian 91, N Boje 86)
Nottinghamshire (4 pts) won by five wickets

Champions Kent, at Edgbaston, were revisiting the scene of the victory which clinched their title triumph the previous September, but this time they left the ground with a sour taste in their mouths as Warwickshire took the four points on a Duckworth-Lewis calculation. It was rough luck for Kent, who saw this game as their best chance to haul

themselves back into contention near the top of the division. Instead, they saw Warwickshire move into a four-point lead at the top of the table. Kent, choosing to bat first, compiled an excellent 266 for 9 from their 45 overs with three partnerships of substance – a 56-run opening stand between Amjad Khan and Rob Key, 60 in 12 overs between David Fulton and Matthew Walker, and then a buccaneering 86 in 12 overs between Walker and Mark Ealham, who top scored with 53 from 45 balls. Drizzle, however, began to fall before the end of the Kent innings, and persisted through the starting overs of the Warwickshire reply. Sensing a deterioration in the weather, Warwickshire sensibly strove to keep ahead of the Duckworth-Lewis figure and, despite losing three wickets in the process, they were still in credit when, with the score 126 for 3 after 20.1 overs, umpires Trevor Jesty and John Steele adjudged what was by now steady rainfall as being too much for the game to be able to continue.

Warwickshire's cause was also helped by Worcestershire's nine-wicket defeat against Durham at Worcester, also on a Duckworth-Lewis ruling. But there could be little quibbling with this decision after Worcestershire, previously unbeaten, were bowled out for just 144. Graeme Bridge took 3 for 22 and, for Worcestershire, only Ben Smith (54) and David Leatherdale (30) prospered as they added 84 for the fourth wicket. Rain then meant that an initial target of 114 from 29 overs became 62 from 13 – even though 3.4 of them had already been bowled. Nicky Peng and Gordon Muchall, however, were more than equal to the task in an unbroken stand of 53, which featured mature strokeplay and sensible running in quite awful conditions.

At Taunton there was a dramatic, but controversial, victory for Glamorgan, who scrambled home when Somerset were penalized by a six-run penalty for bowling a slow over-rate. Somerset had earlier totalled 220 for 9 from their full 45 overs, with Mike Burns and Matthew Wood both contributing half-centuries to resurrect an innings which had subsided to 40 for 4. Two short weather interruptions then brought Glamorgan's target down to 209 from 39 overs, but the cut-off time for Somerset to have begun the final over was 7.18pm. When they failed to meet that deadline, umpires Barry Dudleston and Barrie Leadbeater invoked the penalty. The result was Glamorgan needing six runs, and not 12, from the over about to be bowled by Steffan Jones – Mike Kasprowicz then hit a four and a single from the first two deliveries, and last man Andrew Davies managed to scamper the winning single from the penultimate ball. Somerset's players, officials and supporters were understandably livid – arguing that it was precisely because they had managed to take nine of the Welsh county's wickets, producing a wait for the new batsman each time, that had caused them to miss the cut-off. Before the controversy, Glamorgan were indebted to a responsible 63 from Adrian Dale to keep their hopes up after an initial slump to 47 for 4.

Jason Gallian and Nicky Boje, captain and overseas player, combined to inspire Nottinghamshire to a five-wicket win against Leicestershire in a high-scoring affair at Trent Bridge. Leicestershire's 259 for 7 was built around Vince Wells' 68 and a hard-hit 54 by Darren Stevens. In reply Notts were reeling at 11 for 3, their top three cut down by the new-ball attack of Devon Malcolm and Phil DeFreitas, before Gallian (91) and Boje (86) added a club one-day league record 190 for the third wicket. Kevin Pietersen and Chris Read then saw Notts home with three balls to spare.

Division Two
at Gloucester
Essex 215 for 9 (42.3 overs) (A Flower 80, ML Pettini 75)
Gloucestershire 187 for 9 (35 overs) (MW Alleyne 76, AJ Clarke 4 for 30)
Essex (4 pts) won by 12 runs (DL Method: Gloucestershire target 200 from 35 overs)

at Arundel
Sussex 125 (41.4 overs)
Middlesex 126 for 2 (38.5 overs)
Middlesex (4 pts) won by eight wickets

at Old Trafford
Surrey 152 for 3 (31 overs) (AD Brown 56)
Lancashire did not bat
Match abandoned – 2 pts each

A brave 76 off 60 balls by Mark Alleyne, the Gloucestershire captain, almost pulled off victory against the odds at Gloucester. Essex, however, eventually won the day by just 12 runs in a match which started late, at 2pm, because of the World Cup football final, was interrupted by the weather and ended at 8.18pm on a cold, grey evening. Essex had made 215 for 9 from 42.3 overs when the first rain arrived, the innings revolving around a stand of 116 in 22 overs between Andy Flower (80 off 85 balls) and Mark Pettini, who took a maiden one-day 50 on to 75. Set a revised target of 200 from 35 overs, Gloucestershire were seemingly down and out

at 42 for 4, and then at 113 for 6. But Alleyne continued to believe, taking his side closer than could have been expected when 70 were required from the last six overs.

A grey, chilly and windy day at Arundel was also more to be endured than enjoyed by spectators – especially as a slow, seaming pitch made stroke-making a difficult exercise. Sussex first struggled to 125 all out from 41.4 overs and then saw Middlesex edge their way cautiously to an eight-wicket win. Owais Shah did at least enliven proceedings with some fine shots towards the end of his unbeaten 41.

Lancashire, meanwhile, were grateful for the rain which set in after Surrey had moved with ominous ease to 152 for 3 after only 31 overs at Old Trafford. Alistair Brown initiated the early momentum with 56 from 42 balls, and Mark Ramprakash was 39 not out when bad weather brought a premature end – and, with it, two points apiece to the participants.

7 July 2002: Division One
at Taunton
Somerset 269 for 8 (45 overs) (ID Blackwell 55, M Burns 54, RJ Turner 53*)
Worcestershire 270 for 2 (40.2 overs) (GA Hick 141*, BF Smith 64*, VS Solanki 58)
Worcestershire (4 pts) won by eight wickets

at Maidstone
Kent 244 for 9 (44 overs) (RWT Key 58, JB Hockley 58)
Durham 79 (28.2 overs) (DD Masters 5 for 20)
Kent (4 pts) won by 165 runs

at Swansea
Glamorgan 220 for 8 (45 overs) (A Dale 78*, PAJ DeFreitas 4 for 24)
Leicestershire 221 for 5 (44.2 overs) (IJ Sutcliffe 67)
Leicestershire (4 pts) won by five wickets

Worcestershire moved back to the top of the table, on the same number of points as Warwickshire but ahead of them on run rate, by thrashing Somerset by eight wickets at Taunton. Graeme Hick was the considerable difference between the two teams on yet another beautiful pitch, and his 141 not out from only 114 balls, with two sixes and 17 fours, was his highest score in the one-day league. On the ground where, in 1988, he made his famous 405 not out, Hick was joined in stands of 127 and 139 by Vikram Solanki (58) and Ben Smith (64 not out) as Worcestershire breezed past Somerset's 45-over score of 269 for 8 with a comfortable 4.4 overs to spare. No bowler could find an answer to Hick's complete dominance as he went past 50 from just 34 balls and completed his century from 81. By contrast, no Somerset batsman could play the big innings: Ian Blackwell and Mike Burns tried hard with 55 and 54 respectively, while Rob Turner, supported in his benefit match by John Cleese, a proud Somerset member and a fellow product of Weston-super-Mare, improvised entertainingly with an unbeaten 53 from 45 deliveries.

Kent's crushing 165-run win over Durham at Maidstone was a personal triumph for David Masters. The fast bowler from Chatham took three wickets in four balls during his fourth over and blew away the Durham top order with a hostile, career-best one-day spell of 5 for 20. Durham never recovered and were bowled out for 79 in reply to Kent's 244 for 9, in which Rob Key and James Hockley both made excellent 58s.

Phil DeFreitas and Neil Burns, just two of the ageing, but still enthusiastic and valuable, members of the Leicestershire side, made the difference at Swansea as Glamorgan were beaten by five wickets. DeFreitas took 4 for 24 as Glamorgan were held to 220 for 8 despite Adrian Dale's unbeaten 78, and then the former England paceman launched the Leicestershire reply with 25 from 16 balls in his role as pinch-hitter. Iain Sutcliffe anchored the innings with 67, but Burns' know-how was needed in the closing two overs, with 16 still required. Walking across his stumps, he flicked successive Darren Thomas deliveries for a six and a four to a vacant long leg, and finished on 38 not out.

Division Two
at Southgate
Middlesex 194 for 8 (42 overs) (OA Shah 74)
Surrey 197 for 2 (40.2 overs) (MR Ramprakash 87*, R Clarke 62*)
Surrey (4 pts) won by eight wickets (DL Method: Surrey target 194 from 42 overs)

at Derby
Gloucestershire 161 (40.3 overs) (G Welch 5 for 18)
Derbyshire 154 for 9 (45 overs)
Gloucestershire (4 pts) won by 7 runs

at Southampton Rose Bowl
Hampshire 203 (45 overs) (NC Johnson 92, BV Taylor 4 for 22)
Sussex 110 (34.2 overs) (SD Udal 4 for 31)
Hampshire (4 pts) won by 93 runs

at Northampton
Northamptonshire 261 for 8 (45 overs) (JW Cook 102, DJG Sales 64)
Lancashire 199 (41.2 overs) (AJ Swann 61)
Northamptonshire (4 pts) won by 62 runs

An unbroken stand of 121 between Mark Ramprakash and Rikki Clarke, who ended up on 87 and 62 not out respectively, guided Surrey to victory by eight wickets against Middlesex at Southgate. The win, achieved with ten balls to spare, kept Surrey on top of Division Two. Owais Shah scored 74 for Middlesex, who totalled 194 for 8, but the home side knew the game was up when Paul Weekes dropped his former colleague Ramprakash on 42 at long on.

Gloucestershire stayed level on points with Surrey, but behind on net run rate, by displaying all their famed limited-overs expertise at Derby to beat Derbyshire by seven runs. The home side should have won after bowling out their visitors for 161 and then reaching the final three overs needing 16 to win with five wickets in hand. But Ian Harvey and Mark Alleyne continued to bowl with accuracy and variation which perplexed the Derbyshire batsmen, and in the end James Averis began the final over knowing that he only had to concede less than 12 for victory. Defeat was hard to take for Graeme Welch, who had earlier taken career-best one-day figures of 5 for 18 from his nine overs.

Neil Johnson hit 92 from 110 balls to give Hampshire early command against Sussex at Southampton, and the innings proved to be the basis of their eventual 93-run victory. Billy Taylor claimed 4 for 22 to peg Hampshire back to 203 all out, but then James Tomlinson, a 20-year-old, left-arm fast bowler, grabbed two early wickets as Sussex slumped to 15 for 3. When Shaun Udal (4 for 31) sent back both Chris Adams and Murray Goodwin, after they had added 51 for the fourth wicket, the game was up for Sussex, who were bowled out for 110. To complete a good day for Hampshire, Shane Warne was also at the Rose Bowl for discussions about a future return to the county.

Power-hitting from Jeff Cook, whose second 50 in an 84-ball 102 took him just 29 deliveries, boosted the Northamptonshire total to 261 for 8 at Wantage Road – and beyond the reach of Lancashire. The visitors were later bowled out for 199, to lose by 62 runs, with Cook taking a further toll with 3 for 16 at the end. Alec Swann, playing against his former county, made 61, but the day belonged to Cook, who put on 109 with David Sales (64) and 95 with

Tony Penberthy (38 not out) while striking four sixes and nine fours.

14 July 2002: Division One
at Canterbury
Kent 224 for 7 (45 overs) (MJ Walker 94, PA Nixon 60)
Worcestershire 226 for 5 (43 overs) (VS Solanki 57, BF Smith 54*)
Worcestershire (4 pts) won by five wickets

at Leicester
Warwickshire 189 (45 overs) (NV Knight 86)
Leicestershire 193 for 6 (35.5 overs) (MG Bevan 66*)
Leicestershire (4 pts) won by four wickets

at Trent Bridge
Nottinghamshire 220 (45 overs)
Glamorgan 224 for 2 (36.5 overs) (MP Maynard 80*, DL Hemp 55*)
Glamorgan (4 pts) won by eight wickets

at Scarborough
Yorkshire 283 for 9 (45 overs) (C White 64, A McGrath 59, PS Jones 4 for 72)
Somerset 148 (27 overs) (C White 5 for 19)
Yorkshire (4 pts) won by 135 runs

Kent's grip on the Norwich Union League title was further loosened by Worcestershire, who became leaders out on their own by winning by five wickets in Canterbury while Warwickshire were losing at Leicester. Kent had a dreadful start, sliding to 21 for 4 as Matt Mason exploited early moisture in the pitch. Matthew Walker (94) and Paul Nixon (60) fashioned a fine recovery with a sixth-wicket stand of 116, a record for the county in this competition, but it could only paper over the fact that Kent's 224 for 7 was below par in the conditions. Worcestershire's top order paced their reply perfectly, Vikram Solanki (57) and Graeme Hick (44) making solid contributions before Ben Smith, dropped on 12, stayed on to see his side home with an unbeaten 54.

Warwickshire's four-wicket defeat at Grace Road was brought about by a late-order collapse to 189 all out – and their failure to dismiss Michael Bevan. Nick Knight's 86 was the highlight of the Warwickshire innings, but Leicestershire were in danger of losing their way at 87 for 5 after Phil DeFreitas had gone in first to thrash 49 from 37 balls. Neil Burns, however, survived a 'life' on 12 to score 40 and help the cool Bevan to add a decisive 102 for the sixth wicket. As for Bevan, he once more

The big-hitting Jeff Cook who savaged Lancashire's attack at Wantage Road.

underlined his worldwide reputation as the best one-day finisher in the business with 66 not out.

Glamorgan, meanwhile, served notice of their intention to chase Worcestershire all the way by sweeping Nottinghamshire aside by eight wickets at Trent Bridge. Although eight points adrift of the leaders, following this win, they still had two games in hand. Nottinghamshire's innings lost much of its momentum after Paul Johnson was run out for 26, by Dean Cosker's direct hit, and their 220 all out was easily overhauled. Robert Croft, the acting captain, set the tone with 36 of the first 52 runs, and by the end of their unbroken 117-run partnership,

Matthew Maynard (80 not out) and David Hemp (55 not out) were doing much as they pleased.

Yorkshire kept themselves level with Glamorgan in third place by overwhelming Somerset by 135 runs at Scarborough – amazingly, their first win inside the county boundary since 10 September of the previous year. It all made for wonderful entertainment for the locals as Craig White, the beneficiary and local favourite, followed up his 64 from 63 balls by taking career-best one-day figures of 5 for 19 as Somerset folded for 148 in the face of Yorkshire's 283 for 9. There were nine sixes in all in the Yorkshire innings as the top seven all got past 20, with Anthony McGrath going on to 59.

Division Two

at Southgate
Gloucestershire 272 for 7 (45 overs) (MW Alleyne 93, CM Spearman 78)
Middlesex 194 for 8 (45 overs) (PN Weekes 53*)
Gloucestershire (4 pts) won by 78 runs

at Southend
Essex 200 for 9 (45 overs) (Aftab Habib 50, CT Tremlett 4 for 25)
Hampshire 195 for 8 (45 overs) (NC Johnson 83, JD Middlebrook 4 for 33)
Essex (4 pts) won by 5 runs

at Blackpool
Derbyshire 169 (44.5 overs) (SA Selwood 52)
Lancashire 170 for 9 (40.4 overs) (D Byas 78)
Lancashire (4 pts) won by one wicket

at Hove
Sussex 185 for 6 (45 overs)
Northamptonshire 147 (38.3 overs)
Sussex (4 pts) won by 38 runs

Gloucestershire clinically disposed of Middlesex by 78 runs at Southgate to go four points clear at the top of the Division Two table. Craig Spearman set them on their way with a run-a-ball 78, and then Mark Alleyne (93) and Alex Gidman (48) put on 114 for the fifth wicket to boost the total to 272 for 7. In reply, Middlesex ran up against typically tight Gloucestershire out-cricket and only Paul Weekes, with an unbeaten 53 when the game was all but over, escaped from the straitjacket. Ian Harvey, who for him had a quiet match, nevertheless pulled off an extraordinary leaping boundary catch to dismiss Owais Shah.

Essex pulled off a miracle of their own at Southend where Hampshire, needing 24 off the last five overs with eight wickets in hand, contrived to lose by five runs. Aftab Habib top scored with 50 in an Essex total of 200 for 9, and Chris Tremlett was in outstanding form with the ball as he took 4 for 25. Neil Johnson then plundered 83 and his third-wicket stand of 57 with John Crawley took Hampshire to 177 for 2. Then Crawley charged the medium pace of Graham Napier and was stumped, and suddenly the game changed. James Middlebrook, the off spinner, finished with 4 for 33 and Hampshire ended up with an inadequate 195 for 8.

A defiant 78 by David Byas, easily the best innings of a low-scoring contest, set up an exciting finish at Blackpool. Peter Martin, the Lancashire No. 11, marched in with four runs needed from four balls to overhaul Derbyshire's 169 – and sliced his first ball, a full toss from Jason Kerr, to the third-man boundary. Derbyshire's innings had been sustained by 52 from Steve Selwood, but it was the stand of 55 for the seventh wicket between Byas and Gary Yates, after Lancashire had struggled to 82 for 6 on a bowler-friendly surface, that swung the match.

Sussex gained only their second league victory of the season on an unusually sluggish pitch at Hove, with Northamptonshire being bowled out for 147 in reply to the home side's moderate total of 185 for 6. Will House struck the first ball of the match for six, but there were few fireworks after that grand opening statement. The Sussex bowlers, however, were amply rewarded for their greater discipline.

18 July 2002: Division Two

at Cheltenham
Gloucestershire 296 for 9 (45 overs) (CM Spearman 107, MGN Windows 76, DA Mascarenhas 4 for 67)
Hampshire 225 for 9 (45 overs) (SD Udal 58, JD Francis 51)
Gloucestershire (4 pts) won by 71 runs

Craig Spearman went from 50 to 100 in just 15 scoring shots at Cheltenham as Gloucestershire powered past Hampshire by 71 runs to stretch their lead at the top of Division Two to eight points. Spearman was eventually out for 107, from 85 balls and with four sixes and 13 fours, while Matt Windows also entertained the home crowd royally as Gloucestershire ran up an intimidating 296 for 9 from their 45 overs. In reply there were good half-centuries from Shaun Udal and John Francis, but also an excellent nine overs from Mike Smith, in which he took 3 for 25, as Hampshire were pegged to 225 for 9.

21 July 2002: Division One
at Chester-le-Street
Leicestershire 266 for 7 (45 overs)
(DI Stevens 125)
Durham 181 (40.2 overs)
Leicestershire (4 pts) won by 85 runs

An innings of 125 by Darren Stevens, including 17 fours, proved too hot for Durham to handle at Chester-le-Street. In reply to Leicestershire's 266 for 7, they slipped to an 85-run defeat at 181 all out, with Phil DeFreitas picking up 3 for 25.

22 July 2002: Division Two
at Chelmsford (floodlit)
Middlesex 209 for 8 (45 overs) (AJ Strauss 58, OA Shah 54)
Essex 168 (37.4 overs)
Middlesex (4 pts) won by 41 runs

The first floodlit match staged at Chelmsford ended in disappointment for the home supporters as Essex were beaten by 41 runs on a sluggish surface. Half-centuries from Andy Strauss and Owais Shah lifted Middlesex to 209 for 8, and it was too steep a hill for the Essex batsmen to climb as they made it only as far as 168 all out from 37.4 overs.

23 July 2002: Division Two
at Southampton Rose Bowl (floodlit)
Lancashire 163 (39.1 overs) (SG Law 66)
Hampshire 147 (37.4 overs)
(KW Hogg 4 for 20)
Lancashire (4 pts) won by 16 runs

A match reduced to 40 overs per side at the Rose Bowl was decided in Lancashire's favour by a sparky 66 from 77 balls by Stuart Law. It was, by some distance, the biggest innings of a floodlit fixture in which batting proved to be a difficult business. Lancashire, mainly through Law's skill, totalled 163 and Hampshire, despite being given a rapid start by Neil Johnson's 27, fell away to 147 all out and defeat by 16 runs as Kyle Hogg picked up 4 for 20 from his eight overs.

Darren Stevens, Leicestershire's elegant middle-order batsman, scored 125 against Durham at Chester-le-Street. He averaged 43 in the National League.

24 July 2002: Division Two
at Northampton (floodlit)
Derbyshire 143 (43.5 overs)
Northamptonshire 146 for 3 (27.5 overs)
(MEK Hussey 72*)
Northamptonshire (4 pts) won by seven wickets

Northamptonshire overwhelmed Derbyshire by seven wickets at Wantage Road to dent the visitors' promotion hopes. Jason Kerr's 45 was the only innings of note in an inadequate Derbyshire total of 143, and Mike Hussey's no-nonsense 72 not out made short work of the run chase. Northants, in fact, got home with 17.1 overs in hand.

28 July 2002: Division One
at Chester-le-Street
Durham 275 for 3 (45 overs) (PD Collingwood 118*, MA Gough 57)
Nottinghamshire 231 (44.4 overs) (KP Pietersen 85, N Boje 60)
Durham (4 pts) won by 44 runs

at Leicester
Leicestershire 206 for 9 (45 overs) (DL Maddy 50*)
Kent 189 for 8 (45 overs)
Leicestershire (4 pts) won by 17 runs

at Edgbaston
Glamorgan 300 for 8 (45 overs) (IJ Thomas 72, A Dale 63, MP Maynard 63)
Warwickshire 238 (39.4 overs) (IR Bell 86, RDB Croft 4 for 40)
Glamorgan (4 pts) won by 62 runs

at Worcester
Yorkshire 207 for 8 (45 overs) (DS Lehmann 56)
Worcestershire 208 for 4 (42 overs) (BF Smith 92*, GJ Batty 54*)
Worcestershire (4 pts) won by six wickets

An unbeaten 118 at Chester-le-Street by Paul Collingwood, surprisingly for an England one-day specialist his first limited-overs century, inspired Durham to a rare win – and a much-needed boost to their collective morale. Collingwood's 100-ball effort, in addition to a solid opening stand of 63 between Nicky Peng and Michael Gough (57), propelled Durham to 275 for 3. Nottinghamshire began poorly, but a fifth-wicket partnership of 136 between Kevin Pietersen and Nicky Boje (60) looked threatening until Collingwood popped up again to have Pietersen caught behind for 85. In the end, Notts were

bowled out for 231 with Collingwood, appropriately, wrapping things up with the wicket of Andrew Harris.

A professional performance by Leicestershire stifled Kent on a sluggish surface at Grace Road and, despite a late 47 not out from James Golding, produced victory by 17 runs. The home side's 206 for 9 was built around 48 from 72 balls by Darren Stevens and then an unbeaten 50 from 48 deliveries by Darren Maddy, coming in low down at No. 8. Steady spells from the Leicestershire seamers, the pick of whom was Jamie Grove with 3 for 29, left Kent unable to score the 36 they still required from the last four overs. The visitors finished on 189 for 8.

Glamorgan won an important victory over Warwickshire at Edgbaston, before a crowd of 6,000, and their 62-run win looked likely right from the start of an entertaining afternoon. Robert Croft and Ian Thomas thumped 63 from the first eight overs before Croft was bowled for 34, but the tempo had been set. Thomas went on to score 72, his highest in limited-overs cricket, while Matthew Maynard and Adrian Dale both exploited a short boundary on one side to hit 63s. A total of 300 for 8 was a challenging one, and three early strikes from Alex Wharf made Warwickshire's task even harder. Ian Bell, with 86 from 77 balls, was joined by Jim Troughton (48) in a stand worth 104 in 16 overs, but Croft's 4 for 40 put paid to home hopes.

Worcestershire maintained their eight-point lead at the head of the division by disposing of another of their title rivals, Yorkshire, at New Road. After restricting the visitors to 207 for 8, of which Darren Lehmann made a bright 56, Worcestershire stuttered to 99 for 4 in the first half of their innings before being steered home with three overs to spare by Ben Smith (92 not out from 104 balls) and Gareth Batty (54 not out).

Division Two
at Cheltenham
Sussex 116 (30.5 overs) (MCJ Ball 4 for 15)
Gloucestershire 118 for 4 (17.2 overs) (IJ Harvey 68*)
Gloucestershire (4 pts) won by six wickets

at Guildford
Surrey 310 for 7 (45 overs) (MR Ramprakash 74, IJ Ward 62, JD Ratcliffe 53)
Essex 237 (40.1 overs) (ML Pettini 51, A Flower 50, JD Ratcliffe 4 for 44)
Surrey (4 pts) won by 73 runs

Bottom club Sussex were mauled by six wickets at Cheltenham as Division Two leaders Gloucestershire underlined their total superiority in the art of one-day cricket. Dismissed for just 116, with Martyn Ball ending up with 4 for 15 after the seamers had wreaked early havoc, Sussex were then battered by Ian Harvey's 28-ball 50 as the Australian all-rounder went on to 68 not out.

Jason Ratcliffe, one of the unsung members of the strong Surrey squad, emerged as the match-winner at Guildford as Essex were beaten by 73 runs. Early runs from Ian Ward (62) and Mark Ramprakash (74) teed up Ratcliffe to provide the late acceleration with a 31-ball 53. Essex were then threatening at 194 for 4, following a 99-run stand between Andy Flower (50) and Mark Pettini (51), before Ratcliffe's medium pacers removed both, and the veteran all-rounder went on to finish with 4 for 44 from his eight overs.

30 July 2002: Division One
at Canterbury (floodlit)
Kent 217 for 9 (45 overs) (MJ Walker 75)
Warwickshire 130 (21.2 overs) (MV Fleming 4 for 22)
Kent (4 pts) won by 13 runs (DL Method: Warwickshire target 144 from 22 overs)

A thunderstorm at Canterbury, which followed Kent's innings of 217 for 9, left Warwickshire requiring 144 from 22 overs under the Duckworth-Lewis regulations. That they fell 13 runs short, at 130 all out, was largely due to the waspish seamers of Matthew Fleming and some accomplished glovework by Paul Nixon, the Kent wicketkeeper. Fleming took 4 for 22 from his five overs, with Nixon taking two lightning stumpings to get rid of the dangerous duo Nick Knight and Ian Bell. Nixon also caught Trevor Penney off Fleming and Jim Troughton for 24 off Andrew Symonds. Kent's total, after a frenetic start, owed much to Symonds' strokeplay in his 46 and a calm 75 by Matthew Walker in the middle-order anchor role.

3 August 2002: Division One
at Chester-le-Street
Durham 153 for 8 (37 overs)
Kent 154 for 5 (31.3 overs)
Kent (4 pts) won by five wickets

at Cardiff
Somerset 245 for 7 (43.3 overs) (KA Parsons 70)
Glamorgan 118 (22.1 overs) (MLP Bulbeck 4 for 39)
Somerset (4 pts) won by 107 runs (DL Method: Glamorgan target 226 from 34 overs)

at Headingley
Nottinghamshire 124 for 1 (35 overs) (JER Gallian 63*)

Yorkshire 143 for 6 (25 overs)
Yorkshire (4 pts) won by four wickets (DL Method: Yorkshire target 143 from 26 overs)

Kent bounced back impressively from their Cheltenham and Gloucester Trophy semi-final defeat to inflict a convincing, five-wicket beating on Durham at the Riverside. Mark Ealham took 3 for 18 from his eight overs and James Golding 3 for 23 as, in a match reduced to 37 overs per side, Durham were pegged to 153 for 8. In reply, Matthew Fleming hit 37 off 22 balls and Kent enjoyed a comfortable pursuit of their victory target after the captain's early blows.

Glamorgan's title challenge was dealt a heavy blow as they were tumbled out for just 118 and trounced by 107 runs by Somerset at Cardiff. Keith Parsons, with 70, and some good late-order batting enabled Somerset to reach 245 for 7 from 43.3 overs when rain intervened. Set a revised target of 226, however, Glamorgan were soon in trouble against Matt Bulbeck (4 for 39) and Mike Burns (3 for 22).

Another rain-hit match at Headingley was won by Yorkshire, after Nottinghamshire had their innings cut short at 124 for 1 from 35 overs. Set a Duckworth-Lewis target of 143 from 25 overs, Yorkshire were indebted to opener Craig White's 48 from 30 balls and a boisterous 29 from Chris Silverwood, who was promoted to No. 3. In the end, victory arrived by four wickets with an over in hand.

Division Two
at Derby
Hampshire 143 for 9 (40 overs) (N Pothas 50*)
Derbyshire 137 for 8 (39 overs)
Derbyshire (4 pts) won by two wickets (DL Method: Derbyshire target 137 from 40 overs)

at Bristol
Lancashire 183 for 9 (45 overs) (SG Law 55, WK Hegg 54, IJ Harvey 4 for 41)
Gloucestershire 185 for 5 (35 overs) (IJ Harvey 56, CM Spearman 54)
Gloucestershire (4 pts) won by five wickets

at Whitgift School
Northamptonshire 277 for 5 (40 overs) (MB Loye 101*, DJG Sales 67, ME Cassar 54)
Surrey 162 (27 overs) (DM Ward 78)
Northamptonshire (4 pts) won by 102 runs (DL Method: Surrey target 265 from 29 overs

Derbyshire scraped past Hampshire by two wickets

Northamptonshire's Mal Loye made the most of a weakened Surrey attack at Whitgift School.

holding up the home bowlers for long as the visitors struggled to 183 for 9. Ian Harvey then made 56 from just 37 balls, to go with his 4 for 41 earlier, and put on a quickfire 85 with Craig Spearman (54) as Gloucestershire cruised to their target with ten overs to spare.

An unbeaten 101 from Mal Loye anchored Northamptonshire's 277 for 5 from 40 overs against a weakened Surrey at Whitgift School, Croydon – a total that proved far too many after a weather interruption had left Surrey needing 265 off 29 overs. At least the schoolboys present had the chance to see their cricket master, the 41-year-old former Surrey stalwart David Ward, smash 78 off 52 balls before the home side crumbled to 162 all out and defeat by 102 runs. Ward, who last played for the county in 1996, was one of several emergency call-ups after Surrey opted to leave their entire first-team squad in Leeds to prepare for the re-scheduled Cheltenham and Gloucester trophy semi-final against Yorkshire.

4 August 2002: Division One
at Worcester
Worcestershire 202 for 9 (45 overs)
Glamorgan 108 for 3 (22.1 overs)
Glamorgan (4 pts) won by 22 runs
(DL Method: Glamorgan needed to have 87 from 22.1 overs when rain stopped play)

at Edgbaston
Leicestershire 250 for 6 (45 overs)
(IJ Sutcliffe 98)
Warwickshire 206 for 3 (30.4 overs)
(DP Ostler 103*, JO Troughton 66*)
Warwickshire (4 pts) won by seven wickets (DL Method: Warwickshire target 203 from 36 overs)

Glamorgan grabbed a vital, and slightly fortuitous, 22-run victory over title rivals Worcestershire at New Road in a match badly disrupted by rain. The home side's 202 for 9 from 45 overs looked to be more than useful when Glamorgan slumped to 28 for 3 in reply, but then Shane Lee, Worcestershire's latest overseas 'locum', found his three overs of

in a tense, low-scoring match at Derby. At one stage 50 for 7, Hampshire were hauled up to 143 for 9 off 40 overs by Nic Pothas' unbeaten 50. Dominic Cork's eight overs cost him just nine runs, but batting was not easy for Derbyshire either as the Hampshire seamers won regular success. Michael Di Venuto's 37 gave the home side early impetus, but the presence of 23 wides in the Derbyshire total was probably the biggest deciding factor.

Leaders Gloucestershire swept aside Lancashire's challenge at Bristol by five wickets, with only half-centuries from Stuart Law and Warren Hegg

medium pace being thrashed for 39 as Matthew Maynard and Steve James regained the initiative. There was still some way for Glamorgan to go, however, at 108 for 3 from 22.1 overs, when the heavens opened to leave the Welsh county well ahead of the relevant Duckworth-Lewis computation.

Warwickshire also stepped up the pressure on leaders Worcestershire with a seven-wicket win over Leicestershire at Edgbaston – again on Duckworth-Lewis calculations. This time, however, there was little argument that Warwickshire were well worth the victory. Iain Sutcliffe's 98, and a 40-ball 44 not out from Phil DeFreitas, had seen Leicestershire to 250 for 6 from their 45 overs, but an unbroken partnership between Dominic Ostler and Jim Troughton of 139 took the home side to a target further reduced by a heavy shower. On the resumption, with nine overs removed from their team's allocation, Ostler and Troughton had been left requiring another 50 off 9.3 overs. It proved a simple task, with Ostler completing his century off exactly 100 balls with the stroke that confirmed victory. Troughton's unbeaten 66 took just 60 deliveries.

Division Two
at Lord's
Essex 194 for 8 (41.5 overs) (WI Jefferson 111*)
Middlesex 77 for 8 (9.5 overs)
Middlesex (4 pts) won by two wickets (DL Method: Middlesex target 77 from 10 overs)

at Northampton
Hampshire 133 (41.3 overs)
Northamptonshire 52 for 0 (14.4 overs)
Northamptonshire (4 pts) won by 16 runs (DL Method: Northamptonshire needed to have 36 from 14.4 overs when rain stopped play)

An unbeaten 111 by Will Jefferson was, in the end, not enough for Essex as they were beaten, cruelly, by two wickets in a match badly hit by the weather at Lord's. Opener Jefferson had played an almost lone hand, facing 112 balls for his maiden one-day hundred, as Essex reached 194 for 8 from 41.5 overs. But then rain intervened to leave Middlesex requiring 77 from ten overs. This they achieved with only one ball to spare, even after Owais Shah had struck 25 from 13 deliveries to give them a flying start. When Graham Napier took three wickets in the sixth over it slowed Middlesex, and they ended up needing 11 from the last 12 balls and then four from two. Paul Weekes finally got them there by

driving Ashley Cowan to the pavilion rails.

Northamptonshire's promotion prospects were further enhanced at Wantage Road where, 24 hours after they had taken advantage of Surrey's decision to field a second team against them, they made it eight points for the weekend by beating Hampshire by 16 runs. The visitors batted raggedly to be bowled out for 133 in 41.3 overs, with only John Crawley and Nic Pothas staying long, and Northants were 52 without loss from 14.4 overs, with Mal Loye 31 not out, when heavy rain terminated the match. Spectators were left puzzled as to why the official margin of victory was 16 runs and not ten wickets – but that's Duckworth-Lewis for you!

5 August 2002: Division One
at Headingley (floodlit)
Yorkshire 222 (45 overs) (VJ Craven 59, GM Fellows 50)
Durham 194 (43.5 overs) (GJ Pratt 84*, A Pratt 59, GM Fellows 4 for 19)
Yorkshire (4 pts) won by 28 runs

A brave stand of 88 between the Pratt brothers, Gary and Andrew, saved face for Durham in their floodlit visit to Headingley but not the match. That was won by Yorkshire by 28 runs, who totalled 222 thanks to half-centuries from Vic Craven and Gary Fellows, and were then further boosted by a fiery new-ball spell from Chris Silverwood who took 3 for 10 in seven overs. It was Silverwood, too, who ended Andrew Pratt's 59, with the score on 141, with a catch at long on and although younger brother Gary went on to finish on 84 not out, Durham were bowled out for 194 with Fellows picking up the last four wickets at a cost of just 19 runs.

Division Two
at Hove (floodlit)
Sussex 8 for 0 (1.4 overs)
Gloucestershire did not bat
Match abandoned – 2 pts each

Only ten balls were possible at the start of the match between Sussex and Gloucestershire at Hove before two torrential storms, within 90 minutes of each other, washed out further play. Sussex had reached eight without loss in a match in which James Kirtley, their fast bowler injured while on England one-day duty, was to have made a comeback.

6 August 2002: Division Two
at Whitgift School
Middlesex 274 for 8 (45 overs) (OA Shah 110,

AJ Strauss 74)
Surrey 209 (38.1 overs) (AD Brown 94)
Middlesex (4 pts) won by 65 runs

at Old Trafford (floodlit)
Hampshire 188 for 8 (45 overs) (JS Laney 71)
Lancashire 189 for 6 (44.4 overs) (MJ Chilton 66, SG Law 64)
Lancashire (4 pts) won by four wickets

Surrey suffered their third limited-overs defeat in four days as Middlesex won the London derby at Whitgift School by an emphatic 65 runs. Only Alistair Brown, with a typically adventurous 94 off 63 balls, made any impression on the Middlesex bowlers – with off spinners Paul Weekes and Jamie Dalrymple especially effective – as Surrey were bowled out for 209. Earlier, Andrew Strauss had got his Middlesex team off to a flying start with 74 from 81 balls, and Owais Shah first helped his captain to put on 90 for the third wicket before motoring on to reach 110 from 93 balls with four sixes and eight fours. Despite Brown's best efforts, which amounted to 15 fours and two sixes (one of which caused mayhem as it thudded into a table full of wine glasses in a hospitality tent!), Middlesex's 274 for 8 always looked likely to be a winning score. It was Middlesex's first one-day league win over their keenest rivals for 15 years.

Lancashire had to battle hard to overcome a spirited Hampshire side by four wickets under the Old Trafford lights. Victory eventually came with just two balls in hand, Warren Hegg settling the match with a thunderous lofted on-drive for four. Four young fast bowlers impressed in the contest, however: James Anderson, 19, and 20-year-old Sajib Mahmood, on debut, for Lancashire; and two more 20-year-olds, Chris Tremlett and James Tomlinson, for Hampshire. Jason Laney's 71 was the bedrock of Hampshire's 188 for 8, while Lancashire seemed to be cruising at 120 for 1 after a 116-run stand between Mark Chilton (66) and Stuart Law (64). In the end, however, after Chilton fell to Tomlinson and Law was run out, it needed all Hegg's experience of tight situations to steer his side across the finishing line.

7 August 2002: Division One
at Worcester (floodlit)
Worcestershire 230 for 8 (45 overs) (VS Solanki 81)
Nottinghamshire did not bat
Match abandoned – 2 pts each

There was frustration for the league leaders,

Worcestershire, when their match against Nottinghamshire at New Road was abandoned at the halfway mark because of rain. The home side would have been confident of defending 230 for 8, too, after an 81 from 101 balls by Vikram Solanki and a quickfire 36 from Shane Lee which included three sixes.

Division Two
at Hove
Sussex 194 for 7 (45 overs) (CJ Adams 60, KJ Innes 50*, ESH Giddins 4 for 39)
Surrey 195 for 4 (39.2 overs) (N Shahid 74*, MR Ramprakash 60)
Surrey (4 pts) won by six wickets

Surrey hauled themselves back into the Division Two promotion race with a comfortable six-wicket success against Sussex at Hove. Despite 60 from Chris Adams, the home side were struggling at 110 for 7 before an unbroken stand of 84 between Kevin Innes (50 not out) and Mark Davis took them to 194 for 7. Ed Giddins was Surrey's best bowler with 4 for 39 against his former county, and although James Kirtley took two early wickets with the new ball, there were few other problems for the visitors as Mark Ramprakash (60) and Nadeem Shahid (74 not out) took control.

11 August 2002: Division One
at Canterbury
Kent 238 for 6 (45 overs) (ET Smith 83)
Somerset 112 (32.5 overs)
Kent (4 pts) won by 126 runs

at Leicester
Leicestershire 230 (44.4 overs) (VJ Wells 56, DI Stevens 54, N Killeen 4 for 12)
Durham 231 for 5 (43.5 overs) (GJ Pratt 60*, MA Gough 54, JJB Lewis 52)
Durham (4 pts) won by five wickets

at Cardiff
Glamorgan 149 for 6 (22 overs)
Yorkshire 153 (21.2 overs) (CEW Silverwood 55, DA Cosker 4 for 17)
Glamorgan (4 pts) won by 21 runs (DL Method: Yorkshire target 171 from 22 overs)

Kent gained a modicum of revenge for their Cheltenham and Gloucester Trophy semi-final defeat against Somerset by beating the West Countrymen in front of a partisan Canterbury Week crowd. Ed Smith held the innings together with a competition-best 83 from 114 balls, while Matthew

Fleming (31), Matthew Walker (45) and Mark Ealham (44 not out) all provided added impetus as Kent totalled 238 for 6. Martin Saggers then removed the Somerset top order with three new-ball strikes – and also ran out Jamie Cox for 14 as the visitors slumped to 41 for 5. Nor did things improve much for Somerset after that as they slid to 112 all out.

Outstanding medium-pace bowling from Neil Killeen, who took 4 for 12 from his nine-over allocation at Grace Road, helped Durham to record only their third league victory of the season. Both Darren Stevens and Vince Wells got past 50 for Leicestershire, but Durham's bowlers kept taking wickets and, in the end, a total of 230 proved inadequate. Michael Gough's 54 sustained Durham's top-order effort, but the five-wicket win was sealed when Gary Pratt (60 not out) came together with Jon Lewis (52) in a fifth-wicket stand worth 85.

Spinners Dean Cosker and Robert Croft spearheaded Glamorgan's 21-run win over Yorkshire in a rain-affected contest at Cardiff. Croft and Ian Thomas had earlier kick-started Glamorgan's 22-over score of 149 for 6 by putting on 84 for the first wicket, but not even a hard-hit 55 from Chris Silverwood, at the head of the Yorkshire order, could insure them against the wiles of Cosker and Croft as they were bowled out for 153 in search of the 171 runs from 22 overs that the Duckworth-Lewis formula had set them. Slow left-armer Cosker finished with 4 for 17 and off spinner Croft 3 for 27.

Division Two
at Derby
Essex 209 for 7 (45 overs) (A Flower 52, KJ Dean 4 for 33)
Derbyshire 160 (37.3 overs)
Essex (4 pts) won by 49 runs

at Lord's
Northamptonshire 286 for 7 (45 overs) (MEK Hussey 110, JW Cook 61, MB Loye 56)
Middlesex 72 (24 overs) (DM Cousins 5 for 22)
Northamptonshire (4 pts) won by 214 runs

Essex kept their promotion ambitions very much alive at the expense of close rivals Derbyshire at Derby, winning by 49 runs. Andy Flower's 52 and a thumping 45 not out from Jon Dakin lifted Essex to 209 for 7 after Kevin Dean had taken 4 for 33, and the Derbyshire reply never got going against the visiting seamers.

The West Australian, Mike Hussey, has proved to be an outstanding signing by Northamptonshire in both forms of the game.

Middlesex, promotion contenders themselves before the day began, disintegrated to a shameful 72 all out in the face of an imposing Northamptonshire total of 286 for 7 at Lord's. Mike Hussey (110) dominated a 125-run opening stand with Mal Loye (56), and Jeff Cook led a late charge with four sixes and three fours in his violent 37-ball 61. Darren Cousins, though still troubled by sore feet, shredded the Middlesex top order to finish with one-day best figures of 5 for 22.

13 August 2002: Division Two
at Bristol (floodlit)
Gloucestershire 274 for 6 (45 overs) (MGN Windows 112*, IJ Harvey 52, JW Cook 4 for 35)
Northamptonshire 219 (42 overs) (AL Penberthy 64, DJG Sales 51)
Gloucestershire (4 pts) won by 55 runs

A remarkable 112 not out by Matt Windows hauled up Gloucestershire to a total of 274 for 6 and out of the reach of Northamptonshire at Bristol. Windows, dropped at long on when he was on 16, was scratchy at first and took 82 balls to reach 50. Then, however, he faced just 30 more balls for his next 62 runs and completed his hundred with the first of three successive sixes struck during a final over that cost Mike Cawdron, formerly of Gloucestershire, 24 runs. Ian Harvey's 52 from 36 balls, and a steady 43 from Mark Alleyne, were the other main contributions to the Gloucestershire cause. Tony Penberthy (64) and David Sales (51) batted spiritedly as Northants replied with 219.

14 August 2002: Division One
at Chester-le-Street (floodlit)
Durham 161 (42.5 overs)
Glamorgan 163 for 7 (34.5 overs) (SP James 55*)
Glamorgan (4 pts) won by three wickets

Glamorgan went to the top of Division One with a three-wicket win over Durham at Chester-le-Street which owed much to a controlled innings of 55 not out from their captain, Steve James. Earlier, Durham had totalled 161, with Michael Gough hitting 42 and Darren Thomas taking 3 for 31.

18 August 2002: Division One
at Leicester
Yorkshire 229 for 6 (45 overs)
(MTG Elliott 109, A McGrath 78)
Leicestershire 231 for 5 (44.4 overs)
(DI Stevens 85, Mohammad Kaif 60*)
Leicestershire (4 pts) won by five wickets

at Trent Bridge
Nottinghamshire 239 for 9 (45 overs)
(KP Pietersen 122)
Somerset 170 (38.4 overs) (BM Shafayat
4 for 35)
Nottinghamshire (4 pts) won by 69 runs

Leicestershire took the first four Yorkshire wickets for just one run at Grace Road, but still had to wait until Phil DeFreitas swung a six from the fourth ball of their own 45th over to beat them. The reason was a fine Yorkshire recovery to 229 for 6, led by Matthew Elliott's 109 and assisted in a fifth-wicket stand of 181 by Anthony McGrath's 78. Darren Stevens then hit a sparkling 85 from just 71 balls, but Leicestershire made rather heavy weather of scoring 68 from the last 15 overs despite an unbeaten 60 from Mohammad Kaif on his one-day

county debut. In the end, eight runs were needed from the last over – and DeFreitas settled matters by hitting a ball from Tim Bresnan into the car park.

Kevin Pietersen, dropped because of poor form just a month previously, continued to wreak havoc with a maiden one-day league century as Nottinghamshire beat Somerset by 69 runs at Trent Bridge. The talented Pietersen, suddenly in the form of his 22-year-old life, followed up his championship 254 not out against Middlesex three days earlier by scoring a spectacular 122 from only 100 balls. His second 50 took only 30 deliveries and he hit Ian Blackwell's left-arm spin for four of his five sixes. There were nine fours besides, and Chris Read helped him to add 98 for the fifth wicket as Notts reached 239 for 9. Left-arm seamer David Lucas then took three wickets in six balls with the new ball to reduce Somerset to 11 for 4, and from there it was merely a question of damage limitation. Eventually, the visitors totalled 170 with Bilal Shafayat picking up 4 for 35 with his medium pacers at the end of a week in which he had become the

Matthew Elliott arrived to play for Yorkshire in place of Darren Lehmann in cracking form.

first England player to score a hundred and a double-hundred in the same Under 19 international (against India Under 19).

Division Two
at Southampton Rose Bowl
Essex 227 for 4 (45 overs) (A Flower 54, DDJ Robinson 51)
Hampshire 228 for 5 (44 overs) (JD Francis 84*, WS Kendall 51)
Hampshire (4 pts) won by five wickets

at The Oval
Surrey 190 (44.4 overs) (MR Ramprakash 78)
Derbyshire 193 for 6 (38.5 overs) (SA Selwood 50)
Derbyshire (4 pts) won by four wickets

John Francis, a 21-year-old batsman with a year's studying left to do at Loughborough University, scored an impressive 84 not out to lift some of the gloom beginning to surround Hampshire cricket. With acting captain Will Kendall also hitting 51, Hampshire defeated Essex by five wickets at the Rose Bowl after the visitors had totalled 227 for 4 from their 45 overs. Chris Tremlett broke down with a foot injury at the start of his second over, but the Hampshire attack coped well enough without him.

Despite reaching 43 for no wicket from their first four overs, Surrey managed not only to reach a below-par 190, but also to lose to Derbyshire with more than six overs remaining at The Oval. Mark Ramprakash's 78 was the only innings of note for Surrey, but a more even Derbyshire batting effort included a fine 50 from Steve Selwood and a merry 34 not out from Jason Kerr.

19 August 2002: Division One
at Taunton
Nottinghamshire 296 for 7 (45 overs) (KP Pietersen 147, BM Shafayat 66)
Somerset 237 (38.3 overs) (KA Parsons 73, MJ Wood 61)
Nottinghamshire (4 pts) won by 59 runs

at Edgbaston
Warwickshire 216 for 8 (45 overs) (MA Wagh 84, DA Leatherdale 4 for 37)
Worcestershire 219 for 2 (39.2 overs) (VS Solanki 91, A Singh 71*)
Worcestershire (4 pts) won by eight wickets

Somerset were beginning to get sick of the sight of Kevin Pietersen long before he was finally out for a magnificent 101-ball 147 at Taunton. Just 24 hours

after hitting their bowlers for 122 at Trent Bridge in the same competition, Pietersen thrashed five sixes – two of them out of the ground – and 12 fours, reaching his hundred from just 78 deliveries. Bilal Shafayat (66) helped him to add 158 for the fourth wicket, and a total of 296 for 7 proved beyond Somerset's reach after they slumped to 35 for 4 despite a violent 25 at the top of the order by Richard Johnson. Keith Parsons (73) and Matthew Wood (61) batted bravely in a sixth-wicket partnership of 91 to prolong the entertainment for a big floodlit crowd.

Worcestershire, meanwhile, climbed back above Glamorgan at the head of the Division One table as Vikram Solanki spearheaded an eight-wicket triumph over West Midlands rivals and fellow title-chasers Warwickshire at Edgbaston. After restricting the home side to 216 for 8, in which Mark Wagh made a one-day best 84 and David Leatherdale picked up 4 for 37, Worcestershire were propelled almost all the way to victory by an opening stand of 183 between Solanki and Anurag Singh. Solanki's 91 was a joy to watch, though no doubt a bittersweet experience for the majority of the 9,000 crowd. He hit 14 fours and a six over extra-cover, and looked an international-class batsman as he scored all round the wicket. Singh, though not as fluent, also struck some memorable strokes and saw Worcestershire over the finishing line with 71 not out.

20 August 2002: Division Two
at Hove (floodlit)
Sussex 169 (45 overs)
Lancashire 171 for 6 (44.1 overs)
Lancashire (4 pts) won by four wickets

Lancashire won an attritional contest under the Hove lights when Chris Schofield played a spirited innings of 36 from 50 balls – a positively rapid knock in a contest dominated by the seaming ball. Sussex managed to reach 169 only through some sensible batting from their lower order, and Lancashire needed Schofield's spark after Stuart Law and David Byas had both been bowled following a 56-run third-wicket partnership. Schofield pulled Kevin Innes for the only six of the match when 32 runs were still required from the final six overs, and when he was finally bowled attempting another unorthodox stroke it cleared the stage for John Wood to clump the winning blows. Victory was clinched when Wood swung the first ball of the final over to the midwicket boundary.

21 August 2002: Division One
at Canterbury (floodlit)
Leicestershire 168 for 7 (45 overs)
Kent 172 for 5 (44.4 overs) (SR Waugh 59*)
Kent (4 pts) won by five wickets

A marvellous, fighting 59 not out by Steve Waugh, on his Kent debut, made it a night to remember at Canterbury. A crowd of 7,000 saw Waugh in classic mode as the cold-eyed cricketing assassin after Kent had slipped to 52 for 4 in reply to Leicestershire's 168 for 7 on a sluggish St Lawrence Ground pitch. Gradually, first in a stand of 48 with Mark Ealham, and then in an increasingly free-wheeling partnership worth 72 in 12 overs with Paul Nixon, the Australian Test captain pulled the game out of the hat to earn himself instant hero status in the hop county. One slog-sweep for six off Darren Stevens' medium pace brought a lost ball, as it disappeared into the darkness way beyond the famous lime tree standing sentinel inside the boundary, and Waugh then sealed the five-wicket win in style by cracking the fourth ball of the final over, bowled by old Ashes adversary Phil DeFreitas, to the extra-cover ropes.

Division Two
at The Oval (floodlit)
Surrey 262 (44.5 overs) (MR Ramprakash 50,
DA Mascarenhas 4 for 45)
Hampshire 192 (41.3 overs) (AJ Hollioake 5 for 43)
Surrey (4 pts) won by 70 runs

A 40-ball 49 from Alistair Brown, and a seventh half-century from his last eight one-day innings by Mark Ramprakash, provided the twin base of Surrey's comfortable 70-run win over Hampshire at The Oval. Dimitri Mascarenhas took 4 for 45, but Surrey reached 262 before bowling out their visitors for 192 as Adam Hollioake bagged figures of 5 for 43.

25 August 2002: Division One
at Taunton
Somerset 188 (43.4 overs) (J Cox 64, ID Blackwell 51,
SM Pollock 4 for 36)
Warwickshire 191 for 2 (35 overs) (DP Ostler 77*)
Warwickshire (4 pts) won by eight wickets

Shaun Pollock gave the Taunton crowd yet more evidence of his all-round prowess as Warwickshire all but sentenced Somerset to relegation with a comfortable eight-wicket win. Pollock first took 4 for 36 as Somerset were bowled out for 188, despite 64 from Jamie Cox and 51 from Ian Blackwell. Then, after

Nick Knight's 45, Pollock jogged along with 43 not out in support of Dominic Ostler's 66-ball unbeaten 77 as victory was gained with ten overs in hand.

Division Two
at Colchester
Northamptonshire 167 for 8 (45 overs)
Essex 168 for 6 (41.5 overs) (A Flower 57*)
Essex (4 pts) won by four wickets

at Lord's
Derbyshire 243 for 8 (45 overs) (MJ Di Venuto 94)
Middlesex 211 for 6 (45 overs) (AJ Strauss 70)
Derbyshire (4 pts) won by 32 runs

An unbeaten 57 from Andy Flower guided Essex to a hard-working win over Northamptonshire at Colchester, after they had restricted their visitors to 167 for 8 from the 45-over allocation. John Stephenson picked up 3 for 21, and there were three wickets as well for fellow medium pacer Tony Penberthy in the Essex reply.

Michael Di Venuto narrowly missed a third Lord's hundred within a week when he was dismissed for 94, off just 80 balls, during Derbyshire's 32-run victory against Middlesex. But Di Venuto's innings, which followed his two centuries in the championship fixture between the two teams, proved to be the decisive influence on the outcome – alongside an opening spell of 7-2-8-1 by Derbyshire captain Dominic Cork. Andy Strauss scored 70, but Middlesex could only reach 211 for 6 in reply to Derbyshire's 243 for 8.

26 August 2002: Division One
at Colwyn Bay
Nottinghamshire 226 for 7 (45 overs) (DJ Bicknell 51)
Glamorgan 227 for 5 (43 overs) (IJ Thomas 64,
SP James 54*)
Glamorgan (4 pts) won by five wickets

Glamorgan put the destiny of the Norwich Union League title into their own hands by beating Nottinghamshire by five wickets at Colwyn Bay to go back to the top of the table. With three games left, the Welsh county knew that three more victories would guarantee them only their second one-day league title, following their 1993 success. Notts, who totalled 226 for 7 with Darren Bicknell top scoring with 51, lost Kevin Pietersen to a leg injury. Glamorgan's reply was launched by an aggressive 64 from Ian Thomas, the burly left-handed opener, and they were guided home with two overs to spare by an unbroken stand of 54 between Steve James (54 not out) and Mark Wallace (37 not out).

27 August 2002: Division Two
at Colchester (floodlit)
Gloucestershire 97 (33.4 overs)
Essex 98 for 5 (36.1 overs)
Essex (4 pts) won by five wickets

A poor-quality pitch at Colchester left an expectant floodlit crowd feeling rather short-changed, even though Essex kept their own promotion hopes up by defeating leaders Gloucestershire by five wickets. Both Joe Grant and John Stephenson took three cheap wickets as Gloucestershire struggled to 97 all out in 33.4 overs. It then took a dedicated 44 by Stephenson to ensure there were no major alarms in the Essex innings, which rather limped to its target as the home side reached 98 for 5 in 36.1 overs.

1 September 2002: Division One
at Worcester
Kent 213 for 8 (45 overs) (MV Fleming 68)
Worcestershire 217 for 7 (44.1 overs)
(GA Hick 77*, MJ Saggers 4 for 37)
Worcestershire (4 pts) won by three wickets

at Edgbaston
Warwickshire 238 for 9 (45 overs) (IR Bell 54)
Nottinghamshire 187 (41.4 overs) (CMW Read 69)
Warwickshire (4 pts) won by 51 runs

Worcestershire ended Kent's hopes of a Division One title defence by beating the 2001 champions by three wickets in a tense contest at New Road. Graeme Hick, the Worcestershire captain, kept his head to finish on 77 not out as the equation to overhaul Kent's 213 for 8 came down from 59 off 11 overs to 18 off three. With Ben Smith (46), Hick had added 94 in 24 overs – but Worcestershire's victory, which eventually arrived from the first ball of the final over, also owed much to Vikram Solanki's quickfire 46, containing ten fours, at the top of the order. Martin Saggers took 4 for 37 for Kent and David Fulton made 41 not out, but they ultimately paid the price for not building sufficiently on the start given to them by Matthew Fleming (68 from 60 balls, with 12 fours) and Rob Key (46) in an opening partnership worth 101.

A fine innings of 54 by Ian Bell was the highlight of Warwickshire's emphatic 51-run win over Nottinghamshire at Edgbaston. Facing a total of 238

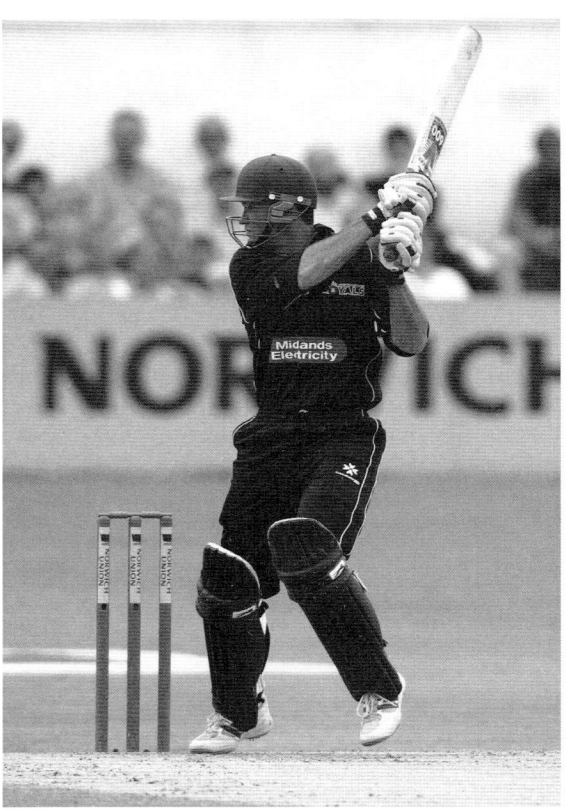

Graeme Hick is still one of the best one-day batsmen in the country, but is continually overlooked.

for 9, Notts began well – but a collapse to 187 all out followed when Chris Read, who hit 69 from 70 balls and added 74 for the second wicket with Usman Afzaal (45), was caught at deep midwicket.

Division Two
at Southampton Rose Bowl
Hampshire 241 for 7 (45 overs) (WS Kendall 110*, SD Udal 58)
Middlesex 217 for 7 (45 overs) (BL Hutton 63)
Hampshire (4 pts) won by 24 runs

at Old Trafford
Lancashire 153 for 9 (45 overs)
Essex 154 for 3 (34.1 overs) (DDJ Robinson 54)
Essex (4 pts) won by seven wickets

at Northampton
Northamptonshire 195 for 8 (45 overs)
Sussex 197 for 4 (43.4 overs) (CJ Adams 64*)
Sussex (4 pts) won by six wickets

A first one-day century in his 110th match from Will Kendall inspired Hampshire to a 24-run victory against Middlesex at the Rose Bowl. Kendall finished on 110 not out, and Shaun Udal hit 58, as Hampshire totalled 241 for 7. Ben Hutton (63), Ed Joyce (43) and Jamie Dalrymple (42) all batted well in reply, but none could go on to play an innings of match-winning proportions and, in the end, Middlesex fell short at 217 for 7.

Essex continued their push for promotion by getting much the better of Lancashire on a sluggish, often-difficult pitch at Old Trafford. Off spinner James Middlebrook starred with 3 for 14 from his nine overs as Lancashire struggled to 153 for 9 from their 45 overs. Darren Robinson then hit 54, and Andy Flower a typically assured 37 not out, as Essex won by seven wickets with more than ten overs remaining.

Steady innings from Bas Zuiderent (39) and Murray Goodwin (38) provided the base for Chris Adams, 64 not out, to play the decisive innings at Northampton where Sussex defeated Northamptonshire by six wickets. There were eight balls to spare when Sussex past Northants' total of 195 for 8.

2 September 2002: Division One
at Headingley
Yorkshire 167 (44.3 overs) (DS Harrison 5 for 26)
Glamorgan 168 for 1 (24.1 overs) (RDB Croft 59, IJ Thomas 55*)
Glamorgan (4 pts) won by nine wickets

at Chester-le-Street
Somerset 204 for 9 (45 overs) (KP Dutch 64)
Durham 208 for 4 (44 overs) (GJ Muchall 81, BJ Hodge 77)
Durham (4 pts) won by six wickets

It was quite a day for David Harrison at Headingley as Glamorgan breezed past Yorkshire by nine wickets to step up their drive to the Norwich Union League title. Harrison's 5 for 26 undermined the Yorkshire innings to such an extent that it took a last-wicket stand of 64 between Richard Blakey (47) and Ryan Sidebottom (30 not out) to haul them up to 167. Then, after a belligerent 59 by Robert Croft in his favoured pinch-hitting role, all-rounder Harrison came in to smash 37 not out and help Ian Thomas (55 not out) to bring victory as early as the first ball of the 25th over.

Marcus Trescothick confirmed his return to fitness with 41, and Keith Dutch made 64 after being promoted to No. 3, but otherwise there was again little for out-of-sorts Somerset to cheer as Durham beat them by six wickets at the Riverside. Brad Hodge

(77) and Gordon Muchall (81) were outstanding in a third-wicket stand of 128 as the home side eased past Somerset's 204 for 9 with an over to spare.

Division Two
at Derby (floodlit)
Derbyshire 213 (45 overs) (NRC Dumelow 52, DG Cork 51, AJ Hollioake 4 for 23)
Surrey 214 for 9 (44.4 overs) (R Clarke 98*)
Surrey (4 pts) won by one wicket

Rikki Clarke defied a nasty blow on the inside of his knee, causing him to hobble for most of his innings, to guide Surrey to an exciting floodlit win at Derby. Clarke was denied a century, finishing on 98 not out, but that did not worry him in the slightest. In the end, when Clarke smashed Dominic Cork through extra-cover for the clinching boundary, there were just two balls to spare and one Surrey wicket left – and he had played his almost lone hand to perfection. Derbyshire's 213 was built around half-centuries from Nathan Dumelow and Cork, but the night belonged to Clarke – one of the best young talents to emerge in the English game in 2002 and voted Young Cricketer of the Year by the Cricket Writers' Club three days earlier.

3 September 2002: Division One
at Cardiff (floodlit)
Glamorgan 280 for 8 (45 overs) (MP Maynard 87, MJ Powell 71)
Worcestershire 177 (36.3 overs) (DA Leatherdale 53)
Glamorgan (4 pts) won by 103 runs

An ecstatic crowd of 5,200 saw Glamorgan demolish close rivals Worcestershire by 103 runs at Cardiff and put one hand on the Norwich Union League trophy. Matthew Maynard (87) and Michael Powell (71) provided most of the fireworks in an imposing total of 280 for 8 by adding 133 in just 19 overs, while skipper Steve James contributed 43. Then, despite a fighting 53 from David Leatherdale, the Glamorgan spinners Robert Croft and Dean Cosker combined to send Worcestershire spiralling disappointingly to 177 all out in reply.

Division Two
at Hove (floodlit)
Hampshire 126 (33 overs) (KJ Innes 4 for 26)
Sussex 127 for 3 (25.1 overs) (MW Goodwin 76*)
Sussex (4 pts) won by seven wickets

Will House, the 26-year-old former Kent batsman, signed off his professional career by hitting the six which wrapped a Sussex win by seven wickets against Hampshire at Hove. The left-hander swung a ball from medium pacer Jimmy Adams over the midwicket boundary to provide the undoubted highlight of an otherwise forgettable match. Kevin Innes had earlier taken 4 for 26 in a wretched Hampshire slide to 126 all out, while the Sussex batting effort revolved around Murray Goodwin's 76 not out – until House stole the curtain call.

4 September 2002: Division One
at Trent Bridge (floodlit)
Nottinghamshire 229 for 6 (45 overs) (Usman Afzaal 75, DJ Bicknell 64)
Durham 232 for 3 (41.5 overs) (BJ Hodge 91*, AM Thorpe 53)
Durham (4 pts) won by seven wickets

An unbeaten 91 off 105 balls from Brad Hodge, including 11 boundaries, swept Durham to a seven-wicket win over Nottinghamshire at Trent Bridge. Ashley Thorpe also impressed with 53, as the visitors were untroubled by having to chase a Nottinghamshire total of 229 for 6, which featured fine knocks of 75 by Usman Afzaal and 64 from Darren Bicknell.

8 September 2002: Division One
at Taunton
Somerset 244 for 6 (45 overs) (PCL Holloway 112*)
Kent 126 (34 overs) (SR Waugh 53, ID Blackwell 4 for 24, RJ Turner 1ct, 4st)
Somerset (4 pts) won by 118 runs

at Scarborough
Yorkshire 153 (44.2 overs) (RJ Blakey 60)
Leicestershire 157 for 4 (18.4 overs) (IJ Sutcliffe 54*)
Leicestershire (4 pts) won by six wickets

Kent's hopes of finishing second in the one-day league they won in 2001 were dashed by a deflating 118-run defeat against Somerset at Taunton. Piran Holloway's 112 not out was the basis of the home side's 244 for 6 and, even though they reached 79 for 1 with Steve Waugh going on to 53, Kent were never in the hunt as they were bowled out for 126. Ian Blackwell took 4 for 24 with his left-arm spin.

Leicestershire crushed Yorkshire at Scarborough, where only a county league record stand of 89 for the eighth wicket by Richard Blakey (60) and Richard Dawson (41) enabled the home side to escape with any sort of honour. Javagal Srinath and Phil DeFreitas used the seaming ball expertly to leave Yorkshire plunging, early on, to 45 for 7.

Through Blakey and Dawson they recovered somewhat to 153 all out – but then the Leicestershire batsmen reached their target in a remarkable 18.4 overs to complete victory by six wickets. Iain Sutcliffe anchored the chase with 54 not out, while Darren Stevens thumped 30 off 19 balls and Vince Wells took just 33 balls to score 48, which included two sixes and eight fours.

Division Two
at Chelmsford
Surrey 162 (43.3 overs) (AP Cowan 4 for 16)
Essex 160 (38.2 overs)
Surrey (4 pts) won by 2 runs

at Bristol
Gloucestershire 292 for 8 (45 overs) (CM Spearman 81, MW Alleyne 54)
Derbyshire 240 (41.4 overs) (SA Selwood 93, CWG Bassano 61)
Gloucestershire (4 pts) won by 52 runs

at Old Trafford
Lancashire 270 for 5 (45 overs) (SG Law 133, MJ Chilton 61)
Northamptonshire 173 (41.2 overs) (JJ Haynes 4ct, 1st)
Lancashire (4 pts) won by 97 runs

Saqlain Mushtaq's 28 was the top score in a Surrey total of 162 at Chelmsford – but they still won by two runs as Essex, alarmingly, lost their last five wickets for 15 runs in 32 balls to be bowled out themselves for 160. Adam Hollioake snatched 3 for 11 in 3.2 overs and a perfect weekend for county champions Surrey ended with them also assured of promotion to Division One of the Norwich Union League.

Gloucestershire, meanwhile, learned joyously about Essex's late collapse because it confirmed their status as Division Two champions following their victory by 52 runs against Derbyshire at Bristol. Craig Spearman (81) had been joined by Jack Russell (42) in an opening stand of 100 from only 12 overs that launched Gloucestershire to an eventual 292 for 8. Tim Hancock (45) and Mark Alleyne (54) also helped build a total that was too hot for Derbyshire to handle, although the visitors battled bravely to 240 with Steve Selwood again impressing with 93.

Stuart Law gave Old Trafford spectators a batting master class with his league-best 133 during Lancashire's 97-run victory over shell-shocked Northamptonshire. Queenslander Law completed his hundred from 81 balls and, overall, faced just 99 while hitting three sixes and 17 fours. Neil Fairbrother and Graham Lloyd, in their final appearances, were applauded all the way to the wicket by the Lancashire crowd. Law then picked up three wickets as Northants were dismissed for 173 in reply to the home team's 270 for 5.

10 September 2002: Division One
at Edgbaston (floodlit)
Warwickshire 191 for 6 (45 overs) (DR Brown 82*)
Yorkshire 194 for 2 (27.3 overs) (MJ Lumb 73)
Yorkshire (4 pts) won by eight wickets

Warwickshire's hopes of finishing second were wrecked by a Yorkshire team spearheaded by the youngest pair of opening bowlers ever fielded in the competition. Tim Bresnan and Nick Thornicroft, both 17, helped to restrict Warwickshire to 191 for 6 from their 45 overs – a total only boosted by an unbeaten 82 from 85 balls by Dougie Brown. Yorkshire then fairly sprinted to victory, by eight wickets, as Michael Lumb (with a one-day best 73) and Richard Blakey (48 not out) swept them home in just 27.3 overs.

11 September 2002: Division One
at Leicester (floodlit)
Leicestershire 215 for 9 (45 overs) (IJ Sutcliffe 104*)
Somerset 216 for 7 (44.2 overs) (J Cox 52, DL Maddy 4 for 36)
Somerset (4 pts) won by three wickets

Iain Sutcliffe (104 not out) reached his hundred with a six off the last ball of the Leicestershire innings at Grace Road, but the home side's 215 for 9 did not prove to be enough as Somerset – following a rain interruption – won by six wickets. Sutcliffe hit 11 fours and three sixes, including that last blow off Matt Bulbeck, while 20-year-old Damien Brandy impressed with 35 on his debut. Darren Maddy then took 3 for 25, but Somerset's chase was kicked off by Jamie Cox (52) and successfully continued by the middle order.

15 September 2002: Division One
at Canterbury
Glamorgan 226 for 7 (45 overs) (MJ Powell 74)
Kent 222 for 9 (45 overs) (MA Ealham 75)
Glamorgan (4 pts) won by 4 runs

at Trent Bridge
Worcestershire 251 for 6 (45 overs) (DA Leatherdale 66, BF Smith 61, CE Shreck 5 for 35)
Nottinghamshire 170 (40.5 overs) (GJ Batty 4 for 36)
Worcestershire (4 pts) won by 81 runs

Glamorgan clinched the Norwich Union League title in grand style at Canterbury, beating the holders Kent by just four runs in a thrilling encounter. Michael Powell's 74, and a hard-hit 43 from Adrian Dale, took Glamorgan to a reasonable total of 226 for 7, but Mark Ealham looked as if he was going to inspire a Kent victory as he thumped 75 from No. 3 in the order. Paul Nixon took up the baton, following Ealham's dismissal, but with ten still needed from the final over Nixon was run out for a 44-ball 49 trying to steal a second run to third man.

Charlie Shreck, a six foot seven inches tall swing bowler, took 5 for 35 on his county debut but still finished up on the losing side as Nottinghamshire were beaten by 81 runs by Worcestershire at Trent Bridge. Ben Smith's 61 and a 71-ball 66 from David Leatherdale were the basis of Worcestershire's 251 for 6, and Gareth Batty's off breaks brought him 4 for 36 as Notts were bowled out for 170 in reply.

Division Two
at Shenley
Middlesex 198 for 5 (45 overs) (NRD Compton 86*, BL Hutton 71*)
Lancashire 199 for 4 (40.4 overs) (MJ Chilton 84*, CP Schofield 52)
Lancashire (4 pts) won by six wickets

at Northampton
Essex 258 for 9 (45 overs) (WI Jefferson 102)
Northamptonshire 216 (43.1 overs) (AL Penberthy 54, GL Brophy 54)
Essex (4 pts) won by 42 runs

at Hove
Derbyshire 240 for 8 (45 overs) (CWG Bassano 55, BV Taylor 4 for 39)
Sussex 166 (41.4 overs)
Derbyshire (4 pts) won by 74 runs

Nick Compton, the grandson of Denis, scored 86 not out in just his fourth one-day appearance for Middlesex, including a six and seven fours, to help Ben Hutton – grandson of Sir Leonard – to add a fighting and unbroken 142 in 23 overs for the sixth wicket at Shenley. Hutton finished on 71 not out, but Middlesex's recovery from 56 for 5 to 198 for 5 was not enough to prevent them from being beaten by six wickets by Lancashire. Mark Chilton anchored the run chase with an unbeaten 84, while Chris Schofield produced a 50-ball 52 as victory arrived with more than four overs in hand.

Will Jefferson hit 102 from 107 deliveries as Essex continued their quest for promotion with a 42-run win over Northamptonshire at Wantage Road. Jefferson's ton, plus 46 from Aftab Habib, took Essex to a challenging 258 for 9 – and Northants fell away for 216 in reply despite a brace of 54s from Tony Penberthy and Gerry Brophy.

Derbyshire were too good for Sussex at Hove, first reaching 240 for 8 from their 45 overs with Chris Bassano top scoring with 55, and then bowling out the home side for 166 even though they had initially moved smoothly to 78 for 1 through Murray Goodwin (45) and Tony Cottey (43). Nathan Dumelow's off breaks earned him 3 for 24.

22 September 2002: Division One:
at Worcester
Worcestershire 255 for 8 (45 overs) (DA Leatherdale 60*, Kadeer Ali 57)
Leicestershire 227 (44.2 overs) (DI Stevens 54)
Worcestershire (4 pts) won by 28 runs

at Cardiff
Warwickshire 275 for 9 (45 overs) (DP Ostler 97, DR Brown 73)
Glamorgan 201 (35.3 overs) (MP Maynard 54)
Warwickshire (4 pts) won by 74 runs

at Headingley
Yorkshire 299 for 3 (45 overs) (MTG Elliott 115*, A McGrath 85*)
Kent 220 (37 overs) (AKD Gray 4 for 34)
Yorkshire (4 pts) won by 79 runs

at Taunton
Somerset 254 for 6 (45 overs) (MJ Wood 88*, M Burns 54)
Durham 79 (21.2 overs)
Somerset (4 pts) won by 175 runs

Worcestershire confirmed themselves as runners-up to Glamorgan by beating Leicestershire by 28 runs at Worcester. A stylish 57 from Kadeer Ali and an unbeaten 60 from the ever-reliable David Leatherdale took them to 255 for 8 and loyal servant Stuart Lampitt, taking a typically steady 3 for 33 in his last match for the county, helped restrict the visitors to 227.

Glamorgan, the champions, paraded the trophy at Cardiff but were then beaten by Warwickshire, who finished third. Dominic Ostler's 97 from 84 balls was the highlight of Warwickshire's 275 for 9, although Dougie Brown also hit an entertaining 73. In reply, Matthew Maynard's 54 was not

enough as Glamorgan faded to 201 all out.

An unbroken partnership for the fourth wicket of 198 between Matthew Elliott and Anthony McGrath – the second-best stand in Yorkshire's one-day league history – provided the inspirational basis of a 79-run win over Kent at Headingley. Elliott finished on 115 not out from 100 balls, while McGrath's unbeaten 85 took him just 74 deliveries. McGrath then took 3 for 39 with his medium pacers, and off spinner Andrew Gray 4 for 34, as Kent were bowled out for 220 as they tried to overhaul Yorkshire's 299 for 3.

Durham were skittled for 79 at Taunton, with Pete Trego finishing with 3 for 14, as Somerset completed a crushing victory by 175 runs. An unbeaten 88 from Matthew Wood, and 54 by Mike Burns, helped push Somerset's 45-over total up to 254 for 6.

Division Two
at The Oval
Surrey 263 for 8 (45 overs) (GP Thorpe 114, AM Smith 5 for 30)
Gloucestershire 184 (39.2 overs) (AJ Hollioake 4 for 24)
Surrey (4 pts) won by 79 runs

at Chelmsford
Essex 189 (38 overs) (Aftab Habib 53)
Sussex 158 (38.3 overs) (MW Goodwin 55)
Essex (4 pts) won by 29 runs (DL Method: Sussex target 188 from 42 overs)

at Derby
Derbyshire 210 for 8 (45 overs) (SA Selwood 81*)
Middlesex 188 (43.3 overs) (EC Joyce 58, JWM Dalrymple 52, G Welch 6 for 31)
Derbyshire (4 pts) won by 22 runs

at Southampton Rose Bowl
Northamptonshire 285 for 6 (45 overs) (DJG Sales 93, MJ Powell 64)
Hampshire 289 for 4 (44.3 overs) (JD Francis 103*, NC Johnson 73, JP Crawley 52)
Hampshire (4 pts) won by six wickets

Surrey beat Division Two champions Gloucestershire by 79 runs at The Oval to earn themselves an £11,000 cheque for coming second in the table. Graham Thorpe scored 114 from 105 balls in Surrey's 263 for 8, while Adam Hollioake capped an emotional season as captain by taking 4 for 24 as Gloucestershire collapsed from 68 without loss to 184 all out.

Essex finished third and beat Sussex by 30 runs at Chelmsford, following a slight Duckworth-Lewis recalculation triggered by a short rain delay early in the home side's innings. Essex wasted four overs of their rescheduled 42 by being bowled out for 189, but only Murray Goodwin (55) and, to a lesser extent, Neil Turk, in a debut innings of 36, caused the home attack any concern. Sussex were eventually dismissed for 158.

Derbyshire's season ended with a victory over Middlesex at Derby, with Steve Selwood again underlining his rich promise with an unbeaten 81 from 112 balls. Selwood's heroics helped Derbyshire reach 210 for 8, and after slumping to 34 for 4 Middlesex could not even be revived by a fifth-wicket stand of 98 between Ed Joyce (58) and Jamie Dalrymple (52). Graeme Welch returned career-best limited-overs figures of 6 for 31 as Middlesex were bowled out for 188.

There was a popular result at the Rose Bowl, meanwhile, as Robin Smith's fifth and final year as captain ended with a thrilling Hampshire win by six wickets against Northamptonshire. A Northants total of 285 for 6, based on 93 from David Sales and Mark Powell's 64, looked a formidable one. But Neil Johnson hit 73 at the top of the order, John Crawley made a crisp 52 and John Francis, 21, finally emerged as a hero symbolic of Hampshire's hope for the future by finishing on 103 not out. It was his first hundred for the county, and victory came with just three balls remaining.

DIVISION ONE FINAL RESULTS

	P	W	L	Tie	NR	Pts
Glamorgan	16	12	3	1	–	50
Worcestershire	16	11	3	–	2	48
Warwickshire	16	9	6	–	1	38
Yorkshire	16	8	7	–	1	34
Kent	16	7	8	1	–	30
Leicestershire	16	7	8	–	1	30
Somerset	16	5	10	–	1	22
Durham	16	5	11	–	–	20
Nottinghamshire	16	3	11	–	2	16

DIVISION TWO

	P	W	L	Tie	NR	Pts
Gloucestershire	16	10	4	–	2	44
Surrey	16	10	5	–	1	42
Essex	16	10	6	–	–	40
Derbyshire	16	8	7	–	1	34
Lancashire	16	7	7	–	2	32
Northamptonshire	16	7	8	–	1	30
Hampshire	16	6	9	–	1	26
Sussex	16	4	10	–	2	20
Middlesex	16	4	10	–	2	20

FEATURES OF NATIONAL LEAGUE 2002

HIGHEST TOTAL

317-8 (45 overs)	Kent v. Nottinghamshire at Trent Bridge	16 June

HIGHEST TOTAL BATTING SECOND

306-8 (45 overs)	Somerset v. Yorkshire at Taunton	12 May

LOWEST TOTAL

68 (20.4 overs)	Lancashire v. Surrey at The Oval	12 May

HIGHEST INDIVIDUAL SCORE

147 KP Pietersen	Nottinghamshire v. Somerset at Taunton	19 August

25 centuries were scored in the competition

SIX WICKETS IN AN INNINGS

6-31 G Welch	Derbyshire v. Middlesex at Derby	22 September

There were 59 instances of four wickets in an innings

TIED MATCHES

Glamorgan tied with Kent at Cardiff	9 June

WINNING BY ONE WICKET

Gloucestershire beat Surrey at The Oval	19 May
Glamorgan beat Somerset at Taunton	30 June
Lancashire beat Derbyshire at Blackpool	14 July
Surrey beat Derbyshire at Derby	2 September

WINNING BY 150 RUNS

214	Northamptonshire beat Middlesex at Lord's	11 August
175	Somerset beat Durham at Taunton	22 September
165	Kent beat Durham at Maidstone	7 July

There were 12 instances of a side winning by more than 100 runs

WINNING BY ONE RUN

Yorkshire beat Somerset at Taunton	12 May

NO PLAY POSSIBLE

Lancashire v. Middlesex at Old Trafford	26 May
Hampshire v. Derbyshire at Southampton Rose Bowl	9 June
Northamptonshire v. Gloucestershire at Northampton	9 June
Nottinghamshire v. Yorkshire at Trent Bridge	9 June
Warwickshire v. Somerset at Edgbaston	9 June

NATIONAL LEAGUE AVERAGES

DERBYSHIRE

Batting	M	Inns	NO	HS	Runs	Av	100	50	c/st
SA Selwood	14	13	2	93	426	38.72	-	4	5
DG Cork	9	9	2	51	215	30.71	1	1	5
SD Stubbings	10	10	1	98*	245	27.22	-	1	2
MJ Di Venuto	13	13	0	94	325	25.00	-	2	2
NRC Dumelow	5	5	0	51	124	24.80	-	1	-
CWG Bassano	11	11	0	61	233	21.18	-	2	2
T Lungley	7	5	3	12*	42	21.00	-	-	1
JID Kerr	15	13	2	65*	227	20.63	-	1	5
MP Dowman	14	13	1	45	195	16.25	-	-	1
AI Gait	8	8	0	30	102	12.75	-	-	3
LD Sutton	14	12	3	29	109	12.11	-	-	17/2
DR Hewson	5	5	0	32	56	11.20	-	-	-
G Welch	14	13	4	23	95	10.55	-	-	-
KJ Dean	12	8	3	16*	46	9.20	-	-	4
LJ Wharton	9	4	2	11*	15	7.50	-	-	-

Also batted (2 matches): SMA Bukhari 2, 10*; NEL Gunter 0.
Did not bat in one match: KM Krikken (2ct, 1st).

Bowling	O	M	Runs	W	Av	Best	4i
DG Cork	79.1	15	222	13	17.07	2-20	-
MP Dowman	79	5	312	17	18.35	3-38	-
G Welch	117.3	14	517	23	22.47	6-31	2
KJ Dean	92	12	422	18	23.44	4-33	1
NRC Dumelow	28.4	0	129	5	25.80	3-24	-
LJ Wharton	52.5	2	219	8	27.37	2-30	-
T Lungley	48.4	1	225	8	28.12	2-29	-
JID Kerr	106.4	4	441	15	29.40	3-27	-

Also bowled: SMA Bukhari 14-0-66-4; NEL Gunter 12-0-91-0.

DURHAM

Batting	M	Inns	NO	HS	Runs	Av	100	50	c/st
BJ Hodge	3	3	1	91*	195	97.50	-	2	3
PD Collingwood	6	6	1	118*	195	39.00	1	-	5
JJB Lewis	13	12	3	52	282	31.33	-	1	3
GJ Muchall	9	9	1	81	228	28.50	-	1	3
GJ Pratt	16	16	4	84*	306	25.50	-	3	6
NG Hatch	3	2	1	20*	25	25.00	-	-	-
AM Thorpe	4	4	0	53	83	20.75	-	1	-
MA Gough	11	11	0	57	226	20.54	-	2	4
A Pratt	16	13	3	59	192	19.20	-	1	19/6
MJ Symington	5	2	0	22	35	17.50	-	-	3
ML Love	3	3	0	36	50	16.66	-	-	2
N Killeen	16	10	6	22*	56	14.00	-	-	3
N Peng	14	14	1	38	178	13.69	-	-	6
GD Bridge	7	6	1	24	59	11.80	-	-	-
AM Davies	16	11	3	31*	77	9.62	-	-	6
DR Law	11	9	0	28	84	9.33	-	-	1
ID Hunter	10	6	0	16	43	7.16	-	-	4
NC Phillips	9	5	0	17	32	6.40	-	-	3

Also batted (3 matches): SJ Harmison 3.
Also batted (1 match): I Pattison 0.

Bowling	O	M	Runs	W	Av	Best	4i
N Killeen	131.4	15	562	30	18.73	4-12	2
PD Collingwood	30.4	2	152	8	19.00	2-29	-
MJ Symington	21	1	98	5	19.60	2-11	-
GD Bridge	53	2	205	9	22.77	3-22	-
SJ Harmison	26	0	117	5	23.40	2-39	-
NC Phillips	77	0	384	15	25.60	3-38	-
AM Davies	112	8	464	16	29.00	3-41	-
MA Gough	51.1	1	263	6	43.83	3-26	-
ID Hunter	71	5	387	7	55.28	2-42	-

Also bowled: NG Hatch 19-1-134-2; BJ Hodge 7-0-29-1; DR Law 44.1-0-321-4;
I Pattison 4-1-29-0; AM Thorpe 11-0-67-2.

ESSEX

Batting	M	Inns	NO	HS	Runs	Av	100	50	c/st
A Flower	14	14	4	80	506	50.60	-	6	16/4
JM Dakin	14	11	4	45*	250	35.71	-	-	4
WI Jefferson	13	13	1	111*	421	35.08	2	-	8
RC Irani	10	10	3	51*	235	33.57	-	2	2
Aftab Habib	8	6	0	53	162	27.00	-	2	4
DDJ Robinson	14	14	0	76	369	26.35	-	3	7
AP Grayson	8	5	1	29	97	24.25	-	-	3
ML Pettini	9	8	0	75	179	22.37	-	2	2

NATIONAL LEAGUE AVERAGES

ESSEX cont.

Batting	M	Inns	NO	HS	Runs	Av	100	50	c/st
JP Stephenson	15	13	2	44	204	18.54	-	-	8
GR Napier	15	12	2	50	150	15.00	-	1	7
ME Waugh	2	2	0	26	28	14.00	-	-	-
AP Cowan	11	7	2	21	63	12.60	-	-	4
JD Middlebrook	14	9	2	19	65	9.28	-	-	4
RS Clinton	3	3	1	11	15	7.50	-	-	2
TJ Phillips	4	4	2	6	14	7.00	-	-	1
JS Foster	3	3	0	14	20	6.66	-	-	5/1
JB Grant	6	2	0	2	2	1.00	-	-	3

Also batted (4 matches): JE Bishop 2*, 6*; AJ Clarke 0 (2ct).
Also batted (3 matches): AC McGarry 1.
Also batted (2 matches): RS Bopara 0, 0.

Bowling	O	M	Runs	W	Av	Best	4i
AJ Clarke	32.3	1	124	10	12.40	4-30	1
JB Grant	37	4	127	8	15.87	3-13	-
AP Cowan	84	7	302	19	15.89	4-33	1
JD Middlebrook	81	6	320	19	16.84	4-33	1
RC Irani	75.2	9	324	16	20.25	3-29	-
AP Grayson	45.3	2	167	8	20.87	3-27	-
JD Stephenson	57.4	1	295	12	24.58	3-14	-
GR Napier	90	6	446	18	24.77	3-10	-
JE Bishop	22	0	134	5	26.80	3-39	-
JM Dakin	76	5	334	11	30.36	2-32	-

Also bowled: AC McGarry 17.3-1-125-2; TJ Phillips 22-0-114-4; ME Waugh 3.3.0-14-3.

GLAMORGAN

Batting	M	Inns	NO	HS	Runs	Av	100	50	c/st
DS Harrison	5	4	3	37*	55	55.00	-	-	1
MP Maynard	14	13	2	87	482	43.81	-	4	14/-
SP James	12	11	3	86	305	38.12	-	3	2
AG Wharf	4	3	2	18	34	34.00	-	-	1
MJ Powell	15	13	1	74	393	32.75	-	2	7
A Dale	16	13	2	78*	354	32.18	-	3	1
IJ Thomas	11	11	1	72	310	31.00	-	3	4
RDB Croft	16	16	0	59	327	20.43	-	1	6
SD Thomas	11	9	2	28*	137	19.57	-	-	2
DL Hemp	11	11	1	55*	195	19.50	-	1	6
MA Wallace	15	12	3	37*	157	17.44	-	-	17/6
MS Kasprowicz	11	7	3	13	58	14.50	-	-	4
DA Cosker	13	3	2	5	8	8.00	-	-	7
AP Davies	11	3	1	11*	15	7.50	-	-	2

Also batted (5 matches): OT Parkin 14* (1ct). Also batted (1 match): J Hughes 9; .K Newell 4.

Bowling	O	M	Runs	W	Av	Best	4i
RDB Croft	117.2	2	550	28	19.64	4-40	1
DS Harrison	37	2	185	9	20.55	5-26	1
A Dale	84	2	377	17	22.17	3-28	-
MS Kasprowicz	89.2	6	359	16	22.43	4-28	1
AP Davies	110.2	6	518	21	24.66	4-33	1
DA Cosker	89.5	3	373	13	28.69	4-17	1
OT Parkin	34.3	2	179	6	29.83	2-44	-
AG Wharf	27	0	164	5	32.80	3-39	-
SD Thomas	60.4	2	339	10	33.90	3-31	-

GLOUCESTERSHIRE

Batting	M	Inns	NO	HS	Runs	Av	100	50	c/st
IJ Harvey	10	9	1	68*	348	43.50	-	4	7
CM Spearman	15	14	0	107	542	38.71	1	4	3
MW Alleyne	14	13	2	93	423	38.45	-	3	5
MGN Windows	12	12	1	112*	333	30.27	1	1	2
J Lewis	6	4	2	27*	51	25.50	-	-	-
JN Snape	9	8	2	38*	137	22.83	-	-	2
APR Gidman	10	8	1	48	137	19.57	-	-	4
MCJ Ball	11	7	2	45	81	16.20	-	-	4
RC Russell	15	10	1	42	138	15.33	-	-	21/5
THC Hancock	7	6	0	45	86	14.33	-	-	3
MA Hardinges	6	6	2	29	51	12.75	-	-	3
J Angel	3	2	1	10*	12	12.00	-	-	-
KJ Barnett	7	7	0	66	82	11.71	-	1	4
AM Smith	13	6	4	12*	22	11.00	-	-	3
CG Taylor	10	9	0	23	97	10.77	-	-	2
JMM Averis	12	7	3	20*	34	8.50	-	-	3
ID Fisher	3	3	1	6	10	5.00	-	-	-

Also batted (1 match): AN Bressington 22; RJ Silence 11.

NATIONAL LEAGUE AVERAGES

GLOUCESTERSHIRE cont.

Bowling	O	M	Runs	W	Av	Best	4i
AM Smith	100.1	14	353	24	14.70	5-30	1
IJ Harvey	68.4	5	288	17	16.94	4-41	1
MCJ Ball	66.2	1	273	15	18.20	4-15	1
J Lewis	49	6	231	9	25.66	4-22	1
MW Alleyne	82	2	337	13	25.92	3-30	-
JMM Averis	87	3	438	16	27.37	3-44	-
JN Snape	35	3	140	5	28.00	2-36	-
MA Hardinges	45	2	202	5	40.40	2-37	-

Also bowled: J Angel 25-1-118-4; AN Bressington 2-0-22-0; ID Fisher 21.1-0-111-3; APR Gidman 7-0-46-3.

HAMPSHIRE

Batting	M	Inns	NO	HS	Runs	Av	100	50	c/st
N Pothas	13	12	7	53*	280	56.00	-	2	19/1
JD Francis	10	10	2	103*	339	42.37	1	2	2
WS Kendall	15	14	2	110*	367	30.58	1	1	5
JS Laney	7	7	0	71	197	28.14	-	1	1
NC Johnson	15	15	0	92	408	27.20	-	3	13
JP Crawley	9	9	0	52	211	23.44	-	1	1
DA Kenway	8	8	0	50	164	20.50	-	1	2
SD Udal	15	13	3	58	197	19.70	-	2	4
AD Mascarenhas	15	14	3	39*	171	15.54	-	-	3
GW White	7	7	0	30	99	14.14	-	-	3
AD Mullally	8	5	3	9*	19	9.50	-	-	1
JHK Adams	3	3	0	17	28	9.33	-	-	2
CT Tremlett	9	7	2	18	44	8.80	-	-	3
JRC Hamblin	6	6	0	13	34	5.66	-	-	2
RA Smith	2	2	0	8	11	5.50	-	-	2
LR Prittipaul	12	9	1	20	43	5.37	-	-	-
JA Tomlinson	9	4	2	6	7	3.50	-	-	1

Also batted (2 matches): I Brunnschweiler 0 (3ct).

Bowling	O	M	Runs	W	Av	Best	4i
CT Tremlett	62.1	6	240	13	18.46	4-25	1
AD Mascarenhas	126.2	13	506	24	21.08	5-27	3
SD Udal	104.2	2	467	17	27.47	4-31	1
JA Tomlinson	65.2	3	319	10	31.90	2-15	-
NC Johnson	77	3	396	12	33.00	3-42	-
AD Mullally	65	7	244	7	34.85	2-17	-
LR Prittipaul	68.1	3	356	9	39.55	3-33	-

Also bowled: JHK Adams 0.1-0-6-0; JRC Hamblin 17-0-107-2; WS Kendall 9-0-57-1.

KENT

Batting	M	Inns	NO	HS	Runs	Av	100	50	c/st
MJ Walker	13	13	2	94	444	40.36	-	3	2
RWT Key	13	13	1	114	483	40.25	1	3	2
SR Waugh	5	5	1	59*	159	39.75	-	2	2
JM Golding	12	8	4	47*	128	32.00	-	-	3
PA Nixon	16	16	4	60	341	28.41	-	1	20/6
MA Ealham	13	12	1	75	291	26.45	-	2	4
MV Fleming	14	14	0	68	332	23.71	-	2	3
ET Smith	6	6	0	83	134	22.33	-	1	-
DP Fulton	10	10	1	41*	192	21.33	-	-	2
JB Hockley	11	11	0	58	213	19.36	-	1	6
GO Jones	7	7	2	28	96	19.20	-	-	1
A Symonds	11	11	0	46	195	17.72	-	-	6
AGR Loudon	2	2	0	21	32	16.00	-	-	-
DD Masters	8	5	3	8*	30	15.00	-	-	-
Amjad Khan	3	2	0	21	27	13.50	-	-	-
MM Patel	3	2	1	12*	13	13.00	-	-	1
JC Tredwell	11	9	4	3*	10	2.00	-	-	4
MJ Saggers	13	5	2	4*	6	2.00	-	-	5
BJ Trott	4	3	1	1*	1	0.50	-	-	-

Did not bat in one match: JP Hewitt.

Bowling	O	M	Runs	W	Av	Best	4i
JM Golding	72	4	324	18	18.00	3-23	-
MA Ealham	95.1	5	397	20	19.85	3-18	-
MJ Saggers	104.1	8	467	20	23.35	4-37	1
A Symonds	39.2	1	192	8	24.00	2-23	-
JC Tredwell	53.5	2	265	11	24.09	3-28	-
MV Fleming	97.2	6	419	14	29.92	4-22	1
DD Masters	51	2	282	6	47.00	5-20	1

Also bowled: Amjad Khan 20-1-100-3; JP Hewitt 2-0-20-1; MM Patel 21.2-4-80-4; BJ Trott 32-1-183-3; SR Waugh 10-0-74-2.

NATIONAL LEAGUE AVERAGES

LANCASHIRE

Batting	M	Inns	NO	HS	Runs	Av	100	50	c/st
SG Law	12	12	1	133	561	51.00	1	4	2
MJ Chilton	15	14	1	84*	453	34.84	-	4	4
CP Schofield	10	9	2	52	188	26.85	-	1	2
KW Hogg	12	8	3	24	103	20.60	-	-	3
WK Hegg	12	10	1	54	167	18.55	-	1	15/1
AJ Swann	7	6	0	61	109	18.16	-	1	-
GD Lloyd	12	11	2	41	160	17.77	-	-	6
D Byas	12	11	0	78	193	17.54	-	1	7
G Yates	5	5	1	32	61	15.25	-	-	1
G Chapple	14	12	2	33	125	12.50	-	-	-
PJ Martin	12	7	3	23*	47	11.75	-	-	3
J Wood	13	7	3	13	46	11.50	-	-	3
JJ Haynes	3	2	1	7*	9	9.00	-	-	8/1
RC Driver	5	4	0	25	30	7.50	-	-	-
NH Fairbrother	10	9	0	14	34	3.77	-	-	1

Also batted (2 matches): A Flintoff 3, 1; TW Roberts 0, 14 (1ct).
Also batted (1 match): G Keedy 10*; TM Rees 7* (1ct); MP Smethurst 1*.
Did not bat in two matches: JM Anderson.
Did not bat in one match: SI Mahmood.

Bowling	O	M	Runs	W	Av	Best	4i
JM Anderson	18	3	83	5	16.60	3-42	-
PJ Martin	90	11	310	18	17.22	3-18	-
J Wood	103	5	418	22	19.00	5-49	1
KW Hogg	79.5	6	343	15	22.86	4-20	1
G Chapple	94.4	8	417	11	37.90	3-26	-
CP Schofield	53.1	1	286	6	47.66	2-38	-

Also bowled: MJ Chilton 25.4-0-121-3; RC Driver 35-2-162-0; NH Fairbrother 2-0-17-0; A Flintoff 10-0-60-1; G Keedy 14-0-78-3; SG Law 8.2-0-41-3; SI Mahmood 8-0-31-0; MP Smethurst 6-0-45-0; AJ Swann 1-0-16-0 ; G Yates 34-2-149-2.

LEICESTERSHIRE

Batting	M	Inns	NO	HS	Runs	Av	100	50	c/st
MG Bevan	5	5	2	66*	182	60.66	-	1	1
DI Stevens	16	15	0	125	651	43.40	1	5	5
IJ Sutcliffe	16	16	3	104*	512	39.38	1	4	3
AS Wright	4	2	1	20	38	38.00	-	-	-
PAJ DeFreitas	13	12	4	49	237	29.62	-	-	-
VJ Wells	10	10	0	68	256	25.60	-	2	3
DL Maddy	15	14	5	50*	225	25.00	-	1	5
DG Brandy	2	2	0	35	50	25.00	-	-	-
MJA Whiley	12	5	4	14*	25	25.00	-	-	4
ND Burns	16	15	2	40	308	23.69	-	-	15/5
CE Dagnall	5	3	0	28	58	19.33	-	-	-
TR Ward	16	16	1	91	285	19.00	-	2	10
RJ Cunliffe	8	5	0	28	70	14.00	-	-	3
GW Flower	3	2	0	19	22	11.00	-	-	-
CD Crowe	14	6	2	8	22	5.50	-	-	3
JO Grove	14	6	1	13	22	4.40	-	-	4

Also batted (2 matches): J Srinath 2* (3ct).
Also batted (1 match): DS Brignull 1; Mohammad Kaif 60* (1ct).
Did not bat in two matches: DE Malcolm.
Did not bat in one match: RD Stemp.

Bowling	O	M	Runs	W	Av	Best	4i
PAJ DeFreitas	95.2	9	342	18	19.00	4-24	1
JO Grove	104	8	481	17	28.29	3-29	-
CE Dagnall	41	2	179	6	29.83	3-56	-
CD Crowe	90.2	0	484	16	30.25	3-40	-
VJ Wells	66.2	4	291	9	32.33	2-17	-
DL Maddy	88.2	3	461	9	51.22	4-36	1
MJA Whiley	60.2	3	321	6	53.50	2-37	-

Also bowled: MG Bevan 6-0-38-2; DS Brignull 9-0-52-2; GW Flower 14.2-0-62-1; DE Malcolm 18-2-96-3; J Srinath 18-2-48-3; RD Stemp 7-1-39-1; DI Stevens 22-1-114-2.

MIDDLESEX

Batting	M	Inns	NO	HS	Runs	Av	100	50	c/st
NRD Compton	4	4	3	86*	123	123.00	-	1	5
OA Shah	13	12	1	110	439	39.90	1	2	5
DC Nash	9	6	3	32*	111	37.00	-	-	10/-
AJ Strauss	12	11	0	74	356	32.36	-	4	1
BL Hutton	9	8	1	71*	177	25.28	-	2	3
JWM Dalrymple	11	10	1	52	227	25.22	-	1	8
CB Keegan	11	5	4	12*	20	20.00	-	-	3
PN Weekes	15	13	4	53*	159	17.66	-	1	8

NATIONAL LEAGUE AVERAGES

MIDDLESEX cont.

Batting	M	Inns	NO	HS	Runs	Av	100	50	c/st
EC Joyce	14	13	0	58	224	17.23	-	1	5
AW Laraman	8	7	1	28	82	13.66	-	-	-
SG Koenig	12	11	1	43*	104	10.40	-	-	3
SJ Cook	12	9	1	21	76	9.50	-	-	2
Abdur Razzaq	8	6	0	24	49	8.16	-	-	1
RMS Weston	3	3	0	21	22	7.33	-	-	-
TF Bloomfield	5	4	1	10	16	5.33	-	-	3
D Alleyne	7	6	1	12	26	5.20	-	-	3/-

Also batted in 7 matches: I Jones 6 (3ct).
Also batted (3 matches): TA Hunt 0 (1ct).
Also batted in one match: MJ Brown 18; AJ Coleman 14* (1ct).

Bowling	O	M	Runs	W	Av	Best	4i
TF Bloomfield	39	2	170	8	21.25	3-28	-
Abdur Razzaq	55.1	5	236	11	21.45	3-19	-
PN Weekes	95.5	7	441	19	23.21	3-17	-
SJ Cook	83	5	367	12	30.58	3-28	-
JWM Dalrymple	59	1	306	10	30.60	2-25	-
CB Keegan	87.2	7	416	13	32.00	2-22	-
I Jones	41.1	1	211	6	35.16	2-32	-
AW Laraman	50	4	251	7	35.85	2-25	-
BL Hutton	38	0	226	6	37.66	2-34	-

Also bowled: AJ Coleman 3-0-31-0; NRD Compton 5-0-20-0; TA Hunt 15-0-80-1.

NORTHAMPTONSHIRE

Batting	M	Inns	NO	HS	Runs	Av	100	50	c/st
MEK Hussey	10	10	2	110	394	49.25	1	3	6
TMB Bailey	15	11	6	44*	217	43.40	-	-	19/6
MB Loye	12	12	2	101*	410	41.00	1	2	2
MJ Powell	2	2	0	64	66	33.00	-	1	-
AL Penberthy	15	13	3	64	329	32.90	-	3	5
DJG Sales	15	14	0	93	459	32.78	-	5	7
DM Cousins	10	2	1	21	30	30.00	-	-	4
JW Cook	15	13	1	102	356	29.66	1	1	3
ME Cassar	9	8	1	54	177	25.28	-	1	3
RSG Anderson	2	2	1	22	23	23.00	-	-	-
JF Brown	13	4	3	16	17	17.00	-	-	1
GL Brophy	4	4	0	54	61	15.25	-	1	2
DE Paynter	2	2	0	18	29	14.50	-	-	-
RA White	5	5	0	18	70	14.00	-	-	-
RJ Warren	3	3	1	17	26	13.00	-	-	1
GP Swann	11	9	1	19	66	8.25	-	-	3
CG Greenidge	12	7	0	20	45	6.42	-	-	3
MWH Inness	5	3	1	2*	4	2.00	-	-	-

Also batted (3 matches): MJ Cawdron 0*, 0 .
Also batted (1 match): MS Panesar 16*.
Did not bat in one match: JAR Blain.

Bowling	O	M	Runs	W	Av	Best	4i
JW Cook	78.5	0	385	22	17.50	4-35	1
DM Cousins	63.2	6	257	14	18.35	5-22	2
GP Swann	42.5	0	194	9	21.55	3-16	-
CG Greenidge	90.3	10	448	17	26.35	3-22	-
AL Penberthy	123	9	473	16	29.56	3-31	-
JF Brown	95.4	7	406	13	31.23	3-30	-
MWH Inness	43	3	197	5	39.40	2-28	-

Also bowled: RSG Anderson 11-0-71-4; JAR Blain 9-0-42-1; ME Cassar 19.5-0-116-1;
MJ Cawdron 22-1-137-2; MS Panesar 9-0-26-0; DE Paynter 2-0-27-1; RA White 6-0-37-2.

NOTTINGHAMSHIRE

Batting	M	Inns	NO	HS	Runs	Av	100	50	c/st
KP Pietersen	11	10	2	147	515	64.37	2	1	6
DJ Bicknell	7	6	0	64	199	33.16	-	2	1
N Boje	9	8	0	86	251	31.37	-	2	5
Usman Afzaal	13	12	0	75	370	30.83	-	3	1
JER Gallian	12	12	1	91	307	27.90	-	2	2
PJ Franks	9	7	2	60	131	26.20	-	1	1
CMW Read	15	13	1	69	297	24.75	-	1	12/7
BM Shafayat	9	9	0	66	219	24.33	-	1	4
MN Malik	6	4	3	11	17	17.00	-	-	3
SJ Randall	11	7	3	25	67	16.75	-	-	4
P Johnson	12	10	0	36	151	15.10	-	-	-
WR Smith	3	2	0	16	25	12.50	-	-	1
AJ Harris	10	6	3	16*	34	11.33	-	-	1
GE Welton	7	7	0	18	68	9.71	-	-	4

NATIONAL LEAGUE AVERAGES

NOTTINGHAMSHIRE cont.

Batting	M	Inns	NO	HS	Runs	Av	100	50	c/st
RJ Logan	8	4	1	15	24	8.00	-	-	3
GJ Smith	7	6	1	16*	33	6.60	-	-	-
SCG MacGill	4	3	1	6	12	6.00	-	-	3
DS Lucas	7	3	1	8	8	4.00	-	-	1

Also batted (1 match): GD Clough 22; S Patel 18; CE Shreck 1* (1ct).

Bowling	O	M	Runs	W	Av	Best	4i
CE Shreck	9	1	35	5	7.00	5-35	1
DS Lucas	49	3	289	12	24.08	3-13	-
BM Shafayat	36.4	1	194	8	24.25	4-35	1
Usman Afzaal	24	0	169	6	28.16	3-48	-
N Boje	74	4	328	11	29.81	2-26	-
GJ Smith	58	8	283	9	31.44	3-41	-
PJ Franks	60.2	1	350	10	35.00	3-31	-
SJ Randall	88	2	399	8	49.87	2-37	-
RJ Logan	54	3	359	6	59.83	2-31	-
AJ Harris	73.5	3	457	6	76.16	2-47	-

Also bowled: GD Clough 3-0-28-0; SCG MacGill 29-1-125-3; MN Malik 37-1-229-1;
S Patel 8-1-44-3; KP Pietersen 14.1-0-106-2.

SOMERSET

Batting	M	Inns	NO	HS	Runs	Av	100	50	c/st
KA Parsons	13	13	1	73	383	31.91	-	3	7
RJ Turner	14	13	5	53*	246	30.75	-	1	17/6
M Burns	12	12	1	54*	330	30.00	-	4	8
J Cox	10	10	0	99	298	29.80	-	3	3
MJ Wood	13	12	1	88*	324	29.45	-	3	3
ID Blackwell	13	13	0	79	312	24.00	-	3	1
PCL Holloway	8	8	1	112*	163	23.28	1	-	-
GD Rose	3	3	1	20*	43	21.50	-	-	3
SRG Francis	10	6	3	27	64	21.33	-	-	-
ME Trescothick	2	2	0	41	41	20.50	-	-	1
KP Dutch	15	14	3	64	210	19.09	-	1	10
PD Bowler	11	11	0	53	198	18.00	-	1	5
MPL Bulbeck	11	6	2	24*	71	17.75	-	-	-
AV Suppiah	4	4	0	22	45	11.25	-	-	1
PS Jones	12	9	5	10	36	9.00	-	-	2
PD Trego	6	5	1	24	36	9.00	-	-	1
AR Caddick	2	2	0	11	15	7.50	-	-	-

Also batted (2 matches): WJ Durston 0, 0; RL Johnson 25.
Also batted (1 match) PW Jarvis 0. Did not bat in one match: M Parsons.

Bowling	O	M	Runs	W	Av	Best	4i
RL Johnson	16	1	60	5	12.00	3-41	-
PD Trego	26	3	140	6	23.33	3-14	-
MPL Bulbeck	74	5	378	16	23.62	4-39	1
PS Jones	87.4	5	532	22	24.18	4-72	1
M Burns	25	0	150	6	25.00	3-22	-
SRG Francis	70	5	384	13	29.53	4-60	1
ID Blackwell	69.1	4	384	11	34.90	4-24	1
KP Dutch	99.4	4	457	12	38.08	2-0	-

Also bowled: AR Caddick 18-1-86-2; WJ Durston 2-0-19-0; PW Jarvis 8-0-54-2;
KA Parsons 54-2-253-4; M Parsons 5-1-26-0; GD Rose 23-1-110-2; AV Suppiah 11-0-62-2.

SURREY

Batting	M	Inns	NO	HS	Runs	Av	100	50	c/st
MR Ramprakash	15	15	3	87*	537	44.75	-	5	3
R Clarke	11	11	2	98*	316	35.11	-	3	5
AJ Hollioake	12	10	2	42*	214	26.75	-	-	9
N Shahid	15	14	3	74*	293	26.63	-	2	4
AD Brown	15	15	0	94	392	26.13	-	4	7
ESH Giddins	14	7	6	13*	26	26.00	-	-	4
SA Newman	3	3	0	37	71	23.66	-	-	-
IJ Ward	15	15	0	62	335	22.33	-	2	3
JN Batty	13	8	1	30	116	16.57	-	-	19/2
IDK Salisbury	9	7	2	21	80	16.00	-	-	5
MA Carberry	3	3	1	19	28	14.00	-	-	2
Saqlain Mushtaq	5	5	1	28	51	12.75	-	-	2
MP Bicknell	9	7	1	19*	58	9.66	-	-	1
AJ Stewart	3	3	0	11	27	9.00	-	-	6/1
PJ Sampson	3	2	0	16	17	8.50	-	-	-
TJ Murtagh	9	6	2	14*	32	8.00	-	-	3
AJ Tudor	5	3	1	6	11	5.50	-	-	-

Also batted (2 matches): JD Ratcliffe 53.
Also batted (1 match): RM Amin 0*; JGE Benning 10; GP Butcher 9; DR Miller 1;

NATIONAL LEAGUE AVERAGES

SURREY cont.

Mushtaq Ahmed 16; BJM Scott 4; GP Thorpe 114; DM Ward 78 (1ct).
Did not bat in two matches: J Ormond (1ct). Did not bat in one match: Azhar Mahmood.

Bowling	O	M	Runs	W	Av	Best	4i
AJ Hollioake	64.2	2	319	23	13.86	5-43	3
JD Ratcliffe	17	0	85	6	14.16	4-44	1
ESH Giddins	107	10	435	30	14.50	5-20	2
MP Bicknell	70.1	10	267	15	17.80	5-26	1
TJ Murtagh	77.3	3	353	13	27.15	3-38	-
IDK Salisbury	49.1	0	236	7	33.71	3-44	-
Saqlain Mushtaq	68	4	242	6	40.33	1-17	-
R Clarke	59.2	3	306	7	43.71	2-32	-

Also bowled: RM Amin 3-0-33-0; Azhar Mahmood 1.4-0-10-1; JGE Benning 7-0-58-2;
GP Butcher 7-0-49-2; DR Miller 7-0-32-0; Mushtaq Ahmed 9-2-19-1; J Ormond 9-0-25-0; MR
Ramprakash 5.2-0-32-2; PJ Sampson 17-0-100-3; AJ Tudor 33-1-169-2; IJ Ward 1-0-8-0.

SUSSEX

Batting	M	Inns	NO	HS	Runs	Av	100	50	c/st
KJ Innes	12	8	3	50*	193	38.60	-	1	3
CJ Adams	10	10	1	64*	303	33.66	-	2	6
MW Goodwin	16	15	2	76*	350	26.92	-	2	6
RSC Martin-Jenkins	16	12	1	50	206	18.72	-	1	2
MJ Prior	10	8	0	73	141	17.62	-	1	4/1
MJG Davis	15	10	3	28	116	16.57	-	-	5
MH Yardy	6	6	1	31	82	16.40	-	-	2
RR Montgomerie	14	14	2	31	178	14.83	-	-	4
PA Cottey	8	7	0	43	101	14.42	-	-	1
WJ House	13	12	2	31	138	13.80	-	-	4
B Zuiderent	5	4	0	39	53	13.25	-	-	-
RJ Kirtley	9	4	2	19*	26	13.00	-	-	1
TR Ambrose	12	10	1	33*	113	12.55	-	-	9/-
MA Robinson	5	4	2	7*	15	7.50	-	-	-
CD Hopkinson	2	2	0	12	14	7.00	-	-	1
PM Hutchison	2	2	0	12	13	6.50	-	-	2
JR Carpenter	2	2	0	8	11	5.50	-	-	2
BV Taylor	16	9	2	16	22	3.14	-	-	2
JD Lewry	2	2	1	1	1	1.00	-	-	2

Also batted (1 match): NRK Turk 36.

Bowling	O	M	Runs	W	Av	Best	4i
BV Taylor	107.2	12	416	22	18.90	4-22	2
RJ Kirtley	57.2	8	229	12	19.08	3-49	-
MJG Davis	105.2	4	423	17	24.88	3-40	-
KJ Innes	62.1	5	284	10	28.40	4-26	1
MA Robinson	28	3	201	6	33.50	2-38	-
RSC Martin-Jenkins	107.5	19	384	11	34.90	2-21	-

Also bowled: CJ Adams 2-0-15-0; PA Cottey 12-0-50-0; CD Hopkinson 2-0-16-1;
PM Hutchison 15-1-76-3; WJ House 10.5-0-40-2; JD Lewry 13.2-1-66-1; MH Yardy 23-1-107-4.

WARWICKSHIRE

Batting	M	Inns	NO	HS	Runs	Av	100	50	c/st
SM Pollock	10	8	3	111*	332	66.40	1	1	4
DP Ostler	13	13	2	103*	465	42.27	1	2	5
TL Penney	6	5	1	50	132	33.00	-	1	-
IR Bell	14	13	1	86	369	30.75	-	3	1
JO Troughton	10	10	3	66*	215	30.71	-	1	1
MA Wagh	6	6	0	84	181	30.16	-	1	-
T Frost	6	3	2	17	29	29.00	-	-	7/-
DR Brown	15	11	1	82*	263	26.30	-	2	1
NV Knight	10	10	0	86	255	25.50	-	1	3
MJ Powell	13	11	1	39	219	21.90	-	-	11
NM Carter	11	11	4	24	86	12.28	-	-	3
NMK Smith	15	12	3	23*	104	11.55	-	-	2
KJ Piper	7	5	1	17	46	11.50	-	-	8/4
A Richardson	4	2	1	8	9	9.00	-	-	1
MA Sheikh	11	5	2	9	15	5.00	-	-	-
AF Giles	4	2	1	2	3	3.00	-	-	1

Also batted (3 matches): IJ Clifford 1 (5ct); GG Wagg 2 (2ct).
Also batted (1 match): HR Jones 6; NA Warren 2.
Did not bat in one match: SE Bond; DW Fleming.

Bowling	O	M	Runs	W	Av	Best	4i
SM Pollock	79.2	10	273	21	13.00	4-36	1
GG Wagg	22	1	106	6	17.66	4-50	1
MJ Powell	35	1	203	8	25.37	3-44	-

NATIONAL LEAGUE AVERAGES

WARWICKSHIRE cont.

Bowling	O	M	Runs	W	Av	Best	4i
NM Carter	83.4	4	440	17	25.88	5-31	1
DR Brown	111.2	7	551	19	29.00	3-43	-
MA Sheikh	83	5	411	12	34.25	2-19	-
NMK Smith	90.3	2	451	13	34.69	3-25	-

Also bowled: SE Bond 9-2-32-0; DW Fleming 4-0-25-0; AF Giles 29.1-1-127-4;
A Richardson 29-1-178-3; MA Wagh 15-0-71-0; NA Warren 5-0-34-3.

WORCESTERSHIRE

Batting	M	Inns	NO	HS	Runs	Av	100	50	c/st
BF Smith	16	15	5	92*	654	65.40	-	7	5
GA Hick	15	14	2	141*	482	40.16	1	2	6
VS Solanki	16	15	1	119*	555	39.64	1	4	8
S Lee	3	2	0	41	77	38.50	-	-	1
A Singh	11	10	1	75*	282	31.33	-	2	2
DA Leatherdale	16	13	1	66	347	28.91	-	3	1
SJ Rhodes	12	7	3	42	94	23.50	-	-	10/4
GJ Batty	16	13	3	54*	206	20.60	-	1	5
SR Lampitt	14	6	5	10*	20	20.00	-	-	1
SD Peters	9	8	0	29	107	13.37	-	-	2
Kabir Ali	16	9	2	24	86	12.28	-	-	2
DJ Pipe	4	4	1	20	36	12.00	-	-	3/4
MS Mason	9	3	1	6	11	5.50	-	-	1
AJ Bichel	5	3	0	12	13	4.33	-	-	2

Also batted (7 matches): A Sheriyar 0*. Also batted (3 matches): AA Donald 0.
Also batted (1 match): Kadeer Ali 57; MJ Rawnsley 1*. Did not bat in one match: DC Catterall.

Bowling	O	M	Runs	W	Av	Best	4i
DA Leatherdale	63.3	4	283	15	18.86	5-9	1
AJ Bichel	37.4	2	152	7	21.71	3-30	-
MS Mason	58.5	3	250	11	22.72	3-37	-
Kabir Ali	109	9	557	21	26.52	5-36	2
SR Lampitt	97.1	9	419	15	27.93	3-33	-
GJ Batty	78	0	414	13	31.84	4-36	1
DA Leatherdale	63.3	4	458	14	32.71	5-9	2
A Sheriyar	47.2	3	229	7	32.71	3-30	-

Also bowled: AA Donald 15.4-3-54-2; GA Hick 6-0-37-1; S Lee 3-0-39-0;
MJ Rawnsley 11.4-0-39-3; BF Smith 2-0-15-0; VS Solanki 2-0-17-0.

YORKSHIRE

Batting	M	Inns	NO	HS	Runs	Av	100	50	c/st
MTG Elliott	5	5	3	115*	266	88.66	2	-	-
DS Lehmann	7	7	1	104	354	59.00	1	3	4
SM Katich	2	2	1	39*	39	39.00	-	-	2
A McGrath	14	13	2	85*	376	34.18	-	3	4
RJ Blakey	15	12	4	60	246	30.75	-	1	17/5
GM Fellows	15	12	4	50	243	30.37	-	1	6
C White	11	11	0	64	309	28.09	-	1	2
MJ Lumb	11	11	1	73	275	27.50	-	1	5
CEW Silverwood	7	7	0	58	182	26.00	-	2	2
MJ Wood	15	13	1	105*	258	21.50	1	-	8
RJ Sidebottom	12	6	4	30*	36	18.00	-	-	2
VJ Craven	6	6	0	59	105	17.50	-	1	1
TJ Bresnan	13	7	3	22	53	13.25	-	-	1
RKJ Dawson	13	10	0	41	100	10.00	-	-	1
MP Vaughan	3	3	0	20	20	6.66	-	-	-
AKD Gray	5	2	0	6	7	3.50	-	-	1
SP Kirby	4	2	0	1	2	1.00	-	-	-

Also batted (3 matches): MJ Hoggard 0 (1ct); ND Thornicroft 0* (1ct).
Also batted (1 match): CJ Elstub 4*.

Bowling	O	M	Runs	W	Av	Best	4i
MJ Hoggard	27	5	100	7	14.28	3-44	-
C White	43.2	1	204	14	14.57	5-19	1
AKD Gray	25	1	131	7	18.71	4-37	1
RKJ Dawson	66	0	333	13	25.61	4-36	1
CEW Silverwood	51	6	227	8	28.37	3-15	-
DS Lehmann	42	0	206	7	29.42	2-23	-
A McGrath	56	3	259	7	37.00	3-39	-
TT Bresnan	78.5	4	389	10	38.90	2-27	-
RJ Sidebottom	75	7	344	8	43.00	2-27	-
GM Fellows	33.5	2	220	5	44.00	4-19	1

Also bowled: VJ Craven 2-0-21-1; CJ Elstub 7-2-31-1; SP Kirby 33.4-1-197-3;
ND Thornicroft 15-2-89-3.

BENSON AND HEDGES CUP
By Mark Baldwin

NORTH DIVISION

28 April 2002
at Trent Bridge
Yorkshire 225 (47.4 overs) (DS Lehmann 89, GJ Smith 5 for 39)
Nottinghamshire 68 for 3 (13 overs)
Yorkshire (2 pts) won by 2 runs (DL Method: Yorkshire target 71 from 13 overs)
Gold Award: GJ Smith

at Derby
Lancashire 17 for 2 (4.3 overs)
Derbyshire did not bat
Match abandoned – 1 pt each

Yorkshire held their nerve to deny Nottinghamshire, and Lance Klusener, in a match finally decided on the Duckworth-Lewis method at Trent Bridge. Yorkshire had first been bowled out for 225, wastefully leaving 14 balls unbowled, their total mainly due to a fifth-wicket stand of 109 between Darren Lehmann (89) and Anthony McGrath (48). Notts had then scored 35 for 1 from eight overs when more rain meant a final target of 71 from 13 overs. Richard Dawson, entrusted with two of the remaining five overs, had Jason Gallian stumped and conceded just seven runs – but Klusener, on his one-day debut for Notts, then pulled Craig White for six. In a breathless finish, the big-hitting Klusener was faced with needing a four from the final ball. He swung, but could only edge White for a single.

Only 4.3 overs were possible at Derby, with Lancashire limping to 17 for 2 as Kevin Dean and Dominic Cork each struck blows with the new ball. However, following six inspections, the match was abandoned at 3.50pm.

29 April 2002
at Leicester
Leicestershire 316 for 6 (50 overs) (TR Ward 127, MG Bevan 113)
Durham 284 for 8 (50 overs) (N Peng 67, GD Bridge 50*)
Leicestershire (2 pts) won by 32 runs
Gold Award: TR Ward

Trevor Ward and Michael Bevan each hit punishing centuries as Leicestershire beat Durham by 32 runs in a high-scoring affair at Grace Road. Ward hit 127 and Bevan, who reached three figures from 96 balls,

113, and their partnership of 206 for the second wicket was the considerable base upon which Leicestershire eventually totalled 316 for 6. Nicky Peng responded with a fine 67 and Graeme Bridge, at the other end of the innings, finished with 50 not out. But Durham, despite totalling 284 for 8 themselves, were never in the hunt.

30 April 2002
at Trent Bridge
Derbyshire 72 for 7 (10 overs)
Nottinghamshire 75 for 0 (8.2 overs)
Nottinghamshire (2 pts) won by ten wickets
Gold Award: GJ Smith

After a 4.55pm start, following rain, Nottinghamshire trounced Derbyshire by ten wickets in a match reduced to the minimum ten overs per side. Derbyshire's total of 72 for 7 looked reasonably competitive, despite impressive left-arm paceman Greg Smith hitting the stumps three times in five deliveries with searing yorkers. But then Chris Read and Lance Klusener, with 35 and 39 not out respectively, knocked off the runs with ten balls to spare.

1 May 2002
at Headingley
Leicestershire 221 for 7 (46 overs) (IJ Sutcliffe 65)
Yorkshire 214 for 8 (45 overs) (C White 93)
Leicestershire (2 pts) won by 6 runs (DL Method: Yorkshire target 221 from 45 overs)
Gold Award: MG Bevan

at Chester-le-Street
Durham 166 for 7 (44 overs)
Lancashire 154 (41 overs)
Durham (2 pts) won by 16 runs (DL Method: Lancashire target 171 from 42 overs)
Gold Award: GD Bridge

Leicestershire went to the top of the group with a gutsy and exciting six-run win against Yorkshire at Headingley. A third-wicket stand of 97 between Iain Sutcliffe and Michael Bevan, and a late thrash from Neil Burns, whose unbeaten 44 took just 29 balls, helped Leicestershire to 221 for 7 from the 46 overs that the weather allowed. Yorkshire, their own target slightly adjusted to 221 from 45 overs, were themselves boosted by a third-wicket partnership – Craig White (93) and Michael Lumb (43) adding 110. But Leicestershire, despite a weakened attack, kept chipping away with off spinner Carl Crowe impressive during a spell of 3 for 35 from eight overs. Yorkshire began the last five overs needing only 27 to win with six wickets in hand, but they lost vital wickets and White's dismissal, bowled by Bevan in the final over, sealed matters.

Durham displayed a similarly steely nerve in their tense, 16-run win over Lancashire at Chester-le-Street, bravely batting first on a tricky pitch and then refusing to panic despite being reduced to 20 for 3 and 67 for 6. An unbroken eighth-wicket stand of 58 between the aggressive Graeme Bridge (37 not out) and Michael Gough, who hit the final ball of the innings for six to reach an unbeaten 32, enabled Durham to total 166 for 7 from 44 overs. Lancashire, needing 171 following a Duckworth-Lewis recalculation, lost wickets regularly against a Durham attack in which seamers Neil Killeen and Mark Davies were outstanding. Killeen took 3 for 12 from eight overs and Davies an equally miserly 1 for 12 from nine to crank up the pressure, while Gold Award winner Bridge also picked up two important wickets with his left-arm spin as Lancashire were eventually dismissed for 154 with three overs remaining.

2 May 2002
at Chester-le-Street
Yorkshire 271 for 7 (50 overs) (DS Lehmann 72, C White 71)
Durham 147 (44.4 overs)
Yorkshire (2 pts) won by 124 runs
Gold Award: C White

Yorkshire overwhelmed Durham by 124 runs at Chester-le-Street to give themselves a good chance of qualification from the northern group. The respective scores at the 15-over mark tell the story of the match – Yorkshire 100 for 2, and then Durham 37 for 3. In the end, it was Yorkshire's 271 for 7 against Durham's 147 all out, and Craig White took the Gold Award by opening up with 71. Darren Lehmann then cruised to 72 and later took three cheapish wickets.

3 May 2002
at Old Trafford
Lancashire 297 for 5 (50 overs) (MJ Chilton 102, G Chapple 50)
Nottinghamshire 138 (26 overs) (J Wood 4 for 31)
Lancashire (2 pts) won by 76 runs (DL Method: Nottinghamshire target 215 from 27 overs)
Gold Award: MJ Chilton

at Derby
Leicestershire 119 for 2 (32 overs) (IJ Sutcliffe 52*)

Derbyshire 51 for 2 (5.1 overs)
Match abandoned – 1 pt each

Lancashire, thanks in the main to Mark Chilton's mature maiden one-day hundred, defeated both Nottinghamshire and the elements at Old Trafford to revive their hopes of quarter-final qualification. Chilton's 102, plus aggressive contributions from Glen Chapple, Stuart Law and Graham Lloyd, saw Lancashire to an imposing 50-over total of 297 for 5. Nottinghamshire's bowling was wayward and their ground-fielding sloppy, but their batting was little better when Duckworth-Lewis calculations left them needing 215 from 27 overs following a rainstorm between innings. A series of ill-judged swipes, resulting in boundary catches, saw them fall to 138 all out with John Wood (4 for 31) one of the chief beneficiaries.

Derbyshire were undone by the bad weather at Derby, where heavy drizzle caused the abandonment of their game against Leicestershire when they required just 31 more runs to win in 4.5 overs with

Mark Chilton scored his first one-day century in Lancashire's victory over Nottinghamshire.

eight wickets standing. Leicestershire had earlier been restricted to 119 for 2 from 32 overs and Derbyshire set out needing 82 from ten overs for victory. Dominic Hewson was 26 not out when the umpires deemed the conditions unplayable for the final time.

4 May 2002
at Derby
Yorkshire 288 for 6 (50 overs) (MJ Wood 115rh, C White 77)
Derbyshire 157 (37.3 overs) (SA Selwood 62, RKJ Dawson 4 for 13)
Yorkshire (2 pts) won by 131 runs
Gold Award: MJ Wood

at Trent Bridge
Nottinghamshire 224 for 6 (50 overs) (L Klusener 68, JER Gallian 56)
Durham 219 (49.4 overs) (N Peng 72, AJ Harris 4 for 42)
Nottinghamshire (2 pts) won by 5 runs
Gold Award: L Klusener

Matthew Wood, one of the successes of the National Academy in Australia the previous winter, emerged as a bloodied hero for Yorkshire in their 131-run win over Derbyshire at Derby. A fine 115, his maiden one-day hundred, was ended by a short ball from skiddy left-arm seamer Mohammad Ali which squeezed between the peak of his helmet and the grille to strike him a sickening blow near the left temple. Stretchered off and taken to the Derbyshire Royal Infirmary, where he had nine stitches, he returned in his blood-spattered whites to later pick up the Gold Award. With Craig White, his opening partner, hitting 77 from 79 balls, however, the match had been all but won when Wood was hurt and Yorkshire's 288 for 6 was too much for the home side. Steve Selwood offered some resistance with 62, but Chris Silverwood picked up three early wickets and Richard Dawson finished things off by taking 4 for 13 in 21 balls.

Lance Klusener signed off from his temporary Nottinghamshire overseas player duties by hitting an 89-ball 68 and then taking 2 for 31 from his ten overs as Durham were beaten by five runs in a tense finish at Trent Bridge. Klusener's power boosted the Notts total to 224 for 6 after Jason Gallian had laboured for 37 overs to make 56, and Chris Read contributed a handy 36 not out as he and Klusener added 68 at the end of the innings. Nicky Peng launched the Durham reply with another eye-

Matthew Wood made 115 before retiring hurt against Derbyshire.

catching knock, his 72 coming from 82 balls with 11 fours, but although Andrew Pratt scored 38, the Durham innings lost its way. In the end, six runs were needed from the last three balls and with the last-wicket pair at the crease. Andy Harris, however, proved too much for last man Steve Harmison, who was bowled for nought. Harris finished with 4 for 42, but Klusener was given the Gold Award.

5 May 2002
at Old Trafford
Leicestershire 175 for 9 (50 overs) (IJ Sutcliffe 58)
Lancashire 158 (47.2 overs) (VJ Wells 4 for 32, DL Maddy 4 for 34)
Leicestershire (2 pts) won by 17 runs
Gold Award: DL Maddy

On a dry Old Trafford pitch of uneven bounce, the medium pace of Darren Maddy and Vince Wells saw Leicestershire to a tense 17-run victory against Lancashire that put them back on top of the Northern Division table. Maddy took 4 for 34 and Wells 4 for 32 as Lancashire were bowled out for 158 in reply to Leicestershire's 175 for 9. There were still 16 balls of the match remaining when Wells had Chris Schofield caught at the wicket. Only two batsmen played anything approaching a dominant innings in the conditions – Iain Sutcliffe for Leicestershire with 58, his third successive half-century in the competition, and Andy Flintoff with 47 in his first county appearance of the season.

6 May 2002
at Headingley
Yorkshire 81 (27.2 overs) (A Flintoff 4 for 11)

Lancashire 82 for 2 (10.5 overs)
Lancashire (2 pts) won by eight wickets
Gold Award: G Chapple

at Leicester
Nottinghamshire 95 (21.4 overs)
Leicestershire 98 for 2 (18.1 overs)
Leicestershire (2 pts) won by eight wickets
Gold Award: CD Crowe

at Chester-le-Street
Derbyshire 172 (48.2 overs)
Durham 174 for 6 (46.5 overs) (PD Collingwood 51)
Durham (2 pts) won by four wickets
Gold Award: PD Collingwood

Lancashire squeezed into the quarter-finals by
thrashing Roses rivals Yorkshire – on the day that
former Tykes captain David Byas returned to
Headingley. Byas was there at the end, at 2.15pm,
when Lancashire completed an eight-wicket win with
the little matter of 39.1 overs to spare! Glen Chapple
thumped 42 in just 26 balls as Lancashire raced to their
victory target of 82. Yorkshire, bowled out for 81 in
27.2 overs, displayed a worrying lack of pride in their
performance – something which was so conspicuous
during the captaincy reign of Byas that had culminated
with the 2001 county championship title. Andy Flintoff
took 4 for 11 and John Wood 3 for 33.

Leicestershire topped the group, ahead of
Yorkshire, and the early finish at Leeds meant that
they already knew they had a guaranteed home tie in
the last eight before their match – a reduced affair of
22 overs per side – against Nottinghamshire could
get under way at 3.15pm. Nottinghamshire,
however, batted with such ineptitude that they were
bowled out for just 95 with two balls unbowled and
Leicestershire, mainly through Iain Sutcliffe and
Darren Stevens, had little trouble in knocking off
the runs required.

Paul Collingwood's 51 was one of the few bright
spots in an otherwise dull contest at Chester-le-
Street between two teams who could not progress in
the competition. Derbyshire totalled 172, with
Dominic Hewson top scorer with 46, and Durham
eventually got home with 19 balls to spare, despite
Tom Lungley's 3 for 29.

Midlands/West/Wales Division

28 April 2002
at Northampton
Glamorgan 122 (30.5 overs)

Northamptonshire 124 for 2 (26.1 overs)(MB Loye 53*)
Northamptonshire (2 pts) won by eight wickets
Gold Award: JW Cook

at Edgbaston
Warwickshire 263 for 6 (41 overs)(NV Knight 126*)
Somerset 78 for 5 (19 overs)
Warwickshire (2 pts) won by 94 runs (DL Method:
Somerset target 173 from 19 overs)
Gold Award: NV Knight

Glamorgan, beaten finalists in 2000, took their
miserable losing streak in the competition to seven
matches after being tumbled out for just 122 in 30.5
overs at Northampton. Five zonal defeats last season
were followed by this eight-wicket defeat as Mal
Loye led Northants to a sauntering victory with 53
not out. Poor batting was at the root of Glamorgan's
demise, with Tony Penberthy (3 for 6) and Jeff Cook
(3 for 19) the main beneficiaries.

Warwickshire, meanwhile, maintained their B and H
mastery over Somerset at Edgbaston – a sixth win
out of six meetings in the competition being built
around a magnificent, unbeaten 126 from Nick
Knight. On a tricky pitch, and after Somerset had

**Nick Knight on the way to another Benson and Hedges Gold
Award against Somerset.**

won the toss, Knight took 12 balls to get off the mark and nine overs to strike his first boundary. But then Knight struck 15 more and a soaring six, as Warwickshire reached an imposing 263 for 6 from their allotted 41 overs. Another weather interruption meant Somerset's target was reduced to 222, from 27 overs, but within four overs Dougie Brown and Shaun Pollock had shared three key wickets and Somerset's challenge was spent. There was still time, though, for a hailstorm and another recalculation, but, in the end, Somerset finished on 78 for 5 from 19 overs and Warwickshire were deserved winners by 94 runs.

29 April 2002
at Worcester
Worcestershire 70 (22 overs) (IJ Harvey 4 for 21, J Lewis 4 for 41)
Gloucestershire 71 for 4 (18.2 overs)
Gloucestershire (2 pts) won by six wickets
Gold Award: IJ Harvey

Gloucestershire humbled Worcestershire at New Road, with Ian Harvey and Jon Lewis taking dramatic advantage of seaming conditions after Mark Alleyne had won the toss by reducing the home side first to 14 for 6, then 28 for 7, and finally 40 for 8. James Averis and Alleyne himself then both claimed a wicket in their very first overs to leave Worcestershire a sorry 70 all out in just 22 overs. Harvey ended with 4 for 21 and Lewis 4 for 41 and the only Worcestershire player who could hold up his head at the end of a six-wicket defeat was Kabir Ali, who followed up his breezy 27 from No. 10 by taking 3 for 21 to make Gloucestershire sweat just a little before crossing the finishing line at 1.50pm. It was, by 22 minutes, the earliest finish to a match in the 31-year history of the Benson and Hedges Cup.

1 May 2002
at Bristol
Gloucestershire 240 for 6 (43 overs) (CG Taylor 93, MGN Windows 86)
Warwickshire 91 (28.4 overs) (IJ Harvey 4 for 12 including a hat-trick)
Gloucestershire (2 pts) won by 149 runs
Gold Award: CG Taylor

at Northampton
Northamptonshire 232 for 7 (50 overs) (MEK Hussey 58, AL Penberthy 53, JW Cook 50, AJ Bichel 4-38)
Worcestershire 233 for 5 (47.3 overs) (SD Peters 52, VS Solanki 50)

Worcestershire (2 pts) won by five wickets
Gold Award: AL Penberthy

Gloucestershire's quest to reach a fourth-successive Benson and Hedges Cup final was fortified further by an emphatic 149-run win over Warwickshire at Bristol. Batting first, Gloucestershire totalled 240 for 6 from 43 overs thanks mainly to a run-a-ball stand of 144 between the diminutive pair of Chris Taylor (93) and Matt Windows (86). Ian Harvey then dismantled the Warwickshire top order with a hat-trick – Nick Knight, Neil Smith and Ian Bell all edging his wobbly seamers – before having Dougie Brown caught at cover to leave the visitors down and out at 13 for 4. Jack Russell, who caught Knight and Bell standing up to the wicket and later snared Trevor Penney too, boosted Gloucestershire supporters further by announcing that he had signed an extension to his contract and committed himself to county cricket until the end of the 2004 season.

Andy Bichel just about outdid Tony Penberthy in the all-rounder stakes as Worcestershire overcame Northamptonshire by five wickets at Northampton. Bichel took 4 for 38 and then hit an unbeaten 27 as Worcestershire successfully overhauled Northants' 232 for 7 with 15 balls to spare. But Penberthy's 53 and 2 for 18 from ten overs still earned him the consolation of the Gold Award and, if Northants had not lost Ben Phillips to a shoulder injury after he had bowled just two overs, the result could have been different. Penberthy had added 68 for the sixth wicket with Jeff Cook (50) after Mike Hussey (58) had single-handedly glued together the first half of the innings. Worcestershire's reply was based on a fine opening stand of 95 between Stephen Peters and Vikram Solanki, who both scored half-centuries.

3 May 2002
at Cardiff
Glamorgan 171 for 8 (50 overs) (DL Hemp 62)
Gloucestershire 173 for 2 (29.1 overs) (CM Spearman 73)
Gloucestershire (2 pts) won by eight wickets
Gold Award: CM Spearman

at Taunton
Northamptonshire 299 for 6 (50 overs) (MEK Hussey 87, DJG Sales 76, MB Loye 56)
Somerset 154 (34.1 overs) (GP Swann 4 for 29)
Northamptonshire (2 pts) won by 145 runs
Gold Award: MEK Hussey

at Edgbaston
Warwickshire 130 (44.4 overs) (AJ Bichel 4 for 24)

Worcestershire 131 for 7 (48.3 overs) (A Richardson 4 for 21)
Worcestershire (2 pts) won by three wickets
Gold Award: DA Leatherdale

Gloucestershire made it three wins out of three with a crushing eight-wicket win over Glamorgan at Cardiff. Despite David Hemp's 62, Glamorgan were overwhelmed by the zest of Gloucestershire's out-cricket as they were restricted to 171 for 8 from their 50 overs. To make matters worse, Matthew Maynard retired hurt with a broken bone in his hand after being hit by a Mark Alleyne lifter. Ian Harvey took 3 for 32 and later added an unbeaten 29 as Gloucestershire reached their target in just 29.1 overs, but the visitors romped home, mainly due to Craig Spearman. The New Zealander with a Welsh mother and a British passport thumped the Welsh bowlers to all parts in his 60-ball 73.

Losing Jamie Cox to the third ball of their innings seemed to take all the fight out of Somerset at Taunton. On a batsman's paradise of a pitch, and against one of the less frightening of county attacks, they were bowled out for a pitiful 154 in reply to Northamptonshire's imposing 299 for 6, in which Mike Hussey led the way with 87, Mal Loye hit 56 and David Sales 76 off 73 balls that included a six which broke a window in the pavilion bar.

A poor pitch at Edgbaston made for a nail biter of a contest that was won, in the end, by Worcestershire's highly-experienced but unsung all-rounders David Leatherdale and Stuart Lampitt. Gloves were rapped all day as the seamers made the ball nip and lift from a surface offering both movement and inconsistent bounce, and Andy Bichel took 4 for 24 as Warwickshire were bowled out for 130. Ian Bell's 40 looked like being the top score in the match by some distance until Leatherdale was joined by Lampitt with Worcestershire seemingly in the mire at 73 for 7. Alan Richardson had taken 4 for 21, but Leatherdale and Lampitt held firm and, like some Chinese water torture, the drip-drip of runs began to bring the target closer. In the end, victory arrived with nine balls to spare – Leatherdale, 43 not out from 92 balls, won the Gold Award while Lampitt remained unbeaten on 20.

5 May 2002
at Bristol
Gloucestershire 270 for 5 (50 overs) (KJ Barnett 67)
Somerset 231 (45.5 overs) (M Burns 61, IJ Harvey 5 for 20)
Gloucestershire (2 pts) won by 39 runs
Gold Award: IJ Harvey

at Edgbaston
Northamptonshire 226 (48.5 overs) (MEK Hussey 84, MB Loye 57)
Warwickshire 228 for 4 (49.1 overs) (MJ Powell 101*, IR Bell 56)
Warwickshire (2 pts) won by six wickets
Gold Award: MJ Powell

at Worcester
Glamorgan 191 for 8 (50 overs)
Worcestershire 192 for 5 (39.4 overs) (VS Solanki 90)
Worcestershire (2 pts) won by five wickets
Gold Award: VS Solanki

Gloucestershire made it four wins out of four in this division by overpowering Somerset by 39 runs in the West Country derby at Bristol. A fine contest, full of runs, was settled when Ian Harvey returned for his second spell deep into the Somerset innings and took 3 for 6 in 11 balls to finish with overall figures of 5 for 20. Before Harvey's return, however, Somerset's seventh-wicket pair of Rob Turner and Keith Dutch had added 86 runs in nine overs to take the visitors to within 42 of Gloucestershire's challenging 270 for 7. Kim Barnett anchored the Gloucestershire innings with 67, but it was Mark Alleyne (47), Jeremy Snape and Martyn Ball who provided the late acceleration. Marcus Trescothick and Mike Burns (61) put on 83 for the Somerset third wicket.

Warwickshire kept alive their hopes of a quarter-final spot by beating Northamptonshire by six wickets at Edgbaston and moving past them into third place in the group table on run rate. Mike Powell, the young captain, was the Warwickshire hero with an unbeaten 101 – his maiden one-day century. Opener Powell put on 89 for the third wicket with Ian Bell (56) and then stayed to see the job through with five balls to spare. Earlier, Northants had batted sloppily to allow themselves to be bowled out for 226 – and with seven deliveries unused – following a second-wicket stand of 123 between Mike Hussey (84) and Mal Loye (57).

Worcestershire stayed second in the group table by romping to a five-wicket victory over hapless Glamorgan at New Road. Seamers Andy Bichel and Matt Mason, a fellow Australian who is 'English'-qualified due to his Irish links, undermined the Glamorgan innings by sharing six wickets, and only some lower-order resistance from Adrian Dale, Mark Wallace and Mike Kasprowicz pulled the Welsh county up to 191 for 8. But with conditions easing as the pitch got drier, Vikram Solanki made sure of

Glamorgan's fate by hitting a high-class 90 and adding 112 for the first wicket with Stephen Peters.

6 May 2002
at Cardiff
Warwickshire 261 for 8 (50 overs) (MJ Powell 74, SM Pollock 64)
Glamorgan 203 (47 overs) (MJ Powell 51, SM Pollock 4 for 12)
Warwickshire (2 pts) won by 58 runs
Gold Award: SM Pollock

at Northampton
Northamptonshire 212 for 5 (44 overs) (RJ Warren 78*)
Gloucestershire 94 (24 overs) (JAR Blain 5 for 30)
Northamptonshire (2 pts) won by 118 runs
Gold Award: JAR Blain

at Taunton
Somerset 126 for 9 (32 overs)
Worcestershire 122 for 3 (19 overs)
Worcestershire (2 pts) won by seven wickets
(DL Method: Worcestershire target 121 from 32 overs)
Gold Award: AJ Bichel

Warwickshire succeeded in their quest for a quarter-final place at Cardiff, consigning Glamorgan to consecutive seasons without a win in the Benson and Hedges Cup with a 58-run victory. Michael Powell (74) and Shaun Pollock (64) set up Warwickshire's eventual total of 261 for 8 by putting on 109 in 24 overs for the second wicket, and the promising Jim Troughton hit out attractively to reach 42 and provide middle-order acceleration. Then Pollock seized the new ball to help reduce Glamorgan to 22 for 3, returning later to finish off the innings for 203 and give himself overall figures of 4 for 12 from nine overs.

John Blain undermined group winners Gloucestershire at Wantage Road, claiming 5 for 30 as the competition favourites were tumbled out for 94. Northamptonshire, who had earlier totalled 212 for 5 in a match reduced to 44 overs per side, had won by 118 runs. It was their third group victory, too, but they were still pipped to the coveted third-placed spot by Warwickshire. The Northants total was built around an excellent, unbeaten 78 off 93 balls by Russell Warren, who added an unbroken 116 with Jeff Cook.

In a 32-over match at Taunton it was the superior batting of Worcestershire's Vikram Solanki and Graeme Hick that made all the difference. Somerset batted poorly in reaching a mere 126 for 9, but

Solanki (48*) and Hick (39) attacked the new ball with relish to speed Worcestershire into the last eight.

South Division

28 April 2002
at Chelmsford
Essex 206 for 9 (50 overs) (RJ Kirtley 5 for 33)
Sussex 120 for 6 (31 overs) (CJ Adams 54, RC Irani 5 for 36)
Essex (2 pts) won by 20 runs (DL Method: Sussex target 141 from 31 overs)
Gold Award: RC Irani

at Lord's
Surrey 123 (38 overs) (MA Butcher 51, AA Noffke 4 for 34)
Middlesex 124 for 2 (30.2 overs) (OA Shah 50*)
Middlesex (2 pts) won by eight wickets
Gold Award: MA Butcher

Ronnie Irani inspired Essex to an unlikely 20-run victory over Sussex at Chelmsford, starring with both bat and ball to rescue them from two crisis moments. First, after Essex had reeled at 18 for 4 against the pace of James Kirtley, who finished with 5 for 33, Irani struck 47 to spearhead a recovery to 206 for 9. Aftab Habib (46) and Paul Grayson (49 not out) also played their part, but when Sussex were cruising along at 103 for 1 in reply, it was Irani alone who turned the match on its head once more. He took 5 for 36, including Chris Adams for 54 and his last four wickets in the space of 15 balls, to reduce Sussex to 114 for 6 and when rain set in soon afterwards, Essex were comfortably ahead on Duckworth-Lewis regulations. Sussex, helpless on 120 for 6 from 31 overs and with opener Richard Montgomerie still unbeaten on 44, felt mugged.

Holders Surrey came unstuck in spectacular fashion on a seaming pitch at Lord's, the scene of their triumph over Gloucestershire ten months earlier. With Ashley Noffke taking 4 for 34 and Chad Keegan 3 for 24, Middlesex bowled out their London rivals for 123 in just 38 overs. Mark Butcher was the only one of Surrey's ten internationals to make any impression – with 51 – before Noffke clipped his off stump with the ball of the day. Despite a couple of short rain interruptions, Middlesex then made serene progress to their target, winning by eight wickets with Owais Shah ending up with an exuberant, unbeaten 50.

29 April 2002
at Southampton Rose Bowl

Kent 183 for 8 (50 overs)
Hampshire 115 (37.2 overs)
Kent (2 pts) won by 68 runs
Gold Award: PA Nixon

Kent did well to recover from being 25 for 4 on a seaming pitch at the Rose Bowl, eventually totalling 183 for 8 from their 50 overs and then bowling out Hampshire for only 115 to win by 68 runs. Matthew Walker (35), Paul Nixon (42) and James Golding (34 not out) all made useful contributions with the bat before Matthew Fleming, with 3 for 12 from six overs and the scalps of Neil Johnson, John Crawley and Robin Smith, delivered the decisive spell.

1 May 2002
at The Oval
Hampshire 243 (50 overs) (RA Smith 64)
Surrey 242 for 7 (50 overs) (AJ Stewart 52, Azhar Mahmood 50, SJ Udal 4 for 36)
Hampshire (2 pts) won by 1 run
Gold Award: SD Udal

at Canterbury
Sussex 282 for 3 (50 overs) (MW Goodwin 85*, RR Montgomerie 71, TR Ambrose 64)
Kent 156 (41 overs)(RSC Martin-Jenkins 4 for 22, RJ Kirtley 4 for 34)
Sussex (2 pts) won by 126 runs
Gold Award: MW Goodwin

In a tightly-contested group, Hampshire squeezed past Surrey by just one run at The Oval to leave the Cup holders at the bottom of the table. In a thrilling finish, Alex Tudor needed to hit the final ball, bowled by Chris Tremlett, for three. He managed just a single. Victory was no more than Hampshire deserved, however, after an inspired spell of bowling from Shaun Udal. The off spinner took 4 for 36 to pluck the heart out of the Surrey top order, before Azhar Mahmood took the home side to the very brink of victory themselves with an explosive 50. He and Tudor added 87 in just ten overs before the Pakistan all-rounder was run out by Will Kendall after he had given the occasional medium pacer the charge and had got the ball tangled up between his pads leaving himself stranded as he looked to see where it had gone. Earlier Alec Stewart (52) and Mark Ramprakash had threatened to make a nonsense of Hampshire's total of 243 with a classy second-wicket stand of 70, and earlier still on a great day's cricket, it had been Hampshire captain Robin Smith, defying back spasms to hit a reviving 64, who had been the hero.

Murray Goodwin and Robin Martin-Jenkins, aided by James Kirtley, led the slaughter of Kent at Canterbury. Sussex totalled 282 for 3 from their 50 overs, and Kent were bowled out for 156 in 41. It was Kent's heaviest defeat to their neighbours and rivals in 18 Benson and Hedges Cup meetings. Richard Montgomerie (71) and Tim Ambrose (64) provided the base for Sussex's challenging score with an opening partnership of 137 from 31 overs – Goodwin, supported by Chris Adams in a third-wicket stand of 128 in 18 overs, then provided the polish with a glorious unbeaten 85 from 62 balls, including four legside sixes. Kent's reply was wrecked by Martin-Jenkins, who took 4 for 22 in ten overs with the new ball, while Kirtley delivered an unplayable leg-cutter to remove Rob Key's off stump. Kent, at 65 for 5, had nowhere to go, and Kirtley later returned to join in the mopping up process and finished with figures of 4 for 34.

2 May 2002
at Chelmsford
Surrey 223 (49.2 overs) (MR Ramprakash 70*, MA Butcher 62, RC Irani 4 for 38)
Essex 224 for 6 (45.2 overs) (A Flower 98)
Essex (2 pts) won by four wickets
Gold Award: A Flower

at Canterbury
Middlesex 133 for 6 (19 overs)
Kent 139 for 3 (18.4 overs) (MV Fleming 50)
Kent (2 pts) won by seven wickets (DL Method: Kent target 139 from 19 overs)
Gold Award: JB Hockley

Sean Udal picked up four wickets, and the Gold Award, as Hampshire defeated Surrey by just one run.

Star-studded Surrey took another tumble at Chelmsford with a third successive defeat in this competition, while Essex underlined their re-emergence from an unhappy 2001 by completing a handsome four-wicket win with almost five overs in hand. Ronnie Irani, the Essex captain, once again set the tone for his side by taking 4 for 38 in the Surrey innings of 223 (in which Mark Ramprakash remained 70 not out after facing just 18 balls in the final 11 overs of the innings), and he later hit 30 as Essex, guided by Andy Flower's magnificent 98 from 114 balls, went to the top of the group table. Graham Napier rode his luck to contribute a rapid 41 after Martin Bicknell had removed both home openers early on. Flower was joined in stands of 51 and 52 by Irani and Aftab Habib.

A match greatly shortened by bad weather at Canterbury ended with Kent romping home by seven wickets against Middlesex. The visitors, who had initially set out thinking they were in a 31-overs-per-side affair, found their innings reduced by more rain to just 19 overs – in which they totalled 133 for 6 with Simon Cook striking 39 from 28 balls. Kent, required by Duckworth-Lewis computations to then make 139 in 19 overs, were given a marvellous start by one-day skipper Matthew Fleming, whose 40-ball 50 contained five fours and a six. The target eventually came down to 41 from the last five overs, and James Hockley claimed the Gold Award for a composed 33 not out from 32 balls to see Kent home with two deliveries to spare.

Zimbabwean Andy Flower guides his adopted Essex to a six-wicket win over Hampshire.

3 May 2002
at Hove
Hampshire 203 for 9 (50 overs)
Sussex 204 for 4 (49 overs) (CJ Adams 80*, PA Cottey 61)
Sussex (2 pts) won by six wickets
Gold Award: CJ Adams

Chris Adams produced a innings of great quality at Hove, guiding his Sussex team to victory by six wickets against Hampshire with an unbeaten 80. Adams was joined by Tony Cottey (61) in a match-winning stand of 95 in 23 overs after Dimitri Mascarenhas, with three wickets, had left Sussex wobbling on 51 for 3 as they chased a workmanlike Hampshire total of 203 for 9. Billy Taylor and James Kirtley were the pick of the home attack, picking up three wickets apiece.

4 May 2002
at The Oval
Surrey 257 for 9 (50 overs) (AD Brown 73, GP Thorpe 61)
Kent 213 (45.3 overs) (RWT Key 59)
Surrey (2 pts) won by 44 runs
Gold Award: AD Brown

Kent's chances of a quarter-final berth were dealt a severe blow by previously winless Surrey at The Oval. Given a typically robust start by Alistair Brown's 73 off 58 balls, Surrey totalled 257 for 9 from their 50 overs with Graham Thorpe scoring 61 in his first innings of the new season. Rob Key, with 59, did his best to keep Kent in the hunt early on, but Philip Sampson, a Manchester-born but South Africa-raised seamer, took 3 for 42 on his Cup debut and innings of 42 from David Fulton and 41 not out from Matthew Walker were not enough as Kent were bowled out for 213 with Alex Tudor cleaning up the tail.

5 May 2002
at Chelmsford
Hampshire 174 (46 overs) (RC Irani 5 for 28)
Essex 176 for 4 (39.4 overs) (A Flower 79*)
Essex (2 pts) won by six wickets (DL Method: Essex target 174 from 47 overs)
Gold Award: A Flower

at Lord's
Sussex 252 for 6 (50 overs) (RR Montgomerie 85, TR Ambrose 56)
Middlesex 224 (48.3 overs) (DC Nash 67, AA Noffke 58, BV Taylor 5 for 28)
Sussex (2 pts) won by 28 runs
Gold Award: BV Taylor

Essex stayed at the top of the Southern Division, and ensured themselves a place in the last eight, by strolling to a six-wicket victory against Hampshire at Chelmsford. Ronnie Irani spearheaded a fine Essex performance in the field by taking 5 for 28 as Hampshire were dismissed for 174. John Stephenson's nagging seamers also brought him three cheap scalps and Andy Clarke, too, picked up a couple of valuable wickets. Nasser Hussain, in his first game of the season, opened up with an aggressive 47 and Andy Flower, who remained 79 not out, guided Essex home after Hussain and Irani had both fallen to Shaun Udal's off breaks.

There was a sad farewell for the retiring Angus Fraser at Lord's, with Middlesex being soundly beaten by Sussex and seeing a quarter-final place seep away. Sussex, by contrast, moved into the last eight with a confident performance that brought them victory by 28 runs. Batting first, Sussex ran up 252 for 6 from their 50 overs – a total based on an opening partnership of 139 between Richard Montgomerie (85) and Tim Ambrose (56).

Then, in reply, Middlesex were soon in disarray at 62 for 7, with Robin Martin-Jenkins picking up 3 for 27. A recovery was fashioned by David Nash (67) and Ashley Noffke (58), who hit out merrily in a stand of 112 for the eighth wicket, but Billy Taylor was on hand to snuff out all chances of a complete turnabout. Taylor ended up with 5 for 28 and the Gold Award and Fraser's last act was to walk out at No. 11 to a guard of honour from the Sussex players. A little matter of 30 runs were needed by now from just 11 balls, and it was not to be Fraser's day.

6 May 2002
at Canterbury
Kent 231 for 9 (50 overs) (DP Fulton 80, MJ Walker 64, AJ Clarke 4 for 44)
Essex 234 for 8 (49.2 overs) (RC Irani 50*)
Essex (2 pts) won by two wickets
Gold Award: RC Irani

at Hove
Surrey 220 (44.4 overs) (AD Brown 97, BV Taylor 4 for 23 including a hat-trick)
Sussex 220 for 9 (46 overs) (RR Montgomerie 66, Azhar Mahmood 4 for 34)
Sussex (2 pts) won by virtue of losing fewer wickets
Gold Award: MJG Davis

at Southampton Rose Bowl
Hampshire 237 for 5 (50 overs) (JP Crawley 103*, GW White 60)

Middlesex 234 for 9 (50 overs) (EC Joyce 53)
Hampshire (2 pts) won by 3 runs
Gold Award: JP Crawley

Ronnie Irani maintained his sparkling early-season all-round form to confirm Essex as the winners of this Division, and usher Kent out of the competition at Canterbury. An exciting match ended with Irani hitting a 32-ball unbeaten half-century, with a six and four boundaries, to see Essex home by two wickets with four balls to spare. It was rough on Kent, who had earlier fought back strongly from being 43 for 4 with a fifth-wicket partnership of 120 in 29 overs between David Fulton (80) and Matthew Walker (64). And, when Nasser Hussain was lbw to Matthew Fleming for 42 and Andy Flower bowled by James Golding for 32, it soon seemed as though Essex would have trouble matching a growing asking rate as further wickets tumbled. But, in the end, and thanks mainly to their never-say-die captain, Essex scrambled 69 from the last ten overs to win.

Another exciting affair at Hove saw Sussex finish runners-up in the group table by beating Surrey because they had lost fewer wickets in a tied match. Surrey's 220 was based on Alistair Brown's superb 97, and also featured another fine spell of bowling from the in-form Billy Taylor (4 for 23) – which included a hat-trick of tail-enders to round off the innings in dramatic style. But even greater drama was to follow at the end of the Sussex reply, which was built on Richard Montgomerie's solid 66. Needing 18 from the last two overs, Sussex were boosted when Mark Davis struck ten from the first three deliveries of the 45th over – the penultimate one in a match reduced to 46 overs per side. Four were then required from the 46th, and after the scores drew level from the fifth ball, Azhar Mahmood's dismissal of James Kirtley from the last ball could not affect the result.

The Southern Division also saw a third nail-biter of a match at Southampton, where Hampshire squeezed past Middlesex by just three runs after totalling 237 for 5 with John Crawley (103 not out) and Giles White (60) putting on 127 for the fourth wicket. Angus Fraser, in his final game for Middlesex, took a creditable 2 for 34 from his ten-over allocation, but much later could not hit the penultimate ball of the game for six to bring his side victory. He missed, and a scrambled bye was all that came from his last piece of action in county cricket. That Middlesex got so close, however, was due to battling innings from Owais Shah (47), Ed Joyce (53) and Simon Cook (48).

21–22 May 2002

QUARTER-FINALS

at Bristol
Gloucestershire 203 for 8 (50 overs) (MW Alleyne 52,
KJ Barnett 51)
Worcestershire 204 for 2 (41.4 overs) (AJ Bichel 94*,
GA Hick 66)
Worcestershire won by eight wickets
Gold Award: AJ Bichel

at Chelmsford
Yorkshire 237 for 9 (50 overs) (DS Lehmann 59,
CEW Silverwood 56)
Essex 239 for 3 (45 overs) (N Hussain 136*)
Essex won by seven wickets
Gold Award: N Hussain

at Hove
Sussex 196-7 (50 overs) (TR Ambrose 87,
RR Montgomerie 57)
Warwickshire 197-6 (48.4 overs) (IR Bell 85*)
Warwickshire won by four wickets
Gold Award: IR Bell

at Leicester
Leicestershire 163 for 8 (50 overs) (MG Bevan 67)
Lancashire 164 for 6 (47.4 overs) (D Byas 91)
Lancashire won by four wickets
Gold Award: D Byas

When the forecast rain duly arrived at around 3pm
on the scheduled first day, Gloucestershire, having
been put in, were 193 for 7 with eight balls of their
innings remaining. Kim Barnett had made a canny
51, his 90th half-century in one-day cricket, and
Mark Alleyne a more aggressive 52. Their eventual
total of 203 for 8, when the match resumed at
3.30pm the following day, looked a useful one, but
Worcestershire's Andy Bichel made it seem
inconsequential with a brilliant unbeaten 94. Sent in
first, he first scythed away in the traditional pinch-
hitter's fashion, but later settled down to play more
conventionally in a second-wicket stand of 127 in 24
overs with Graeme Hick (66). Anurag Singh, a
member of the 1998 British Universities side who
last won a Benson and Hedges tie against
Gloucestershire at Bristol, 13 matches previously,
had also scored a good 30 and victory arrived for
Worcestershire by the unexpected margin of eight
wickets and with more than eight overs to spare.
Bichel faced 127 balls and hit 11 fours.

Andy Bichel
enjoyed his
pinch-hitting role
at Bristol where
he scored a
match-winning
94 not out.

A truly
commanding
innings of 136
not out, off just
144 balls, by
Nasser Hussain,
swept Essex
into the last
four teams in
the Benson and
Hedges Cup.
On a true pitch
at Chelmsford,
which exposed
the undisciplined bowler, Essex overwhelmed
Yorkshire by seven wickets. Yorkshire, asked to bat
first by Ronnie Irani, posted a reasonable score of
237 for 9 – thanks mainly to a pinch-hitting innings
of 56 from 42 balls by Chris Silverwood and a
controlled 59 from Darren Lehmann. But Hussain,
surely reaching his full maturity as a batsman of high
class, pulverized the Yorkshire bowling as he
dominated successive half-century stands with
Darren Robinson, John Stephenson and Andy Flower.

Ian Bell, perhaps the outstanding batting talent of
England's up-and-coming generation, played an
impressive innings at Hove to steer Warwickshire to
a tense four-wicket win over Sussex. Coming in at
No. 4, Bell was soon contemplating a scoreboard
reading 8 for 3 as Robin Martin-Jenkins sliced off
the top of the Warwickshire order. But, first with
Dominic Ostler and Trevor Penney, and later in
decisive stands of 53 and 48 with Dougie Brown and
Neil Smith, Bell calmly set about anchoring
Warwickshire's reply to a Sussex total of 196 for 7.
The 20-year-old tyro finished on 85 not out as
victory was clinched with eight balls to spare and, as
he maintained his composure through two stoppages
for rain as well, Bell demonstrated that he truly
possesses an old head on young shoulders. Earlier,
Sussex paid the price for not building sensibly on an
opening stand of 99 between Richard Montgomerie
(57) and Tim Ambrose, who went on to reach 87.

Leicestershire's decision to bat first in gloomy
conditions backfired when they could only total 163

for 8 from their 50 overs at Grace Road, despite Michael Bevan's careful 67. Still, without a superb 91 from David Byas, who opened the innings and batted with great skill and controlled aggression, Lancashire would have got nowhere near even this tempting target. Finally sixth out and just 17 runs short of the finishing line, after a crucial 48-run stand with Warren Hegg, Byas was the only possible winner of the Gold Award as Lancashire clinched victory by four wickets.

SEMI-FINALS

6–7 June 2002
at Chelmsford
Essex 262 for 9 (50 overs) (RC Irani 57, Kabir Ali 4 for 34)
Worcestershire 124 (33.4 overs)
Essex won by 138 runs
Gold Award: RC Irani

7 June 2002
at Old Trafford
Lancashire 211 for 9 (50 overs) (MJ Chilton 101, SM Pollock 4 for 27)
Warwickshire 213 for 9 (50 overs)
Warwickshire won by one wicket
Gold Award: MJ Chilton

Essex upset the odds at Chelmsford by romping to a 138-run win over Worcestershire, despite losing what looked to be a vital toss when the match eventually got under way in the early afternoon following heavy overnight rain and steady morning drizzle. Nasser Hussain, however, ignored the greenish pitch and gave his county a roistering start with 35 from 40 balls. Darren Robinson and Andy Flower hit 46 and 45 respectively to maintain Essex's early momentum, before Ronnie Irani drove three sixes in a powerful 57 from just 55 deliveries. The result was a more than useful total of 262 for 9, despite Kabir Ali's impressive 4 for 34, and by the close Worcestershire were a hopeless 26 for 4 in reply as the irrepressible Irani struck three hammer blows with the new ball and Ashley Cowan also removed Vikram Solanki. The next morning brought only the defiance of Steve Rhodes' 41, and Worcestershire were soon all out for 124 with Andy Clarke picking up three cheap late wickets.

One of the most thrilling finishes at Old Trafford in the venerable history of the Benson and Hedges Cup saw as audacious a last-ball stroke that can ever have been played to decide a limited-overs contest. Neil Carter, the Warwickshire No. 11, was the

batsman who played it – and Glen Chapple of Lancashire was the gob-smacked bowler who saw Carter sweep a winning boundary with a pre-meditated stroke to a perfectly serviceable delivery. Carter, who had marched out to face that dramatic final ball with Warwickshire 209 for 9 in reply to Lancashire's 211 for 9, sprinted off the field whirling his bat above his head in triumph. He was engulfed by team-mates pouring out from the dressing room. All Lancashire could do was sink to the grass in despair, probably wishing they had not set a field with their long leg up inside the circle. It was a defeat particularly hard to take for Mark Chilton, the Lancashire opener, who had earlier anchored the home side's innings with a dedicated 146-ball 101. Andy Flintoff had also weighed in with 40, but Shaun Pollock's 4 for 27 had helped keep Lancashire's total to reasonable proportions and Warwickshire were always in the hunt as Ian Bell, Jim Troughton, Dougie Brown and Neil Smith all made important contributions. Eight runs were needed from the final over, but then Brown was narrowly run out for 42 from a bullet-like throw from the boundary by Flintoff from the fifth ball. Chapple and Lancashire were celebrating then …

Shaun Pollock took four wickets as Warwicks beat Lancs in a nail-biting semi-final.

but moments later Carter had snatched the prize of a Lord's final away from them.

15 July 2002

FINAL

The 31st and last Benson and Hedges Cup final was not one of the most memorable, but at least it saw in Ian Bell's masterly unbeaten 65 a true vision of England's cricket future.

Bell, the 20-year-old Warwickshire prodigy, was joined by Jim Troughton, 23, in a match-clinching third-wicket stand of 84 after their team, having restricted Essex to 181 for 8, had slid to 21 for 2 in reply. Troughton, a stylish left-hander tipped alongside Bell for imminent England honours by Bob Woolmer, Warwickshire's coach, scored 37. Shaun Pollock, next in at No. 5, then struck a no-nonsense 34, before leaving the stage free for Bell, who faced 89 balls, to accept the plaudits.

Victory came by 5.10pm, by five wickets and with more than 13 overs to spare, and Bell, the last winner of a Benson and Hedges Gold Award, said:

'I wasn't overawed. The situation demanded that I just went out and batted. While Jim looked to hit it, I like to rotate the strike. I back my own ability against anyone who bowls at me. I want a career playing for England – that's what I want to do.' Bell's innings meant he had top scored for Warwickshire in the quarter-final, the semi-final and, now, the final.

For Essex, the pre-match favourites, it was a depressing day as they failed to do themselves justice on the big occasion. It started badly, with England captain Nasser Hussain departing to a Pollock leg-cutter from the second ball of the match.

Suddenly shorn of the batsman who had done so much to propel them to the final with a series of rapid innings from the head of the order, Essex then batted as if they did not quite know what to do next. The needless run out of Graham Napier, who had pulled Pollock's sixth ball for six, hardly helped. Andy Flower, probably coming in too low at No. 5, briefly hinted at leading a revival with 30, but Ronnie Irani had already skied to mid-off and when Aftab Habib, definitely too far down the order at No. 7, was caught for 19, it was left to the

Ian Bell won the Gold Award for his innings of 65 which was the high point in an otherwise disappointing season for the Warwickshire youngster.

FINAL – ESSEX v. WARWICKSHIRE
14 July 2002 at Lord's

ESSEX

Batting

N Hussain	c Piper b Pollock	0
DDJ Robinson	c Brown b Carter	18
GR Napier	run out (Troughton)	17
JR Stephenson	b Carter	0
A Flower*	c Piper b Smith	30
RC Irani (capt)	c Smith b Brown	8
Aftab Habib	c Knight b Giles	19
AP Grayson	not out	38
JM Dakin	c Powell b Brown	12
AP Cowan	not out	27
AJ Clarke		
Extra	lb 4, w 4, nb 3	12
	(50 overs)	**181**

Bowling

	O	M	R	W
Pollock	10	1	32	1
Carter	10	1	45	2
Brown	10	0	32	2
Giles	10	1	28	1
Smith	10	0	40	1

Fall of Wickets
1-0, 2-33, 3-33, 4-40, 5-61, 6-86, 7-109, 8-134

WARWICKSHIRE

Batting

MJ Powell (capt)	c Flower b Cowan	11
NV Knight	c Flower b Irani	9
IR Bell	not out	65
JO Troughton	c Flower b Napier	37
SM Pollock	c Dakin b Irani	34
TL Penney	lbw b Stephenson	0
DR Brown	not out	12
NMK Smith		
KJ Piper*		
AF Giles		
NM Carter		
Extras	lb 6, w 8	14
	(36.2 overs) (5 wickets)	**182**

Bowling

	First innings			
	O	M	R	W
Irani	10	2	40	2
Cowan	8	0	37	1
Clarke	2	0	20	–
Dakin	2	0	22	–
Grayson	4	0	11	–
Napier	5.2	0	31	1
Stephenson	5	0	15	1

Fall of Wickets
1-19, 2-21, 3-105, 4-158, 5-159

Umpires: B Dudleston & JH Hampshire (TV: B Leadbeater)
Toss: Warwickshire
Gold Award: IR Bell

Warwickshire won by five wickets

dependable Paul Grayson to manage a tail-end damage-limitation exercise alongside the splendidly uncomplicated Ashley Cowan.

Bell apart, it was a low-key end – on the field – to one of British sport's most enduring sponsorships. Off it, however, Benson and Hedges certainly went out with a bang as dozens of special guests were invited to Lord's to join in the 'leaving party', including the past winning captains who formed a Gold Award Panel under Raymond Illingworth's chairmanship to choose the recipient of the final Man of the Match medallion. A glossy, 48-page souvenir issue match programme had been commissioned, and even the three umpires who officiated were linked to the competition's proud history.

John Hampshire, Barry Dudleston and Barrie Leadbeater all played in the very first final in 1972 when Leicestershire, under Illingworth, beat Yorkshire in a tense, low-scoring affair.

For 31 seasons, the Benson and Hedges Cup final has been a focal point of high summer and a feature of the English cricket calendar. Great names have seized the moment at Lord's, from Gooch to Richards, from Wasim to Aravinda, and from D'Oliveira to Ben Hollioake. Sadly, there can be no more under the Benson and Hedges banner.

Coach Bob Woolmer joins his Warwickshire team on the podium as they celebrate their comprehensive victory over Essex in the last Benson and Hedges Cup final at Lord's.

CHELTENHAM & GLOUCESTER TROPHY
By Mark Baldwin

First Round: 29 August 2001
Note: First-round ties played in the previous season.

at Dunstable
Bedfordshire 367 for 3 (50 overs) (*DR Clarke 176*,
AR Roberts 113)
Derbyshire Cricket Board XI 182 (36.3 overs)
(JR Benstead 65, AR Roberts 5 for 40)
Bedfordshire won by 185 runs
Man of the Match: AR Roberts

at Dinton CC
Buckinghamshire 224 for 7 (50 overs)
Worcestershire Cricket Board XI 185 (47 overs)
Buckinghamshire won by 39 runs
Man of the Match: ZA Sher (Buckinghamshire)

at Chester Boughton Hall
Lancashire Cricket Board XI 128 (46.2 overs)
Cheshire 131 for 2 (19.4 overs) (RG Hignett 54*)
Cheshire won by eight wickets
Man of the Match: CS Lamb (Cheshire)

at Millom
Warwickshire Cricket Board XI 212 for 7 (50 overs)
(JO Troughton 115*)
Cumberland 195 (48.4 overs) (AA Metcalfe 50,
SJ O'Shaughnessy 50, JO Troughton 4 for 23)
Warwickshire Cricket Board XI won by 17 runs
Man of the Match: JO Troughton

at Chelmsford
Essex Cricket Board XI 237 for 9 (50 overs) (GW
Ecclestone 66, AC Richards 64, RG Halsall 4 for 34)
Sussex Cricket Board XI 243 for 4 (44 overs)
(DJ Hussey 118*, GRA Campbell 65)
Sussex Cricket Board XI won by six wickets
Man of the Match: DJ Hussey

at Welwyn Garden City
Staffordshire 268 (49.2 overs) (PF Shaw 62, GF Archer 53)
Hertfordshire 107 (34.4 overs) (RA Cooper 5 for 42,
D Follett 4 for 17)
Staffordshire won by 161 runs
Man of the Match: D Follett

at Godmanchester
Huntingdonshire Cricket Board XI 180 for 8
(50 overs) (W Larkins 50)
Gloucestershire Cricket Board XI 183 for 5

(42.1 overs) (NA Stovold 75)
Gloucestershire Cricket Board XI won by five wickets
Man of the Match: NA Stovold

at Barwell
Northamptonshire Cricket Board XI 212 (49 overs)
Leicestershire Cricket Board XI 213 for 3 (33.3 overs)
(NJ Pullen 88, NG Patel 62*)
Leicestershire Cricket Board XI won by seven wickets
Man of the Match: NJ Pullen

at Lincoln
Lincolnshire 243 for 8 (50 overs) (J Trower 76, MA Fell
75*, JK Barrow 4 for 31)
Berkshire 157 (41.5 overs) (RP Davis 56, RJ Chapman
4 for 18)
Lincolnshire won by 86 runs
Man of the Match: MA Fell

at Southgate
Scotland 245 for 8 (50 overs) (NJ MacRae 83,
DG Wright 55)
Middlesex Cricket Board XI 221 (50 overs) (SJ Price
85, SJ Davidson 4 for 43)
Scotland won by 24 runs
Man of the Match: DG Wright

at Manor Park, Hellesdon
Norfolk 245 for 3 (50 overs) (CJ Rogers 139*,
JR Walker 76)
Holland 245 (50 overs) (HJC Mol 56, DJ Reekers 53,
PJ Bradshaw 4 for 30)
Norfolk won by virtue of losing fewer wickets
Man of the Match: CJ Rogers

at Christ Church College, Oxford
Nottinghamshire Cricket Board XI 248 for 5 (50
overs) (CM Tolley 78, MW Creed 77)
Oxfordshire 249 for 5 (47.3 overs) (CA Haupt 126*)
Oxfordshire won by five wickets
Man of the Match: CA Haupt

at Copdock
Denmark 112 (28.4 overs) (ID Graham 4 for 17)
Suffolk 114 for 3 (33.4 overs)
Suffolk won by seven wickets
Man of the Match: DJ Callaghan (Suffolk)

at South Wiltshire
Ireland 247 (50 overs) (D Joyce 67, PG Gillespie 66)
Wiltshire 162 (40.2 overs) (PJK Mooney 4 for 34)
Ireland won by 85 runs
Man of the Match: PG Gillespie

Second Round: 13 and 14 September 2001
Note: Second-round ties played in the previous season.

at Beaconsfield
Buckinghamshire 187 (47.3 overs) (PD Atkins 50,
MJ North 4 for 26)
Durham Cricket Board XI 166 (46.1 overs)
Buckinghamshire won by 21 runs
Man of the Match: PD Atkins

at March
Warwickshire Cricket Board XI 232 (49.1 overs) (IJ
Westwood 55, JO Troughton 51, Ajaz Akhtar 4 for 29)
Cambridgeshire 157 for 9 (40 overs) (RJ Rollins 50)
Warwickshire Cricket Board XI won by 75 runs
Man of the Match: T Mees (Warwickshire Cricket
Board XI)

at Toft
Cornwall 216 for 8 (45 overs) (BP Price 74, SC Pope
59, A Kuruvilla 4 for 21)
Cheshire 151 (43.3 overs) (NT Wood 50)
Cornwall won by 65 runs
Man of the Match: SC Pope

at Exmouth
Bedfordshire 266 for 8 (50 overs) (NA Stanley 69,
AR Roberts 50)
Devon 268 for 7 (46.2 overs) (RI Dawson 88,
AR Roberts 4 for 26)
Devon won by three wickets
Man of the Match: RI Dawson

at Bristol
Gloucestershire Cricket Board XI 185 for 9 (50 overs)
(CRJ Budd 65, SJ Foster 5 for 33)
Yorkshire Cricket Board XI 186 for 6 (49.1 overs)
Yorkshire Cricket Board XI won by four wickets
Man of the Match: SJ Foster

at Southampton Rose Bowl
Ireland 241 for 7 (50 overs) (AC Botha 75, D Heasley 66*)
Hampshire Cricket Board XI 209 (50 overs)
Ireland won by 32 runs
Man of the Match: AC Botha

at Hinckley
Kent Cricket Board XI 280 for 9 (50 overs) (MJ Banes
82, AGR Loudon 53, LJP Jenkins 50*, NJ Pullen 4 for 61)
Leicestershire Cricket Board XI 81 (26.5 overs)
(RJ Minter 6 for 8)
Kent Cricket Board XI won by 189 runs
Man of the Match: RJ Minter

at Bourne
Lincolnshire 244 for 9 (50 overs) (OE Burford 55)
Surrey Cricket Board XI 150 (31 overs)
Lincolnshire won by 94 runs
Man of the Match: OE Burford

at Manor Park, Hellesdon
Norfolk 173 (48.1 overs) (MPL Bulbeck 5 for 18)
Somerset Cricket Board XI 61 for 2 (22 overs)
Norfolk won on faster scoring rate
Man of the Match: MPL Bulbeck

at Jesmond
Northumberland 233 for 9 (50 overs) (JA Graham 55,
JB Windows 52*)
Staffordshire 234 for 3 (45.1 overs) (OD Gibson 102*,
GF Archer 89*)
Staffordshire won by seven wickets
Man of the Match: GF Archer

at Linlithgow
Dorset 101 (43 overs)
Scotland 103 for 0 (15.5 overs) (DG Wright 53*)
Scotland won by ten wickets
Man of the Match: DG Wright

at Shifnal
Shropshire 200 for 8 (50 overs)
Oxfordshire 192 for 9 (50 overs)
Shropshire won by 8 runs
Man of the Match: AB Byram (Shropshire)

at Bury St Edmund's
Suffolk 254 for 7 (50 overs) (CJ Warn 52*)
Herefordshire 151 (41.4 overs) (CW Boroughs 59*)
Suffolk won by 103 runs
Man of the Match: CJ Warn

at Hastings
Wales Minor Counties 238 (50 overs) (PV Simmons
51, RW Sylvester 51, AJ Jones 50, JR Morgan
4 for 55)
Sussex Cricket Board XI 235 (49.3 overs)
(GRA Campbell 57, J Snashall 56)
Wales Minor Counties won by 3 runs
Man of the Match: PV Simmons

Third Round: 24, 29 and 30 May 2002

at Beaconsfield
Sussex 268 for 6 (50 overs) (TR Ambrose 95,
B Zuiderent 50)

Buckinghamshire 143 for 7 (50 overs) (ZA Sher 55*)
Sussex won by 125 runs
Man of the Match: TR Ambrose

at Boscawen Park, Truro
Worcestershire 125 for 7 (30 overs) (CE Shreck
5 for 19)
Cornwall 76 (29.2 overs) (Kabir Ali 4 for 2)
Worcestershire won by 49 runs
Man of the Match: CE Shreck

at Exmouth
Yorkshire 259 for 5 (50 overs) (C White 87,
DS Lehmann 54*)
Devon 116 (39.4 overs) (DS Lehmann 4 for 26,
RKJ Dawson 4 for 34)
Yorkshire won by 143 runs
Man of the Match: C White

at Chelmsford
Middlesex 291 for 5 (50 overs) (SG Koenig 116,
PN Weekes 76*)
Essex 295 for 5 (48.1 overs) (N Hussain 96, RC Irani 86*)
Essex won by five wickets
Man of the Match: RC Irani

at Dublin
Ireland 164 (50 overs)
Nottinghamshire 166 for 2 (37.2 overs) (Usman Afzaal
64*)
Nottinghamshire won by eight wickets
Man of the Match: Usman Afzaal

at Folkestone
Kent Cricket Board XI 145 (47.5 overs)
Hampshire 150 for 2 (26.3 overs) (DA Kenway 76,
NC Johnson 66*)
Hampshire won by eight wickets
Man of the Match: DA Kenway

at Old Trafford
Derbyshire 167 (46.2 overs) (DR Hewson 63)
Lancashire 169 for 0 (28.1 overs) (G Chapple 81*,
MJ Chilton 76*)
Lancashire won by ten wickets
Man of the Match: MJ Chilton

at Sleaford
Lincolnshire 154 (46.5 overs) (S Webb 55, AP Davies
5 for 19)
Glamorgan 157 for 4 (37.4 overs)
Glamorgan won by six wickets
Man of the Match: S Webb

at Manor Park, Hellesdon
Kent 341 for 6 (50 overs) (RWT Key 77, DP Fulton 62,
MV Fleming 56)
Norfolk 150 for 8 (50 overs)
Kent won by 191 runs
Man of the Match: MV Fleming

at Raeburn Place, Edinburgh
Surrey 246 for 2 (50 overs) (MR Ramprakash 101*, N
Shahid 65*, IJ Ward 58)
Scotland 63 for 4 (24.1 overs)
*Surrey won by 55 runs (DL Method: Scotland needed
to have 119 from 24.1 overs when rain stopped play)*
Man of the Match: MR Ramprakash

at Shrewsbury School
Shropshire 98 (30.2 overs) (MA Hardinges 4 for 19)
Gloucestershire 99 for 3 (27.2 overs) (KJ Barnett 54*)
*Gloucestershire won by seven wickets (DL Method:
Gloucestershire target 97 from 32 overs)*
Man of the Match: MA Hardinges

at Stone
Warwickshire 192 (50 overs) (NV Knight 54)
Staffordshire 142 (45.4 overs) (A Richardson 5 for 35)
Warwickshire won by 50 runs
Man of the Match: SM Pollock

at Bury St Edmund's
Suffolk 128 for 9 (50 overs)
Northamptonshire 132 for 9 (39.2 overs) (AJ Hall
4 for 33)
Northamptonshire won by one wicket
Man of the Match: KG Shaw (Suffolk)

at Cardiff
Durham 301 for 5 (50 overs) (MA Gough 132,
GJ Pratt 89)
Wales Minor Counties 65 for 2 (25 overs)
*Durham won by 49 runs (DL Method: Wales Minor
Counties target 115 from 25 overs)*
Man of the Match: MA Gough

at Coventry & North Warwickshire CC
Leicestershire 208 for 7 (50 overs)
Warwickshire Cricket Board XI 182 for 8 (50 overs)
(HR Jones 72)
Leicestershire won by 26 runs
Man of the Match: HR Jones

at Scarborough
Somerset 255 for 9 (55 overs) (PD Bowler 104, J Cox
64, RM Pyrah 5 for 50)

Yorkshire Cricket Board XI 168 for 8 (50 overs)
Somerset won by 87 runs
Man of the Match: RM Pyrah

In the two matches between first-class counties, Essex beat Middlesex by five wickets in a high-scoring affair at Chelmsford, while Lancashire trounced Derbyshire by ten wickets at Old Trafford.

Sven Koenig hit 116, Paul Weekes an unbeaten 76 and Simon Cook 39 not out from only 15 deliveries, as Middlesex totalled 291 for 5 from their 50 overs. Essex however, with Nasser Hussain kicking off with 96 from 99 balls, romped home with almost two overs to spare thanks to Ronnie Irani's five legside sixes in a 79-ball 86 not out. Andy Flower (45) sensibly chose to play second fiddle to both Hussain, in a stand of 74, and Irani, with whom he added 76.

Dominic Hewson's 63 was the only real resistance to the Lancashire bowlers as Derbyshire were bundled out for 167 on an Old Trafford pitch of both pace and bounce. The only sour note for the home side, as they cantered to victory through Mark Chilton (76 not out) and Glen Chapple (81 not out from 69 balls), was a broken hand suffered by David Byas.

There were a few alarms for first-class counties against the minnows, but no shocks. The Warwickshire Board team, at Coventry, had perhaps the best chance of causing an upset against Leicestershire on a slow pitch. But, after restricting Leicestershire to 169 for 6 from 47 overs, they allowed them to reach 208 for 7 with Vince Wells (49 not out) and Phillip DeFreitas plundering vital late runs. In reply, and despite a mature 72 from 99 balls by Oxford student Huw Jones, the Board team fell short by 26 runs.

Staffordshire put up a brave fight against Warwickshire at Stone, bowling out the first-class county for 192 in damp, slow conditions. but then being dismissed for 142 themselves.

Elsewhere, Charles Shreck's 5 for 19 against Worcestershire, which earned him the Man of the Match award at Truro, could not prevent a 49-run defeat for Cornwall in a game reduced by bad weather to 30 overs per side. All the other games resulted in comfortable wins for the first-class counties.

Fourth Round: 19 June 2002

at The Oval
Surrey 438 for 5 (50 overs) (AD Brown 268, IJ Ward 97)
Glamorgan 429 (49.5 overs) (RDB Croft 119, DL Hemp 102, SD Thomas 71*, A J Hollioake 5 for 77)

Surrey won by 9 runs
Man of the Match: AD Brown

at Taunton
Hampshire 262 for 5 (50 overs) (JP Crawley 113*, NC Johnson 52)
Somerset 265 for 4 (45.1 overs) (ME Trescothick 133)
Somerset won by six wickets
Man of the Match: ME Trescothick

at Trent Bridge
Nottinghamshire 262 for 5 (50 overs) (JER Gallian 69, CMW Read 51*)
Worcestershire 265 for 2 (44 overs) (GA Hick 117*, VS Solanki 108)
Worcestershire won by eight wickets
Man of the Match: VS Solanki

at Canterbury
Kent 328 for 9 (50 overs) (JB Hockley 121, RWT Key 64, MJ Powell 5 for 40)
Warwickshire 200 (37.1 overs) (IR Bell 50)
Kent won by 128 runs
Man of the Match: JB Hockley

at Chelmsford
Lancashire 166 (46.5 overs) (AP Cowan 4 for 27)
Essex 167 for 1 (28.3 overs) (N Hussain 83*, DDJ Robinson 59)
Essex won by nine wickets
Man of the Match: N Hussain

at Bristol
Durham 179 (47.3 overs) (MW Alleyne 4 for 27)
Gloucestershire 180 for 2 (26 overs) (CM Spearman 104*)
Gloucestershire won by eight wickets
Man of the Match: CM Spearman

at Leicester
Leicestershire 233 (49.1 overs) (TR Ward 112, DI Stevens 83, BV Taylor 4 for 37)
Sussex 234 for 4 (47.3 overs) (RR Montgomerie 126*, MH Yardy 52)
Sussex won by six wickets
Man of the Match: RR Montgomerie

at Northampton
Yorkshire 303 for 3 (50 overs) (MJ Wood 91, MP Vaughan 63*, CEW Silverwood 61)
Northamptonshire 254 (48.2 overs) (JW Cook 70)
Yorkshire won by 49 runs
Man of the Match: CEW Silverwood

Perhaps the most remarkable of all the one-day cricket matches that have been played around the world in modern times illuminated the fourth round of this competition. Only the bowlers who took part in the meeting of Surrey and Glamorgan at The Oval will want to forget the day when a total of 867 runs were plundered from 99.5 overs. That astonishing aggregate was, unsurprisingly, one of the host of world records that were set in a match which Surrey won, breathlessly, by just nine runs. Their winning margin was indeed a mere drop in the ocean of a contest which contained no fewer than 87 fours and 28 sixes.

Man of the Match was Surrey's Alistair Brown, who hit 12 of those sixes – just one short of the one-day record of 13 set by Ian Botham in 1986 – and 30 fours besides. Brown's amazing 268, made off 160 balls in a phenomenal exhibition of controlled hitting, easily surpassed the previous world record individual one-day innings, the 222 scored by Graeme Pollock for Eastern Province against Border in 1974. The Surrey beneficiary dominated a first-wicket stand of 286 with Ian Ward, who made 97, before finally being bowled by Mike Kasprowicz.

Surrey's 438 for 5 from their 50 overs was a world record one-day team total, and Darren Thomas' 3 for 108 from nine overs was the most expensive bowling analysis ever recorded in limited-overs cricket. The most incredible aspect of an incredible day, however, was that Thomas – and Glamorgan – almost had the last laugh.

So true was Paul Brind's pitch, and so tempting the 60-yard boundary on the gas holder side of the ground, that Glamorgan looked for most of

Alistair Brown hit 12 sixes on an extraordinary day at The Oval. Brown scored 268!

their reply to be perfectly capable of doing the seemingly impossible and overhauling Surrey's huge score.

Robert Croft, the acting Glamorgan captain, marched out to open the Welsh county's innings and proceeded to dispatch each of the first five deliveries for four off an increasingly bemused Martin Bicknell. Croft kept on hitting, too, with a largely straight bat, as he went on to score 119 out of his side's first 162 runs. It inspired his team to the extent that, in the end, Thomas' brilliant 71 not out off just 41 balls all but snatched the match. David Hemp (102) and Adrian Dale (49) had also played their part, with a quickfire fourth-wicket stand of 98, but it was Thomas' strong striking, which included three more sixes, that kept the dream alive until the fourth ball of the final over.

Crucially for Surrey, he then lost the strike and left Dean Cosker, the No. 11, needing to hit a six and four from the final two balls of this remarkable day. To the relief of Adam Hollioake, the bowler and Surrey captain, Cosker swung and missed and heard his stumps being spread-eagled behind him.

Glamorgan, their brave chase ultimately in vain, were all out for 429. The overall match aggregate beat, by 113 runs, the previous one-day world record – the 754 scored between India and India B at Madras in 2000–01 – and afterwards Brown said: 'I felt in good form and my feet were moving right. And it's 268 more than I scored against Scotland! But I was very nervous when Martin Bicknell's first five deliveries were all hit so easily for four, even though I didn't think they could keep it up. I never thought they would get anywhere near as close as that.'

The events at The Oval took much of the attention away from the seven other matches in the round, but there was still some fine cricket elsewhere.

None more so than at Taunton where Somerset, boosted by the sheer power of Marcus Trescothick's 133, cruised effortlessly past a Hampshire total of 262 for 5. John Crawley made an unbeaten 113 for Hampshire, but Trescothick, skippering his county, dominated a first-wicket partnership of 130 in 23 overs with Peter Bowler to set up an eventual six-wicket canter.

At Trent Bridge, too, Nottinghamshire were unable to defend exactly the same total as Hampshire's – with their 262 for 5 built upon half-centuries from Jason Gallian (69) and Chris Read (51 not out). Allan Donald's ten overs, costing just 24 runs, were also a factor in a Worcestershire victory that arrived with six overs to spare courtesy

Marcus Trescothick scored 133 for Somerset against Hants, but was injured in the quarter-final.

of a second-wicket stand worth 195 in 30 overs between Vikram Solanki (108) and Graeme Hick (117 not out). For the home side, an eight-wicket defeat increased the mutterings of discontent about Clive Rice, the cricket manager.

A brilliant innings of 121 by James Hockley, from 107 balls and with three sixes and 14 fours, enabled Kent to sweep aside Warwickshire at Canterbury. Hockley was joined in a second-wicket partnership of 157 in 25 overs by Rob Key, his fellow 23-year-old, who hit 64. Despite five wickets for Michael Powell with his occasional seamers, Kent reached an intimidating 328 for 9 from their 50 overs and incisive new-ball spells from Amjad Khan and Martin Saggers then settled matters. Warwickshire eventually reached 200 all out.

Nasser Hussain's aggressive, unbeaten 83, which included three sixes, highlighted Essex's crushing nine-wicket win over Lancashire at Chelmsford. Hussain put on 142 for the first wicket with Darren Robinson, who scored 59, and Essex romped past Lancashire's 166 all out with more than 21 overs to spare. Ashley Cowan produced a highly disciplined display of seam bowling, in more helpful conditions earlier in the day, to finish with 4 for 27. Home fans were also treated to the sight of Ronnie Irani, the Essex captain, shinning up a tree at the Hayes Close End of the ground to retrieve the ball after Andy Flintoff, who top scored for Lancashire with 45, had struck Andy Clarke for a straight six.

Gloucestershire took even fewer overs than Essex to complete their overwhelming eight-wicket victory over Durham at Bristol. Mark Alleyne took 4 for 27 and Ian Harvey 3 for 25 as Durham were restricted to 179 all out. Craig Spearman, the Gloucestershire opener, then thrashed an unbeaten 104 from just 77 balls to underline the home side's superiority.

Leicestershire had only themselves to blame at Grace Road for the manner of their six-wicket defeat against Sussex, for whom Richard Montgomerie scored a well-paced and match-winning 126 not out. From 204 for 1 in the 43rd over, following a 171-run stand for the second wicket by Trevor Ward (112) and Darren Stevens (83), Leicestershire contrived to lose their remaining nine wickets for just 29 runs in 38 balls. They even wasted five precious deliveries of their allotted 50 overs, with Billy Taylor finishing off the innings with a hat-trick by having Grant Flower caught at long on, yorking Darren Maddy and then seeing Devon Malcolm also holing out in the deep. Tight bowling by Flower, whose left-arm spin brought him 2 for 33 from his ten overs, pegged back Sussex in the middle of their innings, but, with 69 being needed from the last ten overs, Will House hit out profitably in an important little contribution down the order and Montgomerie concentrated on being there at the end.

Yorkshire won a high-scoring contest at Northampton by 49 runs, though an aggregate of 557 runs was mere chicken feed compared to the sumptuous banquet on offer at The Oval. Matthew Wood laid solid foundations for Yorkshire's 303 for 3 with 91, while Chris Silverwood responded to being promoted to pinch-hit by swiping 61 off 75 balls. Michael Vaughan, with an unbeaten 63 from 50 balls, then added a further 104 with Simon Katich, whose 40 not out occupied 41 deliveries. Effective new-ball bowling by Silverwood and Matthew Hoggard, supported by Craig White, then prevented the Northants reply from building up any sort of lasting momentum. David Sales did hit 44, and Jeff Cook a violent 70 off 59 balls with four sixes, but the home side were soon chasing a lost cause.

Quarter-Finals: 16 and 17 July 2002

at Chelmsford
Essex 283 for 9 (50 overs) (A Flower 75, DDJ Robinson 52)
Yorkshire 283 for 5 (50 overs) (A McGrath 72*, GM Fellows 68*)
Yorkshire won by virtue of losing fewer wickets
Man of the Match: A McGrath

at Canterbury
Gloucestershire 232 for 8 (50 overs) (KJ Barnett 108, RC Russell 66)

Kent 238 for 5 (44.2 overs) (MV Fleming 53)
Kent won by five wickets
Man of the Match: KJ Barnett

at The Oval
Surrey 337 for 3 (50 overs) (AJ Hollioake 117*,
MR Ramprakash 107*, R Clarke 55)
Sussex 323 for 8 (50 overs) (MW Goodwin 110*,
RR Montgomerie 88)
Surrey won by 14 runs
Man of the Match: AJ Hollioake

at Taunton
Worcestershire 271 (49 overs) (BF Smith 85*,
VS Solanki 53)
Somerset 273 for 6 (47.3 overs) (KA Parsons 121)
Somerset won by four wickets
Man of the Match: KA Parsons

Yorkshire reached what they hoped would prove to
be a turning point in a wretched season when,
through the efforts of Anthony McGrath and Gary
Fellows, they beat Essex in a remarkable tied game
at Chelmsford. Yorkshire went through because they
had lost just five wickets, compared to Essex's nine,
and after McGrath had scored the three runs from
the final over needed to level the scores, Fellows
blocked the last ball. It completed a dramatic match,
in which Yorkshire had slipped to 155 for 5 in reply
to Essex's 283 for 9 before McGrath and Fellows
seized the moment to build an unbroken partnership
of 128 in 18 overs. McGrath won the Man of the
Match award for his unbeaten 72 from 70 balls, yet
it could easily have gone instead to Fellows, whose
68 not out had taken him just 59 deliveries. Essex
were left to reflect that they should have totalled
around 300 after offsetting the early loss of Nasser
Hussain with some excellent top-order batting.
Andy Flower made 75 after an aggressive 52 from
Darren Robinson, while both Ronnie Irani and
Aftab Habib also scored freely against an all-Test-
class attack containing Darren Gough.

It was a tale of oldies but goldies at Canterbury
where Gloucestershire's Kim Barnett and Jack Russell
almost single-handedly made a game of it against
Kent. In the end, with 37-year-old Kent one-day
captain Matthew Fleming to the fore, the home side
won at a canter by five wickets, but not before
Barnett, 42, and Russell, a month away from 39, had
demonstrated that age has yet to diminish their
powers. Martin Saggers took three wickets in his
third over to leave Gloucestershire tottering at 17
for 3, but opener Barnett remained calm and in a

succession of stands with Mark Alleyne, Alex
Gidman and Russell, pulled the innings around. In
the end, after adding 100 in only 14 overs for the
sixth wicket with Russell (66), Barnett was bowled
by Fleming for 108. Gloucestershire's 232 for 8 was
the sort of total they would have backed themselves
to defend not so long ago, but Fleming launched the
Kent reply by tearing into the bowling of Ian Harvey
and James Averis and making 53 out of the first 72
runs scored. After that, all Kent's batsmen had to do
was bat properly and, although Andrew Symonds was
run out for 47, David Fulton kept a cool head and
was joined in an unbroken stand of 60 by Paul Nixon.

Perhaps there was more than a touch of Ben out
there with him, but Adam Hollioake played the
most astonishing innings of his cricketing life to
inspire Surrey to a 14-run victory against a brave
Sussex side at Hove. Just 48 hours after being
overwhelmed with emotion at the service of
thanksgiving at Southwark Cathedral for his younger
brother, killed in a car crash in Perth in March,
Hollioake plundered 117 not out from a mere 52
balls to send Surrey hurtling on to 337 for 3 from
their 50 overs. From the moment he came in at 189
for 3 in the 36th over, following the fall of Rikki
Clarke for a worthy 55, Hollioake batted like a man
possessed. He struck five sixes and 11 fours and
succeeded with almost every outrageous shot he
tried. The pull-
drive, with plenty
of bottom hand,
was especially
effective and
afterwards
Hollioake spoke of
his pleasure that
his parents, John
and Daria, were at
the ground to
witness the
innings. A classy,
unbeaten 107 by
Mark Ramprakash
was completely
overshadowed by
the Hollioake
pyrotechnics –
unsurprising given
that Ramprakash's
share of the 148-
run fourth-wicket
partnership was
just 31. The worth

Adam Hollioake, in a difficult
summer, was Man of the Match
in Surrey's quarter-final win
over Sussex.

of Hollioake's effort was only put into proper perspective, however, when Sussex came so close to overhauling the Surrey score. Murray Goodwin made a brilliant hundred of his own, coming in at 127 for 2 after the precocious Clarke had removed both Tim Ambrose and Chris Adams. Goodwin put on 47 with opener Richard Montgomerie, who reached 50 from just 44 balls and went on to 88 before being caught at the wicket, and remained 110 not out at the end after completing his century from 78 deliveries. Hollioake, of course, assumed responsibility with the ball as the Sussex chase became more frantic, and took two wickets to make the Man of the Match award a formality. But the bowling of Saqlain Mushtaq was another factor, as Sussex were held, just, to 323 for 8.

A first limited-overs century by Keith Parsons, the Somerset hero of their Cheltenham & Gloucester Trophy final triumph at Lord's in 2001, swept the county into the last four before a delirious crowd at Taunton. Facing a Worcestershire total of 271, in which Vikram Solanki made 53 and Ben Smith an unbeaten 85, Somerset also knew that they would have to get past that demanding target without their best batsman. Marcus Trescothick broke his left thumb trying to stop a thunderous Graeme Hick drive at cover, and Parsons came in with Somerset at 36 for 2 and in desperate need of someone to lift them. Parsons lost Mike Burns at 87, but then added 58 with Ian Blackwell and a decisive 106 for the fifth wicket with Rob Turner (47). When he was finally out for 121, driving at Matt Mason, there were only another 22 runs required, and Somerset soon completed a four-wicket win with 15 balls to spare. Parsons faced just 100 balls, hitting a six and 15 fours, and earlier in the game had bowled Hick for 39, had Gareth Batty caught, held two catches and scored a direct hit from distance for a run out. Man of the Match? The name the Taunton crowd were chanting left it in no doubt.

Semi-Finals: 1 and 4 August 2002

at Taunton
Somerset 344 for 5 (50 overs) (ID Blackwell 86, M Burns 72, PD Bowler 70)
Kent 339 (49.1 overs) (MV Fleming 63, A Symonds 55,

Keith Parsons enjoyed a fine all-round match as Somerset beat Worcestershire by four wickets in the quarter-final.

KA Parsons 4 for 55)
Somerset won by 5 runs
Man of the Match: ID Blackwell

at Headingley
Surrey 173 for 8 (48 overs) (MR Ramprakash 63, C White 4 for 35)
Yorkshire 167 for 0 (24.1 overs) (C White 100*, MJ Wood 57*)
Yorkshire won by ten wickets (DL Method: Yorkshire target 167 from 42 overs)
Man of the Match: C White

Somehow, even chasing Somerset's mammoth 344 for 5, Kent managed to throw away this wonderful semi-final match on a batsman's paradise of a pitch

Ian Blackwell, the Somerset big-hitter, who was picked for the Champions Trophy at the end of the season.

at sunny Taunton. Needing just nine more runs from the last 15 deliveries, having reached 336 for 6 through an even, if sometimes profligate, batting display, Kent found themselves bowled out for 339 and with five balls of the innings still unused. How cricket can surprise, and how it can elate and deflate! Kent captain Matthew Fleming, hoping for a Lord's final appearance in his last county season, chose to bowl first on the correct assumption that – in the blissful conditions – it would be better to know exactly how many runs equated to a winning score. Steady bowling by Mark Ealham helped Kent to keep some sort of control, but then Ian Blackwell added a violent 86 from 53 balls to the 70 and 72 by Peter Bowler and Mike Burns, respectively, that had provided the base for Somerset's challenging score. Fleming, however, set up the Kent chase by going in first and hitting 63 from 48 balls – and Kent seemed in complete mastery of their own destiny once they had reached 188 for 3 by the halfway stage. Andrew Symonds, however, got himself out for 54 with a careless shot, as did David Fulton for 48 and Matthew Walker for 35. Order seemed to have been restored by Ealham and Paul Nixon, who added 74 in ten overs for the seventh wicket, but then Nixon rashly charged down the pitch backing-up, and was run out by Keith Dutch's direct hit from midwicket when Ealham rightly sent him back. James Golding was spectacularly run out from mid-off by another direct hit from the sprawling Simon Francis (on as a substitute for cramp victim Richard Johnson), and David Masters was bowled first ball by Matt

Bulbeck. With six required from the final over, bowled by Steffan Jones, Ealham clipped a low full toss straight to midwicket. Cue cider, and tears.

After a wait of four days and 30 minutes, and a re-writing of the competition rules by the ECB, the semi-final meeting between Yorkshire and Surrey at Headingley got under way on a green pitch – and, controversially, not the original. A bowl-out should have determined the outcome after the scheduled three days set aside for the match were washed out. But, after pleas from both sides, the Board agreed to the game being staged outside that 'window', for the first time in the 40-year history of the knock-out competition. Surrey, after struggling on a seaming surface to 173 for 8 from 48 overs, must have wished they had opted for the bowl-out – and what

Controversy reigned at Headingley where, after four days of rain, Craig White's Yorkshire thrashed Surrey by ten wickets in the semi-final.

they must have been thinking after then seeing Craig White smash 100 not out from 78 balls in reply, to lead Yorkshire to a crushing ten-wicket victory, would not bear repeating. More rain had left Yorkshire chasing 167 from 42 overs, but White, dropped at slip on nought off Alex Tudor, made a mockery of the Duckworth-Lewis target by hitting a shocked Surrey attack to all parts. White, who had earlier taken 4 for 35 as only a superb technical innings of 63 by Mark Ramprakash kept Yorkshire's bowlers at bay, struck a six and 16 fours in a remarkable performance. Given the conditions, it was an astonishing effort as White and Matthew Wood (57 not out from 69 balls) steered Yorkshire home by ten wickets and with almost 18 overs to spare.

Final: 31 August 2002 at Lord's

Matthew Elliott stole the show on a sun-blessed day at Lord's, hitting a brilliant, unbeaten 128 as Yorkshire wrested the Cheltenham & Gloucester Trophy out of the hands of Somerset, the holders, by a margin of six wickets

Elliott's runs came from 125 balls, and there were 16 fours. Apart from some early uneasiness against a superb new-ball spell by Richard Johnson, who was easily the pick of the Somerset bowlers, Elliott was completely in control on the ground where, in 1997, he hit a Test century for Australia against England.

Somerset, anchored by Peter Bowler's 67 and given a morale-boosting flying start by fit-again Marcus Trescothick's 25-ball 27, reached 256 for 8 from their 50 overs as Keith Parsons, with 41, did his best to inspire the lower middle order.

Trescothick, having recovered from a broken thumb, played the shot of the day when he drove a perfectly decent length ball from Matthew Hoggard straight into the Lord's pavilion.

Three early wickets by Johnson, who comprehensively out-bowled the disappointing Andrew Caddick, left Yorkshire a little wobbly at 64

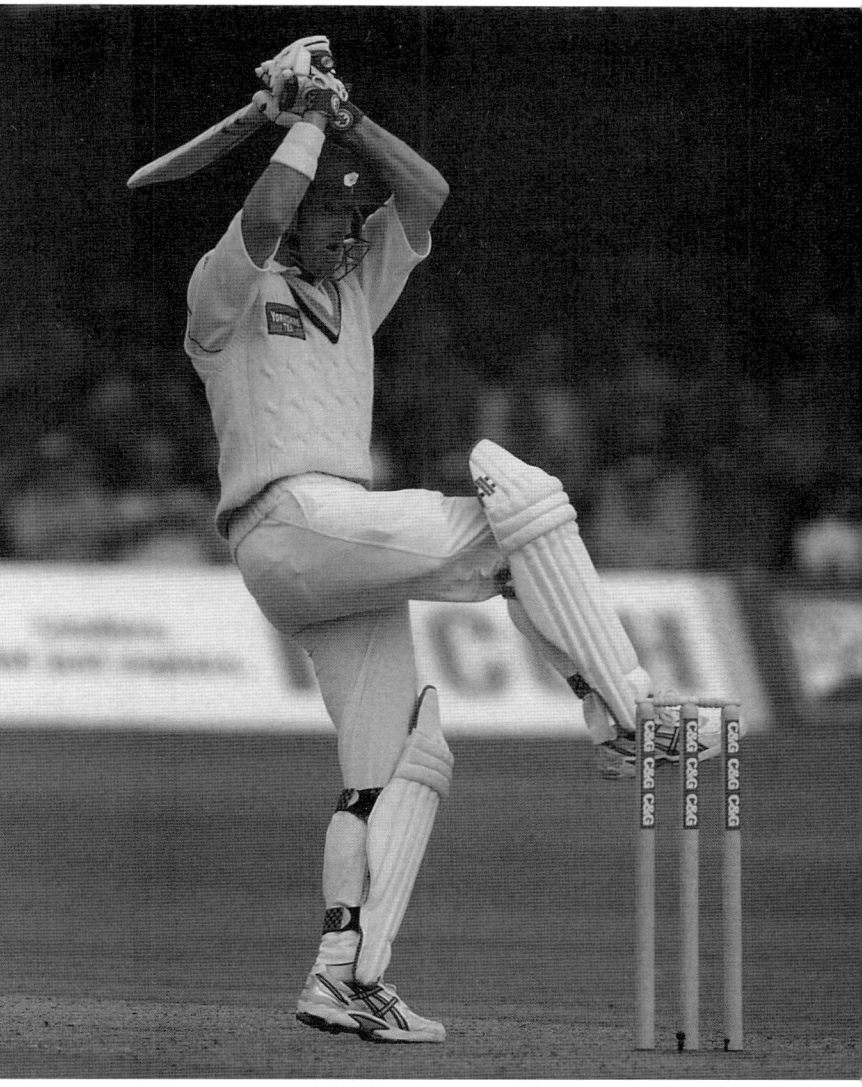

Matthew Elliott stepped in to appear for Yorkshire in the C&G final and responded with a magnificent century.

for 3, but, first with Michael Vaughan and then Anthony McGrath, Elliott imposed himself on the occasion.

He reached his century from 110 balls, and was warmly applauded from all sections of the capacity crowd. It was the first hundred by an overseas player in the final of this competition since Viv Richards for Somerset in 1979.

Sometimes taking a couple of steps down the pitch against both quicker and slower bowlers alike, Elliott batted with class and a calm authority – as if to underline, in the lead-up to an Ashes winter, just how much strength in depth the Australians possess.

Vaughan was perhaps unlucky to be adjudged lbw for 31, before he had really got into his stride, but McGrath looked in prime form as soon as he joined Elliott and finished on 46 not out to add to his useful nine-over bowling stint earlier in the day.

Elliott and McGrath, in the end, added an unbroken 103 for the fifth wicket and victory arrived on a golden evening with two full overs in hand. It was Yorkshire's first knock-out cup title since 1969 and only their fourth domestic success since then.

Richard Blakey holds the C&G Cup aloft to end a turbulent season for Yorkshire.

FINAL – SOMERSET v. YORKSHIRE
31 August 2002 at Lord's

SOMERSET

Batting

PD Bowler	c Blakey b Hoggard	67
ME Trescothick	c Vaughan b Hoggard	27
J Cox (capt)	lbw b McGrath	34
M Burns	lbw b Hoggard	21
ID Blackwell	b Sidebottom	12
KA Parsons	c Sidebottom b Hoggard	41
*RJ Turner	c White b Sidebottom	20
RL Johnson	b Hoggard	2
KP Dutch	not out	13
AR Caddick	not out	0
PS Jones		
Extras	b 1, lb 6, w 6, nb 6	19
	50 overs (8 wickets)	256

Bowling

	O	M	R	W
Silverwood	8	1	30	–
Hoggard	10	0	65	5
Sidebottom	9	0	49	2
McGrath	9	0	37	1
Dawson	10	0	48	–
Vaughan	4	0	20	–

Fall of Wickets
1-41, 2-122, 3-159, 4-171, 5-191, 6-230, 7-233, 8-250

YORKSHIRE

Batting

C White	c Turner b Johnson	12
MJ Wood	b Johnson	19
CEW Silverwood	b Johnson	0
MTG Elliott	not out	128
MP Vaughan	lbw b Jones	31
A McGrath	not out	46
GM Fellows		
*RJ Blakey (capt)		
RKJ Dawson		
RJ Sidebottom		
MJ Hoggard		
Extras	lb 7, w 15, nb 2	24
	48 overs (4 wickets)	260

Bowling

	O	M	R	W
Caddick	9	0	53	–
Johnson	10	2	51	3
Parsons	6	0	31	–
Jones	9	0	45	1
Dutch	8	0	43	–
Blackwell	6	0	30	–

Fall of Wickets
1-19, 2-19, 3-64, 4-157

Umpires: JW Holder & G Sharp (TV: K Palmer)
Toss: Somerset
Man of the Match: MTG Elliott

Yorkshire won by six wickets

INDIA

England in India
Zimbabwe in India
India Domestic First-Class Season
India Domestic One-Day Season
India First-Class Averages

ENGLAND IN INDIA
By Jonathan Agnew

FIRST TEST
3–6 December 2001 at Mohali, Chandigarh

In many ways, it was a miracle this match was ever played at all. Coming less than three months after the terrorist attacks on New York and Washington, northern India was heavily involved in supporting the allied operation in Afghanistan and was considered, by some, to be too dangerous to visit. These included Robert Croft and Andrew Caddick who, given the opportunity not to travel to India by the England and Wales Cricket Board, decided that they would 'put their families first' and opt out of the tour. This was received more sympathetically in some quarters than in others, but their move resulted in late call-ups for Martyn Ball and Richard Johnson, neither of whom, it transpired, bowled a ball in anger on the trip!

The war in Afghanistan was not the only cloud that hung over this Test match: there was trouble much closer to home in the form of Jagmohan Dalmiya, the erstwhile president of the ICC who had, to the surprise and horror of many, returned to cricket politics as the president of the Indian Cricket Board. Never a man to miss an opportunity to confront England over any issue which could swiftly be manipulated into an example of racism, Dalmiya had seized upon the actions of the match referee, Mike Denness, who had banned Virender Sehwag for one Test during India's recent series with South Africa (see pages 272–75). The fact that Sehwag's appeals for catches in that match were nothing less than blatant attempts to cheat was conveniently and completely ignored by Mr Dalmiya, who turned the incident into a personal crusade against the ICC. Absurdly, he insisted that Sehwag, who sat out the following unofficial Test, should be cleared to play at Mohali. The ECB disagreed and, acting with the ICC, stated that if Sehwag were selected by India, England would fly home immediately. It was typical Dalmiya brinkmanship, and a situation he could not possibly win. Sehwag was not chosen, but the uncertainty the distraction had created was reflected both by the poor ticket sales and the lack of organization at the Punjab Stadium, which is the most efficient and hospitable cricket ground in India.

Previous page: Try as they might to blunt the mastery of Sachin Tendulkar with negative bowling, England still saw the little maestro average 76.75 as India won the three-match series 1–0.

Wisely, Mr Dalmiya stayed away from the area throughout the match.

This was to be England's first experience of batting against Harbhajan Singh, the Indian off spinner who had created such excitement against the Australians the previous winter. Anil Kumble was a well-known threat, but Harbhajan was a different prospect altogether, and the fact that India's pace attack was comprised of three uncapped youngsters was widely overlooked. Indeed, this was the case when Saurav Ganguly won the toss (the tenth consecutive time Nasser Hussain had lost the toss in a Test match) and invited England to bat first.

At 129 for 1, this had all the makings of having been a disastrous decision. Trescothick and Hussain appeared to be in little trouble as they recovered from the early loss of Butcher to Yohannan. Their partnership of 125 was cut short when Trescothick played no stroke and was bowled for 66. Thorpe and Hussain took the score along to 172, when Thorpe was caught at slip for 23, starting a collapse in which England lost eight wickets for 66 runs; their last six for only 14! Only England can produce foul-ups quite as spectacular as this and, as we had feared, the man who caused the chaos was Harbhajan, who, in benign conditions, took 5 for 6 in 7.3 overs.

The Turbanator, Harbhajan Singh, condemned England to a heavy defeat at Mohali.

Richard Dawson deputized in Robert Croft's absence, and took four wickets on his debut.

England's only hope of staying in the game was to bowl India out cheaply, but they were thwarted by a painstaking century by Deep Dasgupta, their opening batsman and wicketkeeper. He batted five-and-a-half hours for 100 and when he was third out for 212, the stage was set for his more flamboyant colleagues to stamp India's authority on the game. However, Hussain and Fletcher had been doing their homework and frustrated Rahul Dravid and Sachin Tendulkar with some well-directed, if negative, bowling aimed a foot outside the off stump with eight fielders on the offside and only one on the leg. Once or twice, Tendulkar showed his brilliance by knocking deliveries through midwicket, but the tactic kept the Indian scoring rate in check. Dravid's 86 took five hours, and Tendulkar's 88 nearly four, but when Tendulkar edged Hoggard to Foster (who had earlier dropped Dravid on 33, and was to miss a straightforward stumping offered by Ganguly) India's lead was already 135, and looking ominous. Ganguly scored 47 – but the Indian press still claimed he was out of form – Laxman 28 and Bangar 36 as the home side was finally bowled out shortly before the close of play on the third day for 469 – an imposing lead of 231.

England lost only three wickets before lunch on the fourth day, but India had wrapped up the match before the close of play. Again, Trescothick looked comfortable in scoring 46, but Kumble made amends for having played second fiddle in England's first innings by running through the middle order. Only Thorpe stood firm – he was ninth out for 62 – and the last seven wickets fell for only 76 runs as Kumble took 6 for 81. It was, indeed, a worrying beginning to England's series, made all the more so by the lack of any cricket between the Tests. They would have only five days to get this heavy defeat out of their minds before meeting the same bowlers in Ahmedabad.

FIRST TEST – INDIA v. ENGLAND
3–6 December 2001 at Mohali, Chandigarh

ENGLAND

	First innings		Second innings	
MA Butcher	c Laxman b Yohannan	4	c sub (JJ Martin) b Yohannan	18
ME Trescothick	b Yohannan	66	c Siddiqui b Yohannan	46
N Hussain (capt)	c Laxman b Kumble	85	b Kumble	12
GP Thorpe	c Laxman b Siddiqui	23	c & b Kumble	62
MR Ramprakash	c Das b Harbhajan Singh	17	lbw b Kumble	28
A Flintoff	c Kumble b Harbhajan Singh	18	c Ganguly b Kumble	4
C White	c Dravid b Kumble	5	c Dasgupta b Harbhajan Singh	22
*JS Foster	lbw b Harbhajan Singh	0	lbw b Harbhajan Singh	5
J Ormond	not out	3	b Kumble	0
RKJ Dawson	c Laxman b Harbhajan Singh	5	b Kumble	11
MJ Hoggard	c sub (CC Williams), b Harbhajan Singh	0	not out	0
Extras	lb 7, nb 5	12	b 10, lb 13, w 1, nb 3	27
		238		**235**

	First innings				Second innings			
	O	M	R	W	O	M	R	W
Yohannan	18	3	75	2	17	3	56	2
Siddiqui	11	2	32	1	8	3	16	-
Bangar	5	2	17	-				
Kumble	19	6	52	2	28.4	6	81	6
Tendulkar	4	3	4	-				
Harbhajan Singh	19.3	4	51	5	24	9	59	2

Fall of Wickets
1-4, 2-129, 3-172, 4-200, 5-224, 6-227, 7-229, 8-229, 9-238
1-68, 2-82, 3-87, 4-159, 5-163, 6-196, 7-206, 8-207, 9-224

INDIA

	First innings		Second innings	
SS Das	b Butcher	2		
*D Dasgupta	b White	100	not out	0
A Kumble	c Foster b Dawson	37		
R Dravid	lbw b Ormond	86		
SR Tendulkar	c Foster b Hoggard	88		
SC Ganguly (capt)	c Thorpe b Hoggard	47		
VVS Laxman	c Hussain b Dawson	28		
SB Bangar	c & b Dawson	36		
Harbhajan Singh	lbw b Dawson	1		
IR Siddiqui	b Hoggard	24	(1) not out	5
T Yohannan	not out	2		
Extras	lb 12, w 2, nb 4	18		
		469	(0 wicket)	**5**

	First innings				Second innings			
	O	M	R	W	O	M	R	W
Hoggard	32	9	98	3	0.2	0	5	-
Ormond	28	8	70	1				
Butcher	7	1	19	1				
Flintoff	34	11	80	-				
White	25	8	56	1				
Dawson	43	6	134	4				

Fall of Wickets
1-23, 2-76, 3-212, 4-290, 5-370, 6-378, 7-430, 8-436, 9-449

Umpires: SA Bucknor & S Venkataraghavan
Toss: India
Test Debut: SB Bangar, IR Siddiqui, T Yohannan (India); RKJ Dawson, JS Foster (England)
Man of the Match: A Kumble

India won by ten wickets

SECOND TEST
11–15 December 2001 at Ahmedabad

The Sardar Patel Stadium in Ahmedabad is as far removed from the glorious Punjab Stadium as it is possible to be. Frankly, it is barely fit for human habitation, so it was little wonder that England, who produced a magnificent fightback after their early defeat, could not quite find the inspiration amongst the filthy, pigeon-soiled, decaying walls to level the series. Indeed, had Hussain summoned the courage to declare a little earlier on the fourth day, India might not have been able to cling on for their draw.

England's preparations were hit on the opening morning when it was announced that Graham Thorpe was to fly home immediately in an attempt to save his failing marriage. Since England were already woefully inexperienced, Thorpe's departure left a gaping hole in the side and Hussain found himself without his trusty second lieutenant. Michael Vaughan was drafted in at No. 4, and Ashley Giles (who had been injured for the first Test) returned at the expense of James Ormond.

At least England won the toss for a change and, by lunch, had reached 79 for no wicket. Butcher and Trescothick extended their partnership to 124 when Butcher became the first of Kumble's seven wickets in the innings. Eighteen overs later, England had slipped to 180 for 5 – with Kumble taking all of

them – and another familiar collapse was in full swing. The fourth victim was Trescothick, who joined the unenviable list of Test batsmen to be dismissed on 99, but the situation was retrieved by Craig White who was dropped three times and also survived a stumping chance on his way to his maiden Test century. There are few more genial men in the game than 'Chalky', and his landmark was warmly appreciated as much in the press box as in the England dressing room.

Ramprakash, with 37, and Foster, who made a promising 40 in a stand of 105, kept White company, and as England staggered to 409, the last five wickets had added 227. Kumble finished with the mighty impressive figures of 7 for 115, while his spin partner Harbhajan managed just 1 for 78.

By the close of the second day, India had reached 71 for 2 with Tendulkar on 2 not out. The next morning, the barren stadium was buzzing with thousands of spectators who crammed into the dusty ground to watch their hero bat. He did not let them down either, giving a masterful display of how to blunt Hussain's negative tactics with breathtaking ease. The field set by Hussain was identical to the one which had been mildly successful in Mohali, with eight men on the offside, and just one – a wide mid-on – on the leg. No matter how accurately Hoggard and Flintoff bowled wide of the off stump, Tendulkar still managed to flick the ball across the line and, after one encounter with Hoggard which produced two fours and a three, Hussain conceded defeat. He would return at Bangalore with an even more dastardly plan but, for now, Tendulkar had won the day.

As India lost eight wickets for 220 in the day – with Giles taking 5 for 67 – Tendulkar duly reached his century, with his second 50 runs coming from only 55 balls. England found themselves with a lead of 116, but, by now, illness had struck the camp. Butcher batted bravely despite great discomfort, taking four-and-a-quarter hours over his 92. Hussain scored exactly 50, but the innings drifted as the captain feared the 'Tendulkar factor' might make a mockery of a more generous declaration than the 374 India were set to win from 94 overs. This was a curious paradox in that

Craig White, one of the most popular England cricketers, scored his first Test century in the second Test at Ahmedabad.

Although England tried to tie him down by bowling wide of the off stump, Sachin Tendulkar was still able to score a century in India's first innings.

Hussain's captaincy throughout the match had been nothing short of inspirational. Carefully thought-through field placements were complimented by lengthy discussions with the bowlers and an air of being thoroughly in charge. The contrast with his opposite number, Ganguly, could not have been more obvious. Aloof and apparently disinterested, Ganguly was far from impressive. This, however, is in no way a criticism of his refusal to chase Hussain's target on the final day.

It is possible that Hussain realized, too late, that he had batted on for too long because his captaincy became frenetic on the final morning. It is one thing to tinker with the field as situations develop and change, but it is quite another to change the bowling virtually non-stop and adjust the fielders' positions almost constantly. Poor Richard Dawson, the young off spinner who would probably have been England's most potent weapon given half a chance, found himself bowling no fewer than five spells before lunch in which he bowled a total of nine overs! It was manic cricket and gave the youngster no opportunity to settle into a rhythm.

At least Dawson had the satisfaction of dismissing the great Tendulkar before the game drifted to sleep – he popped up a catch to Vaughan at square leg – but Das and Dasgupta had long since earned India their draw by putting together an opening stand of 119, and England were now faced with the prospect of having to win the final Test to save the series.

SECOND TEST – INDIA v. ENGLAND
11–15 December 2001 at Ahmedabad

ENGLAND

	First innings		Second innings	
MA Butcher	c Dasgupta b Kumble	51	c Dravid b Harbhajan Singh	92
ME Trescothick	c Dasgupta b Kumble	99	c Das b Srinath	12
N Hussain (capt)	lbw b Kumble	1	c Sehwag b Harbhajan Singh	50
MP Vaughan	c Sehwag b Kumble	11	(7) not out	31
MR Ramprakash	b Tendulkar	37	(4) c Tendulkar b Harbhajan Singh	19
A Flintoff	c Laxman b Kumble	0	(5) b Kumble	4
C White	b Harbhajan Singh	121	(6) run out (Yohannan/Harbhajan Singh)	18
*JS Foster	c Tendulkar b Kumble	40	c Yohannan b Kumble	3
AF Giles	b Kumble	7	c Das b Harbhajan Singh	8
RKJ Dawson	c Dasgupta b Srinath	9	c Tendulkar b Kumble	2
MJ Hoggard	not out	4	c Das b Harbhajan Singh	1
Extras	b 6, lb 15, w 1, nb 5	27	b 6, lb 8, nb 3	17
		407		**257**

	First innings				Second innings			
	O	M	R	W	O	M	R	W
Srinath	29	7	105	1	9	2	24	1
Yohannan	17	2	57	–	4	0	25	–
Harbhajan Singh	35.3	9	78	1	30.2	6	71	5
Kumble	51	13	115	7	38	5	118	3
Tendulkar	10	0	27	1				
Sehwag	2	1	4	–	2	0	5	–

Fall of Wickets
1-124, 2-144, 3-172, 4-176, 5-180, 6-239, 7-344, 8-360, 9-391
1-21, 2-133, 3-178, 4-183, 5-183, 6-225, 7-231, 8-247, 9-253

INDIA

	First innings		Second innings	
SS Das	c Butcher b Flintoff	41	run out (Giles/Foster)	58
*D Dasgupta	c Hussain b Giles	17	c Butcher b Dawson	60
R Dravid	c Foster b Hoggard	7	not out	26
SR Tendulkar	c Hussain b Hoggard	103	c Vaughan b Dawson	26
SC Ganguly (capt)	c sub (MCJ Ball) b Flintoff	5	not out	16
VVS Laxman	c Butcher b Giles	75		
V Sehwag	lbw b White	20		
A Kumble	b Giles	5		
Harbhajan Singh	c Flintoff b Giles	0		
J Srinath	c Butcher b Giles	0		
T Yohannan	not out	3		
Extras	b 5, lb 6, w 1, nb 3	15	b 12	12
		291	(3 wickets)	**198**

	First innings				Second innings			
	O	M	R	W	O	M	R	W
Hoggard	28	7	65	2	17	6	33	–
Flintoff	22	7	42	2	8	4	17	–
Giles	43.3	16	67	5	31	12	57	–
Dawson	15	0	73	–	32	9	72	2
White	12	2	33	1	9	5	7	–

Fall of Wickets
1-54, 2-64, 3-86, 4-93, 5-211, 6-248, 7-268, 8-272, 9-274
1-119, 2-124, 3-168

Umpires: ID Robinson & AV Jayaprakash
Toss: England
Man of the Match: C White

Match drawn

THIRD TEST
19–23 December 2001 at Bangalore

Bangalore is the prettiest of India's many cities, but a mysterious tropical cyclone lurking to the east in the Bay of Bengal produced murky, miserable conditions that blighted much of the match. When it was not raining, the floodlights were fully on at all times and the last two days were all but completely obliterated.

Apparently a turgid draw, then, in which England had the upper hand, but, in fact, the match was anything but dull as Hussain unveiled a controversial tactic that was designed purely to frustrate Tendulkar. It was, in fact, a development of the Ahmedabad theme in which England's bowlers had directed the ball wide of the off stump with an almost non-existent legside field. Tendulkar's brilliance had thwarted them there and, clearly, England's think-tank had sat down and wondered how it could contain the little genius. The result was a policy so dreadful and so negative that, if allowed to persist, will kill cricket stone dead within a decade.

Rather than bowl outside the off stump – which at least gave Tendulkar a chance of hitting the ball – Hussain directed his bowlers – including his seamers – to fire the ball deliberately wide of the leg stump, which prevented Tendulkar from hitting the ball at all. The nearest thing to a Bodyline field was set, and everyone sat and watched in utter boredom and mounting despair as ball after ball was propelled down the legside. The umpiring was nothing short of pathetic: Messrs de Silva and Jayaprakash could have nipped this in the bud immediately by calling a wide or two, but nothing was done. This is not a way for cricket to be played at any level; it kills it both as a contest and as a spectacle, and you certainly will not find me hailing Hussain's tactic as 'innovative' as some did that day. And all this despite the fact that Hussain could justify his move by the fact that Tendulkar, in desperation, came down the pitch and, for the first time in his Test career, was stumped with his score on 90. To claim credit for that, though, is to miss the point entirely.

For the second time on the trot, England won the toss and decided to bat. India had surprised their supporters by going into the match with only one seamer, despite the conditions, preferring Sarandeep Singh (an off spinner with a decidedly dubious action) to Yohannan. England kept the same team that had made strides at Ahmedabad

The tactic changed at Bangalore with deliberate legside bowling. Here Tendulkar seizes a rare opportunity to drive during his innings of 90.

and, although the floodlights produced an eerie half light, they made a good fist of their first innings.

The most productive partnership was of 113 between Ramprakash and Vaughan. When they were separated, for 58 and 64 respectively, Flintoff played one of the most gormless strokes in Test history to reduce England to 206 for 5. Taking a pace down the pitch, he casually flicked Sarandeep straight to Tendulkar at midwicket for his second duck of the series, in which he averaged just five with the bat.

Foster and White pulled things around, just as they had done in the previous match, with Foster making his highest Test score of 48. He and Giles added a further 63 and, shortly after lunch on the second day, an increasingly desperate Kumble, who had bowled needing one wicket throughout the innings for his 300th victim in Test cricket, finally trapped the No. 11, Hoggard, lbw and England were bowled out for 336.

India were soon 121 for 5 thanks to a mixture of incisive and negative bowling by Flintoff and Hoggard. While Tendulkar remained, and the weather continued to frustrate, a draw was always the most likely outcome, and the only real interest centred on whether or not Tendulkar could overcome England's plot and reach his hundred. However, all mortals have a breaking point and England should claim not an ounce of credit that, having been at the crease for four-and-three-quarter hours for his 90, Tendulkar simply had enough and aimed a slog at Giles from a yard or two down the pitch. England celebrated, but the only reason to rejoice was the fact that we would not be forced to sit and watch the latest 'leg theory' any more.

Hoggard and Flintoff took four wickets each, but England were unable to build upon their lead of 98 because time simply ran out, and the players flew home for a Christmas break before returning to India for the one-day series.

Matthew Hoggard, leading the attack, put in a spirited performance in Bangalore, picking up four wickets under the floodlights.

THIRD TEST – INDIA v. ENGLAND
19–23 December 2001 at Bangalore

ENGLAND

	First innings		Second innings	
MA Butcher	run out (Dravid/Dasgupta)	27	not out	23
ME Trescothick	c Laxman b Srinath	8	not out	9
N Hussain (capt)	c Dasgupta b Srinath	43		
MP Vaughan	handled the ball	64		
MR Ramprakash	c Dravid b Sarandeep Singh	58		
A Flintoff	c Tendulkar b Sarandeep Singh	0		
C White	c Das b Srinath	39		
*JS Foster	c Dasgupta b Srinath	48		
AF Giles	lbw b Sarandeep Singh	28		
RKJ Dawson	not out	0		
MJ Hoggard	lbw b Kumble	1		
Extras	b 8, lb 9, nb 3	20	b 1	1
		336	(0 wicket)	**33**

	First innings				Second innings			
	O	M	R	W	O	M	R	W
Srinath	29	9	73	4	4	0	19	–
Ganguly	13	3	39	–	3	0	12	–
Kumble	29.3	6	74	1				
Harbhajan Singh	27	7	59	–	0.1	0	1	–
Sarandeep Singh	21	5	54	3				
Tendulkar	3	0	19	–				
Sehwag	1	0	1	–				

Fall of Wickets
1-21, 2-68, 3-93, 4-206, 5-206, 6-219, 7-271, 8-334, 9-334

INDIA

	First innings	
SS Das	b Flintoff	28
*D Dasgupta	c Trescothick b Flintoff	0
VVS Laxman	b Flintoff	12
SR Tendulkar	st Foster b Giles	90
R Dravid	c Foster b Hoggard	3
SC Ganguly (capt)	c Butcher b Hoggard	0
V Sehwag	c Foster b Hoggard	66
A Kumble	c Trescothick b Flintoff	14
Harbhajan Singh	c Hussain b Hoggard	8
Sarandeep Singh	run out (Vaughan)	4
J Srinath	not out	2
Extras	b 4, lb 4, nb 3	11
		238

	First innings			
	O	M	R	W
Hoggard	24.3	7	80	4
Flintoff	28	9	50	4
Giles	34	18	74	1
White	8	2	26	–

Fall of Wickets
1-8, 2-22, 3-88, 4-121, 5-121, 6-173, 7-218, 8-228, 9-235

Umpires: EAR de Silva & AV Jayaprakash
Toss: England
Man of the Match: A Flintoff
Player of the Series: SR Tendulkar

Match drawn

TEST MATCH AVERAGES
India v. England

INDIA

Batting	M	Inns	NO	HS	Runs	Av	100	50	c/st
SR Tendulkar	3	4	0	103	307	76.75	1	2	4
D Dasgupta	3	5	1	100	177	44.25	1	1	6/-
V Sehwag	2	2	0	66	86	43.00	–	1	2
R Dravid	3	4	1	86	122	40.66	–	1	3
VVS Laxman	3	3	0	75	115	38.33	–	1	6
SS Das	3	4	0	58	129	32.25	–	1	5
SC Ganguly	3	4	1	47	68	22.66	–	–	1
A Kumble	3	3	0	37	56	18.66	–	–	2
Harbhajan Singh	3	3	0	8	9	3.00	–	–	–
J Srinath	2	2	1	2*	2	2.00	–	–	–

Also batted in two Tests: T Yohannan 2*, 3* (1 ct)
Also batted in one Test: SB Bangar 36; IR Siddiqui 24, 5* (1 ct); Sarandeep Singh 4

Bowling	Overs	Mds	Runs	Wkts	Av	Best	10m	5/inn
A Kumble	166.1	36	440	19	23.15	7-115	1	2
Harbhajan Singh	136.3	35	319	13	24.53	5-51	–	2
J Srinath	71	18	221	6	36.83	4-73	–	–
T Yohannan	56	8	213	4	53.25	2-56	–	–

Also bowled: SB Bangar 5-2-17-0; SC Ganguly 16-3-51-0; Sarandeep Singh 21-5-54-3;
V Sehwag 5-1-10-0; IR Siddiqui 19-5-48-1; SR Tendulkar 17-3-50-1

ENGLAND

Batting	M	Inns	NO	HS	Runs	Av	100	50	c/st
MP Vaughan	2	3	1	64	106	53.00	–	1	1
ME Trescothick	3	6	1	99	240	48.00	–	2	2
MA Butcher	3	6	1	92	215	43.00	–	2	5
C White	3	5	0	121	205	41.00	1	–	–
N Hussain	3	5	0	85	191	38.20	–	2	4
MR Ramprakash	3	5	0	58	159	31.80	–	1	–
JS Foster	3	5	0	48	96	19.20	–	–	5/1
AF Giles	2	3	0	28	43	14.33	–	–	–
RKJ Dawson	3	5	1	11	27	6.75	–	–	1
A Flintoff	3	5	0	18	26	5.20	–	–	1
MJ Hoggard	3	5	2	4*	6	2.00	–	–	–

Also batted in one Test: J Ormond 3*, 0; GP Thorpe 23, 62 (1 ct)

Bowling	Overs	Mds	Runs	Wkts	Av	Best	10m	5/inn
MJ Hoggard	101.5	29	281	9	31.22	4-80	–	–
A Flintoff	92	31	189	6	31.50	4-50	–	–
AF Giles	108.3	46	198	6	33.00	5-67	1	–
RKJ Dawson	90	15	279	6	46.50	4-134	–	–

Also bowled: MA Butcher 7-1-19-1; J Ormond 28-8-70-1; C White 54-17-122-2

ONE–DAY INTERNATIONALS

Not content with merely disrupting the start of the Test series with his absurd stance over the ban handed to Virender Sehwag during India's recent series against South Africa, Jagmohan Dalmiya, the president of the Indian Board, caused further ructions over his demand that England should play an extra one-day international. Failure to do so, he insisted, would mean that India would not play the fourth Test in England the following summer, although this had already been agreed in writing and tickets had already been sold in advance.

The England management were aghast at this demand, because it would have an effect not only on the time spent at home at Christmas, but also the amount of preparation they would have in New Zealand, where the team was due to travel immediately after the short one-day series.

The ECB had little option but to give in to Dalmiya's blackmail and an extra match was scheduled for Cuttack – one of the least accessible grounds in India, and home of the Orissa Cricket Association which was now handsomely rewarded for having backed Dalmiya's challenge for the presidency.

In fact, the series was highly entertaining with England coming from 3–1 behind to square the rubber 3–3. The highlight was the explosive batting of Tendulkar and Sehwag, who formed the opening pair in the third match which Ganguly had to miss through injury. Stands of 107, 134, 39 and 36 were made at an extraordinary rate, with Sehwag scoring 206 runs in those four games from only 185 balls! It was devastating batting that thoroughly intimidated England's bowlers, and it was largely due to the batting of Trescothick – who averaged 53 – and Knight, who scored a very good century in the penultimate match, that England were able to level the series.

The opening game was staged at Eden Gardens, Calcutta, in front of an estimated crowd of 100,000. It was, indeed, an extraordinary spectacle and England were deprived of victory by a simply appalling umpiring error by Mr Sharma who despatched Trescothick lbw for 121 when he was steering England to their target of 282.

Incisive bowling by Gough helped the visitors to level things up at Cuttack where England won another high-scoring match by 16 runs, but India romped into the lead on a hot and sticky night in Madras. Hollioake and Snape scuttled between the wickets in a partnership of 70 for the seventh wicket, but

Marcus Trescothick was guiding England to victory at Eden Gardens when an appalling umpiring error stopped both him and the tourists in their tracks.

England's total of 217 was at least 30 runs short, and was overtaken with more than three overs to spare.

The fourth match, in Kanpur, was so embarrassingly one-sided that one wondered how England would ever recover from the mauling. Defending only 219 was always going to be difficult, but India reached their target with more than 20 overs to spare, thanks to Tendulkar and Sehwag who put on 134 in just 17 overs! However, thanks to Knight's hundred, England were able to post an impressive 272 for 5 in Delhi, thanks to a remarkable spell of 5 for 14 by Giles that derailed the middle order, India failed by only three runs to clinch the series.

So everything was to play for in the last game in Bombay. England's 255 was by no means impregnable, and although Ganguly made a welcome return to form with 80, India needed 11 from the final over bowled by Gough and fell six runs short.

Sachin Tendulkar formed an explosive opening partnership with Virender Sehwag. In the fourth match of the series they notched up 134 in just 17 overs.

Match One
19 January 2002 at Eden Gardens, Calcutta (floodlit)
India 281 for 8 (50 overs) (D Mongia 71)
England 259 (44 overs) (ME Trescothick 121)
India won by 22 runs
Man of the Match: ME Trescothick

Match Two
22 January 2002 at Barabati Stadium, Cuttack
England 250 for 7 (50 overs) (PD Collingwood 71*, MP Vaughan 63)
India 234 (48.4 overs)
England won by 16 runs
Man of the Match: PD Collingwood

Match Three
25 January 2002 at MA Chidambaram Stadium, Chennai (floodlit)
England 217 (48 overs) (AB Agarkar 4 for 34)
India 221 for 6 (46.4 overs) (SR Tendulkar 68, V Sehwag 51)
India won by four wickets
Man of the Match: SR Tendulkar

Match Four
28 January 2002 at Green Park, Kanpur
England 218 for 7 (39 overs) (NV Knight 74)
India 219 for 2 (29.4 overs) (SR Tendulkar 87*, V Sehwag 82)
India won by eight wickets
Man of the Match: V Sehwag

Match Five
31 January 2002 at Feroz Shah Kotla, Delhi
England 271 for 5 (50 overs) (NV Knight 105, A Flintoff 52)
India 269 for 8 (50 overs) (SC Ganguly 74, AF Giles 5 for 57)
England won by 2 runs
Man of the Match: AF Giles

Match Six
3 February 2002 at Wankhede Stadium, Mumbai (floodlit)
England 255 (49.1 overs) (ME Trescothick 95, Harbhajan Singh 5 for 43)
India 250 (49.5 overs) (SC Ganguly 80)
England won by 5 runs
Man of the Match: ME Trescothick
Player of the Series: SR Tendulkar

ZIMBABWE IN INDIA
By Qamar Ahmed

FIRST TEST
21–25 February 2002 at Nagpur

India found it plain sailing in the first of the two Tests as they outplayed Zimbabwe to win by a margin of an innings and 101 runs. For the Zimbabweans it was their fourth successive defeat, having already been whitewashed in Sri Lanka. Following on 283 runs behind on the first innings Zimbabwe were out for 182 in their second as Harbhajan Singh (with 4 for 46) and Anil Kumble (with 5 for 63) spun them out. Only Trevor Gripper, with 60 runs to his credit, showed any resistance to the Indian spin duo.

Zimbabwe, having won the toss, decided to bat first. Despite losing Gripper early to Zaheer Khan, they were rallied by a second-wicket record partnership of 106 between Stuart Carlisle (77)

Sachin Tendulkar was one of three Indian centurions at Nagpur as Zimbabwe were put to the sword.

and Alistair Campbell (57). From 118 for 1 Zimbabwe then slumped to 287 all out with Travis Friend unbeaten on 60.

India were soon amongst the runs. Opener Shiv Sunder Das struck 105, his second Test century both of which had been scored against Zimbabwe, before Rahul Dravid and Sachin Tendulkar mauled the Zimbabwe attack on the third day. Dravid was out for 65, but Tendulkar reached his 28th Test century and went on to score 176 on the fourth day before Price had him caught at the wicket – he had faced 316 balls. Sanjay Bangar, another talented young player, scored his maiden century in only his second Test and India declared on

FIRST TEST – INDIA v. ZIMBABWE
21–25 February 2002 at Nagpur

ZIMBABWE

	First innings		Second innings	
SV Carlisle (capt)	run out (Das/Harbhajan Singh)	77	lbw b Khan	28
TR Gripper	c Dasgupta b Khan	5	c sub (V Sehwag) b Harbhajan Singh	60
ADR Campbell	c Laxman b Kumble	57	c Laxman b Kumble	30
A Flower	b Khan	3	c Dravid b Kumble	8
GJ Rennie	c sub (V Sehwag) b Srinath	9	c sub (V Sehwag) b Kumble	25
GW Flower	c Dravid b Kumble	14	(7) lbw b Kumble	1
HH Streak	c Das b Kumble	24	(8) lbw b Kumble	8
*T Taibu	b Kumble	1	(9) c sub (V Sehwag) b Harbhajan Singh	0
TJ Friend	not out	60	(10) not out	6
RW Price	run out (Kumble/Dasgupta)	18	(6) c Dravid b Harbhajan Singh	4
BT Watambwa	c Laxman b Kumble	0	c Tendulkar b Harbhajan Singh	1
Extras	b 6, lb 11, nb 2	19	b 1, lb 8, nb 2	11
		287		**182**

	First innings				Second innings			
	O	M	R	W	O	M	R	W
Srinath	22	6	65	1	6	3	20	–
Khan	15	3	46	3	8	1	33	1
Bangar	8	3	20	–				
Kumble	32.5	12	81	4	37	15	63	5
Harbhajan Singh	26	8	58	–	31.4	9	46	4
Tendulkar					6	2	11	–

Fall of Wickets
1-12, 2-118, 3-125, 4-151, 5-175, 6-182, 7-194, 8-227, 9-286
1-32, 2-80, 3-103, 4-147, 5-156, 6-159, 7-161, 8-167, 9-181

INDIA

	First innings	
SS Das	c Campbell b Price	105
*D Dasgupta	b Price	33
R Dravid	b Streak	65
SR Tendulkar	c A Flower b Price	176
SC Ganguly (capt)	c GW Flower b Price	38
VVS Laxman	c Rennie b Price	13
SB Bangar	not out	100
Z Khan	b Watambwa	0
A Kumble	not out	13
J Srinath		
Harbhajan Singh		
Extras	b 16, lb 2, w 3, nb 6	27
	(7 wickets dec.)	**570**

	First innings			
	O	M	R	W
Streak	34	9	108	1
Watambwa	25.5	6	87	1
Price	68	18	182	5
Friend	22	3	61	–
GW Flower	30	8	96	–
Gripper	5	0	18	–

Fall of Wickets
1-79, 2-209, 3-247, 4-344, 5-376, 6-547, 7-547

Umpires: DR Shepherd & S Venkataraghavan
Toss: Zimbabwe
Man of the Match: A Kumble

India won by an innings & 101 runs

570 for 7 to give their bowlers five sessions in which to bowl Zimbabwe out for the second time.

At the end of the fourth day, Zimbabwe had made reasonable progress to 152 for 4, but then lost their last six wickets for only 26 runs on the final morning. Kumble took his 19th five-wicket haul in a Test, finishing with match figures of 9 for 145 in his comeback match following surgery to a shoulder injury.

SECOND TEST
28 February–4 March 2002 at Delhi

The two-match series was wrapped up at lunch on the fifth and final day, and India's four-wicket win was well deserved. Set 122 runs to win India, 36 for 3 overnight, suddenly collapsed to 105 for 6 before reaching the required runs without any further ado. Sachin Tendulkar made 42 and Shiv Sunder Das 31, but left-arm spinner Raymond Price nabbed the prized wickets of Tendulkar and Rahul Dravid to bring the Zimbabweans back into the reckoning. Harbhajan Singh then dashed their unlikely aspirations with some lusty hitting to win the match for India.

India were more than pleased to record their fourth successive home win in a Test series after Zimbabwe, having won the toss, had made 329 in their first innings. Andy Flower was out for 92 and Dion Ebrahim also missed out on his hundred when Javagal Srinath had him leg before for 94.

India, in reply, were 171 for 4 at the end of the second day with the Indian captain, Saurav Ganguly, unbeaten on 78: his first 50 in 12 innings. Zimbabwe had their moments – Tendulkar failed to score for almost an hour after tea before being leg before to Price for 36 and, two balls later, Dravid was run out by a direct throw from Travis Friend. However, following

a rain-marred third day, India had consolidated their position by finishing on 319 for 6, of which Ganguly had scored 135. He added 120 for the fifth wicket with Virender Sehwag (74), but added only one more run to his overnight score before holing out to spinner Price who finished with the creditable figures of 3 for 108.

Having taken a marginal first-innings lead of 25 runs, India's spinners, Harbhajan Singh and Anil Kumble, then bowled superbly to devastate the visitors by bowling them out for only 146. Stuart Carlisle, 37, and Grant Flower, 49, did their best as Harbhajan took 6 for 62 and Kumble 4 for 58 to leave India a mere 122 to win. They made rather heavy weather of it, but got home in the end by four wickets.

At Delhi, it was Saurav Ganguly's turn to register a century as India sealed the series, 2–0.

SECOND TEST – INDIA v. ZIMBABWE
28 February–4 March 2002 at Delhi

ZIMBABWE

	First innings		Second innings	
SV Carlisle (capt)	b Srinath	0	c & b Harbhajan Singh	37
TR Gripper	c Dravid b Khan	8	c Dravid b Harbhajan Singh	10
ADR Campbell	c Dravid b Khan	16	c Dravid b Harbhajan Singh	2
A Flower	c Das b Harbhajan Singh	92	c Das b Harbhajan Singh	0
DD Ebrahim	lbw b Srinath	94	lbw b Kumble	22
GW Flower	run out (Kumble)	30	c Harbhajan Singh b Kumble	49
HH Streak	b Kumble	0	lbw b Kumble	9
TJ Friend	c Tendulkar b Harbhajan Singh	0	b Harbhajan Singh	43
*T Taibu	lbw b Kumble	13	c Bangar b Kumble	10
RW Price	b Kumble	0	c Das b Kumble	3
BT Watambwa	not out	3	not out	1
Extras	b 5, lb 16, nb 9	30	b 2, nb 1	3
		329		**146**

	First innings				Second innings			
	O	M	R	W	O	M	R	W
Srinath	18	4	37	2	4	0	12	–
Khan	22	4	76	2	3	0	12	–
Bangar	7	1	25	–				
Kumble	34	13	88	3	29.3	8	58	4
Harbhajan Singh	27.5	5	70	2	31	5	62	6
Sehwag	1	0	6	–				
Tendulkar	1	0	6	–				

Fall of Wickets
1-0, 2-11, 3-65, 4-181, 5-246, 6-246, 7-289, 8-310, 9-310
1-23, 2-31, 3-31, 4-69, 5-95, 6-113, 7-114, 8-129, 9-142

INDIA

	First innings		Second innings	
SS Das	c Taibu b Streak	13	lbw b Streak	31
*D Dasgupta	lbw b Friend	19	run out (Streak/Taibu)	1
SC Ganguly (capt)	c Gripper b Price	136	lbw b GW Flower	20
SR Tendulkar	lbw b Streak	36	(5) lbw b Price	42
R Dravid	run out (Friend)	1	(6) c A Flower b Price	6
V Sehwag	lbw b Streak	74		
SB Bangar	run out (Carlisle/Taibu)	4	not out	3
A Kumble	not out	34	(4) c Gripper b GW Flower	0
J Srinath	c Gripper b Price	0		
Harbjahan Singh	lbw b Streak	9	(8) not out	14
Z Khan	b Streak	8		
Extras	b 9, lb 6, w 1, nb 4	20	lb 4, nb 5	9
		354	(6 wickets)	**126**

	First innings				Second innings			
	O	M	R	W	O	M	R	W
Streak	37.2	11	92	4	16.5	4	53	1
Watambwa	18	5	47	–				
Friend	19	2	75	1	3	0	17	–
Price	50	16	108	3	19	9	24	2
GW Flower	5	0	17	–	6	3	22	2
Gripper					1	0	6	–

Fall of Wickets
1-24, 2-58, 3-142, 4-144, 5-264, 6-280, 7-321, 8-331, 9-340
1-3, 2-36, 3-36, 4-93, 5-103, 6-105

Umpires: EAR de Silva & AV Jayaprakash
Toss: Zimbabwe
Man of the Match: Harbhajan Singh
Player of the Series: A Kumble

India won by four wickets

Zimbabwe could not cope with Anil Kumble who claimed 16 wickets in the two Tests.

TEST MATCH AVERAGES
India v. Zimbabwe

INDIA

Batting	M	Inns	NO	HS	Runs	Av	100	50	c/st
SB Bangar	2	3	2	100*	107	107.00	1	–	1
SR Tendulkar	2	3	0	176	254	84.66	1	–	2
SC Ganguly	2	3	0	136	194	64.66	1	–	1
SS Das	2	3	0	105	149	49.66	1	–	4
A Kumble	2	3	2	34*	47	47.00	–	–	–
R Dravid	2	3	0	65	72	24.00	–	1	7
Harbhajan Singh	2	2	1	14*	23	23.00	–	–	2
D Dasgupta	2	3	0	33	53	17.66	–	–	1
Z Khan	2	2	0	8	8	4.00	–	–	–

Also batted: J Srinath (2 Tests) 0
Also batted in one Test: VVS Laxman 13 (3 ct); V Sehwag 74

Bowling	Overs	Mds	Runs	Wkts	Av	Best	10m	5/inn
A Kumble	133.2	48	290	16	18.12	5-63	–	1
Harbhajan Singh	116.3	27	236	12	19.66	6-62	–	1
Z Khan	48	8	167	6	27.83	3-46	–	–

Also bowled: SB Bangar 15-4-45-0; V Sehwag 1-0-6-0; J Srinath 50-13-134-3; SR Tendulkar 7-2-17-0

ZIMBABWE

Batting	M	Inns	NO	HS	Runs	Av	100	50	c/st
TJ Friend	2	4	2	60*	109	54.50	–	1	–
SV Carlisle	2	4	0	77	142	35.50	–	1	–
ADR Campbell	2	4	0	57	105	26.25	–	1	1
A Flower	2	4	0	92	103	25.75	–	1	2
GW Flower	2	4	0	49	95	23.50	–	–	1
TR Gripper	2	4	0	60	83	20.75	–	1	3
HH Streak	2	4	0	24	41	10.25	–	–	–
RW Price	2	4	0	18	25	6.25	–	–	–
T Taibu	2	4	0	13	24	6.00	–	–	1
BT Watambwa	2	4	2	3*	5	2.50	–	–	–

Also batted in one Test: DD Ebrahim 94, 22; GJ Rennie 9, 25 (1 ct)

Bowling	Overs	Mds	Runs	Wkts	Av	Best	10m	5/inn
RW Price	137	43	314	10	31.40	5-182	–	1
H Streak	88.1	24	253	6	42.16	4-92	–	–

Also bowled: GW Flower 41-11-135-2; TJ Friend 44-5-153-1; TR Gripper 6-0-24-0; BT Watambwa 43.5-11-134-1

ONE-DAY INTERNATIONALS

India were pushed hard for their series victory having trailed by two matches to one. Having lost the first match at Faridabad, India levelled the series in the second at Chandigarh, but then lost the third at Kochin. That really put them in a corner, but they bounced back in the last two matches, played at Hyderabad and Gauhati, with the help of scintillating batting by the youngsters Dinesh Mongia, Yuvraj Singh and Mohammad Kaif.

At Faridabad, Douglas Marillier hit a riotous 50 in just 21 balls, the fastest half-century for his country, to win the match. Zimbabwe, chasing 275 to win, had lost two wickets for 21, but were helped by a third-wicket partnership of 111 between the two former captains, Andy Flower (71) and Alistair Campbell (84). Marillier then came into bat with 65 runs needed from 34 deliveries, and hit ten fours and a six to pull off a remarkable victory.

India recovered at Mohali with a 64-run victory after making 319 for 6 and then bowling Zimbabwe out for 255. Ganguly hit 86 in 83 balls, Laxman 52 and Rahul Dravid 66. Zimbabwe found themselves penalized for a slow over rate and had to reach to their target in only 49 overs. They lost a wicket in the second over, but were rescued by a partnership of 134 between Campbell and Friend. But once the stand was broken by Harbhajan, who claimed Campbell for 62 and then Friend for 63, the slide to defeat continued for the visitors.

India were dismissed for 191 at Kochin as they chose to bat first. Mohammad Kaif, with 56, confirmed his potential, before medium pacer Douglas Hondo took 4 for 37. Zimbabwe reached their target in only the 45th over as Campbell stuck 71 with seven fours and a six from 119 balls.

Another promising Indian youngster, Yuvraj Singh, made an unbeaten 80 from 60 deliveries to guide India to a five-wicket win at Hyderabad, which levelled the series with one to play. He hammered eight fours and a six and, with Mohammad Kaif (68), added 94 for the fifth wicket after India had lost three wickets for 56. Zimbabwe had earlier scored 240 for 8 with Andy Flower scoring 89.

In the final match at Gauhati, India made an imposing 333 for 6 – their highest score against Zimbabwe – of which Dinesh Mongia made 159 not out, his maiden one-day century. He shared an explosive 158-run fifth-wicket partnership with Yuvraj which took the game away from Zimbabwe. Yuvraj had made 75 off 52 balls and, to make

Zimbabwe's task all the more difficult, they were docked two overs for a slow over rate. Not surprisingly, they fell well short and were bowled out for 232 in the 43rd over, chaotically losing their last five wickets for only five runs.

Match One
7 March 2002 at Nahar Singh Stadium, Faridabad
India 274 for 6 (50 overs) (VVS Laxman 75, SC Ganguly 57)
Zimbabwe 276 for 9 (49.4 overs) (ADR Campbell 84, A Flower 71, DA Marillier 56*, Z Khan 4 for 47)
Zimbabwe won by one wicket
Man of the Match: DA Marillier

Match Two
10 March 2002 at Punjab CA Stadium, Mohali, Chandigarh (floodlit)
India 319 for 6 (50 overs) (SC Ganguly 86, R Dravid 66*, VVS Laxman 52)
Zimbabwe 255 (43.3 overs) (TJ Friend 63, ADR Campbell 62)
India won by 64 runs
Man of the Match: SC Ganguly

Match Three
13 March 2002 at Nehru Stadium, Kochin
India 191 (48.3 overs) (M Kaif 56, DT Hondo 4 for 37)
Zimbabwe 197 for 4 (44.2 overs) (ADR Campbell 71)
Zimbabwe won by six wickets
Man of the Match: DT Hondo

Match Four
16 March 2002 at Lal Bahadur Shastri Stadium, Hyderabad (floodlit)
Zimbabwe 240 for 8 (50 overs) (A Flower 89, AB Agarkar 4 for 32)
India 244 for 5 (48.1 overs) (Yuvraj Singh 80*, M Kaif 68)
India won by five wickets
Man of the Match: Yuvraj Singh

Match Five
19 March 2002 at Nehru Stadium, Gauhati
India 333 for 6 (50 overs) (D Mongia 159*, Yuvraj Singh 75)
Zimbabwe 232 (42.1 overs) (Harbhajan Singh 4 for 33)
India won by 101 runs
Man of the Match: D Mongia
Player of the Series: D Mongia

India won the one-day series 3–2. Their captain, Saurav Ganguly, top scored with 86 in the second match at Mohali.

INDIA DOMESTIC FIRST-CLASS CRICKET
By Qamar Ahmed, R. Mohan and Utpal Shuvro

A maiden triumph for Indian Railways represented a huge achievement for an under-rated side. Admitted into the Ranji fold in 1958, when the late Lala Amarnath was hired as the star professional to build up the team, Railways made their first entry into the final in 2000–01 when they were beaten controversially by 21 runs by Baroda in the five-day match.

There was sweet revenge for Railways, who as a government institution has always struggled to retain its best players, who get far more incentives to play for the private sector. Headquartered in Delhi but

playing in the Central Zone, Railways forced their way into the final of the knock-out competition which they dominated, despite making only a moderate total in the first innings.

The win on their home turf at the Karnal Singh Stadium, a stone's throw from the New Delhi railway station, was emphatic. The victory margin of 277 runs tells the tale of the dominance of the Railway bowlers. The left-arm spinner, Murali Kartik, killed off all chances of a Baroda fightback as he took 5 for 51 in Baroda's total of 169 in reply to Railways' total of 253.

Kartik also top scored for his side at a time when Railways' chances of not making enough in the second innings was a distinct possibility. Kartik's 69 settled the issue, with the defending champions finally falling well short of a fourth-innings target of 391.

Kartik bagged 37 wickets from eight Ranji matches. Opener Amit Pagnis and all-rounder Sanjay Bangar were two Railways batsmen who figured in the top 15 of the national first-class averages.

Baroda had beaten Railways in all three previous meetings in the Ranji Trophy and Railways were very much the underdogs going into the final. Their meeting at the summit for the second time in two years presented more evidence of how lesser-known teams have progressed in national cricket, while the more famous teams have suffered from a surprising lack of commitment to domestic cricket by their Test and international players.

West Zone, the most consistent side throughout the season, won the Duleep Trophy. East Zone had to win their last match against West in order to wrest the trophy from the leaders, but in the unusually wet conditions in April, West remained content to draw the rain-interrupted game and get hold of the handsome cup that they had last won outright in 1985–86. West had been joint winners twice, in 1988–89 with North and in 1997–98 with Central. The cricket in the Duleep Trophy was sufficiently in focus for Yuvraj Singh of North Zone to be called back to the one-day side. He batted on to make a double hundred before leaving the match he was playing in.

There was another huge score from VVS Laxman, who was playing in his sixth consecutive Irani Trophy match, which just goes to show how even a batsman with a Test best of 281 can be under pressure from the national selectors. Having scored 167 against Mumbai the previous season in the match between the Rest of India and the Ranji Trophy champions, Laxman, just returning after a knee injury sustained during the Test tour of Sri Lanka, left his mark on the game with an innings of 145 that took Rest of India to victory over Baroda. With scores of 125 and 90*, Dinesh Mongia was Man of the Match.

INDIA DOMESTIC ONE–DAY CRICKET
By Qamar Ahmed, R. Mohan and Utpal Shuvro

There is always a fair deal of confusion over limited-overs cricket in India. There is no clear definition of priorities. The NPK Salve Trophy that is invariably seen as a trial for probables for selection to the national team before the start of any international series is clearly gaining ground as the premier tournament. Played under lights at one centre, with a sponsor to boot, the competition is the nearest India has to a national event, but it is one that is played among three teams chosen from the whole national pool of players.

The Indian senior team met its Waterloo in Bangalore, where the second string had the better of them. In a season which did not really see the best of the national XI in the Test series against England and the shared one-day series, the senior national side was humbled in the Challenger Series with India A producing an inspired performance in the final.

The senior players have to make themselves available for the Challenger Series making it an attractive event, but similar conditions do not apply to the Ranji Trophy one-day tournament that is played round the year at various venues with teams treating the matches more as a warm-up for the four-day first-class match that follows. A properly run national one-day tournament involving the state sides could be an ideal sponsored event which would also attract spectator interest.

The zonal tournament played for the Deodhar Trophy could also be promoted in a far superior way. The BCCI is, however, too busy organizing the more lucrative international cricket to bother too much about domestic cricket, which is inevitably thought of as a selection platform to fill the fringe places in the national team.

South Zone won the inter-zonal Deodhar Trophy with 14 points from four games, one better than West Zone's tally of 13 points. South made only a modest 223 in their last league match against North

Zone who were also in with a chance of claiming the title. However, North were bowled out for 176 in 45 overs. Central Zone were relegated to third place after having a chance to actually win the trophy with victory in their last match against West.

The Ranji format is to be changed into a two-tier competition next season with an elite group and a plate group with promotions and relegations between the two groups, as in the English county championship. The success of such changes remains to be seen. It is also not clear what format the one-day events will take. Indian cricket has always aped the English system without any of the monetary benefits trickling down to those who play only national cricket.

VVS Laxman returned from injury to play for the Rest of India against Baroda. In excellent form, Laxman scored 145 to lead his team to victory.

FIRST-CLASS AVERAGES
India

BATTING

	M	Inns	NO	HS	Runs	Av	100	50
PM Mullick	9	14	4	207*	806	80.60	2	5
W Jaffer	7	11	1	178	786	78.60	4	3
G Gambhir	7	11	0	218	818	74.36	3	2
D Mongia	7	11	1	178	743	74.30	3	4
RS Gavaskar	8	11	2	166	653	72.55	2	3
AA Pagnis	8	13	1	133*	800	66.66	3	3
S Sriram	12	20	1	149	1263	66.47	5	6
Yashpal Singh	7	13	3	202	660	66.00	1	5
V Rathore	7	12	1	249	716	65.09	3	1
Kavaljit Singh	6	12	1	206	713	64.81	1	6
S Sharath	12	18	3	141*	928	61.86	4	3
A Chopra	11	19	3	143	983	61.43	3	5
AV Kale	6	10	1	122	552	61.33	2	3
SB Bangar	9	14	4	212	605	60.50	2	2
RV Bharadwaj	8	10	1	207*	535	59.44	1	2
Sangram Singh	8	14	1	215*	767	59.00	3	3
CC Williams	8	14	0	157	806	57.57	3	3
JJ Martin	6	10	1	271	504	56.00	1	1
SG Das	10	14	1	129	725	55.76	2	5
SS Raul	10	15	1	210	777	55.50	2	3
ND Modi	7	14	2	118	661	55.08	1	5
TP Singh	7	11	0	186	601	54.63	2	2
AA Muzumdar	6	10	2	133	437	54.62	1	2
Y Goud	13	24	6	190*	977	54.27	4	3
Yuvraj Singh	9	15	0	209	802	53.46	3	4
HK Badani	9	12	2	124	534	53.40	1	4
HH Kanitkar	9	14	0	197	747	53.35	3	–
KR Powar	6	11	2	111	475	52.77	3	1
P Dharmani	9	13	2	127*	579	52.63	3	–
DJ Gandhi	8	10	0	146	521	52.10	2	1
P Chawla	6	10	2	142	413	51.62	1	3
RVC Prasad	8	10	1	150	461	51.22	1	3
SS Das	9	14	0	253	702	50.14	2	3
Shafiq Khan	9	15	0	146	729	48.60	1	5
NR Mongia	12	19	3	164	763	47.68	1	5
PH Sutane	6	12	1	108*	508	46.18	2	2
GK Khoda	11	20	1	167	877	46.15	2	5
Jyoyi P Yadav	9	18	1	117	769	45.23	2	4
AS Yadav	8	14	2	155	539	44.91	1	3
Raja Ali	10	17	1	148	715	44.68	3	2
RR Parida	11	17	0	127	756	44.47	2	4
S Somasunder	4	8	0	119	355	44.37	1	3
M Manhas	10	17	2	193	657	43.80	3	–
Rajiv Kumar	6	10	1	113	394	43.77	2	–
D Vinay Kumar	11	17	2	126	652	43.46	2	2
A Nand Kishore	8	14	1	214	555	42.69	1	3
NA Godbole	5	8	0	186	337	42.12	1	1
N Hussain	5	9	0	85	374	41.55	–	3
Jai P Yadav	12	22	4	120*	745	41.38	1	5
D Dasgupta	11	17	1	137	657	41.06	3	3
Tanvver Jabbar	5	10	1	107	369	41.00	1	4
PK Das	8	13	0	83	526	40.46	–	6
DS Manohar	7	12	2	111	401	40.10	2	1
BBCC Mohapatra	6	9	0	114	357	39.66	1	2
KA Damani	6	11	1	118	399	39.90	1	2
SR Nair	5	9	1	87*	316	39.50	–	4
SC Ganguly	7	9	1	136	309	38.62	1	–
D Bundela	6	12	2	116*	372	37.20	2	1
KD Aphale	5	8	0	76	297	37.12	–	4
A Ratra	6	11	1	72*	334	37.11	–	3
SV Bahutule	9	12	1	105	400	36.36	1	2
RS Ricky	8	15	4	100	392	35.63	1	2
Nischal Gaur	5	10	0	99	354	35.40	–	3
MR Ramprakash	5	9	0	105	318	35.33	1	1
TK Chanda	4	8	0	62	281	35.12	–	1
C Sachdev	4	8	0	99	279	34.87	–	2
MA Butcher	5	10	1	92	309	34.33	–	2
SH Kotak	6	10	2	96	274	34.25	–	2
I Ganda	5	9	1	109	273	34.12	1	1
LR Shukla	11	12	2	58	338	33.80	–	3
RR Powar	9	11	1	110	334	33.40	1	1
Manish Sharma	8	15	2	99	429	33.00	–	4

FIRST-CLASS AVERAGES
India

BATTING

	M	Inns	NO	HS	Runs	Av	100	50
VK Sharma	6	11	0	122	361	32.81	1	2
Jasvir Singh	5	10	0	114	327	32.70	1	3
TN Varsani	6	11	1	118	325	32.50	1	2
Sandeep Sharma	6	12	0	80	388	32.33	–	3
Chetan Sharma	5	9	1	73	257	32.12	–	1
SZ Zuffri	7	11	0	69	350	31.81	–	2
NS Doru	5	9	1	124*	253	31.62	1	–
CD Thomson	5	9	1	64	252	31.50	–	1
CH Kumar	7	10	0	59	315	31.50	–	3
M Saif	5	9	1	79	251	31.37	–	1
AP Bhoite	9	14	1	85	406	31.23	–	3
PMS Reddy	5	10	0	77	309	30.90	–	2
VA Saxena	5	9	0	66	277	30.77	–	1
A Kakkar	5	8	0	97	246	30.75	–	2
TR Arasu	8	11	2	78	275	30.55	–	2
H Joshipura	4	8	0	113	243	30.37	1	1
AC Bedade	7	12	1	77	330	30.00	–	3
SS Parab	6	11	0	74	324	29.45	–	3
R Shamshad	5	10	0	69	294	29.40	–	3
TB Arothe	7	12	0	106	348	29.00	1	1
MH Parmar	6	11	1	89	282	28.20	–	1
M Kartik	8	11	3	69	221	27.62	–	2
M Kaif	4	8	0	55	219	27.37	–	2
S Ramesh	8	13	2	126*	299	27.18	1	–
Anirudh Singh	7	12	0	124	326	27.16	1	–
AS Pathak	6	9	0	68	244	27.11	–	1
U Chatterjee	11	13	4	69	242	26.88	–	1
AA Velaskar	5	9	0	87	236	26.22	–	1
S Verma	4	8	0	73	209	26.12	–	2
MSK Prasad	11	16	1	104	391	26.06	1	1
SD Chowdhury	4	8	0	76	204	25.50	–	2
N Chopra	5	9	1	49*	201	25.12	–	–
NK Patel	6	12	0	133	301	25.08	1	–
A Sattar	4	8	0	69	200	25.00	–	2
HR Jadhav	5	8	0	91*	200	25.00	–	1
VC Naidu	4	8	0	78	198	24.75	–	1
VV Kolambkar	5	10	1	74*	221	24.55	–	1
G Gopal	6	9	1	62	196	24.50	–	1
C White	5	9	0	121	214	23.77	1	–
AR Khurasiya	4	8	0	64	188	23.50	–	2
RR Singh	8	9	0	58	211	23.44	–	1
SB Saikia	5	9	1	48	186	23.25	–	–
Abhay Sharma	8	11	2	65	208	23.11	–	1
KS Sahabuddin	8	10	1	54	200	22.22	–	1
ND Ali	5	10	0	41	220	22.00	–	–
Sarabjit Singh	5	9	0	49	197	21.88	–	–
SC Oasis	5	9	0	47	196	21.77	–	–
Harvinder Singh	10	15	5	34*	215	21.50	–	–
AN Kudva	5	9	1	46	172	21.50	–	–
D Mahajan	4	8	0	46	169	21.12	–	–
RJ Kanwat	7	13	0	63	274	21.07	–	2
AR Kapoor	8	10	2	44	165	20.62	–	–
J Gokulakrishnan	5	9	0	52	182	20.22	–	1
MS Dhoni	4	8	0	96	161	20.12	–	1

Qualification: 8 completed innings, average 20.00

BOWLING

	Overs	Mds	Runs	Wkts	Av	Best	10m	5/inn
PL Mhambrey	167.1	62	336	20	16.18	4-83	–	–
M Kartik	357.5	127	691	38	18.18	5-33	–	3
BKV Prasad	215	65	474	26	18.23	6-35	–	1
Z Khan	213.2	32	783	40	19.57	6-25	2	5
DS Mohanty	275	70	692	35	19.77	5-26	–	1
L Balaji	302.2	80	759	37	20.51	5-42	–	2
KS Parida	432.3	127	1069	52	20.55	8-65	2	4
GK Pandey	157.4	49	310	15	20.66	5-33	–	1
S Joshi	127	31	374	18	20.77	3-30	–	–
A Kumble	299.3	84	730	35	20.85	7-115	1	3
HH Watekar	310.4	94	742	35	21.20	5-163	–	1
SV Bahutule	339.5	89	837	39	21.46	5-56	–	2

FIRST-CLASS AVERAGES
India

BOWLING

	Overs	Mds	Runs	Wkts	Av	Best	10m	5/inn
Harbhajan Singh	335	78	816	38	21.47	6-62	-	3
M Suresh Kumar	274.5	60	709	33	21.48	5-54	1	4
Shakti Singh	296	94	718	33	21.69	5-78	-	1
SK Satpathy	188.1	51	522	24	21.75	5-11	-	1
RR Powar	281.5	78	690	31	22.25	6-30	-	2
A Mishra	242.1	67	649	29	22.37	6-95	-	2
IK Pathan	217.4	52	629	28	22.46	6-72	1	1
IR Siddiqui	195.2	46	585	25	23.40	7-91	-	3
A Bhandari	212.2	44	705	30	23.50	7-92	-	2
J Gokulakrishnan	159	49	402	17	23.64	5-25	-	1
Sarandeep Singh	499.1	120	1356	57	23.78	6-47	-	4
U Chatterjee	579.3	186	1194	50	23.88	7-32	1	4
AI Aware	168.1	47	479	20	23.95	5-58	-	2
AW Zaidi	181.5	47	442	18	24.55	4-67	-	-
Vijay Sharma	141	31	467	19	24.57	5-67	-	2
BN Mehta	244.2	47	661	26	25.42	6-53	-	3
S Narwal	157.1	31	460	18	25.55	5-103	-	1
S Vidyut	138.2	34	437	17	25.70	6-24	-	1
V Sharma	406.4	94	1211	47	25.76	6-59	-	3
A Barik	175.2	27	648	25	25.92	5-18	-	1
Gagandeep Singh	201.3	43	528	20	26.40	4-32	-	-
SK Sharma	185	41	485	18	26.94	6-55	-	1
NSC Aiyappa	144.3	26	488	18	27.11	5-112	-	1
RR Singh	136.3	43	306	11	27.81	3-12	-	-
RJ Kanwat	253.1	60	668	24	27.83	5-74	-	1
SB Bangar	171.4	39	529	19	27.84	5-32	-	1
S Pandey	256.1	51	838	30	27.93	8-132	1	1
LA Patel	215.3	53	561	20	28.05	6-77	1	1
D Ganesh	266.3	72	788	28	28.14	4-47	-	-
A Uniyal	153.5	25	565	20	28.25	4-56	-	-
SLV Raju	309	105	610	21	29.04	6-42	1	2
MR Shrinivas	261.4	62	765	26	29.42	5-57	-	1
SV Ghag	238.5	61	653	22	29.68	5-105	-	1
NP Singh	262.1	79	658	22	29.90	5-27	-	1
MB Triparthi	147.3	40	401	13	30.84	3-42	-	-
JS Yadav	305.3	87	729	23	31.69	5-91	-	1
Arun Singh	168.5	54	478	15	31.86	4-70	-	-
SS Lahiri	484	117	1356	42	32.28	6-73	-	2
N Chopra	208	57	550	17	32.35	5-83	-	1
M Faiq	165.2	50	423	13	32.53	5-52	1	2
AP Bhoite	177.4	22	590	18	32.77	4-31	-	-
KS Sahabuddin	322.5	87	788	24	32.83	5-92	-	1
Sukhvinder Singh	196.2	66	432	13	33.23	6-73	-	1
S Ganesh Kumar	140	26	443	13	34.07	6-103	-	1
Harvinder Singh	264	54	833	24	34.70	4-66	-	-
RB Patel	238.5	47	707	20	35.35	5-154	-	1
AR Kapoor	279	72	750	21	35.71	3-20	-	-
Jai P Yadav	296.2	85	715	20	35.75	4-94	-	-
RVC Prasad	151	42	430	12	35.83	3-14	-	-
SK Sanwal	195.1	30	541	15	36.06	4-116	-	-
HAS Khalid	152	31	419	11	38.09	4-95	-	-
V Bhatia	244	52	728	19	38.31	4-40	-	-
ND Hirwani	206.5	27	654	17	38.47	4-137	-	-
Jagtar Singh	194	42	575	15	38.33	5-54	-	1
LR Shukla	276	78	734	18	40.77	3-53	-	-
R Ramkumar	191.2	53	513	12	42.75	4-62	-	-
VN Buch	249.4	59	779	17	45.82	5-94	-	1
Sandeep Sharma (HP)	152.3	36	472	10	47.20	5-68	-	1
M Madhukar	192.5	44	523	11	47.54	3-42	-	-
A Sharma (Servs)	224.4	51	691	14	49.35	5-39	-	1

FIRST-CLASS AVERAGES
India

BOWLING

	Overs	Mds	Runs	Wkts	Av	Best	10m	5/inn
T Yohannan	174.4	33	644	13	49.53	3-100	-	-
RL Sanghvi	350	69	1163	23	50.56	5-69	-	1

Qualification: 10 wickets in 8 innings

The following players took 10 wickets in fewer than 8 innings:

	Overs	Mds	Runs	Wkts	Av	Best	10m	5/inn
N Aggarwal	55.3	11	194	10	19.40	4-56	-	-
PV Gandhe	191.3	65	380	19	20.00	6-55	1	1
Babloo Kumar	77.3	25	205	10	20.50	4-72	-	-
A Flintoff	126	42	263	12	21.91	4-50	-	-
ND Kambli	86.4	22	245	11	22.27	4-49	-	-
Shahid Khan	152.5	33	380	15	25.33	5-83	-	1
Ashwani Gupte	125	23	365	14	26.07	4-33	-	-
RV Pawar	114.3	34	267	10	26.70	4-41	-	-
L Jain	118.5	28	296	11	26.90	4-34	-	-
A Nehra	184.1	58	456	16	28.50	5-46	-	1
S Vishnuvardhan	90.1	15	315	11	28.63	6-148	-	1
MJ Hoggard	124.5	33	332	11	30.18	4-80	-	-
SS Raul	163.2	32	403	13	31.00	2-12	-	-
SG Bhatt	144.4	31	450	14	32.14	7-43	-	1
M Manhas	115.2	23	397	12	33.08	3-31	-	-
M Diwakar	157	23	490	14	35.00	5-139	-	1
MJV Ingty	184.4	40	639	17	37.58	5-119	-	1
RW Price	173	50	459	12	38.25	5-182	-	1

FIELDING

39 - NR Mongia (35ct, 4st); 31 - RB Jhalani (26ct, 5st); 27 - D Dasgupta (23ct, 4st);
25 - P Dharmani; 24 - PP Vora (23ct, 1st); 23 - TR Arasu (20ct, 3st), MSK Prasad (21ct, 2st);
21 - A Ratra (16ct, 5st), Abhay Sharma (19ct, 2st); 22 - VVS Laxman; 19 - G Gopal (18ct,1st),
SZ Zuffri (16ct, 3st); 15 - VST Naidu (14ct, 1st), Ravikant Sharma, Sarabjit Singh (13ct, 2st),
AA Velaskar (13ct, 2st); 14 - JS Foster (13ct, 1st), Sangram Singh, Shafiq Khan, Yuvraj Singh;
13 - AP Bhoite, V Dahiya (11ct, 2st), N Haldipur, M Srinivas (11ct, 2st); 12 - A Chopra, SS Dighe
(11ct, 1st), Y Goud, A Nand Kishore, SK Sanwal; 11 - A Bhatt (11ct, 2st), P Chawla (10ct, 1st),
U Chatterjee, SS Das, M Manhas, VC Naidu, S Nath (10ct, 1st), SC Oasis, RR Parida, V Rathore,
SS Raul, S Satbhai (9ct, 1st); 10 - R Dravid, VR Mane

Qualification: 10 or more catches

NEW ZEALAND

Bangladesh in New Zealand
England in New Zealand
New Zealand Domestic First-Class Season
New Zealand Domestic One-Day Season
New Zealand First-Class Averages

BANGLADESH IN NEW ZEALAND
By Bryan Waddle

Bangladesh had made previous tours of New Zealand before they achieved Test match status, but that experience did not help them greatly in their first official Test series.

They opened with two three-day games, but it was not an auspicious beginning. They were rained out without batting in the opening encounter, a non-first-class fixture against a Regional Selection, before losing outright by an innings and 193 runs to Auckland just prior to the first Test.

FIRST TEST
18–22 December 2001 at Hamilton

Despite numerous delays and interruptions caused by the unusually wet 'summer', New Zealand completed an emphatic clean sweep over cricket's new boys. It was a victory that was demanded by New Zealand captain Stephen Fleming after his side returned home from the drawn three-Test series with Australia. Fleming's strong, imaginative leadership had almost stolen the deciding third Test off Australia. Without being disrespectful, Fleming realistically predicted a two-nil series win over Bangladesh, to challenge his side to maintain its professional standards against the world's bottom-ranked side.

For a while, in the first Test at Hamilton, they were under pressure to do that. Sent into bat after the first two days had been washed out, New Zealand were 19 for 3 and 51 for 4 against some lively seam bowling from Mashrafe Mortaza and Manjurul Islam, who did not let their inexperience and the New Zealanders' reputations dictate to them. It was the only session Bangladesh won in the entire series, but it was enough encouragement for them to face the immediate future with confidence. Craig McMillan and Mark Richardson extricated New Zealand with some dashing strokeplay that produced a fifth-wicket stand of 190 in the space of 40 overs in three hours. McMillan, as ever, was the aggressor, reaching his fifth Test hundred off just 136 balls.

Chris Cairns continued where McMillan had left off and the ferocious assault on the Bangladesh bowlers continued before New Zealand declared on 365 for 9 from just 77 overs. While lacking in finesse and discipline, the Bangladesh batsmen were not shy when it came to playing extravagant strokes. Their approach was more suited to the one-day game that forms a major part of their domestic programme. The top order struggled to cope with the bounce extracted by the pacy New Zealand attack. Cairns, Bond and Martin exposed weaknesses in technique that will need to be addressed if Bangladesh are to advance in the Test match arena. Reluctant to get into line, they flailed away, successful at times with some attractive cut strokes and neat deflections.

They almost avoided the follow-on, missing out by 11 runs, despite some attractive strokeplay from Habibul Bashar and Sanwar Hossain on his Test debut, while Khaled Mahmud had a less cultured, but dangerously effective, approach. Al Sahariar supplied the substance to the second innings that lasted just 46.2 overs as Chris Cairns regained his pace, hostility and, more importantly, his accuracy to secure his second seven-wicket bag at Hamilton's Westpactrust Stadium. He had previously demolished the West Indies' batting two years earlier for his career best figures of 7 for 27.

Mark Richardson, New Zealand's opening batsman, rescued his team from embarrassment in the first Test against Bangladesh. NZ were reduced to 51 for 4 on the first morning at Hamilton.

Previous page: Nathan Astle produced one of the greatest knocks in Test history, a remarkable 222 from only 168 balls, but England still emerged victorious in the first Test at Christchurch.

FIRST TEST – NEW ZEALAND v. BANGLADESH
18–22 December 2001 at Hamilton

NEW ZEALAND

	First innings	
MH Richardson	c & b Mohammad Sharif	143
L Vincent	c & b Mashrafe Mortaza	0
MS Sinclair	c Khaled Mashud b Manjural Islam	7
SP Fleming (capt)	c Khaled Mashud b Mashrafe Mortaza	4
NJ Astle	c Al Sahariar b Manjural Islam	5
CD McMillan	c Manjural Islam b Mashrafe Mortaza	106
CL Cairns	b Mohammad Sharif	48
*AC Parore	b Mohammad Sharif	20
DL Vettori	lbw b Khaled Mahmud	0
SE Bond	not out	4
CS Martin		
Extras	b 2, lb 18, w 5, nb 3	28
	(9 wickets dec.)	365

	First innings			
	O	M	R	W
Mashrafe Mortaza	27	3	100	3
Manjural Islam	18	5	66	2
Mohammad Sharif	20.1	2	114	3
Khaled Mahmud	9	0	40	1
Mohammad Ashraful	3	0	25	-

Fall of Wickets
1-1, 2-19, 3-29, 4-51, 5-241, 6-330, 7-357, 8-359, 9-365

BANGLADESH

	First innings		Second innings	
Javed Omar	c Richardson b Cairns	9	lbw b Martin	15
Al Sahariar	c Sinclair b Bond	15	c Parore b Cairns	53
Habibul Bashar	c Martin b Vettori	61	c Parore b Cairns	1
Aminul Islam	c Parore b Bond	14	b Cairns	0
Mohammad Ashraful	c Sinclair b Vettori	1	c sub (CJ Drum) b Bond	6
Sanwar Hossain	c Vincent b McMillan	45	b Bond	12
*Khaled Mashud (capt)	c Bond b McMillan	6	c Fleming b Cairns	6
Khaled Mahmud	c Richardson b Bond	45	c Sinclair b Cairns	0
Mohammad Sharif	b Martin	0	not out	4
Mashrafe Mortaza	lbw b Bond	3	c Vincent b Cairns	2
Manjural Islam	not out	0	c Fleming b Cairns	1
Extras	lb 1, nb 5	6	lb 4, nb 4	8
		205		108

	First innings				Second innings			
	O	M	R	W	O	M	R	W
Cairns	11	0	55	1	18.2	2	53	7
Bond	13.1	2	47	4	15	4	28	2
Martin	11	4	38	1	4	1	6	1
McMillan	8	1	39	2				
Vettori	15	4	25	2	9	4	17	-

Fall of Wickets
1-24, 2-32, 3-92, 4-95, 5-121, 6-146, 7-155, 8-156, 9-204
1-39, 2-42, 3-42, 4-68, 5-90, 6-98, 7-98, 8-104, 9-107

Umpires: DL Orchard & AL Hill
Toss: Bangladesh
Test Debut: Sanwar Hossain (Bangladesh)
Man of the Match: MH Richardson

New Zealand won by an innings & 52 runs

Craig McMillan scored a typically pugnacious innings at Wellington where his 70 came from only 71 balls.

SECOND TEST
26–30 December 2001 at Basin Reserve, Wellington

Wellington's weather was even less charitable for the Boxing Day Test as New Zealand continued their uncompromising push for a series victory. The Basin Reserve pitch might not have been at its best, due to the lack of adequate preparation, but the tourists should have fared better than their first-innings total of 132. Apart from Aminul Islam, who faced 134 balls reaching 42, there was a lack of discipline and patience against a New Zealand attack that was only steady rather than menacing. Five other batsmen reached double figures, with Al Sahariar's 18 the second top score. Chris Cairns provided the initial danger with two wickets in his second over, the third of the match. Chris Drum, Daniel Vettori and Shane Bond conceded little to a side that was trying desperately to change from its attacking style to the more controlled Test match approach.

After the second day washout, New Zealand were urgent and determined in establishing a lead, fearing the weather might impede their progress. McMillan was the spark once again, scoring 70 from 71 balls, and, with Fleming, added 130 in 25 overs to totally demoralize Bangladesh. Mark Richardson continued his remarkable run in Test cricket with yet another half-century. Fleming had such confidence in his side that he was prepared to declare with an advantage of just 209.

He was justified, however, as Bond's pace unsettled the tentative Bangladesh batsmen and by stumps on day three, they were 67 for 5 with Bond having taken 3 for 13. It took just 41 overs to end the match with Bond, who ended with 4 for 54,

SECOND TEST – NEW ZEALAND v. BANGLADESH
26–30 December 2001 at Wellington

BANGLADESH

	First innings		Second innings	
Javed Omar	c Vincent b Cairns	0	lbw b Bond	12
Al Sahariar	c Bond b Vettori	18	c Horne b Bond	0
Habibul Bashar	c Sinclair b Cairns	6	lbw b Drum	32
Aminul Islam	c Vincent b Bond	42	c Vettori b Bond	4
Mohammad Ashraful	c Fleming b Cairns	11	lbw b Vettori	10
Sanwar Hossain	run out (Vincent/Vettori)	10	b Bond	7
Khaled Mahmud	c Parore b Drum	10	run out (McMillan/Parore)	4
*Khaled Mashud (capt)	not out	10	not out	19
Hasibul Hossain	c Vincent b Drum	4	c Parore b Vettori	7
Manjural Islam	b Vettori	0	(11) c Sinclair b Cairns	0
Mashrafe Mortaza	run out (McMillan)	8	(10) b Cairns	29
Extras	lb 4, w 1, nb 8	13	lb 7, w 1, nb 3	11
		132		**135**

	First innings				Second innings			
	O	M	R	W	O	M	R	W
Cairns	15	7	24	3	6	1	27	2
Bond	13	4	21	1	15	5	54	4
Drum	11	1	26	2	3	0	9	1
Vettori	25	6	57	2	17	8	38	2

Fall of Wickets
1-0, 2-6, 3-49, 4-81, 5-92, 6-108, 7-114, 8-118, 9-119
1-5, 2-28, 3-41, 4-62, 5-64, 6-75, 7-79, 8-86, 9-135

NEW ZEALAND

	First innings	
MH Richardson	c Mashrafe Mortaza b Hasibul Hossain	83
MJ Horne	c Khaled Mashud b Manjural Islam	38
L Vincent	c Khaled Mashud b Mashrafe Mortaza	23
SP Fleming (capt)	c Khaled Mashud b Manjural Islam	61
CD McMillan	run out (Mashrafe Mortaza)	70
MS Sinclair	not out	19
CL Cairns	c Habibul Bashar b Manjural Islam	36
*AC Parore		
DL Vettori		
SE Bond		
CJ Drum		
Extras	b 1, lb 6, w 1, nb 3	11
	(6 wickets dec.)	**341**

	First innings			
	O	M	R	W
Mashrafe Mortaza	16	1	57	1
Manjural Islam	29	5	99	3
Hasibul Hossain	21	3	88	1
Aminul Islam	7	0	37	-
Khaled Mahmud	12	2	42	-
Mohammad Ashraful	3	0	11	-

Fall of Wickets
1-104, 2-148, 3-153, 4-283, 5-285, 6-341

Umpires: DJ Harper & BF Bowden
Toss: New Zealand
Man of the Match: CD McMillan

New Zealand won by an innings & 74 runs

Cairns and Vettori dominating the reluctant batting order. Habibul Bashar showed some resistance and Mashrafe Mortaza displayed a willingness to attack towards the end, but it hardly delayed the inevitable. Fleming's imaginative captaincy was rewarded with his 15th Test victory as captain, a record for New Zealand, who recorded their 49th win in Test cricket

The series was always destined to be lopsided, but a resolute attitude was expected from the tourists. They failed to display the commitment required, with their best effort an innings that lasted just 64 overs – the first innings of the Basin Reserve Test. While they returned home badly beaten, there was enough to suggest that players like Habibul, Sanwar, and Al Sahariar possess the ingredients to compete at the highest level, but they will need to make technical adjustments to balance off the potential evident in their game. Mashrafe and Manjurul, while not of express pace, are persistent seam bowlers with the aggressive attitude and bowling skills to form the basis of a potent attack.

TEST MATCH AVERAGES
New Zealand v. Bangladesh

NEW ZEALAND

Batting	M	Inns	NO	HS	Runs	Av	100	50	c/st
MH Richardson	2	2	0	143	226	113.00	1	1	2
CD McMillan	2	2	0	106	176	88.00	1	1	-
CL Cairns	2	2	0	48	84	42.00	-	-	-
SP Fleming	2	2	0	61	65	32.50	-	1	3
MS Sinclair	2	2	1	19*	26	26.00	-	-	5
L Vincent	2	2	0	23	23	11.50	-	-	5

Also batted in two Tests: SE Bond 4* (2 ct); AC Parore 20 (5 ct)
Also batted in one Test: NJ Astle 5; MJ Horne 38 (1 ct); DL Vettori 0 (1 ct)
CJ Drum and CS Martin played in one Test but did not bat

Bowling	Overs	Mds	Runs	Wkts	Av	Best	10m	5/inn
CL Cairns	50.2	10	159	13	12.23	7-53	-	1
SE Bond	56.1	15	150	11	13.63	4-47	-	-
DL Vettori	66	22	137	6	22.83	2-25	-	-

Also bowled: CJ Drum 14-1-35-3; CD McMillan 8-1-39-2; CS Martin 15-5-44-2

BANGLADESH

Batting	M	Inns	NO	HS	Runs	Av	100	50	c/st
Habibul Bashar	2	4	0	61	100	25.00	-	1	1
Al Sahariar	2	4	0	53	86	21.50	-	1	1
Khaled Mashud	2	4	2	19*	41	20.50	-	-	5/-
Sanwar Hossain	2	4	0	45	74	18.50	-	-	-
Aminul Islam	2	4	0	42	60	15.00	-	-	-
Khaled Mahmud	2	4	0	45	59	14.75	-	-	-
Mashrafe Mortaza	2	4	0	29	42	10.50	-	-	2
Javed Omar	2	4	0	15	36	9.00	-	-	-
Mohammad Ashraful	2	4	0	11	28	7.00	-	-	-
Manjural Islam	2	4	1	1	1	0.33	-	-	1

Bowling	Overs	Mds	Runs	Wkts	Av	Best	10m	5/inn
Manjural Islam	47	10	165	5	33.00	3-99	-	-

Also bowled: Aminul Islam 7-0-37-0; Hasibul Hossain 21-2-88-1; Khaled Mahmud 21-2-82-1;
Mashrafe Mortaza 43-4-157-4; Mohammad Ashraful 6-0-36-0; Mohammad Sharif 20.1-2-114-3

ENGLAND IN NEW ZEALAND
By Jonathan Agnew

ONE-DAY INTERNATIONALS

After their rousing fightback in India, where England's one-day team launched a spirited comeback to square the six-match series, this entirely floodlit contest – which preceded the Test series – raised more questions than answers. New Zealand were worthy winners, not least because they were more organized and seemed far better equipped for the shortened form of the game. England, on the other hand, dropped too many catches and, because the balance of their batting order was adversely affected by Nasser Hussain's

determination to bat at No. 3, collapses were commonplace. Hussain simply is not capable of scoring quickly enough in that key position and this is an area that must be reassessed as quickly as possible before the serious planning for the 2003 World Cup can begin in earnest.

It was a typically spectacular collapse that cost England the opening match at Christchurch. After Hussain and Nick Knight – who was England's player of the tournament – had taken the score to 156 for 2 in the 28th over, the remaining eight wickets fell in a heap for the addition of only 40 runs. It was mind-blowing stuff as Daniel Vettori took 3 for 17 from eight overs, and although Darren Gough – who was on a mission to remain in New Zealand for the Test series – took four wickets in two overs, it was too late and New Zealand cruised to a four-wicket win with more than 11 overs in hand.

Three days later, at the new WestpacTrust Stadium in Wellington, England decided that playing James Foster as a specialist wicketkeeper was a luxury they could ill afford and handed the gloves to Marcus Trescothick. The strengthened batting line-up proceeded to record their second lowest score in one-day internationals – a miserable 89 all out in reply to New Zealand's 244 for 8. In a thoroughly insipid performance, in which Andre Adams swung the ball to great effect, England slumped to 65 for 7 in the 27th over after Craig McMillan had top scored for New Zealand with 69.

Despite the talk now being of a five-nil whitewash, England played an unchanged team at McLean Park in Napier and, finally, won a match. Knight top scored once again, and although Hussain's 24 had come from 48 balls, Thorpe gave a masterful demonstration of how to score at a run a ball without resorting to slogging. Stephen Fleming made 76 not out as New Zealand chased 245 to win, but Paul Collingwood found some swing under the lights and took 4 for 38 as New Zealand found themselves 43 runs short.

It was inevitable that Messrs Duckworth and Lewis should stamp their authority on at least one match in this series, and their opportunity came at Auckland in the fourth game. England's 193 for 6 from 40 overs was reassessed to give New Zealand the revised target of 223 to win. The locals were

Darren Gough was only available for the one-day internationals that preceded the Test series in New Zealand. His burst of four wickets in two overs at Christchurch was not enough to prevent an England defeat.

outraged, and it did seem that England had benefited rather more than they deserved, especially since batting second had created problems throughout the series. Andrew Flintoff picked up four wickets as New Zealand slipped to 86 for 5 and finished 34 runs short of their target.

So, from two nil down, England had levelled the series with the final match to play at Dunedin.

Batting first, Hussain and Owais Shah took too long compiling their half-centuries and the total of 218 for 8 was at least 40 runs light. Astle gave a difficult chance early on and steered New Zealand to victory with a 150-ball 122 not out.

Match One
13 February 2002 at Jade Stadium, Christchurch (floodlit)
England 196 (40.2 overs) (NV Knight 73)
New Zealand 198 for 6 (38.3 overs) (NJ Astle 67*, CJ Nevin 55, D Gough 4 for 44)
New Zealand won by four wickets
Man of the Match: NJ Astle

Match Two
16 February 2002 at WestpacTrust Stadium, Wellington (floodlit)
New Zealand 244 for 8 (50 overs) (CD McMillan 69)
England 89 (37.2 overs)
New Zealand won by 155 runs
Man of the Match: AR Adams

Match Three
20 February 2002 at McLean Park, Napier (floodlit)
England 244 for 5 (50 overs) (NV Knight 80, GP Thorpe 52)
New Zealand 201 (46.3 overs) (SP Fleming 76*, PD Collingwood 4 for 38)
England won by 43 runs
Man of the Match: PD Collingwood

Match Four
23 February 2002 at Eden Park, Auckland (floodlit)
England 193 for 6 (40 overs) (GP Thorpe 59*, MP Vaughan 59)
New Zealand 189 (38 overs) (CL Cairns 58, A Flintoff 4 for 17)
England won by 33 runs (DL Method: New Zealand target 223 from 40 overs)
Man of the Match: A Flintoff

Match Five
26 February 2002 at Carisbrook, Dunedin (floodlit)
England 218 for 8 (50 overs) (OA Shah 57, N Hussain 50)
New Zealand 223 for 5 (48.5 overs) (NJ Astle 122*)
New Zealand won by five wickets
Man of the Match: NJ Astle

One-day cricket might have been invented for Nathan Astle. He sealed England's fate in the final game with a century in the deciding match at Dunedin.

First Test
13–16 March 2002 at Christchurch

History will record the mundane fact that England won the opening Test in Christchurch by 98 runs, but that tells only a fraction of the story of a truly remarkable match. It would also require more than merely a cursory glimpse at the result to observe that New Zealand seriously threatened to overhaul a fourth-innings target of 550, although the reality of that will probably only be appreciated by those of us who were lucky enough to be at Lancaster Park on the fourth afternoon.

At tea, New Zealand, on 270 for 6, were heading for their predictable defeat. Nathan Astle was providing some plucky resistance, but since both Adam Parore and Daniel Vettori had been

Back in whites, Astle played an astonishing innings of 222 in New Zealand's second innings at Christchurch.

promoted above the injured Chris Cairns, it seemed as if England's mopping up operation after the break would be made all the easier by the inability of the big-hitting all-rounder to bat. Twenty one overs later, however, when England's battered and increasingly bewildered players ran from the ground in an equal measure of triumph and relief, 181 runs had been scored – 139 of them by Astle – in what must be the most exhilarating exhibition of clean-hitting ever seen in Test cricket.

It was the second new ball that appeared to get the quiet Cantabrian's dander up. Matthew Hoggard, whose seven wickets in New Zealand's first innings had assisted greatly in setting up England's dominant position, was smashed for 90 runs from 60 balls. A unique new-ball field was set: three slips and everyone else on the boundary rope. In the commentary box it was suggested that it should now be included in the MCC coaching manual, and known henceforth as 'the Hoggard', should there ever be the need for a despairing captain to resort to it again.

Meanwhile, Andy Caddick had taken six second-innings wickets – including the ninth to fall, which brought the limping Cairns to the crease – but he was despatched equally ruthlessly with 66 runs coming from 30 deliveries, including three towering sixes from the first three balls of his 25th over. It was simply awesome, but it was made all the more astonishing by the absence of any slogging: each of Astle's 11 sixes was the result of a genuine, lofted drive ranging through an arc from deep extra-cover to long on. In 55 minutes, Astle and Cairns added 118 and as the victory 'target' plummeted from 217 to 99, the game was rushing away from England with such a force that one really began to wonder if they could possibly retrieve the situation.

The entertainment finally ended when Astle edged a flailing drive at Hoggard, having scored 222 from only 168 balls, with 182 coming in boundaries. His double century was timed at 217 minutes, only three minutes more than the fastest-ever recorded by Sir Donald Bradman at Leeds in 1930. Sadly, it is not possible to assess accurately how many deliveries the Don faced that day, but the tempo at which the game was played in that era leads me confidently to wager with anyone that he received comfortably more than the 153 that were bowled Astle's way. Had there not been two breaks in play while the umpires searched their dressing room for balls to replace those that had been launched out of the ground, Astle's innings would unquestionably have been the fastest of all time, in all respects.

Another attempt to put it into perspective is to remember that the quickest Test century was scored by Viv Richards from 56 balls, and people who witnessed it – not least the bowlers – still speak about it in awe. Astle's second hundred came from just 39 deliveries.

Having absorbed all of that excitement, I must now disclose that it was merely the brief finale to a plot that twisted and turned throughout a match that was staged on a controversial 'drop-in' pitch that, on the opening morning, was as green and lush as a cow meadow in early May. It is an exciting innovation, and quite necessary when you consider that the Canterbury Crusaders and the Auckland Blues rugby teams had been gouging lumps out of one another on the same square only four days before the start of the Test match. The 'drop-in' pitch lives in a metal frame on the practice area behind the main ground and was lovingly eased into place by Chris Lewis, the groundsman, with the help of an enormous machine, thus enabling cricket and rugby to co-exist. 'But at what cost?' we wondered, as the damp, green strip was unveiled for the first time. 'The toss will decide the match'. And after five balls England – put in to bat by Stephen Fleming – were duly 0 for 2. Shades of Wanderers in 1999.

Marcus Trescothick and Mark Butcher had both departed with the air of men who had been cruelly betrayed by the pitch, but the first sign of this being no ordinary Test match occurred immediately when Michael Vaughan responded by hooking two sixes and dashing to 27 from only 31 balls before becoming Cairns' third victim. Graham Thorpe's firm-footed drive at Chris Drum contributed further to England's misery and, at lunch, they were on an uncertain 83 for 4.

Shortly after the interval, New Zealand committed their first of a series of howlers in the field. Nasser Hussain, digging in, had reached a noble half-century when Fleming dropped a straightforward offering at slip. Mark Ramprakash, playing in his 50th Test, added 56 with his captain who, despite being tortured for a time by Astle's medium-paced wobblers, began to cash in on his rare good fortune. Andrew Flintoff's ghastly 14-ball duck appeared merely to confirm that he was apparently heading for a career of opening the bowling and batting at No. 11; James Foster's 82-minute resistance prompted his stock to rise, and when Hussain was the

last man out for 106 to a borderline lbw decision by the newly promoted Asoka de Silva, England's 228 was a healthy total under the trying circumstances.

With Darren Gough restored to the bosom of his family, there was great interest in how England's attack would respond to his absence and, in the case of Caddick in particular, to the increased responsibility that went with it. That he has great ability has never been questioned, but he blows hot and cold and there is evidence that he rarely succeeds in the first innings of Test matches. With no Gough in the side, Caddick was now returning to the city where he was both born and raised as England's senior bowler.

On the second day he kicked and pawed at the ground increasingly fretfully as Hoggard rose to the challenge from the Port Hills End. Urged on by the increasingly voluble Barmy Army massed directly behind him, the young Yorkshireman took the first five wickets to fall in a manner that would have made Fred Trueman purr with pleasure. Pitching the ball up and swinging it away at an honest pace, Hoggard was supported by a superb catch at fourth slip by Thorpe to dispose of Matt Horne and, in an unchanged spell of 20 overs, he took 5 for 59, including the wicket of the dangerous nightwatchman, Vettori, for 42. Caddick replaced him and, in his second over, took three wickets that drove home England's superiority. Parore's first-ball lbw decision looked high, but had Craig White, who was on as a substitute for Hoggard, not dropped McMillan on the third-man boundary, New Zealand

would have slipped from 117 for 5 to 117 for 9. The reprieved McMillan made a pugnacious 40, but Hoggard returned to wrap up the tail to finish with 7 for 63, and England's lead of 81 was all the better for the fact that the pitch was still assisting the seamers, albeit to a lesser degree. Their advantage was stretched to 144 by the close of the second day.

I remember suggesting to my radio listeners that England's batsmen should play 'carefully' on the third day in order to build, steadily and sensibly, a lead of 400 by stumps. In 81 overs, they scored 405 at a rate of five runs per over, enabling Hussain to declare with 21 overs remaining with a lead of 549! Although Fleming was unable to call on the injured Cairns to bowl, that is the extent of the sympathy New Zealand deserve because, once again, crucial mistakes were made in the field; none more so than the slip catch that Astle dropped when Thorpe had made just four. This came at a moment when New Zealand were threatening to fight back, having reduced the visitors to 106 for 5 with the lead at 187, but, even so, no one had a right to expect what happened next. Flintoff's batsmanship this winter has ranged from the bizarre to the downright gormless. Now, presented with a series of tempting half volleys, he hit five fours and a six from his first 12 balls, and Freddie's adrenalin was racing.

How England supporters have longed to see an innings like this from a No. 7! It was everything that Flintoff had promised to produce, but our hopes that he would oblige were fading day by day. Powerful drives straight down the ground were accompanied by savage blows to leg – one six off Ian Butler over midwicket was a classic – and, happily, there were even intelligently-taken quick singles as he and Thorpe dismembered New Zealand's pitifully inexperienced attack.

Vettori was brought on too late to apply the brakes and their partnership of 281 was the fourth highest for the sixth wicket in Test cricket; just another of a mass of statistics that blew around Lancaster Park like confetti in a howling gale.

Thorpe's unbeaten 200 from 231 balls – his Test best and, again, one of the fastest ever – earned him the Man of the Match award, and the fact that he was embarrassed to receive it reveals more about the quality and lasting impression of Astle's breathtaking innings than statistics ever could.

Graham Thorpe also made a double century at Christchurch. Here he aims a sweep at Vettori on his way to the 200 not out that earned him the Man of the Match award.

FIRST TEST – NEW ZEALAND v. ENGLAND
13–16 March 2002 at Christchurch

ENGLAND

	First innings		Second innings	
ME Trescothick	c Parore b Cairns	0	c Vettori b Butler	33
MP Vaughan	c Parore b Cairns	27	b Butler	0
MA Butcher	c Butler b Cairns	0	hit wicket b Butler	34
N Hussain (capt)	lbw b Drum	106	c Parore b Drum	11
GP Thorpe	c Fleming b Drum	17	not out	200
MR Ramprakash	c Parore b Astle	31	b Drum	11
A Flintoff	lbw b Astle	0	c sub (MN McKenzie) b Astle	137
*JS Foster	lbw b Drum	19	not out	22
AF Giles	c Drum b Butler	8		
AR Caddick	lbw b Butler	0		
MJ Hoggard	not out	0		
Extras	b 1, lb 10, nb 9	20	b 6, lb 4, nb 10	20
		228	(6 wickets dec.)	**468**

	First innings				Second innings			
	O	M	R	W	O	M	R	W
Cairns	15	4	58	3	4	0	8	0
Drum	20.2	8	36	3	32	6	130	2
Butler	16	2	59	2	23	2	137	3
NJ Astle	18	10	32	2	5.4	0	20	1
Vettori	9	1	26	–	22	3	97	–
McMillan	3	1	6	–	10	–	66	–

Fall of Wickets
1-0, 2-0, 3-46, 4-83, 5-139, 6-151, 7-196, 8-214, 9-226
1-11, 2-50, 3-81, 4-85, 5-106, 6-387

NEW ZEALAND

	First innings		Second innings	
MH Richardson	lbw b Hoggard	2	c Foster b Caddick	76
MJ Horne	c Thorpe b Hoggard	14	c Foster b Caddick	4
DL Vettori	c Foster b Hoggard	42	(8) c Flintoff b Giles	12
L Vincent	b Hoggard	12	(3) c Butcher b Caddick	0
SP Fleming (capt)	c Giles b Caddick	12	(4) c Foster b Flintoff	48
NJ Astle	lbw b Hoggard	10	(5) c Foster b Hoggard	222
CD McMillan	c Vaughan b Hoggard	40	(6) c & b Caddick	24
CL Cairns	c Flintoff b Caddick	0	(11) not out	23
*AC Parore	lbw b Caddick	0	(7) b Caddick	1
CJ Drum	not out	2	(9) lbw b Flintoff	0
IG Butler	c Hussain b Hoggard	0	(10) c Foster b Caddick	4
Extras	lb 5, nb 8	13	b 9, lb 11, w 1, nb 16	37
		147		**451**

	First innings				Second innings			
	O	M	R	W	O	M	R	W
Caddick	18	8	50	3	25	8	122	6
Hoggard	21.2	7	63	7	24.3	5	142	1
Flintoff	12	2	29	–	16	1	94	2
Giles					28	6	73	1

Fall of Wickets
1-4, 2-50, 3-65, 4-79, 5-93, 6-117, 7-117, 8-117, 9-146
1-42, 2-53, 3-119, 4-189, 5-242, 6-252, 7-300, 8-301, 9-333

Umpires: EAR de Silva & BF Bowden
Toss: New Zealand
Test Debut: IG Butler (New Zealand)
Man of the Match: GP Thorpe

England won by 98 runs

SECOND TEST
21–25 March 2002 at Wellington

After rain and gale-force winds lopped off the first day and three-quarters of the match, this was always destined to be a Test in which proceedings in the middle did not amount to very much. When, on the third morning, news of Ben Hollioake's tragic death in a car crash in Perth devastated his England team-mates of only a month before, the cricket became utterly irrelevant.

Hollioake was a delightfully charismatic, laid-back individual who, therefore, was hugely popular with

both the players and media alike. He was immensely talented, too; his languid, deceptively powerful batting at No. 7 was supported by his medium-paced bowling, while his fielding at backward point was breathtaking. Hollioake was, though, becoming increasingly aware of the danger that this ability could be unfulfilled and had seriously contemplated a move away from Surrey, where his brother, Adam, is captain.

In the end he signed another one-year's extension to his contract but, after a winter spent with the England one-day squad in India and New Zealand, he still had not nailed down a permanent place in the team. Hollioake's last appearance for England was on 28 January in Kanpur, and following the series in New Zealand he left for Perth to visit his parents.

There was the ghastly situation in which three England players, including his very close Surrey friends, Mark Butcher and Graham Thorpe, were batting, oblivious to the news that had quickly circulated through the now-silent crowd. The flags all around the Basin Reserve were solemnly lowered to half mast while the game continued. It was only when the batsmen were dismissed – and Nasser Hussain had returned to the dressing room at lunch – that the dreadful news was broken to them.

England would never offer this as an excuse, but it was hardly surprising, therefore, that they were bowled out after the interval, losing six wickets for 81 runs with their minds, very obviously, elsewhere.

This gave New Zealand the opportunity to fight back into the series. Stephen Fleming had won the toss and asked England to bat first on a pitch that had seen only one first-class total in excess of 200 in ten innings this year. There was a little movement for the seamers early on and it was quickly evident that it would be the spinners at the end of the game who were likely to pose the greatest threat.

A minute's silence preceded the start of play on the fourth day and, again, it was a thoroughly moving spectacle. Both teams lined up in front of the dressing rooms and, as they broke away to take to the field immediately afterwards, a number of England's cricketers had been reduced to tears. At least they were all in the middle together and, as is so often the case, this had a galvanizing effect. Although it took England an hour or so to focus

The news of the death of Ben Hollioake (pictured here with brother Adam in last year's B and H final) cast a shadow over proceedings in Wellington. He had appeared for England in a one-day international in India only two months earlier.

themselves and get into the game, they did so spectacularly. Ashley Giles started the fightback when Lou Vincent, who had enjoyed the most outrageous good luck, top edged a sweep and was caught by Thorpe at short fine leg for 57 and this opened the way for Andy Caddick to produce a terrific rhythmical spell in which, in unhelpful conditions, he captured five wickets either side of lunch to finish with 6 for 63. Giles captured the other four to fall in the innings and England found themselves with a lead of 62.

They were hardly in a frame of mind to be positive under the circumstances, but in a display that speaks volumes for the hard, professional attitude that has been instilled by Hussain and Duncan Fletcher, the lead was stretched to 246 by the close thanks to aggressive batting from Butcher, Marcus Trescothick and Michael Vaughan.

Butcher and Trescothick were both reprieved by umpire Steve Dunn – who had a thoroughly wretched match – and when Butcher was dismissed for 60 early on the fifth morning, Andrew Flintoff was promoted to No. 4 and responded with an innings of sheer brutality. He raced to his 50 from only 33 deliveries and finished with 75 from only 44 balls, including two sixes and ten fours. It was precisely the injection of urgency that Hussain required to declare before lunch and set New Zealand a target of 356 to win from a minimum of 86 overs which, even by their Christchurch standards, was unlikely in the extreme.

England's task, though, was hampered by the return of the strong wind. Since Giles needed to bowl from the southern end to exploit the wearing pitch, this meant that the faster bowlers had to set off into the gale. Richardson was nipped out early by Giles, and Flintoff removed Horne for 38, but Vincent was, again, absurdly fortunate to be given not out by Dunn when on four, and James Foster erred for the third time in the match by dropping Fleming when he was on one. This enabled New Zealand to consolidate, and they lost only one wicket between lunch and tea which, effectively, saved the game.

Matthew Hoggard who, surprisingly, did not bowl during that time, took two wickets in two overs – Vincent for 71 and Fleming, whose 11 took nearly two-and-a-half hours. Nathan Astle and Craig McMillan negotiated the time that remained to ensure that the match ended in quiet, subdued circumstances which reflected the mood of everyone at the Basin Reserve.

SECOND TEST – NEW ZEALAND v. ENGLAND
21–25 March 2002 at Wellington

ENGLAND

	First innings		Second innings	
ME Trescothick	c Vincent b Vettori	37	c Richardson b Vettori	88
MP Vaughan	c Fleming b Drum	7	c Drum b Vettori	34
MA Butcher	c Astle b Drum	47	c Martin b Drum	60
N Hussain (capt)	c Astle b Vettori	66	(5) not out	13
GP Thorpe	c Fleming b Martin	11	(6) not out	1
MR Ramprakash	b Butler	24		
A Flintoff	c Drum b Butler	2	(4) c & b Vettori	75
*JS Foster	not out	25		
AF Giles	c McMillan b Butler	10		
AR Caddick	c Richardson b Martin	10		
MJ Hoggard	c Parore b Butler	7		
Extras	b 4, lb 2, w 6, nb 22	34	b 5, lb 13, nb 4	22
		280	(4 wickets dec.)	293

	First innings				Second innings			
	O	M	R	W	O	M	R	W
Butler	18.3	2	60	4	6	0	32	-
Drum	24	6	85	2	16	2	78	1
Martin	17	3	58	2	7	1	40	-
Vettori	25	3	62	2	24	1	90	3
Astle	1	0	1	-	9	4	18	-
McMillan	3	0	8	-	3	0	17	-

Fall of Wickets
1-26, 2-63, 3-133, 4-163, 5-221, 6-221, 7-223, 8-238, 9-250
1-79, 2-194, 3-209, 4-291

NEW ZEALAND

	First innings		Second innings	
MH Richardson	c Giles b Caddick	60	c Thorpe b Giles	4
MJ Horne	b Caddick	8	c Foster b Flintoff	38
L Vincent	c Thorpe b Giles	57	lbw b Hoggard	71
SP Fleming (capt)	c Thorpe b Caddick	3	b Hoggard	11
NJ Astle	c Hussain b Giles	4	not out	11
CD McMillan	lbw b Caddick	41	not out	17
*AC Parore	c Ramprakash b Giles	0		
DL Vettori	c Thorpe b Caddick	11		
CJ Drum	c Trescothick b Giles	2		
IG Butler	c Foster b Caddick	12		
CS Martin	not out	0		
Extras	b 2, lb 9, nb 9	20	b 3, lb 1, nb 2	6
		218	(4 wickets)	158

	First innings				Second innings			
	O	M	R	W	O	M	R	W
Caddick	28.3	7	63	6	17	6	31	-
Hoggard	13	5	32	-	13	4	31	2
Giles	37	3	103	4	33	11	53	1
Flintoff	10	4	9	-	16	6	24	1
Vaughan					5	1	15	-

Fall of Wickets
1-16, 2-135, 3-138, 4-143, 5-147, 6-149, 7-178, 8-201, 9-207
1-28, 2-65, 3-128, 4-131

Umpires: DB Hair & RS Dunne
Toss: New Zealand
Man of the Match: AR Caddick

Match drawn

THIRD TEST
30 March–3 April 2002 at Auckland

England's precious lead in the series was wantonly surrendered first by some abject bowling under the floodlights that enabled New Zealand to set them 312 to win and then, in the most unlikely pursuit of that target, a last-day batting performance so woeful that it beggared belief. That the build-up to the Test had been overshadowed by the funeral of Ben Hollioake might well have been a contributing factor to the lack of resolve and, especially, the overall impression given by the players that a mere cricket series had little value in the greater scheme of things; all of which is understandable to an extent. It was, nonetheless, a hugely disappointing way for an entire winter of hard work to end.

The pitch was another of the drop-in variety, but one which looked less grassy than had been the case at Christchurch, and more 'conventional' than the wispy-haired strip that England and New Zealand had used at Eden Park for a one-day international. Dank, miserable weather restricted the first day to only 54 overs and completely washed out the second, which had begun with the news of the death of the Queen Mother. Even the third day was restricted to two, two-and-a-half hour sessions because of a large, wet patch at long leg.

A draw – and with it a one-nil victory – seemed assured. Even looking back now, it is still inconceivable that England contrived to lose from this point. During the third day, they managed to complete New Zealand's first innings; bowling them out for 202, of which Chris Harris – restored to the ranks – made a painstaking 71. It was a good recovery from 86 for 5, but was hardly an innings to dominate a Test match. In the final six overs of the day, however, England had slipped to 12 for 3 as Daryl Tuffey – a rangy seam bowler – removed Trescothick and Butcher for ducks and Hussain was caught at slip off Drum. Thorpe reached 42 on the fourth morning and appeared to be restoring some calm with Flintoff when the latter received a decision for caught behind from umpire Doug Cowie so ghastly that it stopped everyone in their tracks. The bowler, Andre Adams, did not even appeal and replays clearly showed that Flintoff's bat was several inches from making contact with the ball. Still, inexplicably, the finger was raised and while a bemused Flintoff sat and contemplated life in the dressing room, England's innings was rapidly mopped up for 160 to give New Zealand a small lead of 42.

Restored to New Zealand's ranks, the evergreen Chris Harris made a doughty 71 in difficult circumstances.

The fourth day – as is so often the case – proved to be the pivotal day of the match. It ended a full half an hour after sunset with the floodlights doing their best to compensate for the almost total darkness. In fact, they were inadequate and play only continued because it was very much in the interests of the batting team for it to do so. For the fielders – who claimed that they could not see the red ball against the dark background - it was an unhappy experience and Hussain attempted more than once to argue the case with the umpires.

In the meantime, Nathan Astle and Craig McMillan were busy dismembering England's attack,

Opposite: Andre Adams literally jumps for joy as he celebrates the fall of James Foster as England head for defeat and a drawn series.

which was wholly ineffective despite the conditions, which had earlier helped Tuffey to claim 6 for 54. Hussain appeared reluctant to turn to Caddick – by far his most experienced bowler – and it was left to Flintoff and Hoggard to try to stem the flow of runs. Astle raced to 65 from 51 balls, including eight fours and two sixes while McMillan's half-century came at a run a ball. Parore, in his final international innings, chimed in with 36 and the declaration came as the players returned to the ground on the fifth and final morning.

Stephen Fleming had thought through the possibilities with great care. He knew that if England batted throughout the day, they would win. He also must have had grave concerns about his inexperienced attack that had performed so heroically in the first innings. He must have suspected, too, that England would try and intimidate Tuffey, Drum and Adams by getting after them in a positive fashion.

That was, indeed, the approach that England adopted, but rather than merely positive, it became thoroughly reckless to the extent of the lower order virtually handing the game to the Kiwis.

At 122 for 2, England appeared to be well in the hunt for their target of 312 to win in 105 overs. The innings resembled a one-day international in that after 15 overs, England were 73 for 2. Suddenly they lost three wickets for three runs in two overs including Thorpe, who had been dropped second ball. While Hussain continued to bat aggressively, Ramprakash fell shortly after lunch for two and England still needed 157 to win. Surely it was now time to settle for a draw and return home with the series intact? Not a bit of it. Foster scored 23, as he and Hussain added 49 in a little over an hour before Adams struck two crucial blows.

First, Foster was caught behind and then, three runs later, Hussain drove a return catch which Adams seized low to his left. Hussain's 82 had come from 119 balls and now New Zealand could sense victory. Far from resisting bravely and defending their series lead, Caddick's dismissal was shameful. Slogging a catch to mid-on for four, he departed with the air of a man who could not wait to get on the plane home, and when Hoggard was snapped up at slip to give Adams his third wicket, even the New Zealanders could not believe how easy their task had been. This defeat meant that England slipped to fifth in the world Test championship and were overtaken by New Zealand who moved to fourth.

THIRD TEST – NEW ZEALAND v. ENGLAND
30 March–3 April 2002 at Auckland

NEW ZEALAND

	First innings		Second innings	
MH Richardson	b Caddick	5	c sub (Usman Afzaal) b Butcher	25
L Vincent	b Caddick	10	(9) c Giles b Hoggard	10
SP Fleming (capt)	c Ramprakash b Hoggard	1	b Hoggard	1
CZ Harris	lbw b Flintoff	71	lbw b Butcher	43
NJ Astle	c Thorpe b Caddick	2	c Butcher b Flintoff	65
CD McMillan	lbw b Caddick	41	not out	50
*AC Parore	c sub (Usman Afzaal) b Flintoff	45	(2) c Thorpe b Hoggard	36
DL Vettori	lbw b Hoggard	3	c Foster b Flintoff	0
AR Adams	c Giles b Flintoff	7	(7) b Flintoff	11
DR Tuffey	c Butcher b Hoggard	0	b Hoggard	5
CJ Drum	not out	2		
Extras	lb 10, nb 5	15	b 3, lb 9, w 1, nb 10	23
		202	(9 wickets dec.)	**269**

	First innings				Second innings			
	O	M	R	W	O	M	R	W
Caddick	25	5	70	4	11	3	41	-
Hoggard	28.2	10	66	3	19.1	3	68	4
Flintoff	16	6	49	3	23	1	108	3
Butcher	5	3	6	-	9	2	34	2
Giles	1	0	1	-	1	0	6	-

Fall of Wickets
1-12, 2-17, 3-17, 4-19, 5-86, 6-172, 7-191, 8-198, 9-200
1-53, 2-55, 3-91, 4-166, 5-217, 6-232, 7-234, 8-262, 9-269

ENGLAND

	First innings		Second innings	
ME Trescothick	lbw b Tuffey	0	b Drum	14
MP Vaughan	c Parore b Adams	27	c Fleming b Drum	36
MA Butcher	c Richardson b Tuffey	0	c sub (BGK Walker) b Astle	35
N Hussain (capt)	c Fleming b Drum	2	c & b Adams	82
GP Thorpe	b Tuffey	42	c Parore b Tuffey	3
MR Ramprakash	c Parore b Tuffey	9	(7) b Tuffey	2
A Flintoff	c Parore b Adams	29	(6) b Tuffey	0
*JS Foster	not out	16	c Parore b Adams	23
AF Giles	lbw b Tuffey	0	not out	21
AR Caddick	b Tuffey	20	c Vettori b Drum	4
MJ Hoggard	c Fleming b Adams	0	c Astle b Adams	2
Extras	b 1, lb 11, nb 3	15	b 1, lb 8, nb 2	11
		160		**233**

	First innings				Second innings			
	O	M	R	W	O	M	R	W
Tuffey	19	6	54	6	16	3	62	3
Drum	10	3	45	1	10	0	52	3
Adams	15.4	2	44	3	15.5	3	61	3
McMillan	1	0	5	-				
Astle					19	6	44	1
Vettori					2	0	5	-

Fall of Wickets
1-0, 2-0, 3-11, 4-60, 5-75, 6-118, 7-122, 8-124, 9-159
1-23, 2-73, 3-122, 4-125, 5-125, 6-155, 7-204, 8-207, 9-230

Umpires: S Venkataraghavan & DB Cowie
Toss: New Zealand
Test Debut: AR Adams (New Zealand)
Man of the Match: DR Tuffey

New Zealand won by 78 runs

TEST MATCH AVERAGES
New Zealand v. England

NEW ZEALAND

Batting	M	Inns	NO	HS	Runs	Av	100	50	c/st
NJ Astle	3	6	1	222	314	62.80	1	1	3
CD McMillan	3	6	2	50*	213	53.25	-	1	1
MH Richardson	3	6	0	76	172	28.66	-	2	3
L Vincent	3	6	0	71	160	26.66	-	2	1
AC Parore	3	5	0	45	82	16.40	-	-	10/-
MJ Horne	2	4	0	38	64	16.00	-	-	-
DL Vettori	3	5	0	42	68	13.60	-	-	3
SP Fleming	3	6	0	48	76	12.66	-	-	6
IG Butler	2	3	0	12	16	5.33	-	-	1
CJ Drum	3	4	2	2*	6	3.00	-	-	3

Also batted in one Test: AR Adams 7, 11 (1ct); CL Cairns 0, 23*; CZ Harris 71, 43;
CS Martin 0* (1ct); DR Tuffey 0, 5

Bowling	Overs	Mds	Runs	Wkts	Av	Best	10m	5/inn
DR Tuffey	35	9	116	9	12.88	6-54	-	1
AR Adams	31.4	5	105	6	17.50	3-44	-	-
IG Butler	63.3	6	288	9	32.00	4-60	-	-
CJ Drum	112.2	25	426	12	35.50	3-36	-	-
DL Vettori	82	8	280	5	56.00	3-90	-	-

Also bowled: NJ Astle 52.4-20-115-4; CL Cairns 19-4-66-3; CD McMillan 20-1-102-0;
CS Martin 24-4-98-2

ENGLAND

Batting	M	Inns	NO	HS	Runs	Av	100	50	c/st
GP Thorpe	3	6	2	200*	274	68.50	1	-	7
N Hussain	3	6	1	106	280	56.00	1	2	2
JS Foster	3	5	3	25*	105	52.50	-	-	9/-
A Flintoff	3	6	0	137	243	40.50	1	1	2
MA Butcher	3	6	0	60	176	29.33	-	1	3
ME Trescothick	3	6	0	88	172	28.66	-	1	1
MP Vaughan	3	6	0	36	131	21.83	-	-	1
MR Ramprakash	3	5	0	31	77	15.40	-	-	2
AF Giles	3	4	1	21*	39	13.00	-	-	4
AR Caddick	3	4	0	20	34	8.50	-	-	1
MJ Hoggard	3	4	1	7	9	3.00	-	-	-

Bowling	Overs	Mds	Runs	Wkts	Av	Best	10m	5/inn
AR Caddick	124.3	37	377	19	19.84	6-63	-	2
MJ Hoggard	119.2	34	402	17	23.64	7-63	-	1
A Flintoff	93	20	313	9	34.77	3-49	-	-
AF Giles	100	20	236	6	39.33	4-103	-	-

Also bowled: MA Butcher 14-5-40-2; MP Vaughan 5-1-15-0

NEW ZEALAND DOMESTIC FIRST-CLASS CRICKET
By Bryan Waddle

Wellington came close to the unimaginable – a clean sweep of the three trophies in New Zealand domestic cricket – but were denied the chance to complete the treble by rain in the season's final first-class fixture.

After comprehensive victories in the limited-over competitions, the State Shield, and the 20-over-a-side State Max tournament, Wellington needed an outright win over Auckland in the final match of the season to grab the first-class title. They did their best to contrive a result after much of the second day of their four-day match had been washed out, with a strange declaration, but in the end, it wasn't to be.

Wellington started six points behind Auckland heading into the final match, and, with six points available for an outright victory, the series would be decided by net run rate in the event of a tie.

They scored an impressive 409 in the first innings, built on solid batting throughout, and restricted Auckland to 215 for 9 in the first innings for a lead of 194. But that took up three days, leaving Wellington with little hope of an outright result. So, rather than enforce the follow-on, Wellington opted to set Auckland a target in the hope of bowling them out quickly enough to secure the title on net average run rate.

They batted for 19 overs before declaring at 48 for 1, leaving Auckland a target of 243, but in order to win the title on the net run rate formula, they had to dismiss them for 169. They couldn't do either and Auckland took the title despite failing to record an outright result.

In fact, rain played a big part in the two matches between the leading two teams. Their first-round match at Wellington's Basin Reserve was restricted to only 101.5 overs on the first day with none possible on the subsequent three days.

There is no doubt that Auckland and Wellington were the best sides in the competition, with Auckland winning six of their ten games outright and Wellington winning five. Both sides suffered just one defeat.

Central Districts were in contention for a while, recording five outright wins, but they missed out on any bonus points gained for a first-innings success.

At the other end of the scale, Otago had a woeful season, losing their first nine games outright before scoring a consolation win over third-placed Central Districts on the final day of the season.

Auckland's return to the winners circle – New Zealand's largest province had not won since the 1995–96 season – was achieved by a solid all-round performance rather than reliance on one or two stars. With their international players away for much of the season, their provincial depth was tested and Auckland were able to develop a consistent side.

Only two of the squad scored over 500 runs in the season, Tim McIntosh and Matt Horne, while Rob Nicol contributed 489 runs to their cause. Leading bowlers Chris Drum and Andre Adams just made the top-ten wicket-takers, but Drum underlined his consistency in the domestic game with 28 wickets at an average of 10.71.

Canterbury's Michael Papps was leading run scorer with an impressive 756 runs at 54 including two centuries. He was one of a number of players who displayed outstanding form for a team that failed to threaten for the title.

Scott Styris, and identical twins James and Hamish Marshall, were dominant with the bat for Northern Districts, despite their side finishing second last in the ten-team competition.

James Marshall scored 706 runs at an average of just under 40, including the highest score of the season and a record for his province, 235, just a week after Styris had bettered Graham Hick's record score by a Northern batsman with an innings of 212 not out.

Central District's English professional Ben Smith was the only other double centurion with 201 not out against Canterbury. Smith and discarded international Mathew Sinclair had to carry the responsibility for Central's batting following the departure of Craig Spearman to English county side Gloucestershire and an injury to their captain Jacob Oram.

Wellington's batting was left to former

Chris Harris' outstanding form for Canterbury earned him a recall to the Test team. The left-hander ended the season with an average of 85.

Test opener Matthew Bell and Richard Jones. Although neither could match their previous year's efforts, they still played a significant role in Wellington's title challenge. As the leading scorers, they were called on a number of times to steer their side to victory from tight situations.

In another rain-affected match against Otago in Dunedin, Wellington had to create an opportunity for victory, declaring 149 behind to encourage Otago to set a target. Otago responded by leaving Wellington a demanding 352 for victory at a rate in excess of four runs an over, which they achieved for the loss of just two wickets. Jones and Bell set about the chase aggressively and completed an opening stand of 299 from 70 overs.

Wellington had to scramble for victory in their next match against Northern Districts. On a difficult pitch they faced a less demanding chase for 242 to win, the highest score in a low-scoring match. With nine wickets down and 20 runs needed, No. 11 Jeetan Patel joined James Franklin to help steer his side to victory in the final over. Wellington almost made a habit of featuring in tight finishes.

Auckland, on the other hand, won matches in a more measured fashion. The champions did feature in the dramatic turnaround in fortunes as the season drew to a close. Sent into bat by Central Districts, Auckland were dismissed for 71 in 26 overs conceding a first-innings lead of 102 on the first day on which 21 wickets fell. Opener Matt Horne had the dubious distinction of being dismissed twice on the first day of a match.

Auckland's second innings was vastly better, as they reached 290 to set a target of 189 by tea on the second day. Central, despite the presence of international players Sinclair, Oram and Glenn Sulzberger, as well as Ben Smith, succumbed for 72 an hour into the third day. It was that resilience, coupled with general consistency, that ensured Auckland its first title in six seasons.

NEW ZEALAND DOMESTIC ONE-DAY CRICKET
By Bryan Waddle

Wellington's ability to capture major trophies was justifiably questioned through the 1990s, but they dispelled any doubts when they added the State Shield one-day title to the first-class trophy they had won the previous year.

More than any other province, Wellington had been subjected to much light-hearted banter about their capacity to win finals, so victory came as sweet revenge for the Wellington 'Firebirds'. The taste of success was even sweeter with an emphatic win over Canterbury after they had lost to them regularly during the 1990s.

Wellington deserved the title having qualified top after ten matches, two complete rounds. They lost only once, ironically to Canterbury, the side they were to beat in the final.

Third-placed qualifiers Canterbury were forced to play a semi-final against Northern Districts. Northern had won seven from their ten games to finish three points behind Wellington in the round robin. Canterbury's place in the final wasn't determined until the last over and it was a case of youth and enthusiasm over experience, with newcomer Cleighton Cornelius playing a vital role. After completing his ten overs for 38 runs and two wickets as Northern were dismissed for 209, Cornelius also went on to play a significant innings in his debut match.

He went to the crease with 26 still required from six overs with four wickets remaining. Two wickets fell at 201 in the 48th leaving Cornelius, the senior partner, to steer his side to its tenth final in 11 years with two balls to spare.

Hometown advantage played a big part in Wellington's success in the final at the Basin Reserve, but it wasn't a hometown lad who won the Man of the Match award. Northants professional David Sales produced a dashing innings of 62 from 83 balls to help Wellington to a total of 200, although that did not appear to be a challenging score for a while.

Sales had been playing club cricket in Wellington as part of an ongoing exchange programme with English county side Northamptonshire. Promoted to opener, he batted with authority, adding 117 for the second wicket with Richard Jones before Wellington lost seven wickets in the space of 13 overs for just 46 runs. Chasing a modest target of 201, Canterbury faltered after a promising start, 101 for 3 in the 28th over, to be all out for 147 in the 45th.

Auckland opener Matt Horne was the leading run scorer with 428 at 42.8 and a strike rate of 96.39, but his success was not translated into the team's results. Auckland finished last, with just two wins from their ten games.

Wellington's seam bowler Paul Hitchcock was the top bowler with 22 wickets at 14.54 and his second lucrative season with the ball earned him selection for the New Zealand one-day team that toured the West Indies.

FIRST-CLASS AVERAGES
New Zealand

BATTING

	M	Inns	NO	HS	Runs	Av	100	50
CZ Harris	8	12	3	155*	770	85.55	2	7
CD McMillan	5	8	2	106	389	64.83	1	2
N Hussain	5	9	0	106	349	58.16	1	3
MH Richardson	10	15	1	143	779	55.64	3	5
MJ Horne	11	17	2	178	798	53.20	3	1
MHW Papps	10	19	4	158*	793	52.86	2	4
GP Thorpe	4	8	2	200*	285	47.50	1	-
NJ Astle	5	8	1	222	325	46.42	1	1
RJ Nicol	10	13	1	109*	489	44.45	2	1
SB Styris	10	17	2	212*	662	44.13	1	4
MS Sinclair	9	15	2	171	573	44.07	2	-
MP Vaughan	4	7	0	156	287	41.00	1	-
RM Frew	7	14	1	115	529	40.69	1	4
PG Fulton	5	9	2	84	280	40.00	-	2
JAH Marshall	10	18	0	235	706	39.22	2	4
MD Bell	7	14	2	131*	465	38.75	1	2
BF Smith	9	16	2	201*	533	38.07	1	3
ME Parlane	6	10	0	146	373	37.30	1	2
SP Fleming	7	11	1	115	372	37.20	1	2
RA Jones	9	16	0	171	576	36.00	2	3
NKW Horsley	9	13	1	106*	410	34.16	1	2
TG McIntosh	10	17	1	123	524	32.75	2	2
BB McCullum	8	16	0	142	510	31.87	1	2
MR Jefferson	3	5	0	53	155	31.00	-	1
RG Hart	10	15	3	102*	370	30.83	1	2
TK Canning	9	12	3	56*	277	30.77	-	1
ME Trescothick	4	8	0	88	246	30.75	-	2
CB Gaffaney	11	22	2	126*	608	30.40	1	3
Aminul Islam	3	6	1	79*	147	29.40	-	1
A Flintoff	5	9	0	137	260	28.88	1	1
GP Sulzberger	8	13	0	61	375	28.84	-	3
CD Cumming	11	22	1	111	591	28.14	1	4
JW Sheed	3	6	1	64	140	28.00	-	2
HJH Marshall	10	17	1	92	443	27.68	-	1
JEC Franklin	10	16	4	73	331	27.58	-	1
SL Stewart	9	17	0	60	454	26.70	-	4
BBJ Griggs	10	17	2	76	395	26.33	-	1
BP Martin	9	12	5	45	184	26.28	-	-
GJ Hopkins	11	19	3	79*	418	26.12	-	1
MA Butcher	4	9	0	60	235	26.11	-	1
CR Pryor	11	21	4	59	439	25.82	-	1
GR Stead	11	19	2	62	437	25.70	-	3
GT Donaldson	10	18	3	52	384	25.60	-	2
L Vincent	7	11	0	75	280	24.45	-	3
AI Sahariar	3	6	0	53	145	24.16	-	1
MDJ Walker	8	11	2	100*	212	23.55	1	-
AC Barnes	8	11	1	95	230	23.00	-	2
AJ Hore	7	14	1	70	283	21.76	-	3
CJ Nevin	7	10	2	50	174	21.75	-	1
AR Adams	9	13	0	72	280	21.53	-	3
MJ Mason	10	16	5	44	233	21.18	-	-
JDP Oram	4	8	1	50	148	21.14	-	1
AM Schwass	9	14	1	44	272	20.92	-	-
PJ Ingram	6	12	1	43	226	20.54	-	-
AJ Penn	10	15	4	66	226	20.54	-	1
PJ Wiseman	10	14	2	59	246	20.50	-	1
PD McGlashan	3	5	0	65	100	20.00	-	1
JAF Yovich	10	15	2	90	248	19.07	-	2
LJ Woodcock	5	10	1	48	169	18.77	-	-
MD Bailey	4	8	1	31	129	18.42	-	-
RS Scragg	4	7	0	54	128	18.28	-	1
DP Kelly	8	15	0	114	271	18.06	1	1
RA Young	11	13	2	86	190	17.27	-	1
MN Hart	9	17	1	51	276	17.25	-	1
CJM Furlong	7	12	0	88	206	17.16	-	1
Habibul Bashar	3	6	0	61	102	17.00	-	1
AC Parore	5	6	0	45	102	17.00	-	-
WAS Silva	3	5	0	33	83	16.60	-	-
BGK Walker	11	13	0	63	215	16.53	-	1
AJ Redmond	8	15	0	101	242	16.13	1	-
RT King	3	6	0	31	96	16.00	-	-
KD Mills	5	6	0	42	96	16.00	-	-
GE Bradburn	8	15	2	53	205	15.76	-	1
MR Ramprakash	5	8	0	42	125	15.62	-	-
Sanwar Hossain	3	6	0	45	92	15.33	-	-
ND Morland	7	13	3	27	152	15.20	-	-
RA Lawson	9	18	0	63	270	15.00	-	1

FIRST-CLASS AVERAGES
New Zealand

BATTING

	M	Inns	NO	HS	Runs	Av	100	50
JS Patel	9	10	4	23	86	14.33	-	-
SJ Blackmore	6	10	0	32	143	14.30	-	-
LK Germon	4	7	0	23	93	13.28	-	-
MG Croy	8	16	1	58*	197	13.13	-	1
SP Beare	5	9	0	60	114	12.66	-	1
JI Englefield	6	11	0	57	137	12.45	-	1
GW Aldridge	8	10	1	33	112	12.44	-	-
RD Burson	7	11	1	39	120	12.00	-	-
AR Caddick	5	7	1	20	71	11.83	-	-
SJ Waide	3	5	0	17	57	11.40	-	-
RGT Smith	6	10	1	21	102	11.33	-	-
DL Vettori	5	6	0	42	68	11.33	-	-
DR Tuffey	5	7	1	29	67	11.16	-	-
WA Wisneski	7	8	2	23	64	10.66	-	-
DG Sewell	10	16	9	24	74	10.57	-	-
Khaled Mahmud	3	6	0	45	63	10.50	-	-
MR Gillespie	4	6	0	21	63	10.50	-	-

Qualification: 5 completed innings

BOWLING

	Overs	Mds	Runs	Wkts	Av	Best	10m	5/inn
AM Schwass	259.2	71	663	45	14.73	7-36	-	3
CJ Drum	317.3	94	817	53	15.41	6-34	1	3
SB Styris	202.2	59	477	28	17.03	5-18	-	1
AR Caddick	192.3	59	546	31	17.61	6-63	-	3
AJ Penn	304.3	93	722	40	18.05	8-21	1	2
LJ Hamilton	319.4	95	770	42	18.33	6-32	-	3
AR Adams	308.4	78	781	42	18.59	5-44	-	2
WA Cornelius	221.4	66	649	34	19.08	7-53	1	3
MR Gillespie	102.3	24	315	16	19.68	5-50	-	1
KP Walmsley	280.1	73	810	39	20.76	5-51	-	1
GS Shaw	148	26	475	21	22.61	4-12	-	-
GW Aldridge	213	60	527	23	22.91	4-43	-	-
DR Tuffey	164.5	40	528	23	22.95	7-69	-	2
BE Hefford	170	49	431	18	23.94	4-20	-	-
MDJ Walker	249.1	87	505	21	24.04	4-25	-	-
TK Canning	292.3	86	651	26	25.03	5-35	-	2
ND Morland	176.3	44	477	19	25.10	4-26	-	-
MJ Mason	328.1	90	806	32	25.18	5-22	1	1
BGK Walker	315.4	100	716	28	25.57	4-46	-	-
JAF Yovich	316.2	59	1057	40	26.42	6-102	1	2
WA Wisneski	172	30	583	22	26.50	5-74	-	1
RD Burson	225.4	73	566	21	26.95	4-65	-	-
IG Butler	198.4	41	706	26	27.15	4-46	-	-
MJ Hoggard	152.2	40	498	18	27.66	7-63	-	1
JEC Franklin	280	62	802	27	29.70	4-59	-	-
BP Martin	212.4	63	508	17	29.88	3-24	-	-
GP Sulzberger	190.4	62	459	15	30.60	4-52	-	-
CR Pryor	275.5	53	1001	32	31.28	5-45	-	2
DG Sewell	309	72	974	31	31.41	7-64	-	2
PJ Wiseman	347.1	77	940	29	32.41	5-99	-	1
AJ Redmond	164	40	395	12	32.91	4-35	-	-
DL Vettori	148	30	417	11	37.90	3-90	-	-
A Flintoff	119	27	381	10	38.10	3-49	-	-
JS Patel	179.2	56	482	12	40.16	3-49	-	-
KD Mills	149	33	426	10	42.60	2-30	-	-
CS Martin	181	52	546	11	49.63	3-67	-	-
RGT Smith	186.2	37	598	12	49.83	3-21	-	-

Qualification: 10 wickets in 8 innings

The following bowlers took 10 wickets in fewer than 8 innings:

CL Cairns	69.2	14	225	16	14.06	7-53	-	1
SE Bond	88.4	22	243	16	15.18	5-37	-	1
SJ Cunis	124.1	35	266	10	26.60	3-40	-	-

FIELDING

34 - RG Hart (33ct,1st), RA Young (32ct,2st); 31 - BBJ Griggs; 28 - GJ Hopkins (25ct,3st); 25 - MG Croy (23ct,2st); 20 - MS Sinclair; 16 - CJ Nevin; 15 - AC Parore; 13 - CJM Furlong; 12 - GA Howell, SB Styris, GP Sulzberger; 10 - DJ Drew, SP Fleming, JS Foster, CZ Harris, Khaled Mashud, JAH Marshall, MHW Papps, MH Richardson.

Qualification: 10 catches or more

AUSTRALIA

PAKISTAN IN AUSTRALIA
By Jim Maxwell

SUPER CHALLENGE II

Was this so called Super Challenge Australia's winter of discontent? Australian, and particularly Melbourne's, sports pundits are used to watching Australian Rules football in June. It's cold and far away from the flannelled foolery of perspiring nights under lights in January. The ACB's second attempt at out-of-season scheduling was certainly not a failure, making a profit out of television rights and sponsorship, but the mediocre crowds, and Australia's off-season form, posed questions about where and when such matches should be played in future.

While another movie remake about bushranger Ned Kelly was nearby in the making, the Pakistanis ambushed Australia to grab some psychological succour for the World Cup. On the evidence of Shoaib Akhtar's outstanding fast bowling, Pakistan have the weaponry to blast out any team. Under Waqar Younis' leadership, Pakistan were a far more cohesive side than the opposition Australia had trounced at Lord's in 2001 in the World Cup final.

Shoaib's match-winning spell in the deciding match at the Gabba was spectacularly destructive. Late in-swing at 150kph is unplayable, and the ball that knocked over Ponting was a gem. Two of Shoaib's rockets leapt past the batsman's nose, soaring over wicketkeeper Latif's head for four byes apiece. His other victims included Martyn, uppercutting to third man, Lehmann, bowled first up exposing his leg stump, Bevan, caught when Shoaib went around the wicket, and Gillespie, struck plumb lbw by another in-swinger. Shoaib's deadly spell wrecked Australia's batting after Gilchrist had been wastefully run out after failing to beat Yohanna's throw from mid-on. Shoaib, Wasim and Waqar supported by Azhar Mahmood and Shahid Afridi comprised a potent, balanced attack, with Saqlain and Abdur Razzaq absent on county duty.

Pakistan had batted attractively to set a difficult target. Imran Nazir attacked the new ball and, despite a middle-order slump including two shambolic run outs, Yohanna and the 36-year-old veteran Wasim Akram added 88, including 58 from the last five overs. Twenty-three of those runs came

Previous page: The Australian team show off the Wisden Trophy. After back-to-back series wins over South Africa, Australia still remain the team to beat.

from McGrath's final over, with consecutive sixes hit down the ground by Wasim. Australia had developed an unhappy habit of going for ten an over in the happy hour in South Africa, a situation that was usually rescued by their batsmen, but this time they could not respond.

The fanfare for the series promoted a showdown between Shoaib Akhtar and Brett Lee to establish who was the fastest bowler. Alas, the marketing men did not have a hotline to the selectors, because Lee was not chosen in the first match, and Shoaib cried off with hip soreness ten minutes before play started under the roof at Melbourne's Colonial Stadium. Only 11,671 fans braved the chilly weather to watch a lopsided spectacle, won by Australia with 17.1 overs and seven wickets to spare. Andy Bichel, preferred to Lee, and fresh from regular county cricket, led the charge on the bouncy drop-in pitch, taking 3 for 30 as Pakistan wavered to a poor 176 for 8. Gilchrist and Hayden smashed 101 from 97 balls, dispatching some wayward bowling, mainly to the offside boundary.

Pakistan levelled the series after Australia lost Gilchrist and Ponting within Wasim's first three balls, and stumbled to 167, watched by a marginally improved Saturday crowd of 16,891. Akhtar warmed up for his Gabba blitz with two wickets and a few missiles faster than 150kph, Lee was a mixture of scythe and wides, while Younis Khan guided the chase successfully with seven balls and a couple of wickets in hand.

At the end of the series the ACB said they would reassess their winter commitment to cricket. Tight schedules could encourage matches against Bangladesh and other minnows to be staged in the warmer climes of Cairns or Darwin in mid-year. Certainly cricket was not designed to be played in thermal underwear, nor when an event called the World Cup (football) was grabbing most of the audience.

Match One
12 June 2002 at Colonial Stadium, Melbourne (floodlit)
Pakistan 176 for 8 (50 overs)
Australia 177 for 3 (32.5 overs) (AC Gilchrist 56)
Australia won by seven wickets
Man of the Match: AC Gilchrist

Match Two
15 June 2002 at Colonial Stadium, Melbourne (floodlit)
Australia 167 (45.4 overs) (DR Martyn 56)
Pakistan 168 for 8 (45 overs) (Younis Khan 56*)
Pakistan won by two wickets
Man of the Match: Younis Khan

Match Three
19 June 2002 at
Woolloongabba,
Brisbane (floodlit)
Pakistan 256 for 7
(50 overs)
(Imran Nazir 66,
Yousuf Youhana 61*)
Australia 165 (40 overs)
(Shoaib Akhtar 5 for 25)
Pakistan won by 91 runs
Man of the Match:
Shoaib Akhtar
Player of the Series:
Shoaib Akhtar

Shoaib Akhtar has had to
endure endless speculation
about his bowling action,
but he has never given up.
He was the Man of the
Super Challenge series.

NEW ZEALAND IN AUSTRALIA
By Jim Maxwell

FIRST TEST
8–12 November 2001 at Brisbane

A match that was heading for a waterlogged wipe-out came to life on the final day thanks to some imaginative captaincy. Needing 20 runs from the last two overs to win, with Cairns in blazing form, New Zealand's chase was on target to pull off a shock victory. In partnership with the eager McMillan, Cairns had already struck two huge sixes, and aiming a drive towards long on he found Ponting clutching the ball just inside the boundary. McGrath had put the pressure on Cairns, bowling the previous over full outside the off stump, but within the allowable width, frustrating McMillan who could not score. And with 15 needed from the last over, McGrath again bowled a miserly line, restricting McMillan and Parore to just five runs, and the drawn result.

New Zealand were launched by Richardson's 57 from 69 balls, and when Fleming was in control with Astle, they needed 97 from the last 15 overs with seven wickets in hand. Astle took on his perennial nemesis Shane Warne and skied a catch to Gillespie at mid-off. Steve Waugh's direct-hit run out disposed of Fleming by a third-umpire photo finish, setting up the climactic Cairns-McMillan charge.

The exciting finish was a million to one chance earlier in the day when New Zealand still needed 16 runs to avoid the follow-on, at 271 for 8. Steve Waugh had just taken his 100th Test catch, to give the impressive Lee his fifth wicket. Next ball Vettori edged straight to Warne at first slip, who muffed the chance. Vettori and Nash hit out, and as soon as the follow-on mark was passed, Fleming declared. Their innings had been revived from a calamitous 55 for 4 by Astle, McMillan and Cairns, who had smashed 61 from 70 balls with eight screaming fours.

Taking up Fleming's challenge, Steve Waugh promoted Gilchrist to open the innings, but he was out to Cairns' slower ball in the fifth over with the score on 30 for 1. Attacking a weakened line-up, without Nash and O'Connor who had both suffered back injuries, Australia raced on for 14 overs, to 84 for 2, with Waugh's declaration leaving New Zealand 57 overs to make 284.

Fleming's initial decision to send Australia in under high cloud should have paid an early dividend when Cairns struck

The weather ruined the opening Test of the series at Brisbane, but Brett Lee served notice of what was to follow with 5 for 67 in New Zealand's first innings.

Langer's pads with the fifth ball of the match. Umpire Harper shook his head, and although he later admitted his error, it was no comfort to the Kiwis, because the first wicket fell at 224.

Langer and Hayden smacked the wayward, underpitched offerings, to cement their opening combination. It must have looked easy from the dressing room, because the middle order succumbed quickly to some loose shots once the left-handers were separated. McMillan hurled down some sucker balls, in the style, if not the skill, of a latter day Botham.

Going into the second day with a new ball, New Zealand could not get the breakthrough quickly enough to prevent another Gilchrist assault. Brett Lee also struck attractively as the innings rolled into the third day between showers, helping Gilchrist to his fourth Test century in a stand worth 135.

Brisbane's wet weather wiped out the equivalent of two days' play, so the pitch never developed the wear and footmarks for Warne to exploit. On the run of play a draw was a fortunate outcome for New Zealand, but they almost achieved the improbable thanks to both captains' enterprise.

Matt Hayden was one of three Australian centurions at the Gabba. Hayden top scored with 136 as he and Justin Langer put on 224 for the first wicket.

FIRST TEST – AUSTRALIA v. NEW ZEALAND
8–12 November 2001 at Brisbane

AUSTRALIA

	First innings		Second innings	
JL Langer	c Vettori b McMillan	104	(4) not out	18
ML Hayden	c Richardson b Cairns	136	(2) run out (sub L Vincent)	13
RT Ponting	c Vettori b Cairns	5	(3) not out	32
ME Waugh	lbw b Astle	0		
SR Waugh (capt)	c Parore b McMillan	3		
DR Martyn	c Vettori b McMillan	4		
*AC Gilchrist	c sub (L Vincent) b Cairns	118	(1) b Cairns	20
SK Warne	c Sinclair b Cairns	22		
B Lee	c Parore b Cairns	61		
JN Gillespie	not out	20		
GD McGrath				
Extras	lb 4, w 1, nb 8	13	nb 1	1
	(9 wickets dec.)	486	(2 wickets dec.)	84

	First innings				Second innings			
	O	M	R	W	O	M	R	W
Cairns	37	8	146	5	5	1	29	1
Nash	30	6	93	-				
O'Connor	17.2	4	67	-				
Vettori	13.4	0	65	-	2	0	8	-
Astle	19	7	46	1				
McMillan	14	1	65	3	7	0	47	-

Fall of Wickets
1-224, 2-233, 3-235, 4-256, 5-260, 6-263, 7-302, 8-437, 9-486
1-30, 2-39

NEW ZEALAND

	First innings		Second innings	
MH Richardson	lbw b Gillespie	26	lbw b Warne	57
M Bell	c Ponting b Gillespie	6	lbw b McGrath	5
MS Sinclair	c Ponting b Lee	3	st Gilchrist b Warne	23
SP Fleming (capt)	c Gilchrist b Gillespie	0	run out (SR Waugh)	57
NJ Astle	c Gilchrist b Lee	66	c Gillespie b Warne	49
CD McMillan	c Warne b Lee	45	not out	23
CL Cairns	c SR Waugh b Lee	61	c Ponting b Lee	43
*AC Parore	c SR Waugh b Lee	11	not out	3
DJ Nash	not out	25		
DL Vettori	not out	3		
SB O'Connor				
Extras	lb 15, nb 26	41	b 1, lb 9, w 1, nb 3	14
	(8 wickets dec.)	287	(6 wickets dec.)	274

	First innings				Second innings			
	O	M	R	W	O	M	R	W
McGrath	26	6	80	-	20	4	66	1
Gillespie	18.4	6	56	3	8	0	48	-
Lee	23	6	67	5	10	0	53	1
Warne	18	2	61	-	18	2	89	3
Ponting	3	0	8	-				
ME Waugh					1	0	8	-

Fall of Wickets
1-36, 2-51, 3-55, 4-55, 5-147, 6-242, 7-243, 8-271
1-33, 2-89, 3-90, 4-190, 5-213, 6-264

Umpires: SA Bucknor & DJ Harper
Toss: New Zealand
Man of the Match: B Lee

Match drawn

SECOND TEST
22–26 November 2001 at Hobart

Rain wrecked Australia's chances of pushing for victory, as New Zealand struggled towards avoiding the follow-on mark on the final day.

Fleming gambled on bowling Australia out cheaply when he won the toss again, but another dominant opening partnership set up an unassailable position for the home side. Langer's cutting and pulling rushed him to his third hundred in as many Tests, a feat last achieved by David Boon, the local marketing executive and corporate lunch organizer, in 1993. Langer whistled past 50 from 49 balls hitting ten fours, while Hayden happily waited to pounce, scoring just two runs in this early mayhem. Langer's first scoring shot could have been terminal, but Bell at backward point spilt a head-high chance from the unlucky Tuffey. Tuffey and Cantabrian constable Shane Bond, making his debut, had replaced the injured Nash and O'Connor.

Hayden maintained his prolific form, battering the two four-ball-an-over bowlers. A measure of New Zealand's waywardness and Australia's potency was the statistic of 76 fours and five sixes, or 342 runs out of the innings of 558 runs. The New Zealand pace bowling was indisciplined, earning the justifiable description, 'they're bowling pies'.

Ponting relished the opportunity to produce a substantial performance in front of his admirers, despite another middle-order hiccup that included leg before ducks to Steve Waugh padding up and Martyn missing an arm ball. Australia's momentum was unaffected by the loss of key wickets, and by stumps they had amassed 411 for 6. Warne and Lee continued the plunder after Ponting had completed

Ricky Ponting tucked into the wayward New Zealand attack to complete his first Test century at the Bellerive Oval in Hobart: his home town.

SECOND TEST – AUSTRALIA v. NEW ZEALAND
22–26 November 2001 at Hobart

AUSTRALIA

	First innings	
JL Langer	c Vettori b Cairns	123
ML Hayden	c Bond b Vettori	91
RT Ponting	not out	157
ME Waugh	b Vettori	12
SR Waugh (capt)	lbw b Bond	0
DR Martyn	lbw b Vettori	0
*AC Gilchrist	b Vettori	39
SK Warne	b Astle	70
B Lee	c McMillan b Vettori	41
JN Gillespie		
GD McGrath		
Extras	b 3, lb 5, w 2, nb 15	25
	(8 wickets dec.)	558

	First innings			
	O	M	R	W
Cairns	28	3	122	1
Tuffey	15	1	74	–
Bond	28	0	135	1
Vettori	36	5	138	5
McMillan	8	0	51	–
Astle	9	0	30	1

Fall of Wickets
1-223, 2-238, 3-253, 4-266, 5-267, 6-336, 7-481, 8-558

NEW ZEALAND

	First innings	
MH Richardson	lbw b Gillespie	30
M Bell	c Gilchrist b Warne	4
MS Sinclair	b Gillespie	23
SP Fleming (capt)	lbw b McGrath	71
NJ Astle	c Warne b ME Waugh	11
CD McMillan	b Gillespie	55
CL Cairns	c Gilchrist b McGrath	20
*AC Parore	not out	10
DL Vettori	not out	10
DR Tuffey		
SE Bond		
Extras	lb 1, nb 8	9
	(7 wickets dec.)	243

	First innings			
	O	M	R	W
McGrath	27	12	46	2
Gillespie	28	14	45	3
Warne	24.2	3	70	1
Lee	19	5	51	–
ME Waugh	7	1	30	1

Fall of Wickets
1-11, 2-53, 3-76, 4-100, 5-197, 6-219, 7-223

Umpires: SA Bucknor & SJ Davis
Toss: New Zealand
Test debut: SE Bond (New Zealand)
Man of the Match: RT Ponting

Match drawn

a scintillating maiden Bellerive Test hundred. Four hours of play were lost to rain on the second day and when the New Zealanders finally began their innings on day three, their openers struggled to score against the sustained pace attack.

The players were curious about the appearance of third umpire John Smeaton, deputizing for Steve Davis, who had a mishap overnight. Attempting to scale a fence well after stumps on the previous evening, Davis landed more heavily than his colleagues and ended up in hospital with a badly wounded knee.

Bell was hopelessly out of touch and Warne's introduction induced a premeditated sweep shot that deflected the ball off an apparent jumble of bat and glove to Gilchrist, and novitiate umpire Smeaton struck. The Kiwis had their minds on survival and their eyes on the clouds as Gillespie rattled through Sinclair first ball after lunch. Rain wiped out the rest of the day with New Zealand on 71 for 2.

Fleming and McMillan defied and counter-attacked on day four after Richardson was unluckily leg before to Gillespie via a faint inside edge and Warne grabbed a wonderful catch to remove Astle. Fleming passed 50 for the 32nd time in his career, and when the rain tumbled down again he was on 71 and McMillan 51 with the visitors on 197 for 4.

The main interest on the final day was whether Fleming could reach his century. Going around the wicket, McGrath caused an immediate kafuffle when Fleming shouldered arms to the day's first ball, and after a typically agonizing wait, umpire Bucknor squirted the decision. McMillan too did not play at a Gillespie off cutter and the innings was fading away when, without a hint of surprise, it rained again. Nil all – showdown at the WACA.

THIRD TEST
30 November–4 December 2001 at Perth

A high-scoring, entertaining match fluctuated on the final day with both teams pushing for victory. A couple of crucial umpiring decisions went against New Zealand after they had set Australia 440 to win. Steve Waugh survived a caught behind shout off the persevering Vettori when he was on 13, and Gillespie appeared to glove a catch before he had scored, with 5.5 overs remaining and the score on 355 for 7.

Umpire Robinson later admitted that he had made an error, reckoning that he never heard the

Some typical fireworks from Nathan Astle, who scored 156, enabled New Zealand to score 534 in their first innings at Perth and put Australia under pressure.

snick of confirmation, but New Zealand had profited from some other favourable umpiring decisions earlier in the match.

The irony of the drawn series was that the much-vaunted Australian attack did not take ten New Zealand wickets in an innings, and New Zealand, whose bowling line-up was reckoned incapable of knocking Australia over, dismissed Australia in the first innings in Perth, taking a lead of 183 runs.

New Zealand's patient, disciplined batting upset Australia's hopes of dominating the contest with their pace bowling. Sure of the bounce on a WACA pitch that had little of the sideways movement that traditionally produces three-day finishes, Vincent, Fleming and Astle played on length, frequently, allowing deliveries to pass over or just outside the off stump. McGrath was defused, and could not find the fuller length or luck for his regular slip-catching dismissals.

Vincent became the first Kiwi-born player to make a hundred on debut against Australia, although begrudging Aussies reminded their neighbours that Vincent had played all of his youth cricket in Australia before moving back to Auckland. He cut, drove and pulled confidently, using his feet well to attack Warne's tempters.

Fleming also enjoyed the true bounce, scoring his first Test hundred against Australia, after labouring in the 90s for 45 minutes. Vincent, who had only opened the batting once before in his first-class career, hit 15 fours and a six as he shared a 199-run stand with his captain. The second new ball ripped out four wickets, but Parore played the innings of his career to resist, and helped the able Astle to attack, carrying the record-breaking partnership of 253 beyond tea on the second day. For the first time four New Zealanders made hundreds in a Test innings, as the world champions struggled for a breakthrough.

Using the breeze skillfully, Vettori threatened to force a rare Australian follow-on when Gilchrist was caught at short leg on 192 for 6. Warne and Martyn played sensibly after Astle dropped the budding all-rounder on ten. Warne's calculated hitting seemed certain to bring him his maiden Test hundred, but he was spectacularly caught by Richardson at deep midwicket for 99, aiming another hoick from Vettori.

Vincent again showed his mettle, cracking seven fours in a run-a-ball 54, launching New Zealand to a potential winning position, when Fleming closed the day leaving a day and 17 overs to bowl Australia out for less than 439. Australia have little reputation for batting out draws, and the undersung Kiwi attack were sustained both by Vettori's accuracy and the occasional wicket.

Steve Waugh and Gilchrist gave no hint of a final assault until Gilchrist, on cue, smashed 18 from a Vettori over, leaving the home side to make 123 from the final 15 overs. Gilchrist plundered Cairns for 14 in the next over, and ears were pricking to the broadcast again when another Gilchrist thump was deflected by Vettori onto the bowler's stumps, running out Waugh for 67. Warne continued the attack, but a mix-up run out brought a halt to a potentially spectacular finish, as Gilchrist and Gillespie played out time.

Daniel Vettori then took 6 for 87 as Australia were bowled out for 351.

THIRD TEST – AUSTRALIA v. NEW ZEALAND
30 November–4 December 2001 at Perth

NEW ZEALAND

	First innings		Second innings	
MH Richardson	b Gillespie	9	run out (SR Waugh)	30
L Vincent	c ME Waugh b Warne	104	c ME Waugh b Lee	54
MS Sinclair	lbw b McGrath	2	c Gilchrist b McGrath	29
SP Fleming (capt)	lbw b Lee	105	(5) b Warne	4
NJ Astle	not out	156	(6) c Langer b Gillespie	40
CD McMillan	lbw b Gillespie	4	(7) c Warne b Gillespie	19
DL Vettori	c Martyn b Gillespie	2	(9) c SR Waugh b Lee	3
CL Cairns	c Gilchrist b Lee	8	(4) c Warne b Lee	42
*AC Parore	c McGrath b Lee	110	(8) not out	16
SE Bond	b Lee	0	b Lee	8
CS Martin				
Extras	b 4, lb 15, w 2, nb 13	34	b 1, lb 6, nb 4	11
	(9 wickets dec.)	534	(9 wickets dec.)	256

	First innings				Second innings			
	O	M	R	W	O	M	R	W
McGrath	27	11	72	1	17	4	63	1
Gillespie	40	7	112	3	17	0	55	2
Lee	32.5	5	125	4	16	3	56	4
Warne	43	9	135	1	21	3	75	1
Martyn	10	0	44	–				
ME Waugh	6	1	26	–				
Ponting	4	3	1	–				

Fall of Wickets
1-12, 2-19, 3-218, 4-264, 5-269, 6-272, 7-281, 8-534, 9-534
1-77, 2-90, 3-128, 4-151, 5-199, 6-208, 7-241, 8-246, 9-256

AUSTRALIA

	First innings		Second innings	
JL Langer	c Parore b Cairns	75	c Vettori b Bond	0
ML Hayden	c Vincent b Bond	0	c Sinclair b Vettori	57
RT Ponting	c Parore b Martin	31	b Cairns	26
ME Waugh	c Bond b Vettori	42	b McMillan	86
SR Waugh (capt)	c Parore b Vettori	8	run out (Vettori)	67
DR Martyn	c Fleming b Cairns	60	b Vettori	30
*AC Gilchrist	c Richardson b Vettori	0	not out	83
SK Warne	c Richardson b Vettori	99	run out (Sinclair)	10
B Lee	c McMillan b Vettori	17		
JN Gillespie	c Parore b Vettori	0	(9) not out	1
GD McGrath	not out	0		
Extras	lb 2, w 1, nb 16	19	lb 3, w 2, nb 16	21
		351	(7 wickets)	381

	First innings				Second innings			
	O	M	R	W	O	M	R	W
Cairns	23	5	86	2	15	2	72	1
Bond	18	2	74	1	21	3	80	1
Martin	23	4	88	1	12	0	51	–
Vettori	34.4	7	87	6	45	11	142	2
Astle	5	1	14	–	12	5	18	–
McMillan					5	2	15	1

Fall of Wickets
1-3, 2-61, 3-122, 4-137, 5-191, 6-192, 7-270, 8-342, 9-346
1-1, 2-52, 3-130, 4-195, 5-244, 6-339, 7-355

Umpires: ID Robinson & DB Hair
Toss: New Zealand
Test Debut: L Vincent (New Zealand)
Man of the Match: DL Vettori
Player of the Series: JL Langer

Match drawn

TEST MATCH AVERAGES
Australia v. New Zealand

AUSTRALIA

Batting	M	Inns	NO	HS	Runs	Av	100	50	c/st
RT Ponting	3	5	2	157*	251	83.66	1	–	3
JL Langer	3	5	1	123	320	80.00	2	1	1
AC Gilchrist	3	5	1	118	260	65.00	1	1	6/1
ML Hayden	3	5	0	136	297	59.40	1	2	–
SK Warne	3	4	0	99	201	50.25	–	2	4
B Lee	3	3	0	61	119	39.66	–	1	–
ME Waugh	3	4	0	86	140	35.00	–	1	2
DR Martyn	3	4	0	60	94	23.50	–	1	1
JN Gillespie	3	3	2	20*	21	21.00	–	–	1
SR Waugh	3	4	0	67	78	19.50	–	1	3

Also batted: GD McGrath (3 Tests) 0* (1 ct)

Bowling	Overs	Mds	Runs	Wkts	Av	Best	10m	5/inn
B Lee	100.5	19	352	14	25.14	5-67	–	1
JN Gillespie	111.4	27	316	11	28.72	3-45	–	–
GD McGrath	117	37	327	5	65.40	2-46	–	–
SK Warne	124.2	19	430	6	71.66	3-89	–	–

Also bowled: DR Martyn 10-0-44-0; RT Ponting 7-3-9-0; ME Waugh 14-2-64-1

NEW ZEALAND

Batting	M	Inns	NO	HS	Runs	Av	100	50	c/st
NJ Astle	3	5	1	156*	322	80.50	1	1	–
AC Parore	3	5	3	110	150	75.00	1	–	6/-
SP Fleming	3	5	0	105	237	47.40	1	2	1
CD McMillan	3	5	1	55	146	36.50	–	1	2
CL Cairns	3	5	0	61	174	34.80	–	1	–
MH Richardson	3	5	0	57	152	30.40	–	1	3
MS Sinclair	3	5	0	29	80	16.00	–	–	2
DL Vettori	3	5	2	10*	18	9.00	–	–	5
MD Bell	3	3	0	6	15	5.00	–	–	–

Also batted: SE Bond (2 Tests) 0, 8 (2 ct); DJ Nash (1 Test) 25*; L Vincent (1 Test) 104, 54 (1 ct)
CS Martin, SB O'Connor and DR Tuffey played in one Test but did not bat

Bowling	Overs	Mds	Runs	Wkts	Av	Best	10m	5/inn
DL Vettori	131.2	23	440	13	33.84	6-87	–	2
CL Cairns	108	19	455	10	45.50	5-146	–	1

Also bowled: NJ Astle 45-13-108-2; SE Bond 67-5-289-3; CD McMillan 34-3-178-4;
CS Martin 35-4-139-1; DJ Nash 30-6-93-0; SB O'Connor 17.2-4-67-0; DR Tuffey 15-1-74-0

SOUTH AFRICA IN AUSTRALIA
By Jim Maxwell

FIRST TEST
14–18 December 2001 at Adelaide

The most anticipated match of the season was well fought until Australia took control on the fourth day and vanquished South Africa by 246 runs.

South Africa went into this important clash without ace fast bowler Allan Donald, who was struggling with a foot injury. Donald's injury and lack of match preparation at the age of 35, threw the burden onto Makhaya Ntini, the wayward Nantie Hayward, plus Shaun Pollock, who struggled to bowl at his best and rarely moved the ball. It was an ominous beginning, and on a dry Adelaide pitch Australia were well set within an hour, as Hayden and Langer maintained their confident association.

Klusener had Hayden caught at cover, but Ponting, having survived a miss by Kirsten at third slip on six, was serenely in control. His run out to Dippenaar's direct hit from cover was the result of a poor call from Langer, who completed his fourth Test century in six innings. The run out cued one of those middle-order hiccups that Gilchrist normally arrests. For once he failed, falling to left-armer Claude Henderson, whose turn and bounce reduced Australia from 182 for 1 to 248 for 6, abetted by Mark Waugh's loose dismissal to Hayward.

South Africa, who must have fancied their chances of keeping Australia under 300, could not curb Martyn and Warne. Martyn had been cruelly dropped from the team in 1994 after a failed run chase in Sydney. He made amends with a poised, skillfully crafted innings, helped by the reliable blocks and bangs from Warne, and then Lee. Partnerships of 84 and 77 frustrated not only South Africa, but also Graeme Pollock, who was a guest radio commentator, and a South African selector. Shaun's uncle was forthright in his criticism of predictable and formulaic tactics. Pollock himself could not penetrate with the new ball, and Australia's bankable total of 439 looked ideal for the wiles of Warne's leg spin.

Warne had been challenged in the match build-up by Stuart MacGill, and there was speculation about playing both spinners. It was a policy that had failed in the Caribbean in 1999, and the selectors conservatively stuck with the reliable mix of Warne and three pace bowlers. Steve Waugh introduced Warne after four overs, but Kirsten and Gibbs were in good touch, taking 87 runs from the expectant bowlers.

Another Waugh tactic paid off when McGrath went around the wicket and his first ball to Kirsten was an in-swinging full toss, that he failed to spot as it whacked his pads in front. Australia pounced. Tyro No. 3 Dippenaar aimed a square drive at McGrath's bouncing off-stump attack, and saw Ponting haul in a miraculous left-handed catch in the slips.

Nightwatchman Henderson supported Gibbs, but Lee's smart return removed Henderson, and Gibbs had a brain explosion, rushing down the pitch towards the taunting Warne. Kallis, in at No. 5 instead of No. 3 where he could have taken Australia on, was cut short by McGrath's reverse swing. McKenzie and Boucher revived the innings, before another novel move from Waugh led to Martyn taking his first Test wicket. Warne cleaned up, bagging his first five-wicket return in Adelaide.

Australia's useful 65-run lead grew handsomely on the fourth day via Hayden's dominating strokes. Like Martyn, Hayden had some memories of failure against the Proteas, and as he lashed Henderson's over-the-wicket lobs

Shane Warne celebrates another five-wicket haul in the new manner by showing the ball to the Adelaide crowd.

towards and beyond the legside boundaries; commentator Pollock remarked that Claude had wanted to go around the wicket at Hayden, but his captain had insisted he keep aiming at the footmarks.

In a productive partnership with Mark Waugh, Hayden raced to 99, waited nervously for three overs, then reached his fourth Test century, guiding Australia to a lead of 374.

By stumps South Africa were teetering. Gibbs went bat pad to McGrath, and with the timing of a legendary actor in his pomp, Warne dismissed Kirsten with the final ball of the day.

The Adelaide pitch was showing its usual variable tendencies, and Australia's prime bowlers, McGrath and Warne, were eager for wickets after the disappointment of a drawn series against New Zealand. McGrath disconcerted Dippenaar with a short ball that barely rose above the stumps. Soon he was edging to Warne, and McKenzie followed quickly, padding up to an off cutter from McGrath. Umpire Venkat may still have been recovering from a blow to his leg on the previous day when he could not avoid a Ponting pull shot at square leg, because the inevitable replays suggested the ball was not doing enough to hit.

Kallis held out, and Klusener had more luck than McKenzie, scything and edging around the slip cordon. Gillespie replaced McGrath, finding the outside edge to Gilchrist to dispatch Klusener, and then Boucher off the glove down the legside. Either side of lunch, Warne collected wickets as easily as devouring a vegemite sandwich, and Lee made amends for a burst of no-balls and some intemperate first-innings intimidation of the tail, by taking the last two wickets. Kallis resolutely remained unbeaten on 65, watching his team-mates fold depressingly. Warne with eight wickets was the Man of the Match and Australia had won with a knock-out punch that suggested they would win again unless South Africa could get Donald back to full fitness for the second Test.

Brett Lee celebrates as he captures the wicket of Nantie Hayward to give Australia victory in the first Test at Adelaide.

FIRST TEST – AUSTRALIA v. SOUTH AFRICA
14–18 December 2001 at Adelaide

AUSTRALIA

	First innings		Second innings	
JL Langer	c Pollock b Henderson	116	c Boucher b Pollock	1
ML Hayden	c Ntini b Klusener	31	b Kallis	131
RT Ponting	run out (Dippenaar/Boucher)	54	lbw b Kallis	25
ME Waugh	c Boucher b Hayward	2	c Boucher b Henderson	74
SR Waugh (capt)	c McKenzie b Henderson	8	(6) c Pollock b Henderson	13
DR Martyn	not out	124	(7) not out	6
*AC Gilchrist	c Kallis b Henderson	7	(5) c McKenzie b Kallis	22
SK Warne	b Klusener	41	b Henderson	6
B Lee	c McKenzie b Hayward	32		
JN Gillespie	c Boucher b Henderson	3		
GD McGrath	b Hayward	5		
Extras	lb 6, nb 10	16	b 8, lb 16, nb 7	31
		439	(7 wickets dec.)	**309**

	First innings				Second innings			
	O	M	R	W	O	M	R	W
Pollock	28	8	64	-	12	4	38	1
Hayward	31	5	108	3	10	0	32	-
Ntini	19	7	64	-	8	3	13	-
Kallis	16	1	37	-	15	2	45	3
Klusener	14	4	44	2	4	0	27	-
Henderson	33	4	116	4	29.1	1	130	3

Fall of Wickets
1-80, 2-182, 3-199, 4-211, 5-238, 6-248, 7-332, 8-409, 9-434
1-8, 2-66, 3-247, 4-273, 5-291, 6-303, 7-309

SOUTH AFRICA

	First innings		Second innings	
HH Gibbs	st Gilchrist b Warne	78	c Langer b McGrath	9
G Kirsten	lbw b McGrath	47	c Ponting b Warne	7
HH Dippenaar	c Ponting b McGrath	4	c Warne b McGrath	0
CW Henderson	run out (McGrath/Lee)	30	(9) c Ponting b Warne	3
JH Kallis	lbw b McGrath	5	(4) not out	65
ND McKenzie	lbw b Martyn	87	(5) lbw b McGrath	0
L Klusener	b Warne	22	(6) c Warne b Gillespie	18
*MV Boucher	c Langer b Warne	64	(7) c Gilchrist b Gillespie	0
SM Pollock (capt)	c Gilchrist b Warne	0	(8) c Ponting b Warne	1
M Ntini	c Ponting b Warne	9	b Lee	4
M Hayward	not out	0	c Gilchrist b Lee	12
Extras	b 8, lb 9, nb 11	28	b 4, lb 1, w 1, nb 3	9
		374		**128**

	First innings				Second innings			
	O	M	R	W	O	M	R	W
McGrath	33	10	94	3	14	8	13	3
Gillespie	23	7	57	-	11	4	23	2
Warne	39.4	9	113	5	29	7	57	3
Lee	19	2	81	-	12	3	29	2
ME Waugh	3	0	9	-				
Martyn	4	2	3	1	1	0	1	-

Fall of Wickets
1-87, 2-93, 3-155, 4-178, 5-178, 6-214, 7-355, 8-356, 9-365
1-12, 2-17, 3-21, 4-21, 5-54, 6-58, 7-67, 8-74, 9-111

Umpires: S Venkataraghavan & SJA Taufel
Toss: Australia
Man of the Match: SK Warne

Australia won by 246 runs

SECOND TEST
26–29 December 2001 at Melbourne

Australia's convincing nine-wicket win with a day to spare left South Africa gasping. Like the proverbial bunnies in the headlights, the Proteas were overrun by a confident, disciplined team, and their batting crumbled when their bowlers lost control of the game.

Boxing day at the MCG has become a special occasion. It is also invariably wet, and with bushfires raging around Sydney, Melbourne was a contrast of grey skies and showers. A crowd numbering 61,796 was left wondering and waiting when play would begin, and, sensing that the moist conditions might favour his pace attack, Steve Waugh kept South Africa on the run by electing to bowl.

Andy Bichel, the perennial 12th man, replaced Gillespie, who withdrew with a shoulder injury at the 11th hour, and although he was less than fully fit, Allan Donald came in for Ntini.

In the 40 overs possible between showers on day one, South Africa wobbled to 89 for 3. Well-directed bowling and brilliant catching kept Australia bubbling. Ponting in the slips and then Hayden in the gully swooped athletically, and McGrath again removed Kirsten, this time with his

After making a century at Adelaide, Matt Hayden scored another days later in Melbourne.

second ball from around the wicket. Kallis survived the usual assault of throat-thrusting cannonballs, hooking one of the missiles through Lee's clutches at long leg.

Kallis and McKenzie had eased the total on to 131 on a brighter second morning, and as Bichel effervescently hurled another out-swinger past Kallis, a yelp from the slip cordon was enough for Eddie Nicholls to raise his finger. The telltale replays showed that Kallis had missed the ball by a good margin, and, celebrating his good fortune, Bichel immediately grabbed a superb return left-handed catch off Klusener.

It was Bichel's day. He caught Boucher at mid-off from a wide Mark Waugh offering, and ran out Henderson with a direct hit from cover. Pollock added 44 for the last wicket with Hayward, but 277 looked inadequate on a pitch that was playing evenly.

By stumps the Langer/Hayden duo had continued their confident rampage, and the South African

attack seemed innocuous, lacking both a plan and patience to cope with the left-handers.

The plunder sailed past 200, and Hayden passed Bob Simpson's record for the most Test runs by an Australian in a calendar year. South Africa needed to take every chance, and when Langer was caught at square leg, and then Hayden holed out to long-on, after the aggressive Hayward had Ponting caught off his glove at slip, Donald stirred Steve Waugh with a few lifters. Twice Waugh fended balls towards Dippenaar at short leg, and twice he failed to hold on.

The innings was racing to a substantial lead, as Waugh and Martyn enjoyed the true bounce of an excellent pitch, and some tiring bowlers. With Waugh set for another MCG hundred, Martyn took on Gibbs at cover, and as Waugh scrambled to beat the throw, Darrell Hair saw the bails drop and immediately gave Waugh out. Waugh had his back turned, and sensing that Hair had called for third-umpire assistance, he hovered. Replays indicated that Boucher may have dislodged the bails before the throw hit the stumps, and as Hair came in to repair the stumps he realized that Waugh had not seen his judgment, and told a somewhat miffed Australian captain that he had to go. Waugh was fined 50 per cent of his match fee for his reluctant departure. It was his tenth Test score in the 90s, one more than the recently vanquished Michael Slater.

For once the tail did not wag, but the lead was still 210, and the third-day crowd had watched Australia score 361.

Hopes of a South African fightback were dashed when Kirsten edged to Ponting at third slip, and Gilchrist grabbed an inside snick from Gibbs in his left glove. Dippenaar's wretched run continued when Hayden held a full-blooded shot at short leg as the ball settled in his midriff.

Kallis played a lone hand, watching McKenzie nick a big Warne leg break and the out-of-form Klusener miss a full-length McGrath special. No partnership was sustained, and as Kallis moved closer to a deserved hundred, he ran out his captain on a poor call to Martyn at cover, and, on 98, with the last man in, Kallis played to backward point, slipped slightly as he turned for a second run, and failed to beat a brilliant Martyn throw to Gilchrist.

Needing ten to win Australia at last lost an early wicket when Langer edged into the slips. But Hayden scored the winning runs to complete a tally of 1,391 for the calendar year. It had been three years since South Africa had lost successive Tests, and with the third Test due to start in five days, they faced the prospect of an embarrassing series whitewash.

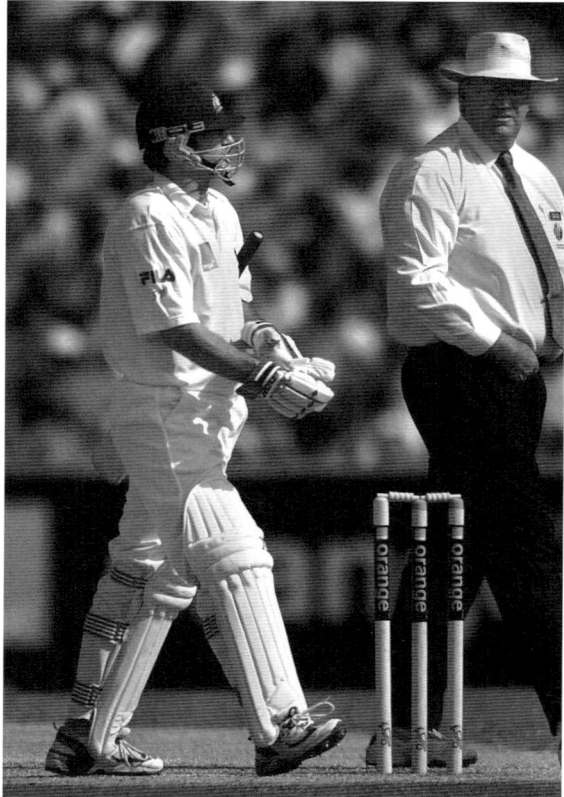

Apparently on course for another hundred, Steve Waugh was fined 50 per cent of his match fee after appearing to ignore the run out decision by Umpire Darryl Hair.

SECOND TEST – AUSTRALIA v. SOUTH AFRICA
26–29 December 2001 at Melbourne

SOUTH AFRICA

	First innings		Second innings	
HH Gibbs	c Ponting b McGrath	14	c Gilchrist b Lee	21
G Kirsten	b McGrath	10	c Ponting b Lee	10
HH Dippenaar	c Hayden b Lee	26	c Hayden b Warne	23
JH Kallis	c Gilchrist b Bichel	38	run out (Martyn/Gilchrist)	99
ND McKenzie	lbw b Lee	67	c Gilchrist b Warne	12
L Klusener	c & b Bichel	0	lbw b McGrath	7
*MV Boucher	c Bichel b ME Waugh	43	c ME Waugh b Warne	0
SM Pollock (capt)	not out	42	run out (Martyn)	18
CW Henderson	run out (Bichel)	5	c ME Waugh b McGrath	16
AA Donald	c Ponting b Lee	0	b Bichel	7
M Hayward	c ME Waugh b Bichel	14	not out	0
Extras	b 1, lb 10, nb 7	18	b 4, nb 2	6
		277		**219**

	First innings				Second innings			
	O	M	R	W	O	M	R	W
McGrath	26	8	70	2	21	6	43	2
Lee	31	10	77	3	18	5	52	2
Bichel	19.5	6	44	3	12.1	0	52	1
Warne	19	3	56	-	24	3	68	3
ME Waugh	8	1	19	1				

Fall of Wickets
1-24, 2-36, 3-59, 4-131, 5-131, 6-198, 7-220, 8-225, 9-233
1-24, 2-37, 3-74, 4-107, 5-120, 6-121, 7-157, 8-192, 9-215

AUSTRALIA

	First innings		Second innings	
JL Langer	c Klusener b Donald	85	c Henderson b Pollock	7
ML Hayden	c Donald b Henderson	138	not out	3
RT Ponting	c Kallis b Hayward	22	not out	0
ME Waugh	b Donald	34		
SR Waugh (capt)	run out (Gibbs)	90		
DR Martyn	c Kallis b Pollock	52		
*AC Gilchrist	not out	30		
SK Warne	c Kirsten b Donald	1		
B Lee	c McKenzie b Hayward	3		
AJ Bichel	c Boucher b Pollock	5		
GD McGrath	lbw b Pollock	0		
Extras	lb 17, w 1, nb 9	27		
		487	(1 wicket)	**10**

	First innings				Second innings			
	O	M	R	W	O	M	R	W
Donald	29	5	103	3	2	0	4	-
Pollock	31	3	84	3	1	0	6	1
Hayward	26	1	109	2				
Kallis	17	3	55	-				
Henderson	29	3	108	1				
Klusener	7	1	11	-				

Fall of Wickets
1-202, 2-267, 3-267, 4-348, 5-429, 6-462, 7-463, 8-470, 9-475
1-7

Umpires: EA Nicholls & DB Hair
Toss: Australia
Man of the Match: ML Hayden

Australia won by nine wickets

THIRD TEST
2–5 January 2002 at Sydney

Australia completed another comprehensive victory over South Africa, winning by ten wickets with a day in hand. On the back of another massive left-handed opening partnership, Australia's spin duo of Warne and MacGill prevailed on a favourable, but fair, pitch. Gary Kirsten revived the Proteas' hopes with a seven-hour epic, before the left-handers resumed business to finish off the series in style.

On a hazy day, with bushfire smoke shrouding Sydney and a crowd of almost 36,000 packing into a renovated SCG, Hayden and Langer began more soberly than they had in the previous two Tests, and Langer was fortunate to survive a few miscues over the slip cordon.

Given the shambolic state of the South African selection process, it was surprising that their bowlers could maintain their concentration, nay their sanity, after the decision to veto the originally nominated XI. In a lengthy circumlocution on the radio, Percy Sonn, the United Cricket Board president, tried to explain why the belated inclusion of Justin Ontong

Australia's openers had a prolific series. Here, in Sydney, Justin Langer celebrates his second century with Matt Hayden, who averaged 107 against the South Africans.

over the better qualified Jacques Rudolph, was based on merit rather than political motivation.

The quota policy called for at least one coloured player to be selected, and Herschelle Gibbs was the regular choice. However, as the series had been lost, and Klusener was wretchedly out of form, it was expedient, perhaps opportunistic, to extend the quota. According to the UCB logic, Ontong was a specialist No. 6, and Rudolph a specialist No. 3. So Ontong, who had registered an undistinguished pair in his only first-class match on the tour, got the nod over Rudolph, who had made 52 and 28 in the same match. Anticipating an SCG 'turner', South Africa included the recently arrived Boje to partner left-arm spinner Claude Henderson.

Having weathered the early assault from Donald and Pollock, the left-handed accumulation gathered pace, and Dippenaar did not help by spilling a chance off a Hayden sweep shot when he was 68. The duo maintained their century opening stand average, going past 1,000 runs in ten innings since they had joined forces at The Oval in the Ashes series.

Hayden blazed a straight drive for his third hundred in as many Tests, and as the mob applauded another 200 partnership, the commentators wondered if Pollock had forgotten about Boje's selection. He eventually got involved taking four wickets, but Australia had no trouble in marching powerfully past 500, as Martyn played another impressive innings. He blossomed from patience and care, to exotic strokeplay, including an elegant reverse sweep when Henderson dispensed with his point fieldsman. The tail-enders cheerfully hit out, and showed how comfortable the pitch had become in the process.

That trend changed dramatically when McGrath ran in. For the third time in the series he dismissed Kirsten, who edged to Ponting at third slip. Dippenaar was bowled neck and crop, and when Waugh tossed the ball to MacGill ahead of Warne, the local leg spinner produced a cobra-spitting leg break that Kallis instinctively prodded at, nicking to Gilchrist. Gibbs was caught at slip, and from 93 for 4 at stumps, the innings fell apart so rapidly on day three, that South Africa were batting again before lunch.

Novitiate Ontong did well to survive overnight, but when McKenzie did not play at Warne's

Sydney has always been a happy hunting ground for Shane Warne. He picked up six wickets in the match as Australia thumped South Africa 3–0 to confirm their status as No. 1 in the world.

straighter leg break, the youngster froze on the crease, and Warne's yelp was rewarded.

In the follow-on, Lee burst through Gibbs' defence, suggesting that Waugh's decision to give the new ball to McGrath and Warne was speculatively errant. Kirsten should also have fallen to Lee when he was on 12, but Mark Waugh spilt the chance at second slip.

Dippenaar got set for a change, and at last the Proteas created some resistance in a worthy partnership. Kirsten was the anchorman, driving and cutting in a defiant performance that carried his team close to avoiding an innings defeat. It was left to Pollock to provide some clout in a last-wicket stand of 49 with Donald.

Warne and MacGill shared 13 wickets between them, and Australia needed 53 to complete the task. In complimenting the South Africans for their spirited fightback, Steve Waugh acknowledged the all-round excellence of his team, and generously donated the team's winning prize money to the relief fund set up for Sydney's bushfire victims.

THIRD TEST – AUSTRALIA v. SOUTH AFRICA
2–5 January 2002 at Sydney

AUSTRALIA

	First innings		Second innings	
JL Langer	c McKenzie b Boje	126	not out	30
ML Hayden	c Kallis b Pollock	105	not out	22
RT Ponting	run out (Ontong/Boucher)	14		
ME Waugh	c Boucher b Donald	19		
SR Waugh (capt)	b Pollock	30		
DR Martyn	c McKenzie b Boje	117		
*AC Gilchrist	c Boucher b Kallis	34		
SK Warne	b Pollock	37		
B Lee	b Boje	29		
SCG MacGill	c Henderson b Boje	20		
GD McGrath	not out	1		
Extras	b 4, lb 8, w 1, nb 9	22	lb 2, nb 1	3
		554	**(0 wicket)**	**54**

	First innings				Second innings			
	O	M	R	W	O	M	R	W
Donald	31	6	119	1	3	0	12	–
Pollock	37	11	109	3	3	1	11	–
Kallis	22	1	129	1				
Henderson	27	3	112	–	2	0	14	–
Boje	25.2	6	63	4	2.1	0	15	–
Ontong	2	0	10	–				

Fall of Wickets
1-219, 2-247, 3-253, 4-302, 5-308, 6-356, 7-439, 8-502, 9-542

SOUTH AFRICA

	First innings		Second innings	
HH Gibbs	c ME Waugh b MacGill	32	b Lee	10
G Kirsten	c Ponting b McGrath	18	b MacGill	153
HH Dippenaar	b McGrath	3	c Ponting b MacGill	74
JH Kallis	c Gilchrist b MacGill	4	c Gilchrist b Warne	34
ND McKenzie	b Warne	20	c MacGill b Lee	38
JL Ontong	lbw b Warne	9	lbw b Warne	32
*MV Boucher	c Ponting b Warne	35	c Gilchrist b McGrath	27
SM Pollock (capt)	c Martyn b McGrath	6	not out	61
N Boje	run out (Langer/McGrath)	7	b MacGill	1
CW Henderson	c McGrath b MacGill	9	b MacGill	2
AA Donald	not out	2	c Lee b Warne	2
Extras	lb 8, nb 1	9	b 8, lb 7, nb 3	18
		154		**452**

	First innings				Second innings			
	O	M	R	W	O	M	R	W
McGrath	17	6	35	3	28	5	95	1
Lee	6	2	13	–	19	5	62	2
MacGill	20.2	6	51	3	45	13	123	4
Warne	19	5	47	3	42.5	8	132	3
ME Waugh					6	1	14	–
Ponting					1	0	11	–

Fall of Wickets
1-37, 2-43, 3-56, 4-77, 5-93, 6-98, 7-111, 8-121, 9-148
1-17, 2-166, 3-211, 4-282, 5-356, 6-372, 7-392, 8-393, 9-403

Umpires: DR Shepherd & DJ Harper
Toss: Australia
Test Debut: JL Ontong
Man of the Match: ML Hayden

Australia won by ten wickets

TEST MATCH AVERAGES
Australia v. South Africa

AUSTRALIA

Batting	M	Inns	NO	HS	Runs	Av	100	50	c/st
DR Martyn	3	4	2	124*	299	149.50	2	1	1
ML Hayden	3	6	2	138	430	107.25	3	–	2
JL Langer	3	6	1	126	365	73.00	2	1	2
SR Waugh	3	4	0	90	141	35.25	–	1	–
ME Waugh	3	4	0	74	129	32.25	–	1	4
AC Gilchrist	3	4	1	34	93	31.00	–	–	9/1
RT Ponting	3	5	1	54	115	28.75	–	1	11
B Lee	3	3	0	32	64	21.33	–	–	1
SK Warne	3	4	0	41	85	21.25	–	–	2
GD McGrath	3	3	1	5	6	3.00	–	–	1

Also batted in one Test: AJ Bichel 5 (2 ct); JN Gillespie 3; SCG MacGill 20 (1 ct)

Bowling	Overs	Mds	Runs	Wkts	Av	Best	10m	5/inn
GD McGrath	139	43	350	14	25.00	3-13	–	–
SK Warne	173.3	35	473	17	27.82	5-113	–	1
B Lee	105	27	314	9	34.88	3-77	–	–
SCG MacGill	65.2	19	174	7	24.85	4-123	–	–

Also bowled: AJ Bichel 32-6-96-4; JN Gillespie 34-11-80-2; DR Martyn 5-2-4-1;
RT Ponting 1-0-11-0; ME Waugh 17-2-42-1

SOUTH AFRICA

Batting	M	Inns	NO	HS	Runs	Av	100	50	c/st
JH Kallis	3	6	1	99	245	49.00	–	2	4
G Kirsten	3	6	0	153	245	40.83	1	–	1
ND McKenzie	3	6	0	87	224	37.33	–	2	6
SM Pollock	3	6	2	61*	128	32.00	–	1	4
MV Boucher	3	6	0	64	169	28.16	–	1	7/-
HH Gibbs	3	6	0	78	164	27.33	–	1	–
HH Dippenaar	3	6	0	74	130	21.66	–	1	–
M Hayward	2	4	2	14	26	13.00	–	–	–
L Klusener	2	4	0	22	47	11.75	–	–	1
CW Henderson	3	6	0	30	65	10.83	–	–	–
AA Donald	2	4	1	7	11	3.66	–	–	1

Also batted in one Test: N Boje 7, 1; M Ntini 9, 4 (1 ct); JL Ontong 9, 32

Bowling	Overs	Mds	Runs	Wkts	Av	Best	10m	5/inn
SM Pollock	112	27	312	8	39.00	3-84	–	–
M Hayward	67	6	249	5	49.80	3-108	–	–
CW Henderson	120.1	11	480	8	60.00	4-116	–	–

Also bowled: N Boje 27.3-6-78-4; AA Donald 65-11-238-4; JH Kallis 70-7-266-4;
L Klusener 25-5-82-2; M Ntini 27-10-77-0; JL Ontong 2-0-10-0

VB SERIES
(Australia, New Zealand and South Africa)
By Jim Maxwell

For only the third time in 23 seasons Australia failed to reach the finals of the annual tri-nations one-day tournament. South Africa convincingly defeated New Zealand in the deciding matches, after they had topped the points table in the preliminary round of 12 matches.

Tough decisions were taken after a disappointing series for the home team. The Waugh twins were dropped, and Ricky Ponting named as the one-day captain of Australia.

The home team batted poorly to lose its first three matches, and ultimately fell foul of the experimental bonus points system after recovering some poise to finish level with South Africa and New Zealand on four wins each.

Designed to enliven run chases, with the attraction of a bonus point for a run rate 1.25 times more than its opponents, the experiment ran into trouble in the penultimate match. The New Zealand captain, Stephen Fleming, admitted that his side had deliberately conceded a bonus point to boost New Zealand's chances of qualifying for the finals.

Australia needed a victory and a bonus point in the last match, and requiring 284 to win, South Africa settled for ensuring that they passed 226 to deny Australia their vital point. The system had worked well in the domestic six-team format, but was proved to be open to manipulation in a three-team competition.

South Africa had won three of their four qualifying matches against New Zealand, increasing their record to 15 wins from 16 matches against them, going into the finals.

It was a psychological hurdle that New Zealand could not overcome, and South Africa won both matches with both wickets and overs in hand.

Two of the best matches in the preliminaries produced outstanding centuries from Chris Cairns and, later, from Michael Bevan. At the Gabba, Cairns' explosive attack lifted New Zealand from a shaky 98 for 5 to a win with five balls to spare, running down South Africa's 241 with 102 not out from 123 balls.

At the MCG – in a match Australia had to win to keep their finals hopes alive – Bevan guided his team from a perilous 82 for 6, aiming for a 246-run target.

Bevan's skillful 102 not out wobbled Australia to a two-wicket, three-balls-to-spare win, and left New Zealand bewildered at a great escape.

South Africa's improvement, following a disastrous Test series, was a consolation for Pollock's battered squad, but Australia played carelessly, lacking the opening partnerships and zest in the field that had marked previous campaigns. The selectors' response was swift and unforgiving. The experienced Waugh twins were dropped, and Ricky Ponting was given the chance to establish himself as the captain in the lead up to the 2003 World Cup.

Match One
11 January 2002 at Melbourne Cricket Ground (floodlit)
New Zealand 199 for 8 (50 overs) (CZ Harris 63*)
Australia 176 (42 overs)

New Zealand (4 pts) won by 23 runs
Man of the Match: CZ Harris

Match Two
13 January 2002 at Melbourne Cricket Ground
(floodlit)
Australia 198 (48.5 overs) (SR Waugh 62, RT Ponting 51)
South Africa 199 for 6 (48.3 overs)
South Africa (4 pts) won by four wickets
Man of the Match: SM Pollock

Match Three
15 January 2002 at Bellerive Oval, Hobart
South Africa 257 for 7 (50 overs) (G Kirsten 97)
New Zealand 231 for 9 (50 overs) (SP Fleming 85)
South Africa (4 pts) won by 26 runs
Man of the Match: G Kirsten

Match Four
17 January 2002 at Sydney Cricket Ground (floodlit)
New Zealand 235 for 9 (50 overs)
Australia 212 (47.2 overs) (MG Bevan 66)
New Zealand (4 pts) won by 23 runs
Man of the Match: CZ Harris

Match Five
19 January 2002 at Woolloongabba, Brisbane (floodlit)
South Africa 241 (48.3 overs) (JH Kallis 65,
MV Boucher 51, SE Bond 4 for 37)
New Zealand 244 for 6 (49.1 overs) (CL Cairns 102*)
New Zealand (4 pts) won by four wickets
Man of the Match: CL Cairns

Match Six
20 January 2002 at Woolloongabba, Brisbane (floodlit)
Australia 241 for 4 (50 overs) (DR Martyn 104*,
RT Ponting 80)
South Africa 214 (48.4 overs) (ND McKenzie 68,
GD McGrath 4 for 30)
Australia (4 pts) won by 27 runs
Man of the Match: DR Martyn

Match Seven
22 January 2002 at Sydney Cricket Ground
South Africa 106 (38.3 overs) (AJ Bichel 5 for 19)
Australia 107 for 2 (18.4 overs) (ME Waugh 55*)
Australia (5 pts) won by eight wickets
Man of the Match: AJ Bichel

Match Eight
26 January 2002 at Adelaide Oval (floodlit)
New Zealand 242 for 5 (50 overs) (NJ Astle 95,
L Vincent 55)

Australia 165 (45.2 overs) (SE Bond 5 for 25)
New Zealand (5 pts) won by 77 runs
Man of the Match: SE Bond

Match Nine
27 January 2002 at Adelaide Oval (floodlit)
South Africa 253 for 5 (50 overs) (HH Gibbs 89,
MV Boucher 57*, JN Rhodes 55)
New Zealand 160 (45.2 overs) (N Boje 4 for 31)
South Africa (5 pts) won by 93 runs
Man of the Match: MV Boucher

Match Ten
29 January at Melbourne Cricket Ground (floodlit)
New Zealand 245 for 8 (50 overs) (CL Cairns 55,
SP Fleming 50)
Australia 248 for 8 (49.3 overs) (MG Bevan 102*,
SE Bond 4 for 38)
Australia (4 pts) won by two wickets
Man of the Match: MG Bevan

Match Eleven
1 February 2002 at WACA Ground, Perth (floodlit)
South Africa 270 for 5 (50 overs) (JN Rhodes 107*,
SM Pollock 69*, MV Boucher 58)
New Zealand 203 for 8 (50 overs)
South Africa (5 pts) won by 67 runs
Man of the Match: JN Rhodes

Match Twelve
3 February 2002 at WACA Ground, Perth
Australia 283 for 7 (50 overs) (B Lee 51*)
South Africa 250 for 5 (50 overs) (JH Kallis 104*)
Australia (4 pts) won by 33 runs
Man of the Match: JH Kallis

First Final
6 February 2002 at Melbourne Cricket Ground (floodlit)
New Zealand 190 (47.5 overs) (CD McMillan 73,
SP Fleming 50, M Ntini 5 for 31)
South Africa 191 for 2 (45.1 overs) (HH Dippenaar 79*,
JH Kallis 59*)
South Africa won by eight wickets
Man of the Match: M Ntini

Second Final
8 February 2002 at Sydney Cricket Ground (floodlit)
New Zealand 175 (41.1 overs) (CL Cairns 57)
South Africa 173 for 4 (38.1 overs) (JN Rhodes 61*)
South Africa won by six wickets
(DL Method: South Africa target 172 from 46 overs)
Man of the Match: JN Rhodes
Player of the Series: SE Bond

AUSTRALIAN DOMESTIC FIRST–CLASS CRICKET – PURA CUP
By Jim Maxwell

Queensland won a third successive title with an emphatic 235-run win over Tasmania in the final. For most of the season the tantalizing question was who would play Queensland in the decider, after the Bulls charged into the lead with an outright win over Tasmania in the shortest time ever in Australian four-day cricket. The December match at the Gabba lasted only nine-and-a-half hours, with accusations of a substandard pitch bombarding Queensland officials. Jamie Cox, the Tasmanian captain, simply said the pitch was 'bloody hard to bat on'.

A month later, Tasmania dramatically turned Queensland over at Bellerive, winning by an innings, the first of four outright wins at home that rushed them towards the final.

For a team generally written off at the season's outset because their bowling appeared to be underwhelming, it was a tremendous comeback from the humiliation at the Gabba. However, the home-ground confidence of the Bulls proved too powerful, and the victory was their fifth in eight seasons, underlining their reputation as the most accomplished team in the country.

Queensland's performance was led by some wonderful batting from Jimmy Maher and Martin Love, who both scored over 1,000 runs in the Pura Cup. And Michael Kasprowicz was the season's leading bowler, taking 49 wickets at 22.08.

Maher and emerging off spinner Nathan Hauritz were absent in South Africa for the final, but replacement opener Brendan Nash with 96, and all-rounder Andrew Symonds, who made 91 and took six match wickets, exemplified Queensland's depth of talent. Kasprowicz bagged nine wickets, taking five in the first innings as Tasmania were dismissed for 141, to trail by 161. Queensland pressed home their advantage by compiling 368 in their second innings, leaving Tasmania to score 530 to win.

Another outstanding display in the field around persistent bowling dominated the

final innings and the match was over just after lunch on the final day.

Scott Jurgensen's bowling effort, taking 11 wickets in the final, was a reminder of how much the Tasmanian attack had improved, and surprised their detractors during the season.

Curiously, Tasmania's leading bowlers were all imports. Jurgensen, with 36 wickets, had gone from NSW to WA en route to Tasmania, David Saker, 38 wickets, had originally made his mark for Victoria, Damien Wright, 22 wickets, sprang from Sydney, and the talented all-rounder, Shane Watson, 23 wickets, was a spurned Queenslander. Another emerging talent was Shawn Clingeleffer, a homegrown wicketkeeper who scored 517 runs and grabbed 36 catches.

In the push for final qualification both WA and SA had their chances. WA's failure to beat NSW, the wooden spooners, in both matches, proved costly. In Sydney, a Michael Bevan double century saved the Blues after WA had led by 363 runs on the first innings, and at the WACA, NSW were 311 for

Queensland's Martin Love enjoyed a productive season, scoring over 1,000 runs in the Pura Cup which his team won for the third successive time.

9 in their second innings, after WA had elected not to enforce the follow-on, setting NSW 406 runs to win. Australian aspirants Simon Katich and Michael Hussey had mediocre seasons, averaging under 40, and the batting was inconsistent.

The relationship between coach Mike Veletta and captain Katich fell apart, and Katich, who lost his Australian contract, decided to move to NSW for the following season. Again Jo Angel shouldered most of the bowling workload, taking 44 wickets.

SA lost two of their last three matches and hung on for a draw against WA after a magnificent outright win at the Gabba seemed as though it would sustain their run to the final.

Greg Blewett and Darren Lehmann scored regularly, supported by left-hander Ben Johnson, and fast medium bowler Paul Rofe took 41 wickets in a promising debut season.

Victoria won only two matches, despite strong batting from Brad Hodge and Matthew Elliott. Hodge and Jimmy Maher shared the Player of the Season award.

NSW relied on Michael Bevan too much, and Michael Slater fell so far out of form that he was dropped late in the season. Their bright hopes were Stuart Clark with 45 wickets, and Michael Clarke, a young, middle-order batsman.

The Pura Cup table, with NSW and Victoria on the bottom, indicated a new order in Australian cricket, and Queenslanders could scoff at the old adage, 'when NSW and Victoria are strong, Australia is strong'.

AUSTRALIAN DOMESTIC ONE-DAY CRICKET – ING CUP
By Jim Maxwell

NSW successfully defended their one-day title with a rugged victory over Queensland in the final. In a match where most batsmen succumbed to the pressure of the occasion, NSW prevailed by 19 runs to repeat their success of the previous season.

On a Gabba pitch that appeared chock-full of runs, Queensland failed to overhaul a modest NSW total of 204. The assorted, varied bowling, with Shawn Bradstreet taking four wickets and Dominic Thornely three, was brilliantly supported in the field as the Bulls lost their last five wickets for 36 runs.

While Love had been moving easily to 53, the Queensland innings looked prosperous, after match winners Maher, Law and Symonds had all gone cheaply. Perren (36) and Carseldine (29) added 48 for the sixth wicket, until they fell to a combination of rash and ambitious strokes.

NSW's recovery in the field matched their early dominance with the bat when an opening partnership of 82 seemed certain to create a healthy score. Pace bowlers Hopes and Noffke, backed up by Hauritz's off spin, produced panic in the middle order, opened up by Stuart Law's running, diving catch at deep mid-on to remove Haddin for 45. Phelps (31) and Thornely (20 not out) rallied for important, and what turned out to be critical, runs to push NSW towards respectability.

The Blues had scraped into the final by three runs against WA, on the back of Corey Richards' exuberant, if lucky, score of 151 at the WACA. He was dropped three times as he raced to his career-best one-day score from just 147 deliveries.

In the WA chase, NSW became sloppy in the field, with Brad Hogg (39 not out) keeping the contest throbbing until Bradstreet was caught behind with three balls remaining. Hussey's earlier revival innings of 45 for WA included a rich consolation prize for his team when a sweep shot for six struck a sponsor's sign worth $200,000.

In their final preliminary match in Adelaide, Queensland defeated SA to qualify at the top of the points table, winning by five wickets. Love and Perren added 97, with Love scoring 64 from 79 balls. SA had scrambled to 194 for 8 thanks to all-rounder Brad Young, who made 58 from 58 balls.

During the home and away series, WA's Jo Angel became the leading wicket-taker in domestic one-day cricket, passing Tom Moody's mark of 70 wickets.

Darren Lehmann was named Player of the Competition, polling 22 votes and defeating team-mate Greg Blewett. Lehmann, who won for the second year running, scored 374 runs at a strike rate of 82.02. This consistent form earned him a recall to the Australian one-day team.

Darren Lehmann was recalled to the national team after being named Player of the ING Competition which was won by NSW.

FIRST-CLASS AVERAGES
Australia

BATTING

	M	Inns	NO	HS	Runs	Av	100	50
ML Hayden	10	17	2	147	1244	82.93	6	4
MG Bevan	8	14	2	203*	868	72.33	4	3
JL Langer	10	18	3	133	1030	68.66	5	3
DR Martyn	8	11	2	189	616	68.44	3	2
RT Ponting	8	14	3	157*	733	66.63	3	2
JP Maher	10	19	1	209	1194	66.33	3	6
GB Hogg	7	11	3	90	525	65.62	-	6
ML Love	12	22	3	202rh	1189	62.57	2	6
BA Johnson	7	14	3	138*	653	59.36	3	2
DS Lehmann	8	14	0	246	823	58.78	4	1
BJ Hodge	10	18	3	140	858	57.20	4	2
GS Blewett	11	21	3	169*	1025	56.94	5	3
IJ Harvey	7	11	2	87	432	48.00	-	4
AC Gilchrist	8	12	2	118	477	47.70	1	2
SG Clingeleffer	11	15	4	141*	517	47.00	2	1
ND McKenzie	4	8	0	114	373	46.62	1	2
MV Boucher	5	9	1	134	372	46.50	1	1
ME Waugh	8	11	0	168	500	45.45	1	3
G Kirsten	5	10	0	153	454	45.40	1	2
MJ North	9	15	1	200*	633	45.21	3	1
BP Nash	5	10	1	157	395	43.88	1	2
MTG Elliott	10	20	2	135*	780	43.33	1	6
HH Gibbs	5	9	0	145	386	42.88	1	2
J Moss	5	9	0	109	378	42.00	1	3
RJ Campbell	9	15	1	121	576	41.14	1	4
GJ Mail	8	14	1	150*	528	40.61	1	5
MG Dighton	10	15	0	126	594	39.60	2	3
MJ Clarke	9	18	1	132	663	39.00	2	2
J Cox	11	18	1	174	660	38.82	2	3
CJ Davies	5	9	1	119*	306	38.25	1	1
MW Goodwin	8	13	0	141	474	36.46	1	2
SM Katich	11	18	0	131	651	36.16	1	4
MEK Hussey	11	19	1	100	621	34.50	1	4
DG Wright	11	15	3	63	409	34.08	-	4
CD McMillan	5	9	1	55	272	34.00	-	2
MA Higgs	10	18	3	80	490	32.66	-	4
S Young	5	8	0	84	259	32.37	-	3
BJ Haddin	10	18	2	102	515	32.18	1	3
CJ Richards	5	10	1	74	276	30.66	-	1
MJ Nicholson	9	14	3	101*	334	30.36	1	1
SK Warne	8	11	1	99	296	29.60	-	2
DS Berry	10	16	3	148	382	29.38	1	1
SR Watson	7	11	1	58*	292	29.20	-	3
BH Higgins	10	18	2	80	467	29.18	-	5
DJ Marsh	11	17	2	97	433	28.86	-	2
JL Arnberger	8	16	2	70*	401	28.64	-	2
DA Fitzgerald	8	15	0	139	426	28.40	1	1
M Klinger	7	11	2	58	251	27.88	-	2
AA Noffke	11	13	3	73	275	27.50	-	1
SR Waugh	6	8	0	90	219	27.37	-	2
A Symonds	10	17	2	91	405	27.00	-	2
MJ Slater	7	13	1	58*	314	26.16	-	2
BE Young	9	16	0	122	406	25.37	1	-
SG Law	10	16	3	70	316	24.30	-	2
B Lee	7	8	0	61	191	23.87	-	1
MP Mott	9	16	0	87	378	23.62	-	2
SW Meuleman	8	13	0	109	307	23.61	1	1
JL Cassell	5	9	0	86	211	23.44	-	1
DF Hills	4	8	0	136	186	23.25	1	-
BP van Deinsen	4	8	0	61	182	22.75	-	2
SA Deitz	4	8	0	86	178	22.25	-	1
MS Sinclair	5	9	0	80	200	22.22	-	1
GA Manou	10	16	1	62	312	20.80	-	1
SR Mason	7	10	1	41	187	20.77	-	-
MH Richardson	5	9	0	57	187	20.77	-	1
MJ Smith	8	15	2	46	270	20.76	-	-
SCG MacGill	8	11	2	53	177	19.66	-	1
CL White	5	8	0	91	144	18.00	-	1
S Lee	6	10	0	41	172	17.20	-	-
J Angel	10	15	4	61	180	16.36	-	1
NW Bracken	8	14	5	38	145	16.11	-	-
CT Perren	8	14	3	47*	173	15.72	-	-

FIRST-CLASS AVERAGES
Australia

BATTING

	M	Inns	NO	HS	Runs	Av	100	50
SR Clark	9	15	5	31*	145	14.50	-	-
ML Lewis	7	11	2	54*	130	14.44	-	1
L Klusener	4	8	0	50	105	13.12	-	1
NM Hauritz	7	9	1	41	102	12.75	-	-
CW Henderson	5	8	0	30	102	12.75	-	-
PE McIntyre	6	12	2	40	121	12.10	-	-
WA Seccombe	12	18	3	49	171	11.40	-	-

Qualification: 8 completed innings, average 10.00

BOWLING

	Overs	Mds	Runs	Wkts	Av	Best	10m	5/inn
MWH Inness	214.5	61	597	31	19.25	7-19	1	1
SJ Jurgensen	290	85	710	36	19.72	6-65	2	4
SR Clark	387	108	1047	45	23.26	5-42	-	4
SR Watson	126.4	20	514	22	23.36	6-32	1	2
MS Kasprowicz	378.5	87	1239	51	24.29	5-44	-	2
J Angel	412	124	1074	44	24.40	6-52	-	1
JN Gillespie	243.4	60	689	28	24.60	8-50	1	1
PC Rofe	441.4	152	1060	41	25.85	7-52	1	3
B Lee	228.5	51	763	29	26.31	5-56	-	2
DJ Saker	366.3	103	1003	38	26.39	5-53	-	1
A Symonds	226.5	62	588	22	26.72	4-45	-	-
AJ Bichel	166	40	508	19	26.73	4-54	-	-
BA Williams	279	72	906	32	28.31	4-34	-	-
MJ Nicholson	299.4	62	936	33	28.36	5-68	-	1
AA Noffke	380.4	97	1110	39	28.46	5-31	-	2
DW Fleming	124.2	39	391	13	30.07	3-34	-	-
NM Hauritz	178	37	484	16	30.25	4-119	-	-
MJ Smith	273.2	54	917	29	31.62	7-98	-	1
NW Bracken	248.5	55	763	24	31.79	4-10	-	-
GB Hogg	182.5	42	575	17	33.82	3-95	-	-
IJ Harvey	207.4	49	623	17	36.64	3-53	-	-
GD McGrath	340.5	107	880	24	36.66	3-13	-	-
JH Dawes	238.4	64	706	19	37.15	3-4	-	-
ML Lewis	184.4	43	621	16	38.81	4-64	-	-
SK Warne	373	63	1156	29	39.86	5-113	-	1
DG Wright	346.3	114	932	23	40.52	3-15	-	-
MA Harrity	335.2	67	1106	27	40.96	5-65	-	1
PE McIntyre	225.4	42	741	18	41.16	6-75	-	1
SCG MacGill	328.1	70	1124	27	41.62	5-132	-	1
DA Nash	259	60	909	21	43.28	4-59	-	-
BE Young	299.2	61	864	14	61.71	3-21	-	-
CW Henderson	206.1	33	748	11	68.00	4-116	-	-

Qualification: 10 wickets in 8 innings

The following bowlers took 10 wickets in fewer than 8 innings:

	Overs	Mds	Runs	Wkts	Av	Best	10m	5/inn
WN Carr	94.2	28	276	16	17.25	6-46	-	1
DL Vettori	189.5	38	580	22	26.36	6-80	-	3
PR Reiffel	100.3	24	280	10	28.00	4-71	-	-
CL Cairns	140	24	565	15	37.66	5-71	-	2

FIELDING

52 - WA Seccombe; 36 - RJ Campbell, SG Clingeleffer;
35 - DS Berry (32ct, 1st), GA Manou (33ct, 2st); 28 - BJ Haddin (27ct,1st);
24 - AC Gilchrist (22ct, 2st); 20 - DJ Marsh; 16 - MEK Hussey;
15 - MTG Elliott, RT Ponting; 13 - JP Maher; 12 - AC Parore (11ct, 1st);
11 - MJ North, CT Perren; 10 - MV Boucher, S Lee, ML Love.

Qualification: 10 or more catches

PAKISTAN

West Indies in Pakistan
New Zealand in Pakistan
Pakistan Domestic First-Class Season
Pakistan Domestic One-Day Season
First-Class Averages

WEST INDIES IN PAKISTAN
By Tony Cozier

FIRST TEST
31 January–4 February 2002 at Sharjah

The Pakistan Cricket Board (PCB), reluctantly, but inevitably, accepted the West Indies' concern over the potential threat to their security posed by the military hostilities in Afghanistan to the west and Kashmir to the east, and shifted their ICC-scheduled series to Sharjah instead.

It was another significant financial setback for the PCB, for there was little local interest in the reduced schedule of two Tests and three one-day internationals.

More attention was shown by the ICC's Anti-Corruption Unit whose head, Lord Condon, had identified Sharjah as one of the centres of illegal gambling on the game in an earlier report.

In a scenario that might have been developed by the CIA, KGB and MI5 at the height of the Cold War, two members of the unit, both former Scotland Yard detectives, were dispatched to Sharjah, and were later joined by Lord Condon himself. Small video cameras were placed outside the teams' dressing rooms and in the hotel foyers and players were banned from using mobile phones in the stadium.

Yet there were rarely more than 500 spectators in the stadium that became Test cricket's 82nd venue and the site of yet another disaster for the West Indies, whose two comprehensive defeats brought their record to 23 losses in 27 overseas Tests.

Pakistan also clinched the one-day series by comfortably winning the first two matches before the West Indies gained the consolation of victory in the last to carry back home.

The pitches were as bare and flat as they had been for the 184 one-day internationals previously staged at the stadium and capably stood the test of the longer game. Pakistan's batsmen took ample advantage, amassing first-innings totals of 493 and 472 that placed immediate pressure on opponents without the injured Brian Lara and Ramnaresh Sarwan and bereft of self-belief following their thrashing in the three Tests in Sri Lanka only a few months earlier.

Previous page: Politics and cricket should not stand side by side, but after being forced to play a series against the West Indies in neutral Sharjah, Pakistan's series against New Zealand came to an abrupt halt when a bomb exploded outside the teams' hotel in Karachi.

Pakistan's Shoaib Akhtar warms up before meeting West Indies in the first Test series at Sharjah, a neutral ground. Akhtar took 5 for 24 in the second innings.

Lara was still recovering from his elbow injury sustained towards the end of his prolific tour of Sri Lanka. Sarwan, the only other batting success from Sri Lanka, developed a back problem and withdrew from the team only a week before departure.

Even in the absence of Wasim Akram, whose only appearance after recovering from injury was in a solitary one-day international, Pakistan also possessed not only strong batting but well-balanced bowling, spearheaded by the stirring pace of Shoaib Akhtar, that was never far away from a breakthrough.

The contest would have been far keener, even if the outcome was likely to have been the same, had the West Indies not been so abysmal in the field. They missed a staggering 17 catches in the two Tests, varying in degrees from improbable to laughable, as each of the four Pakistani century-makers escaped on the way to his landmark. Shahid Afridi was missed four times in his typically swashbuckling 107 in the second Test during a second-wicket partnership of 190 with Younis Khan that left the West Indies in a shambolic state by tea on the first day.

The fact that Pakistan batted first was also indicative of the West Indies' state of mind. Hooper won the toss and chose to bowl, even though the leg spinner Dinanath Ramnarine was in the XI and Pakistan had scored 493 going in first after Waqar Younis won the toss in the opening Test. It seemed, and probably was, a faint-hearted response to Shoaib's demolition of the batting on the last day of the previous Test three days earlier.

There were times, as there were in Sri Lanka and not infrequently in the recent past, that the West Indies gained a favourable position only to let it slip through poor cricket and an inferiority complex brought on by their succession of defeats.

Pakistan were 94 for 4 and 178 for 5 on the first day of the first Test, but still reached 493. They owed their recovery to a sixth-wicket partnership of

FIRST TEST – PAKISTAN v. WEST INDIES
31 January–4 February 2002 at Sharjah

PAKISTAN

	First innings		Second innings	
Taufeeq Umar	b Hooper	24	run out (Jacobs)	23
Naved Latif	lbw b Dillon	0	c Jacobs b Dillon	20
Younis Khan	c Gayle b Hooper	53	c Jacobs b Cuffy	32
Inzamam-ul-Haq	c Jacobs b Dillon	10	c Hooper b Dillon	48
Yousuf Youhana	b Cuffy	146	c Dillon b Cuffy	12
Abdur Razzaq	c Jacobs b WW Hinds	34	c Ganga b Collins	29
*Rashid Latif	b Gayle	150	not out	47
Saqlain Mushtaq	c & b Dillon	17		
Waqar Younis (capt)	not out	25		
Shoaib Akhtar	b Gayle	20		
Danish Kaneria	c & b Gayle	0		
Extras	b 6, lb 7, w 1	14	nb 3	3
		493	(6 wickets dec.)	**214**

	First innings				Second innings			
	O	M	R	W	O	M	R	W
Dillon	42	10	141	3	17	3	46	2
Collins	33	3	96	-	14.4	1	56	1
Cuffy	35	10	75	1	19	3	78	2
Hooper	32	7	85	2	5	0	23	-
RO Hinds	4	0	31	-				
WW Hinds	8	1	26	1	2	0	11	-
Gayle	7.5	0	27	3				

Fall of Wickets
1-3, 2-45, 3-80, 4-94, 5-178, 6-382, 7-438, 8-457, 9-493
1-35, 2-54, 3-101, 4-134, 5-146, 6-214

WEST INDIES

	First innings		Second innings	
D Ganga	lbw b Saqlain Mushtaq	20	b Shoaib Akhtar	34
CH Gayle	b Saqlain Mushtaq	68	b Shoaib Akhtar	66
SL Campbell	lbw b Danish Kaneria	6	run out (Rashid Latif)	20
WW Hinds	st Rashid Latif b Danish Kaneria	59	c Rashid Latif b Shoaib Akhtar	8
CL Hooper (capt)	lbw b Abdur Razzaq	56	lbw b Abdur Razzaq	13
S Chanderpaul	b Waqar Younis	66	c Rashid Latif b Abdur Razzaq	0
RO Hinds	c Rashid Latif b Waqar Younis	62	not out	9
*RD Jacobs	c Danish Kaneria b Waqar Younis	6	lbw b Abdur Razzaq	0
M Dillon	run out (Rashid Latif/ Saqlain Mushtaq)	5	b Shoaib Akhtar	0
CE Cuffy	b Waqar Younis	0	b Shoaib Akhtar	0
PT Collins	not out	1	b Abdur Razzaq	12
Extras	b 1, lb 3, w 1, nb 12	17	b 1, lb 1, nb 7	9
		366		**171**

	First innings				Second innings			
	O	M	R	W	O	M	R	W
Waqar Younis	25.3	4	93	4	9	2	35	-
Shoaib Akhtar	18	4	68	-	16	7	24	5
Abdur Razzaq	18	2	49	1	7.5	0	25	4
Danish Kaneria	26	5	75	2	19	7	55	-
Saqlain Mushtaq	36	12	71	2	11	5	30	-
Taufeeq Umar	2	0	6	-				

Fall of Wickets
1-88, 2-96, 3-126, 4-180, 5-231, 6-352, 7-353, 8-362, 9-363
1-76, 2-115, 3-125, 4-146, 5-149, 6-150, 7-150, 8-155, 9-155

Umpires: G Sharp & Riazuddin
Toss: Pakistan
Test Debut: Naved Latif (Pakistan), RO Hinds (West Indies)
Man of the Match: Shoaib Akhtar

Pakistan won by 170 runs

Rashid Latif, Pakistan's wicketkeeper, scored 150 in the first innings to set up victory for his team.

204 between Yousuf Youhana, whose 146 was his third hundred in successive Tests against the West Indies, and the wicketkeeper Rashid Latif, whose 150 was his maiden Test hundred.

The West Indies were 352 before they lost their sixth wicket, but their infamously fragile tail-end then caved in, as it had repeatedly done in Sri Lanka and continued to do here. The last five wickets fell for 14 in the first innings, the last seven for 25 in the second innings on the final day to Shoaib and Abdur Razzaq when they had a real chance of holding out for a draw.

SECOND TEST
7–10 February 2002 at Sharjah

In the second Test, the West Indies were up against it when Pakistan ended the first day on 344 for 3 and did not have the heart to make a fight of it. Without Saeed Anwar, the quality left-handed opener who was still not fit, Pakistan had problems only with their opening partnership and that was born out by their first-wicket partnerships throughout the series – 3, 35, 12 and 0. In spite of his hundred, Afridi did not seem the answer to the problem.

Inzamam-ul-Haq had a quiet series, but Younis Khan, Youhana, Razzaq and Rashid took up the slack. Waqar, short of the pace of his salad days but not the guile, and the persistent Razzaq were ideal foils to the speed of Shoaib and Saqlain's off spin and Danish Kaneria's leg spin were ideal contrasts.

There was some encouragement for the West Indies from some of their younger batsmen but, overall, their batting lacked consistency and their bowling penetration. What was most glaringly wanting was self-belief.

The left-handed opener Chris Gayle hit the ball as hard as anyone during half-centuries in both innings of the first Test and in the first two one-day internationals. Daren Ganga, his altogether more subdued right-handed partner, batted solidly in the Tests and Ryan Hinds, the 20-year-old left-hander, showed both a compact style and a refreshing temperament in his debut series.

As he was in Sri Lanka, Merv Dillon was the West Indies' best bowler, but he had little support from either the other bowlers, in spite of Cameron Cuffy's control, or, especially, from his fielders.

Captain Hooper had the personal satisfaction of ending the trip with an unbeaten 112 and victory in the last one-day international, but it was hardly consolation for another disappointing campaign.

Runs continued to flow for Pakistan's batsmen in the second Test. Younis Khan reached 153 before being dismissed by Pedro Collins.

With a huge lead behind them, the stage was set for Pakistan's bowlers – led by Waqar Younis – to rout West Indies and complete a 2-0 victory.

SECOND TEST – PAKISTAN v. WEST INDIES
7–10 February 2002 at Sharjah

PAKISTAN

	First innings		Second innings	
Taufeeq Umar	c Ganga b Dillon	8	(2) lbw b Dillon	69
Shahid Afridi	b Cuffy	107	(1) c Jacobs b Dillon	0
Younis Khan	c Ganga b Collins	153	c Ganga b Dillon	71
Inzamam-ul-Haq	c Hooper b Ramnarine	36	c sub (D Brown) b Collins	6
Yousuf Youhana	b Dillon	60	not out	52
Abdur Razzaq	not out	64	run out (Hooper)	16
*Rashid Latif	c Hooper b Ramnarine	16	not out	2
Saqlain Mushtaq	b Cuffy	5		
Waqar Younis (capt)	lbw b Ramnarine	2		
Shoaib Akhtar	c & b Cuffy	4		
Danish Kaneria	c Gayle b Cuffy	0		
Extras	b 12, lb 2, nb 3	17	lb 6, w 1, nb 2	9
		472	**(5 wickets dec.)**	**225**

	First innings				Second innings			
	O	M	R	W	O	M	R	W
Dillon	27	6	63	2	18	2	57	3
Collins	30	5	99	1	14	2	56	1
Cuffy	29	3	82	4	20	3	52	-
Ramnarine	36	5	137	3	12	1	39	-
Hooper	7	0	41	-				
RO Hinds	5	1	24	-	12	3	15	-
Gayle	1	0	12	-				

Fall of Wickets
1-12, 2-202, 3-272, 4-364, 5-393, 6-416, 7-447, 8-454, 9-463
1-0, 2-144, 3-145, 4-175, 5-216

WEST INDIES

	First innings		Second innings	
D Ganga	b Shahid Afridi	65	lbw b Shoaib Akhtar	21
CH Gayle	b Shoaib Akhtar	6	lbw b Waqar Younis	4
WW Hinds	b Saqlain Mushtaq	25	c Taufeeq Umar** b Saqlain Mushtaq	34
CL Hooper (capt)	not out	84	lbw b Saqlain Mushtaq	1
S Chanderpaul	c Yousuf Youhana b Danish Kaneria	16	lbw b Abdur Razzaq	19
M Dillon	c Taufeeq Umar b Shoaib Akhtar	0	(8) lbw b Abdur Razzaq	0
RO Hinds	lbw b Abdur Razzaq	11	(6) lbw b Waqar Younis	46
*RD Jacobs	b Saqlain Mushtaq	31	(7) not out	35
D Ramnarine	b Shoaib Akhtar	0	b Abdur Razzaq	0
CE Cuffy	b Shoaib Akhtar	4	b Waqar Younis	15
PT Collins	c Inzamam-ul-Haq b Saqlain Mushtaq	1	b Waqar Younis	0
Extras	b 7, lb 8, w 6	21	b 2, lb 6, nb 6	14
		264		**189**

	First innings				Second innings			
	O	M	R	W	O	M	R	W
Waqar Younis	9	1	24	-	10	2	44	4
Shoaib Akhtar	18	3	63	4	8	3	23	1
Danish Kaneria	13	2	34	1	11	2	25	-
Saqlain Mushtaq	21.5	4	75	3	19	8	42	2
Shahid Afridi	15	0	34	1	2	0	14	-
Abdur Razzaq	8	1	13	1	11	2	33	3

** Taufeeq Umar deputy wicketkeeper

Fall of Wickets
1-19, 2-88, 3-116, 4-159, 5-170, 6-189, 7-236, 8-237, 9-247
1-19, 2-46, 3-47, 4-84, 5-114, 6-161, 7-162, 8-162, 9-189

Umpires: DB Hair & Shakeel Khan
Toss: Pakistan
Man of the Match: Younis Khan
Players of the Series: Abdur Razzaq & M Dillon

Pakistan won by 244 runs

TEST MATCH AVERAGES
Pakistan v. West Indies

PAKISTAN

Batting	M	Inns	NO	HS	Runs	Av	100	50	c/st
Rashid Latif	2	4	2	150	240	120.00	1	–	3/1
Yousuf Youhana	2	4	1	146	270	90.00	1	2	–
Younis Khan	2	4	0	153	309	77.25	1	2	–
Shahid Afridi	1	2	0	107	107	53.50	1	–	–
Abdur Razzaq	2	4	1	64*	143	47.66	–	1	–
Taufeeq Ahmed	2	4	0	69	124	31.00	–	1	2
Waqar Younis	2	2	1	25*	27	27.00	–	–	–
Inzamam-ul-Haq	2	2	0	48	100	25.00	–	–	1
Shoaib Akhtar	2	2	0	20	24	12.00	–	–	–
Saqlain Mushtaq	2	2	0	17	22	11.00	–	–	–
Naved Latif	1	2	0	20	20	10.00	–	–	–

Also batted in two Tests: Danish Kaneria 0, 0 (1 ct)

Bowling	Overs	Mds	Runs	Wkts	Av	Best	10m	5/inn
Abdur Razzaq	44.5	6	126	9	14.00	4-25	–	–
Shoaib Akhtar	60	17	178	10	17.80	5-24	–	1
Waqar Younis	53.3	9	196	8	24.50	4-44	–	–
Saqlain Mushtaq	87.5	29	218	7	31.14	3-75	–	–

Also bowled: Danish Kaneria 69-16-189-3; Taufeeq Umar 2-0-6-0; Shahid Afridi 17-0-48-1

WEST INDIES

Batting	M	Inns	NO	HS	Runs	Av	100	50	c/st
CL Hooper	2	4	1	84*	154	51.33	–	2	3
RO Hinds	2	4	1	62	128	42.66	–	1	–
CH Gayle	2	4	0	68	144	36.00	–	2	3
D Ganga	2	4	0	65	140	35.00	–	1	4
WW Hinds	2	4	0	59	126	31.50	–	1	–
S Chanderpaul	2	4	0	66	101	25.25	–	1	–
RD Jacobs	2	4	1	35*	72	24.00	–	–	5/-
CE Cuffy	2	4	0	15	19	4.75	–	–	1
PT Collins	2	4	1	12	14	4.66	–	–	–
M Dillon	2	4	0	5	5	1.25	–	–	2

Also batted in one Test: SL Campbell 6, 20; D Ramnarine 0, 0

Bowling	Overs	Mds	Runs	Wkts	Av	Best	10m	5/inn
M Dillon	104	21	306	10	30.60	3-57	–	–
CE Cuffy	103	19	287	7	41.00	4-82	–	–

Also bowled: PT Collins 91.4-11-307-3; CH Gayle 8.5-0-39-3; RO Hinds 21-4-70-0; WW Hinds 10-1-37-1; CL Hooper 44-7-149-2; D Ramnarine 48-6-176-3

ONE–DAY INTERNATIONALS

Pakistan extended their superiority from the Tests into the one-day internationals, confirming their resilience and depth that the West Indies lacked. They won the first two matches before the West Indies ended their otherwise unhappy tour with a clear-cut victory in the last. As in the Tests, the West Indies got themselves into favourable situations, but could not press the advantage home.

In the first match, they lost their last five wickets for 29 and did not use 1.3 of their 50 allocated overs to be all out for 190. Yet their bowlers, with Merv Dillon and Cameron Cuffy to the fore, and their fielders kept Pakistan on such a tight rein they were four down for 62 in the 22nd over and 110 for 5 after 31. It was then that Abdur Razzaq, their outstanding all-rounder who was Man of the Series, stepped in to make an unbeaten 46 off 41 balls as Pakistan won with 3.5 overs to spare.

Pakistan were again in trouble at 51 for 4 in the 17th over batting first in the second match. This time Shoaib Malik, previously a tail-end off spinner pushed up to No. 4 purely on the evidence of his batting in the nets, changed the course of the innings and the match with an unbeaten 111 off 130 balls that led Pakistan to 232 all out.

When the explosive Chris Gayle blasted three sixes and eight fours in 63 off 46 balls in a stand of 101 off 14 overs with fellow Jamaica left-hander Wavell Hinds, the West Indies appeared on the way to levelling the series. But Shoaib removed them both in a fiery second spell and the West Indies' challenge subsided. Fast bowler Mohammad Sami, in his first match of the tour, spectacularly ended the match with a hat-trick – lbw, bowled, bowled.

Roles were reversed in the final match. It was the West Indies who recovered from the faltering start to build a demanding total and Pakistan who could not make an adequate reply.

The West Indies were 61 for 4 in the 14th over with the elongated tail close at hand when Hooper and Shivnarine Chanderpaul, their two most experienced players, finally showed their worth.

When Chanderpaul was out for 67 with 5.4 overs remaining, they had added 154 off 30.5 overs. Hooper continued to the end with 112, from 127 balls with four sixes and eight fours. It was his seventh hundred in such matches and gave the West Indies something to work with.

Pakistan, possibly complacent with the series secure, were quickly 18 for 3, then 51 for 4, and the recovery that always materialized in earlier matches, in both forms of the game, never came. Gayle completed an excellent series by snaring the last four wickets, zeroing in on middle stump with his flat, full-length off spin.

Match One
14 Februry 2002 at Sharjah CA Stadium (floodlit)
West Indies 190 (48.3 overs) (CH Gayle 50)
Pakistan 193 for 6 (46.1 overs)
Pakistan won by four wickets
Man of the Match: Abdur Razzaq

Match Two
15 February 2002 at Sharjah CA Stadium (floodlit)
Pakistan 232 (49 overs) (Shoaib Malik 111*)
West Indies 181 (34.4 overs) (CH Gayle 63, Mohammad Sami 4 for 44, including a hat-trick)
Pakistan won by 51 runs
Man of the Match: Shoaib Malik

Match Three
17 February 2002 at Sharjah CA Stadium
West Indies 260 for 5 (50 overs) (CL Hooper 112*, S Chanderpaul 67)
Pakistan 150 (40.2 overs) (CH Gayle 4 for 19)
West Indies won by 110 runs
Man of the Match: CL Hooper
Player of the Series: Abdur Razzaq

West Indies had a miserable experience in Sharjah, but their captain, Carl Hooper, scored 112 not out in the final one-day match to earn a consolation victory.

NEW ZEALAND IN PAKISTAN
By Bryan Waddle

ONE-DAY INTERNATIONALS

Pakistan's one-day cricket form may have been open to question in the lead up to the three-match series with New Zealand. They were under the microscope for a lack of consistency, despite a well-balanced, quality side.

Pakistan answered those queries in an emphatic fashion with a side that produced not only consistent performances but also continuity in selection, which has been rare.

After winning the three-nation Sharjah Cup which also involved New Zealand and Sri Lanka, they hosted New Zealand in the first home series since New Zealand cancelled its scheduled tour because of the US-led invasion of Afghanistan.

The tour took place in the stifling heat of April-May, when most teams resist playing in Pakistan – New Zealand unwillingly accepted.

They felt the heat from the outset losing the opening encounter by 153 runs. Yousuf Youhana and Younis Khan produced a partnership of 151 to demoralize the limited New Zealand attack.

Youhana, a classy, elegant right-hander compiled his second consecutive century, following up his match-winning innings in Sharjah with 125 from 155 deliveries.

New Zealand had 50 up in nine overs but once Nathan Astle was dismissed, they never looked likely to reach the imposing target. Not for the first time they were dismantled by the pace of Shoaib Akhtar who took six wickets in his nine overs. The New Zealand innings of 122 lasted just 30 overs.

Punishing New Zealand batsman Craig McMillan ensured Pakistan had no easy path to a series clean sweep with a sparkling century in the second match in Rawalpindi.

In less demanding conditions, McMillan scored 105 from 116 balls to steer New Zealand to 277 for 5. McMillan and Matt Horne provided the foundation with a 96-run second-wicket partnership.

Pakistan stumbled early, 6 for 2 in the second over, but Shahid Afridi played a typically belligerent innings to upset the early New Zealand momentum. Younis Khan and Abdur Razzaq negotiated the path to victory with a fourth-wicket stand of 93 from 17 overs, the win achieved with 17 balls to spare.

After playing an unchanged side for six matches, Pakistan experimented with a new opener in the final encounter in Lahore. Shoaib Malik eagerly accepted the challenge with a century built from unorthodox but confident strokeplay. Youhana, Razzaq and debutant batsman Misbah ul-Haq ensured Pakistan reached a challenging total of 278.

Without their leading batsman, Nathan Astle, New Zealand failed to reproduce the type of batting form we had seen from them in Rawalpindi.

Horne, McMillan, Chris Harris and Lou Vincent made impressive starts, but McMillan's 38, the highest score of the innings, tells its own story.

Malik bowled as impressively as he had batted with 3 for 37 from ten overs with good support from Mohammad Sami and Shahid Afridi.

Pakistan's enthusiasm to establish Shoaib Akhtar as the fastest bowler in the world was given technological support with a radar reading that displayed 161kph – much to the delight of the local fans. However the technology was unreliable and was contradicted by the TV readings. The ICC decided that Akhtar's claim to be the fastest bowler in the world should remain just that, an unofficial claim.

Match One
21 April 2002 at National Stadium, Karachi (floodlit)
Pakistan 275 for 6 (50 overs) (Yousuf Youhana 125, Younis Khan 69)
New Zealand 122 (30 overs) (Shoaib Akhtar 6 for 16)
Pakistan won by 153 runs
Man of the Match: Shoaib Akhtar

Match Two
24 April 2002 at Rawalpindi Cricket Stadium (floodlit)
New Zealand 277 for 5 (50 overs) (CD McMillan 105, MJ Horne 62)
Pakistan 278 for 7 (47.1 overs) (Abdur Razzaq 86, Younis Khan 70)
Pakistan won by three wickets
Man of the Match: Abdur Razzaq

Match Three
27 April 2002 at Gaddafi Stadium, Lahore (floodlit)
Pakistan 278 for 5 (50 overs) (Shoaib Malik 115, Yousuf Youhana 53)
New Zealand 212 (45.4 overs)
Pakistan won by 66 runs
Man of the Match: Shoaib Malik

Yousuf Youhana led the way for Pakistan's one-day victory over New Zealand with a brilliant 125 in the opening match of the series in Karachi.

FIRST TEST
1–3 May 2002 at Lahore

For a while, on a steaming hot day in Lahore, Inzamam-ul-Haq threatened the individual Test scoring record of Brian Lara.

In oppressive 40-degree temperatures, on a benign pitch, Inzamam made New Zealand's toothless bowling attack appear second rate. He first passed his highest Test score and proceeded not only to threaten Lara's 375, but went close to surpassing the highest score by a Pakistan Test batsman.

Had it not been for cramp and the rapid decline in the Pakistan first innings, he might well have beaten Hanif Mohammed's 337 made against the West Indies in 1957–58.

Pakistan had not enjoyed much home success leading up to this series, in fact they had lost the previous four, although they had recently been successful in Sharjah over a puzzling West Indies outfit. Inzamam, too, had experienced a slump in form which belied his status as one of the world's best batsmen.

Even allowing for New Zealand's injury-depleted bowling attack, Inzamam's 329 from 436 deliveries was an innings of majestic quality.

The toss was as much a determining factor in the match as Inzamam's innings. A slow, lifeless pitch gave

The mighty, yet graceful Inzamam in action at Lahore where he scored 329: the tenth highest score in Test history, and the second highest by a Pakistani.

Darryl Tuffey some encouragement in the first over when he had Shahid Afridi caught behind by new wicketkeeper Rob Hart.

When Younis Khan was out from the bowling of Daniel Vettori, 57 for 2 was as good as it got for New Zealand.

Inzamam and Imran Nazir added 204 for the third wicket in the most telling partnership of the innings. There were modest contributions from the rest of the Pakistan order, but each partnership with Inzamam added to New Zealand's misery.

The Test match was beyond New Zealand at the end of the first day. Despite numerous opportunities created by Vettori, Pakistan had reached 355 for 4.

Inzamam ultimately batted for nine-and-a-half hours, hitting 38 fours and nine sixes and hardly missing a beat as he compiled a record partnership for the ninth wicket against New Zealand – 78 with Shoaib Akhtar – following the 111 he had added with Saqlain Mushtaq for the seventh wicket.

Facing an imposing total of 643, New Zealand were only batting to save the Test, and rather than offer much resistance New Zealand suffered the largest defeat in their Test history.

By stumps on the second day, New Zealand had slumped to 56 for 6 with Matt Horne, Mark Richardson, Stephen Fleming and Chris Harris all bowled by Shoaib who ended the day with 4 for 11.

New Zealand were dismissed for 73 early on day three with Shoaib adding two further wickets to his haul for career-best figures of 6 for 11 from 8.2 overs.

Akhtar bowled with great pace and hostility and the New Zealanders had little answer to it, almost resigning themselves to an early defeat. There were also thinly veiled signs that the New Zealand batsmen were unconvinced that Akhtar's action was any better than it was when he had been cited by umpires Dunne and Cowie on Pakistan's previous tour of New Zealand.

There was a little more resistance in the second innings as New Zealand followed on 570 runs behind. Horne went cheaply for the second time, but the top five produced some encouraging innings. Vincent and Richardson added 66 for the second wicket and Vincent and Fleming took the score past 100 before the third wicket fell. Vincent played some delightful attacking strokes until he became the first of leg spinner Danish Kaneria's five wickets.

Without Shoaib Akhtar, who had sprained an ankle during the first innings, and with captain Waqar Younis bowling just nine overs on a lifeless pitch, it was left to the spinners to continue the destruction of New Zealand.

At one stage, 186 for 3 was looking much more promising. There was little likelihood of saving the Test, but a fifth day became a much greater probability.

Once Kaneria got into the groove with his leg spin on a dry, deteriorating pitch, it became only a matter of time, and the last seven wickets fell for 53 runs with the leg spinner ending with figures of 5 for 110.

Not only was it the largest defeat for New Zealand it was fourth largest innings defeat in the history of Test cricket, and Inzamam was the obvious choice for Man of the Match.

Reeling from Inzamam's onslaught, New Zealand were then routed by Shoaib Akhtar who claimed 6 for 11.

FIRST TEST – PAKISTAN v. NEW ZEALAND
1–3 May 2002 at Lahore

PAKISTAN

	First innings	
Imran Nazir	c Richardson b McMillan	127
Shahid Afridi	c Hart b Tuffey	0
Younis Khan	c Fleming b Vettori	27
Inzamam-ul-Haq	c Tuffey b Walker	329
Yousuf Youhana	c Fleming b Martin	29
Abdur Razzaq	lbw b Tuffey	25
*Rashid Latif	c & b Harris	7
Saqlain Mushtaq	b McMillan	30
Waqar Younis (capt)	c & b McMillan	10
Shoaib Akhtar	st Hart b Walker	37
Danish Kaneria	not out	4
Extras	b 1, lb 8, w 1, nb 8	18
		463

	First innings			
	O	M	R	W
Tuffey	25	7	94	2
Martin	31	12	108	1
Vettori	40	4	178	1
Walker	14.5	3	97	2
Harris	29	3	109	1
McMillan	18	1	48	3

Fall of Wickets
1-1, 2-57, 3-261, 4-355, 5-384, 6-399, 7-510, 8-534, 9-612

NEW ZEALAND

	First innings		Second innings	
MH Richardson	b Shoaib Akhtar	8	c Rashid Latif b Saqlain Mushtaq	32
MJ Horne	b Shoaib Akhtar	4	c Rashid Latif b Waqar Younis	0
L Vincent	c Rashid Latif b Danish Kaneria	21	c Rashid Latif b Danish Kaneria	57
SP Fleming (capt)	b Shoaib Akhtar	2	c sub (Mohammad Sami) b Danish Kaneria	66
CZ Harris	b Shoaib Akhtar	2	lbw b Abdur Razzaq	43
CD McMillan	c Shahid Afridi b Saqlain Mushtaq	15	lbw b Danish Kaneria	2
*RG Hart	lbw b Waqar Younis	4	b Danish Kaneria	0
DL Vettori	c Waqar Younis b Saqlain Mushtaq	7	c sub (Shoaib Malik) b Abdur Razzaq	5
BGK Walker	lbw b Shoaib Akhtar	0	not out	15
DR Tuffey	not out	6	c Younis Khan b Danish Kaneria	12
CS Martin	b Shoaib Akhtar	0	c sub (Shoaib Malik) b Saqlain Mushtaq	0
Extras	lb 1, nb 3	4	b 4, lb 6, nb 4	14
		73		**246**

	First innings				Second innings			
	O	M	R	W	O	M	R	W
Waqar Younis	10	6	21	1	9	1	38	1
Shoaib Akhtar	8.2	4	11	6				
Danish Kaneria	6	1	19	1	32	3	110	5
Saqlain Mushtaq	6	1	21	2	17.3	3	38	2
Abdur Razzaq					14	2	47	2
Shahid Afridi					4	1	3	–

Fall of Wickets
1-12, 2-17, 3-19, 4-21, 5-53, 6-57, 7-66, 8-67, 9-73
1-3, 2-69, 3-101, 4-186, 5-193, 6-193, 7-204, 8-227, 9-245

Umpires: SA Bucknor & RE Koertzen
Toss: Pakistan
Test Debut: RG Hart (New Zealand)
Man of the Match: Inzamam-ul-Haq

Pakistan won by an innings & 324 runs

AN EYE-WITNESS ACCOUNT OF THE KARACHI BOMB
By Bryan Waddle

It started as a typical day on tour: that unwelcome early morning wake-up call. 'It's the office, just checking on the weather for the start of play,' they said, unsure of the time zone and blissfully unaware that Karachi in early May is never anything other than stinking hot. A few moments of contemplation time, shared with the sounds of traffic in the street below – the incessant horn-blowing and six lanes of vehicular traffic trying to fit into the two which are ill-suited for the Karachi rush hour.

I remember wondering what the day would hold when the traffic noise was overpowered by a deafening explosion, swiftly followed by shattered glass which ripped through ageing sun-filters and flew past me like large gunshot pellets. Then an eerie silence, before the sound of screams merged with the traffic noise and the distant whine of emergency sirens. I knew the sound immediately, having experienced blasts on two previous trips to Sri Lanka – it was the all-too-familiar sound of a bomb.

Dressed as I had slept in boxer shorts and a T-shirt, I trod cautiously over the shattered glass to reach my shoes and cellphone and headed for the uncertainty of the emergency exit. Sartorial elegance was the least of my worries as I joined other guests on the sixth floor of the Pearl Continental Hotel – many were dressed equally unfashionably. Many had been awoken by the blast without understanding what was happening, and there did not appear to be any organized evacuation process.

It was a slow trip down the fire escape along with the frightened, the panic-stricken and the orderly, all eager to reach the ground and what we hoped would be safety from any further blast.

On the way down, I encountered the New Zealand team's security officer, Reg Dickason. He was on the second floor, busily ensuring that the entire New Zealand party assembled in one place and with a forthright reminder of the urgency. The bomb had exploded at precisely the time that the players from both teams were due to depart for the National Stadium and, for a short but worrying time, not all were accounted for.

Thankfully, there was only one minor external injury. The New Zealand team physio, Dayle Shackel, sustained a cut from flying glass as he waited alone in the New Zealand team bus.

As everyone assembled it was immediately evident that the tour was finished – the nervous chatter between the players centred on the time of the next flight out.

Despite some positive rhetoric and criticism of New Zealand's decision from the Pakistan Board, there is little doubt that it was the right decision. The Pakistan players were as unsettled by the explosion as the New Zealanders and were even apologetic that something they had no control over should end the series.

The random act of terrorism killed 14 innocent civilians, and made Pakistan a no-go area for touring cricket teams. New Zealand had been reluctant to go in the first place, and the West Indies had previously played Pakistan's home series in Sharjah, such was their concern.

New Zealand were persuaded to accept the trip, so long as there was a heavy security presence. There were armed police escorts to and from the grounds and the airport. There was a limit imposed on the players' ability to move freely outside the team hotel and, in Rawalpindi, the players left the ground past two lines of heavily armed security forces.

But is this the answer? Cricket is a social game, its character is enhanced by the interaction between players and supporters, a fact that was totally lost behind security cordons and the need to employ a security specialist in the official tour party.

Many confused and bewildered players left Karachi with a terrifying mental picture of a suicide car-bomb explosion. Even the most hardened individual was left with a lasting memory of death, destruction and mayhem that is far removed from cricket and it is a memory that will not easily be erased.

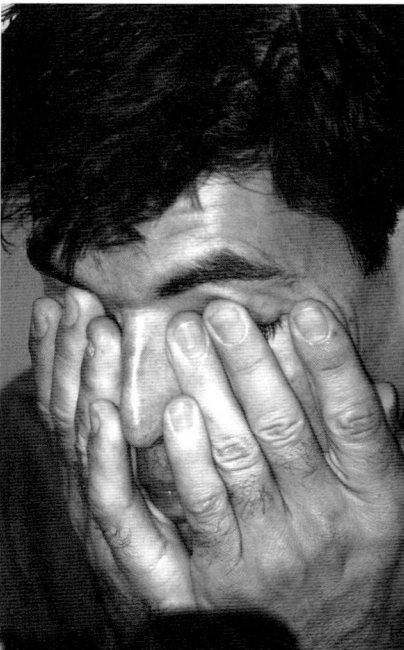

It was a harrowing experience for everyone concerned. New Zealand's captain, Stephen Fleming, broke down in the press conference to explain his team's decision to abandon the tour.

PAKISTAN DOMESTIC FIRST–CLASS CRICKET
By Qamar Ahmed

In a season lasting nearly nine months, Pakistan hosted Bangladesh and Sri Lanka for the Asian Test championship matches and, in late April, New Zealand arrived to honour their commitment after cancelling their original scheduled tour for security reasons. The continued uncertainty forced Pakistan to play a home Test series on the neutral ground at Sharjah against the West Indies. In a hectic season, an under-19 team from Sri Lanka toured Pakistan, losing the series to the Pakistan's junior string by a margin of 1–4.

On the domestic front, as many as 120 first-class games were played in the first-class tournaments: 20 more than in the previous year. That included 71 matches in the Quaid-e-Azam Trophy and 45 in the Patron's Trophy Grade One. In a revamped format, the Pakistan Cricket Board (PCB) invited teams from the district areas to participate in order to provide opportunities for cricketers from remote regions of the country. The PCB added four combined teams along with 14 district teams to the Quaid-e-Azam Trophy. Baluchistan, the rest of Punjab, the rest of Sind and the rest of North West Frontier formed teams comprising of players within these provinces who had played in Grade Two matches.

Karachi Whites were the winners of the tournament for the 17th time by defeating Peshawar by eight wickets. Gujranwala, Sargodha and Karachi Blues also performed creditably in the competition. In the final, held at Karachi, Peshawar were dismissed for 158 in their first innings and Karachi, having taken a first-innings lead of 102, allowed the opposition to recover admirably by scoring 354 in the second innings, which included 171 by Yasir Hameed.

Left with a target of 252 to win, Karachi achieved their goal with the loss of only two wickets as opener Ghulam Ali made 113 not out.

National Bank emerged as the champions of the Patron's Trophy Grade One by topping the ten-team league table with 18 points over second-placed Khan Research Laboratories (KRL). The former holders of the trophy, Pakistan Customs, failed to rediscover last season's form and finished sixth.

As usual, the batsmen flourished in helpful conditions. Eleven batsmen – Misbah-ul-Haq, Ijaz Ahmed Junior, Hasan Raza, Mohammad Ramzan, Saeed Bin Nasir, Usman Tariq, Farhan Adil, Zahoor Elahi, Bilal Asad, Imran Farhat and Ghulam Ali – reached 1,000 runs during the season. However, the more familiar figure of Inzamam-ul-Haq – who played only four matches including three Tests topped the averages with 628 runs (at an average of 157.00) which included his 329 against New Zealand in the first Test at Lahore. Fazl-e-Akbar of PIA and Peshawar took 95 wickets in 15 matches at 17 each, while other notable bowling feats were performed by Asif Mujtaba, Faisal Irfan and Jaffer Nazir who all took hat-tricks.

PAKISTAN DOMESTIC ONE–DAY CRICKET
By Qamar Ahmed

Twenty eight teams from the length and breadth of Pakistan competed in the only one-day tournament played during the season. The teams consisted of the 18 city and district associations who had played in the Quaid-e-Azam Trophy Grade One, and ten departmental and commercial organizations formed teams which had already played in the Patron's Trophy Grade One.

In the four preliminary pool matches, it was the Pakistan International Airlines (PIA) and Habib Bank teams who emerged unscathed by winning all six matches in their group. They were to meet in the final which PIA won by the narrow margin of only six runs in a floodlit match at the Gaddafi Stadium in Lahore. This was PIA's eighth win in a one-day domestic championship. PIA had left a target of 237 for the Habib Bank to win the tournament.

In PIA's innings of 236, Test cricketers Faisal Iqbal and Shoaib Mohammad both made half-centuries. In reply, Salim Elahi scored 64 useful runs in 75 balls, but, in the run chase, Habib Bank lost six wickets for 86. The Test opener, Taufiq Umar, rallied his team with an attractive 95, but the off spinner Shoaib Malik dashed their aspirations when he struck twice in the final over to finish with figures of 2 for 15.

The losing semi-finalists were National Bank – who were defeated by nine runs by PIA – and the Water and Power Development Authority, who were easily disposed of by Habib Bank by 139.

Left-handed opener Taufiq Umar won the award for best batsman, wrist spinner Danish Kaneria picked up the best bowler prize while the best wicketkeeper of the competition was Atiq-uz-Zaman – all three represented Habib Bank.

Next page: Now aged 36, and with 400 wickets in both Test cricket and one–day internationals behind him, the inspirational Wasim Akram is now contemplating his retirement from the game.

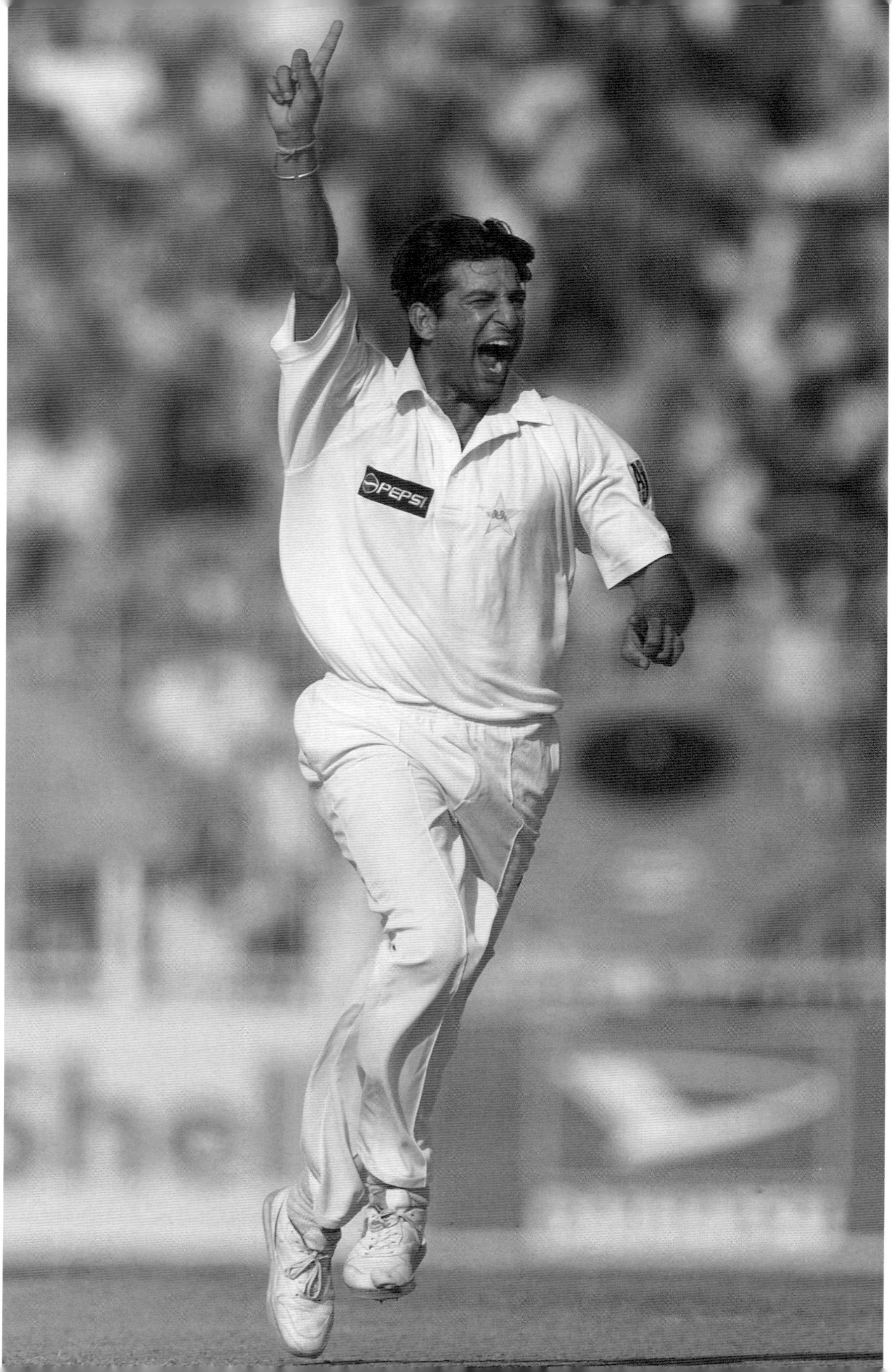
PEPSI

FIRST-CLASS AVERAGES
Pakistan

BATTING

	M	Inns	NO	HS	Runs	Av	100	50
Misbah-ul-Haq	18	24	3	204*	1386	66.00	4	7
Rehan Rafiq	11	17	4	197*	800	61.53	3	2
Babar Naeem	7	14	0	227	832	59.42	2	5
Imran Javed	10	14	3	134	630	57.27	2	3
Ijaz Ahmed, jr	15	22	2	116	1087	54.35	5	5
Mohammad Ramzan	16	27	3	162	1297	54.04	4	4
Hasan Raza	18	28	7	256	1096	52.19	2	3
Saeed Bin Nasir	17	30	7	133	1162	50.52	3	7
Usman Tariq	17	28	3	210	1183	47.32	1	9
Atif Rauf	5	9	1	133*	373	46.62	1	1
Faisal Iqbal	11	19	2	171	785	46.17	3	3
Agha Sabir	6	10	0	196	455	45.50	2	-
Asim Kamal	14	20	2	160	817	45.38	3	4
Naved Latif	6	10	2	80	363	45.37	-	4
Arif Mahmood	8	10	2	105*	363	45.37	1	3
Farhan Adil	16	25	2	124	1041	45.26	3	3
Asim Munir	7	11	2	157*	407	45.22	2	-
Younis Khan	6	11	0	117	483	43.90	1	3
Yousuf Youhana	8	13	2	102*	477	43.36	1	3
Zahoor Elahi	17	30	2	108	1202	42.92	2	10
Sajid Ali	8	13	2	123*	463	42.09	3	1
Bilal Asad	17	32	2	112	1260	42.00	3	6
Imran Farhat	17	30	1	204	1200	41.37	3	4
Asif Mujtaba	8	14	1	122*	522	40.15	1	3
Iqbal Imam	9	15	2	114	522	40.15	1	2
Shadab Kabir	12	19	0	137	760	40.00	2	4
Mohammad Hafeez	15	23	0	177	919	39.95	3	4
Mohammad Javed	9	14	5	79*	358	39.77	-	2
Ghulam Ali	18	32	1	113*	1228	39.61	2	6
Aamer Malik	6	10	2	113*	306	38.25	1	1
Akhtar Sarfraz	13	21	2	89	714	37.57	-	2
Sufyan Munir	7	14	2	127*	449	37.41	2	2
Taufeeq Umar	6	10	0	113	374	37.40	2	1
Majid Jahangir	13	22	1	104	785	37.38	1	5
Naved-ul-Hasan	14	20	3	117	625	36.76	1	4
Ali Naqvi	12	19	0	137	687	36.15	1	3
Naseer Khan	7	12	1	85	393	35.72	-	4
Rizwan Qureshi	8	15	3	67	428	35.66	-	2
Saeed Anwar, jr	13	25	3	144*	779	35.40	2	4
Sami-ul-Haq	5	9	0	80	318	35.33	-	4
Inam-ul-Haq	15	28	1	101	944	34.96	1	7
Atiq-uz-Zaman	14	20	2	115	629	34.94	2	3
Abdur Rahim	7	13	2	68	384	34.90	-	5
Abdur Razzaq	7	11	2	110*	314	34.88	1	1
Kashif Siddiq	13	22	0	103	762	34.63	2	4
Salim Mughal	12	20	2	128*	623	34.61	1	3
Shahid Qambrani	7	13	1	105	415	34.58	1	3
Bilal Khilji	13	20	1	150*	654	34.42	1	5
Mian Nafees	7	14	2	81	417	34.75	-	4
Bazid Khan	16	28	0	127	962	34.35	1	7
Mohammad Masroor	6	9	0	94	308	34.22	-	3
Rafatullah Mohmand	10	17	1	97	545	34.06	-	3
Intikhab Alam	11	18	3	69	510	34.00	-	4
Rizwan Ahmed (2)	8	16	0	102	543	33.93	1	2
Hammad Tariq	6	9	0	138	299	33.22	1	-
Tariq Mahmood	7	13	1	90*	391	32.58	-	3
Wajahatullah Wasti	14	22	1	101	684	32.57	1	4
Naved Ashraf	7	14	1	95	422	32.46	-	5
Imran Abbas	12	18	1	165	546	32.11	2	-
Imran Nazir	17	29	3	127	833	32.03	1	4
Salim Elahi	14	25	1	168	753	31.37	1	5
Kamran Akmal	17	29	3	120	810	31.15	2	3
Moin Khan	11	15	1	119	436	31.14	1	2
Aftab Alam	7	12	1	95	342	31.09	-	2
Imran Khan	6	11	0	124	341	31.00	1	1
Yasir Hameed	15	27	2	171*	774	30.96	1	3
Naseer Ahmed	5	10	0	91	308	30.80	-	1
Tariq Haroon	11	18	1	92	521	30.64	-	3
Tariq Javed	7	11	3	60*	245	30.62	-	2
Taimur Khan	9	14	0	74	428	30.57	-	4
Faisal Khan	5	8	0	113	244	30.50	1	-
Mohammad Wasim	10	16	0	123	484	30.25	1	3

FIRST-CLASS AVERAGES
Pakistan

BATTING

	M	Inns	NO	HS	Runs	Av	100	50
Asmatullah Mohmand	8	15	2	106*	388	29.84	1	2
Mohammad Hussain	14	26	0	126	773	29.73	1	3
Afsar Nawaz	10	19	0	156	561	29.52	1	2
Zulfiqar Jan	13	21	4	100*	498	29.29	1	2
Sohail Idrees	15	26	1	154	732	29.28	1	4
Azizullah Khan	8	16	1	79	439	29.26	-	4
Naumanullah	14	23	0	114	670	29.13	1	4
Mohammad Nawaz	14	20	2	107	516	28.66	1	2
Aamer Hanif	6	9	1	73	229	28.62	-	2
Tahir Mughal	12	20	5	68*	427	28.46	-	3
Rizwan Ahmed (1)	7	14	0	95	397	28.35	-	3
Azhar Shafiq	9	14	0	106	396	28.28	1	2
I Mohammad	10	18	0	107	507	28.16	1	2
Ijaz Shah	4	8	0	85	219	27.37	-	1
Humayun Farhat	16	27	0	69	737	27.29	-	7
Nasim Khan	14	26	1	104	678	27.12	1	3
Yasir Arafat	17	28	4	60	650	27.08	-	4
Adil Nisar	12	24	4	85	535	26.75	-	3
Rizwan Malik	13	24	1	100*	615	26.73	1	3
Qaiser Abbas	15	25	0	90	665	26.60	-	4
Kashif Rasheed	4	8	0	68	209	26.12	-	1
Ahmed Said	8	15	1	78*	359	25.64	-	3
Saad Wasim	7	12	1	132	282	25.63	1	1
Majid Majeed	6	10	0	57	256	25.60	-	1
Sohail Jaffar	6	12	1	65	276	25.09	-	1
Maqsood Raza	8	13	0	68	326	25.07	-	2
Riaz Shaikh	13	22	3	74	476	25.05	-	2
Iqbal Sheikh	4	8	0	68	199	24.87	-	2
Hanif-ur-Rehman	11	21	1	79	495	24.75	-	4
Akram Khan	4	8	0	106	197	24.62	1	-
Aamer Iqbal	9	16	3	69	318	24.46	-	2
Shoaib Khan	7	13	2	79*	262	23.81	-	2
Azhar Mahmood	5	9	0	51	214	23.77	-	1
Wasim Majeed	4	8	0	81	187	23.37	-	1
Ahmed Hayat	10	14	3	77	256	23.27	-	1
Ghaffar Kazmi	7	12	0	79	279	23.25	-	1
Irfan Fazil	10	17	4	51*	300	23.07	-	2
Javed Khan	5	10	2	50	183	22.87	-	1
Mushtaq Ahmed	11	15	1	68	317	22.64	-	2
Ali Hussain	6	11	1	54	226	22.60	-	1
Mujahid Jamshed	7	10	0	86	225	22.50	-	1
Khalid Mahmood	9	13	0	141	291	22.38	1	-
Naeem Akhtar	11	19	4	55	335	22.33	-	1
Abid Mahmood	5	9	1	78	178	22.25	-	1
Mohtashim Ali	8	16	0	77	355	22.18	-	1
Zia-ur-Rehman	11	20	2	61	398	22.11	-	3
Shahid Nazir	13	17	5	45	265	22.08	-	-
Mohammad Fazil	8	15	2	45	283	21.76	-	-
Mohammad Bilal	8	15	2	68	281	21.61	-	1
Waqar Younis	6	8	0	64	172	21.50	-	1
Aamer Bashir	14	23	0	115	491	21.34	1	2
Mohammad Zahid	9	13	4	43	192	21.33	-	-
Jaffar Nazir	15	19	2	80	359	21.11	-	3
Abdur Rehman	10	15	3	58*	252	21.00	-	1
Faisal Naved	11	20	0	102	414	20.70	1	-
Tariq Aziz	8	16	1	109	310	20.66	2	-
Kabir Khan	14	19	7	66*	243	20.25	-	1
Akhtar Bangash	5	9	0	72	177	19.66	-	1
Shahid Anwar	8	14	0	63	270	19.28	-	1
Adnan Ameer	4	8	0	51	153	19.12	-	1
Fareed Butt	5	9	0	81	170	18.88	-	1
Naeem Akhtar (2)	5	10	1	57*	168	18.66	-	1
Shahid Afridi	8	14	0	70	260	18.57	-	3
Iftikhar Anjum	15	28	8	55	371	18.55	-	2
Kashif Raza	12	20	3	64	315	18.52	-	-
Adnan Raees	5	10	0	68	185	18.50	-	2
Shoaib Malik	8	12	0	100	222	18.50	1	-
Faisal Athar	7	14	0	41	253	18.07	-	-
Zahid Umar	6	11	1	51	178	17.80	-	1
Shahnawaz Malik	7	13	0	51	221	17.30	-	1
Azam Khan	4	8	0	44	138	17.25	-	-
Sarfraz Ahmed	11	17	1	48*	270	16.87	-	-

FIRST-CLASS AVERAGES
Pakistan

BATTING

	M	Inns	NO	HS	Runs	Av	100	50
Javed Hayat	6	12	0	53	202	16.83	-	1
Saad Janjua	7	13	1	39	201	16.75	-	-
Faisal Irfan	13	22	8	50	230	16.42	-	1
Arshad Khan	17	25	3	59	356	16.18	-	1
Ibrahim Afridi	8	15	1	72*	214	15.28	-	1
Ata-ur-Rehman	7	10	0	36	150	15.00	-	-
Tanvir Ahmed	15	20	1	44	285	15.00	-	-

Qualification: 8 completed innings, average 15.00

BOWLING

	Overs	Mds	Runs	Wkts	Av	Best	10m	5/inn
Ijaz Ahmed, jr	166	56	338	25	13.52	6-74	1	1
Irfan Fazil	193.3	32	419	28	14.96	4-32	-	-
Tahir Mughal	396.3	74	1308	83	15.75	7-63	3	6
Kabir Khan	320.1	63	930	56	16.60	4-21	-	-
Mohammad Javed	242.4	61	688	41	16.78	5-63	1	3
Shahid Afridi	86.5	26	224	13	17.23	3-41	-	-
Fazl-e-Akbar	508.4	98	1656	95	17.43	8-68	3	9
Mohammad Zahid (2)	408.1	115	873	48	18.18	6-106	1	5
Naeem Akhtar	333.1	72	933	51	18.29	6-53	1	3
Waqar Ahmed	426.1	74	1523	80	19.03	6-46	1	8
Jaffar Nazir	464.1	95	1324	69	19.18	7-43	1	5
Shahid Nazir	319.1	76	924	48	19.25	5-46	-	1
Azhar Mahmood	172.5	35	583	30	19.43	7-55	1	2
Mushtaq Ahmed	343.5	74	1207	62	19.46	6-79	-	5
Waqas Ahmed	308.1	60	994	51	19.49	7-84	2	5
Danish Kaneria	292	61	871	44	19.79	6-42	1	4
Azhar Abbas	220.3	46	731	36	20.30	6-38	1	2
Fahad Masood	229.4	55	670	33	20.30	5-49	-	2
Yasir Arafat	485.3	71	1853	91	20.36	7-102	2	6
Sarfraz Ahmed	343.3	80	816	40	20.40	5-24	1	2
Shabbir Ahmed	456.3	104	1249	61	20.47	5-21	-	2
Mohammad Hussain	548.4	187	1306	64	20.73	6-60	2	6
Raees Amjad	288.5	48	978	46	21.26	6-35	-	3
Wasim Khan	308.3	49	1129	53	21.30	6-60	1	5
Shoaib Akhtar	157	33	520	24	21.66	6-11	-	1
Abdur Rauf	499.5	86	1855	84	22.08	8-40	1	3
Saad Janjua	195.4	28	727	32	22.71	5-39	-	1
Sajid Shah	357.4	52	1280	56	22.85	5-74	1	1
Zahid Saeed	320.1	52	1127	49	23.00	5-73	-	1
Faisal Irfan	384.1	86	1042	44	23.68	4-44	-	-
Ali Raza	293.4	45	956	40	23.90	7-52	-	1
Murtaza Hussain	292.1	63	747	31	24.09	7-33	-	5
Rajesh Ramesh	217.5	32	785	32	24.53	5-68	-	1
Nadeem Afzal	201.4	39	676	27	25.03	5-51	-	1
Tanvir Ahmed	563.4	103	1878	75	25.04	7-75	2	6
Waqar Younis	156.4	33	603	24	25.12	4-19	-	-
Iftikhar Anjum	458.1	94	1546	61	25.34	7-80	-	3
Ahmed Hyat	278.2	29	1017	40	25.42	6-42	1	3
Qaiser Abbas	137.3	44	283	11	25.72	3-21	-	-
Arif Mahmood	173	33	442	17	26.00	5-43	-	1
Naved-ul-Hasan	391.4	54	1486	57	26.07	7-49	1	2
Kashif Raza	311.5	70	861	33	26.09	4-46	-	-
Mubashir Nazir	323.1	61	1091	41	26.60	5-27	-	2
Abdur Razzaq	181.2	28	667	25	26.68	4-50	-	-
Imran Farhat	117.1	8	485	18	26.94	3-62	-	-
Arshad Khan	523.3	136	1335	49	27.24	8-80	1	2
Aqib Javed	251.5	68	629	23	27.34	5-73	-	1
Mohammad Zahid (1)	211	47	658	24	27.41	5-61	-	1
Asim Butt	124	15	505	18	28.05	4-37	-	-
Tabish Nawab	318.4	77	898	32	28.06	6-39	-	3
Sohail Hashmi	134	27	452	16	28.25	5-61	-	1
Aamer Nazir	245.5	33	918	32	28.68	4-55	-	-
Aqeel Ahmed	293.4	53	1011	35	28.88	6-61	1	2
Shoaib Malik	136.5	26	438	15	29.20	3-21	-	-
Abdur Rehman	392.2	125	921	31	29.70	5-120	-	1
Mohammad Sarfraz	222.5	40	705	23	30.65	4-63	-	-
Riaz Shaikh	391.3	64	1323	43	30.76	5-36	-	1
Imran Javed	178	44	464	15	30.93	2-13	-	-

FIRST-CLASS AVERAGES
Pakistan

BOWLING

	Overs	Mds	Runs	Wkts	Av	Best	10m	5/inn
Rizwan Saeed	188	42	567	18	31.50	4-56	-	-
Shakeel-ur-Rehman	159	33	536	17	31.52	6-44	-	1
Kashif Pervez	174.4	34	574	18	31.88	5-39	-	1
Mohammad Sami	295.5	54	1028	32	32.12	5-59	-	1
Faisal Afridi	230.4	42	778	24	32.41	3-24	-	-
Rizwan Qureshi	240.2	69	681	21	32.42	5-58	-	1
Ali Naqvi	214	47	649	20	32.45	5-34	-	1
Waqas Chughati	346.4	60	1238	38	32.57	7-75	1	1
Naseer Khan	175	38	524	16	32.75	5-104	-	1
Bilal Asad	222	33	796	24	33.16	3-35	-	-
Tariq Haroon	180	38	541	16	33.81	3-22	-	-
Tahir Maqsood	174.3	35	555	16	34.68	3-30	-	-
S John	127.4	19	499	14	35.64	5-59	-	1
Rizwan Ahmed	216	28	860	23	37.39	6-101	1	2
Azhar Shafiq	217.5	40	713	18	39.61	4-93	-	-
Mohammad Asif	215.1	48	568	14	40.57	5-26	-	1

Qualification: 10 wickets in 8 innings

The following bowlers took 10 wickets in fewer than 8 innings:

	Overs	Mds	Runs	Wkts	Av	Best	10m	5/inn
Wasim Akram	61	15	155	11	14.09	4-39	-	-
Noor-ul-Amin	158.4	50	385	26	14.80	6-49	1	3
Tariq Mahmood	89.1	16	254	16	15.87	6-43	-	1
Taimur Khan	84	27	217	12	18.08	5-35	-	1
Ashraf Bashir	107.1	42	210	11	19.09	4-5	-	-
Naved Arif	136.1	35	366	19	19.26	5-28	-	1
Shahid Khan	154	36	502	24	20.91	7-50	1	1
Irfanuddin	88.4	21	212	10	21.20	3-53	-	-
Mohammad Aslam	119.2	28	331	15	22.06	5-33	1	2
Mohammad Hasnain	114.4	16	442	20	22.10	6-45	1	1
Umair Khan	88.3	10	364	16	22.75	4-54	-	-
Imran Adil	71.1	13	242	10	24.20	3-42	-	-
Mohammad Asif (2)	130.5	28	430	17	25.29	6-34	-	1
Sajid Ali	162.1	31	482	18	26.77	4-37	-	-
Rauf Akbar	66.2	10	275	10	27.50	5-63	-	1
Aamer Wasim	140.3	26	415	15	27.66	3-16	-	-
Moazzam Ali	94.1	17	283	10	28.30	5-120	-	1
Salman Fazal	135.5	44	286	10	28.60	5-86	-	1
Kamran Hussain	128.3	32	402	14	28.71	3-91	-	-
Hanif-ur-Rehman	128.3	35	352	11	32.00	4-51	-	-
Ikranullah	121.3	19	363	11	33.00	3-61	-	-
Mohammad Hafeez	196.3	44	472	14	33.71	3-53	-	-
Nadeem Iqbal	165.3	32	497	14	35.50	3-62	-	-
Hasnain Kazim	139	24	520	14	37.14	4-106	-	-
Ata-ur-Rehman	160.4	31	499	12	41.58	3-30	-	-

FIELDING

67 - Humayan Farhat (55ct, 1st); 60 - Kamran Akmal (52ct, 8st); 46 - Atiq-uz-Zaman (45ct, 1st); Moin Khan (45ct, 1st); 41 - Zulfiqar Jan; 31 - Mutahir Shah (29ct, 2st); 30 - Nadeem Hussain (28ct, 2st); 29 - Aamer Iqbal, Mohammad Fazil (28ct, 1st); 27 - Khalid Mahmood; 26 - Ahmed Said (22ct, 4st), Hanif Malik (24ct, 2st), Zahid Umar; 23 - Nadeem Abbasi; 20 - Ijaz Ahmed, jr; 19 - Abid Mahmood (18ct, 1st); 18 - Naumanullah, Rashid Latif; 17 - Ali Raza (14ct, 3st), Inam-ul-Haq Rashid (12ct, 5st); 16 - Ahmed Zeeshan (15ct, 1st), Bazid Khan, Mohammad Salman, Sarfraz Kazmi (13ct, 3st), Shakeel Ansar (13ct, 3st); 14 - Ghulam Ali, Hasan Raza; 15 - Afsar Nawaz, Imran Nazir, Mohammad Hafeez, Shadab Kabir; Inam-ul-Haq, Mohammad Wasim; 13 - Farhan Iqbal, Imran Farhat, Yasir Hameed, Zahoor Elahi; 12 - Asim Kamal, Malik Khaleq (11ct, 1st), Misbah-ul-Haq, Mohammad Islam, Mohammad Kashif, Mohtashim Ali, Naseer Ahmed, Wajatullah Wasti; 11 - Aftab Alam, Bilal Asad, Bilal Khilji, Mohammad Ramzan, Salim Elahi, Shahid Mahmood, Tariq Aziz; 10 - Aamer Bashir, Adnan Raees, Mohammad Shehbaz, Saeed Anwar, jr, Saeed Bin Nasir, Shoaib Khan

Qualification: 10 or more catches

SOUTH AFRICA

Triangular Tournament
India in South Africa
Australia in South Africa
South Africa Domestic First-Class Season
South Africa Domestic One-Day Season
First-Class Averages

TRIANGULAR TOURNAMENT
(South Africa, India and Kenya)
By Marcus Prior

South Africa's six-wicket win over India in the Durban final confirmed the home side's obvious superiority for the most part of what had been a largely predictable and uninspiring triangular tournament.

For the ninth time in succession, India lost the final of a one-day tournament leaving captain Saurav Ganguly at a loss to explain why his team could find no way of snapping out of their woeful streak. At least they have a habit of making finals, though. For gutsy Kenya, that is still a distant dream.

The Kenyans did at least manage a victory, and that without captain Maurice Odumbe, banned for two matches after some colourful thoughts to the press on the attitude of an unspecified umpire towards his players during their Kimberley defeat to South Africa. It was probably a deserved suspension, but Odumbe's passionate pleas for more opportunities for his side at the highest level were a recurring theme of the tournament. They were offered not so much as an excuse, but with legitimate concern for the future of the sport in his country.

The win came over India in Port Elizabeth, where Kenya comfortably defended a total of 246 for 6 to win by 70 runs, largely thanks to some brilliant fielding and a superb spell of bowling from seamer Joseph Angara, who finished with 4 for 30 from his ten overs. That Angara was forced to miss the rest of the tournament following the death of his mother, only underlined Kenya's constant struggle to compete.

The tenor of the tournament was set from the first encounter between South Africa and India at the Wanderers. Centuries from Ganguly and Sachin Tendulkar in an opening partnership of 193 helped India to an impressive 279 for 5, but on a gloriously true batting surface Gary Kirsten responded with an unbeaten 133 as South Africa won by six wickets with ten balls to spare.

India's Port Elizabeth embarrassment meant a win-or-bust final game against the Kenyans in Paarl, but despite fears of a cataclysmic wheel-wobble, India applied themselves fully and outclassed the

East Africans – Tendulkar and Ganguly both scoring centuries again as India won by 186 runs.

Durban, the venue for the final, was enduring one of its wetter spells as match-day approached, and although the game proceeded without interruption, the conditions were very much in favour of bowlers looking to swing and seam the ball. An important toss was won by South Africa and India, put into bat, struggled from the moment Tendulkar and Ganguly were both back in the pavilion with just 31 runs on the board. Despite Rahul Dravid's 77, India were dismissed for 183, ten balls short of their allotted 50 overs. That it never looked defendable was largely down to another fine innings from Kirsten, who took his series average to 93.25 with a typically solid and unfussy 87, as South Africa reached their target with nearly eight overs to spare.

Match One
5 October 2001 at Johannesburg (floodlit)
India 279 for 5 (50) (SC Ganguly 127, SR Tendulkar 101)
South Africa 280 for 4 (48.2 overs) (G Kirsten 133*)
South Africa (4 pts) won by six wickets
Man of the Match: G Kirsten

Match Two
7 October 2001 at Benoni
Kenya 159 for 7 (50 overs) (SO Tikolo 68*)
South Africa 160 for 3 (33.4 overs) (JH Kallis 54)
South Africa (5 pts) won by seven wickets
Man of the Match: SM Pollock

Match Three
10 October 2001 at Centurion (floodlit)
India 233 (48.5 overs) (R Dravid 54, SM Pollock 5 for 37)
South Africa 192 (46.2 overs)
India (4 pts) won by 41 runs
Man of the Match: Harbhajan Singh

Match Four
12 October 2001 at Bloemfontein (floodlit)
Kenya 90 (37.1 overs) (AB Agarkar 4 for 27)
India 91 for 0 (11.3 overs) (V Sehwag 55*)
India (5 pts) won by ten wickets
Man of the Match: AB Agarkar

Match Five
14 October 2001 at Kimberley
Kenya 229 for 7 (50 overs) (MO Odumbe 60, RD Shah 55, TM Odoyo 53)
South Africa 230 for 1 (41.1 overs) (L Klusener 75*, HH Dippenaar 74*, HH Gibbs 70)

Previous page: Shane Warne marked his 100th Test with a Man of the Match performance in Cape Town. The spin king bowled 98 overs in the match, snaring eight South African wickets in the process as Australia underlined their superiority with a four-wicket win to take an unassailable 2–0 series lead.

South Africa (4 pts) won by nine wickets
Man of the Match: HH Gibbs

Match Six

17 October 2001 at Port Elizabeth (floodlit)
Kenya 246 for 6 (50 overs) (KO Otieno 64,
TM Odoyo 51, RD Shah 50)
India 176 (46.4 overs)
Kenya (5 pts) won by 70 runs
Man of the Match: JO Angara

Match Seven

19 October 2001 at East London (floodlit)
South Africa 283 for 4 (50 overs) (HH Dippenaar 81)
India 236 (44.4 overs) (SC Ganguly 85, R Dravid 71*)
South Africa (4 pts) won by 46 runs
Man of the Match: SC Ganguly

**Two centuries and 87 in the final from experienced opener
Gary Kirsten eased South Africa to victory.**

Match Eight

22 October 2001 at Cape Town (floodlit)
South Africa 354 for 3 (50 overs) (ND McKenzie 131*,
G Kirsten 124, MV Boucher 51* and 4 catches)
Kenya 146 (45.3 overs) (CK Langeveldt 4 for 21)
South Africa (5 pts) won by 208 runs
Man of the Match: ND McKenzie

Match Nine

24 October 2001 at Paarl (floodlit)
India 351 for 3 (50 overs) (SR Tendulkar 146,
SC Ganguly 111, V Sehwag 55*)
Kenya 165 for 5 (50 overs)
India (5 pts) won by 186 runs
Man of the Match: SR Tendulkar

Final

26 October 2001 at Durban (floodlit)
India 183 (48.2 overs) (R Dravid 77)
South Africa 187 for 4 (42.1 overs) (G Kirsten 87)
South Africa won by six wickets
Man of the Match: SM Pollock
Player of the Series: G Kirsten

INDIA IN SOUTH AFRICA
By Marcus Prior

FIRST TEST
3–7 November 2001 at Bloemfontein

A series that would end in acrimony and controversy got off to a blistering start in Bloemfontein as South Africa went one up in the series thanks to a nine-wicket win. It was, as it sounds, a thoroughly conclusive display from the home side, but India's failure to capitalize on their pulsating performance with the bat on day one ultimately cost them the match.

After being put into bat by South African captain Shaun Pollock, India reached 372 for 7 at stumps. Surely not even the most cynical of Indian fans steeped in the knowledge of his side's woeful record away from home could have believed South Africa would celebrate victory inside four days.

So it proved, with Pollock himself spearheading South Africa's resurgence and claiming ten wickets for the first time in his 59th Test. The victory gave South Africa an edge they would never surrender in the remainder of the series.

The psychological contest looked to have been won by the Indians in spectacular style on day one. After

Shaun Pollock's dogged line and length proved too much for the Indians in the first Test and earned the South African captain ten wickets in the match.

Pollock and the recalled Mornantau Hayward made the most of favourable early conditions to reduce India to 68 for 4, Sachin Tendulkar and debutant Virender Sehwag majestically rebuilt the innings.

There were some Indian greats looking on at Goodyear Park who felt Tendulkar's 155 was perhaps the best innings they had seen the maestro play. Tendulkar himself insisted afterwards that he never rated any knock better than another, but his 26th Test hundred – taking him level with Steve Waugh behind Sunil Gavaskar's 34 – was a gem.

By the time he was caught in the deep by Neil McKenzie off the bowling of Makhaya Ntini, Tendulkar had faced just 184 balls, hitting 23 fours and a six. He had also shared in a fifth-wicket partnership of 220 with Sehwag as the pair tore South Africa's bowling apart with 132 runs between lunch and tea.

There was still plenty of work to be done, however, and after Tendulkar's departure Sehwag grew in confidence. Back in India, Sehwag is nicknamed 'the poor man's Tendulkar', and for good reason. Stocky and compact, he presented an eerily familiar straight bat when he looked to drive as well as that singular flourish of the wrists when working the ball through the legside.

Sehwag (105) was out shortly before the close, bowled by a beauty from Pollock that seamed between bat and pad to clip the off stump.

The game turned on its head on day two. South Africa required just five overs and one ball to wrap up the Indian innings, with Pollock finishing with 4 for 91.

Herschelle Gibbs scored his fourth Test century and his first on home soil as he and the ever-reliable Gary Kirsten (73) got South Africa's reply off to a confident start. When Kirsten was bowled off the bottom edge by Anil Kumble for 73 after the pair had added 189 for the first wicket, it was the third successive innings the openers had combined for a hundred runs or more.

Gibbs was in richly entertaining form, reaching his hundred with a towering six pulled contemptuously over midwicket off Zaheer Khan, but fell shortly afterwards, the over after Kirsten's departure, when he drove Javagal Srinath tamely to mid-off. Although Boeta Dippenaar again failed to build on a useful start, Neil McKenzie confirmed his growing maturity with a confident 68 and Jacques Kallis was 49 not out as South Africa reached the close on 327 for 3.

When Ashish Nehra finally induced an edge from Kallis on 68 the next morning, it was the first success by any bowler against South Africa's most consistent batsman in 1,241 minutes – nearly 21 hours – of Test cricket, a new world record.

But for all the cussed resistance of Kallis, day three belonged to Lance Klusener. The all-rounder who took the 1999 World Cup by storm was in perhaps the deepest trough of form of his professional life. In 11 innings since scoring 97 against Sri Lanka ten months earlier, Klusener had managed only 110 runs at an average of just over 12.

Although he was clearly not back to his best, Klusener was still brutal in the way he dealt with the Indian attack, clubbing 18 fours and a six as he joined Gibbs on the four Test century mark. The only disappointment was that he felt his innings was not worth talking about to the media afterwards, preferring instead to head for the nets with coach Graeme Ford – and that on a day when fewer than a thousand spectators paid their way into the ground.

For one Indian at least, there was something to celebrate. When Shaun Pollock was caught at short leg fending off a rising delivery from Srinath, he presented the Indian seamer with his 200th Test wicket. Srinath is just the fifth Indian bowler to have reached the landmark and he finished the innings with 5 for 140.

India's second batting effort was a cameo of their troubles away from home. Despite reaching the close of day three on 96 for 1, the tumble to defeat on the resumption was as ignominious as it was predictable. Only Shiv Sunder Das passed 50, and the Indians were undone by little more than Pollock's dogged pursuance of what he does best – that nagging line and length on or around off stump.

The South African captain had to wait for his tenth wicket of the match, however, as Ntini put down a difficult running chance offered by Nehra. The ten were finally complete with the game's coup de grace – Srinath caught at long on by McKenzie to give Pollock figures of 6 for 56 in the innings and a match analysis of 10 for 147.

There was another landmark for Kallis, too. Tendulkar's loose drive to point handed the South African his 100th Test wicket. In the process, Kallis became just the eighth player in the history of the game to score 3,000 runs and take 100 wickets in Tests, alongside Gary Sobers, Kapil Dev, Imran Khan, Ian Botham, Richard Hadlee, Tony Greig and Ravi Shastri.

FIRST TEST – SOUTH AFRICA v. INDIA
3-7 November 2001 at Bloemfontein

INDIA

	First innings		Second innings	
SS Das	b Hayward	9	(2) c Boucher b Hayward	62
R Dravid	c Kallis b Pollock	2	(1) c Kirsten b Pollock	11
VVS Laxman	c Boucher b Hayward	32	c Kallis b Pollock	29
SR Tendulkar	c McKenzie b Ntini	155	c Gibbs b Kallis	15
SC Ganguly (capt)	c Kirsten b Kallis	14	c Boucher b Ntini	30
V Sehwag	b Pollock	105	b Pollock	31
*D Dasgupta	c Boucher b Pollock	34	c Boucher b Pollock	4
A Kumble	c Boucher b Kallis	6	lbw b Hayward	4
J Srinath	c Gibbs b Hayward	1	c McKenzie b Pollock	16
Z Khan	c Boucher b Pollock	0	c Boucher b Pollock	0
A Nehra	not out	0	not out	17
Extras	lb 7, w 7, nb 7	21	b 4, lb 8,nb 6	18
		379		**237**

	First innings							
	O	M	R	W				
Pollock	27	8	91	4	21.4	10	56	6
Hayward	20.3	5	70	3	23	8	74	2
Kallis	22	6	87	2	15	3	56	1
Ntini	14.4	2	71	1	10	3	39	1
Klusener	6	1	32	–				
Boje	5	1	21	–				

Fall of Wickets
1-74, 2-43, 3-51, 4-68, 5-288, 6-351, 7-372, 8-378, 9-379
1-29, 2-108, 3-108, 4-154, 5-188, 6-195, 7-202, 8-206, 9-206

SOUTH AFRICA

	First innings		Second innings	
HH Gibbs	c Khan b Srinath	107	lbw b Kumble	1
G Kirsten	b Kumble	73	not out	30
JH Kallis	c Laxman b Nehra	68	not out	21
ND McKenzie	lbw b Kumble	68		
HH Dippenaar	b Srinath	20		
L Klusener	c & b Kumble	108		
SM Pollock (capt)	c Das b Srinath	0		
*MV Boucher	c Dravid b Srinath	47		
N Boje	c Dasgupta b Nehra	6		
M Ntini	c Dasgupta b Srinath	23		
M Hayward	not out	0		
Extras	b 12, lb 11, w 4, nb 16	43	nb2	2
		563	(1 wicket)	**54**

	First innings				Second innings			
	O	M	R	W	O	M	R	W
Srinath	33	6	140	5	5	1	13	–
Nehra	22	3	121	2	3	0	9	–
Khan	26	7	98	–	2.4	0	9	–
Kumble	50	12	132	3	4	0	23	1
Tendulkar	7	0	27	–				
Sehwag	5	0	22	–				

Fall of Wickets
1-189, 2-197, 3-327, 4-359, 5-377, 6-377, 7-498, 8-517, 9-548
1-6

Umpires: EAR Silva & DL Orchard
Toss: South Africa
Test Debut: D Dasgupta, V Sehwag
Man of the Match: SM Pollock

South Africa won by nine wickets

SECOND TEST
16–20 November 2001 at Port Elizabeth
By Telford Vice

Mike Denness has been long retired as a player, but there was something amiss with him not being named, for better or worse, Man of the Match after an extraordinary game in which events off the field, and even thousands of kilometres away, assumed greater importance than what happened between the boundaries.

India showed fine character in forcing a draw despite the storm unleashed above their heads after Denness found six of their players had transgressed the International Cricket Council's (ICC) code of conduct. Among their number was the iconic Sachin Tendulkar, whom Denness found guilty of 'interfering with the match ball, thus changing its condition'. Tendulkar, a prince among players, a ball tamperer, a cheat? That was sure to inflame passions wherever cricket was cared about, and there was no surprise when it was reported that an effigy of Denness was being burned in India.

A press conference called on the final morning to announce Denness' decisions rapidly degenerated into farce. Denness was present, but refused to answer questions. Which prompted Ravi Shastri to ask: 'We know what he looks like – why is he here.' United Cricket Board (UCB) chief executive Gerald Majola was left to deal with the angry pack of reporters, whose annoyance was fuelled by the fact that the story had leaked early and consequently their editors were on their backs. 'I know where you're coming from.' Majola was reduced to bleating as the assembled media's heckles rose. 'Yes,' snapped veteran cricket writer Dicky Rutnagur. 'I'm from the *Daily Telegraph*.'

But the real fire was not ignited by Tendulkar's fate. He was one of five players handed fines and a suspended sentence. The sixth, Virender Sehwag, was banned for one match for dissent and intimidating the umpire. That put Sehwag out of the third Test, and raised the ire of Indian cricket supremo, Jagmohan Dalmiya.

Dalmiya threatened to pull his team out of the tour unless Denness was replaced, or unless the ICC agreed to hold his decisions in abeyance. Neither of Dalmiya's demands found favour at Lord's, and, for an awful moment, India's premature departure from South Africa was alarmingly imminent. The UCB, faced with a financial catastrophe if the third Test in Centurion did not go ahead, took a backward step in saying it would prevent Denness from fulfilling

His performance may have been overshadowed by events off the pitch, but Herschelle Gibbs sparkled during his innings of 196.

his duties at St George's Park. But ultimately the South African authorities followed a course of action suggested to them by none other than the ICC, who had rightly said the third Test would be unofficial if Sehwag took the field.

Sehwag was selected, the third Test was declared unofficial and South Africa were 1–0 series winners. The UCB appointed Dave Orchard as an umpire and Denis Lindsay as referee – largely, it seemed, to prevent further problems if the match was subsequently declared official – and a meaningless match ensued in Centurion.

It took Clive Lloyd to pull the bigger picture into focus: 'We've had the match-fixing scandal and we've just come back to normality. We could have done without this.' Such unpleasantness was unimaginable on a first day at St George's Park that saw Herschelle Gibbs' considerable talents on sparkling display. Saurav Ganguly's decision to put South Africa in perhaps had more to do with protecting his batsmen from the home side's seam attack on a green-tinged pitch than affording his attack the opportunity to make the most of the conditions.

But India made headway nonetheless. Javagal Srinath struck in the seventh over when he had Gary Kirsten caught in the slip cordon. Several near misses followed, and Kallis played on to Srinath five balls before lunch having scored 24 in a second-wicket stand of 70. Neil McKenzie was then bowled by a cunningly flighted delivery from Harbhajan Singh as South Africa slipped to 116 for 3.

Never one to let the pressure build, Gibbs was 56 not out at lunch. And there was no holding him back when the conditions eased in the afternoon and he was able to unfurl his full array of strokes – in particular a range of cut shots that grew more outrageous as his score mounted.

Like Kallis before him, Boeta Dippenaar was content to play second fiddle to Gibbs and he scored just 29 out of their partnership of 105. By the close, Gibbs had scored 155 out of South Africa's total of 237 for 5. He was dismissed 20 minutes

Veteran pace bowler, Javagal Srinath, took 6 for 76 in the South Africa innings of 376.

SECOND TEST – SOUTH AFRICA v. INDIA
16–20 November 2001 at Port Elizabeth

SOUTH AFRICA

	First innings		Second innings	
HH Gibbs	c Sehwag b Tendulkar	196	b Agarkar	12
G Kirsten	c Laxman b Srinath	4	c Laxman b Srinath	5
JH Kallis	b Srinath	24	not out	89
ND McKenzie	b Harbhajan Singh	12	c Dasgupta b Srinath	2
HH Dippenaar	c Dasgupta b Agarkar	29	c Sehwag b Harbhajan Singh	28
L Klusener	c Laxman b Srinath	9	c Sehwag b Harbhajan Singh	29
SM Pollock (capt)	c Harbhajan Singh b Srinath	3	not out	55
*MV Boucher	not out	68		
N Boje	lbw b Kumble	1		
M Ntini	c Das b Srinath	10		
M Hayward	b Srinath	0		
Extras	lb 2, nb 4	6	b 3, lb 3, nb 7	13
		362	(5 wickets dec.)	**233**

	First innings				Second innings			
	O	M	R	W	O	M	R	W
Srinath	30	6	76	6	17	9	28	2
Agarkar	22	2	85	1	23	3	71	1
Ganguly	2	0	21	–	5	0	17	–
Kumble	29	10	67	1	9	0	22	–
Harbhajan Singh	34	6	89	1	20	2	79	2
Tendulkar	4	0	22	1	4	0	10	–

Fall of Wickets
1-17, 2-87, 3-116, 4-221, 5-230, 6-244, 7-324, 8-325, 9-353
1-14, 2-22, 3-26, 4-91, 5-139

INDIA

	First innings		Second innings	
SS Das	lbw b Pollock	1	c Boucher b Pollock	0
*D Dasgupta	b Ntini	13	c Kallis b Hayward	63
R Dravid	b Pollock	2	c Boucher b Hayward	87
SR Tendulkar	c Klusener b Pollock	1	not out	22
SC Ganguly (capt)	b Pollock	42	not out	4
VVS Laxman	lbw b Pollock	89		
V Sehwag	c Kirsten b Kallis	13		
AB Agarkar	c Boucher b Kallis	1		
Harbhajan Singh	run out (Boucher)	0		
A Kumble	c Kirsten b Hayward	28		
J Srinath	not out	0		
Extras	b 3, w 2, nb 6	11	b 10, lb 7, w 1, nb 12	30
		201	(3 wickets)	**206**

	First innings				Second innings			
	O	M	R	W	O	M	R	W
Pollock	16	3	40	5	26	11	39	1
Hayward	17	5	45	1	25	6	58	2
Ntini	14	3	49	1	12	4	25	–
Kallis	10	2	50	2	11.2	5	15	–
Boje	4	2	8	–	14	4	33	–
Klusener	1	0	6	–	7	3	15	–
McKenzie					1	0	4	–

Fall of Wickets
1-5, 2-13, 3-15, 4-47, 5-69, 6-111, 7-119, 8-119, 9-199
1-0, 2-171, 3-184

Umpires: RB Tiffin & IL Howell
Toss: India
Man of the Match: HH Gibbs

Match drawn

before lunch the next day, cutting Tendulkar's fifth ball to gully, for 196.

Mark Boucher, who shared 80 runs for the seventh wicket with Gibbs, maintained the momentum with a quickfire 68 off 70 balls before South Africa were dismissed in the second over after lunch. Srinath wrapped up the tail to finish with 6 for 76.

Stumps found India on a mournful 182 for 8, and dependent on rearguard action by VVS Laxman and Anil Kumble.

Shaun Pollock crippled India's reply by removing Shiv Sunder Das, Rahul Dravid and Tendulkar in the space of the first 20 balls he bowled. India were dismissed in the eighth over of the third morning with Laxman trapped in front for a fighting 89 to earn Pollock his fifth wicket and complete an impressive display of tight seam bowling by the South African captain.

Kallis and Pollock then mounted the partnership South Africa needed to take control of the match. It swelled to an unbroken 94 before Pollock declared with a lead of 394, his decision complicated by light taking 14 overs from the third day and rain washing out almost the entire morning session of the fourth day.

Rain saw less than five overs bowled between lunch and tea, and light prevented a further 23 overs of play. That left India on 28 for 1 at the close, and not many would have bet on them surviving the final day after the dramas described above.

But makeshift opener Deep Dasgupta and Dravid showed steely composure and straight bats, and were entrenched until the second over before tea. Their stand endured for more than five hours and yielded 171 runs, and earned India grudging respect from the bristling South Africans.

UNOFFICIAL TEST – SOUTH AFRICA XI v. INDIA
23–27 November 2001 at Centurion
By Craig Ray

On a grey November morning, South African captain Shaun Pollock bowled the first delivery of the match against India at Centurion Park to Shiv Sunder Das, who let it go gently past to wicketkeeper Mark Boucher. If a passer-by had cast a cursory glance at the field there would have been nothing terribly unusual about the scene.

But beneath the tranquility of 13 players in white flannels gathered for a game of cricket, a massive political storm was raging in the corridors of power that was threatening to tear the sport apart.

What should have been the first ball of a thrilling Test series decider between two closely matched teams had become a farce. The fact that the players were on the field at all was a major achievement.

Pollock's first delivery handed South Africa a 1–0 series triumph, although there were still five days of cricket to be played on the ground in the outskirts of Pretoria.

It was a hollow victory claimed at the start of a desperately sad day for international cricket – a day when appeasement triumphed over common sense and, more tellingly, over the ethos of sport.

With the match stripped of its official Test status by the International Cricket Council (ICC) all records and statistics from the scorebook would be downgraded to first class.

It was an unprecedented move by the ICC, forced by the United Cricket Board of South Africa's (UCBSA) decision to remove English match referee Mike Denness and deny him access to the ground in an effort to appease the Board of Control for Cricket in India (BCCI).

Jacques Kallis' patient, five-hour 110 seemed irrelevant as a storm raged through cricket's governing body.

Denness had censured six Indian players during the drawn second Test in Port Elizabeth. The misdemeanours ranged from excessive appealing to dissent, but the punishment handed to India's star batsman Sachin Tendulkar was too much for the BCCI to bear. Tendulkar was accused of ball-tampering and subsequently handed a suspended one-match ban by Denness for his indiscretion while middle-order batsman Virender Sehwag was given a one-match ban.

Jagmohan Dalmiya, president of the BCCI, found the situation unacceptable and threatened to call off the tour if Denness was not removed from his post for the third Test.

The UCBSA were backed into a corner and opted to replace Denness with South African Denis Lindsay at Centurion Park leaving the ICC with little option but to strip the match of its Test status, despite calls by Dalmiya for the game to have its status reinstated at a later date.

So the rest of the tour and the unofficial Test went ahead in an almost surreal atmosphere, with South Africa duly winning at Centurion by an innings and 71 runs as news off the field overshadowed events on it.

The usual 'buzz' that surrounds a Test venue, the players dressing room and the press box on the first morning was glaringly absent as most present felt as if they had just been asked to take their sister to the prom.

Pollock won the toss and asked counterpart Rahul Dravid to bat. Dravid was making his first appearance as Indian captain following the late withdrawal of Saurav Ganguly who developed a mysterious shoulder injury between the final net on Thursday and the start of play on Friday.

India made three changes to the team from Port Elizabeth with debutant Connor Williams replacing Sehwag, left-arm fast bowler Ashish Nehra coming in for Ajit Agarkar and seamer Venkatesh Prasad taking over from Ganguly. South Africa made just one change by bringing in Pretoria youngster Jacques Rudolph for Boeta Dippenaar.

Das and Williams opened the batting, taking almost an hour before striking the first boundary. Williams was eventually dislodged for five by an in-swinging delivery from Lance Klusener which trapped him leg before. India went to lunch with only 44 runs on the board.

After the interval South Africa enjoyed the better of the mid-afternoon session as Jacques Kallis removed the dangerous Tendulkar for 27 and VVS Laxman for 14. This followed the dismissal of

Dravid soon after lunch, when fast bowler Makhaya Ntini had him lbw for five.

India survived to stumps on 221 for 8 forcing South Africa into the field for a second day.

They added just 11 runs on the second morning as Nantie Hayward claimed his fourth wicket of the innings by removing Nehra. The visitors were only nine down, but a hand injury to Javagal Srinath prevented him from batting.

South Africa's response was emphatic on a pitch that became easier to bat on as the day wore on. The home side posted a massive 566 for 8 thanks to some fine individual performances.

Gary Kirsten and Herschelle Gibbs put on 135 in a partnership for the first wicket which laid the foundations for a big score.

Gibbs scored 59 while Kirsten went on to score 90. But it was first Kallis and then Pollock who carried the match to a point where only South Africa could win.

Kallis scored a patient 110 which took nearly five hours to compile while Pollock blazed a brilliant 113 not out from just 109 balls in a little over two hours, which included nine fours and seven sixes.

It was one of the finest displays of clean ball striking seen in South Africa, but coming as it did in this match, it will be denied the honour of being added to Pollock's impressive Test batting statistics. With Ntini swinging merrily for 34 runs at the end, Pollock declared the innings closed after the third day with South Africa enjoying a 334-run first-innings lead.

With two days to go it appeared inevitable that the superior South African pace attack had the firepower to win the match by an innings.

But Williams and Das were defiant throughout the morning session on day four. Williams (42) was eventually caught by Kallis at slip off Klusener with the last ball of the 31st over with the total on 92. Das (48) followed 13 overs later, bowled by Pollock with the score on 116 as the innings started to unravel.

Rain brought an early end to the fourth day with Dravid and Tendulkar at the wicket giving the tourists hope of saving the match. But Dravid went for 23 on the fifth morning and Tendulkar, who was dropped by Kirsten when he had 16, eventually made 40 before being bowled by Ntini.

His wicket signalled a collapse as the rest of the India batting line-up tumbled quickly as South Africa won a match where the result was of little consequence.

SOUTH AFRICA XI v. INDIA
23–27 November 2001 at Centurion

INDIA

	First innings		Second innings	
SS Das	c Gibbs b Hayward	46	b Pollock	48
CC Williams	lbw b Klusener	5	c Kallis b Klusener	42
R Dravid (capt)	lbw b Ntini	5	b Hayward	23
SR Tendulkar	c Boucher b Kallis	27	b Ntini	40
VVS Laxman	c Kirsten b Kallis	14	c Gibbs b Ntini	23
*D Dasgupta	c Rudolph b Hayward	36	lbw b Kallis	27
A Kumble	b Hayward	27	c Boje b Pollock	8
Harbhajan Singh	run out (Ntini)	29	c Boucher b Hayward	30
J Srinath	retired hurt	8	absent injured	–
BKV Prasad	not out	11	absent injured	–
A Nehra	c Boje b Hayward	4	(9) not out	0
Extras	b 1, lb 12, nb 7	20	b 2, lb 11, nb 7	20
		232		**261**

	First innings				Second innings			
	O	M	R	W	O	M	R	W
Pollock	20	11	21	–	14	2	40	2
Hayward	28.4	8	74	4	17	3	61	2
Ntini	17	3	78	1	18	6	27	2
Klusener	12	6	11	1	12	6	30	1
Kallis	13	7	15	2	14.1	4	45	1
Boje	7	2	20	–	7	2	34	–
Rudolph					2	0	11	–

Srinath retired hurt at 210 for 7

Fall of Wickets
1-16, 2-49, 3-90, 4-100, 5-107, 6-158, 7-197, 8-221, 9-232
1-92, 2-116, 3-130, 4-188, 5-197, 6-212, 7-259, 8-261

SOUTH AFRICA

	First innings	
HH Gibbs	c Harbhajan Singh b Srinath	59
G Kirsten	c Dravid b Nehra	90
JA Rudolph	run out (sub: AB Agarkar/ Kumble)	21
JH Kallis	b Kumble	110
ND McKenzie	c Laxman b Tendulkar	33
L Klusener	c Laxman b Srinath	33
*MV Boucher	b Nehra	19
SM Pollock (capt)	not out	113
N Boje	st Dasgupta b Harbhajan Singh	20
M Ntini	not out	34
M Hayward		
Extras	b 11, lb 2, w 2, nb 14, pen 5	34
	(8 wickets dec.)	**566**

	First innings			
	O	M	R	W
Srinath	27	3	94	2
Nehra	30	5	123	2
Prasad	21	6	71	–
Harbhajan Singh	34.1	10	104	1
Kumble	34	4	102	1
Tendulkar	11	0	54	1

Fall of Wickets
1-135, 2-171, 3-195, 4-261, 5-321, 6-395, 7-395, 8-445

Umpires: RE Koertzen & DL Orchard
Toss: South African XI

South African XI won by an innings & 73 runs

TEST MATCH AVERAGES
South Africa v. India

SOUTH AFRICA

Batting	M	Inns	NO	HS	Runs	Av	100	50	c/st
MV Boucher	2	2	1	68*	115	115.00	–	1	11/-
JH Kallis	2	4	2	89*	202	101.00	–	2	3
HH Gibbs	2	4	0	196	316	79.00	2	–	2
L Klusener	2	3	0	108	146	48.66	1	–	1
G Kirsten	2	4	1	73	112	37.33	–	1	4
SM Pollock	2	3	1	55*	58	29.00	–	1	–
ND McKenzie	2	3	0	68	82	27.33	–	1	2
HH Dippenaar	2	3	0	29	77	25.56	–	–	–
M Ntini	2	2	0	23	33	16.50	–	–	–
N Boje	2	2	0	6	7	3.50	–	–	–

Also batted: M Hayward (2 Tests) 0*, 0

Bowling	Overs	Mds	Runs	Wkts	Av	Best	10m	5/inn
SM Pollock	90.4	32	226	16	14.12	6-56	1	2
M Hayward	85.3	24	247	8	30.87	3-70	–	–
JH Kallis	58.2	16	208	5	41.60	2-50	–	–

Also bowled: N Boje 23-7-62-0; L Klusener 14-4-53-0; ND McKenzie 1-0-4-0;
M Ntini 50.4-12-184-3

INDIA

Batting	M	Inns	NO	HS	Runs	Av	100	50	c/st
SR Tendulkar	2	4	1	155	193	64.33	1	–	–
VVS Laxman	2	3	0	89	150	50.00	–	4	4
V Sehwag	2	3	0	105	149	49.66	1	–	3
SC Ganguly	2	4	1	42	90	30.00	–	–	–
D Dasgupta	2	4	0	63	114	28.50	–	1	4
R Dravid	2	4	0	87	102	25.50	–	1	1
SS Das	2	4	0	62	72	18.00	–	1	2
A Kumble	2	3	0	28	38	12.66	–	–	1
J Srinath	2	3	1	16	17	8.50	–	–	–

Also batted in one Test: AB Agarkar 1; Harbhajan Singh 1 (1 ct); Z Khan 0, 0 (1 ct);
A Nehra 0*, 17*

Bowling	Overs	Mds	Runs	Wkts	Av	Best	10m	5/inn
J Srinath	85	22	257	13	19.76	6-76	–	2
A Kumble	92	22	244	5	48.80	3-132	–	–

Also bowled: AB Agarkar 45-5-156-2; SC Ganguly 7-0-38-0; Harbhajan Singh 54-8-168-3;
Z Khan 28.4-7-107-0; A Nehra 25-3-130-2; V Sehwag 5-0-22-0

AUSTRALIA IN SOUTH AFRICA

FIRST TEST
22–24 February 2002 at Johannesburg
By Marcus Prior

Any thoughts South Africa may have harboured that the Australians would be a different prospect on home soil were unceremoniously swept aside by a performance of overwhelming authority from the world champions.

After taking a 3–0 pummeling in Australia, the South Africans returned home in the knowledge that a drawn series would take them to the top of the world Test rankings, largely thanks to their 2000 series win in India. That they were totally unqualified for such a lofty status was underlined in bold at the Wanderers ground in Johannesburg.

The innings-and-360-run defeat handed out by Australia was the second largest margin of victory in the history of Test cricket, second only to the innings-and-579-run defeat England inflicted on the Australians at The Oval in 1938, when Len Hutton scored 364. But it was not so much the size of the defeat as the manner of South Africa's capitulation which was so disturbing for watching fans. South Africa lost 14 wickets on the Sunday to lose inside three days, the final nine second-innings wickets claimed in 14.3 overs for just 44 runs by the magnificent Glenn McGrath (five) and Shane Warne (four).

In mitigation? Captain Shaun Pollock was ruled out of the side after suffering a side strain in a provincial match on his return from Australia, leaving deputy Mark Boucher to stand in the breach. And once again the pre-Test period was bedeviled by controversy over selection. When Justin Ontong was ruled out with a hamstring injury, 12th man Graeme Smith and the serially unfortunate Jacques Rudolph might have considered themselves at the head of the queue, but black left-hander Ashwell Prince was called into the side instead. The fact that Prince was a high achiever on the domestic scene was conveniently brushed aside, however, by some of the country's more reactionary cricket commentators.

As if that were not distraction enough, South Africa then had to cope with the breakdown of Allan Donald on the first afternoon. When Donald, for so long the heart and soul of South Africa's attack, left the field on the shoulders of physiotherapist Craig Smith, it was hard to avoid the sense of a great career that had come to a shuddering end.

Donald's demise came only after he and all the other South African bowlers had taken a fearful hiding from the Australians when Steve Waugh won the toss and chose to bat first on a true Wanderers surface which still offered plenty of encouragement to the bowlers.

Matthew Hayden continued the sublime run of form that started in the first Test in Adelaide with his fourth consecutive hundred against the South Africans. In doing so, he joined compatriots Sir Donald Bradman, Jack Fingleton and Neil Harvey as well as Sunil Gavaskar, two other Sirs, Everton Weekes and Clyde Walcott, and Ken Barrington as the only players to have achieved the feat.

Hayden's hundred was the centrepiece of a day on which all the Australian top order contributed as the tourists closed on 331 for 5. Australia's continued supremacy proved too much for a few boorish individuals, who took it upon themselves to spit at Steve Waugh and throw beer over not out batsmen Damien Martyn and Adam Gilchrist as they headed for the dressing room.

But Martyn and Gilchrist would have their revenge on day two, and how sweet it must have

The magnificent Australian fast bowler, Glenn McGrath topped the bowling averages at the end of the series that Australia won 2–1.

tasted. The pair combined for a sixth-wicket stand of 317 – the second highest by any team in the history of Test cricket – as South Africa were put to the sword. Gilchrist led the charge, smashing the fastest double century of all time off just 212 balls, with 19 fours and eight sixes. Although New Zealand's Nathan Astle would soon surpass his record, the sheer contempt with which Gilchrist treated the South African attack was breathtaking.

As he and Martyn took 190 runs off the 27 overs between lunch and tea, Gilchrist took aim – in the middle of a Test match, no less – at a target set a hundred metres back in the crowd at deep midwicket. The prize for striking it was a gold bar worth over £80,000 and when one huge hit off the occasional medium pace of Neil McKenzie passed within inches as Gilchrist willed it on from the crease, South Africa's humiliation was complete.

Martyn took longer to join in the fun, but when he realized just how easily Gilchrist was picking off the South African bowlers, he decided on some belligerence and improvisation of his own. It brought him his second 50 in the space of just 37 balls and his fifth Test century.

Steve Waugh's declaration with Australia 652 for 7 and Gilchrist still cocking the trigger was as merciful as it was mercenary. It was also no more than a stay of execution.

By the close South Africa had limped to 111 for 4, with Prince defying his critics with a gutsy, unbeaten 47. However, Prince would add only two more runs on the third morning before aiming an injudicious slash at Jason Gillespie and seeing Matthew Hayden in the gully deny him a 50 on his Test debut. It would prove the highest score by any South African batsman in the match. The first innings folded swiftly and although Herschelle Gibbs (47) and Prince (28) briefly threatened a second-innings fightback, McGrath and Warne ruthlessly finished things off. 'I wasn't surprised. We bowled extremely well and South Africa bowled poorly,' Warne said after moving into second place on the all-time wicket-taker's list with 436, two ahead of Kapil Dev but still 83 behind Courtney Walsh. 'To make 600 on that wicket, South Africa bowled poorly. That was their problem in Australia as well.'

For the South Africans, it was next to impossible to find positives. Donald gone, perhaps for ever, selection still dogged by political controversy and the team vanquished as it had never been before. Only two months previously contenders for the crown of world champions, now they were desperate just to compete at all.

Adam Gilchrist, with an unbeaten 204, was in devastating form as 190 runs were scored by Australia in one session at the Wanderers.

FIRST TEST – SOUTH AFRICA v. AUSTRALIA
22–24 February 2002 at Johannesburg

AUSTRALIA

	First innings	
JL Langer	lbw b Donald	28
ML Hayden	c Boucher b Nel	122
RT Ponting	c Boucher b Nel	39
ME Waugh	c Boucher b Ntini	53
SR Waugh (capt)	c Gibbs b Kallis	32
DR Martyn	c Kirsten b Kallis	133
*AC Gilchrist	not out	204
SK Warne	c McKenzie b Boje	12
B Lee	not out	4
JN Gillespie		
GD McGrath		
Extras	b 2, lb 14, w 4, nb 5	25
	(7 wickets dec.)	652

	First innings			
	O	M	R	W
Donald	15.2	2	72	1
Ntini	33	8	124	1
Kallis	24	1	116	2
Nel	30.4	6	121	2
Boje	35	4	153	1
McKenzie	8	0	50	–

Fall of Wickets
1-46, 2-113, 3-224, 4-272, 5-293, 6-610, 7-643

SOUTH AFRICA

	First innings		Second innings	
HH Gibbs	lbw b Warne	34	st Gilchrist b Warne	47
G Kirsten	c Warne b McGrath	1	c Martyn b Gillespie	12
AG Prince	c Hayden b Gillespie	49	b Warne	28
JH Kallis	c Warne b Lee	3	c Gilchrist b McGrath	8
ND McKenzie	c Gillespie b McGrath	16	not out	27
HH Dippenaar	c Gilchrist b McGrath	2	lbw b Warne	1
*MV Boucher (capt)	c Gilchrist b Lee	23	b Warne	1
N Boje	c ME Waugh b Gillespie	0	c Ponting b McGrath	5
M Ntini	c SR Waugh b Lee	9	b McGrath	0
A Nel	lbw b Warne	7	c Langer b McGrath	0
AA Donald	not out	3	c Hayden b McGrath	0
Extras	b 4, lb 3, nb 5	12	w 1, nb 3	4
		159		133

	First innings				Second innings			
	O	M	R	W	O	M	R	W
McGrath	14	6	28	3	12.3	4	21	5
Gillespie	15	5	58	2	4	1	13	1
Warne	9	0	26	2	12	3	44	4
Lee	10	1	40	3	10	2	55	–

Fall of Wickets
1-11, 2-51, 3-55, 4-108, 5-113, 6-113, 7-114, 8-146, 9-155
1-20, 2-89, 3-98, 4-98, 5-107, 6-109, 7-122, 8-122, 9-122

Umpires: SA Bucknor & RE Koertzen
Toss: Australia
Test Debut: AG Prince (South Africa)
Man of the Match: AC Gilchrist

Australia won by an innings & 360 runs

SECOND TEST
8–12 March 2002 at Cape Town
By Marcus Prior

Despite a much-improved performance from the South Africans, Australia firmly closed the door on the series at Newlands and in the process ensured their continued status as world Test champions. For the first time in five Tests between the two sides, spectators were treated to a match of genuine ebb and flow, until Australia cruised home on the fifth day.

Shane Warne was named Man of the Match in a memorable 100th Test for the leg spinner. He bowled an astonishing 98 overs in the match – 70 of them in the South African second innings – taking eight wickets and chiming in with 63 at a crucial stage when Australia batted for the first time. Fittingly, he was there at the death, when Ricky Ponting pulled Paul Adams over square leg for six to bring up both his tenth Test century and Australia's victory by four wickets.

Ponting was the linchpin of a sterling Australian run chase, holding the batting together after Justin Langer (58) and Matthew Hayden (96) had shared 102 pulsating runs during a one-sided final session on day four. It was the perfect launch pad for what appeared a daunting target – the 331 runs Australia successfully chased was the tenth highest total to win a Test match. That they did it with such ease spoke powerfully of the place Steve Waugh's all-conquering side have already reserved for themselves in cricket history. Hayden fell four runs short of what would have been a century in five consecutive Tests, all against South Africa. Only Sir Donald Bradman (six), against England between 1936 and 1938, has managed more and Hayden was clearly disgusted with the manner of his dismissal, lured into chasing the widest of several deliberately tempting deliveries from Jacques Kallis and edging to wicketkeeper Mark Boucher.

Another easy Australian victory looked on the cards as early as the first day when South Africa, after winning the toss and deciding to bat, collapsed to 92 for 6 shortly after lunch. Only a street-fighting 70 on debut from all-rounder Andrew Hall took the home side past 200, although he was well supported by the unorthodox batting talents of Paul Adams in a stand of 69 for the eighth wicket.

Hall and the recalled Adams demonstrated the kind of never-say-die attitude that many thought had deserted the South Africans, no more so than with the withdrawal of Daryll Cullinan from the side shortly before the Test.

Recently appointed Australia's one-day captain, Ricky Ponting steered his team to victory in the second Test at Cape Town.

Cullinan had won a recall to the national team and in Shaun Pollock's continued absence was even tipped to skipper the South Africans, but refused to play when his demand for a full year's contract was dismissed out of hand by Cricket Board chief executive, Gerald Majola.

Cullinan was a contrary figure for much of his career, and will now be remembered in South Africa as the man who spurned the opportunity to help his country when they needed him most. It also opened the door to his fiercest critics, who claimed the classy right-hander was simply afraid of the Australians, and Warne in particular, against whom he has a career average of only 12.75. Australia's reply was given a familiarly rapid start before the close as Hayden and Langer smashed their way to 46 without loss amidst a deluge of boundaries. Day two would be a different matter, however, as Adams found a probing length and two wickets for both him and Makhaya Ntini saw Australia stutter to 185 for 6.

Enter Adam Gilchrist. As if the South Africans were not sick of the sight of the Australian wicketkeeper after his blitzkrieg double hundred in Johannesburg two weeks earlier, Gilchrist set about a demolition job equally as destructive and demoralizing. With Warne his sidekick, Gilchrist added 132 for the seventh wicket and then plundered 63 of the last 65 runs as South Africa finally dismissed Australia for 382. Gilchrist finished on 138 not out off 108 balls, striking 22 crisp fours and a pair of sixes.

South Africa's second effort with the bat was out of context with almost everything that had preceded it in the series. Gritty and defiant throughout, all the top order made runs, Gary Kirsten (87) and Herschelle Gibbs (39) at last getting the innings off to a good start with a fluent partnership worth 84 for the first wicket.

20-year-old debutant Graeme Smith made up for his first-innings failure with a mature and composed 68, while Kallis struck an authoritative 73 before he was one of six victims for Warne. On the fourth morning, when South Africa resumed on 307 for 4, Neil McKenzie gave every impression that he was the man to reach three figures before he attempted a very tight single on 99 and was superbly run out by a direct hit from Damien Martyn at cover.

Almost from the start, Warne toiled into the rough outside the right-hander's leg stump, probing away with remarkable control and waiting for a lapse in concentration. It was a phenomenal effort from the slimline 32-year-old, who saw fit to give up beer, pizza and chips in a bid to prolong his career at the highest level.

Warne's 70 overs in the South African second innings were 15 more than he had ever bowled before and afterwards he admitted to being absolutely exhausted, comparing his efforts to a big night out when waiting for a second wind to keep him going for a little longer.

In defiance of Warne's labours, Adams again staged a hugely entertaining last stand with the bat to finish unbeaten on 23 as South Africa claimed a 330-run lead. On most grounds, in most conditions and against most sides it would have been more than ample, but against Steve Waugh's Australians it was probably 30 or 40 runs short of what they required.

Ponting's match-winning knock was well timed, too. Only recently appointed captain of the one-day side at the expense of Steve Waugh to the surprise of many, it was an innings of both courage and maturity. There was a very real sense of a changing of the guard.

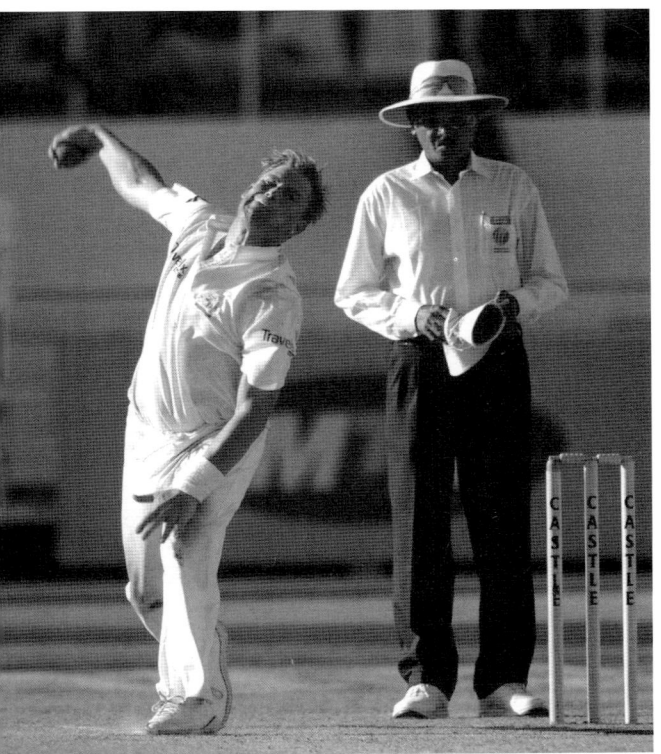

SECOND TEST – SOUTH AFRICA v. AUSTRALIA
8–12 March 2002 at Cape Town

SOUTH AFRICA

	First innings		Second innings	
HH Gibbs	c ME Waugh b Gillespie	12	c Ponting b Warne	39
G Kirsten	c ME Waugh b Lee	7	lbw b Lee	87
GC Smith	c Ponting b McGrath	3	c Gilchrist b Warne	68
JH Kallis	c Gilchrist b McGrath	23	lbw b Warne	73
ND McKenzie	b Warne	20	run out (Martyn)	99
AG Prince	c Gilchrist b McGrath	10	c Ponting b Warne	20
*MV Boucher (capt)	c Gilchrist b Lee	26	lbw b Gillespie	37
AJ Hall	c Gilchrist b Gillespie	70	run out (Lee/Gillespie)	0
PR Adams	c Warne b Gillespie	35	not out	23
M Ntini	c ME Waugh b Warne	14	c Langer b Warne	11
D Pretorius	not out	5	c ME Waugh b Warne	0
Extras	b 5, lb 5, nb 4	14	b 8, lb 3, w 2, nb 3	16
		238		**473**

	First innings				Second innings			
	O	M	R	W	O	M	R	W
McGrath	20	4	42	3	25	7	56	–
Gillespie	15	4	52	3	29	10	81	1
Lee	16	1	64	2	22	3	99	1
Warne	28	10	70	2	70	15	161	6
ME Waugh	1	0	1	–	9	3	34	–
Martyn					4	0	15	–
SR Waugh					3	0	16	–

Fall of Wickets
1-15, 2-18, 3-25, 4-70, 5-73, 6-92, 7-147, 8-216, 9-229
1-84, 2-183, 3-254, 4-284, 5-350, 6-431, 7-433, 8-440, 9-464

AUSTRALIA

	First innings		Second innings	
JL Langer	b Ntini	37	b Pretorius	58
ML Hayden	c Hall b Kallis	63	c Boucher b Kallis	96
RT Ponting	c Boucher b Adams	47	not out	100
ME Waugh	c Gibbs b Ntini	25	c Boucher b Ntini	16
SR Waugh (capt)	b Adams	0	b Adams	14
DR Martyn	c Boucher b Ntini	2	lbw b Adams	0
*AC Gilchrist	not out	138	c McKenzie b Kallis	24
SK Warne	c Kallis b Adams	63	not out	15
B Lee	c Prince b Adams	0		
JN Gillespie	c Kallis b Adams	0		
GD McGrath	lbw b Ntini	2		
Extras	b 2, lb 1, w 2	5	lb 6, nb 5	11
		382	**(6 wickets)**	**334**

	First innings				Second innings			
	O	M	R	W	O	M	R	W
Ntini	22.5	5	93	4	24	4	90	1
Pretorius	11	1	72	–	14	5	60	1
Kallis	16	1	65	2	17	2	68	2
Hall	11	1	47	–	3	0	6	–
Adams	20	1	102	4	21.1	0	104	2

Fall of Wickets
1-67, 2-130, 3-162, 4-168, 5-176, 6-185, 7-317, 8-338, 9-343
1-102, 2-201, 3-251, 4-268, 5-268, 6-305

Umpires: SA Bucknor & RE Koertzen
Toss: South Africa
Test Debut: AJ Hall, D Pretorius, GC Smith (South Africa)
Man of the Match: SK Warne

Australia won by four wickets

South Africa made Australia work harder for their wickets at Newlands, but Shane Warne finished with 6 for 161.

THIRD TEST
15–18 March 2002 at Durban
by Telford Vice

Mike Procter could not quite come to terms with it all. 'We didn't used to get 28 wickets in the first two days even when we didn't cut the grass on this pitch,' he said, his bafflement tempered by fond memories of the days when his venomous pace and Kingsmead's snakepit pitch were a lethal combination.

The surface prepared for this match was fair-minded, and while venomous bowlers lurked in both teams, the quality of the batsmen ranged against them should have ensured a contest. But only on what became the final morning did bat rule ball, and only because by then Australia's bowlers could no longer fool themselves that this match mattered to them. It ended 30 minutes before the scheduled lunch interval on the fourth day when Mark Boucher swept Mark Waugh over midwicket for six. South Africa's total of 340 for 5 was their highest winning score, and it surpassed the 332 for 7 England made in Melbourne in 1928–29 as the most successful run chase against Australia.

Such bits and bobs, significant though they will be to the game's statisticians, were cold comfort to the South Africans. The hidings they were dealt by Australia in the previous five Tests that the teams contested in the southern summer made this a hollow victory. South Africa had embarked for Australia in December regarded, officially and in more sensible circles, as the game's second-best team and in with a real chance of usurping the unchallenged world champions. Alas, by the time the series arrived in Durban, that theory would not have made it onto even J.R.R. Tolkien's wish list.

'Some of us have realized that you can never be bigger than the game itself – we wanted to restore the pride in playing for your country that should always be there,' Boucher said after the match, a clear clue to solving the mystery of where South Africa had gone so comprehensively wrong.

Boucher put Australia in to bat, a decision that furrowed many a brow. They were dismissed for 315, which would seem an indication that Boucher had got it wrong. However, that was Australia's lowest total in the six Test matches at that stage, and it was the first time South Africa had bowled them out in less than three sessions.

David Terbrugge, who last played in a Test against West Indies three years previously, shared the new ball with Makhaya Ntini and was welcomed back to the top flight when he pitched his first delivery of the match outside the off stump of Justin Langer, who mistimed his pull shot and was caught at square leg.

Neil McKenzie held a sharp, low chance at second slip as Jacques Kallis removed Matthew Hayden for 26, but Ricky Ponting and Mark Waugh stifled South African hopes of making further headway with a partnership that swelled to 108 before Ponting carelessly coasted home after Waugh drove Kallis into the covers and was run out by the swooping Herschelle Gibbs.

Ponting's 89 was packed with cameo cuts and pulls, but he should have made more of his opportunity. Ditto Waugh, who edged a drive off Kallis to the slips. Steve Waugh then misread Paul Adams' chinaman to be caught behind and cost Australia their third wicket in seven overs.

And then came Adam Gilchrist, that whirlwind cunningly disguised as a wicketkeeper-batsman. He saw Australia safely past 300, with his trademark blitzkrieg strokeplay, before heaving Adams to deep square leg nine runs short of a century. South Africa would have been significantly more content with their day's work had Gary Kirsten not been caught behind when the fingertips of his glove brushed a legside delivery from Brett Lee – the penultimate ball of the day, as dictated by fading light.

The second day was as close to madness as cricket should be allowed to venture. Seventeen wickets fell

on a sound batting pitch, and to bowling which, while steady, was not exceptional. When the angel dust cleared, Australia's lead stood at 307. Warne and Lee took four wickets each, with the latter profiting from two brilliant catches. Nightwatchman Adams fell to the first, by Hayden in the gully who somehow snared the ball with his left hand after it had seemed fully a yard past him.

The second was even more spectacular, as Damien Martyn at point leapt high and extended his right arm to try and catch Neil McKenzie's hard-hit cut shot. The ball swerved away from Martyn, but just as it was about to veer out of reach he stabbed out his left arm to secure a magical catch.

Gibbs scored an at-times-sublime half-century, but seven balls after raising his bat in acknowledgement he drove loosely at Jason Gillespie's away-swinger to be caught behind. South Africa were dismissed midway through the second session having lost their last five wickets for 48 runs. Australia followed that dubious lead, and by the close they were 159 for 8.

Only Steve Waugh looked like a batsman who had taken guard in a Test match before. Ntini had him well held by Kallis at second slip in the seventh over of the third morning to end two-and-a-half hours of defiance, and the fast bowler's next delivery pitched on middle stump to clip the top of off and bowl Glenn McGrath.

That left South Africa needing to score 335 to win, but Gibbs and Kirsten eased their concern about the monumental task that seemed to lay ahead with a partnership of 142, the first century stand in the six Tests by South Africa.

It was ended in reckless fashion when indecision saw Kirsten run out for 64, but Gibbs refused to be rattled and went on to his sixth Test century. Graeme Smith showed good composure to help Gibbs add 74 before he skied Mark Waugh to Gilchrist. Waugh struck again in his next over to have Gibbs caught at deep midwicket for 104, and when McKenzie spooned Warne to midwicket, South Africa had lost three wickets for 16 runs.

Kallis and Ashwell Prince halted the slide with disciplined batting, and at stumps South Africa were 71 runs away. Had the series still been alive, the fourth day would have been breathless with tension. But Kallis and Prince were not subjected to anything more than the usual pressures as they set about reeling in the target.

Their stand had reached 99 when Prince pushed forward to a leg break from Warne and was caught at slip for 48. Four runs were needed to finish the job, and Boucher went two better than that.

THIRD TEST – SOUTH AFRICA v. AUSTRALIA
15–18 March 2002 at Durban

AUSTRALIA

	First innings		Second innings	
JL Langer	c Kirsten b Terbrugge	11	c Boucher b Terbrugge	18
ML Hayden	c McKenzie b Kallis	28	c Prince b Terbrugge	0
RT Ponting	run out (Gibbs)	89	c Terbrugge b Ntini	34
ME Waugh	c Smith b Kallis	45	b Kallis	30
SR Waugh (capt)	c Boucher b Adams	7	c Kallis b Ntini	42
DR Martyn	b Terbrugge	11	c Boucher b Kallis	0
*AC Gilchrist	c Smith b Adams	91	c Boucher b Kallis	16
SK Warne	c Boucher b Ntini	26	c McKenzie b Adams	13
B Lee	b Ntini	0	(10) not out	23
JN Gillespie	c Boucher b Hall	1	(9) c Kallis b Adams	3
GD McGrath	not out	4	b Ntini	0
Extras	w 2	2	b 1, lb 3, w 1, nb 2	7
		315		**186**

	O	M	R	W	O	M	R	W
Ntini	20	3	87	2	17	2	65	3
Terbrugge	16	2	61	2	4	1	21	2
Kallis	20	3	95	2	11	2	29	3
Hall	9.1	2	35	1	4	1	20	-
Adams	9	0	37	2	13	0	47	2

Fall of Wickets
1-11, 2-61, 3-169, 4-178, 5-182, 6-230, 7-287, 8-289, 9-311
1-4, 2-19, 3-77, 4-90, 5-90, 6-114, 7-128, 8-150, 9-186

SOUTH AFRICA

	First innings		Second innings	
G Kirsten	c Gilchrist b Lee	21	(2) run out (Martyn/Lee)	64
HH Gibbs	c Gilchrist b Gillespie	51	(1) c Martyn b ME Waugh	104
PR Adams	c Hayden b Lee	6		
GC Smith	c Gilchrist b McGrath	1	(3) c Gilchrist b ME Waugh	42
JH Kallis	c & b Warne	16	(4) not out	61
ND McKenzie	c Martyn b Lee	25	(5) c Hayden b Warne	4
AG Prince	c Lee b Warne	0	(6) c ME Waugh b Warne	48
*MV Boucher (capt)	c & b Warne	0	(7) not out	8
AJ Hall	not out	27		
M Ntini	c McGrath b Warne	14		
DJ Terbrugge	c Gilchrist b Lee	0		
Extras	lb 1, w 1, nb 4	6	lb 2, w 2, nb 5	9
		167	(5 wickets)	**340**

	O	M	R	W	O	M	R	W
McGrath	11	4	26	1	28	11	54	-
Lee	17.2	1	82	4	20	2	75	-
Gillespie	14	6	25	1	15	2	58	-
Warne	13	4	33	4	30	6	108	2
ME Waugh					11.5	1	43	2

Fall of Wickets
1-48, 2-74, 3-75, 4-85, 5-109, 6-119, 7-119, 8-148, 9-167
1-142, 2-216, 3-218, 4-232, 5-331

Umpires: S Venkataraghavan & DL Orchard
Toss: South Africa
Man of the Match: HH Gibbs
Player of the Series: AC Gilchrist

South Africa won by five wickets

Left: Finally, at their sixth attempt, South Africa managed to defeat Australia at Durban where Herschelle Gibbs followed his first innings 51 with 104.

TEST MATCH AVERAGES
South Africa v. Australia

SOUTH AFRICA

Batting	M	Inns	NO	HS	Runs	Av	100	50	c/st
AJ Hall	2	3	1	70	97	48.50	-	1	1
HH Gibbs	3	6	0	104	287	47.83	1	1	2
ND McKenzie	3	6	1	99	191	38.20	-	1	4
JH Kallis	3	6	1	73	184	36.80	-	2	4
G Kirsten	3	6	0	87	192	32.00	-	2	2
PR Adams	2	3	1	35	64	32.00	-	-	-
GC Smith	2	4	0	68	114	28.50	-	1	2
AG Prince	3	6	0	49	155	25.83	-	-	2
MV Boucher	3	6	1	37	95	19.00	-	-	13/-
M Ntini	3	5	0	14	48	9.60	-	-	-

Also batted in one Test: N Boje 0, 5; HH Dippenaar 2, 1; AA Donald 3*, 0; A Nel 7, 0;
D Pretorius 5*, 0; DJ Terbrugge 0 (1 ct)

Bowling	Overs	Mds	Runs	Wkts	Av	Best	10m	5/inn
PR Adams	63.1	1	290	10	29.00	4-102	-	-
JH Kallis	88	9	373	11	33.90	3-29	-	-
M Ntini	116.5	22	459	11	41.72	4-93	-	-

Also bowled: N Boje 35-4-153-1; AA Donald 15.2-2-72-1; AJ Hall 27.1-4-108-1;
ND McKenzie 8-0-50-0; A Nel 30.4-6-121-2; D Pretorius 25-6-132-1; DJ Terbrugge 20-3-82-4

AUSTRALIA

Batting	M	Inns	NO	HS	Runs	Av	100	50	c/st
AC Gilchrist	3	5	2	204*	473	157.66	2	1	13/1
RT Ponting	3	5	1	100*	309	77.25	1	1	4
ML Hayden	3	5	0	122	309	61.80	1	2	4
ME Waugh	3	5	0	53	169	33.80	-	1	6
SK Warne	3	5	1	63	129	32.25	-	1	5
JL Langer	3	5	0	58	152	30.40	-	1	2
DR Martyn	3	5	0	133	146	29.20	1	-	3
SR Waugh	3	5	0	42	95	19.00	-	-	1
B Lee	3	4	2	23*	27	13.50	-	-	1
GD McGrath	3	3	1	4*	6	3.00	-	-	1
JN Gillespie	3	3	0	3	4	1.33	-	-	1

Bowling	Overs	Mds	Runs	Wkts	Av	Best	10m	5/inn
GD McGrath	110.3	36	227	12	18.91	5-21	-	1
SK Warne	162	38	442	20	22.10	6-161	-	1
JN Gillespie	92	28	287	8	35.87	3-52	-	-
B Lee	95.2	10	416	10	41.60	4-82	-	-

Also bowled: DR Martyn 4-0-15-0; ME Waugh 21.5-4-78-2; SR Waugh 3-0-16-0

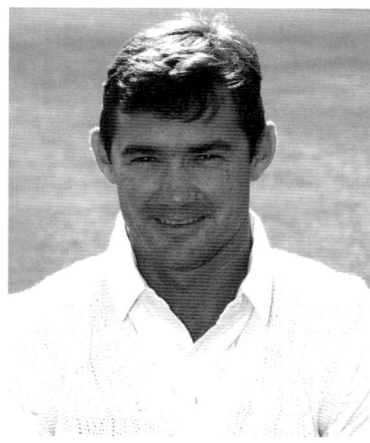

The Queenslander, Jimmy Maher played a major role in Australia's convincing 5–1 victory in the one-day internationals. He top scored with 95 at Centurion Park.

ONE–DAY INTERNATIONALS
By Telford Vice

Australia effortlessly shifted gear after their victorious Test series to ensure that South Africa also ate their dust in the seven-match one-day rubber, which the visitors won 5–1 (with one match tied). South Africa had, with the help of a spot of creative accounting by New Zealand, won the triangular tournament in Australia, despite losing three of their four matches against the world champions.

Once they were back home, however, there were no benevolent Black Caps or pernickety bonus-point systems to hide behind, and it seemed anything South Africa could do Australia could do demonstrably better. The point was best illustrated in the sixth match at St George's Park. South Africa put what seemed to be an insurmountable total of 326 for 3 on the board, the most runs scored against Australia in 501 one-day internationals. Undaunted, Australia replied with 330 for 7 to win with five balls to spare to record the highest successful run chase in one-day international history.

Australia held their nerve in the face of unfavourable odds to win that match, and it is worth pointing out that they had claimed the series by the time the circus pitched its big top in Port Elizabeth. Indeed, the Australians delivered performances in both the Test and one-day series that set benchmarks at least as important as those established by their 1948 vintage.

But it was also true that South Africa were beaten by a team other than the mighty Australians in this series: themselves. While their batting was competitive for the most part, their bowling and fielding often seemed bent on shooting itself in the foot. For example, Australia bowled six no-balls in the seven matches – South Africa sent down 44.

The hamstring injury that limited Lance Klusener's involvement to the first three matches did not help South Africa's cause, but neither did their selectors by inexplicably leaving out Allan Donald after he had returned to fitness in time to play in the final three games. Similarly, Ashwell Prince and David Terbrugge, who made a genuine difference in the Test series, were nowhere to be seen in the one-day games.

South Africa's batting failed to fire in the first two matches, in which Australia had been restricted to sub-par totals, and the third was tied due largely to Shaun Pollock's wooden captaincy. The home side's bowling, their perennial strength, became their most crippling weakness in the next three matches as they lost all semblance of line and length. They regrouped admirably to win the last game at a wet Newlands, though by then the Australians were probably more concerned with their duty-free shopping lists than matters at hand. In fact, by the end of the series, what was not long ago the game's most disciplined, hardest and most-respected limited-overs side had been battered into an amoebic mess. Australia, ably led by Ricky Ponting, who also set a blazing example with the bat, were only too pleased to inherit the mantle.

Match One
22 March 2002 at Johannesburg
Australia 223 for 8 (50 overs)
South Africa 204 (44.4 overs) (L Klusener 83, HH Dippenaar 51)
Australia won by 19 runs
Man of the Match: JN Gillespie

Match Two
24 March 2002 at Centurion
Australia 226 for 8 (50 overs) (JP Maher 95, SM Pollock 4 for 32)
South Africa 181 (46.2 overs) (L Klusener 59, JN Gillespie 4 for 43)
Australia won by 45 runs
Man of the Match: JP Maher

Match Three
27 March 2002 at Potchefstroom
South Africa 259 for 7 (50 overs) (JN Rhodes 83, JH Kallis 71, B Lee 4 for 45)
Australia 259 for 9 (50 overs) (ML Hayden 78, M Ntini 4 for 33)
Match tied
Man of the Match: JP Maher

Match Four
30 March 2002 at Bloemfontein
Australia 290 for 6 (50 overs) (RT Ponting 129)
South Africa 253 (48.1 overs) (ND McKenzie 67, JN Rhodes 56, B Lee 4 for 63)
Australia won by 37 runs
Man of the Match: RT Ponting

Match Five
3 April 2002 at Durban (floodlit)
South Africa 267 for 6 (50 overs) (JN Rhodes 76)
Australia 271 for 2 (47.5 overs) (AC Gilchrist 105, ML Hayden 59)
Australia won by eight wickets
Man of the Match: AC Gilchrist

It was a rare event to see a South African smiling, but Makhaya Ntini's four wickets at Potchefstroom enabled his team to tie the third match.

Match Six
6 April 2002 at Port Elizabeth
South Africa 326 for 3 (50 overs) (GC Smith 84, JH Kallis 80*, JN Rhodes 71*)
Australia 330 for 7 (49.1 overs) (RT Ponting 92, DS Lehmann 91, AC Gilchrist 52)
Australia won by three wickets
Man of the Match: AC Gilchrist

Match Seven
9 April at Cape Town (floodlit)
South Africa 249 for 7 (39 overs) (GC Smith 73)
Australia 185 (32.3 overs) (MG Bevan 55, N Boje 5 for 21)
South Africa won by 65 runs
(DL Method: Australia target 251 from 39 overs)
Man of the Match: N Boje
Player of the Series: RT Ponting

SOUTH AFRICA DOMESTIC FIRST-CLASS CRICKET – SUPERSPORT SERIES 2001–02
By Telford Vice

Had the final at Kingsmead not had the obvious strings attached, Kwazulu-Natal would have deserved more of the criticism launched at them after they drained the life from what should have been the showpiece of the domestic summer. However, Northerns had to win the final to claim the championship – a draw would do for Kwazulu-Natal because they had led the standings after the second stage of league competition.

Who could blame Kwazulu-Natal when they duly engineered a stalemate, particularly as they did so only once their prospects of winning faded. But blame there was in abundance. 'What happened was an absolute disgrace and a pathetic advertisement for cricket,' said no less than Western Province and South Africa A captain HD Ackerman. Spectators trickled out of Kingsmead on the penultimate fourth day – which ended with Kwazulu-Natal 415 runs ahead – vowing never to return.

Lo and behold, they were back the next afternoon applauding Kwazulu-Natal captain Dale Benkenstein as he held the trophy aloft. Perhaps they realized overnight that it was difficult to push for a win on a pitch that refused to deteriorate, with an out-of-form spinner and with Kingsmead's history of producing stupendous fourth innings.

Ackerman's sourness could have had much to do with Kwazulu-Natal beating his team at Newlands in a match that, had it gone the other way, would have put Western Province in the final. The Cape Town game was not short on acrimony, what with the Province Board citing Lance Klusener after his attempt to run out Thami Tsolekile – or more likely to drive him back into his crease – ended with the ball striking the batsman. Klusener apologized immediately, but that was not enough for Province, and the all-rounder was fined R5,000 (about 315 pounds) at a disciplinary hearing. Curiously, neither umpire deemed the Klusener-Tsolekile incident worthy of a written report.

Northerns reached the final on the back of a fine season by Martin van Jaarsveld, who scored 934 runs at an average of 84 with four centuries and three half-centuries. He was deservedly named 'Cavalier', or the Player of the Season. The other contender for that honour was Kwazulu-Natal spearhead Nixon McLean, who took 44 wickets at 16.

Both featured prominently in the final, with van Jaarsveld the epitome of judicious, patient batting for his 155 in Northerns' first innings of 286 scored in reply to Kwazulu-Natal's 214. McLean took 6 for 84 despite bowling off less than half his normal run because of an injured hamstring.

Northerns' lead of 72 looked significant. However, Jonty Rhodes, who scored 74 in the first innings and later said he believed he was playing the cricket of his life, all but took the match and the title away from the visitors with an innings of 154 that would have been snuffed out for ten had the delivery that bowled him not been a no-ball.

Rhodes set the scene for Benkenstein to score a career-best 259, and for Kwazulu-Natal to total 754 – more than any other South African team in a first-class match.

'Come on boys,' Neil McKenzie urged his Northerns team-mates as the match crawled to its conclusion, 'a wicket always falls on 702!'

Would that his joke is caught by administrators who are blind to the idiocy of staging a final after months of hard league competition. But that is a false hope, for the sponsors are also the broadcasters: the real authorities.

SOUTH AFRICA DOMESTIC ONE-DAY CRICKET – THE STANDARD BANK CUP, 2001–02
By Marcus Prior

The question of who was South Africa's premier one-day side was answered in emphatic style for the second year in succession by the KwaZulu-Natal Dolphins as they swept aside the challenge of Western Province in a final played on their home ground. Unbeaten throughout the entire competition, Dale Benkenstein's team swept all before them and no one could argue whether or not they were deserved winners.

In fact, Western Province were the only side who ever looked as though they could muscle in on KwaZulu-Natal's party and in 20-year-old left-handed batsman Graeme Smith, they also possessed the man of the tournament.

Smith showed the kind of form which soon after the final saw him called into the South African Test side, amassing 738 runs in 12 innings, including a century and seven 50s, the runs coming at an average of 67.09. As an added bonus, Smith also claimed 19 wickets with his teasing, but expensive, off spin, only one short of the top wicket-taker in the competition, team-mate Roger Telemachus.

Western Province's passage to the final was sealed with an 89-run victory over North West in Cape Town, where Smith contributed 117 not out. The first match of the three-leg final in Potchefstrom was won almost single-handedly by Lloyd Ferreira, who anchored a tricky run chase with a magnificently belligerent 134 off 117 balls with 15 fours and two sixes. As the innings of the tournament it was hard to beat.

The Dolphins were clinical in seeing off Eastern Province in their own semi-final, winning a Duckworth-Lewis-engineered first match in Port Elizabeth by 17 runs, before returning home and winning again by 16 runs. That neither side required a deciding match to claim their place in the final spoke volumes for their all-round superiority.

Dale Benkenstein's international career has faltered, but he led Kwazulu-Natal to honours in both the first-class and domestic competitions.

FIRST-CLASS AVERAGES
South Africa

BATTING

	M	Inns	NO	HS	Runs	Av	100	50
M van Jaarsveld	11	19	2	182*	1268	74.58	5	5
JN Rhodes	5	8	0	172	499	62.37	2	2
JH Kallis	6	11	3	110	496	62.00	1	4
DM Benkenstein	8	12	0	259	713	59.41	3	1
G Kirsten	7	13	1	244	710	59.16	1	5
HD Ackerman	10	16	4	140*	695	57.91	2	4
HH Gibbs	7	13	0	196	732	56.30	3	3
AG Puttick	9	16	3	229*	720	55.38	2	3
JA Beukes	7	12	2	105	528	52.80	2	2
HM Amla	8	12	2	103	516	51.60	1	5
AJ Hall	8	10	1	153	447	49.66	1	2
G Dros	9	14	3	117*	513	46.63	1	4
MI Gidley	8	16	2	215*	651	46.50	1	3
JJ van der Wath	8	11	4	113*	325	46.42	1	1
A Jacobs	6	10	0	197	463	46.30	2	1
JL Langer	5	8	0	161	370	46.25	1	1
SC Pope	8	15	2	131	591	45.46	1	4
RG Arendse	8	11	2	95	409	45.44	-	4
GC Smith	9	16	1	156	679	45.26	2	2
JA Rudolph	12	21	2	164	839	44.15	3	1
JC Adams	8	12	1	124*	479	43.54	2	1
GFJ Liebenberg	8	14	1	158	554	42.61	2	2
L Klusener	6	8	0	108	340	42.50	1	2
AM Bacher	9	17	0	132	711	41.82	3	3
W Bossenger	6	11	2	124*	364	40.44	1	2
JM Otto	8	15	2	143	524	40.30	2	1
P de Bruyn	7	10	1	185	358	39.77	1	1
BH Tucker	8	16	1	110	561	37.40	1	2
PC Strydom	7	12	2	135*	373	37.30	1	2
DJ Callaghan	7	14	1	100	484	37.23	1	3
DJ Watson	8	14	2	153	439	36.58	1	2
AJ Seymore	9	13	0	89	474	36.46	-	4
H Davids	9	16	3	83	468	36.00	-	5
JA Morkel	7	10	1	87*	324	36.00	-	3
AN Petersen	8	14	1	147	466	35.84	1	3
HH Dippenaar	9	14	2	102*	427	35.58	2	-
LL Bosman	9	15	0	121	527	35.13	1	3
CC Bradfield	7	14	0	80	490	35.00	-	5
JG Myburgh	7	12	1	65	384	34.90	-	4
DJJ de Vos	9	16	1	102	521	34.73	1	3
ND McKenzie	8	13	1	99	416	34.66	-	3
JG Strydom	9	16	1	120	501	33.40	2	2
ELR Stewart	7	10	2	114*	262	32.75	1	-
PPJ Koortzen	8	15	1	164	454	32.42	1	1
D Jennings	8	10	2	67	256	32.00	-	1
WA Dugmore	4	8	0	95	256	32.00	-	3
IJL Trott	8	14	1	93	415	31.92	-	4
ML Bruyns	8	15	1	102*	444	31.71	1	1
BL Reddy	8	11	2	109	262	29.11	1	1
AM Amla	7	9	0	75	259	28.77	-	2
JDC Bryant	7	14	1	90	374	28.76	1	3
LJ Koen	8	12	0	86	343	28.58	-	2
DJ Jacobs	9	17	0	123	484	28.47	2	1
RJ Peterson	9	16	2	108	398	28.42	1	2
MR Street	9	16	2	58*	376	26.85	-	2
JC Kent	6	10	0	92	266	26.60	-	1
CFK van Wyk	9	13	2	51	292	26.54	-	1
MV Boucher	7	11	2	68*	238	26.44	-	1
SC Cook	9	17	1	101*	409	25.56	1	2
AC Thomas	11	18	2	57*	400	25.00	-	3
J Louw	6	11	2	86*	225	25.00	-	1
MJ Powell	6	11	0	75	272	24.72	-	2
SJ Palframan	9	14	2	74*	291	24.25	-	2
MC Venter	9	16	0	85	381	23.81	-	3
BL Bennett	4	8	0	85	187	23.37	-	1
GV Grace	9	17	1	72	364	22.75	-	2
GH Bodi	10	17	1	58	359	22.43	-	2
TL Tsolekile	10	13	3	84	218	21.80	-	1
R Magiet	6	10	1	54	190	21.11	-	2
MR Benfield	5	9	0	39	182	20.22	-	-
JM Henderson	9	17	2	55	298	19.86	-	2
JM Kemp	5	10	1	56	175	19.44	-	2

FIRST-CLASS AVERAGES
South Africa

BATTING

	M	Inns	NO	HS	Runs	Av	100	50
J Botha	7	13	1	52	230	19.16	-	1
GA Roe	9	16	4	26	213	17.75	-	-
EO Moleon	9	16	0	38	281	17.56	-	-
S Abrahams	8	10	1	44	155	17.22	-	-
GT Love	8	13	0	73	209	16.07	-	2
GJP Kruger	7	12	3	26	143	15.88	-	-
T Henderson	6	9	1	45	126	15.75	-	-
TA Bula	7	12	3	39	136	15.11	-	-
M Ntini	8	12	2	34*	148	14.80	-	-
AK Kruger	7	12	2	54	146	14.60	-	1
S Elworthy	8	10	0	48	143	14.30	-	-
CE Eksteen	8	12	0	40	171	14.25	-	-
N Boje	9	11	0	46	144	13.09	-	-
R Bailey	9	12	0	28	146	12.16	-	-
DJ Terbrugge	10	12	3	26	103	11.44	-	-
U Abrahams	5	10	0	52	110	11.00	-	1
NAM McLean	8	12	2	28	109	10.90	-	-
VC Drakes	8	13	2	35	115	10.45	-	-

Qualification: 8 completed innings, average 10.00

BOWLING

	Overs	Mds	Runs	Wkts	Av	Best	10m	5/inn
KC Jackson	107.5	35	276	18	15.33	5-42	-	1
WR Visagie	65.1	23	185	12	15.41	5-49	-	1
NAM McLean	263.4	81	710	44	16.13	6-84	1	3
L Klusener	157.4	55	398	24	16.58	5-51	1	2
A Nel	327.2	97	769	46	16.71	6-25	-	3
SM Pollock	172.4	71	357	21	17.00	6-56	1	2
S Elworthy	321.4	84	942	52	18.11	6-45	1	3
CM Willoughby	333.2	95	849	44	19.29	6-44	-	1
CD de Lange	166.1	55	328	16	20.50	5-65	-	1
DH Townsend	102.5	32	287	14	20.50	4-27	-	-
AC Thomas	362.5	129	935	43	21.74	7-95	-	4
D Pretorius	300.2	70	981	42	23.35	6-49	-	4
MI Gidley	250.2	51	662	28	23.64	6-45	-	2
HS Williams	297.2	96	652	26	25.07	4-45	-	-
DJ Terbrugge	327.2	79	878	35	25.08	6-58	-	1
JA Morkel	173.2	45	477	19	25.10	5-53	-	1
RE Bryson	135.1	36	379	15	25.26	4-45	-	-
AJ Hall	179.5	48	516	20	25.80	5-97	-	1
WJ du Toit	206.2	41	624	24	26.00	5-98	-	1
ANW Tweedie	131.4	36	441	16	27.56	4-48	-	-
M Hayward	218.4	61	620	22	28.18	4-74	-	-
AG Botha	170	59	424	15	28.26	3-17	-	-
BB Kops	110.5	14	459	16	28.68	5-89	-	1
ZA Abrahim	316.5	73	832	29	28.68	5-67	-	1
PR Adams	289.5	45	883	30	29.43	4-54	-	-
JJ van der Wath	275.3	74	710	24	29.58	6-37	-	1
VC Drakes	291.3	78	742	25	29.68	5-25	-	1
B Lee	137.2	16	540	18	30.00	4-37	-	-
J Louw	153.1	28	423	14	30.21	4-33	-	-
CW Henderson	398.2	111	1066	35	30.45	5-129	-	1
N Boje	318	95	708	23	30.78	6-31	-	2
T Henderson	184.4	39	580	18	32.22	4-60	-	-
GJ Kruis	212	52	687	21	32.71	4-40	-	-
CE Eksteen	368	93	867	26	33.34	4-70	-	-
AC Dawson	317.2	99	835	25	33.40	4-27	-	-
JH Kallis	173.3	36	641	19	33.73	3-29	-	-
R Telemachus	156	31	484	14	34.57	3-62	-	-
P Joubert	222	72	590	17	34.70	4-23	-	-
GA Roe	310.3	109	769	22	34.95	5-47	-	1
M Ntini	273.3	57	987	28	35.25	6-37	-	1
JC Kent	127.1	38	354	10	35.40	2-23	-	-
J Botha	175	36	550	15	36.66	3-53	-	-
JM Kemp	167.3	32	517	14	36.92	5-60	-	1
M Zondeki	156.4	50	444	12	37.00	2-34	-	-
EO Moleon	212.5	53	713	19	37.52	5-60	-	1
JN Gillespie	132	42	387	10	38.70	3-52	-	-
GJP Kruger	244.5	38	864	22	39.27	5-139	-	1

FIRST-CLASS AVERAGES
South Africa

BOWLING

	Overs	Mds	Runs	Wkts	Av	Best	10m	5/inn
MF George	214.4	42	719	18	39.94	4-61	-	-
GT Love	366.1	89	971	24	40.45	4-79	-	-
RJ Peterson	232.2	42	814	20	40.70	4-9	-	-
JT Mafa	223.4	61	703	17	41.35	3-37	-	-
AK Kruger	155.4	26	592	14	42.28	4-87	-	-
DJJ de Vos	199.1	44	532	11	48.36	3-37	-	-
S Abrahams	256.5	65	731	15	48.73	3-35	-	-
GH Bodi	182	31	677	11	61.54	2-40	-	-

Qualification: 10 wickets in 8 innings

The following bowlers took 10 wickets in fewer than 8 innings:

	Overs	Mds	Runs	Wkts	Av	Best	10m	5/inn
HC Bakkes	104	44	184	13	14.15	3-25	-	-
GD McGrath	125.3	45	244	17	14.35	5-17	-	2
SK Warne	178	40	501	22	22.77	6-161	-	1
FA Rose	145.5	32	390	17	22.94	6-48	-	1
JE Bastow	102	29	280	12	23.33	4-57	-	-
J Srinath	112	25	351	15	23.40	6-76	-	2
A Mohammed	85	16	285	10	28.50	5-74	-	1
M Kartik	131.3	37	314	10	31.40	6-101	-	1

FIELDING

38 - CFK van Wyk (37ct, 1st); 35 - MR Street (32ct, 3st); 34 - SJ Palframan (32ct, 2st); 33 - MV Boucher (32ct, 1st); 31 - D Jennings (30ct, 1st); 30 - TK Tsolekile (27ct, 3st); 28 - ELR Stewart; 24 - W Bossenger, TA Bula; 21 - AC Gilchrist (20ct, 1st); 20 - AG Puttick (19ct, 1st); 15 - Z Homani (13ct, 2st), DJ Jacobs (14ct, 1st); 13 - PA Patel (11ct, 2st), GC Smith, M van Jaarsveld, MN van Wyk; 12 - NC Johnson; 11 - HD Ackerman, RG Arendse, DN Crookes, GFJ Liebenberg, DJ Watson; 10 - G Dros, A Jacobs, PPJ Koortzen, I Mitchell, JM Otto, JA Rudolph

Qualification: 10 or more catches

The final itself was something of a damp squib – literally. After Western Province won the toss and put the home side into bat, the Dolphins innings was twice interrupted by rain, although not for long enough to force any change in the playing conditions.

Man of the Match Benkenstein rounded off a superb tournament (367 runs at an impressive average of 52.42) with an unbeaten 77, while wicketkeeper Errol Stewart provided the grandstand finish, belting 53 off 39 balls including a six which careened out of Kingsmead to take the Dolphins to 223 for 6 from their 45 overs.

Two early wickets from Ross Veenstra and West Indian Nixon McLean pinned the Western Province run chase back right from the start, and although Andrew Puttick and Alan Dawson at No. 9 both struck half-centuries, the visitors were never truly in the running and fell 28 runs short of their target.

SRI LANKA

WEST INDIES IN SRI LANKA
by Charlie Austin

First Test
13–17 November 2001 at Galle

Sri Lanka produced won of the great fightbacks of modern times during the first Test against West Indies at Galle. In a match that mirrored their 1998 performance against England at The Oval, they clawed their way back into a game after the tourist's batsmen had moved their side within a whisker of impregnability. West Indies, flushed with fresh hope of a Caribbean success after successful recent tours to Zimbabwe and Kenya, departed Galle despondent, disbelieving as to how they could conspire to lose after such a bright start.

As at The Oval three years before, it was a victory fashioned by skillful spin bowling from Muttiah Muralitharan, who claimed 6 for 126 in the first innings and 5 for 44 in the second, finishing with a ten-wicket haul for the third consecutive match. He was backed up by the Sri Lankan top order, who batted for two long days to establish an unlikely first-innings lead, paving the way for Muralitharan to confound and confuse on a worn, final-day pitch.

West Indies lost by ten wickets, despite Brian Lara returning to best form. His selection on the tour had been the source of controversy back home after it was revealed that despite six months out of the game he was still suffering from a groin injury. But it proved to be a wise gamble by the selectors as the 32-year-old Trinidadian scored 178 in the first innings – his 16th Test century and his first for nearly a year – and then 40 in the second. His duel with Muralitharan was a highlight; the left-hander summing up all his skill and experience to play the off spinner expertly.

On the first day, Lara was instrumental in the West Indies grabbing the initiative. Coming to the crease after the fall of opener Daren Ganga (47), with the innings poised on 95 for 2, he sped to a 71-ball 50. Ramnaresh Sarwan, promoted to bat at No. 3, provided an accomplished foil, also playing Muralitharan well. The pair added 145 for the third wicket. Captain Carl Hooper (69) carried on in the same vein afterwards and the West Indies finished the day on 316 for 3.

The visitors could hardly believe their luck after preparations that had been hampered by injuries, poor

Previous page: A golden year for the prolific Muttiah Muralitharan saw him become the youngest player in the history of the game to reach the 400 Test wicket landmark. Who knows how far the off spinner will go.

Brian Lara's brilliant innings of 178 was not enough to prevent West Indies losing the first Test at Galle.

weather and security fears. Lara, basking contentedly on the outfield in the evening sun after the day's play, talked of a score in excess of 500 and a very big hundred – it all sounded very ominous for Sri Lanka.

On the second morning, Hooper and Lara batted on with great alarm. Muralitharan was pulled into the attack after the first hour and the game started to change. He had bowled 40 overs for a solitary wicket the previous day, but grabbed five wickets in 13.4 overs on the second. He first had Hooper caught and bowled (393 for 4) and then claimed the prize wicket of Lara, shortly after the luncheon interval when the left-hander gloved a sweep and

Right: Kumar Sangakkara justified his promotion to No. 3 with 140 in Sri Lanka's first innings.

was smartly caught by wicketkeeper Kumar Sangakkara (423 for 5). His dismissal sparked a collapse; the last five wickets falling for 25 runs as the West Indies were restricted to 448.

Sri Lanka's openers then set off urgently, Sanath Jayasuriya clubbing a rapid 25 before being snatched at point (37 for 1). But that proved to be the last high point of the game for the visitors. It soon became clear that the last-minute withdrawal of Reon King had left a hole in their bowling attack; fellow pace bowler Colin Stuart was short of match fitness having bowled 13 first-class overs in three

months prior to the game and left-arm spinner Neil McGarrell had not bowled a ball all tour outside of the nets. Mervyn Dillon strained every sinew in a courageous effort for his side, on what was an unforgiving surface for pace bowlers, and leg spinner Dinanath Ramnarine bowled accurately, but they were unable to break a confident Sri Lankan batting order. Marvan Atapattu (61) and Sangakkara (140) laid a firm foundation with a 109-run partnership before Mahela Jayawardene (99) played the sparkiest innings of the game by far, cutting the wayward and increasingly tired attack to ribbons. One hundred and sixty-two runs were added in just 42.4 overs and Jaywardene looked destined for his fourth Test hundred in consecutive Tests before being run out as he tried to scramble the final run. After his unfortunate departure the game slowed, with the Sri Lankans preferring to grind out their runs. On the third evening Russel Arnold (33) and Sangakkara added just 35 runs in 17.1 overs to leave Sri Lanka on 343 for 3 at the close of play.

Day four was tortuous to watch: Sri Lanka chiseling away slowly at the West Indies advantage and then even more slowly building a lead. Sangakkara duly completed his second Test hundred, a marathon of concentration and endurance having kept wicket for the first one-and-a-half days before buckling on his pads, and Hashan Tillekeratne (105*) crawled towards his second hundred in three Tests. With similarly adhesive support from Thilan Samaraweera (77), Jayasuriya finally closed the innings on 590 for 9 late in the day. Sri Lanka were criticized for their lack of positive intent, for the fact that their lack of urgency provided the West Indies with a better chance of saving the game. And as Ganga and Sarwan added 67 comfortable runs the following morning the game looked to be petering towards a stalemate. However, the soft dismissal of Ganga, who swept straight into the hands of square leg, was quickly followed by the departure of Sarwan and Hooper, who drove loosely to be caught at short extra-cover. Marlon Samuels was pinned to his stumps by Muralitharan straight after lunch and West Indian hopes rested on Lara's slim shoulders. And he certainly looked in control, easing his way to 40 before disaster struck for the West Indies; Jayasuriya introduced Samaraweera, whose off breaks had looked innocuous in the first innings. Lara relaxed, whistling a catch to midwicket as he tried to hit over the top. It was the end of the road for the visitors, with the last five wickets adding a mere 13 runs.

FIRST TEST – SRI LANKA v. WEST INDIES
13–17 November 2001 at Galle

WEST INDIES

	First innings		Second innings	
D Ganga	c Jayawardene b Vaas	47	c Tillekeratne b Bandaratilleke	33
CH Gayle	c Sangakkara b Vaas	9	c Muralitharan b Vaas	1
RR Sarwan	b Muralitharan	88	c Arnold b Muralitharan	30
BC Lara	c Sangakkara b Muralitharan	178	c Muralitharan b Samaraweera	40
CL Hooper (capt)	c & b Muralitharan	69	c Jayasuriya b Bandaratilleke	6
MN Samuels	b Muralitharan	16	lbw b Muralitharan	2
*RD Jacobs	c Sangakkara b Vaas	8	b Muralitharan	9
NC McGarrel	c Arnold b Muralitharan	4	not out	10
M Dillon	c Jayasuriya b Vaas	5	lbw b Muralitharan	0
D Ramnarine	not out	0	b Vaas	0
CEL Stuart	b Muralitharan	0	c Vaas b Muralitharan	2
Extras	b 8, lb 6, nb 5, pen 5	24	b 2, lb 2, nb 7	11
		448		**144**

	First innings				Second innings			
	O	M	R	W	O	M	R	W
Vaas	31	6	95	4	17	8	20	2
Fernando	18	2	80	–	2	0	10	–
Muralitharan	53.4	11	126	6	31.3	10	44	5
Bandaratilleke	22	3	76	–	19	6	46	2
Jayasuriya	9	2	24	–	5	0	13	–
Samaraweera	6	0	24	–	4	1	7	1
Arnold	2	1	4	–				

Fall of Wickets
1-15, 2-95, 3-240, 4-393, 5-423, 6-434, 7-440, 8-448, 9-448
1-3, 2-70, 3-70, 4-83, 5-93, 6-131, 7-135, 8-138, 9-139

SRI LANKA

	First innings		Second innings	
MS Atapattu	c Lara b Ramnarine	61	(2) not out	0
ST Jayasuriya (capt)	c McGarrell b Dillon	25	(1) not out	6
*K Sangakkara	run out (Ganga/Hooper)	140		
DPMD Jayawardene	run out (Samuels)	99		
RP Arnold	lbw b Ramnarine	33		
HP Tillekeratne	not out	105		
TT Samaraweera	c Jacobs b Stuart	77		
WPUJC Vaas	c Samuels b Dillon	7		
MCN Bandaratilleke	c Jacobs b Ramnarine	4		
M Muralitharan	lbw b Stuart	14		
TCB Fernando				
Extras	b 1, lb 13, w 4, nb 7	25		
	(9 wickets dec.)	**590**	(0 wicket)	**6**

	First innings				Second innings			
	O	M	R	W	O	M	R	W
Dillon	51	11	121	2				
Stuart	37.4	7	138	2	0.4	0	6	–
McGarrell	31	3	95	–				
Ramnarine	58	12	158	3				
Hooper	24	3	59	–				
Samuels	1	0	5	–				

Fall of Wickets
1-37, 2-146, 3-308, 4-358, 5-395, 6-549, 7-562, 8-567, 9-590

Umpires: JH Hampshire & PT Manuel
Toss: West Indies
Test Debut: TCB Fernando (Sri Lanka)
Man of the Match: M Muralitharan

Sri Lanka won by ten wickets

SECOND TEST
21–25 November 2001 at Kandy

The lush, temperate hills of Kandy have gained a reputation for conjuring up the unexpected: in 1999, Steve Waugh and Jason Gillespie were involved in a horrific collision, whilst in 2001, woeful umpiring reduced England's game with Sri Lanka to a farce. And as Sri Lanka approached this game against the West Indies they were openly fretting about a curse that had seen them stumble to three consecutive surprise defeats at the hill-country venue.

Sri Lanka did manage to break free of their superstition with a 131-run victory to seal the series, but otherwise the game was true to Kandy's recent past. It started bizarrely with the West Indies being shorn of half their bowling attack in the space of three overs and ended in high tension as an umpiring blunder opened the way for the hosts in a dramatic final hour.

Sri Lanka batted first after winning the toss and were soon in trouble as Marvan Atapattu shuffled in front of his stumps to be trapped lbw by Mervyn Dillon. But Dillon, the West Indies' most threatening bowler in the first Test, was forced out of the attack after suffering from sudden chest pains in his second over. Three balls later, fast bowler Colin Stuart was barred from bowling again in the innings under Law 42.6 (b) after producing two unintentional, but nevertheless dangerous, beamers.

The West Indies were left with meager bowling resources: left-arm pace bowler Pedro Collins, who had not bowled a single ball under match conditions all tour, leg spinner Dinanath Ramnarine and Carl Hooper, with his part-time off breaks. After the pounding handed out by Sri Lanka's batsmen at Galle, the West Indies would have feared the worst. However, Sri Lanka's top order failed to seize upon their opponents' misfortune, slipping to 53 for 4 before lunch on the first morning.

Polished half-centuries from Mahela Jayawardene (88) – who came into the game with scores of 104, 25, 139, 150, 99 in his previous three Tests – and Hashan Tillekeratne (87) saved Sri Lanka from embarrassment to leave them on 193 for 5 when rain curtailed day one.

The poor weather continued on during the next two days. Between the showers, guided by Tillekeratne, with support from Thilan Samaraweera (29) and Nuwan Zoysa (23), Sri Lanka increased their first innings to 288. In the context of first-innings scores of 253, 297 and 274 in the previous three Tests at Kandy, it appeared to be a reasonable total, but with so much time having been lost to rain the game looked set for a draw.

However, the match developed quickly on day four. West Indies, 39 for 1 when play commenced, were bowled out for 191 after a late-order collapse saw them lose their last five wickets for just 24 runs. Muttiah Muralitharan (4 for 54), playing in front of his home crowd, made the early inroads dismissing

Lara apart, the West Indian batsmen all struggled to cope with Muttiah Muralitharan. The off spinner claimed 24 wickets in the series.

Ramnaresh Sarwan, Carl Hooper and Marlon Samuels, but it was left-arm Chaminda Vaas (4 for 56) that provided the most eye-catching performance in a devastating display of reverse swing bowling during the afternoon.

Brian Lara (74), now playing with regal authority after regaining his best form at Galle, tried his utmost to hold the innings together, protecting his partners from the wiles of Muralitharan by farming the strike. The ploy worked well in a 41-run partnership with Ridley Jacobs (24) until Vaas was brought back into the attack. For the best part of a year, Vaas had been learning the art of reverse swing, studiously watching videos of the old-ball King Wasim Akram, and for the first time in his career he mastered it, claiming four wickets for 12 runs in six overs: Jacobs edged an in-swinger onto his stumps; Dillon feathered a catch behind after playing and missing four times; and both Ramnarine and Collins were trapped lbw.

Sri Lanka, wary that nervy second-innings performances had largely been responsible for their previous three Kandian defeats, built their lead cautiously, with Sanath Jayasuriya (55) and Marvan Atapattu (84) adding 89 for the first wicket. By the close of play they were 128 for 1 with a 225-run lead.

On the final morning they showed greater positive intent, especially Kumar Sangakkara, who sped to 45. But Lara's glorious form delayed a declaration until a lead of 321 runs had been established, leaving West Indies with the task of scoring four runs per over on a pitch offering both the fast bowlers and spinners encouragement.

Sri Lanka's circumspection provided the visitors with an excellent chance of saving the game, a task they came within 16 minutes of achieving. Had it not been for the controversial dismissal of Lara two balls after tea, adjudged to have been caught at short leg when replays showed that he had hit the ball straight into the ground, they would probably have survived. Even so, a stubborn seventh-wicket stand of 59 between Samuels (54) and Dillon (19) carried the visitors well into a gloomy final hour.

With only 42 minutes remaining and with the light fading fast (so much so that Jayasuriya was unable to call upon his fast bowlers), Muralitharan, who claimed 6 for 81 in the innings to record his fourth ten-for in consecutive Tests, broke through as Dillon played over the top of a straight delivery. Ramnarine survived for another 15 minutes before Samuels stretched across his stumps and was adjudged lbw. Pedro Collins was soon bowled by a booming off break and then Stuart, still nursing his pride after

SECOND TEST – SRI LANKA v. WEST INDIES
21–25 November 2001 at Kandy

SRI LANKA

	First innings		Second innings	
MS Atapattu	lbw b Dillon	0	st Jacobs b Ramnarine	84
ST Jayasuriya (capt)	c Gayle b Collins	16	c Gayle b Ramnarine	55
*K Sangakkara	b Ramnarine	15	c Ramnarine b Dillon	45
DPMD Jayawardene	c & b Ramnarine	88	c Stuart b Dillon	16
RP Arnold	b Ramnarine	4	c Dillon b Ramnarine	1
HP Tillekeratne	b Collins	87	not out	7
TT Samaraweera	c Jacobs b Dillon	29	(8) not out	3
WPUJC Vaas	c Hooper b Collins	0	(7) c Ganga b Ramnarine	0
MCN Bandaratilleke	not out	12		
DNT Zoysa	b Collins	23		
M Muralitharan	c Stuart b Dillon	4		
Extras	lb 6, nb 4	10	b 3, lb 6, w 2, nb 2	13
		288	(6 wickets dec.)	**224**

	First innings				Second innings			
	O	M	R	W	O	M	R	W
Dillon	20	4	55	3	19	2	60	2
Collins	27	7	78	4	11	0	52	–
Stuart	0.1	0	2	–	8	1	21	–
Gayle	0.3	0	4	–				
Hooper	21	6	44	–	13	4	16	–
Ramnarine	25	6	81	3	16	2	66	4
Samuels	3	0	18	–				

Fall of Wickets
1-1, 2-27, 3-49, 4-53, 5-169, 6-249, 7-249, 8-249, 9-281
1-89, 2-176, 3-204, 4-206, 5-215, 6-215

WEST INDIES

	First innings		Second innings	
CH Gayle	b Zoysa	44	(2) c Sangakkara b Vaas	0
D Ganga	c Jayawardene b Zoysa	0	(1) b Muralitharan	8
RR Sarwan	b Muralitharan	17	c Arnold b Muralitharan	48
BC Lara	lbw b Muralitharan	74	c Tillekeratne b Bandaratilleke	45
CL Hooper (capt)	lbw b Muralitharan	23	lbw b Bandaratilleke	4
MN Samuels	c Sangakkara b Muralitharan	0	lbw b Muralitharan	54
*RD Jacobs	b Vaas	24	c Sangakkara b Vaas	5
M Dillon	c Sangakkara b Vaas	0	b Muralitharan	19
D Ramnarine	lbw b Vaas	0	not out	0
PT Collins	lbw b Vaas	0	b Muralitharan	0
CEL Stuart	not out	0	b Muralitharan	0
Extras	lb 5, nb 4	9	b 3, lb 2, nb 2	7
		191		**190**

	First innings				Second innings			
	O	M	R	W	O	M	R	W
Vaas	22	8	56	4	13	2	39	2
Zoysa	13	3	34	2	8	4	13	–
Muralitharan	23.4	5	54	4	35.5	16	81	6
Bandaratilleke	4	0	25	–	15	7	29	2
Samaraweera	4	1	17	–	5	2	9	–
Jayasuriya					5	2	13	–
Tillekeratne					2	1	1	–

Fall of Wickets
1-8, 2-51, 3-72, 4-126, 5-126, 6-167, 7-173, 8-173, 9-181
1-3, 2-25, 3-83, 4-107, 5-110, 6-126, 7-185, 8-190, 9-190

Umpires: JH Hampshire & MG Silva
Toss: Sri Lanka
Man of the Match: M Muralitharan

Sri Lanka won by 131 runs

his calamitous first morning, watched in horror as the ball rolled back from an apparently successful defensive shot onto his stumps. Three wickets had fallen in 12 balls and the Sri Lankans had broken their Kandy jinx.

THIRD TEST
29 November–3 December 2001 at Colombo

Despite the sublime batting form of Brian Lara, which peaked in the third Test at the Sinhalese Sports Club where he compiled two masterful centuries, the West Indies were forced to endure the ignominy of a series whitewash after a ten-wicket defeat – a walloping that left them with 21 defeats in their last 25 Tests overseas.

Seldom can a player have performed so prolifically and yet be forced to sit on the losers' bench. Lara's domination, both the hard statistics and the imperious manner in which he played, was astonishing. After scoring 221 and 130 in the game, he finished with 688 runs in the series at an average of 114.66, the second highest aggregate in a three-Test series after Graham Gooch's Indian summer in 1990 (752 runs). But it was the way he shielded his team-mates from the wiles of Muttiah Muralitharan

that proved so impressive. Right from the first day – which the West Indies dominated in similar fashion to the first Test – Lara decided to monopolize the strike, even when he was partnered by as accomplished a player as Ramnaresh Sarwan, who also impressed by scoring 69 and 66.

Lara had unraveled Muralitharan's box of tricks and, like a magician who has had his illusions exposed, the off spinner could only hold up his hands and admit as much afterwards. 'Brian (Lara) won the battle,' said Muralitharan, adding, 'He's the best batsmen I have ever bowled to.'

Lara's secret was his ability to decode his deliveries from the wrist, which allowed him to select his shots with a certainty that others could only dream of. He preyed on Muralitharan's discomfort against left-handers, waiting patiently and invariably seizing upon any opportunity to drive and cut.

Had Chaminda Vaas not been in the most irresistible form of his life then Lara's unselfish tactics could well have saved the game for the West Indies. But Sri Lanka's hard-working left-armer conjured up his own magic. He swung the glistening new ball dangerously, making early incisions in both innings, and also prospered when Sanath Jayasuriya tossed him the tattered old ball, which he rolled out of his fingers or swerved with his wrist. He claimed 14 for 191 in the match, the second-best figures by a Sri Lankan bowler after Muralitharan's 16 for 220 at The Oval in 1998.

Chaminda Vaas has developed into an outstanding fast bowler. His 26 wickets against the West Indies came at only 15 runs each.

And then there was Hashan Tillekeratne, jostling quietly for some limelight after a superb series. The majesty of Lara's performance had grabbed the headlines, but the efficient and disciplined efforts of Tillekeratne were no less heroic. The 34-year-old was dismissed just once in the series, scoring 105 not out at Galle, 87 and seven not out at Kandy, and then a career-best 204 not out here.

Tillekeratne and co. once again overhauled a decent first-innings total of 390, before pressing on to build a match-winning lead, eventually scoring 627 for 9 – the most runs conceded by the West Indies for 23 years. The visitors were left cursing their failure to capitalize on a first-day advantage that had seen them return to the team hotel full of confidence on 327 for 3.

The West Indies had recovered well after a disastrous start. Vaas, exploiting some steamy atmospheric conditions, whisked out both openers to leave the visitors precariously placed on 17 for 2. However, Lara and Sarwan wrestled back the initiative during a 194-run stand for the third wicket. When Sarwan, searching for his first Test century, was run out as Lara tried to grab the strike against Muralitharan, Carl Hooper (56) carried on the momentum.

The following morning, the West Indies started to slide. Vaas, armed with the second new ball, quickly trapped Hooper and Marlon Samuels lbw with his in-dipper and Zoysa clean bowled Ridley Jacobs. Mervyn Dillon became Vaas' fourth lbw victim of the innings and when Vaas swung a delivery through Lara's tired defences the lower order folded. The last seven wickets fell for only 43 runs.

The West Indies quickly dismissed Marvan Atapattu, but Jayasuriya (85) and Kumar Sangakkara (55) were soon into their stride. Atapattu apart, all the Sri Lankan batsmen contributed, with key partnerships between Russel Arnold (65) and Tillekeratne followed by Thilan Samaraweera and Tillekeratne yielding 141 and 165 respectively. With the lower order also contributing, Tillekeratne, hampered with a hamstring injury, was able to complete his first Test double century – a chanceless innings that spanned nine hours.

The West Indies, 237 in arrears when they started their second innings, were soon in trouble. Chris Gayle, who had failed to live up to his high-profile billing before the series, edged nervously to the slips to complete a pair (the fifth time in six innings that Vaas had claimed his wicket) and Daren Ganga fell in identical fashion to the first innings: trapped on the crease by a Vaas in-swinger.

At 20 for 2 and with morale clearly low, a fourth-day finish remained a distinct possibility, a fact not lost on the sponsors, who persuaded Air Force skydivers to deliver the Janashakthi Test Series trophy into the stadium during the tea interval. But Sarwan and Lara fought back for the second time in the game. Taking the attack to Sri Lanka's bowlers they gave the visitors hope of a draw, finishing the day on 145 for 2.

But such hopes rested squarely on the shoulders of Lara after the early dismissal of Sarwan the following morning, and his 130, his second hundred of the game, proved too little to save the game. When Zoysa curved an in-swinging yorker between bat and pad – to widespread surprise – it marked the beginning of the end, and as a final incendiary lower-order collapse ensued, the last five wickets fell for 18 runs.

Hashan Tillekeratne enjoyed an outstanding series, scoring 403 runs and a highest score of 204 not out at SSC, Colombo.

THIRD TEST – SRI LANKA v. WEST INDIES
29 November–3 December 2001 at Colombo

WEST INDIES

	First innings		Second innings	
D Ganga	lbw b Vaas	6	lbw b Vaas	10
CH Gayle	c Sangakkara b Vaas	0	c Jayawardene b Vaas	0
RR Sarwan	run out (Jayawardene)	69	c Sangakkara b Vaas	66
BC Lara	b Vaas	221	b Zoysa	130
CL Hooper (capt)	c Sangakkara b Muralitharan	56	st Sangakkara b Muralitharan	9
MN Samuels	lbw b Vaas	4	c Jayawardene b Muralitharan	4
*RD Jacobs	b Vaas	2	not out	31
M Dillon	lbw b Vaas	2	c sub (UDU Chandana) b Vaas	8
D Ramnarine	c Jayawardene b Muralitharan	0	lbw b Vaas	0
PT Collins	c Samaraweera b Vaas	4	lbw b Vaas	0
MI Black	not out	0	lbw b Vaas	0
Extras	b 5, lb 7, nb 14	26	b 4, lb 1, nb 3	8
		390		**262**

	First innings				Second innings			
	O	M	R	W	O	M	R	W
Vaas	32.2	5	120	7	25	3	71	7
Zoysa	20	4	55	1	11	1	45	1
Samaraweera	8	0	31	–	8	2	23	–
Bandaratilleke	9	2	37	–	2	0	2	–
Muralitharan	37	6	115	1	36	5	116	2
Jayasuriya	3	0	11	–				
Arnold	3	0	8	–				
Tillekeratne	1	0	1	–				

Fall of Wickets
1-2, 2-17, 3-211, 4-347, 5-359, 6-368, 7-376, 8-385, 9-389
1-1, 2-20, 3-161, 4-203, 5-203, 6-240, 7-258, 8-258, 9-262

SRI LANKA

	First innings		Second innings	
MS Atapattu	c Gayle b Collins	4	not out	19
ST Jayasuriya (capt)	c Ramnarine b Black	85	not out	8
*K Sangakkara	c Gayle b Dillon	55		
DPMD Jayawardene	lbw b Dillon	39		
RP Arnold	c Jacobs b Hooper	65		
HP Tillekeratne	not out	204		
TT Samaraweera	run out (Black)	87		
WPUJC Vaas	c Samuels b Collins	23		
DNT Zoysa	b Hooper	10		
MCN Bandaratilleke	c Jacobs b Collins	25		
M Muralitharan	not out	0		
Extras	b 5, lb 14, w 2, nb 5	26		
	(9 wickets dec.)	**627**	(0 wicket)	**27**

	First innings				Second innings			
	O	M	R	W	O	M	R	W
Dillon	46	9	131	2	3	0	12	–
Collins	47	4	156	3	2.3	0	15	–
Black	32	6	123	1				
Ramnarine	17	3	51	–				
Hooper	43	7	112	2				
Gayle	10	1	28	–				
Sarwan	2	0	7	–				

Fall of Wickets
1-5, 2-104, 3-179, 4-204, 5-345, 6-510, 7-550, 8-569, 9-611

Umpires: RB Tiffin & EAR de Silva
Toss: West Indies
Men of the Match: WPUJC Vaas & BC Lara
Player of the Series: BC Lara

Sri Lanka won by ten wickets

TEST MATCH AVERAGES
Sri Lanka v. West Indies

SRI LANKA

Batting	M	Inns	NO	HS	Runs	Av	100	50	c/st
HP Tillekeratne	3	4	3	204*	403	403.00	2	1	2
TT Samaraweera	3	4	1	87	196	65.33	–	2	1
K Sangakkara	3	4	0	140	255	63.75	1	1	9/1
DPMD Jayawardene	3	4	0	99	242	60.50	–	2	5
ST Jayasuriya	3	6	2	85	195	48.75	–	2	2
MS Atapattu	3	6	2	84	168	42.00	–	2	–
RP Arnold	3	4	0	65	103	25.75	–	1	3
MCN Bandaratilleke	3	3	1	25	41	20.50	–	–	–
DNT Zoysa	2	2	0	23	33	16.50	–	–	–
M Muralitharan	3	3	1	14	22	11.00	–	–	3
WPUJC Vaas	3	4	0	23	30	7.50	–	–	1

TCB Fernando played in one Test but did not bat.

Bowling	Overs	Mds	Runs	Wkts	Av	Best	10m	5/inn
WPUJC Vaas	140.2	32	401	26	15.42	7-71	1	2
M Muralitharan	217.4	53	536	24	22.33	6-81	2	3

Also bowled: RP Arnold 5-1-12-0; MCN Bandaratilleke 71-18-215-4; TCB Fernando 20-2-90-0; ST Jayasuriya 22-4-61-0; TT Samaraweera 35-6-110-1; HP Tillekeratne 3-1-2-0; DNT Zoysa 52-12-147-4

WEST INDIES

Batting	M	Inns	NO	HS	Runs	Av	100	50	c/st
BC Lara	3	6	0	221	688	114.66	3	1	1
RR Sarwan	3	6	0	88	318	53.00	–	3	–
CL Hooper	3	6	0	69	167	27.83	–	2	1
D Ganga	3	6	0	47	104	17.33	–	–	1
RD Jacobs	3	6	1	31*	79	15.80	–	–	5/1
MN Samuels	3	6	0	54	76	12.66	–	1	2
CH Gayle	3	6	0	44	54	9.00	–	–	4
M Dillon	3	6	0	19	34	5.66	–	–	1
PT Collins	2	4	0	4	4	1.00	–	–	–
CEL Stuart	2	4	1	2	2	0.66	–	–	2
D Ramnarine	3	6	2	0*	0	–	–	–	3

Bowling	Overs	Mds	Runs	Wkts	Av	Best	10m	5/inn
D Ramnarine	116	23	356	10	35.60	4-66	–	–
M Dillon	139	26	379	9	42.11	3-55	–	–
PT Collins	87.3	11	301	7	43.00	4-78	–	–

Also bowled: MI Black 32-6-123-1; CH Gayle 10.3-1-32-0; CL Hooper 101-20-231-2; NC McGarrell 31-3-95-0; MN Samuels 4-0-23-0; RR Sarwan 2-0-7-0; CEL Stuart 46.3-8-167-2

LG ALBANS TROPHY
(Sri Lanka, West Indies and Zimbabwe)
By Charlie Austin

As Zimbabwe and West Indies limbered up for the LG Albans Trophy in December 2001 they would have been acutely aware of the magnitude of the challenge ahead: Sri Lanka had not been beaten in a one-day series or tournament at home for nearly three-and-a-half years. The hosts never really looked like slipping up either as they became the first team to book a place in the final, a game that they then went on to dominate as well.

Sri Lanka carried burgeoning confidence into the tournament after their Test series win, whereas the West Indies continued to be hampered by injuries, the most serious of which was the dislocated elbow sustained by Brian Lara at Kandy that forced the in-form left-hander out of the tournament. The situation was exacerbated further when the management sent home pace bowler Mervyn Dillon – one of the few success stories of the Test series – for disciplinary reasons.

Zimbabwe, who had already gambled by leaving behind senior players, significantly reduced their chances of success further as the Zimbabwe Cricket Union (ZCU) prevented the tour management from selecting the final XI on merit. Unofficial racial quotas were enforced from Harare and the dissatisfaction within the team was palpable.

And their inexperience was brutally exposed in the first match – the shortest game in the history of one-day cricket. It was a disaster for the sponsors but a godsend for the police, who wanted to impose a countrywide evening curfew in the wake of the general election held just days before. Zimbabwe were bowled out for just 38, the lowest total in one-day international cricket, surpassing the 43 scored by Pakistan against the West Indies at Cape Town in 1992-93. Chaminda Vaas was the chief destroyer claiming 8 for 19, also a record in the shortened version of the game. Exploiting some residual moisture in the Sinhalese Sports Club, Vaas swung the ball wickedly, especially into the right-handers. He struck with his very first delivery and went on to take the first eight wickets to fall, and he looked set to take all ten before Muttiah Muralitharan whipped out the final two batsmen. Sri Lanka quickly knocked off the required runs and the match was concluded in just over two hours.

But despite that humiliation, described as a 'freak' result by captain Stuart Carlisle, Zimbabwe bounced back the following day when they secured a four-wicket victory against the West Indies. It brought to an end an appalling 28-match run in which they had only registered victories against Bangladesh. West Indies were bowled out for 173 with Daren Ganga top scoring with 59. Nevertheless, Carl Hooper's side could still have won had it not been for a sloppy performance in the field. Zimbabwe, their lack of confidence exposed by a nervy run chase, slipped to 145 for 6 at one stage before Andy Flower (47 not out) guided them home.

The tournament then moved on to Premadasa International Stadium, a venue well suited to Sri Lanka's spin-based attack. However, West Indies

In an extraordinary spell, Chaminda Vaas took 8 for 19 as Zimbabwe collapsed to 38 all out. It was the shortest game in international cricket.

managed to spring a surprise in the third game, defeating the hosts by 49 runs. Crucially, Hooper won the toss, batted first and posted a challenging 251 target after half-centuries from Lara (60) and Ganga (50). Fast bowler Corey Collymore, called into the squad as a replacement, then took 5 for 51 as Sri Lanka, who had started well enough with a brisk 92-run opening stand between Jayasuriya (83) and Avishka Gunawardene (38), were bowled out for 201.

The following day Sri Lanka guaranteed their place in the LG final defeating Zimbabwe by 59 runs, a sufficient margin of victory to give them their second bonus point of the tournament. Sri Lanka won the toss and batted, scoring 272 with Gunawardene (90) and Mahela Jayawardene (96) both impressing. Zimbabwe then struggled on a wearing re-used pitch as Jayasuriya employed five spinners to throttle the run chase.

The final two group games of the triangular were staged at Kandy, the first an apparently irrelevant tussle between the West Indies and Sri Lanka, and the second a straight shoot-out between the two visiting teams for a place in the finals. But the first game of the weekend proved crucial as Lara, who had been batting serenely, badly dislocated his elbow after a freak on-field collision with Marvan Atapattu. He was carried off the field and was out of international cricket for three months – it was the West Indies' seventh injury casualty of the tour. It was hardly surprising that the West Indies then produced a below-par total, which was comfortably overhauled by Jayawardene (106*), who scored a 90-ball century, and Atapattu (82*).

West Indies cast aside the loss of Lara the following day, grabbing their place in the final thanks to a particularly feeble batting performance from Zimbabwe, who were bowled out for 154 on a fine batting pitch. Chris Gayle, who had had a hapless tour of Sri Lanka up until then, being dismissed for three consecutive ducks in the Test series, allowed the West Indies to canter home with a ferocious knock of 85 from 79 balls, an innings of remarkable power.

The West Indies chances in the final, played under lights at Premadasa, nose-dived the moment that Jayasuriya won the toss. Both previous games at the venue had been won by the side batting first and whilst Sri Lanka's 253 score might not have appeared to have been formidable, the difficulties of chasing at the venue, when the pace of the wicket slows and the ball spins, were well known – the highest ever total successfully chased in the 48 one-day internationals staged at Premadasa was 243.

Nevertheless, Hooper's side made a decent attempt, as Ganga (50) and Gayle (60) added 111 for the first wicket. But as the ball softened run scoring became markedly harder and soon after off spinner Kumar Dharmasena knocked back Ganga's off stump the pressure started to build. Wickets started to tumble and the run rate spiraled out of control. Despite a cavalier 34 from Hooper, Sri Lanka eventually won comfortably by 34 runs.

Match One

8 December 2001 at Sinhalese Sports Club Ground, Colombo
Zimbabwe 38 (15.4 overs) (WPUJC Vaas 8 for 19, including a hat-trick)
Sri Lanka 40 for 1 (4.2 overs)
Sri Lanka (5pts) won by nine wickets
Man of the Match: WPUJC Vaas

Match Two

9 December 2001 at Sinhalese Sports Club Ground, Colombo
West Indies 173 (49.1 overs) (D Ganga 59)
Zimbabwe 175 for 6 (48.1 overs)
Zimbabwe (4pts) won by four wickets
Man of the Match: SV Carlisle

Match Three

11 December 2001 at R Premadasa Stadium, Khetterama (floodlit)
West Indies 250 for 8 (50 overs) (BC Lara 60, D Ganga 50)
Sri Lanka 201 (43.2 overs) (ST Jayasuriya 83, CD Collymore 5 for 51)
West Indies (4pts) won by 49 runs
Man of the Match: CD Collymore

Match Four

12 December 2001 at R Premadasa Stadium, Khetterama (floodlit)
Sri Lanka 272 for 7 (50 overs) (DPMD Jayawardene 96, DA Gunawardene 90)
Zimbabwe 213 (47.2 overs) (M Muralitharan 4 for 32)
Sri Lanka (5pts) won by 59 runs
Man of the Match: DPMD Jayawardene

Match Five

15 December 2001 at Asgiriya Stadium, Kandy
West Indies 235 (49.5 overs) (CL Hooper 72, D Ganga 52)
Sri Lanka 239 for 2 (43.1 overs) (DPMD Jayawardene 106*, MS Atapattu 82*)
Sri Lanka (4pts) won by eight wickets
Man of the Match: DPMD Jayawardene

Match Six

16 December 2001 at Asgiriya Stadium, Kandy
Zimbabwe 154 (49.2 overs) (HH Streak 57)
West Indies 155 for 2 (34 overs) (CH Gayle 85)
West Indies (5pts) won by eight wickets
Man of the Match: CH Gayle

Final

19 December 2001 at R Premadasa Stadium, Khetterama (floodlit)
Sri Lanka 253 for 8 (50 overs) (ST Jayasuriya 64, DPMD Jayawardene 63)
West Indies 212 for 7 (47 overs) (CH Gayle 60, D Ganga 50)
Sri Lanka won by 34 runs (DL Method: West Indies target 247 from 47 overs)
Man of the Match: ST Jayasuriya
Player of the Series: ST Jayasuriya

ZIMBABWE IN SRI LANKA
By Charlie Austin

FIRST TEST
27–31 December 2001 at Colombo

Zimbabwe's Christmas celebrations were spoilt by the news that their captain, the 25-year-old leg spinner, Brian Murphy, the only specialist slow bowler in the squad, was not sufficiently confident to lead his young charges into battle.

Kumar Sangakkara on his way to a match-winning century against Zimbabwe at Colombo.

It wasn't a total catastrophe – he had bowled dreadfully in the side's only warm-up game, clearly having not made a full recovery from a broken finger – but it stacked the odds against the tourists on a bone-dry Sinhalese Sports Club pitch, perfectly prepared to suit Sri Lanka's spinners, particularly, of course, Muttiah Muralitharan.

Zimbabwe's stand-in captain, Stuart Carlisle, then gambled after winning the toss. Forced to field a four-pronged pace attack, he had hoped to find some moisture lurking beneath the surface – the fact that Zimbabwe had been skittled out for 38 in a one-day game just days before no doubt playing on his mind. But the decision backfired, handing the initiative to Sri Lanka, allowing them to amass a formidable 586 for 6 – a record between the two sides.

Carlisle argued afterwards that it could have been so different. He had a case; Sri Lanka could have lost both openers within the first half hour. Marvan Atapattu was fortunate to survive an appeal for a catch at short leg when he had made just one, whilst Sanath Jayasuriya received the benefit of the doubt when he appeared to have squeezed a catch behind. It wasn't the only misfortune that befell the visitors; several of their batsmen had reason to be aggrieved when it was their turn to bat.

Jayasuriya (92) made the most of his luck, playing a typically buccaneering innings, although he missed out on a deserved century when he gloved a catch behind off the part-time off breaks of Trevor Gripper – Zimbabwe's most penetrative bowler on day one. His dismissal prompted a period of attrition, with Carlisle instructing his bowlers to bowl wide of the off stump so that he could arrange deep-set fields. But Kumar Sangakkara (128) and Russel Arnold refused to self-destruct and survived till the close of play.

Day two promised more drudgery, but Zimbabwe's bowlers could not match the discipline of the previous evening. Sangakkara smashed 12 from the first over and the hosts did not look back thereafter, adding 375 runs in the day. Sangakkara scored his third Test century and Thilan Samaraweera (123 not out), displaying unwavering concentration and impeccable judgment, scored his second. And Hashan Tillekeratne (96) so nearly passed three figures for the fourth time since his international return just months before. In their 35 minutes of batting before the close, Zimbabwe lost their 18-year-old opener, Hamilton Masakadza.

Day three saw a steady fall of wickets throughout the day. Muttiah Muralitharan, the chief wicket-taker, picked up four wickets in the innings and eight in the match, to round off a remarkable year in which he had claimed 80 wickets in 11 games, the highest-ever haul by a spinner in a calendar year. Only Dennis Lillie (85 wickets in 13 games) has taken more. The visitors desperately needed Andy Flower (42), a left-hander and their only world-class batsman, to counter the off spinner. He threatened an innings of resistance during a 41-run partnership – the highest of the innings – with Craig Wishart, but never looked entirely comfortable with his form and eventually departed.

Zimbabwe were forced to follow on 402 runs in arrears and then lost two further wickets before the close of play. The following day was spent by the swimming pool after a government order that no cricket should be played on Full Moon Holidays, but the rest did not revitalize the tourists and on the fourth day they slipped, with a certain sense of inevitability to an innings and 166 runs defeat – Sri Lanka's largest victory in their 19-year history.

Muttiah Muralitharan spun Sri Lanka to an emphatic victory with eight wickets in the match.

FIRST TEST – SRI LANKA v. ZIMBABWE
27–31 December 2001 at Colombo

SRI LANKA

	First innings		
MS Atapattu	c A Flower b Streak		25
ST Jayasuriya (capt)	c A Flower b Gripper		92
*K Sangakkara	c Wishart b Brent		128
DPMD Jayawardene	c Carlisle b Gripper		18
RP Arnold	lbw b Streak		13
HP Tillekeratne	c A Flower b Streak		96
TT Samaraweera	not out		123
WPUJC Vaas	not out		74
DNT Zoysa			
TCB Fernando			
M Muralitharan			
Extras	b 2, lb 4, w 3, nb 8		17
	(6 wickets dec.)		586

	First innings			
	O	M	R	W
Streak	34	5	113	3
Friend	27	8	102	–
Olonga	23	3	103	–
Brent	33	5	82	1
Gripper	22	3	91	2
GW Flower	22	3	89	–

Fall of Wickets
1-78, 2-150, 3-170, 4-249, 5-320, 6-450

ZIMBABWE

	First innings		Second innings	
H Masakadza	c Tillekeratne b Zoysa	3	c Atapattu b Muralitharan	28
TR Gripper	c Jayawardene b Muralitharan	30	c Sangakkara b Muralitharan	10
SV Carlisle (capt)	c Jayasuriya b Vaas	10	c Sangakkara b Fernando	32
GJ Rennie	lbw b Muralitharan	35	(5) c Jayawardene b Fernando	4
*A Flower	b Samaraweera	42	(6) lbw b Zoysa	10
GW Flower	c Tillekeratne b Muralitharan	0	(7) c Tillekeratne b Muralitharan	18
CB Wishart	c Tillekeratne b Zoysa	21	(8) c Tillekeratne b Samaraweera	27
HH Streak	not out	26	(9) not out	36
TJ Friend	lbw b Vaas	6	(4) b Muralitharan	44
GB Brent	b Muralitharan	0	c Jayasuriya b Zoysa	7
HK Olonga	lbw b Fernando	4	c Sangakkara b Vaas	0
Extras	lb 1, nb 6	7	b 4, lb 7, nb 9	20
		184		236

	First innings				Second innings			
	O	M	R	W	O	M	R	W
Vaas	24	6	63	2	21.2	6	76	1
Zoysa	14	6	24	2	15	4	34	2
Muralitharan	26	8	53	4	36	17	35	4
Jayasuriya	1	0	4	–	7	3	22	–
Fernando	9.5	0	32	1	15	3	48	2
Samaraweera	5	1	7	1	7	2	10	1

Fall of Wickets
1-3, 2-29, 3-60, 4-89, 5-105, 6-146, 7-146, 8-166, 9-167
1-40, 2-58, 3-93, 4-105, 5-127, 6-145, 7-165, 8-197, 9-235

Umpires: Riazuddin & PT Manuel
Toss: Zimbabwe
Man of the Match: K Sangakkara

Sri Lanka won by an innings & 166 runs

SECOND TEST
4–7 January 2002 at Kandy

Their feeble performance in the first Test, coupled with the stubborn refusal of their selectors to call for a specialist spinner when it became clear that leg spinner Brian Murphy's bruised confidence and finger would not recover in time, meant that the odds of Zimbabwe leveling the series in the hill-station town of Kandy looked increasingly long as the Test approached.

But then the Asian propensity for self-destruction reared its ugly head, momentarily fueling the tourist's hopes. On the eve of the game, Sri Lanka's selectors summarily announced, against the wishes of the team management and players, that they would be resting vice-captain Marvan Atapattu and young fast bowler Buddhika Fernando. Zimbabwe were so weak, they surmised, without proper consultation or regard for conditions, that the time had come to blood some young players in preparation for a tough year overseas. The team was incensed and Sanath Jayasuriya, backed by his senior players, steadfastly refused to accept their decision. An emergency team meeting was called and a flurry of phone calls between the selectors, the sports minister Johnston Fernando and the team management ensued. Finally, as midnight approached, Fernando stepped in decisively and overruled the selectors, three of whom resigned the following morning.

The next day, emboldened by their show of strength, Sri Lanka went a long way towards another crushing victory and a series win. And the bizarre events of the preceding evening soon faded into the background as Muttiah Muralitharan grabbed the limelight, so nearly surpassing Jim Laker's record

bowling figures of 10 for 53 against the Australians at Manchester in 1956.

Zimbabwe won the toss and, with the mistake of bowling first in the first match still fresh in their minds, elected to bat first. On a fresh-looking surface they started brightly enough, adding 39 for the first wicket. Enter Muralitharan ... to

His action is still questioned in some quarters and, in conditions that suit, Murali is devastating. He was denied taking all ten Zimbabwean wickets at Kandy when Vaas claimed the final victim.

instantaneous success, as Trevor Gripper swept the second ball only to be caught off his bootstraps. Hamilton Masakadza soon followed, misreading the off spinner's cleverly disguised straighter ball. Gavin Rennie was smartly stumped and Andy Flower perished, again whilst sweeping.

And so it continued throughout the day, with wickets falling at regular intervals. With 38 minutes remaining in the day Grant Flower, top scorer with 72, was bowled. Zimbabwe were 201 for 9 and the crowd sensed history. So did the Sri Lankans and the fielders did all they could to ensure Muralitharan claimed the tenth wicket, Atapattu dropping the simplest of catches off Sanath Jayasuriya's left-arm spin. But the tail-end pair of Henry Olonga and Travis Friend batted adhesively before disaster struck, moments before the close: Muralitharan, fielding on the deep-square boundary, dived forward to catch a top-edged sweep only to dislocate the ring finger of his bowling hand.

A diagnosis of torn ligaments looked set to deny Muralitharan the chance of taking all ten the following morning. However, with a doctor on standby armed with a painkilling needle, Muralitharan bowled the first over. His first ball flew off bat and pad towards silly point, but Russel Arnold fumbled the sharp chance. His fifth ball jerked back into Friend's pads only for fellow off-spinner umpire, Venkataraghavan, to rule not out. Then came the anti-climax as Chaminda Vaas, bowling well within himself, watched in horror as Olonga feathered a catch behind. Muralitharan had to settle for the nevertheless remarkable figures of 9 for 51 from 40 overs of trickery – still the fifth best figures of all time.

The rest of the game proved predictable. Sri Lanka's batsmen, led by captain Jayasuriya who scored a sparkling 139, scored 505, the sixth time in their last seven games that they had passed the 500-mark. And then, in the second innings, Muralitharan once again proved a handful, claiming four wickets to finish with 13 for 115 in the game, his tenth Test ten-for – a new world record. Buddhika Fernando played his part, too, with four wickets, fully justifying the insistence of his team-mates that he should play. Zimbabwe were bowled out for 175 in their second innings, losing the game by an innings and 94 runs.

SECOND TEST – SRI LANKA v. ZIMBABWE
4–7 January 2002 at Kandy

ZIMBABWE

	First innings		Second innings	
H Masakadza	b Muralitharan	10	b Vaas	0
TR Gripper	c Jayawardene b Muralitharan	20	lbw b Muralitharan	21
SV Carlisle (capt)	lbw b Muralitharan	20	c Atapattu b Vaas	9
GJ Rennie	st Sangakkara b Muralitharan	0	lbw b Fernando	68
*A Flower	c Sangakkara b Muralitharan	8	lbw b Fernando	11
GW Flower	b Muralitharan	72	c Sangakkara b Fernando	21
CB Wishart	lbw b Muralitharan	26	c Jayasuriya b Muralitharan	3
HH Streak	b Muralitharan	1	not out	14
DA Marillier	b Muralitharan	8	lbw b Muralitharan	9
TJ Friend	not out	29	b Fernando	0
HK Olonga	c Sangaakkara b Vaas	18	c Samaraweera b Muralitharan	1
Extras	b 3, lb 7, nb 14	24	lb 6, nb 12	18
		236		**175**

	First innings				Second innings			
	O	M	R	W	O	M	R	W
Vaas	17	4	58	1	18	5	35	2
Zoysa	15	2	44	–	10	1	30	–
Muralitharan	40	19	51	9	26.4	7	69	4
Fernando	5	2	13	–	12	2	27	4
Samaraweera	8	2	33	–	4	2	2	–
Jayasuriya	12	3	27	–	1	0	3	–
Tillekeratne					1	0	8	–

Fall of Wickets
1-39, 2-45, 3-51, 4-67, 5-83, 6-137, 7-140, 8-166, 9-201
1-0, 2-16, 3-51, 4-109, 5-134, 6-138, 7-160, 8-173, 9-174

SRI LANKA

	First innings	
MS Atapattu	lbw b Friend	9
ST Jayasuriya (capt)	c Gripper b GW Flower	139
*K Sangakkara	hit wicket b Friend	42
DPMD Jayawardene	lbw b GW Flower	56
RP Arnold	c Wishart b GW Flower	71
HP Tillekeratne	lbw b Streak	37
TT Samaraweera	c A Flower b Friend	17
WPUJC Vaas	not out	72
TCB Fernando	c Friend b Masakadza	45
DNT Zoysa	run out (Olonga)	1
M Muralitharan	b Streak	1
Extras	b 3, lb 1, w 1, nb 7	12
		505

	First innings			
	O	M	R	W
Streak	32.5	7	85	2
Friend	26	4	97	3
Olonga	24	2	131	–
Marillier	21	4	75	–
GW Flower	28	4	66	3
Gripper	14	3	38	–
Masakadza	3	0	9	1

Fall of Wickets
1-11, 2-82, 3-202, 4-273, 5-336, 6-365, 7-388, 8-499, 9-503

Umpires: S Venkataraghavan & EAR de Silva
Toss: Zimbabwe
Man of the Match: M Muralitharan

Sri Lanka won by an innings & 94 runs

THIRD TEST
12–15 January 2002 at Galle

Zimbabwe's cricketers would have been forgiven for throwing in the towel: their selectors had not picked the best side, leaving experienced players such as Alistair Campbell at home for non-cricketing reasons; and they had then refused to send a replacement for Brian Murphy, denying them a specialist spinner on typically slow, bowler-friendly pitches. And all the while Robert Mugabe's thugs were whipping up a frenzy of violence at home as the General Election approached. Two innings defeats in a row had knocked the confidence out of the young players and here, in Galle, the odds were stacked in the hosts' favour, as Muttiah Muralitharan, within breathing distance of 400 Test wickets, was gifted a sandpit of a pitch.

In such a context, their performance during the first three days was admirable. They didn't dominate, far from it, but they rolled up their sleeves and worked tirelessly, even desperately, slowly clawing back some respect. On the first day their part-time spinners – Grant Flower and Douglas Marillier – pegged back the hosts, and on day two it needed an eighth-wicket stand of 146 between Upul Chandana (92) and Thilan Samaraweera (76) to lift them to 418 – still a mediocre total by recent Sri Lankan standards. It was followed by an impressive fightback by the tourist's openers. But then, on the fourth day, they snapped. It had all proved too much; the tour had been depressing and they ran out of steam. Fifteen wickets fell for 85 runs and they could muster only 79 runs in their second innings. The only consolation was that they had not lost by an innings, but a 315-run defeat could hardly be called a success.

Strangely it had appeared motivated by the prospect of delaying Muralitharan's entry into 400 Club. Stuart Carlisle (64), promoting himself to open, and Trevor Gripper (83), temporarily gained the upper hand; pushing, prodding, padding and occasionally slog-sweeping their way towards a record 153-run partnership for the first wicket on the third

day. Spectators had poured into the stadium armed with banners, flags and drums; the sponsors prepared a celebratory fireworks display and a branded 'Countdown to 400' scoreboard. But both were forced to wait for another day as Muralitharan took just two wickets, leaving him on 397 scalps.

The following morning Heath Streak and Grant Flower guided Zimbabwe past the follow-on target before a final incendiary collapse. From 232 for 6, they slumped to 236 all out. Muralitharan took three of the five wickets to fall and claimed his 400th when he bowled Henry Olonga to finish the innings. Finally the crowds were able to celebrate his achievement, a remarkable one at that – he was the

At just 29 years old, Muttiah Muralitharan became the youngest player in the history of the game to reach the 400 Test wicket mark.

It is usually Murali who takes the spinners' wickets, but Sanath Jayasuriya grabbed nine in the third Test at Galle to complete a three-nil drubbing over Zimbabwe.

youngest ever to the landmark at 29 years old, two years the junior of Shane Warne, and reached it in just 72 matches, eight games quicker than Sir Richard Hadlee, the previous quickest to the mark.

And as Muralitharan walked of the field, holding the innings ball aloft in jubilation, you could almost feel Zimbabwe's resolve weaken. The Sri Lankan batsmen continued the celebratory mood, clattering 212 for 2 declared in 41 overs, with Marvan Atapattu (100*) scoring an unbeaten hundred. Within three overs Zimbabwe's batsmen were back at the coalface. This time though the openers did not fire, as Sanath Jayasuriya, who had a tremendous match with the ball taking 9 for 74, quickly saw off Gripper and Craig Wishart. Suddenly, a game that appeared destined to last for five days, was diving towards a conclusion as wickets tumbled. Cricket Board officials were soon racing down the motorway from Colombo for the match presentation. And sure enough, after Sri Lanka had claimed an extra half hour, Zimbabwe's resistance came to an end.

THIRD TEST – SRI LANKA v. ZIMBABWE
12–15 January 2002 at Galle

SRI LANKA

	First innings		Second innings	
MS Atapattu	b Rennie b GW Flower	50	not out	100
ST Jayasuriya (capt)	b Friend	28	c Wishart b Olonga	36
*K Sangakkara	b Marillier	29	c Gripper b Friend	56
DPMD Jayawardene	c & b GW Flower	76	not out	17
RP Arnold	c A Flower b Streak	40		
HP Tillekeratne	c A Flower b Marillier	3		
TT Samaraweera	run out (Marillier)	76		
WPUJC Vaas	lbw b Streak	8		
UDU Chandana	c Carlisle b Marillier	92		
TCB Fernando	b Marillier	1		
M Muralitharan	not out	5		
Extras	b 2, lb 5, nb 3	10	lb 1, nb 2	3
		418	(2 wickets dec.)	212

	First innings				Second innings			
	O	M	R	W	O	M	R	W
Streak	32	11	70	2	11	1	35	-
Friend	26	7	58	1	7	0	39	1
Olonga	18	6	52	-	7	0	56	1
GW Flower	39	7	89	2	9	0	38	-
Marillier	34.4	5	101	4	6	0	34	-
Gripper	9	0	41	-				
Rennie					1	0	9	-

Fall of Wickets
1-50, 2-107, 3-125, 4-222, 5-229, 6-236, 7-254, 8-400, 9-413
1-75, 2-170

ZIMBABWE

	First innings		Second innings	
SV Carlisle (capt)	lbw b Muralitharan	64	lbw b Jayasuriya	28
TR Gripper	st Sangakkara b Jayasuriya	83	lbw b Jayasuriya	3
CB Wishart	lbw b Jayasuriya	1	c Samaraweera b Muralitharan	7
GJ Rennie	c Sangakkara b Jayasuriya	6	c Arnold b Jayasuriya	7
*A Flower	c Tillekeratne b Muralitharan	6	c Jayawardene b Jayasuriya	3
GW Flower	lbw b Muralitharan	19	lbw b Jayasuriya	0
HH Streak	b Jayasuriya	33	c Jayasuriya b Muralitharan	7
DD Ebrahim	c Arnold b Jayasuriya	1	not out	5
DA Marillier	not out	0	c & b Muralitharan	15
TJ Friend	b Muralitharan	1	lbw b Vaas	3
HK Olonga	b Muralitharan	0	c Fernando b Vaas	0
Extras	b 11, lb 8, nb 2	21	lb 1, nb 1	2
		236		79

	First innings				Second innings			
	O	M	R	W	O	M	R	W
Vaas	19	7	36	-	7.3	2	17	2
Fernando	11	1	33	-	2	0	6	-
Muralitharan	58.3	26	67	5	16	7	24	4
Jayasuriya	29	10	43	5	18	5	31	4
Chandana	12	4	24	-				
Samaraweera	5	1	14	-				

Fall of Wickets
1-153, 2-155, 3-161, 4-171, 5-171, 6-232, 7-234, 8-235, 9-236
1-17, 2-30, 3-38, 4-45, 5-45, 6-54, 7-56, 8-72, 9-79

Umpires: DR Shepherd & TH Wijewardene
Toss: Sri Lanka
Man of the Match: ST Jayasuriya
Player of the Series: M Muralitharan

Sri Lanka won by 315 runs

TEST MATCH AVERAGES
Sri Lanka v. Zimbabwe

SRI LANKA

Batting	M	Inns	NO	HS	Runs	Av	100	50	c/st
WPUJC Vaas	3	3	2	74*	154	154.00	-	2	-
TT Samaraweera	3	3	1	123*	216	108.00	1	1	2
ST Jayasuriya	3	4	0	139	295	73.75	1	1	4
K Sangakkara	3	4	0	128	255	63.75	1	1	7/2
MS Atapattu	3	4	1	100*	184	61.33	1	1	2
DPMD Jayawardene	3	4	1	76	167	55.66	-	2	4
HP Tillekeratne	3	3	0	96	136	45.33	-	1	6
RP Arnold	3	3	0	71	124	41.33	-	1	2
TCB Fernando	3	2	0	45	46	23.00	-	-	1
M Muralitharan	3	2	1	5*	6	6.00	-	-	1

Also batted: DNT Zoysa (2 Tests) 4; UDU Chandana (1 Test) 92

Bowling	Overs	Mds	Runs	Wkts	Av	Best	10m	5/inn
M Muralitharan	203.1	84	294	30	9.80	9-51	1	2
ST Jayasuriya	68	21	130	9	14.44	5-43	-	1
TCB Fernando	54.5	8	159	7	22.71	4-27	-	-
WPUJC Vaas	106.5	30	285	8	35.62	2-17	-	-

Also bowled: UDU Chandana 12-4-24-0; TT Samaraweera 29-8-66-2; HP Tillekeratne 1-0-8-0;
DNT Zoysa 54-13-131-4

ZIMBABWE

Batting	M	Inns	NO	HS	Runs	Av	100	50	c/st
HH Streak	3	6	3	36*	117	39.00	-	-	-
TR Gripper	3	6	0	83	167	27.83	-	1	2
SV Carlisle	3	6	0	64	163	27.16	-	1	2
GW Flower	3	6	0	72	130	21.66	-	1	1
GJ Rennie	3	6	0	68	120	20.00	-	1	1
TJ Friend	3	6	0	44	83	16.60	-	-	1
CB Wishart	3	6	0	27	85	14.16	-	-	3
A Flower	3	6	0	42	80	13.33	-	-	6/-
DA Marillier	2	4	1	15	32	10.66	-	-	-
H Masakadza	2	4	0	28	41	10.25	-	-	-
HK Olonga	3	6	0	18	23	3.83	-	-	-

Bowling	Overs	Mds	Runs	Wkts	Av	Best	10m	5/inn
HH Streak	109.5	24	303	7	43.28	3-113	-	-
GW Flower	98	14	282	5	56.40	3-66	-	-
TJ Friend	86	16	296	5	59.20	3-97	-	-

Also bowled: GB Brent 33-5-82-1; TR Gripper 45-6-170-2; DA Marillier 61.4-9-210-4;
H Masakadza 3-0-9-1; HK Olonga 72-11-342-1; GJ Rennie 1-0-9-0

BANGLADESH IN SRI LANKA
By Charlie Austin

FIRST TEST
21–23 July 2002 at P. Saravanamuttu Stadium, Colombo

Three days after arriving back from England, a disastrous tour that had shattered the team's confidence, Sri Lanka played Bangladesh at P. Saravanamuttu Stadium in the first match of a two-Test series.

Within hours of the team's return, captain Sanath Jayasuriya became engulfed in a dispute over selection. With a busy schedule leading up to the 2003 World Cup, the three-man selection panel wanted to rest key players, but Jayasuriya was adamant that Bangladesh should be taken seriously.

A compromise was eventually thrashed out with the help of sports minister Johnston Fernando whereby only batsman Hashan Tillekeratne and fast bowlers Chaminda Vaas and Nuwan Zoysa would sit out the first Test. However, in the second game, wholesale changes would be made, with nine established players rested.

In the end, Jayasuriya's reluctance to experiment appeared unwarranted, as Sri Lanka eventually strolled to victory within three days, by an innings and 196 runs, but there were moments of concern for the hosts, especially in the fast bowling department and in the top order.

However, Muttiah Muralitharan, back to full fitness after withdrawing from the NatWest triangular series, and Aravinda De Silva, desperate to prove his fitness to the selectors as they mulled over their World Cup strategy, kept Sri Lanka's blushes to a minimum as they rescued their side with ball and bat respectively. Muralitharan, although clearly rusty, claimed five wickets in both innings to finish with 10 for 98 in the match, his 11th ten-wicket haul in Tests. He also drew level with Sir Richard Hadlee's record 36 five-wicket hauls in Test cricket. Whilst the Sri Lankan pace bowlers struggled with their rhythm, spraying the ball about obligingly, the prolific off spinner was a constant threat as Bangladesh were bowled out for 161 in the first innings.

Sri Lanka's top order was then expected to feed themselves greedily on the world's weakest bowling attack, but Bangladesh's resources are gradually increasing and the opening bowlers, 16-year-old Talha Jubair and 22-year-old Manjural Islam, prompted a flutter of panic on the second morning. Moving the ball through the air after an early start, the pair reduced Sri Lanka to 56 for 3.

Fortunately for the hosts, the experienced De Silva (206) was lurking in the middle order, only too aware that this was an opportunity not to be missed. He played a faultless innings, full of characteristic whips and short-arm jabs through the onside. And although he finished with 28 fours and a six, he hustled between the wickets, pushing his younger partners hard.

After a short partnership with Kumar Sangakkara (75), he teamed up with Jayasuriya (145), the pair adding 234 for the fifth wicket. Whilst Jayasuriya played circumspectly to start with in his unaccustomed middle-order role, the runs flowed

FIRST TEST – SRI LANKA v. BANGLADESH
21–23 July 2002 at P. Saravanamuttu Stadium, Colombo

BANGLADESH

	First innings		Second innings	
Hannan Sarkar	lbw b Jayasuriya	55	lbw b WRS de Silva	1
Al Sahariar	lbw b WRS de Silva	13	c Sangakkara b Muralitharan	67
Ehsanul Haque	b CRD Fernando	2	c TCB Fernando	
			b CRD Fernando	5
Habibul Bashar	lbw b Muralitharan	24	b Muralitharan	34
Akram Khan	c HAPW Jayawardene		c Sangakkara	
	b TCB Fernando	20	b Muralitharan	5
Aminul Islam	c Arnold b Muralitharan	0	c Sangakkara	
			b Muralitharan	0
*Khaled Mashud (capt)	c Jayasuriya		c TCB Fernando	
	b Muralitharan	23	b PA de Silva	26
Enamul Haque	st HAPW Jayawardene		b CRD Fernando	22
	b Muralitharan	1		
Manjural Islam	b TCB Fernando	0	c Sangakkara b Muralitharan	2
Alamgir Kabir	b Muralitharan	0	b WRS de Silva	0
Talha Jubair	not out	0	not out	5
Extras	b 8, lb 4, w 1, nb 10	23	lb 5, w 1, nb 11	17
		161		**184**

	First innings			Second innings		
	O	M	R	W	O	M	R	W
TCB Fernando	10	3	38	2	7	2	34	–
WRS de Silva	13	3	31	1	11	1	35	2
CRD Fernando	10	3	40	1	11	4	25	2
Muralitharan	19.4	6	39	5	25	6	58	5
Jayasuriya	1	0	1	1	10	2	20	–
PA de Silva					2.3	1	7	1

Fall of Wickets
1-32, 2-50, 3-107, 4-111, 5-111, 6-148, 7-151, 8-156, 9-161
1-2, 2-14, 3-91, 4-113, 5-113, 6-124, 7-158, 8-161, 9-166

SRI LANKA

	First innings	
MS Atapattu	b Talha Jubair	20
RP Arnold	c sub (Fahim Muntasir) b Manjural Islam	25
K Sangakkara	run out (Al Sahariar/Enamul Haque)	75
DPMD Jayawardene	b Talha Jubair	0
PA de Silva	lbw b Enamul Haque	206
ST Jayasuriya (capt)	c sub (Mohammad Ashraful) b Enamul Haque	145
*HAPW Jayawardene	c Al Sahariar b Manjural Islam	5
TCB Fernando	not out	31
M Muralitharan	c Al Sahariar b Enamul Haque	0
CRD Fernando	c Habibul Bashar b Enamul Haque	15
WRS de Silva	not out	5
Extras	lb 6, w 2, nb 6	14
	(9 wickets dec.)	**541**

	First innings			
	O	M	R	W
Manjural Islam	25	1	128	2
Talha Jubair	21	0	120	2
Alamgir Kabir	15	1	82	–
Enamul Haque	38	6	144	4
Habibul Bashar	9	0	43	–
Ehsanul Haque	3	0	18	–

Fall of Wickets
1-35, 2-49, 3-56, 4-206, 5-440, 6-447, 7-491, 8-491, 9-524

Umpires: SA Bucknor & DR Shepherd   Toss: Sri Lanka
Test Debut: WRS de Silva (Sri Lanka), Alamgir Kabir, Ehsanul Haque, Hannan Sarkar, Talha Jubair (Bangladesh)
Man of the Match: M Muralitharan

Sri Lanka won by an innings & 196 runs

quickly. By the evening it turned into a torrent as Jayasuriya slammed six sixes, Sri Lanka eventually scoring an incredible 509 runs in the day – the most ever scored by one team in a single day.

Bangladesh were left needing the small matter of 380 runs to make Sri Lanka bat again, a virtually impossible objective for such an inexperienced line-up against Muralitharan on a turning pitch. And after the new-ball bowlers had claimed a wicket apiece, the spin magician rolled up his sleeves. Only opener Al-Sahariar (67) mounted substantial resistance, as the close-in fielders slowly picked off the tourists.

SECOND TEST
28–31 July 2002 at Sinhalese Sports Club Ground, Colombo

Despite resting nine established first-team players, Sri Lanka cruised to victory against Bangladesh in the second Test at their Sinhalese Sports Club; their tenth consecutive Test win on home soil and their first triumph without the assistance of Muttiah Muralitharan since the off spinner made his debut in 1992. The celebrations may have been muted, but the relief to be back on the victory trail was palpable.

Sri Lanka were also grateful to have apparently unearthed new talent – although success against Bangladesh is a questionable barometer of potential – as pace bowler Chamila Gamage (MKGCP Lakshitha), one of three debutantes in Jayasuriya's side, and left-handed opener Michael Vandort stood out from the pack as Test players of the future. Gamage, 23, announced his arrival in emphatic style, clean bowling Mohammad Ashraful with his first delivery, whilst Vandort, 22, a tall left-hander, confirmed his reputation for having a sound temperament as he scored 61 and 140.

The tourists were equally bold in their selection, putting their faith in the younger generation, handing out three new caps, as the experienced trio of Aminul Islam, Akram Khan and Enamul Haque were all shown the door. And after a vigorous, fighting performance on the first day, the changes appeared justified.

Bangladesh won the toss and elected to field first, keen to exploit the most favourable conditions for seam bowlers on the first morning. Although they failed to make early inroads, as Jehan Mubarak (24) and Vandort compiled a 60-run opening stand, they slowly chipped away through the day. Even when Jayasuriya (85) was swinging away merrily in the afternoon, they kept their composure. And when

SECOND TEST – SRI LANKA v. BANGLADESH
28-31 July 2002 at Sinhalese Sports Club Ground, Colombo

SRI LANKA

	First innings		Second innings	
MG Vandort	lbw b Alok Kapali	61	b Talha Jubair	140
J Mubarak	lbw b Tapash Baisya	24	run out (Tapash Baisya/ Khaled Mashud)	31
MN Nawaz	c Khaled Mashud b Fahim Muntasir	21	not out	78
HP Tillekeratne	c & b Fahim Muntasir	18	not out	5
ST Jayasuriya (capt)	c Khaled Mashud b Manjural Islam	85		
TT Samaraweera	c Habibul Bashar b Manjural Islam	58		
*HAPW Jayawardene	c Khaled Mashud b Manjural Islam	0		
UDU Chandana	c Habibul Bashar b Alok Kapali	20		
TCB Fernando	not out	29		
WRS de Silva	c Khaled Mashud b Talha Jubair	5		
MKGCP Lakshitha	c Alok Kapali b Talha Jubair	12		
Extras	b 1, lb 5, nb 6	12	b 4, lb 1, w 1, nb 3	9
		373	(2 wickets dec.)	**263**

	First innings				Second innings			
	O	M	R	W	O	M	R	W
Manjural Islam	23	4	46	3	9	0	28	-
Talha Jubair	21.4	3	74	2	14	1	52	1
Tapash Baisya	12	1	69	1	8	0	40	-
Fahim Muntasir	18	3	46	2	19	3	56	-
Alok Kapali	29	2	122	2	11	0	54	-
Habibul Bashar	3	1	10	-	5	0	28	-

Fall of Wickets
1-60, 2-90, 3-131, 4-133, 5-260, 6-260, 7-298, 8-298, 9-309
1-80, 2-252

BANGLADESH

	First innings		Second innings	
Hannan Sarkar	lbw b Fernando	5	c Jayawardene b de Silva	30
Al Sahariar	c Jayawardene b Jayasuriya	12	b de Silva	6
Habibul Bashar	lbw b Fernando	11	c Jayawardene b Lakshitha	3
Mohammad Ashraful	b Lakshitha	1	c Mubarak b Samaraweera	75
Tushar Imran	lbw b Lakshitha	8	st Jayawardene b Chandana	28
*Khaled Mashud (capt)	c Tillekeratne b Samaraweera	15	(7) not out	13
Alok Kapali	lbw b Jayasuriya	39	(6) c Mubarak b Samaraweera	23
Fahim Muntasir	c & b Samaraweera	7	(9) lbw b de Silva	1
Tapash Baisya	not out	52	(8) c Chandana b de Silva	3
Manjural Islam	c Jayawardene b Jayasuriya	0	c Tillekeratne b Samaraweera	0
Talha Jubair	c Jayawardene b Chandana	0	c Mubarak b Samarweera	0
Extras	lb 4, nb 10	14	lb 1, nb 1	2
		164		**184**

	First innings				Second innings			
	O	M	R	W	O	M	R	W
Fernando	15	3	36	2	5	2	12	-
de Silva	11	2	45	-	13	5	35	4
Jayasuriya	7	2	17	3	9	4	14	-
Lakshitha	12	5	33	2	12	2	48	1
Samaraweera	12	3	18	2	11.4	1	49	4
Chandana	5	1	11	1	10	3	25	1

Fall of Wickets
1-20, 2-28, 3-31, 4-43, 5-51, 6-72, 7-86, 8-123, 9-163
1-27, 2-36, 3-40, 4-99, 5-167, 6-168, 7-171, 8-175, 9-184

Umpires: SA Bucknor & DR Shepherd   Toss: Bangladesh
Test Debut: MKGCP Lakshitha, J Mubarak, MN Nawaz (Sri Lanka), Tushar Imran, Alok Kapali, Tapash Baisya (Bangladesh)
Man of the Match: MG Vandort

Sri Lanka won by 288 runs

TEST MATCH AVERAGES
Sri Lanka v. Bangladesh

SRI LANKA

Batting	M	Inns	NO	HS	Runs	Av	100	50	c/st
ST Jayasuriya	2	2	0	145	230	115.00	1	1	2
MG Vandort	1	2	0	140	201	100.50	1	1	-
MN Nawaz	1	2	1	78*	99	99.00	-	1	-
J Mubarak	1	2	0	31	55	27.50	-	-	3
HP Tillekeratne	1	2	1	18	23	23.00	-	-	2
WRS de Silva	2	2	1	5*	10	10.00	-	-	-
HAPW Jayawardene	2	2	0	5	5	2.50	-	-	5/2

Also batted batted in two Tests: TCB Fernando 31*, 29* (2 ct)
Also batted in one Test: RP Arnold 25 (1 ct); MS Atapattu 20; UDU Chandana 20 (1 ct);
PA de Silva 206; CRD Fernando 15; DPMD Jayawardene 0; MKGCP Lakshitha 40;
M Muralitharan 0; TT Samaraweera 58 (1 ct); K Sangakkara 75 (4 ct)

Bowling	Overs	Mds	Runs	Wkts	Av	Best	10m	5/inn
M Muralitharan	44.4	12	98	10	9.80	5-39	1	2
TT Samaraweera	23.4	4	67	6	11.16	4-49	-	-
ST Jayasuriya	27	8	52	4	13.00	3-17	-	-
WRS de Silva	48	11	146	7	20.85	4-35	-	-
TCB Fernando	37	10	120	4	30.00	2-36	-	-

Also bowled: UDU Chandana 15-4-36-2; PA de Silva 2.3-1-7-1; CRD Fernando 21-7-64-3;
MKGCP Lakshitha 24-7-81-3

BANGLADESH

Batting	M	Inns	NO	HS	Runs	Av	100	50	c/st
Tapash Baisya	1	2	1	52*	55	55.00	-	1	-
Mohammad Ashraful	1	2	0	75	76	38.00	-	1	-
Alok Kapali	1	2	0	39	62	31.00	-	-	1
Khaled Mashud	2	4	1	26	77	25.66	-	-	4
Al Sahariar	2	4	0	67	98	24.50	-	1	2
Hannan Sarkar	2	4	0	55	91	22.75	-	1	-
Habibul Bashar	2	4	0	34	72	18.00	-	-	3
Tushar Imran	1	2	0	28	36	18.00	-	-	-
Akram Khan	1	2	0	20	25	12.50	-	-	-
Enamul Haque	1	2	0	22	23	11.50	-	-	-
Fahim Muntasir	1	2	0	7	8	4.00	-	-	1
Ehsanul Haque	1	2	0	5	7	3.50	-	-	-
Talha Jubair	2	4	2	5*	5	2.50	-	-	-
Manjural Islam	2	4	0	2	2	0.50	-	-	-

Also batted in one Test: Alamgir Kabir 0, 0; Aminul Islam 0, 0

Bowling	Overs	Mds	Runs	Wkts	Av	Best	10m	5/inn
Enamul Haque	38	6	144	4	36.00	4-144	-	-
Manjural Islam	57	5	202	5	40.40	3-46	-	-
Talha Jubair	56.4	4	246	5	49.20	2-74	-	-

Also bowled: Alamgir Kabir 15-1-82-0; Alok Kapali 40-2-176-2; Ehsanul Haque 3-0-18-0;
Fahim Muntasir 37-6-102-2; Habibul Bashar 17-1-81-0; Tapash Baisya 20-1-109-1

Bangladesh were soon in trouble with the bat, losing two wickets in the 39 minutes of play before lunch. Gamage, bowling in-swingers that occasionally held their line off the seam, struck a double blow immediately after lunch and the visitors were soon reeling on 87 for 8. Two of the debutantes, leg-spinning all-rounder Alok Kapali (39) and fast bowler Tapash Baisya (52*), then ensured a modicum of respectability with useful lower-order contributions before Bangladesh were finally bowled out for 164.

Jayasuriya opted not to enforce the follow-on after a hot day in the field, preferring instead to watch his top order amass an unassailable lead. Vandort cashed in on his chance, as did left-hander Naveed Nawaz (78*) with a gritty, business-like innings, and Sri Lanka eventually set Bangladesh 473 runs to win – an improbable target for any side, let alone a team that had failed to pass 200 in their ten previous innings.

Sri Lanka needed just two of the seven sessions available to bowl out Bangladesh, as only 17-year-old Mohammad Ashraful (75) mounted serious resistance, with some support from Kapali (23). But when the fifth-wicket pair were separated, midway through the fourth morning, the tail collapsed – the last six wickets falling for just 17 runs as left-arm Sujeewa de Silva and off spinner Thilan Samaraweera picked up four wickets apiece.

ONE-DAY INTERNATIONALS

After the controversial exploratory flirtation with younger players during the Test series, Sri Lanka's selectors fielded a full-strength side against Bangladesh during a three-match one-day series.

Nevertheless, looking forward to the ICC World Cup in South Africa next year, the selectors made nine changes to the squad that had performed so poorly during the NatWest triangular series in England. Out went the charismatic wicketkeeper batsman Romesh Kaluwitharana, left-arm fast bowler Nuwan Zoysa, burly opener Avishka Gunawardene, all-rounder Thilan Samaraweera, as well a handful of fringe players. And in came veteran Aravinda De Silva, for the first time in 18 months, as the selectors admitted that their predecessors faith in young players during the past two years had unearthed no batsman with the class to match Sri Lanka's most capped limited overs player.

Crucially, the selectors reverted to Sri Lanka's Test batting line-up, acknowledging the potential folly of a pinch-hitting partner for Sanath Jayasuriya during the fast approaching World Cup. Kumar Sangakkara

left-armer Manjural Islam produced a perfect out-swinger to dismiss the Sri Lanka captain, they finished the day on a high, grabbing four late wickets in all to leave the game evenly poised with Sri Lanka on 305 for 8.

Unfortunately for the visitors, they were unable to finish off the Sri Lankan tail the following morning. They grabbed the ninth wicket within eight minutes, but Charitha Buddika Fernando (29*) and Gamage (40) added 64 runs for the final wicket, swinging the initiative firmly to Sri Lanka.

bedded down at No. 3 whilst Marvan Atapattu opened the innings. Unfortunately, for Bangladesh, and indeed the sponsors, the series turned out to be predictably one-sided. At no stage did the tourists look capable of winning a game, their greatest triumph coming when Sri Lanka's middle order wobbled in the final game of the series.

Captain Khaled Mashud won the Man of the Tournament award, but only because the television commentators adjudicating admired his guts and tenacity in face of such a sorry performance by his young team, which had been bolstered by the inclusion of several one-day specialists.

Mashud won the toss in the first game and elected to bat first, a brave decision at the Sinhalese Sports Club. And, in front of a small Sunday crowd in carnival mood, Bangladesh performed creditably after losing early wickets with Mashud (54) and Imran Tushar (61) both scoring half-centuries. But the 227-run target was between 30 to 50 runs short of being competitive, as Sri Lanka's batsmen played freely. Jayasuriya smashed an entertaining 40 from 32 balls and his opening partner, Atapattu, eased the hosts home with 83 from 101 balls.

The following day Bangladesh once again batted first. This time, however, they were humiliated, slumping to 76 all out with 23-year-old all-rounder Hasantha Fernando claiming 3 for 12 with his gentle medium pace. Sri Lanka, despite losing two early wickets, wrapped up the series in 15.4 overs.

The final game proved the most entertaining, with Sri Lanka scoring 258 having been put into bat. At one stage, though, they were in considerable trouble as they slipped to 115 for 4 before Tillekeratne Dilshan (50) and Russel Arnold (62) added 100 for the fifth wicket.

Bangladesh would have had to break a venue record to win the game – the highest total ever chased successfully at Premadasa International Stadium being 246 – and they never looked likely to do that. But fighting innings from Habibul Bashar (52), Mashud (37) and Khaled Mahmud (39) prevented further embarrassment at the end of another disappointing tour for the tourists.

Match One

4 August 2002 at Sinhalese Sports Club Ground, Colombo
Bangladesh 226 for 8 (50 overs) (Tushar Imran 61, Khaled Mashud 54)
Sri Lanka 228 for 5 (44.4 overs) (MS Atapattu 83)
Sri Lanka won by five wickets
Man of the Match: MS Atapattu

Match Two

5 August 2002 at Sinhalese Sports Club Ground, Colombo
Bangladesh 76 (30.1 overs)
Sri Lanka 77 for 2 (15.4 overs)
Sri Lanka won by eight wickets
Man of the Match: CRD Fernando

Match Three

7 August 2002 at R. Premadasa Stadium, Khetterama
Sri Lanka 258 for 6 (50 overs) (RP Arnold 62, TM Dilshan 50)
Bangladesh 200 (47.2 overs) (Hasibul Bashar 52)
Sri Lanka won by 58 runs
Man of the Match: RP Arnold

Marvan Atapattu enjoyed a one-sided tournament with Bangladesh which, predictably, Sri Lanka won 3–0.

SRI LANKA DOMESTIC FIRST–CLASS CRICKET
By Charlie Austin

Colts Cricket Club won a new-look Premier League tournament in 2001–02 when they cruised to an eight-wicket victory against the Sinhalese Sports Club (SSC) in the tournament final, completing an unbeaten season and reclaiming a trophy they last won in the 1999–2000 season.

They did so despite the exceptional form of SSC batsman Mahela Jayawardene, who scored 137 and 99 in the final, to follow a masterful 274 in the semi-final, the highest first-class score ever in Sri Lankan domestic cricket. The 25-year-old right-hander finished the season having scored a staggering 867 runs at an average of 108.37. But Jayawardene's innings apart, Colts CC had dominated the game, their fast bowlers grabbing the initiative on the first day, bundling out SSC for 216. Off-spinning all-rounder Muthumudalige Pushpakumara, adjudged Man of the Match, also played a significant part, taking four lower-order wickets.

Colts then scored 411 thanks to a solid top-order performance with half-centuries from Chaminda Mendis (52), Sajith Fernando (72) and Romesh Kaluwitharana (74). And when SSC collapsed in the second innings, slipping from 192 for 4 to 234 all out, Colts only required 40 to win.

Colts had faced a sterner test in the semi-final stage when they secured a tense win against Nondescripts Cricket Club (NCC), the defending champions, in a closely fought game. They eventually won by two wickets, thanks to

Mahela Jayawardene was in commanding form during the final of the Premier League. His 274 in the semi-final is the highest score in Sri Lankan domestic cricket.

Kaluwitharana's 84 and a nerveless 31 not out from Chaminda Vaas. SSC had also limped through to the final by the skin of their teeth, despite scoring 561 in their first innings after centuries from Jayawardene and WSM Perera. Set an apparently innocuous 109-run target, they collapsed to 73 for 7 before Thilan Samaraweera (46*) rescued the run chase and guided them home.

The final knock-out between the big four (Colts, SSC, Tamil Union and NCC) followed a half-baked reform of the tournament structure. Desperate to raise the standard of domestic cricket in Sri Lanka, which is hampered by too many clubs and poor facilities, the Board of Control for Cricket in Sri Lanka (BCCSL) dreamt up a complicated, three-stage competition.

A two-division structure was the favoured solution amongst administrators, but the clubs were scared of languishing in the second division and were reluctant to accept such a radical change. Instead, in a political compromise, the top four teams were creamed off the top into a 'Super Group' whilst the remaining 12 sides battled out for the four remaining places in a 'Super League' stage. The top four sides in that then qualified for a place in the semi-finals. The remaining eight teams were then joined by the top two sides in the second division to contest a Plate competition.

The BCCSL was also forced to abandon proposals to redistribute players, a centralized plan that would have been treacherously difficult to administer, which was designed to raise interest in rural areas and prevent the apparently inexorable migration of talented cricketers to Colombo.

Chilaw Marians Sports Club, only promoted last year, were the most improved domestic team, winning the Premier League Plate competition. Ragama Cricket Club, also promoted last year, were runners-up.

Moratuwa Sports Club won the P. Sara tournament (second division) to gain promotion into the Premier League whilst Antonians Sports Club were relegated.

Right-arm seamer Chamila Gamage (MKGCP Lakshitha), who plays for Air Force Sports Club, was the highest wicket-taker in the year, taking 64 wickets at 11.64. Left-arm spinner Nushika Rupasinghe, from Colts Cricket Club, also impressed with 59 wickets at 21.29. Bhathiya Perera just outscored Jayawardene to be the year's highest aggregate run scorer, finishing with 895 runs at an average of 55.93.

FIRST-CLASS AVERAGES
Sri Lanka

BATTING

	M	Inns	NO	HS	Runs	Av	100	50
HP Tillekeratne	13	14	6	204*	942	117.75	3	5
DPMD Jayawardene	12	18	2	274	1426	89.12	4	7
TT Samaraweera	15	16	4	123*	723	60.25	2	4
ST Jayasuriya	9	14	2	139	721	60.08	1	5
PA de Silva	9	13	1	194	691	57.58	2	3
WMB Perera	12	20	4	111*	895	55.93	3	4
LPC Silva	10	16	1	127*	816	54.40	2	4
CU Jayasinghe	9	15	2	100*	692	53.23	1	6
K Sangakkara	9	13	0	140	691	53.15	2	3
UA Fernando	7	8	0	108	418	52.25	2	2
TM Dilshan	10	12	1	165*	570	51.81	1	4
YN Tillakaratne	5	8	0	153	390	48.75	1	2
UDU Chandana	9	10	0	194	487	48.70	1	3
MG Vandort	11	14	0	144	639	45.64	1	5
MS Atapattu	11	18	3	201	661	44.06	2	3
PC Jayasundera	11	17	3	112*	611	43.64	2	3
RP Hewage	10	14	2	102*	514	42.83	1	3
AS Polonowita	10	16	2	95	585	41.78	–	5
RS Kaluwitharana	8	13	1	84	496	41.33	–	5
RP Arnold	9	11	0	110	445	40.45	1	3
KAS Jayasinghe	8	15	0	175	606	40.40	1	4
MN Nawaz	10	17	1	139	642	40.12	1	4
RHS Silva	11	16	0	169	642	40.12	1	4
JSK Peiris	9	15	3	90*	476	39.66	–	4
UC Hathurasinghe	11	18	2	133	634	39.62	2	4
HDPK Dharmasena	10	13	1	90	475	39.58	–	5
KLR Fernando	8	12	1	79	433	39.36	–	2
GRP Peiris	12	21	1	97	778	38.90	–	5
EFMU Fernando	11	20	0	133	765	38.25	1	7
CS Fernando	8	14	4	70	374	37.40	–	3
MC Mendis	11	17	1	95	590	36.87	–	7
SI Fernando	11	17	0	94	626	36.82	–	5
NT Paranavitana	9	12	1	105	401	36.45	1	2
WPUJC Vaas	12	15	5	74*	365	36.50	–	1
SN Wijesinghe	10	16	2	114	501	35.78	1	2
MMDNRG Perera	10	16	1	152	535	35.66	2	1
HAPW Jayawardene	11	16	3	101	462	35.53	1	3
KHRK Fernando	11	18	2	103	551	34.43	2	2
IC Soysa	6	10	1	65	309	34.33	–	3
S Jayantha	9	14	2	137	411	34.25	1	2
WMG Ramayakumara	8	13	2	103*	371	33.72	1	3
WAI Wanigasekera	8	11	1	154*	337	33.70	1	1
DM Ramanayake	8	13	0	125	434	33.38	1	3
BSM Warnapura	8	14	1	88	434	33.38	–	4
SI de Saram	12	22	1	108	701	33.38	1	6
RSA Palliyaguruge	11	18	2	147	530	33.12	1	2
DP Samaraweera	9	12	2	71	329	32.90	–	2
WASNB Peiris	8	15	0	58	491	32.73	–	4
JWHD Boteju	9	14	1	89	412	31.69	–	4
DA Gunawardene	8	14	1	138	410	31.53	1	2
RGD Sanjeewa	8	13	1	107	378	31.50	2	–
DA Ranatunga	8	15	0	133	472	31.46	2	–
S Rodrigo	11	17	3	100*	440	31.42	1	3
UNK Fernando	8	11	0	113	342	31.09	1	1
KADM Fernando	10	12	2	76*	310	31.00	–	1
TMI Mutaliph	9	15	1	142*	431	30.78	1	2
ST Tittagalla	9	15	1	103	428	30.57	1	2
GI Daniel	12	17	2	108	451	30.06	1	3
WMSM Perera	11	18	1	123	504	29.64	2	2
KPPB Seneviratne	12	21	2	91	562	29.57	–	5
WDDS Perera	12	16	1	64	440	29.33	–	2
AP Dalugoda	11	20	2	85	516	28.66	–	3
PSAN Shiroman	11	20	0	67	571	28.55	–	6
WP Wickrama	11	17	2	75	427	28.46	–	2
LHD Dilhara	11	19	2	104	479	28.17	1	1
DK Liyanage	7	10	2	69	225	28.12	–	1
MN Silva	8	13	3	125	281	28.10	1	1
LJP Gunaratne	11	19	2	143	475	27.94	1	1
KADJ Siriwardene	6	10	0	112	276	27.60	1	2
MS Sampan	10	16	2	84	384	27.42	–	2
NHV Chinthaka	8	15	0	116	409	27.26	1	3
NANN Perera	5	10	0	79	269	26.90	–	2

FIRST-CLASS AVERAGES
Sri Lanka

BATTING

	M	Inns	NO	HS	Runs	Av	100	50
CH Gayle	5	8	0	120	215	26.87	1	-
SKL de Silva	9	15	0	80	402	26.80	-	4
WADAP Perera	11	20	1	69	502	26.42	-	4
BDAP Ranaweera	8	14	2	43	317	26.41	-	-
HM Maduwantha	11	19	3	47*	422	26.37	-	-
WJMR Dias	13	23	3	75*	525	26.25	-	4
SHT Kandamby	10	14	0	96	361	25.78	-	2
MTP Fernando	11	16	1	66	381	25.40	-	2
WMPN Wanasinghe	6	12	1	43	278	25.27	-	-
MNR Cooray	10	17	1	139	404	25.25	1	1
ASA Perera	8	11	2	44	224	24.88	-	-
WCR Tissera	9	15	0	77	371	24.73	-	2
BARS Priyadarshana	11	20	1	106*	468	24.63	1	2
SEDR Fernando	11	19	0	131	464	24.42	1	2
MCR Fernando	12	18	0	97	436	24.22	-	3
S Kalavitigoda	11	17	1	169	382	23.87	1	-
RS Kalpage	10	12	1	56	262	23.81	-	1
DN Hunukumbura	6	11	1	60	238	23.80	-	2
WR Fernando	9	15	0	96	357	23.80	-	2
S Arangalla	11	20	1	83	451	23.73	-	2
PB Ediriweera	9	15	0	80	356	23.73	-	2
N Weeraman	10	18	0	99	426	23.66	-	3
RC Rupasinghe	8	16	0	74	378	23.62	-	3
MDK Perera	12	21	0	134	495	23.57	1	1
KS Lokuarachchi	10	12	0	43	282	23.50	-	-
MK Gajanayake	12	22	2	91	470	23.50	-	2
RPAH Wickramaratne	6	10	0	53	230	23.00	-	1
MH Wijesinghe	7	14	0	61	321	22.92	-	2
EMI Galagoda	12	21	3	59	409	22.72	-	2
J Mubarak	10	17	1	70	358	22.37	-	2
HGP Ranaweera	5	8	0	56	177	22.12	-	1
S Madanayake	11	19	3	79	354	22.12	-	2
LL Fernando	9	14	3	78	239	21.72	-	2
M Pushpakumara	10	13	0	81	281	21.61	-	1
HMRKB Herath	12	12	2	43	216	21.60	-	-
HGJM Kulatunga	8	12	0	60	258	21.50	-	3
GST Perera	8	13	0	64	278	21.38	-	2
HSSMK Weerasiri	6	11	0	57	234	21.27	-	2
SHSN de Silva	6	10	1	34	191	21.22	-	-
DTB Kolugala	8	14	3	48	233	21.18	-	-
GE Randiligama	5	8	0	56	168	21.00	-	1
CD Fernando	8	14	2	80	252	21.00	-	2
ARRA Amunugama	11	17	4	68*	272	20.92	-	1
KMH Perera	7	9	1	86	167	20.87	-	1
CM Bandara	9	11	2	36	187	20.77	-	-
DMGS Dissanayake	10	12	3	46	187	20.77	-	-
BCMS Mendis	8	13	0	54	270	20.76	-	1
NMT Shantha	7	14	1	66*	267	20.53	-	2
MCN Bandaratilleke	12	18	2	58	325	20.31	-	2
DK Ranaweera	9	15	0	63	304	20.26	-	2
DNT Zoysa	10	11	1	60*	202	20.20	-	2
RR Tissera	7	11	0	84	221	20.09	-	2
D Ganga	5	8	0	54	158	19.75	-	1
MS Villavarayan	9	12	2	38	194	19.40	-	-
CM Withanage	10	19	1	54*	349	19.38	-	1
PK Siriwardene	11	21	1	47	386	19.30	-	-
MMM Rameez	8	14	0	58	270	19.28	-	2
DT de Zoysa	8	15	1	68	269	19.21	-	1
MKPB Kularatne	9	16	5	49*	210	19.09	-	-
RN Weerasinghe	4	8	0	78	151	18.87	-	1
GAS Perera	11	17	1	45*	301	18.81	-	-
ICD Perera	11	20	0	64	376	18.80	-	4
KADC Silva	11	21	0	62	395	18.80	-	1
WRD Dissanayake	11	19	0	163	356	18.73	1	-
DD Wickramasinghe	8	14	3	59	206	18.72	-	1
DN Pathirana	9	16	2	55	256	18.28	-	1
KSD Kumara	11	20	0	53	363	18.15	-	1
IS Gallage	8	13	3	43	181	18.10	-	-
RC Galappathy	5	10	2	29	144	18.00	-	-
SA Burke	5	9	0	47	159	17.66	-	-
HAHU Tillekeratne	9	18	0	103	317	17.61	1	-
RHTA Perera	11	19	1	60	317	17.61	-	1

FIRST-CLASS AVERAGES
Sri Lanka

BATTING

	M	Inns	NO	HS	Runs	Av	100	50
AS Wewalwala	5	9	0	48	157	17.44	-	-
MNTH Kumara	8	11	3	31	137	17.12	-	-
WAL Chaturanga	6	11	1	48	171	17.10	-	-
K Weeraratne	7	11	1	46	171	17.10	-	-
MGDJ Pradeep	8	16	0	77	273	17.06	-	1
SC Gunasekera	6	12	2	51	170	17.00	-	1
KA Kumara	8	13	0	50	215	16.53	-	1
CRP Galappathy	6	12	0	55	198	16.50	-	1
ALDM Deshapriya	5	8	0	56	131	16.37	-	1
KLS Gamage	10	17	0	41	278	16.35	-	-
GG Ranga Yasalal	11	21	0	56	341	16.23	-	1
DCPD Wickramanayake	7	14	0	46	226	16.14	-	-
DV Gunawardene	9	15	0	62	240	16.00	-	1
S Chandana	10	18	3	40*	240	16.00	-	-
PN Ranjith	12	18	7	29	175	15.90	-	-
NG Peiris	6	9	0	44	142	15.77	-	-
KGN Randika	5	9	1	30	126	15.75	-	-
I Amithakeerthi	4	8	0	80	125	15.62	-	1
LDI Perera	11	15	6	36	140	15.55	-	-
GS Dananjaya	10	17	3	41*	217	15.50	-	-
SHSMK Silva	9	13	2	48	164	14.90	-	-
MI Palihakkara	7	12	0	71	175	14.58	-	1
J Arnolda	8	15	0	48	207	13.80	-	-
KNS Fernando	7	13	0	54	179	13.76	-	1
B de Silva	9	16	1	70	204	13.60	-	1
DA Marage	7	8	0	42	107	13.37	-	-
RD Dissanayake	11	19	4	44*	199	13.26	-	-
KSC de Silva	9	12	3	29	118	13.11	-	-
KEA Upashantha	10	13	0	28	169	13.00	-	-
DWAND Vitharana	7	10	1	43	114	12.66	-	-
MTS de Zoysa	8	16	0	60	202	12.62	-	1
HMS Jayawardene	7	13	0	33	162	12.46	-	-
KRRK Wimalasena	10	17	1	50	198	12.37	-	1
CPH Ramanayake	9	15	1	31	172	12.28	-	-
MKGCP Lakshitha	10	17	3	43	166	11.85	-	-
WPA Ariyadasa	4	8	0	26	94	11.75	-	-
WT Abeyratne	9	14	2	44	131	10.91	-	-
KMN Tharanga	5	10	0	26	107	10.70	-	-
RW Gunaratne	9	17	2	34	154	10.26	-	-
PTS Fernando	7	11	1	34	102	10.20	-	-

Qualification: 8 completed innings, average 10.00

BOWLING

	Overs	Mds	Runs	Wkts	Av	Best	10m	5/inn
MKGCP Lakshitha	299	66	745	64	11.64	7-23	3	8
M Muralitharan	555	177	1172	87	13.47	9-51	6	10
TP Gamage	96	9	426	29	14.68	8-32	-	3
CPH Ramanayake	196.2	50	435	29	15.00	6-25	-	1
DMGS Dissanayake	202.3	57	481	30	16.03	5-7	-	2
MNTH Kumara	129.3	31	371	23	16.13	6-38	-	1
WP Wickrama	97.3	17	308	19	16.21	6-57	-	1
KHRK Fernando	225.5	38	720	43	16.74	5-10	-	1
LDI Perera	267.2	51	891	53	16.81	6-42	-	4
PN Ranjith	255.5	57	847	49	17.28	7-55	-	3
S Arangalla	223.3	52	650	37	17.56	6-41	1	2
UC Hathurasinghe	251.2	89	537	30	17.90	4-32	-	-
CM Hathurasingha	208.3	32	703	39	18.02	7-29	1	4
WRD Dissanayake	294.1	71	741	41	18.07	6-70	-	2
HM Maduwantha	264	79	651	36	18.08	7-51	-	2
LS Malinga	135	14	494	27	18.29	4-37	-	-
HDPK Dharmasena	241.1	65	603	32	18.84	5-57	-	2
WPUJC Vaas	395.1	99	1169	62	18.85	7-71	1	2
MK Gajanayake	92.5	14	359	19	18.89	3-13	-	-
GS Dananjaya	106.1	13	379	20	18.95	6-56	-	2
KS Lokuarachchi	340	82	845	42	20.11	5-103	-	1
WCA Ganegama	159.4	33	506	25	20.24	5-38	-	1
RGD Sanjeewa	107.3	30	245	12	20.41	2-4	-	-
BARS Priyadarshana	261.5	44	927	45	20.60	5-73	-	1
AW Ekanayake	373.4	109	872	42	20.76	7-101	-	3

FIRST-CLASS AVERAGES
Sri Lanka

BOWLING

	Overs	Mds	Runs	Wkts	Av	Best	10m	5/inn
MMDPV Perera	178.5	29	561	27	20.77	4-60	–	–
GP Wickramasinghe	172.4	30	582	28	20.78	5-81	–	1
D Hettiarachchi	282.4	63	811	39	20.79	6-98	1	2
TT Samaraweera	325.3	60	979	47	20.82	6-87	1	4
HGD Nayanakantha	140	25	438	21	20.85	4-57	–	–
KADM Fernando	220	40	758	36	21.05	8-34	1	4
PC Jayasundera	288.1	69	856	40	21.40	5-66	–	1
MKDI Amerasinghe	197.5	42	605	28	21.60	5-50	–	1
NS Rupasinghe	473.3	107	1280	59	21.69	6-94	–	3
KR Pushpakumara	258.1	52	807	37	21.81	5-41	–	1
ASA Perera	136	17	480	22	21.81	5-104	–	1
M Jayasena	191.3	53	525	24	21.87	6-39	–	2
RD Dissanayake	196	48	573	26	22.03	5-33	–	1
SHSMK Silva	268.4	64	777	35	22.20	7-52	1	4
DTB Kolugala	221.5	51	748	33	22.66	7-117	1	3
M Pushpakumara	254.3	54	779	34	22.91	4-43	–	–
JC Gamage	140	28	392	17	23.05	2-18	–	–
KEA Upashantha	174.2	27	623	27	23.07	6-29	–	1
PW Gunaratne	190	33	651	28	23.25	4-18	–	–
RS Kalpage	216	53	558	24	23.25	3-30	–	–
RSA Palliyaguruge	190.2	46	535	23	23.26	4-31	–	–
DK Liyanage	143.1	21	489	21	23.28	5-22	–	1
HMRKB Herath	398.5	98	1030	44	23.40	8-47	1	3
LJP Gunaratne	249	42	775	33	23.48	8-133	1	1
WCR Tissera	118.4	22	400	17	23.52	5-41	–	1
ABT Lakshitha	104.2	26	331	14	23.64	4-21	–	–
IS Gallage	120	25	403	17	23.70	4-53	–	–
GAS Perera	402.1	90	1067	45	23.71	7-68	–	3
MS Villavarayan	249.4	54	760	32	23.75	5-47	–	2
MMDNRG Perera	255	41	962	40	24.05	6-70	1	4
NNN Nanayakkara	98.1	9	440	18	24.44	5-91	–	1
ARRA Amunagama	152.1	28	468	19	24.63	7-47	–	1
MCR Fernando	208.4	53	522	21	24.85	3-36	–	–
UDU Chandana	321.5	82	1029	41	25.09	5-59	–	2
NC Komasaru	225.4	73	509	20	25.45	5-66	–	2
SI Fernando	122.1	27	263	10	26.30	2-21	–	–
DGR Dhammika	139	29	370	14	26.42	6-61	–	1
PDRL Perera	236	27	942	35	26.91	4-41	–	–
S Madanayake	218	33	569	21	27.09	5-48	–	1
THAIK Bandaranayake	107	13	407	15	27.13	3-25	–	–
KGAS Kalum	94	7	436	16	27.25	3-35	–	–
S Chandana	257.5	38	982	36	27.27	5-41	–	1
KSC de Silva	142.2	22	491	18	27.27	4-39	–	–
CRB Mudalige	305.3	58	932	34	27.41	7-29	–	2
KG Perera	280.1	104	579	21	27.57	5-83	–	1
B de Silva	175	28	498	18	27.66	4-23	–	–
S Weerakoon	247.1	84	529	19	27.84	3-46	–	–
RC Rupasinghe	177.5	45	603	21	28.71	5-34	–	1
MDK Perera	319.1	84	867	30	28.90	5-20	–	2
WMPN Wanasinghe	131.1	25	405	14	28.92	4-30	–	–
MCN Bandaratilleke	382.5	81	1144	39	29.33	5-63	–	1
RAP Nissanka	144.4	26	502	17	29.52	6-20	–	1
DNT Zoysa	248	62	683	23	29.69	4-43	–	–
JWHD Boteju	117	23	333	11	30.27	2-27	–	–
ST Jayasuriya	119	27	306	10	30.60	5-43	–	1
AKC Silva	112.3	15	382	12	31.83	4-28	–	–
SP Rupasinghe	135.5	31	382	12	31.83	3-23	–	–
BMSB Nawaratne	143.3	31	471	14	33.64	2-31	–	–
IS Baddegama	152.2	33	560	16	35.00	3-28	–	–
AP Dalugoda	302	83	782	22	35.54	6-80	–	1
LHD Dilhara	178	33	608	16	38.00	3-56	–	–
J Arnolda	123	23	394	10	39.40	3-55	–	–

Qualification: 10 wickets in 8 innings

The following bowlers took 10 wickets in fewer than 8 innings

MMCS Perera	55.2	8	210	19	11.05	5-43	–	2
DM Perumal	50.4	9	159	11	14.45	3-30	–	–
MHA Jabbar	72.1	13	257	14	18.35	5-24	–	1
BCN Amarasinghe	75.3	11	267	14	19.07	5-35	–	2
A Rideegammanagedera	95	23	262	13	20.15	4-27	–	–

FIRST-CLASS AVERAGES
Sri Lanka

BOWLING

	Overs	Mds	Runs	Wkts	Av	Best	10m	5/inn
NT Paranavitana	101.2	17	269	13	20.69	4-39	–	–
PTS Fernando	65.1	7	262	12	21.83	4-26	–	–
AGRMS Ranaweera	107.3	25	330	15	22.00	8-73	1	1
PK Wijetunge	75	11	225	10	22.50	4-73	–	–
KLSL Dias	78.3	14	266	11	24.18	3-20	–	–
WAI Wanigasekera	76.5	13	349	13	26.84	3-14	–	–
WT Abeyratne	103.4	28	280	10	28.00	6-48	–	1
D Ramnarine	145.1	36	410	14	29.28	4-54	–	–
SR Abeywardene	116.3	19	387	12	32.25	5-96	–	1
K Weeraratne	107	18	420	13	32.30	4-37	–	–
CO Obuya	104.3	13	363	11	33.00	4-48	–	–
LL Fernando	101.3	10	420	12	35.00	4-66	–	–
PP Wickramasinghe	137.2	22	385	11	35.00	4-70	–	–
WSP Jayawardene	115.3	10	403	10	40.30	4-98	–	–
WGM Ramayakumara	149.3	22	508	12	42.33	3-36	–	–
CM Bandara	129.5	22	469	11	42.63	3-32	–	–
M Dillon	169	31	455	10	45.50	3-55	–	–
MGPR Pradeep	133.3	31	468	10	46.80	3-68	–	–

FIELDING

35 - KLK Fernando (33ct, 2st); 34 - KLR Fernando (33ct, 1st); 31 - SS Deshabandu (23ct, 8st), WMSM Perera (30ct, 1st); 30 - CS Fernando (29ct, 1st); 29 - MKPB Kularatne (26ct, 3st), K Sangakkara (26ct, 3st); 28 - TM Dilshan (27ct, 1st), EFMU Fernando (27ct, 1st);
26 - EMI Galagoda (23ct, 3st); 22 - HAPW Jayawardene (21ct, 1st); 21 - WR Fernando (19ct, 2st); 20 - WAL Chaturanga (19ct, 1st), RS Kaluwitharana (17ct, 3st), TR Peiris (14ct, 6st), GST Perera (17ct, 3st), MGDJ Pradeep (18ct, 2st); 19 - DM Ramanayake (18ct, 1st);
18 - SKL de Silva (17ct, 1st), DK Ranaweera (17ct, 1st), MS Sampan (17ct, 1st);
17 - DPMD Jayawardene; 16 - RSA Palliyaguruge, WASNB Peiris (15ct, 1st);
15 - UDU Chandana, KHRK Fernando, SS Kalavitigoda, NT Paranavitana, RHS Silva, RR Tissera;
14 - J Mubarak; 13 - DN Pathirana, WMB Perera, PSAN Shiroman; 12 - NHV Chinthaka, RS Kalpage, TMI Mutaliph, M Pushpakumara, N Weeraman; 11 - PB Ediriweera, SEDR Fernando, KLS Gamage, MC Mendis, MDK Perera, MS Villavarayan; 10 - SI de Saram (9ct, 1st), CD Fernando, MTP Fernando, SI Fernando, LPJ Gunaratne, KSD Kumara, ICD Perera, MMDPV Perera, NANN Perera, DWAND Vitharana.

Qualification: 10 or more catches

WEST INDIES

India in the West Indies
New Zealand in the West Indies
West Indies Domestic
First-Class Cricket
West Indies Domestic
First-Class Averages

INDIA IN THE WEST INDIES
By Tony Cozier

The script was obvious, but the West Indies' home series of five Tests against India did not follow it. Brian Lara and Sachin Tendulkar were the anticipated stars, appearing on opposite sides for the first time in Tests since India's previous Caribbean tour five years earlier. In fact, they played only minor parts as the story unfolded.

India arrived with realistic hopes of ending their dismal record away from home, where their last triumph was eight years earlier in Sri Lanka and, outside of the geographical confines of their neighbourhood, 16 years since they won 2–0 in England. They were once more disappointed, comprehensively beaten in the third and fifth Tests by opponents with as shocking a recent overseas account as their own, but are still tough to beat at home.

The loss was all the more galling for India – and, conversely, all the more satisfying for the West Indies – for they took the lead with a hard-fought victory by 37 runs in the second Test at the Queen's Park Oval in Trinidad, venue of their only two wins on seven previous tours. The teams were evenly matched with similar strengths and weaknesses, strong in the middle order, but shaky at top and bottom and limited in bowling. The West Indies won because they compensated better in key situations for the failure of their champion batsman. India lost because they could not overcome their notorious aversion to pitches, at Kensington Oval in Barbados and Sabina Park in Jamaica, bouncier and faster than those they are brought up on.

Unusually, India owed their victory at Queen's Park in part to their three fast bowlers, the veteran Javagal Srinath and the two eager young left-armers, Ashish Nehra and Zaheer Khan. But on livelier surfaces, they conceded first-innings totals of 394 in the third Test and 422 in the fourth, while the four West Indies fast bowlers, with Merv Dillon to the fore, were irresistible. Anil Kumble and Harbhajan Singh, whose contrasting spin is such a force in India, never played together and Kumble returned home early for attention to a fractured jaw. Hit by a bouncer from Merv Dillon in the fourth Test, he bravely sent down 14 overs wrapped in head bandages, like some survivor of a motorway crash, but could not continue.

Previous page: After victory over the touring Indians, defeat to New Zealand, led by Stephen Fleming, soured the season for the new-look West Indies team.

The West Indies reverted to their tried-and-trusted policy of pure pace for the last four Tests and for the first time under Carl Hooper's captaincy. They lacked the menace of the fearsome quartets of a previous era, yet virtually settled the two victories by dismissing India for 102 at Kensington and 214 at Sabina.

The spearhead was Dillon who confirmed himself as the effective new-ball bowler Malcolm Marshall predicted he would be when he first came into the team five years earlier. Cameron Cuffy maintained the pressure, not only with his 17 cheap wickets (21.88), but also with his accuracy that conceded just under two runs an over.

The back-up was provided by the raw newcomer, Adam Sanford, and the left-arm swing bowler Pedro Collins, whose value could not be properly assessed by their unflattering returns (15 wickets at 34.93 for Sanford, nine at 37.88 for Collins) for they repeatedly accounted for the big wickets.

None was bigger than Tendulkar who fell three times to Collins (twice for 0s, second ball and first ball) and twice to Sanford (once for a fourth-ball 0).

Lara, still physically and mentally bothered by the left elbow he dislocated and fractured in December on his prolific tour of Sri Lanka, was a shadow of himself. He had played no cricket for four months while he recuperated and managed only two half-centuries (the highest 55) and an average of 28.85.

Hooper and Man of the Series Shivnarine Chanderpaul, who followed him in the order, filled the breach more than adequately. Each compiled three hundreds and passed 500 runs in a series for the first time, sharing partnerships of 293, 214 and 186. Hooper's 233 and Chanderpaul's 140 in the first Test in their native Georgetown were their personal Test bests.

Hooper was atoning for years of underachievement – Chanderpaul was making up for time lost in the 17 Tests he has missed through one injury or another over the previous three years. The stylish Ramnaresh Sarwan repeated the solidity at No. 3 he had established in Sri Lanka, but continued his frustrating habit of getting out when going well. Only once was he dismissed for less than 35 yet his highest score was 65.

Seeking to solve problems at the top of the order and with the wicketkeeping, the selectors recalled Stuart Williams and Junior Murray three years after they had played in their last Tests. It was, in Sir Garry Sobers' graphic phrase, 'recycling failures'.

They were soon dropped again and immediately Wavell Hinds, the tall Jamaican left-hander, and the reinstated Ridley Jacobs, the doughty wicketkeeper, made a difference.

Hinds' 113 and his opening partnership of 111 with fellow Jamaican left-hander Chris Gayle on the grassiest Sabina Park pitch anyone can remember, were considered by rival captain, Saurav Ganguly, as the most crucial elements in the West Indies' win by 155 runs in the final Test.

Jacobs immediately thumped a belligerent 118 on a featherbed pitch in his native St John's that yielded 1,142 runs for 18 wickets and a maiden hundred by the 20-year-old Indian Ajay Ratra. It was the first time that wicketkeepers on both sides had scored hundreds in a Test. But Jacobs' 59, that helped push the West Indies beyond 400 in their first innings at Sabina, was more valuable than either.

Tendulkar began with scores of 79 in the weather-beaten first Test and 117 in the first innings of the second that set up a strong position that India eventually converted into victory. He finished with a sparkling 86 at Sabina that, for a couple of hours, gave India a glimmer of hope that they might reach an unprecedented winning target of 408. In between, the little maestro's scores were an international dialing code: 0, 8, 0, 0.

During this rare barrenness others did flourish, but only once when it really counted, in the second innings in Port-of-Spain, when Tendulkar's first 0 was followed by a crucial partnership of 151 between Ganguly and VVS Laxman.

When Collins got him for the third time, sneaking through his back foot defence from round the wicket to bowl him for 86 in the final innings of the series, it effectively sealed India's fate. The last seven wickets went down for 82, the last a quarter of an hour before heavy rain that was to last another 11 days and wash out the first two one-day internationals.

Vulnerable at the top of the order, India tried three opening partners for the diminutive Shiv Sunder Das, but they had only one start better than 20. It placed immediate pressure on the middle order and, with Tendulkar's inconsistency, Rahul Dravid, Ganguly and Laxman were left to take up the slack. Each had statistically satisfying series. Laxman applied the consistency that has been missing to his class that was always obvious, compiling 474 runs at an average of 79. Dravid scored 404 runs at 57.71 and Ganguly, after demoting himself down the order, 322 at 53.66. But all

needed to do more when the pressure was on. And, once more, it was the pressure of having to deal with a foreign environment that was India's undoing.

FIRST TEST
11–15 April 2001 at Georgetown, Guyana

Guyana's equatorial weather, that has always been the bane of Test cricket's only venue in South America, changed from breezy, bright sunshine to steady rain 35 minutes before tea on the fourth day. It continued through the night to leave the outfield so soaked that a match drifting to a draw was abandoned the next morning.

There was the significant consolation for the long-suffering Guyanese public of sublime batting by three of their own. Captain Carl Hooper converted his first Test hundred on his home ground into a double century, 233, his highest Test score, and shared a fifth-wicket partnership of 293 with Shivnarine Chanderpaul, whose 140 was also a personal best. Ramnaresh Sarwan, who helped Hooper steady the innings on the opening day with a stand of 113, stroked 53 attractive runs before once more wasting his wicket with a careless stroke.

The West Indies held the advantage after removing Sachin Tendulkar for 79 when he was at his most dangerous and reducing India to 275 for 7 in reply to their 501. But Rahul Dravid was a wall they could not penetrate. He remained unbeaten on 144 when the rain set in, by which time he and the resolute

The first Test ended in a high-scoring draw with West Indies captain, Carl Hooper scoring 233.

No.9, Sarandeep Singh, specially flown out as stand-in for the injured Harbhajan Singh, had defied the West Indies for three hours and 25 minutes. Initially eliminating the threat of the follow-on, they had put on 120 when it was terminally halted.

Hooper's 11th Test hundred led the West Indies out of early trouble that included the loss of Brian Lara without scoring.

On the Bourda ground where they even play their club cricket, Hooper, Sarwan and Chanderpaul combined to thwart the Indians after Javagal Srinath had removed both openers and, dubiously, Lara with only 44 scored.

Hooper's first hundred after six Tests on home soil was worth 108 at the end of the extended opening day, when the West Indies, batting after Hooper won the toss on a hard, dry pitch and lightning fast outfield, were 270 for 4. Hooper was lucky to survive an uncertain start. He was missed by the sprawling wicketkeeper Deep Dasgupta off an inside-edge off Srinath from the first ball he faced and Dravid and VVS Laxman let his edge off the medium pacer Sanjay Bangar bisect them in the slips when he was on ten. These were errors for which India paid dearly.

Sarwan was the more secure of the two until he rifled a careless drive from off spinner Sarandeep ten minutes into the final session directly to mid-off.

Hooper had already overcome his early uncertainty by then and he and Chanderpaul took advantage of a tiring attack on a hot, sunny afternoon. It was a shift from the early exchanges.

Quickly finding the correct line and length, Srinath accounted for openers Chris Gayle (in his second over) and Stuart Williams (in his fourth) and won a short, stirring duel against Lara, who fell without scoring.

In his first match since dislocating and fracturing his left elbow in a one-day international in Sri Lanka on 15 December, Lara was kept on the defensive for ten testing deliveries by Srinath. He played uncertainly at his 11th and Australian Daryl Harper, one of the eight umpires on the new International Cricket Council's so-called elite panel, raised his finger on appeal as wicketkeeper Deep Dasgupta gathered. Lara's disbelief was obvious as he trudged off and the television replays showed that, whatever the ball hit, it wasn't the bat.

Had India made the most of Hooper's chances, the course of the innings would have been different, but the captain advanced to his hundred late in the day with one of his three sixes followed by the 14th of his 29 fours, both off Anil Kumble. Next day, he carried on to his second hundred.

A year after the resurrection of his long and turbulent career, the innings was as critical to his controversial status as West Indies captain as to his team's position. His marathon innings that occupied ten hours 35 minutes and 402 balls surpassed his 178 against Pakistan nine years earlier as his Test best. He eventually fell to a spectacular tumbling catch by Sarandeep at long leg off Kumble.

To the backdrop of typically noisy, joyous celebrations, Hooper gained crucial support from Chanderpaul. They consolidated the West Indies' position by extending their fifth-wicket partnership from 113 at the start to 293, a team record against India. It was ended when Chanderpaul was lbw to the left-arm seamer Zaheer Khan ten minutes before tea.

Chanderpaul was uncharacteristically aggressive, striking 23 fours and taking the attack to the Indians, whose captain Saurav Ganguly occasionally used the rare tactic of placing one legside fielder.

The last three West Indies batsmen raised only seven on the third morning, but managed to push the total above 500. But, on the featureless pitch, they could not capitalize on either an early breakthrough or Tendulkar's timely wicket on the stroke of tea as India responded with 237 for 4 by another day extended by the sluggish over rate.

Dravid and VVS Laxman ensured Tendulkar's loss, lbw, heaving across the line from the quick leg spinner Mahendra Nagamootoo, did not lead to further trouble with a stand worth 119 before it was broken the following day.

Tendulkar had spent two days in the field observing Hooper and Chanderpaul enjoy the conditions and, although it arrived earlier than India would have wanted, he was unlikely to waste his opportunity when it came.

After nibbling uncertainly at his first delivery, India's premier batsman crashed 14 boundaries in all directions before Nagamootoo and the giant fast bowler Cameron Cuffy suddenly curbed his aggression.

He required a mere 95 balls to move into the 70s, but another 47 to add eight before Nagamootoo foxed him with successive balls. The first deflected from his tentative edge onto wicketkeeper Junior Murray's thigh and flew past slip. The next drew his ill-advised cross haul.

Tendulkar was forced to enter the fray at 21 for 2 in the seventh over when Ganguly's limp hook shot off Merv Dillon lobbed to square leg, six overs after opener Dasgupta was lbw to Cuffy without scoring. Tendulkar and the other opener, Shiv Sunder Das, steadied things with a stand of 78 until Adam

FIRST TEST – WEST INDIES v. INDIA
11–15 April 2002 at Georgetown, Guyana

WEST INDIES

	First innings	
GH Gayle	c Dasgupta b Srinath	12
SC Williams	lbw b Srinath	13
RR Sarwan	c Zaheer Khan	
	b Sarandeep Singh	53
BC Lara	c Dasgupta b Srinath	0
CL Hooper (capt)	c Sarandeep Singh b Kumble	233
S Chanderpaul	lbw b Zaheer Khan	140
*JR Murray	lbw b Zaheer Khan	0
MV Nagamootoo	not out	15
M Dillon	lbw b Bangar	0
A Sanford	lbw b Kumble	1
CE Cuffy	run out (Tendulkar/Dasgupta)	0
Extras	b 1, lb 4, w 3, nb 26	34
		501

	First innings			
	O	M	R	W
Srinath	33	8	91	3
Zaheer Khan	32	9	97	2
Bangar	27	6	63	1
Kumble	45.1	7	145	2
Ganguly	2	1	2	–
Sarandeep Singh	21	5	80	1
Tendulkar	3	0	18	–

Fall of Wickets
1-21, 2-37, 3-44, 4-157, 5-450, 6-454, 7-494, 8-494, 9-499

INDIA

	First innings	
SS Das	b Sanford	33
*D Dasgupta	lbw b Cuffy	0
SC Ganguly (capt)	c Nagamootoo b Dillon	5
SR Tendulkar	lbw b Nagamootoo	79
R Dravid	not out	144
VVS Laxman	c Gayle b Cuffy	69
SB Bangar	lbw b Cuffy	0
A Kumble	c Nagamootoo b Sanford	3
Sarandeep Singh	not out	39
J Srinath		
Zaheer Khan		
Extras	b 4, lb 12, w 2, nb 5	23
	(7 wickets)	**395**

	First innings			
	O	M	R	W
Dillon	32.3	5	115	1
Cuffy	27	6	57	3
Sanford	25	5	81	2
Nagamootoo	40	13	103	1
Hooper	12	4	16	–
Gayle	4	2	7	–

Fall of Wickets
1-6, 2-21, 3-99, 4-144, 5-263, 6-270, 7-275

Umpires: EAR de Silva & DJ Harper
Toss: West Indies
Test Debut: A Sanford (West Indies)
Man of the Match: CL Hooper

Match drawn

Rahul Dravid recovered from a blow on the helmet to register his tenth Test century.

Sanford, the policeman on debut, bowled him off the inside-edge for 33 with a ball that bounced steeply.

The next day, Dravid recovered from a numbing blow to the helmet to complete his tenth Test hundred and dispel Indian fears of following on.

The elegant right-hander had added only two to his overnight 57 when he misjudged a bouncer during an aggressive opening spell from Dillon and ducked into a ball that crashed into the grill of his helmet.

It took several minutes of on-field attention before he could resume, but the only noticeable effect was a slight swelling of the jaw.

His concentration remained solid and his strokeplay impeccable as he saw India through a rocky period during which they lost three wickets for 12 before they reached the 302 required to deny the West Indies the option of the follow-on.

Dravid was not the only one to cause the West Indies frustration on a pitch still offering their attack no encouragement. Sarandeep, in only his third Test, came in at 275 for 7, after VVS Laxman, Sanjay Bangar and Anil Kumble had fallen in quick succession, and batted with assurance that belied his position in the order.

In the end, though, the weather rendered it all meaningless.

SECOND TEST
19–23 April at Port-of-Spain, Trinidad

The Queen's Park Oval, to Test cricket what Alfred Hitchcock was to Hollywood, produced another fascinating match with a finish as tense as any the master of the mystery movie directed.

For the second successive season, the West Indies began the last day of the Queen's Park Test with a feeling of optimism. For the second time, it ended in disappointment.

In 2001 against South Africa, they were 32 for 1 chasing a winning total of 232. They fell short by 69. Now they were 131 for 2, 181 away from their target and, with Lara and Hooper together, holding at least an even chance of victory. They lost again, by 37 runs, as India completed their third victory on the only ground on which they have ever won in the Caribbean.

Duped by the notoriously fickle pitch into bowling on winning the toss and defied by an extraordinary batsman, the West Indies were subjected to a frustrating opening day on which India built their platform for victory. The home side were encouraged by neither pace nor bounce and had to contend for the final five-and-a-half hours with Tendulkar, who accumulated his 29th Test hundred, drawing level with Don Bradman, the batsman to whom he has been frequently and flatteringly compared.

The Indian champion was below his best and lucky to escape several narrow shaves during the first half of his stay. But his unbeaten 113 and his third-wicket stand of 121 with Dravid formed the backbone of India's satisfactory 262 for 4 at stumps.

Dravid, reverting to No. 3 from No. 5 in a straight swap with Ganguly, revived the innings in a partnership of 124 with Tendulkar after Das and his makeshift partner Bangar were out by lunch.

Dravid picked up where he had left off in the first Test and played with appreciably more flair and assurance than Tendulkar for 67, before Black beat his on-drive to hit off stump a quarter of an hour before tea.

Ganguly gifted his wicket away when he was on 25 with a loose drive to mid-off from Hooper's off spin. He departed with Tendulkar three short of his landmark, but the little maestro soon passed it before digging in for the next day.

The West Indies missed a chance to dispatch Laxman with the second new ball before the close,

Port-of-Spain is home to Brian Lara, but Sachin Tendulkar stole the honours by scoring 117 as India won the second Test.

but Lara at first slip and Hooper at second let the edge off Cuffy bisect them.

An intense struggle ensued on the second day. The West Indies limited India's total by claiming the last six wickets for 77 runs and replied strongly before Lara, 52 and returning to his best form, was the first of three wickets to fall for one run off nine balls that once more altered proceedings in the closing overs.

India's progress was impeded 45 minutes into the day when Tendulkar was lbw on the back foot to Cuffy after adding only four to his overnight 113. Laxman took on Tendulkar's mantle, but found support from neither the wicketkeeper nor the bowlers as Cuffy, Sanford and Black rounded off the innings with Laxman stranded, undefeated on 69.

The West Indies made a positive reply, but the loss of Williams, snapped up at short leg from Harbhajan the last ball before tea for 43, left them 80 for 2 at the second interval.

Lara overcame a hesitant start, especially against Harbhajan, and he and Sarwan had the measure of the bowling in a stand of 56 when Sarwan's careless drive at Nehra flew from the edge to first slip.

With Lara and Hooper, their two most established batsmen together, the West Indies were sailing along at 179 for 3 with the shadows lengthening when they had the wind taken out of their sails.

Zaheer made the crucial break, clipping Lara's outside edge for a catch to the keeper. Chanderpaul followed to the first ball of the next over from Srinath, victim of a dubious lbw decision to a ball that clearly pitched outside leg stump.

Srinath gained a more straightforward lbw verdict against Murray off the last ball of the over to leave the crowd of around 12,000 stunned and the innings in need of rebuilding.

It took India 22.5 overs and almost two hours to wrap up the West Indies innings on the third morning, but the lead of 94 was still sufficient to put pressure on a team that committed itself to batting last at the toss.

Ganguly and Laxman then slowly and surely restored India's position after the trauma of losing Tendulkar for a fourth-ball duck. Their partnership began at an unsteady 54 for 4, 40 minutes after lunch, and they were still together at 165 when fading light ended play at 165 for 4.

Laxman joined his captain when Tendulkar was lbw aiming to work Sanford to leg, off a ball that seemed likely to rise over middle stump. It was the third wicket to fall for two runs after Bangar's edge to second slip off Sanford and Dravid's legside deflection to the keeper off Cuffy.

The West Indies sensed a complete breakthrough, but lacked the firepower to complete the job.

The contest continued to shift one way then the next over the remaining two days. The last six Indian second-innings wickets tumbled for 13 in ten overs on the fourth day once Dillon's 13th delivery with the second new ball was chopped onto his stumps by Laxman, ending his partnership of 149 with Ganguly. The collapse that ensued characterized the weakness of the lower order of both teams and kept the match wide open once again.

Williams' edge to first slip off Srinath denied the West Indies the sound foundation they were looking for and severe cramp in his forearms forced Gayle to retire with the score on 68 for 1, 35 minutes after tea.

It stirred Lara from his seat in the players' area to join Sarwan who was already established. The left-hander was quickly into his stride and the stand was worth 57, with the light fading, when Sarwan was again the victim of a careless shot, steering Harbhajan's straight ball to slip.

It was a timely wicket for India, but never more than those of Lara and Hooper an hour into the last day, both to Nehra, that all but settled the outcome.

Lara was 40 at the start, but it was immediately evident he was gripped by the tension of the moment. He had not managed a hundred in eight previous Tests at Queen's Park Oval, his home ground since he was a boy, and his signal to the usually boisterous

SECOND TEST – WEST INDIES v. INDIA
19–23 April 2002 at Port-of-Spain, Trinidad

INDIA

	First innings		Second innings	
SS Das	lbw b Dillon	10	lbw b Dillon	0
SB Bangar	c Murray b Sanford	9	c Hooper b Sanford	16
R Dravid	b Black	67	c Murray b Cuffy	36
SR Tendulkar	lbw b Cuffy	117	lbw b Sanford	0
SC Ganguly (capt)	c Dillon b Hooper	25	not out	75
VVS Laxman	not out	69	b Dillon	74
*A Ratra	c Murray b Cuffy	0	lbw b Cuffy	2
Harbhajan Singh	c Cuffy b Sanford	0	c Gayle b Cuffy	0
Zaheer Khan	b Sanford	5	(10) run out (Sarwan/Murray)	4
J Srinath	lbw b Black	18	(9) c Williams b Dillon	2
A Nehra	c Hooper b Black	0	b Dillon	0
Extras	b 4, lb 13, nb 2	19	b 5, lb 2, nb 2	9
		339		**218**

	First innings				Second innings			
	O	M	R	W	O	M	R	W
Dillon	28	7	82	1	21.1	7	42	4
Cuffy	30	12	49	2	20	6	53	3
Sanford	29	5	111	3	17	5	46	2
Black	17.5	7	53	3	14	3	36	–
Hooper	11	4	27	1	17	4	28	–
Sarwan					3	0	6	–

Fall of Wickets
1-18, 2-38, 3-162, 4-218, 5-276, 6-282, 7-287, 8-298, 9-339
1-6, 2-54, 3-54, 4-56, 5-205, 6-210, 7-210, 8-213, 9-218

WEST INDIES

	First innings		Second innings	
CH Gayle	c Das b Srinath	13	(2) c Harbhajan Singh b Zaheer Khan	52
SC Williams	c Das b Harbhajan Singh	43	(1) c Dravid b Srinath	13
RR Sarwan	c Dravid b Nehra	35	c Dravid b Harbhajan Singh	41
BC Lara	c Ratra b Zaheer Khan	52	c Dravid b Nehra	47
CL Hooper (capt)	c Ganguly b Zaheer Khan	50	c Das b Nehra	22
S Chanderpaul	lbw b Srinath	1	not out	67
*JR Murray	lbw b Srinath	0	run out (Ratra/Das)	1
M Dillon	lbw b Nehra	9	b Srinath	0
MI Black	run out (Harbhajan Singh)	6	c Das b Srinath	3
A Sanford	c Tendulkar b Harbhajan Singh	12	b Nehra	1
CE Cuffy	not out	1	c Bangar b Zaheer Khan	4
Extras	b 5, lb 8, w 3, nb 7	23	b 2, lb 5, w 4, nb 13	24
		245		**275**

	First innings				Second innings			
	O	M	R	W	O	M	R	W
Srinath	22	4	71	3	32	9	69	3
Nehra	20	4	52	2	31	8	72	3
Zaheer Khan	14	2	47	2	21.1	5	55	2
Harbhajan Singh	19.5	3	51	2	30	8	66	1
Bangar	2	0	11	–				
Tendulkar					1	0	6	–

Fall of Wickets
1-50, 2-80, 3-136, 4-179, 5-180, 6-180, 7-201, 8-217, 9-232
1-27, 2-125, 3-157, 4-164, 5-237, 6-238, 7-238, 8-254, 9-263

Umpires: EAR de Silva & DJ Harper
Toss: West Indies
Test Debut: A Ratra (India)
Man of the Match: VVS Laxman

India won by 37 runs

'Trini Posse' Stand to mute its music even before facing a ball was indicative of his anxiety.

He spent a nervous hour adding seven before he sparred at Nehra's fourth ball and edged a catch to first slip, much as he had done against Zaheer in the first innings.

In Nehra's next over, Hooper, out of position for a pull shot, tugged a catch low to Das at midwicket.

India celebrated wildly, but they became increasingly muted as Chanderpaul and Gayle got stuck in. They saw off nine overs with the second new ball, forcing Ganguly to replace Nehra with fellow left-armer Zaheer. His first ball was a wide, his second was slapped straight to cover point by Gayle.

It signalled the end. As the last six wickets went down for 38 and Cuffy's stabbed catch to gully off Zaheer formalized the result, the flags fluttering highest and the faces wreathed in smiles were east, not West, Indian.

THIRD TEST
2–5 May 2002 at Bridgetown, Barbados

India were again stricken by their jinx of the Kensington Oval and were comprehensively beaten for the seventh time in their eight Tests on the ground.

They were shaken by a wicket off the first ball of the match after they had been sent in, had Tendulkar fall for his second successive 0 and were all out for 102 in 33.4 overs on the opening day, broken into three parts by rain interruptions.

After that there was no way back as the West Indies amassed 394, mainly on the strength of two more hundreds by Hooper and Chanderpaul, in spite of the customary collapse of the last six wickets for 18 runs.

India did better in their second innings but not by enough and only Zaheer's

merry hitting at No. 9 and Ganguly's second defiant innings of the match saved them the indignity of an innings defeat.

India's problems were immediate. Ganguly called the toss wrong on the truest, bounciest pitch of the series and Das was bowled by Dillon's on-target first delivery. It was a start that would have set off alarm bells in an Indian dressing room already suspicious of Kensington's bogey. The position never got much better on an opening day that was interrupted three times by rain.

In the seventh over, Jaffer, with his feet static, edged Dillon to Jacobs and, three balls later, Tendulkar sparred at Collins' second ball on his return to the team and Jacobs jubilantly claimed the deflection.

Dravid and Ganguly added to India's woes when they hesitated over a run to cover where Chanderpaul's pick-up and return to bowler Cuffy beat Dravid by inches, a verdict reached on the evidence of the television replay.

Ganguly found himself left with wicketkeeper Ratra and the four bowlers when Cuffy breached

West Indies fought back at Barbados with centuries from Carl Hooper and Shivnarine Chanderpaul (right).

Laxman's loose drive to hit off stump. The captain was then on 19 and was responsible for 29 of the 51 runs scored, among them a six over long off from Dillon who had gained revenge of sorts with a breathtaking, overhead catch at third man to end both Ganguly's, and India's, innings.

The West Indies went into the second day 33 for 1, after Williams had been taken at slip off Zaheer the previous afternoon, and strengthened their position, but they had to subdue opponents who fought like Bengal tigers.

After losing Gayle to the fifth ball of the morning to stand on 35 for 2, the West Indies advanced to 314 for 4 by close, an overall lead of 212 with three days remaining.

Their consolidation was based on partnerships of 119 between Sarwan, who made 60 before once more carelessly surrendering his wicket, and Lara, who scored 55, and between Hooper and Chanderpaul with an unbroken stand of 153 at stumps.

But it was not until the heat of the day that a combination of the increasing hopelessness of their situation and a pitch that was approaching perfection finally took their toll on India and their effort in the field flagged.

Lara had to overcome a scratchy start during which he was kept on 24 for 28 balls and over half an hour while Hooper spent 40 minutes and 27 balls adding to his tea-time score of 11.

India's hopes of getting back into contention flickered when Nehra accounted for Lara, who popped a return catch off a slower ball, and Sarwan, who was taken at gully from a sliced drive, in successive overs. They were crestfallen when third umpire Billy Doctrove ruled Hooper in when television replays showed his bat short of his ground on Nehra's deflection from Chanderpaul's drive. It proved a critical moment for Hooper was then on 15 and would go on to add a further 100.

The match went through a succession of contortions on the third day, but it would have taken the flexibility of an Indian yoga master to have turned the situation for India on its head.

At the end of the third day, the West Indies remained as strongly placed as they had when they routed India for 102 on the opening day. They extended their lead to 292 before lunch after Hooper and Chanderpaul accumulated their hundreds and removed the top four in the Indian order for 169 by close, called seven overs early because of fading light.

Had Sarwan been able to cling on to sharp chances at short leg before either Ganguly or

THIRD TEST – WEST INDIES v. INDIA
2–5 May 2002 at Bridgetown, Barbados

INDIA

	First innings		Second innings	
SS Das	b Dillon	0	c Sarwan b Dillon	35
Wasim Jaffer	c Jacobs b Dillon	12	run out (Chanderpaul)	51
R Dravid	run out (Chanderpaul/Cuffy)	17	c Jacobs b Sanford	14
SR Tendulkar	c Jacobs b Collins	0	lbw b Dillon	8
SC Ganguly (capt)	c Dillon b Sanford	48	not out	60
VVS Laxman	b Cuffy	1	c Hooper b Collins	43
*A Ratra	c Jacobs b Dillon	1	lbw b Dillon	13
Harbhajan Singh	c Dillon b Sanford	13	b Cuffy	3
Zaheer Khan	c Sarwan b Sanford	4	c Jacobs b Sarwan	46
J Srinath	lbw b Dillon	0	c Gayle b Sarwan	0
A Nehra	not out	0	c Collins b Dillon	3
Extras	w 2, nb 4	6	lb 6, nb 14	20
		102		**296**

	First innings				Second innings			
	O	M	R	W	O	M	R	W
Dillon	11	1	41	4	31.2	8	82	4
Cuffy	9	4	17	1	24	16	26	1
Collins	8	0	24	1	22	1	78	1
Sanford	5.4	0	20	3	15	3	78	1
Hooper					5	0	11	-
Gayle					3	0	14	-
Sarwan					1	0	1	2

Fall of Wickets
1-0, 2-26, 3-27, 4-50, 5-51, 6-61, 7-78, 8-86, 9-101
1-80, 2-101, 3-117, 4-118, 5-183, 6-208, 7-211, 8-285, 9-285

WEST INDIES

	First innings		Second innings	
SC Williams	c Wasim Jaffer b Zaheer Khan	18	(2) not out	4
CH Gayle	lbw b Zaheer Khan	14	(1) not out	0
RR Sarwan	c Wasim Jaffer b Nehra	60		
BC Lara	c & b Nehra	55		
CL Hooper (capt)	c Tendulkar b Harbhajan Singh	115		
S Chanderpaul	not out	101		
*RD Jacobs	c Ratra b Nehra	0		
M Dillon	c Das b Nehra	6		
PT Collins	b Harbhajan Singh	0		
A Sanford	lbw b Harbhajan Singh	0		
CE Cuffy	run out (Tendulkar/Ratra)	1		
Extras	b 3, lb 8, nb 13	24	nb 1	1
		394	(0 wicket)	**5**

	First innings				Second innings			
	O	M	R	W	O	M	R	W
Srinath	32	7	85	-				
Nehra	32	9	112	4				
Zaheer Khan	29	8	83	2				
Ganguly	7	5	9	-				
Harbhajan Singh	34.5	7	87	3	0.2	0	4	-
Tendulkar	1	0	7	-	1	0	1	-

Fall of Wickets
1-30, 2-35, 3-154, 4-161, 5-376, 6-376, 7-392, 8-393, 9-393

Umpires: EAR de Silva & DJ Harper
Toss: West Indies
Man of the Match: M Dillon

West Indies won by 10 wickets

Carl Hooper on his way to 115 in a stand of 215 with Chanderpaul.

day to a skied offside catch off Harbhajan Singh. Chanderpaul was on 91 and just managed to pass his hundred as wickets fell all around him.

Hooper punctuated his 12th Test hundred that occupied five-and-three-quarter hours with 18 fours. Chanderpaul had 12 in a stay 20 minutes longer as he repeated his maiden hundred on the same ground against India five years earlier.

Although there were a couple of unexpected twists in the tail, the West Indies duly completed their first victory in nine Tests with both time and wickets to spare.

Ganguly and Laxman, the last specialist batsman, carried India's hopes of making a fight of it at the start of the day, but Laxman edged a drive low to second slip off Collins 20 minutes into the day, leaving Ganguly and the tail to summon what they could. After Ratra and Harbhajan went cheaply, Zaheer, a typically belligerent right-handed, lower-order batsman with nothing to lose, smashed a run-a-ball 46. He belted two big legside sixes off Sanford and four fours just when India seemed to be heading for a quick innings defeat.

He dominated a partnership of 74 with Ganguly until Hooper introduced novice leg spinner Sarwan for a speculative last over before lunch. Zaheer cut at his first ball and snicked a catch to Jacobs to signal both the end of his merry little knock and the first session. Continuing his unfinished over on resumption, Sarwan had Srinath taken at gully with his first delivery.

Last man Nehra prevented the unlikely hat-trick, but then skied an outfield catch after Dillon replaced Sarwan, leaving Ganguly unbeaten on 60 and the West Indies needing five runs to complete the task.

It was Dillon's fourth wicket of the innings and his eighth of the match, which was enough to earn him the Man of the Match award.

Laxman had scored, the West Indies might have already completed their job inside three days. As it was, however, the pair added 51 going into the fourth day.

India's slim hopes of getting back into contention flickered as they dispatched the last six West Indies wickets for 18 after removing Hooper for 115 and followed with their best opening partnership of the series of 80. But Jaffer was run out for an aggressive 51 containing ten fours and the diminutive Das fell for 35 to Sarwan's amazing catch off Dillon at short-leg. When Dravid edged Sanford to Jacobs and Tendulkar was lbw to Dillon in successive overs, India were 117 behind with another 28 overs remaining for the day, but Ganguly and Laxman rode their luck to see them out.

The West Indies' stranglehold loosened briefly after Hooper was out an hour and a half into the

FOURTH TEST
10–14 May 2001 at St John's, Antigua

The Recreation Ground, the venue of Brian Lara's highest Test score, Viv Richards' fastest Test hundred and 31 centuries overall since its inauguration in 1981, was again at its most inviting for batting. It produced a meaningless match that added five more hundreds to its list and yielded 1,142 runs for only 18 wickets. Yet the two most eminent players managed four runs between them: Tendulkar out first ball in India's 513 for 9 declared (their highest total in the Caribbean) and Lara for four in the West Indies 629 for 9 declared.

It did give rise to a remarkable piece of trivia as Ratra and Jacobs became the first set of opposing wicketkeepers in the 1,602 Tests played since the first in 1877 to score hundreds in the same match. Less notable was the fact that all 11 Indians bowled in the West Indies' innings as Ratra handed the gloves over to Dravid for one over to complete the dubious set.

More memorable was Kumble's courage and commitment to his team. In spite of both helmet and grill protection, he had his jaw cracked by a bouncer from Dillon batting on the second day, an injury so serious he would fly back to India three days later for a corrective operation. Yet, he insisted on returning to the action for the final session of the third day after Tendulkar made his unpractised leg breaks turn appreciably.

Encased in bandages like a casualty from Kandahar, he sent down the most threatening 14 overs of the match, claiming Lara lbw and foxing Hooper into offering catches, one unaccepted at slip, the other taken at short leg from bat and pad off a no-ball.

Hooper's decision to bowl on winning his third consecutive toss seemed based on no more than speculation and, after Das played on to the fifth ball of Collins' first over, Jaffer and Dravid made use of the placid surface to add 155 for the second wicket.

Collins quickly struck again in his second spell, accounting for Jaffer and Tendulkar to catches by Jacobs off successive balls that cut away on pitching. It was a temporary interruption to India's progress as Dravid and Ganguly consolidated with a partnership worth 58 by the end of the day.

When three wickets went down inside the first hour on the second morning, leaving India on 257 for 6 with only the suspect lower order to accompany Laxman, it seemed as though the West Indies had taken the initiative. Dravid and Ganguly were so stalled against Dillon and Cuffy that they eked out seven runs from the first eight overs, prompting Ganguly to cut Cuffy to point as he attempted to break free.

Three runs later, Dravid dragged Dillon back onto his stumps after a mainly defensive innings that occupied 291 balls and five minutes short of five hours. Kumble soon took his damaging blow and, although he bravely batted on, he understandably stabbed the next lifter that came along to short leg.

It was the last wicket to fall in the day as Laxman and Ratra, whose previous scores in his debut series were 0, 2, 1 and 13, played with few alarms and considerable enterprise. They defied the eight bowlers Hooper used to dislodge them, with Laxman passing his

Ajay Ratra, the Indian wicketkeeper, on his way to his first Test century at the Recreation Ground, Antigua.

third Test hundred the over after Ratra completed his first 50 and carrying India to the security of 462 for 6 by the close of play.

Laxman extended his innings of six hours ten minutes only 20 minutes into the third morning. Fending a short ball from Dillon off his body, he stepped back onto his off stump to end a partnership of 217 with Ratra, a new Indian seventh-wicket record against the West Indies. The 20-year-old keeper was one away from his hundred when Laxman was dismissed, but needed only four more balls to stroke his 12th four to reach his landmark. Ganguly let the innings run until it was past 500 before declaring, but his bowlers found the work as hard as the West Indies' bowlers had done.

There was intermittent encouragement, but it ultimately came to nothing. By the end of the third day, Zaheer had removed Gayle, caught behind off his glove to a rare delivery that bounced, Tendulkar bowled Hinds round his legs with a low full toss and Kumble sent back Lara, lbw on the back foot.

Had Hooper not had his two escapes off successive balls from the brave Kumble when he was on ten, the course of the match might have been different. But he offered few chances after that.

Sarwan fell to Zaheer in the second over of the fourth day – again out without converting a half-century into anything more substantial – after which Hooper and Chanderpaul helped themselves to their third hundreds of the series against bowling clearly handicapped by the absence of Kumble.

Hooper passed 500 runs in the series for the first time in a career that started in 1987 before his wild, tired stroke off Tendulkar lifted a catch to cover. He spent just under six-and-three-quarter hours over his runs, stroking three sixes and 13 fours, and had a further chance at 85 when Ganguly put down a stiff, two-handed return.

Chanderpaul was on 80 when the day ended with his sights clearly on three figures. With the West Indies 108 behind, half their wickets standing and a day remaining, the draw seemed inevitable.

Jacobs ensured it was not a boring finale, entertaining his hometown crowd of no more than a couple of thousand with his robust hitting that brought him five sixes and 11 fours in his second Test hundred. Dillon smashed his Test-best 43 near the end, but Chanderpaul never changed his ultra-cautious approach in gathering his third hundred of the series.

Right: Ratra's opposite number, Ridley Jacobs, responded in kind. This was the first time two wicketkeepers both scored hundreds in Test cricket.

FOURTH TEST – WEST INDIES v. INDIA
10–14 May 2002 at St John's, Antigua

INDIA

First innings

SS Das	b Collins	3
Wasim Jaffer	c Jacobs b Collins	86
R Dravid	b Dillon	91
SR Tendulkar	c Jacobs b Collins	0
SC Ganguly (capt)	c Hinds b Cuffy	45
VVS Laxman	hit wicket b Dillon	130
A Kumble	c Chanderpaul b Dillon	6
*A Ratra	not out	115
Zaheer Khan	c Jacobs b Cuffy	4
J Srinath	c Lara b Cuffy	15
A Nehra	not out	1
Extras	lb 6, w 1, nb 10	17
	(9 wickets dec.)	**513**

First innings

	O	M	R	W
Dillon	51	14	116	3
Cuffy	40	7	87	3
Collins	44	10	125	3
Sanford	32	6	113	-
Hooper	13	4	29	-
Hinds	2	0	9	-
Sarwan	9	3	23	-
Gayle	5	1	5	-

Fall of Wickets
1-13, 2-168, 3-168, 4-233, 5-235, 6-257, 7-474, 8-485, 9-508

WEST INDIES

First innings

CH Gayle	c Ratra b Zaheer Khan	32
WW Hinds	b Tendulkar	65
RR Sarwan	lbw b Zaheer Khan	51
BC Lara	lbw b Kumble	4
CL Hooper (capt)	c Nehra b Tendulkar	136
S Chanderpaul	not out	136
*RD Jacobs	c Laxman b Dravid	118
M Dillon	b Wasim Jaffer	43
PT Collins	c sub (Harbhajan Singh) b Wasim Jaffer	11
A Sanford	c Zaheer Khan b Laxman	2
CE Cuffy	not out	0
Extras	b 10, lb 9, w 6, nb 6	31
	(9 wickets dec.)	**629**

First innings

	O	M	R	W
Srinath	45	19	82	-
Nehra	49	16	122	-
Zaheer Khan	48	14	129	2
Ganguly	12	0	44	-
Tendulkar	34	5	107	2
Kumble	14	5	29	1
Laxman	17	6	32	1
Dravid	9	3	18	1
Wasim Jaffer	11	3	18	2
Das	8	2	28	-
Ratra	1	0	1	-

Fall of Wickets
1-65, 2-121, 3-135, 4-196, 5-382, 6-548, 7-607, 8-625, 9-628

Umpires: DR Shepherd & RB Tiffin
Toss: West Indies
Man of the Match: A Ratra

Match drawn

He spent the day's five-and-a-half hours painstakingly moving from 80 to 136 not out, an innings that lasted 11-and-a-quarter hours and 510 balls. Jaffer, Dravid and Laxman had the day's only successes, each claiming their first Test wickets. It was all as ludicrous as that.

FIFTH TEST
18–22 May 2002 at Kingston, Jamaica

The West Indies defied both the disadvantage of having to bat first on the grassiest Sabina Park pitch anyone could remember and a dramatic late change in the weather to complete a convincing victory that secured the series.

Wavell Hinds, on his home ground at Sabina Park, hits another four on his way to a series-winning 113.

They might have been denied their deserving triumph by a little more resolve from India's last three wickets that fell in just 8.3 overs to the second new ball on the final morning with ominous, dark clouds rolling in from the Blue Mountains.

The start had already been delayed half an hour by heavy overnight rain that returned less than half an hour after Zaheer's incongruous swipe to extra-cover formalized the result. The deluge would continue unabated for another 11 days, causing deadly flooding throughout Jamaica and eliminating Sabina's two one-day internationals.

The Jamaican left-handers, Gayle and Wavell Hinds, claimed the immediate advantage on their home ground with a partnership of 111 that Ganguly, who made the justifiable choice to bowl first on winning the toss, described as the most significant factor in the match. Once that base

had been established, the West Indies were always in control.

There were middle-order stumbles in both innings and Tendulkar made a worrying charge in his last innings of the series, but neither was long enough to alter the balance of the game.

The initial lurch occurred late on the first day as three wickets fell in the space of 18 overs to transform 246 for 1, with 22 overs remaining, to 287 for 4 at close.

Hinds scored 113, an innings of flawless quality, Sarwan 54 and India had long since squandered their chance of bowling on a pitch with early help for the seam bowlers when the equilibrium was shifted by a wanton stroke.

Attempting to hoist Harbhajan for his third six, Hinds only found the fielder precisely placed in that position two overs earlier. The tall left-hander's second Test hundred lasted five minutes short of six hours and contained 14 fours in addition to two sixes.

Hinds was replaced by Lara, who again scratched around uncharacteristically before edging his 25th ball to the keeper off Nehra. When Sarwan was caught at leg-slip off both the edge and pad off Harbhajan in the next over for 65, the spring that had been squeezed out of the Indian step earlier in the day suddenly reappeared. But it was too late.

They were let down by the veteran Srinath and his two young left-arm accomplices, Nehra and Zaheer, who sprayed the new ball in all directions except where it was likely to create any damage.

Even after Gayle, bothered by leg cramps, was caught in the gully off Zaheer for 68, the Indians looked at a loss to know where the next wicket was coming from until Hinds' misjudgment lifted their spirits.

There was an early boost on the second morning when Hooper diverted Srinath's bouncer off the back of the bat high to slip, but the West Indies soon regained the initiative.

A typically robust counter-attack by Jacobs, who clouted two sixes and seven fours in his 59 from 90 balls and shared a sixth-wicket partnership of 109 with the in-form Chanderpaul, re-established their position after Hooper's dismissal within the first 20 minutes.

The two saw the total past 400 before the last five wickets could only cobble together 21 more runs. Harbhajan added three more wickets to those of Hinds and Sarwan, triggering the collapse by bowling Jacobs off the inside edge. Chanderpaul's dismissal came as some little consolation for

Srinath's otherwise lacklustre performance that included an over worth 19, 15 to Jacobs and four byes from a bouncer that cleared the keeper.

There were two immediate setbacks for India as Dillon accounted for Jaffer in the third over and Dravid in the seventh and the dismissals of Tendulkar and Das, after a steadying stand of 69, fortified the West Indies' position by the close of play.

Tendulkar started on the back of successive scores of 0, 0, 8 and 0, but soon reasserted himself. For an hour and 35 minutes either side of tea, he shaped like the genuine article, although he was not flawless. He was on 34 when he offered a low, barely catchable return to Collins' left.

When Collins was replaced by Sanford, Tendulkar drove his first ball past cover for his seventh boundary and, attempting the same stroke, dragged the next ball onto his off stump.

Sabina Park, noisy at the best of times, exploded with a cacophony that could be heard in Montego Bay. The hullabaloo had not died down when Das was Cuffy's clear-cut lbw victim.

It was the West Indies' last wicket for the day as Ganguly and Laxman batted through to the end, with the score on 141 for 4, with few alarms.

Once Ganguly edged Dillon to Jacobs 35 minutes into the third morning to break a partnership of 84, India's fragile lower order once more capitulated.

The last six wickets went down for just 44 runs with Laxman left high and dry on 65. Dillon had taken three of them for his second return of five wickets in a Test innings, five years after his first against Pakistan in 1997.

It earned the West Indies a lead of 210 but, after Hooper chose to bat again, they stuttered to 81 for 5 on Brian Lara's dismissal for 35 and 122 for 7 when Chanderpaul and Collins came together in a solid partnership worth 43 by the close of play.

Aiming to put the match out of India's reach, they lost wickets steadily second time round. Srinath made the breakthrough, dispatching Hinds and Gayle to edged catches in the slips, and Zaheer accounted for both Sarwan and Hooper.

As Zaheer uprooted Lara's off stump off the inside edge, Jacobs fell to Harbhajan and Dillon was bowled, swinging wildly at Nehra, India were back in contention. But Chanderpaul and Collins then blocked them out over the last hour and 55 minutes of the day.

Chanderpaul drove a return catch off Zaheer's fourth ball of the second over the following morning, but Collins, with a mixture of bona fide strokes and tail-ender's swipes, recorded his highest

Merv Dillon also enjoyed returning home to Jamaica. His 5 for 71 in India's first innings gave West Indies a lead of 210.

Test score as the West Indies put on a further 32.

To claim a famous victory and end eight years without a series success overseas, India had to beat their own 406 for 4 that has stood as Test cricket's highest winning total since the Port-of-Spain Test of 1976.

Their target was 408 but, for a couple of magical hours, Tendulkar batted with an authority that suggested he might knock them off on his own, stroking 13 meaty boundaries in all directions during his innings of 86.

Once his master class was ended by Collins' sixth ball after tea that breached his back-foot defence on the angle from round the wicket, the fight went out of India.

The Indian maestro's wicket capped the best day of Collins' 11 Tests. After his heroics with the bat, he returned to have Jaffer smartly caught at short leg by Hinds with his third ball and Shiv Sunder Das lbw with his ninth.

Sanford tightened the West Indies' grip with an lbw decision against Rahul Dravid at 77 for 3. As Tendulkar took charge, dominating a partnership of 93 with Ganguly and passing 8,000 runs in his 96th Test – the tenth player to reach the mark – India could harbor hopes of the improbable. However, they rapidly disappeared once Collins made his crucial intervention.

Once Tendulkar departed, Ganguly and Laxman, India's two most consistent batsmen in the series, fell cheaply to catches off miscued hooks off Sanford, and Harbhajan hoisted a catch to mid-on off Gayle's off spin as the West Indies closed in on their goal.

India scraped through to the end of the day, called four overs early, at 237 for 7, but made no effort to hold on for the help the rain would clearly bring.

FIFTH TEST – WEST INDIES v. INDIA
18–22 May 2002 at Kingston, Jamaica

WEST INDIES

	First innings		Second innings	
CH Gayle	c Wasim Jaffer b Zaheer Khan	68	c Ganguly b Srinath	15
WW Hinds	c Wasim Jaffer		c Laxman b Srinath	6
	b Harbhajan Singh	113		
RR Sarwan	c Das b Harbhajan Singh	65	c Das b Zaheer Khan	12
BC Lara	c Ratra b Nehra	9	b Zaheer Khan	35
CL Hooper (capt)	c Dravid b Srinath	17	c Ratra b Zaheer Khan	6
S Chanderpaul	c Ratra b Srinath	58	c & b Zaheer Khan	59
*RD Jacobs	b Harbhajan Singh	59	c sub (D Mongia)	
			b Harbhajan Singh	16
M Dillon	lbw b Harbhajan Singh	0	b Nehra	4
PT Collins	c Laxman b Nehra	12	b Harbhajan Singh	24
A Sanford	c & b Harbhajan Singh	1	c Ganguly b Harbhajan Singh	5
CE Cuffy	not out	0	not out	3
Extras	b 5, lb 6, w 5, nb 4	20	b 4, nb 8	12
		422		**197**

	First innings				Second innings			
	O	M	R	W	O	M	R	W
Srinath	32	9	111	2	16	3	49	2
Nehra	30	14	72	2	9	2	23	1
Zaheer Khan	24	4	78	1	20	2	79	4
Ganguly	8	4	12	–				
Harbhajan Singh	38	3	138	5	17.2	2	42	3

Fall of Wickets
1-111, 2-246, 3-264, 4-264, 5-292, 6-401, 7-409, 8-411, 9-422
1-17, 2-24, 3-38, 4-60, 5-81, 6-117, 7-122, 8-170, 9-187

INDIA

	First innings		Second innings	
SS Das	lbw b Cuffy	33	lbw b Collins	10
Wasim Jaffer	c Jacobs b Dillon	0	c Hinds b Collins	7
R Dravid	lbw b Dillon	5	lbw b Sanford	30
SR Tendulkar	b Sanford	41	b Collins	86
SC Ganguly (capt)	c Jacobs b Dillon	36	c Sarwan b Sanford	28
VVS Laxman	not out	65	c Dillon b Sanford	23
*A Ratra	c Hinds b Dillon	3	lbw b Cuffy	19
Harbhajan Singh	c Hinds b Dillon	4	c Cuffy b Gayle	17
Zaheer Khan	c Lara b Cuffy	6	c Collins b Dillon	12
J Srinath	c Gayle b Collins	2	b Cuffy	4
A Nehra	run out (Sarwan)	0	not out	0
Extras	lb 6, nb 11	17	b 5, lb 1, w 1, nb 9	16
		212		**252**

	First innings				Second innings			
	O	M	R	W	O	M	R	W
Dillon	24	4	71	5	22.3	6	77	1
Cuffy	22	5	49	2	18	6	34	2
Collins	19	2	54	1	17	4	60	3
Sanford	9	1	27	1	19	8	48	3
Hooper	1	0	5	–	5	1	15	–
Gayle					4	2	7	1
Sarwan					3	0	5	–

Fall of Wickets
1-5, 2-15, 3-84, 4-86, 5-168, 6-178, 7-184, 8-194, 9-197
1-19, 2-25, 3-77, 4-170, 5-176, 6-209, 7-228, 8-242, 9-252

Umpires: DR Shepherd & RB Tiffin
Toss: India
Man of the Match: WW Hinds
Player of the Series: S Chanderpaul

West Indies won by 155 runs

TEST MATCH AVERAGES
West Indies v. India

WEST INDIES

Batting	M	Inns	NO	HS	Runs	Av	100	50	c/st
S Chanderpaul	5	7	3	140	562	140.50	3	3	1
CL Hooper	5	7	0	233	579	82.71	3	1	3
WW Hinds	2	3	0	113	184	61.33	1	1	4
RD Jacobs	3	4	0	118	193	48.25	1	1	10/-
RR Sarwan	5	7	0	65	317	45.28	–	4	3
CH Gayle	5	8	1	68	206	29.42	–	2	4
BC Lara	5	7	0	55	202	28.85	–	2	2
SC Williams	3	5	1	43	91	22.75	–	–	1
PT Collins	3	4	0	24	47	11.75	–	–	2
M Dillon	5	7	0	43	62	8.85	–	–	4
A Sanford	5	7	0	12	22	3.14	–	–	–
CE Cuffy	5	7	4	4	9	3.00	–	–	2

Also batted in one Test: MI Black 6, 3; JR Murray 0, 0, 1 (3 ct); MV Nagamootoo 15* (2 ct)

Bowling	Overs	Mds	Runs	Wkts	Av	Best	10m	5/inn
CE Cuffy	190	62	372	17	21.88	3-53	–	–
M Dillon	221.3	52	626	23	27.21	5-71	–	1
A Sanford	151.4	33	524	15	34.93	3-20	–	–
PT Collins	110	17	341	9	37.88	3-60	–	–

Also bowled: MI Black 31.5-10-89-3; CH Gayle 16-5-33-1; WW Hinds 2-0-9-0;
CL Hooper 64-17-131-1; MV Nagamootoo 40-13-103-1; RR Sarwan 16-3-35-2

INDIA

Batting	M	Inns	NO	HS	Runs	Av	100	50	c/st
VVS Laxman	5	8	2	130	474	79.00	1	4	3
R Dravid	5	8	1	144*	404	57.71	1	2	5
SC Ganguly	5	8	2	75*	322	53.66	–	2	3
SR Tendulkar	5	8	0	117	331	41.37	1	2	2
Wasim Jaffer	3	5	0	86	156	31.20	–	2	4
A Ratra	4	7	1	115*	153	25.50	1	–	6/-
SS Das	5	8	0	35	124	15.50	–	–	7
Zaheer Khan	5	7	0	46	81	11.57	–	–	3
SB Bangar	2	3	0	16	25	8.33	–	–	1
Harbhajan Singh	3	6	0	17	37	6.16	–	–	2
J Srinath	5	7	0	18	41	5.85	–	–	–
A Nehra	4	7	3	3	4	1.00	–	–	2

Also batted in two Tests: A Kumble 3, 6
Also batted in one Test: D Dasgupta 0 (2 ct); Sarandeep Singh 39* (1 ct)

Bowling	Overs	Mds	Runs	Wkts	Av	Best	10m	5/inn
Harbhajan Singh	140.2	23	388	14	27.71	5-138	–	1
A Nehra	171	53	453	12	37.75	4-112	–	–
Zaheer Khan	188.1	44	568	15	37.86	4-79	–	–
J Srinath	212	59	558	13	42.92	3-69	–	–

Also bowled: SB Bangar 29-6-74-1; SS Das 8-2-28-0; R Dravid 9-3-18-1; SC Ganguly 29-10-67-0;
A Kumble 59.1-12-174-3; VVS Laxman 17-6-32-1; A Ratra 1-0-1-0; Sarandeep Singh 21-5-80-1;
SR Tendulkar 40-4-139-2; Wasim Jaffer 11-3-18-2

ONE-DAY INTERNATIONALS
By Tony Cozier

At the last time of asking, India managed to earn a consoling share of the spoils from their West Indies tour. Disappointed by their 2–1 defeat in the Test series by opponents who surprised them with their fighting qualities, the Indians clinched the one-day series by the same margin with their victory by 56 runs in the fifth and final match in Port-of-Spain.

They had been beaten in three previous such series in the Caribbean (2–1 in 1983, 5–0 in 1989 and 3–1 in 1997), but there was no doubt about their superiority this time. After the first two matches at Sabina Park were washed out during Jamaica's 11 days of torrential rain that followed the final Test, their two victories were comprehensive.

The West Indies' only success was in the fourth match, the first of two at the Queen's Park Oval, that was reduced by half to 25 overs an innings by rain.

Both teams saw it as continuing preparation for the World Cup in South Africa, less than a year off. They have been drawn in different pools but neither appeared strong enough to cause the Australians sleepless nights over the security of their title.

'It's a great feeling to win after having lost the Tests,' captain Saurav Ganguly, voted Man of the Series for scores of 41, 39 and 56, said after collecting the Cricket in Caymanite Trophy. 'It's always great to win abroad.'

'It was good for us all, but especially as we have so many young boys in the team,' he said. 'It's important that they get the winning feeling.'

It was India's second successive one-day series triumph, following their 3–2 series win over Zimbabwe in India in March. West Indies captain Carl Hooper was not despondent over the result, his team's third successive loss in a one-day series after falling to Sri Lanka in the final of a triangular tournament in Sri Lanka in December and 2–1 to Pakistan in Sharjah in February.

'The thing is we've got a fairly young side,' he said. 'When you think of people like Sachin Tendulkar, Saurav Ganguly and Rahul Dravid with the wealth of experience they have, then it becomes tough when you don't have experienced bowlers who have played against the likes of these players, especially in the first 15 overs … I thought it was a good experience for our boys,' he added. 'Certainly a good one for me.'

Indian coach John Wright, the former New Zealand opening batsman, saw the series as helping India develop what he called 'the right combination' for the World Cup.

'After the Test series loss, we wouldn't have been able to swallow a one-day defeat and this result has been great,' he said. 'The batting order looks a lot more

After the disappointment of two washouts, India won the one-day series with Sachin Tendulkar scoring 65 in Trinidad to win the Man of the Match award.

measured now with Sachin coming at
No. 4 and Dinesh Mongia and Virender
Sehwag developing well.'

Tendulkar had been used mostly as
an opener in the shorter form of the
game but dropped down the order with
Sehwag taking his place. The jury was
out on the switch following Sehwag's
impetuosity that led to three dismissals
from poor strokes. But Ganguly
confirmed his status as the ideal opener
in the shorter game while the left-
handed Mongia once more proved a
handy No. 3, taking the Man of the
Match award in the first match with
74 off 104 balls.

Significantly, a sore shoulder meant
Tendulkar missed the match that India
lost, when they were bowled out for
123 from their 25 overs. He returned
next day, still handicapped by the
injury, to play a Man of the Match
innings of 65 off 70 balls.

With their two most experienced
bowlers back in India – Javagal Srinath
announcing his retirement and Anil
Kumble having surgery on the jaw he
fractured in the Test series – India had
to rely on their young brigade. Zaheer
Khan, Ashish Nehra, Tinu Yohannan,
Ajit Agarkar and Harbhajan Singh
capably filled the breach.

Yohannan, tall, slim and lively, set up
the win in Bridgetown by removing the
openers in his initial spell and, after a
shaky start, Agarkar finished things off
with the last three wickets for four runs
with yorkers.

Nehra, Zaheer, Agarkar and
Harbhajan shared the wickets in the last
match, but Tendulkar snared the most
crucial, Brian Lara sweeping a low full
toss directly to deep square leg.

India brought in Sehwag, Mongia,
Yohannan, Agarkar, Youvraj Singh and
Mohammed Kaif for the one-day series.
None played in the Tests and their youth and
enthusiasm gave a fresh look to the team in the field.

The West Indies had only one man who did not
appear in the Tests, fast bowler Corey Collymore. In
both their defeats, they were let down by the batting
that had been so reliable in the Tests.

They were bowled out for 186 in 44.5 overs in

Chris Gayle hit 84 in the fourth one-day international at
Queen's Park Oval, Port-of-Spain to give the West Indies
their only victory in the series.

Bridgetown, losing their last seven wickets for 46 as
Hooper was left stranded and unbeaten on 76.

In the deciding match in Port-of-Spain, they were

effectively beaten when Lara was fifth out for 36 in the 25th over at 88 for five chasing a revised target of 248 off 44 overs.

Shivnarine Chanderpaul and Ridley Jacobs raised their hopes with a stand of 71 from 11 overs but, once they fell, their long tail of four fast bowlers contributed little and India were comfortable winners.

A rain delay between innings that lopped six overs off the West Indies innings brought the Duckworth/Lewis system into play for the first time during the series.

With the relevant compact disc incompatible with available computers, two wickets were down and four overs had been bowled before match referee Mike Procter and third umpire Billy Doctrove could decide on the West Indies' target score.

It was an embarrassment, but it made no difference to the outcome.

Match One
25 May 2002 at Sabina Park, Kingston
No play possible – match abandoned without a ball bowled

Match Two
26 May 2002 at Sabina Park, Kingston
No play possible – match abandoned without a ball bowled

Match Three
29 May 2002 at Kensington Oval, Bridgetown
West Indies 186 (44.5 overs) (CL Hooper 76*)
India 187 for 3 (43.5 overs) (D Mongia 74)
India won by seven wickets
Man of the Match: D Mongia

Match Four
1 June 2002 at Queen's Park Oval, Port-of-Spain
India 123 (25 overs)
West Indies 124 for 3 (22.1 overs) (CH Gayle 84)
West Indies won by seven wickets
Man of the Match: CH Gayle

Match Five
2 June 2002 at Queen's Park Oval, Port-of-Spain
India 260 (50 overs) (SR Tendulkar 65, SC Ganguly 56, M Dillon 5 for 52)
West Indies 191 (36.2 overs) (S Chanderpaul 51)
India won by 56 runs (DL Method: West Indies target 248 from 44 overs)
Man of the Match: SR Tendulkar
Player of the Series: SC Ganguly

NEW ZEALAND IN THE WEST INDIES

ONE-DAY INTERNATIONALS
By Tony Cozier

The West Indies' five one-day internationals against New Zealand produced scoring at a rate of 5.02 runs an over, close finishes, controversy and confusion. The West Indies clinched it 3–1 off the last ball of the series at the packed Arnos Vale ground in St Vincent amidst chaos created by what New Zealand captain Stephen Fleming called 'incompetent umpiring'.

Chanderpaul, returning in the penultimate over with a badly bruised left elbow after a blow from Bond that had earlier sent him to hospital, hit three consecutive fours and a single off Daryl Tuffey from the last four balls of the match. The 292 runs scored was the highest total they had ever made chasing a target, but conflicting information from umpires Asoka de Silva, of the ICC elite panel, and Billy Doctrove, the official scorers and the befuddled

An unbeaten 108 from Shivnarine Chanderpaul eased the home side to victory in the second match with five balls to spare.

manually operated scoreboard, left the New Zealanders, in the words of Fleming, 'wild'. They later issued a formal complaint to ICC match referee Wasim Raja.

Not trusting the scoreboard, Fleming repeatedly consulted with the umpires over the number of overs remaining for his bowlers but could get no definite answer. When the confusion led to belated confirmation that Paul Hitchcock, New Zealand's best bowler in his debut series, had completed his ten, Fleming had to turn for the decisive last over to Tuffey, whose opening four overs had cost 34 runs. Hitchcock, in fact, still had one more available.

'It could have cost us the match and the series,' was Fleming's understandable comment.

Even five weeks later, when the tour was done and dusted, Fleming was still fuming. 'That still grates me big time,' he said. 'If we'd won that to make it 2–2 in the one-dayers, to add to the Test series win, that would have made it a very good tour. To lose was very, very annoying in the manner we did so.'

It tarnished the climax of a series that pulsated after the opening match at Sabina Park was abandoned following New Zealand's pedestrian 176 all out from 49.4 overs through the same Jamaican weather that earlier washed out India's first two one-day matches.

The early problems reflected the New Zealanders' rustiness. The rain that caused serious flooding in Jamaica restricted their practice on arrival and their only warm-up match was against a limited University of the West Indies Vice-Chancellor's XI that they won by 85 runs. Inevitably, they improved as they went on.

The West Indies inaugurated the impressive new Beausejours Stadium in St Lucia, nestled beneath rolling hills in the tourist belt in the north of the island, with victories in both weekend matches that earned them an unassailable 2–0 lead.

New Zealand won the third match at the Queen's Park Oval in Port-of-Spain under the perplexing Duckworth/Lewis system that challenged the West Indies to make the same total, 212 from 44.2 overs, as they had off 11.4 fewer overs. The margin in the end was a mere nine runs, but it set up St Vincent's grand finale.

Scott Styris served notice of what was to come in the Test series with 63 not out and 6 for 25 in match four.

Chanderpaul, retaining his form from the preceding Indian series, was promoted to his earlier position as opener and batted through the innings for 108 in St Lucia's first match. It led the West Indies to victory off the first ball of the final over, overhauling New Zealand's 248 for 7 that was based on Fleming's measured 89 and all-rounder Styris' boisterous 85 off 83 balls with three sixes and seven fours. It was the first indication of the impact Styris would have on the tour.

Lara's unbeaten 59, his highest score of an unflattering season, saw the West Indies home with ten overs to spare the next day after New Zealand, batting first as they did in every match, only managed to muster 210 for 7 from their 50 overs. Vincent and Harris shared a fifth-wicket partnership of 90 off 23 overs, but the West Indies kept the lid on the scoring rate with tight bowling and fielding. The results were a bonus for the St Lucia crowd of 12,000, welcoming the West Indies back for international cricket for the first time since Australia played a one-day international in 1984 at Mindoo Philip Park in Castries.

The West Indies were undone in the fourth match in Trinidad by a pair of British mathemeticians by the names of Henry Duckworth and Tony Lewis and by the ebullient Styris.

In an all-round performance matched not even by New Zealand's finest all-rounder, the absent, injured Chris Cairns, Styris belted 63 not out and then claimed the most wickets by a New Zealander in a one-day international, 6 for 25 off seven overs.

Styris and Astle were going along at a rate of five-and-a-half runs an over in a partnership of 122 when rain ended the innings. Astle's unbeaten 91 from 115 balls was his highest score of an inconsistent tour. In spite of Jacobs' unbeaten 60 off 45 balls, the West Indies fell nine runs short of their adjusted goal of 212 from 33 overs.

Ordinary fans, not versed in complicated calculations, were bewildered that New Zealand should have scored 212 for 5 off 44.1 overs and that the West Indies then had to make the identical score off 70 fewer balls to beat them. Yet they nearly did it, Chris Gayle blasting a run-a-ball 60 before Jacobs' closing blitz.

Arnos Vale followed with 583 runs from the day's 100 overs to keep the animated crowd fully entertained – and the confusion at the end to embarrass the umpires.

New Zealand's 291 for 8 was based on Fleming's 65, Craig McMillan's 83 off 87 balls and Lou Vincent's 55 off 73. Once the left-armer Collins went for 26 off one over, 18 by Fleming, the momentum rarely slackened.

The West Indies did well to keep in touch all the way. Gayle, Lara, Hooper and Sarwan all made telling contributions, but they looked likely to fall short before Tuffey's dramatic last over.

Styris and the astute medium pacer Hitchcock, considered such a one-day specialist he only had one first-class match prior to the tour, emerged as two little-known players whose names Sir Richard Hadlee and his selection panel would have already pencilled in for next year's World Cup.

The biggest benefit for the West Indies was the all-round performance of Gayle who thumped 194 runs at an average of 48.5 and a strike rate of 86.99 as left-handed opener and claimed 12 wickets with an economy rate of 4.07 runs an over with his stiff, flat, right-arm off spin.

It was a psychological filip for the West Indies after losing series in Sri Lanka and Sharjah and, two weeks earlier, against India in the Caribbean.

Match One
5 June 2002 at Sabina Park, Kingston
New Zealand 176 (49.4 overs) (CD McMillan 69)
West Indies did not bat
Match abandoned – no result

Match Two
8 June 2002 at Beausejours Stadium, St Lucia
New Zealand 248 for 7 (50 overs) (SP Fleming 89, SB Styris 85)
West Indies 250 for 4 (49.1 overs)
(S Chanderpaul 108*)
West Indies won by six wickets
Man of the Match: S Chanderpaul

Match Three
9 June 2002 at Beausejours Stadium, St Lucia
New Zealand 210 for 7 (50 overs) (L Vincent 58*, CZ Harris 50)
West Indies 211 for 3 (40 overs) (BC Lara 59*)
West Indies won by seven wickets
Man of the Match: BC Lara

Match Four
12 June 2002 at Queen's Park Oval, Port-of-Spain
New Zealand 212 for 5 (44.2 overs) (NJ Astle 91*, SB Styris 63*)
West Indies 202 for 9 (33 overs) (RD Jacobs 60*, CH Gayle 60, SB Styris 6 for 25)
New Zealand won by 9 runs (DL Method: West Indies target 212 from 33 overs)
Man of the Match: SB Styris

Match Five
16 June 2002 at Arnos Vale, St Vincent
New Zealand 291 for 8 (50 overs) (CD McMillan 83, SP Fleming 65, L Vincent 55, CH Gayle 4 for 54)
West Indies 292 for 6 (50 overs) (CH Gayle 67, RR Sarwan 52)
West Indies won by four wickets
Man of the Match: CH Gayle
Player of the Series: CH Gayle

FIRST TEST
21–25 June 2002 at Bridgetown, Barbados

New Zealand's first victory in 12 Tests on their fourth tour of the Caribbean was conclusive and reflected the difference between the teams in discipline, intensity, all-round strength and sheer cricketing common sense.

The West Indies effectively lost for only the fourth

time in 39 Tests at the Kensington Oval through their abysmal batting on the second afternoon that led to an all-out 107 and a deficit of 230. There was no coming back after that on a dry pitch that was never devilish but, at the same time, was never entirely trustworthy.

The signal triumph prompted justifiable celebrations among the New Zealanders in the dressing room and their 50 or so supporters who were rewarded for their long journey. A version of the 'haka' in front of the Sir Garfield Sobers Pavilion had locals bemused.

Captain Fleming's fourth Test hundred, an innings as vital to his team as any in his 70 Tests, led New Zealand from the uncertainty of 117 for 5 to 257 for 6, establishing a solid base after they had been sent in on losing the toss.

The tall left-hander entered the fray after an hour when Vincent provided Dillon with his 100th Test wicket off a sharp leg cutter and occupied the crease for the next four hours and 35 minutes before he

Stephen Fleming's fourth Test hundred eased the Kiwis to their first Test victory in 12 attempts in the Caribbean.

top-edged a cut to slip off Hooper 40 minutes before the close of play.

He guided New Zealand through a difficult period between lunch and tea when they lost four good wickets for 29 against disciplined West Indies fast bowling and found a dogged partner in wicketkeeper Hart, with whom he shared a priceless partnership of 108.

The pitch was not as favourable as Hooper had reckoned it might be, but the West Indies' bowling was as ragged in the first and final sessions as it was controlled in the second. They held a definite advantage when Sanford plucked out Richardson's off stump, removing him for 41, and Harris, Astle, and McMillan fell in quick succession after lunch.

But Fleming was still there to take charge. He survived an uncanny piece of luck at 11 when a ball from Sanford deflected from his pad onto his off stump without removing the bail, but batted with increasing certainty and fluency. His main scoring strokes were 20 fours, mostly off his legs and drives through the offside.

Hart, in his second Test, buckled down to the job of supporting Fleming so carefully that he didn't score a boundary in just over three hours to the close of play.

On Fleming's dismissal, Vettori, another left-hander, came to lash five fours at the end.

The next day, Kensington, for so long the bastion of West Indies cricket, experienced at first hand the harm and humiliation repeatedly inflicted on it at other venues across the globe in recent times.

On the ground where they bowled India out for 102 and trounced them by ten wickets just six weeks earlier, they collapsed for 107 through a succession of reckless, unforgivable strokes. It was their lowest total at Kensington since England bowled them out for 102 on an uncovered, rain-affected pitch in 1935.

Collins removed the left-handed Richardson to a first slip catch in the first of seven overs at the end of the day when New Zealand predictably chose to spurn the follow-on. But it was scant consolation.

Hart's unwavering adherence to the basics that occupied five hours 20 minutes and 220 balls for his unbeaten 57 and No. 8 Tuffey's defiance for an hour and a half for 28 saw to it that New Zealand added a further 80 runs. They should have been examples of the application required in the conditions.

The West Indies took no heed. Eight batsmen were out to catches in the field – four in the deep, four closer to the bat. All were attempting big shots.

They were instantly and initially unsettled by Bond's raw pace, consistently clocked over 90 miles

In Shane Bond the New Zealanders have unearthed a fast bowler of genuine hostility. He took 5 for 78 in the home side's second innings.

an hour on the speed gun. He backed it up with control and was soon on a hat-trick.

Gayle's feet were as heavy as a Mafia victim's as he tamely drove the first ball of Bond's third over into wide cover's lap. Sarwan, who filled the breach, offered an expansive pull from outside off stump next ball but could only get it as far as mid-on from high on the bat. Nor was the sequence of suicide strokemakers at an end.

As soon as Butler took over from Bond, Hooper hooked the first bouncer that came along to long leg. Any recovery from the situation rested with Lara, by now into his stride, and Chanderpaul, the

form batsman of the season. Lara was foxed into dragging an intended cut off Vettori back onto his leg stump after having gone scoreless for 25 balls and, while Chanderpaul remained steadfast, he could find no one to stay with him as the last five batsmen contributed just 13 runs between them.

New Zealand strengthened their position on the third day although, even with Dillon absent for all but six overs with a back strain, the West Indies made a spirited effort to regain lost ground. But it was too little, too late.

They restricted New Zealand's second innings to 243, but it still left them with a winning target of 474 never before reached in any Test.

Only a typically belligerent attack by Astle on the wayward Sanford immediately after lunch broke the pattern of a dour, attritional struggle. Astle hammered four of his 11 fours in Sanford's first over on resumption and three more before Hooper removed the struggling bowler after conceding 35 runs from three overs.

Astle's 77 and his sixth-wicket partnership of 76 with Fleming, batting down the order because of a stiff neck, steadied New Zealand after they had lost their first five wickets for 88.

Astle was one of six deserving wickets for 76 for Collins, who stoically filled the breach left by Dillon. He kept going for 30 overs on a humid, overcast day for his best return in his 12 Tests.

He made an early breakthrough as Vincent misjudged his in-swinger and was lbw offering no stroke, but the West Indies were again held up by Tuffey, batting through to the last over to lunch as nightwatchman until he nudged Hooper's straight ball to slip.

In the afternoon, Collins added McMillan and Astle to his collection, both taken in the slips driving, had Hart lobbing a miscued hook to square leg and finished off the innings with a keeper's catch off Butler.

He should have had a couple more, but Sarwan dropped two sharp chances, the first at short leg off Harris' first ball, the second at cover when Astle was on 12. It was Sarwan's 22nd birthday but, following his first-ball 0 the previous day, he was unlikely to celebrate it with champagne and dinner at one of Barbados' plush hotels.

The other wicket-takers were Sanford, who removed Fleming to a hooked catch on the square-leg boundary and bowled Vettori middle stump, and

FIRST TEST – WEST INDIES v. NEW ZEALAND
21-25 June 2002 at Bridgetown, Barbados

NEW ZEALAND

	First innings		Second innings	
MH Richardson	b Sanford	41	c Lara b Collins	0
L Vincent	c Jacobs b Dillon	14	lbw b Collins	2
SP Fleming (capt)	c Gayle b Hooper	130	(7) c Hinds b Sanford	34
CZ Harris	c Lara b Collins	0	lbw b Powell	19
NJ Astle	c Lara b Dillon	2	c Lara b Collins	77
CD McMillan	lbw b Sanford	6	c Hooper b Collins	1
*RG Hart	not out	57	(8) c Hinds b Collins	24
DL Vettori	c Hinds b Collins	39	(9) b Sanford	11
DR Tuffey	lbw b Powell	28	(3) c Gayle b Hooper	31
SE Bond	b Powell	5	not out	6
IG Butler	run out (Gayle)	3	c Jacobs b Collins	26
Extras	lb 8, nb 4	12	lb 8, w 1, nb 3	12
		337		**243**

	First innings				Second innings			
	O	M	R	W	O	M	R	W
Dillon	28	5	73	2	6	3	11	-
Collins	24	5	80	2	30.4	8	76	6
Powell	21	6	41	2	20	4	61	1
Sanford	28.4	7	101	2	17	5	68	2
Hooper	13	5	21	1	17	8	19	1
Gayle	10	3	12	-				
Sarwan	1	0	1	-				

Fall of Wickets
1-38, 2-88, 3-89, 4-106, 5-117, 6-225, 7-278, 8-323, 9-333
1-0, 2-11, 3-48, 4-69, 5-88, 6-164, 7-181, 8-205, 9-213

WEST INDIES

	First innings		Second innings	
CH Gayle	c Vettori b Bond	3	lbw b Bond	73
WW Hinds	c McMillan b Tuffey	10	c Richardson b Vettori	37
RR Sarwan	c Butler b Bond	0	c Vettori b Bond	18
BC Lara	b Vettori	28	b Bond	73
CL Hooper (capt)	c Tuffey b Butler	6	c Fleming b Tuffey	16
S Chanderpaul	not out	35	c Fleming b Vettori	17
*RD Jacobs	c Astle b Vettori	4	c Astle b Vettori	6
PT Collins	c Vincent b Butler	8	(9) lbw b Bond	8
A Sanford	c Hart b Butler	1	(10) not out	0
DB Powell	c Harris b Butler	0	(8) c Astle b Butler	2
M Dillon	c Fleming b Vettori	0	c Vincent b Bond	0
Extras	lb 4, nb 8	12	b 5, lb 11, w 2, nb 1	19
		107		**269**

	First innings				Second innings			
	O	M	R	W	O	M	R	W
Bond	12	1	34	2	21	7	78	5
Tuffey	7	3	16	1	15	5	43	1
Butler	11	2	26	3	14	0	58	1
Vettori	12.1	2	27	4	19	3	53	3
Astle					5	4	4	-
Harris					9	3	17	-

Fall of Wickets
1-6, 2-6, 3-31, 4-47, 5-62, 6-73, 7-90, 8-93, 9-103
1-68, 2-133, 3-142, 4-179, 5-204, 6-216, 7-222, 8-252, 9-269

Umpires: RE Koertzen & S Venkataraghavan
Toss: West Indies
Test Debut: DB Powell
Man of the Match: SP Fleming

New Zealand won by 204 runs

Powell who won an lbw claim against Harris.

The West Indies set out next morning with all their wickets intact, but New Zealand encountered relevant resistance for only half the day – and from a rampant Lara when it hardly mattered before the result was complete with 11 overs and a day remaining.

Gayle's 73, occupying two hours and 55 minutes, and his successive stands of 68 for the first wicket with Hinds and 65 for the second with Sarwan, carried the West Indies 20 minutes into the second session with only one wicket down.

Vettori had the solitary success before lunch when Hinds edged the left-arm spinner's third ball to short leg from the pad, but Bond made the break in his second spell immediately on resumption, taking care of Sarwan and Gayle.

Sarwan brought the wrath of the few hundred spectators on his head by repeating his fatal hook of the first innings, with the same resulting catch to mid-on, and Gayle, too late in defence, fell lbw, after which only Lara's shot-filled 73, compiled mainly with the tail-enders, delayed New Zealand for long.

Bond had the last laugh after a typical Lara assault, shattering the left-hander's stumps while adding two tail-end wickets to bring his tally to five for the innings.

SECOND TEST
28 June–3 July 2002 in St George's, Grenada

Twice during his debut Test, Styris wrested the advantage from the West Indies, ultimately earning New Zealand the draw that secured them the mini-series, their first such success on four tours of the Caribbean.

New Zealand were 208 for 6 in the second over of the second morning when Styris entered the fray and he proceeded to a hundred in his first Test innings that, with critical help from solid partners, built a strong total of 373.

He again came to the rescue an hour into the final day after three main middle-order wickets had fallen for nine nervous runs and New Zealand, on 157 for 5, and only 60 ahead with a minimum of five hours remaining. By the time the match and the series ended in the anti-climax of rain three hours later, he and the unyielding Hart were still together in a stand worth 99 and New Zealand were safe. Unbeaten on 69, Stryis was the tenth player in the history of the game to mark his debut Test with a hundred and a half-century.

Afterwards, Hooper acknowledged his bowlers had been defied as much by the lifeless pitch for the inaugural match at Test cricket's 84th Test venue as by their determined opponents.

Gayle made the most of a lifeless pitch for a commanding 204 which helped the West Indies to gain a first-innings lead of 97, but the home side, as in the previous Test, did not have the penetration to finish off their opponent's lower order.

Sent in once again after Hooper had won the toss, New Zealand were making steady progress on the opening day until two late wickets fell to the second new ball.

Richardson and Astle were engaged in a trouble-free, fourth-wicket partnership of 124 when Collins removed Richardson for 95 and nightwatchman Vettori to miscued hook shots in the last quarter of an hour.

Richardson had almost batted through the day's six hours before he was denied his third Test hundred by Gayle's spectacular, low, tumbling catch at fine leg.

Scott Styris became only the tenth player in the history of Test cricket to mark his debut with a century and a half-century.

Richardson and Astle came together 20 minutes after lunch to rebuild the innings after Fleming and Harris had fallen within one run of each other to leave New Zealand on 82 for 3. Fleming edged Collins to first slip and Harris was smartly taken by Jacobs off Hooper's bouncing off break. After that, the West Indies seemed resigned to their struggle until Collins intervened.

He did so again with his first ball the following morning after an hour's delay for rain and the absence of a satisfactory mower to shave the pitch. Astle was lbw offering nothing but pad to an in-swinger, but Styris, the strongly built all-rounder from Northern Districts, showed no nerves, only a sound technique and a wide range of strokes, in sharing partnerships of 48 with McMillan, 56 with Hart and 49 with Bond.

Bond arrived after McMillan was smartly held at first slip and Hart gloved his sweep off Hooper to leg-slip. He accompanied Styris from 71 to 100 before Lara, in charge during Hooper's brief absence after tea, gave a bowl to Chanderpaul who promptly had Bond lbw.

Styris was last out after ten minutes short of four hours at the crease during which he struck a six and eight fours off 178 balls.

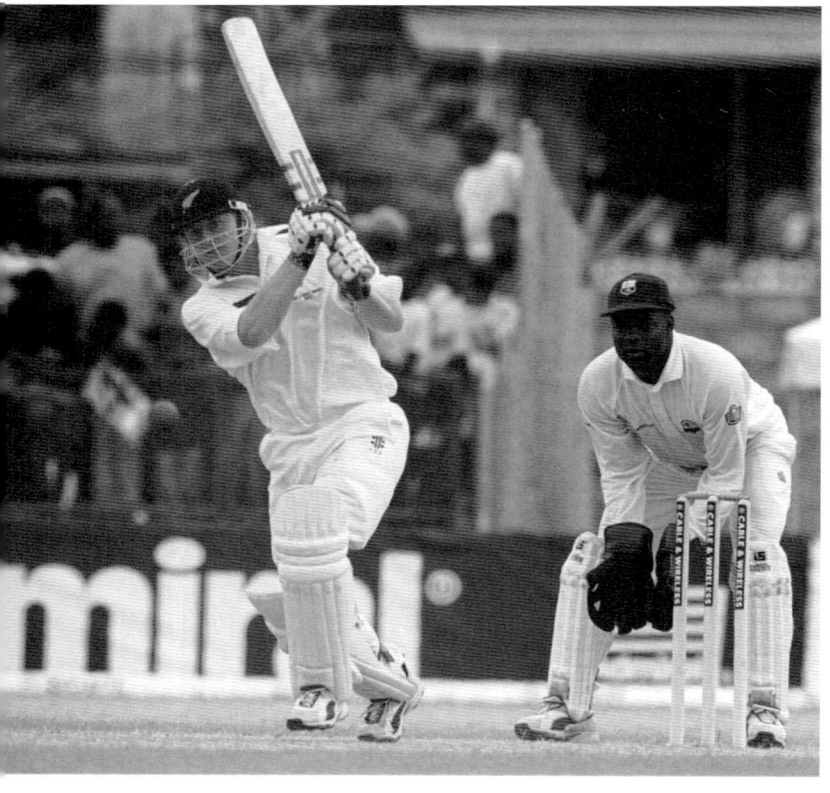

Bond had an early wicket, hitting Hinds' off stump with his speciality, the yorker, in the 21 overs the West Indies batted on the second afternoon, but he and his colleagues had to contend with a Gayle-force assault next day.

The tall left-hander hit the ball with the power of a latter day Clive Lloyd in compiling his second Test hundred. When he was ruled caught behind off Bond 20 minutes before the end, he had two sixes and 29 fours against his name. There was hardly a stroke he did not play and no bowler went unpunished.

He electrified a crowd of 10,000, the largest of the match, with a brutal attack on the second new ball just before tea. After Bond went through Hooper's defence with an in-swinging yorker with his second delivery with the new ball, Gayle hammered successive boundaries off four balls of the next over from Butler.

At the opposite end, he hoisted the first ball of Bond's next over, a no-ball, high over long on for a massive six. His blitz continued as he raised his second hundred from 120 balls – compared to 212 for his first.

He had three strokes of luck – one with a favourable decision when stuck on 94 for 35 minutes and two to missed outfield catches at 136 and 199, both off Bond. Six short of his hundred, his edge to the wicketkeeper off Butler went undetected by umpire Venkatraghavan, to the New Zealanders' disbelief.

He had partnerships of 100 with Sarwan, 75 with Lara, 38 with Hooper and, finally, 143 with Chanderpaul to send the West Indies into the lead.

Sarwan was run out for the sixth time in his 24 Tests, cut off by Harris' diving save at extra-cover and swift return to bowler Vettori.

Lara took 17 from Vettori's first two overs after lunch and was in ominous form when Styris enhanced his debut by drawing a wild slash that flew from the edge to the diving Hart.

Bond's dismissal of Hooper was another psychological boost for the New Zealanders before Gayle embarked on his stunning counter-attack and Chanderpaul presented him with typically solid support.

The West Indies began the fourth day 21 to the good with Chanderpaul seemingly their key man. But Bond conjured up another top delivery, second ball, that he could only edge low to first slip so that Jacobs, the competent left-handed Nagamootoo and, for a change, a couple of fast bowlers, extended the lead to 97. Bond once more had five wickets in the innings, a sign of things to come.

The already unlikely possibility of the West Indies making something of their advantage was fading when they were revived by two wickets in the final 25 minutes of the day and three more in the first hour of the last morning.

After a few early alarms that included two missed slip catches off Collins when Vincent had only a single, the openers had wiped out the arrears and were guiding New Zealand towards safety with a stand of 117 when Hooper summoned Sarwan to try his occasional leg spin.

Chris Gayle's 204 was an innings of electrifying power.

His third ball, quick and flat, breached Vincent's defence to hit off stump, bowling him for 54. Six overs later, Hooper found Fleming's edge for a catch at slip.

Richardson, following his first-innings score of 95 with another dogged innings, was unbeaten on 69 as he and Harris nervously batted through to the close with New Zealand, 139 for 2, 42 ahead. The West Indies made a spirited bid on the last morning for the victory they needed to share the series, with the contrasting spin of Hooper and Nagamootoo creating early havoc, but they could not sustain it.

Richardson survived a chance to Jacobs from an edged cut off Nagamootoo, but fell to a more difficult legside take by the keeper in the leg spinner's next over after adding only two to his overnight 69.

Astle went for no score to Hinds' juggling catch at short leg from inside edge and pad off Hooper's off break and when Harris popped another short-leg catch to the diving Sarwan off Nagamootoo for 17, the West Indies seemed on their way to their goal.

With McMillan demoted in the order because of three stitches in a cut on his left hand, caused by one of Gayle's booming drives, another quick wicket might have effectively settled the issue. But it never came.

SECOND TEST – WEST INDIES v. NEW ZEALAND
28 June–2 July 2002 at St George's, Grenada

TEST MATCH AVERAGES
West Indies v. New Zealand

NEW ZEALAND

	First innings		Second innings	
MH Richardson	c Gayle b Collins	95	c Jacobs b Nagamootoo	71
L Vincent	b Cuffy	24	b Sarwan	54
SP Fleming (capt)	c Lara b Collins	6	c Lara b Hooper	5
CZ Harris	c Jacobs b Hooper	0	c Sarwan b Nagamootoo	17
NJ Astle	lbw b Collins	69	c Hinds b Hooper	0
DL Vettori	c Jacobs b Collins	1		
CD McMillan	c Lara b Cuffy	14		
SB Styris	b Sanford	107	(6) not out	69
*RG Hart	c Hinds b Hooper	20	(7) not out	28
SE Bond	lbw b Chanderpaul	17		
IG Butler	not out	5		
Extras	lb 6, w 2, nb 7	15	lb 7, nb 5	12
		373	(5 wickets)	**256**

	First innings				Second innings			
	O	M	R	W	O	M	R	W
Collins	30	9	68	4	17	7	28	–
Cuffy	35	12	76	2	10	3	20	–
Sanford	22.5	4	74	1	14	3	27	–
Nagamootoo	33	11	88	–	42	16	75	2
Hooper	25	3	44	2	34	10	66	2
Gayle	3	1	5	–	6	2	7	–
Chanderpaul	4	0	12	1	2	2	–	–
Sarwan					6	0	26	1

Fall of Wickets
1-61, 2-81, 3-82, 4-205, 5-206, 6-208, 7-256, 8-312, 9-361
1-117, 2-132, 3-148, 4-149, 5-157

WEST INDIES

	First innings	
CH Gayle	c Hart b Bond	204
WW Hinds	b Bond	10
RR Sarwan	run out (Harris/Vettori)	39
BC Lara	c Hart b Styris	48
CL Hooper (capt)	lbw b Bond	17
S Chanderpaul	c Fleming b Bond	51
*RD Jacobs	c Styris b Butler	17
MV Nagamootoo	c Hart b Styris	32
PT Collins	lbw b Vettori	14
A Sanford	c Butler b Bond	12
CE Cuffy	not out	0
Extras	b 4, lb 2, w 5, nb 15	26
		470

	First innings			
	O	M	R	W
Bond	30.1	7	104	5
Butler	21	4	83	1
Styris	25	3	88	2
Vettori	41	9	134	1
Astle	6	2	15	–
Harris	15	4	40	–

Fall of Wickets
1-28, 2-128, 3-204, 4-242, 5-385, 6-394, 7-441, 8-448, 9-470

Umpires: RE Koertzen & S Venkataraghavan
Toss: West Indies
Test Debut: SB Styris
Man of the Match: CH Gayle
Player of the Series: SE Bond

Match drawn

WEST INDIES

Batting	M	Inns	NO	HS	Runs	Av	100	50	c/st
CH Gayle	2	3	0	204	280	93.33	1	1	3
S Chanderpaul	2	3	1	51	103	51.50	–	1	–
BC Lara	2	3	0	73	149	49.66	–	1	7
RR Sarwan	2	3	0	39	57	19.00	–	–	1
WW Hinds	2	3	0	37	57	19.00	–	–	5
CL Hooper	2	3	0	17	39	13.00	–	–	1
PT Collins	2	3	0	14	30	10.00	–	–	–
RD Jacobs	2	3	0	17	27	9.00	–	–	5/-
A Sanford	2	3	1	12	13	6.50	–	–	–

Also batted in one Test: CE Cuffy 0*; M Dillon 0, 0; MB Nagamootoo 32; DB Powell 0, 2

Bowling	Overs	Mds	Runs	Wkts	Av	Best	10m	5/inn
PT Collins	101.4	29	252	12	21.00	6-76	–	1
CL Hooper	89	26	150	6	25.00	2-44	–	–
A Sanford	82.3	19	270	5	54.00	2-68	–	–

Also bowled: S Chanderpaul 6-2-12-1; CE Cuffy 45-15-96-2; M Dillon 34-8-84-2;
CH Gayle 19-6-24-0; MV Nagamootoo 75-27-163-2; DB Powell 41-10-102-3;
RR Sarwan 7-0-27-1

INDIA

Batting	M	Inns	NO	HS	Runs	Av	100	50	c/st
RG Hart	2	4	2	57*	129	64.50	–	1	4/-
MH Richardson	2	4	0	95	207	51.75	–	2	1
SP Fleming	2	4	0	130	175	43.75	1	–	4
NJ Astle	2	4	0	77	148	37.00	–	2	3
L Vincent	2	4	0	54	94	23.50	–	1	2
DL Vettori	2	3	0	39	51	17.00	–	–	2
IG Butler	2	3	1	26	34	17.00	–	–	–
SE Bond	2	3	1	17	28	14.00	–	–	–
CZ Harris	2	4	0	19	36	9.00	–	–	1
CD McMillan	2	3	0	14	21	7.00	–	–	1

Also batted in one Test: SB Styris 107, 69* (1 ct); DR Tuffey 28, 31 (1 ct)

Bowling	Overs	Mds	Runs	Wkts	Av	Best	10m	5/inn
SE Bond	63.1	15	216	12	18.00	5-78	–	2
DL Vettori	72.1	14	214	8	26.75	4-27	–	–
IG Butler	46	6	167	5	33.40	3-26	–	–

Also bowled: NJ Astle 11-6-19-0; CZ Harris 24-7-57-0; SB Styris 25-3-88-2; DR Tuffey 22-8-59-2

Mahendra Nagamootoo, whose quick leg breaks and googlies helped Guyana achieve the double in the West Indies domestic tournaments.

WEST INDIES DOMESTIC FIRST-CLASS CRICKET
By Tony Cozier

The changing of the guard, so controversially conspicuous at Board level, was affirmed on the field as well as Jamaica and Guyana took over as the new powerhouses of West Indies cricket in the 2001–02 season. There were significant administrative shifts as well.

In keeping with the mandate of West Indies Cricket Board (WICB) president, Wes Hall, to bring prominent past players back into the mainstream, Sir Vivian Richards, as prominent as they come, was appointed head of the selection panel in June. He was joined in what Hall, himself a previous selector, described as a 'thankless' job by another first-timer, Gordon Greenidge, Richards' team-mate during the golden period of the 1980s.

While their predecessors once had an embarrassment of riches from which to choose, especially out of Barbados and the Leeward Islands whose players dominated the West Indies teams of their era, Richards and co. would find their resources limited and, at present, concentrated mainly on Jamaica and Guyana. Seven of the 13 they chose for the two Tests against New Zealand at the end of the longest home season in history were either Jamaican or Guyanese.

It was not surprising that Guyana did the double by winning the Red Stripe Bowl and the Busta International Shield, reversing their loss in the 2001 final to Jamaica who had earlier claimed the Busta Cup. Even without several of their leading players – Courtney Walsh (retired), Jimmy Adams (off in South Africa captaining Free State), Franklyn Rose, Marlon Samuels and Nehemiah Perry (injured) – the Jamaicans swept into the final of the Shield with seven successive victories in eight matches.

It was an unprecedented sequence, but they could not maintain it, losing to Guyana on first innings in a drawn final that was enough for the Shield to change hands. More to the point, they were denied by the Guyana captain, Carl Hooper, who followed his 222 in the semi-final win on first innings over the Leeward Islands with an unbeaten 149 out of 354, batting at No. 7. Along the way, Jamaica clinched the Busta Cup, based on the placings of the six regional teams after the qualifying round of a tournament that, for the second year, also involved a foreign A team, Bangladesh, and West Indies B, the under-23 development combination.

In contrast, Barbados, Busta Cup winners in 2001 and champions 16 times since an annual regional tournament was inaugurated in 1966, were beaten in three successive matches for the first time in their proud history and failed to make it into the semi-finals. It was the second season of the expanded tournament but, while England A had clearly enhanced the competitiveness in 2001, reaching the Shield semis, the Bangladeshi reserves, with an average age of 21, were out of their depth. They lost six of their eight matches, gaining the consolation of one victory, by eight runs, over the Windward Islands.

The tournament began while the West Indies were in Sharjah, engaged in another barren overseas series against Pakistan, but it only kept the leading players out for the first two matches. None made a bigger impact on return than captain Hooper with his big scores in the Shield semi and final. Guyana also had hundreds from Shivnarine Chanderpaul and Lennox Cush, in a third-wicket partnership of 251 against the Leewards in the first round, and Azimul Haniff, 235, and Sewnarine Chattergoon, 143, in an opening partnership of 340 against the hapless Bangladeshis.

But Guyana's main strength lay in the combination of Mahendra Nagamootoo's quick leg breaks and googlies and Neil McGarrell's orthodox left-arm spin. Nagamootoo's tournament-high 50 wickets earned him a recall to the Test team, McGarrell had 35 in support.

Jamaica's triumph in the Cup and advance to the Shield final was based principally on all-round balance and an obvious team spirit engendered by captain Robert Samuels, the left-handed opener who played six Tests in 1996-97, and coach Robert Haynes.

Gareth Breese, 26, a former West Indies youth team captain, epitomized their strength. A stylish right-hander, he averaged 36.72 in the lower half of the order to complement his 44 wickets (at 20.18 runs each) with steady off spin. It was enough to influence his inclusion in the West Indies squad for the subsequent one-day series against India and New Zealand, even though he never got his chance.

Samuels and the opener Leon Garrick both topped 500 runs while Breese had varied support from the lively pace of Darren Powell and Jermaine Lawson, the medium-pace swing of Laurie Williams and the steady left-arm spin of Ryan Cunningham.

Although the former head of selectors, Mike Findlay, the Test wicketkeeper of the late 1960s, repeated his familiar lament over the general standard, a distinct improvement in the scores, both team and individual, was a heartening sign. Cynics countered by noting the weakness of the bowling, but it had been much the same in recent years.

Familiar names were dominant among the heavy-scorers, but several promising young batsmen raised hopes of a bright future. Hooper's 222 in the semi-final was followed by 252 not out by captain Stuart Williams that carried the Leewards to within 49 of Guyana's total, with five wickets standing, when rain ended the match and blocked their path to the final.

Williams also took 195 off Barbados and, three years after his last Test appearance, his tournament-high 974 runs (at 97.4) prompted a recall to the Test team against India. It was a place he could not secure.

The other double hundreds were Haniff's 235 against Bangladesh A and 22-year-old Sylvester Joseph's unbeaten 211 for the Leewards against West Indies B. Those who were dazzled by his

strokeplay with the West Indies under-19s in England the previous summer were not surprised that Devon Smith, the diminutive 20-year-old left-handed Windward Islands' opener from Grenada, was the highest and most consistent scorer in the Busta Cup. His 750 runs, at an average of 62.5, included 143 against Barbados and seven other scores over 50.

Smith's fellow Grenadian, the 34-year-old veteran wicketkeeper Junior Murray, established a Windward Islands' record with four hundreds in the season. Like Stuart Williams, his form won him back his Test place against India but, like Williams, he quickly lost it again.

Two 19-year-olds, Donovan Pagon and Dwayne Bravo, returned from the youth World Cup in New Zealand to immediately make the jump to first-class level.

Pagon, a compact Jamaican right-hander who was second highest scorer in the New Zealand tournament, made 110 for West Indies B in his debut innings against a Guyana attack manned by four Test bowlers (Nagamootoo, McGarrell, Hooper and Reon King). It was a match in which the eventual Shield champions had the embarrassment of following on against the inexperienced youngsters.

Bravo, a dashing right-hander from the same Santa Cruz valley in Trinidad as Brian Lara and long since compared to his brilliant compatriot at a

similar age, required only four matches for his maiden hundred, 122 against the Windward Islands.

Delighted as they are that so many batsmen are suddenly emerging (Chris Gayle, Ramnaresh Sarwan, Marlon Samuels, Daren Ganga and Ryan Hinds are others in their early-20s who have gone into the Test team), the West Indians are keener to find new bowlers of genuine pace and aggression … they are still looking.

Adam Sanford, 24, a strong Antiguan policeman, was impressive enough in his first full season to earn Test selection and retain his place in all seven Tests for the season. A native of Dominica, he is a direct descendant of the Caribs – the indigenous people Christopher Columbus encountered when he first landed in the New World and who gave the region its name – the first such Test cricketer. His speed is better described as stiff rather than express and his Test returns were only moderate.

The Jamaicans, Darren Powell, 24, and Lawson, 24, and the Barbadian Tino Best, a small, energetic 20-year-old, are others of lively pace. All were given their chance on the West Indies A team to England during the summer, another of the WICB's measures to expose and develop players of promise.

As usual, the Red Stripe Bowl was separate from the Busta tournament and staged in October, with the qualifying group matches in Guyana and Jamaica and the semis and final in Jamaica, home of the sponsors.

A lack of finance led to the exclusion of Bermuda, Canada, the United States and the Cayman Islands, who had all competed a year earlier.

The decision to split the Windwards, the 2000 champions, into North and South and the Leewards into Antigua and the Rest weakened them to such an extent that the four teams all lost to the traditional territories.

Trinidad and Tobago's 409 for 6 off 50 overs against Windwards North, with three individual hundreds, was by far the highest in regional limited-overs cricket and proof that the new arrangement was flawed.

Once more demonstrating how evenly matched they are at present, Jamaica and Guyana tied their low-scoring semi-final at 191 for 9 each. Their record in the qualifying round was used to decide that Guyana advanced to meet Barbados in the final where Ramnaresh Sarwan's 80 and Hooper's unbeaten 45 off 27 balls earned them the Bowl with 3.1 overs to spare.

Left: Stuart Williams, from the Leeward Islands, made the highest score (252 not out) in the West Indies' domestic season. Only Carl Hooper scored more first-class runs.

FIRST-CLASS AVERAGES
West Indies

BATTING

	M	Inns	NO	HS	Runs	Av	100	50
S Chanderpaul	12	17	5	140	987	82.25	4	5
MD Ventura	6	7	4	76*	240	80.00	-	3
SC Williams	11	19	5	252*	1065	76.07	3	4
CL Hooper	12	16	1	233	1081	72.06	5	1
VVS Laxman	7	11	3	130	521	65.12	1	4
DS Smith	8	14	1	143	841	64.69	1	8
RS Morton	7	10	0	104	645	64.50	2	5
SL Campbell	3	5	1	107	237	59.25	2	-
RO Hinds	4	5	0	166	278	55.60	1	1
SC Ganguly	6	9	2	75*	374	53.42	-	3
RG Samuels	9	14	3	106*	572	52.00	1	4
RAM Smith	7	12	2	72	514	51.40	-	7
R Dravid	6	9	1	144*	406	50.75	1	2
D Ganga	4	7	1	151*	302	50.33	1	1
SC Joseph	6	9	1	211*	386	48.25	1	2
RD Jacobs	10	13	3	118	473	47.30	1	4
CO Browne	7	12	2	161	471	47.10	1	3
WW Hinds	10	16	1	175	693	46.20	2	2
FL Reifer	7	12	1	127*	488	44.36	1	4
JR Murray	9	15	0	125	643	42.86	4	1
CH Gayle	11	19	1	204	762	42.33	1	5
DJ Bravo	5	9	0	122	380	42.22	1	2
LV Garrick	9	16	2	138	581	41.50	2	2
AR Percival	5	8	2	96	244	40.66	-	1
KJ Wilkinson	7	12	0	135	486	40.50	1	2
LMP Simmons	3	6	2	47*	162	40.50	-	-
RK Currency	4	7	1	82	240	40.00	-	1
LJ Cush	8	12	1	154	438	39.81	2	-
SR Tendulkar	6	9	0	117	349	38.77	1	2
PA Wallace	7	13	1	99	463	38.58	-	5
IH Jan	8	16	1	110	574	38.26	1	4
A Haniff	9	15	0	235	570	38.00	1	3
S Chattergoon	8	13	0	143	483	37.15	1	4
SJ Benn	6	11	2	78	328	36.44	-	3
BC Lara	7	10	0	73	351	35.10	-	3
FA Adams	8	13	1	71	419	34.91	-	5
GR Breese	10	14	2	83	419	34.91	-	4
KI Tittle	6	8	1	101*	237	33.85	1	1
RL Powell	7	11	0	86	372	33.81	-	3
LA Roberts	7	12	0	146	401	33.41	2	-
RIC Holder	7	13	1	112*	395	32.91	1	2
NC McGarrell	9	11	2	56*	292	32.44	-	2
RR Sarwan	10	14	0	65	452	32.28	-	4
Mazharul Haque	7	14	0	90	451	32.21	-	3
Wasim Jaffer	4	7	0	86	218	31.14	-	3
K Arjune	8	15	1	109*	413	29.50	1	1
SM Jeffers	7	13	0	70	381	29.30	-	2
Akram Khan	7	14	0	72	404	28.85	-	2
CF Lopez	5	10	2	37	209	26.12	-	-
A Ratra	5	9	2	115*	182	26.00	1	-
SB Bangar	4	5	1	76*	102	25.50	-	1
KA Mason	8	14	2	68*	306	25.50	-	2
JA Mitchum	4	7	2	59*	125	25.00	-	1
A Ally-Haniff	9	13	3	52	247	24.70	-	2
Hannan Sarkar	7	14	0	69	345	24.64	-	2
KH Hibbert	9	14	2	81	290	24.16	-	1
S Naidoo	3	6	0	89	142	23.66	-	1
H Pooran	4	8	0	72	187	23.37	-	1
MV Nagamootoo	11	15	4	48	254	23.09	-	-
AS Jackson	3	6	1	29	115	23.00	-	-
A Kanhai	3	5	1	39	92	23.00	-	-
RN Lewis	7	12	1	55	237	21.54	-	1
D Dasgupta	3	5	1	54*	86	21.50	-	1
DR Smith	6	11	0	102	235	21.36	1	-
EJ Powell	3	6	2	32*	85	21.25	-	-
RO Cunningham	8	10	4	35	127	21.16	-	-
F Thomas	7	11	4	33	145	20.71	-	-
KN Casimir	6	10	1	57*	184	20.44	-	1
PA Browne	7	13	0	55	264	20.30	-	2
KD Martin	5	10	0	61	201	20.10	-	1
N Deonarine	4	6	1	46	100	20.00	-	-
TA Willett	4	5	0	46	99	19.80	-	-

FIRST-CLASS AVERAGES
West Indies

BATTING

	M	Inns	NO	HS	Runs	Av	100	50
Tareq Aziz	5	10	7	12*	58	19.33	-	-
J Eugene	6	11	0	86	212	19.27	-	1
LR Williams	8	11	1	40	189	18.90	-	-
Ehsanul Haque	7	14	0	50	263	18.78	-	1
Ahsanullah Hasan	3	6	1	37	92	18.40	-	-
Mushfiqur Rahman	7	14	1	57	238	18.30	-	2
AWL Sealy	6	11	5	57*	108	18.00	-	1
AN Mayers	7	13	0	55	232	17.84	-	2
RA Austin	5	8	2	56*	106	17.66	-	1
D James	4	7	0	46	123	17.57	-	-
CJK Hodge	5	9	1	65	135	16.87	-	1
IDR Bradshaw	6	10	0	32	167	16.70	-	-
S Badree	4	8	0	43	133	16.62	-	-
SS Das	7	12	1	35	175	15.90	-	-
IO Jackson	7	11	0	33	172	15.63	-	-
Tushar Imran	6	12	0	79	178	14.83	-	1
Anwar Hossain	7	14	1	44	192	14.76	-	-
D Mohammed	6	9	1	52	116	14.50	-	1
Mosaddek Hossain	6	12	1	63	156	14.18	-	1
D Ramnarine	4	6	1	19	69	13.80	-	-
SM Clarke	4	7	0	42	95	13.57	-	-
KK Sylvester	6	9	0	50	111	12.33	-	1
DK Butler	7	11	2	24*	111	12.33	-	-
CC Alexander	5	10	1	23	110	12.22	-	-
R Griffith	3	5	0	33	61	12.20	-	-
Naimur Rahman	7	14	0	29	165	11.78	-	-
Zaheer Khan	6	8	0	46	92	11.50	-	-
KK Peters	5	9	3	20	68	11.33	-	-
PT Collins	9	10	1	24	100	11.11	-	-
Alamgir Kabir	5	10	1	27*	95	10.55	-	-
DRE Joseph	4	7	0	41	72	10.28	-	-
DB Powell	10	12	2	38	101	10.10	-	-

Qualification: 5 innings, average 10.00

BOWLING

	Overs	Mds	Runs	Wkts	Av	Best	10m	5/inn
LR Williams	185.2	42	499	26	19.19	5-20	-	1
KCB Jeremy	313.4	69	789	41	19.24	6-33	-	3
RO Cunningham	248	94	529	27	19.59	5-51	-	1
GR Breese	408.2	108	948	47	20.17	6-57	1	3
DB Powell	253.2	55	655	29	22.58	5-28	-	2
PT Collins	322	69	865	37	23.37	6-76	-	2
IDR Bradshaw	219.5	41	726	31	23.41	4-61	-	-
MI Black	302	73	944	40	23.60	5-76	-	1
NC McGarrell	374.1	105	845	35	24.14	5-88	-	1
TL Best	110	15	413	17	24.29	5-37	-	1
Harbhajan Singh	189.4	30	516	21	24.57	5-138	-	1
DK Butler	209.1	58	523	21	24.90	3-38	-	-
M Persad	259.3	53	657	26	25.26	7-113	-	1
F Thomas	210.4	29	710	28	25.35	5-65	-	1
IO Jackson	292.4	67	692	27	25.62	5-66	-	1
MV Nagamootoo	554.1	137	1386	53	26.15	6-61	1	3
D Mohammed	143	21	367	13	28.23	2-31	-	-
M Dillon	284.3	71	792	28	28.28	5-71	-	1
SJ Benn	256.2	64	679	24	28.29	5-87	-	2
CE Cuffy	291.5	92	605	21	28.80	3-53	-	-
A Sanford	561.4	109	1827	61	29.95	5-80	-	1
KG Darlington	192.1	34	617	20	30.85	4-49	-	-
RD King	258	58	843	27	31.22	4-27	-	-
Mossadek Hossain	224.5	33	677	21	32.23	5-46	-	2
Zaheer Khan	205.3	47	627	19	33.00	4-79	-	-
AWL Sealy	217	39	631	19	33.21	5-79	-	1
JJC Lawson	182.4	41	514	15	34.26	4-28	-	-
J Srinath	230	63	597	17	35.11	3-69	-	-
Naimur Rahman	251.4	60	628	17	36.94	5-31	-	1
CJK Hodge	186.4	28	571	15	38.06	4-87	-	-

Qualification: 10 wickets in 8 innings

FIRST-CLASS AVERAGES
West Indies

BOWLING

	Overs	Mds	Runs	Wkts	Av	Best	10m	5/inn

The following bowlers took 10 wickets in fewer than 8 innings:

	Overs	Mds	Runs	Wkts	Av	Best	10m	5/inn
SE Bond	63.1	15	216	12	18.00	5-78	-	2
RA Austin	139.1	34	412	16	25.75	5-60	-	2
Anwar Hossain	85	18	262	10	26.20	4-34	-	-
S Shillingford	144.1	35	339	12	28.25	5-71	-	1
KK Peters	137.1	35	319	11	29.00	3-49	-	-
Alamgir Kabir	105	19	363	12	30.25	4-52	-	-
A Kumble	124.4	26	364	12	30.33	5-50	-	1
Tareq Aziz	111	17	405	13	31.15	4-70	-	-
D Ramnarine	143.2	24	447	14	31.92	5-116	-	1
RJ Christopher	115.1	27	353	10	35.30	4-50	-	-
GT Prince	132	19	489	13	37.61	5-96	-	1
A Nehra	171	53	453	12	37.75	4-112	-	-
CC Alexander	98.4	12	410	10	41.10	3-79	-	-

FIELDING

30 - JR Murray (29ct, 1st); 24 - A Ally-Haniff (23ct, 1st), RD Jacobs; 19 - CO Browne (18ct, 1st), KA Mason (18ct, 1st); 15 - KH Hibbert (13ct, 2st); 14 - RG Samuels; 13 - LV Garrick, RS Morton, RAM Smith, SC Williams; 12 - Anwar Hossain; 11 - SS Das, NC McGarrell; 10 - Ehsanul Haque, CH Gayle, WW Hinds, MV Nagamootoo, RL Powell

Qualification: 10 catches or more

ZIMBABWE

South Africa in Zimbabwe
England in Zimbabwe
Zimbabwe Domestic First-Class Season
First-Class Averages

SOUTH AFRICA IN ZIMBABWE
by Telford Vice

FIRST TEST
7–11 September 2001 at Harare

Remove from the equation a cluster of quality bowlers, retain some of the game's finest batsmen, factor in a Harare pitch as featureless as the back of a farmer's khaki shirt, and the batting has to be gluttonous. It duly was, before South Africa won by nine wickets, 40 minutes before the scheduled tea interval on the final day.

South Africa improved their record first-, second- and third-wicket partnerships in matches against Zimbabwe, while the home side did likewise for their fourth – twice – seventh and ninth wickets. Zimbabwe's totals were their biggest against their southern neighbours.

The list of injured players told of what might have been. Allan Donald, his fitness impaired by influenza, was ruled out of both Tests, Bryan Strang was hamstrung, while Andy Blignaut and Brighton Watambwa escaped the team curfew with ankle and knee problems respectively.

At stumps on the first day South Africa were 414 for 1 – within sight of England's record for a day's play of 503 for 2 against South Africa at Lord's in 1924. Herschelle Gibbs scored a mere 147 as Gary Kirsten, 202 not out on the first day, went on to 220 in more than seven hours before driving at a wide delivery from debutant medium pacer Doug Hondo to be taken behind. It was Kirsten's third double century and an innings which took him past 5,000 Test runs, as well as making him the third man, after Sachin Tendulkar and Steve Waugh, to inflict centuries on eight Test-playing countries.

Jacques Kallis ground out an unbeaten 157 in more than six hours, and went to 3,000 runs before Shaun Pollock declared at 600 for 3, 25 minutes before tea on the second day.

Zimbabwe, needing 401 to avoid the follow-on, stumbled to 51 for 3 before Dion Ebrahim and Andy Flower righted them with steady batting. But, seven overs from the close, Ebrahim charged the debutant left-arm spinner, Claude Henderson, and was stumped for an otherwise level-headed 71 to end the stand at 82.

Previous page: Andy Flower continued his sublime run of form throughout the year. An average of 211.00 against South Africa (including an unbeaten 199 in the first Test) signified that he is Zimbabwe's only true world-class batsman.

That left Zimbabwe's fate squarely on Flower's shoulders. The flinty left-hander defied the South Africans for four-and-a-half hours before he was trapped in front for 142 – one of four wickets claimed by galumphing fast bowler Andre Nel, another new cap – to end the innings with Zimbabwe short of their immediate target. By the close on the third day, Zimbabwe were still 217 runs away from making the visitors bat again with Ebrahim, Alistair Campbell and Craig Wishart all back in the hut.

Flower was off the field for just 83 minutes before he found himself taking guard again. He resumed on

South Africa's experienced opener, Gary Kirsten, enjoyed his visit to the Harare Sports Club. He scored 220 out of South Africa's overwhelming total of 600 for 3 declared.

Andy Flower did his best by scoring 142 in Zimbabwe's first innings, but the home team was heavily beaten.

43 not out on the fourth day, and his partnership with Hamilton Masakadza swelled to 186 before the latter was caught at short leg off Henderson – the fourth chance he offered – for 86, shortly after lunch.

Stumps found Flower unbowed and 118 not out to become the first man in 52 years to score centuries in both innings against South Africa, and the second Zimbabwean to do so against any opposition after his brother, Grant. It was a feat worthy of triumph, but South Africa removed the three remaining batsmen before lunch on the final day to leave themselves a victory target of 78.

Cruelly, Flower was 199 not out when Hondo was leg before to Nel to end the innings. He was at the crease for almost ten hours and improved his career average to 55.2, at that stage the third highest among current Test players.

FIRST TEST – ZIMBABWE v. SOUTH AFRICA
7–11 September 2001 at Harare

SOUTH AFRICA

	First innings		Second innings	
HH Gibbs	b Friend	147		
G Kirsten	c A Flower b Hondo	220	not out	31
JH Kallis	not out	157	not out	42
ND McKenzie	c Hondo b Friend	52		
L Klusener	not out	8		
*MV Boucher				
HH Dippenaar			(1) lbw b Friend	0
SM Pollock (capt)				
CW Henderson				
M Ntini				
A Nel				
Extras	lb 2, w 6, nb 8	16	b 5, lb 1	6
	(3 wickets dec.)	600	(1 wicket)	79

	First innings				Second innings			
	O	M	R	W	O	M	R	W
Streak	34	4	120	–	4	2	10	–
Friend	27	2	147	2	7	0	44	1
Hondo	18	0	87	1	1	1	0	–
Price	42	2	192	–	3.2	0	19	–
Whittall	12	2	34	–				
GW Flower	6	0	18	–				

Fall of Wickets
1-256, 2-455, 3-582
1-0

ZIMBABWE

	First innings		Second innings	
DD Ebrahim	st Boucher b Henderson	71	lbw b Pollock	0
ADR Campbell	c Boucher b Nel	0	b Kallis	7
H Masakadza	run out (McKenzie)	13	c Dippenaar b Henderson	85
CB Wishart	c Klusener b Kallis	0	c Klusener b Pollock	6
*A Flower	lbw b Pollock	142	not out	199
RW Price	c Kirsten b Nel	0	(10) c McKenzie b Klusener	4
GW Flower	c Dippenaar b Nel	0	(6) c Dippenaar b Ntini	16
GJ Whittall	b Kallis	16	(7) lbw b Henderson	3
HH Streak (capt)	lbw b Henderson	7	(8) c Kallis b Pollock	19
TJ Friend	c Pollock b Nel	30	(9) b Klusener	17
DT Hondo	not out	1	lbw b Nel	6
Extras	b 4, nb 2	6	b 9, lb 10, nb 10	29
		286		391

	First innings				Second innings			
	O	M	R	W	O	M	R	W
Pollock	22.3	5	62	1	29	5	67	3
Nel	16	6	53	4	14.5	5	33	1
Ntini	13	2	60	–	23	10	48	1
Kallis	12	1	39	2	21	4	52	1
Henderson	24	3	55	2	55	16	122	2
Klusener	3	0	13	–	29	9	50	2

Fall of Wickets
1-2, 2-43, 3-51, 4-133, 5-143, 6-143, 7-188, 8-207, 9-282
1-0, 2-18, 3-25, 4-211, 5-243, 6-260, 7-287, 8-326, 9-344

Umpires: DB Hair & RB Tiffin
Toss: South Africa
Test Debut: Douglas T Hondo (Zimbabwe)
Man of the Match: A Flower

South Africa won by nine wickets

SECOND TEST
14–18 September 2001 at Bulawayo

Rain and a wet outfield led to the abandonment of the entire second day. That drained much of the remaining life from a match that began dying its slow death as early as the second hour, when the ball stopped swinging or deviating off the seam.

The eventual stalemate was hardly enlivened by Jacques Kallis breaking the world record for the most time spent at the crease between dismissals. Nasser Hussain set the previous mark at 1,021 minutes – a shade more than 17 hours – in South Africa in 1999–2000. It was certainly a worthwhile achievement for Kallis, but one that was best applauded with yawns.

The terror attacks in the United States three days before the start of the match saw the players take to the field wearing black armbands and observe a minute's silence before the start of play. That set the tone of a game the Zimbabweans were happy to draw, and in which the South Africans seemed content to sit on the unassailable series lead they had earned by winning the first Test in Harare.

Shaun Pollock's field placings lost attacking intent by the over, and, shortly after the first drinks break, he resorted to the left-arm spin of Nicky Boje.

Alistair Campbell and Dion Ebrahim were not about to waste the breathing space afforded them by South Africa's flaccid tactics, and they denied the visitors success until Campbell lofted one of Lance Klusener's off cutters to point six overs before light forced an early close.

The stand of 152 was the first century opening partnership for Zimbabwe since Gavin Rennie and Grant Flower shared 144 against New Zealand in 1997–98.

Potential catches fell short of slip, gully and short leg, but the only genuine chance was offered when Ebrahim, on 59 with the total on 130, flicked Klusener backward of square only for Herschelle Gibbs to drop a sitter.

Ebrahim edged to slip off Claude Henderson four balls before the enforced close of play, which came with Zimbabwe having meandered to 154 for 2. Andy Flower brightened proceedings when play resumed on the third day, batting with refreshing freedom for his

In a rain-affected draw, Jacques Kallis broke the world record for time spent at the crease between dismissals, beating Nasser Hussain's 17 hours in 1999–2000.

12th score of at least 50 in his previous 15 innings.

Henderson worked hard for his four wickets. He began bowling in the 17th over of the day and wheeled away unchanged for the rest of the innings, which ended when Heath Streak declared with an hour's play remaining. Henderson's 67 overs were the most bowled in a Zimbabwean innings.

South Africa were 26 without loss at the close, and reached their follow-on target of 220 after tea on the fourth day on the back of century stands for both the first and third wickets. They were 119 behind at stumps. Ray Price removed Gibbs and Gary Kirsten both within sight of their centuries, but Kallis and Neil McKenzie seemed destined to reach three figures on what loomed as an academic final day.

Kallis went to his hundred in the seventh over of the final morning, but, two overs later, McKenzie was trapped in front for 88 by Travis Friend's first delivery of the day.

Kallis had improved his career-best score to 189 not out – a ruthlessly clinical innings – when Pollock declared, while Price's 5 for 181 were his best figures. The 79 overs he bowled were the most by a Zimbabwean in an innings.

SECOND TEST – ZIMBABWE v. SOUTH AFRICA
14–18 September 2001 at Bulawayo

ZIMBABWE

	First innings		Second innings	
ADR Campbell	c Gibbs b Klusener	77	c Dippenaar b Henderson	20
DD Ebrahim	c Pollock b Henderson	71	b Henderson	4
H Masakadza	c Boucher b Nel	13	not out	42
SV Carlisle	lbw b Pollock	49	c Ntini b Henderson	4
*A Flower	c McKenzie b Henderson	67	not out	14
GW Flower	run out (Klusener/Henderson)	44		
GJ Whittall	c Pollock b Henderson	16		
HH Streak (capt)	c Klusener b Henderson	31		
PA Strang	not out	38		
TJ Friend	b Pollock	4		
RW Price	not out	0		
Extras	lb 8, nb 1	9	b 4, lb 4, nb 4	12
	(9 wickets dec.)	419	(3 wickets)	96

	First innings				Second innings			
	O	M	R	W	O	M	R	W
Pollock	28	14	40	2	4	1	8	-
Nel	21	3	73	1	3	0	9	-
Ntini	25	9	68	-	3	0	11	-
Klusener	37	10	87	1	12	7	21	-
Henderson	67	24	143	4	18	11	33	3
Kirsten					2	1	6	-

Fall of Wickets
1-152, 2-154, 3-175, 4-261, 5-327, 6-330, 7-377, 8-377, 9-406
1-21, 2-38, 3-58

SOUTH AFRICA

	First innings	
HH Gibbs	c A Flower b Price	74
G Kirsten	st A Flower b Price	65
JH Kallis	not out	189
ND McKenzie	lbw b Friend	88
HH Dippenaar	c GW Flower b Price	11
L Klusener	c Campbell b Price	27
SM Pollock (capt)	c Carlisle b Price	41
*MV Boucher	b Friend	14
CW Henderson	b Friend	0
M Ntini		
A Nel		
Extras	b 3, lb 7	10
	(8 wickets dec.)	519

	First innings			
	O	M	R	W
Streak	25	9	64	-
Friend	30.2	9	87	3
Strang	14.2	2	52	-
Price	79	19	181	5
Whittall	29.4	6	80	-
GW Flower	8	0	45	-

Fall of Wickets
1-117, 2-162, 3-343, 4-368, 5-418, 6-490, 7-513, 8-519

Umpires: JH Hampshire & KC Barbour
Toss: Zimbabwe
Man of the Match: JH Kallis

Match drawn

TEST MATCH AVERAGES
Zimbabwe v. South Africa

ZIMBABWE

Batting	M	Inns	NO	HS	Runs	Av	100	50	c/st
A Flower	2	4	2	199*	422	211.00	2	2	2/1
H Masakadza	2	4	1	85	153	51.00	-	1	-
DD Ebrahim	2	4	0	71	146	36.50	-	2	-
ADR Campbell	2	4	0	77	104	26.00	-	1	1
GW Flower	2	3	0	44	60	20.00	-	-	1
HH Streak	2	3	0	31	57	19.00	-	-	-
TJ Friend	2	3	0	30	51	17.00	-	-	-
GJ Whittall	2	3	0	16	35	11.66	-	-	-
RW Price	2	3	1	4	4	2.00	-	-	-

Also batted in one Test: SV Carlisle 49, 4 (1ct); DT Hondo 1*, 6 (1ct); PA Strang 38*;
CB Wishart 0, 6

Bowling	Overs	Mds	Runs	Wkts	Av	Best	10m	5/inn
TJ Friend	64.2	11	278	6	46.33	3-87	-	-
RW Price	124.2	21	392	5	78.40	5-181	-	1

Also bowled: GW Flower 14-0-63-0; DT Hondo 19-1-87-1; PA Strang 14.2-2-52-0;
HH Streak 63-15-194-0; GJ Whittall 41.4-8-114-0

SOUTH AFRICA

Batting	M	Inns	NO	HS	Runs	Av	100	50	c/st
G Kirsten	2	3	1	220	316	158.00	1	1	1
HH Gibbs	2	2	0	147	221	110.50	1	1	1
ND McKenzie	2	2	0	88	140	70.00	-	2	2
HH Dippenaar	2	2	0	11	11	5.50	-	-	4

Also batted in two Tests: MV Boucher 14 (2ct, 1st); CW Henderson 0; JH Kallis 157*, 42*, 189* (1ct);
L Klusener 8*, 27 (3ct); SM Pollock 41 (3ct)
A Nel and M Ntini (1ct) played in two Tests but did not bat

Bowling	Overs	Mds	Runs	Wkts	Av	Best	10m	5/inn
A Nel	54.5	14	168	6	28.00	4-53	-	-
SM Pollock	83.3	25	177	6	29.50	3-67	-	-
CW Henderson	164	56	353	11	32.09	4-143	-	-

Also bowled: JH Kallis 33-5-91-3; G Kirsten 2-1-6-0; L Klusener 81-26-171-3;
M Ntini 64-21-187-1

ONE-DAY INTERNATIONALS

Jonty Rhodes held probably the world's safest lunch sandwiches in his hands as he clambered aboard the team bus en route to practice minutes after joining the squad in Bulawayo following the Test series.

By the mere act of turning up, Rhodes lightened and lifted the mood of a South African team that has a tendency to lapse into a bleak, business-like funk when it should be at least a little chuffed with its lot as a group of idolized young men paid handsomely to travel the world and play cricket.

Happily, Rhodes was in the thick of things as South Africa won the first two matches by the stupendous margins of 153 and 148 runs, and completed a whitewash by claiming the last game by six wickets.

Rhodes batted twice and scored two of the six half-centuries accumulated by the South Africans, while Herschelle Gibbs' natural audacity ran rampant as he made the only century of the series in the first match.

The dearth of run booty on the other side of the fence illustrated the difference between the teams – Alistair Campbell and Stuart Carlisle were the only Zimbabweans to register half-centuries.

South Africa were at their most devastating in the first match. Their total of 363 for 3 was their highest in one-day international cricket, while Gibbs, dropped on four by Andy Flower off Travis Friend, scored the fastest century by a South African – off 84 balls – on his way to 125. Gibbs and Gary Kirsten launched the innings in some style with a partnership of 153 off 115 balls.

The home side never recovered from their onslaught, and Heath Streak's 1 for 80 were the worst figures ever returned by a Zimbabwean in this form of the game.

Campbell scored a defiant 81, but he struggled to find significant support among his shell-shocked team-mates and Zimbabwe were held to a total of 210 for 5 and a resounding defeat by the margin of 153 runs.

The series then moved to the supposedly livelier pitch of the Harare Sports Club for the second match, but South Africa's batting form remained insatiable as they scored 272 for 7.

Left: Herschelle Gibbs, South Africa's opener, won the Player of the Series award for his century at Bulawayo (125) and his innings of 69 at Harare. South Africa completed a 3–0 whitewash over Zimbabwe.

Zimbabwe's day began badly when their premier bowler, Heath Streak, was forced out of the match with a back spasm. It remained that way for the home side as Gibbs hit the last ball of the first over for six over fine leg, three catches went down in the South African innings, Andy Flower scored just two before playing on, and Zimbabwe's total of 124 was a new low against South Africa. Claude Henderson, meanwhile, took a liking to the Zimbabwean tail and claimed the impressive figures of 4 for 17.

The anti-climactic third match the next day had all the appeal of a hangover, and mercifully it came and went without significant incident. Zimbabwe were restricted to a total of 184 for 6, which South Africa reached with nine overs to spare.

Campbell and Carlisle batted solidly, while Ebrahim showed promising aggressive tendencies. But, particularly with Streak still out, Zimbabwe had little hope of hemming in the lusty South Africans, who were guided to victory by Neil McKenzie's seamless innings of 69 not out.

Match One
23 September 2001 at Queen's Sports Club, Bulawayo
South Africa 363 for 3 (50 overs)
(HH Gibbs 125, JH Kallis 83, G Kirsten 66, JN Rhodes 54*)
Zimbabwe 210 for 5 (50 overs)
(ADR Campbell 81)
South Africa won by 153 runs
Man of the Match: HH Gibbs

Match Two
29 September 2001 at Harare Sports Club
South Africa 272 for 7 (50 overs) (HH Gibbs 69, JN Rhodes 56)
Zimbabwe 124 (40.1 overs)
(CW Henderson 4 for 17)
South Africa won by 148 runs
Man of the Match: JN Rhodes

Match Three
30 September 2001 at Harare Sports Club
Zimbabwe 184 for 6 (50 overs)
(SV Carlisle 51)
South Africa 188 for 4 (41 overs)
(ND McKenzie 69*)
South Africa won by six wickets
Man of the Match: ND McKenzie
Player of the Series: HH Gibbs

ENGLAND IN ZIMBABWE
By Jonathan Agnew

Political uncertainties were cast aside as England set off for Zimbabwe and a much-needed short series in which to rediscover the apparently lost art of winning one-day matches. It had been more than a year since England had last achieved a victory and, in terms of matches played, Zimbabwe's predicament was even worse, having lost their last 12 games in a row. This was hardly going to be a battle of the giants.

Zimbabwean cricket desperately needed this tour. The country was heading towards an acrimonious general election and the white minority, but by far the cricketing majority, was feeling vulnerable. This trip was a tonic and one they did not want to be boycotted for political reasons, no matter how well founded these political reasons may have been.

The series was crushingly one-sided, with England winning every match, and never looking threatened in any of them. New faces had been brought in to enliven the fielding and provide much-needed enthusiasm: James Foster was preferred to Alec Stewart, while James Kirtley, Matthew Hoggard and Owais Shah were given the chance to press a claim for the tours of India and New Zealand and, of course, the World Cup in South Africa in 2003. It was not unnoticed by the powers that be that England's opening match would be played here in Zimbabwe.

The first three games were staged in Harare with the gorgeous mauve jacaranda trees in full bloom. Hussain and Knight, in particular, found these to their liking, while Hoggard took 5 for 49 in the third game and Kirtley's nip caused raised eyebrows in the referee's chamber. Colonel Naushad Ali broke just about every convention going when he announced in the press conference after the second game that he had concerns about Kirtley's action and would be reporting him to the ICC. The fact that he was suspicious about a kink in the arm was quite acceptable, but the manner in which he handled such a delicate matter suggested that his career as a match referee would be a short one.

In fact, England showed their faith in Kirtley by playing him again in the fourth game, which

Left: Nick Knight helped to put England back on track after having failed to win a one-day match for a year. Knight won the Player of the Series for his three half-centuries in the five-match tournament.

England won comfortably in Bulawayo. Whether or not they should have done so was a moot point, since Kirtley should have undergone immediate remedial work, but it showed the young Sussex seamer had some spirit. Again, England won that match by 70 runs with five overs in hand: it really was a dreadfully tedious series, the main interest in which was to guess by how much breakfast would increase in price overnight as inflation ran at more than 100 per cent.

Foster had a very mixed tour that suggested it would be a brave man who would choose him for a Test match just yet. He dropped a couple of sitters, and spectacularly fell out with Andy Flower when the Zimbabwean wicketkeeper declined to walk for a caught-behind appeal.

The vastly experienced Zimbabwean appeared to suggest that young Foster should concentrate on catching the ball before abusing international batsmen of more than a decade and nearly 200 matches' experience.

However, it did get England back on the winning track and that was all they had endeavoured to do when they embarked on this one-day series. As for Zimbabwe, frankly it was difficult to see how they could possibly deteriorate any further.

Match One
3 October 2001 at Harare Sports Club
Zimbabwe 206 (49.1 overs)
(A Flower 59)
England 210 for 5 (46.4 overs)
(N Hussain 73, NV Knight 50)
England won by five wickets
Man of the Match: JN Snape

Match Two
6 October 2001 at Harare Sports Club
Zimbabwe 195 (49.1 overs)
England 196 for 2 (37.3 overs)
(NV Knight 82*, N Hussain 50)
England won by eight wickets
Man of the Match: MJ Hoggard

Match Three
7 October 2001 at Harare Sports Club
Zimbabwe 261 for 8 (50 overs)
(A Flower 142*, HH Streak 56,
MJ Hoggard 5 for 49)
England 265 for 6 (47.3 overs)
England won by four wickets
Man of the Match: A Flower

Match Four

10 October 2001 at Queen's Sports Club, Bulawayo
England 280 for 9 (50 overs)
(PD Collingwood 77, ME Trescothick 52,
DA Marillier 4 for 38)
Zimbabwe 210 (44.3 overs) (GW Flower 96)
England won by 70 runs
Man of the Match: PD Collingwood

Match Five

13 October 2001 at Queen's Sports Club, Bulawayo
Zimbabwe 228 (49.3 overs) (GW Flower 104)
England 229 for 3 (43.4 overs) (NV Knight 80*,
PD Collingwood 56*)
England won by seven wickets
Man of the Match: NV Knight
Player of the Series: NV Knight

Nasser Hussain was delighted with the team's performance in Zimbabwe as an experimental and young side won all five matches, but question marks still remain over his batting position.

ZIMBABWE DOMESTIC FIRST-CLASS CRICKET – 2001–02 LOGAN CUP

Mashonaland and Midlands rode roughshod over the rest of the field with the former emerging as champions. Which was as it should have been, because Mashonaland won all five of their matches. That said, Midlands came close to matching the Harare-based side by winning four matches and drawing the other to finish a marginal four points behind the eventual champions.

The crucial match of the season, then, was Mashonaland's win by 248 runs over Midlands at Harare Sports Club in the third round. Emphatic though that margin seems to indicate, the home side needed Craig Evans' rousing 163 to right a first innings that teetered at 32 for 3. Barney Rogers helped Evans halt the slide with a fourth-wicket partnership of 92, and the hard-hitting stalwart was eventually last out having spent more than four hours at the crease in which he faced 188 balls and hit 19 fours and seven sixes.

Consequently, Mashonaland recovered to a total of 329, and by the close of the first day they had turned the match on its head by reducing Midlands to 43 for 4. Dirk Viljoen's 78 stemmed the flow of wickets as the visitors replied with 211 the next day, and at stumps Mashonaland were 190 for 6 in their second innings.

Thanks largely to a stand of 106 by Rogers and Donald Campbell, Mashonaland added 73 in a furious first hour on the third day before declaring and leaving Midlands a target of 382.

However, only James Cornford, with an unbeaten 69, and Matthew Vaughan-Davies, showed the required application as Midlands crumbled to defeat in just more than two hours with Brighton Watambwa taking 4 for 57.

Ultimately one-sided though the match was, Mashonaland were docked five points for a slow over rate in Midlands' first innings. That meant they had to claim a full house of batting and bowling points in their last match, against the Academy XI, to be sure of claiming the cup. They duly did so as they thrashed the students by an innings and 163 runs inside two days.

The lack of depth which is at the heart of many of Zimbabwe's cricket problems ensured the leading two teams were always significantly ahead of the pack. Mashonaland A finished all of 30 points behind Midlands with two wins, two losses and a draw, while the Academy XI, Matabeleland and Manicaland huddled under a threadbare blanket spread over three points at the foot of the table. The bottom three had one victory, nine defeats and five draws between them.

Evans enjoyed a golden summer with four centuries in six innings and an aggregate of 684 runs at an average of 114. Andy Flower could find the time to play just one match for Mashonaland, but he made it count by making centuries in each innings.

Manicaland's Neil Ferreira scored three hundreds to become the only other player to notch more than one century. Ray Price of Midlands led the bowling averages with 31 wickets at 13.64 apiece.

Andy Flower stood head and shoulders above the rest in Zimbabwe's first–class competition, scoring four hundreds in six innings.

FIRST-CLASS AVERAGES
Zimbabwe

FIRST-CLASS AVERAGES
Zimbabwe

BATTING

	M	Inns	NO	HS	Runs	Av	100	50
A Flower	3	6	3	199*	692	230.66	4	1
CN Evans	4	6	0	210	384	114.00	4	-
J Cornford	5	7	3	98*	314	78.50	-	3
NR Ferreira	5	9	0	210	650	72.22	3	2
GM Strydom	5	10	2	109	537	67.12	1	4
GW Flower	4	7	2	235*	324	64.80	1	-
GM Ewing	5	9	2	106*	412	58.85	1	4
DJR Campbell	5	7	1	79	311	51.83	-	3
MA Vermeulen	4	8	0	180	393	49.12	1	1
GJ Whittall	5	9	0	247	423	47.00	1	1
AJ Mackay	5	7	1	108	275	45.83	1	2
DD Ebrahim	4	7	1	71	264	44.00	-	2
BG Rogers	5	8	0	96	350	43.75	-	3
WT Siziba	5	10	0	103	423	42.30	1	2
TJ Friend	4	5	0	121	195	39.00	1	-
GF Barrett	4	8	0	106	311	38.87	1	1
MJ Vaughan-Davies	5	7	2	86*	194	38.80	-	1
MG McKillop	5	9	1	71*	309	38.62	-	3
AP Hoffman	5	10	0	112	384	38.40	1	2
ST Makunura	3	5	1	62	142	35.50	-	1
SR Walker	3	6	0	75	212	35.33	-	2
HP Rinke	4	8	2	84*	205	34.16	-	1
E Chigumbura	5	9	0	70	306	34.00	-	2
DR Matambanadzo	5	7	0	80	236	33.71	-	1
GC Goosen	4	8	1	101*	236	33.71	1	-
BRM Taylor	5	10	0	82	322	32.20	-	1
T Duffin	5	9	2	89	223	31.85	-	2
RW Sims	3	6	0	75	183	30.50	-	2
LS Malloch-Brown	5	9	0	78	274	30.44	-	2
SM Ervine	5	7	0	55	193	27.57	-	1
A Maregwede	4	8	0	68	219	27.37	-	1
RE Butterworth	4	8	0	42	200	25.00	-	-
C Macmillan	4	5	0	59	124	24.80	-	1
AJC Neethling	3	6	0	64	144	24.00	-	1
KPR Went	5	9	1	57	185	23.12	-	2
TK Mawoyo	4	7	0	38	152	21.71	-	-
ADR Campbell	3	5	0	77	104	20.80	-	1
SV Carlisle	3	6	0	64	124	20.66	-	1
M Kenny	4	8	1	57	144	20.57	-	1
N Chouhan	5	10	0	72	204	20.40	-	1
HH Streak	3	5	0	39	101	20.20	-	-
RJ King	5	10	0	43	190	19.00	-	-
T Mupariwa	3	5	3	16*	38	19.00	-	-
CB Wishart	3	5	1	61	73	18.25	-	1
P Utseya	4	7	1	58	109	18.16	-	1
V Sibanda	4	8	0	35	136	17.00	-	-
IM Chinyoka	4	8	0	52	128	16.00	-	1
C Delport	5	6	0	32	95	15.83	-	-
LJ Soma	5	9	0	75	141	15.66	-	1
DT Mutendera	4	8	2	15*	85	14.16	-	-
CH Brewer	4	8	0	66	104	13.00	-	1
NB Mahwire	5	7	0	44	90	12.85	-	-
RW Price	6	10	1	77	114	12.66	-	1
T Benade	3	6	0	35	72	12.00	-	-
JS Nicolle	5	10	5	20	55	11.00	-	-
KJ Taylor	3	6	2	11*	42	10.50	-	-
CR Williams	5	8	0	27	81	10.12	-	-

Qualification: 6 innings, average 10.00

BOWLING

	Overs	Mds	Runs	Wkts	Av	Best	10m	5/inn
TR Gripper	32.5	6	103	9	11.44	4-44	-	-
GJ Rennie	31	4	76	6	12.66	3-27	-	-
GB Brent	64.4	18	142	10	14.20	5-64	-	1
AP Hoffman	42.1	12	113	7	16.14	3-10	-	-
DA Marillier	37.4	4	130	8	16.25	4-44	-	-
BT Watambwa	48.2	7	154	9	17.11	4-57	-	-
DP Viljoen	76.2	15	189	11	17.18	3-34	-	-
CN Evans	53	15	138	8	17.25	6-37	-	1

BOWLING

	Overs	Mds	Runs	Wkts	Av	Best	10m	5/inn
W Mwayenga	29	5	90	5	18.00	2-17	-	-
MJ Vaughan-Davies	88.5	22	281	14	20.07	4-21	-	-
HK Olonga	32.3	5	103	5	20.60	2-24	-	-
JS Nicolle	132	34	381	18	21.16	4-46	-	-
RW Price	337.3	100	815	36	22.63	8-35	1	4
HP Rinke	88	21	252	11	22.90	4-39	-	-
J Cornford	35	7	115	5	23.00	2-36	-	-
AJ Mackay	148.2	33	465	19	24.47	4-41	-	-
DT Mutendera	99.3	23	306	12	25.50	5-71	-	1
NB Mahwire	98.5	20	335	13	25.76	4-40	-	-
MA Vermeulen	71	19	129	5	25.80	2-40	-	-
GJ Whittall	148.4	41	354	13	27.23	4-38	-	-
KJ Taylor	30.5	1	137	5	27.40	3-42	-	-
A Nel	54.5	14	168	6	28.00	4-53	-	-
T Benade	74.1	13	259	9	28.77	3-51	-	-
LJ Soma	117.3	25	403	14	28.78	4-39	-	-
BG Rogers	81	7	290	10	29.00	4-34	-	-
SM Pollock	83.3	26	177	6	29.50	3-67	-	-
GM Ewing	235.3	65	619	20	30.95	5-80	-	2
IM Chinyoka	59	20	156	5	31.20	2-23	-	-
JM Lewis	96.4	29	319	10	31.90	3-12	-	-
CW Henderson	164	56	353	11	32.09	4-143	-	-
TJ Friend	94.2	19	354	11	32.18	3-22	-	-
C Macmillan	138.4	32	383	11	34.81	3-54	-	-
M Kenny	47	8	175	5	35.00	1-12	-	-
GW Flower	74	14	221	6	36.83	3-60	-	-
Douglas T Hondo	59.2	9	224	6	37.33	5-68	-	1
P Utseya	115.1	23	379	10	37.90	4-72	-	-
KM Dabengwa	111.4	13	447	11	40.63	5-94	-	1
IM Coulson	67	14	257	6	42.83	3-55	-	-
SM Ervine	59	8	222	5	44.40	2-31	-	-
RN Manyande	128	37	312	7	44.57	2-46	-	-
MSL Seager	137.3	24	457	9	50.77	4-128	-	-
HH Streak	115	29	314	6	52.33	5-61	-	1
GM Strydom	124	12	538	10	53.80	4-134	-	-
A Maungwa	96	16	270	5	54.00	2-25	-	-
N Chouhan	71.1	5	291	5	58.20	2-41	-	-
RW Sims	123	18	432	7	61.71	6-132	-	1
MW Townshend	79	15	348	5	69.60	3-61	-	-

Qualification: 5 wickets in 4 innings

FIELDING

16 - NR Ferreira (14ct, 2st); 13 - GC Goosen (10ct, 3st), C Delport (8ct, 5st); 12 - A Maregwede; 11 - DJR Campbell (10ct, 1st); 10 - J Cornford; 9 - SM Ervine; 8 - IM Chinyoka; 6 - TJ Friend, AP Hoffman, MG McKillop, BG Rogers, GM Strydom, SR Walker; 5 - RE Butterworth, KM Dabengwa, A Flower (4ct, 1st), GW Flower, DT Mutendera, DP Viljoen

Qualification: 5 catches or more

BANGLADESH

Zimbabwe in Bangladesh
Pakistan in Bangladesh
Bangladesh Domestic First-Class Cricket
Bangladesh Domestic One-Day Cricket
Bangladesh First-Class Averages

ZIMBABWE IN BANGLADESH
By Qamar Ahmed

First Test
8–11 November 2001 at Dhaka

Incessant rain before and during the match rescued Bangladesh from another defeat in a Test. When the match was abandoned on the final morning, it was the first time in their six Tests to date that Bangladesh were able to avoid a heavy loss. Put in to bat, Bangladesh were reduced to 56 for 8, but managed to score 107 in their first innings. Trailing by 324 runs they were 125 for 3 in their second knock on the third day, requiring 199 more runs to make Zimbabwe bat again, but the fourth and fifth days were washed out.

Only three Bangladesh batsmen, Aminul Islam (12), Naimur Rehman (13) and Enamul Haque (24 not out) reached double figures in the first innings as medium pacers Travis Friend and Henry Olonga bagged 5 for 31 and 3 for 18 respectively to bowl Bangladesh out on the first afternoon. Zimbabwe were reduced to 20 for 2 after losing opener Trevor Gripper without scoring and Dion Ebrahim trapped leg before for three, but the tourists finished the second day at 348 for 7, taking a lead of 241 runs. They had been 89 for 5, but Craig Wishart – who made 94 – added 127 with Douglas Marillier for the sixth wicket and Heath Streak and Travis Friend put on 108 for the eighth. Zimbabwe were finally dismissed for 431 after lunch on the third day.

Faced with an inevitable defeat, Bangladesh put up some bold resistance in their second innings. Having lost their first wicket with the score on six to Travis Friend – who had Al Sahariar caught by Grant Flower – the home team recovered through a second-wicket stand of 102 between opener Javed Omar and Habibul Bashar. Omar made 35 before being caught off the spinner Douglas Marillier. Habibul Bashar's 65 contained ten fours, but torrential rain flooded the ground and Hanumant Singh, the referee, declared the Test abandoned on the fourth afternoon.

Previous page: Yousuf Youhana averaged 276 as Pakistan swept aside Bangladesh 2-0 in the two-Test series. All part of the learning curve. It has been a difficult season for Test cricket's newest nation, but there have been encouraging signs of improvement.

FIRST TEST – BANGLADESH v. ZIMBABWE
8–11 November 2001 at Dhaka

BANGLADESH

	First innings		Second innings	
Javed Omar	b Streak	3	c Olonga b Marillier	35
Al Sahariar	lbw b Friend	4	c GW Flower b Friend	5
Habibul Bashar	c A Flower b Friend	0	c Murphy b Friend	65
Aminul Islam	lbw b Olonga	12	not out	6
Mohammad Ashraful	c Wishart b Olonga	0	not out	0
Khaled Mahmud	c Gripper b Friend	6		
Naimur Rahman (capt)	b Friend	13		
*Khaled Mashud	c Carlisle b Friend	6		
Mashrafe Mortaza	c A Flower b Streak	8		
Enamul Haque	not out	24		
Manjural Islam	c Gripper, b Olonga	9		
Extras	b 3, lb 3, w 1, nb 15	22	b 3, lb 1, nb 10	14
		107	(3 wickets)	**125**

	First innings				Second innings			
	O	M	R	W	O	M	R	W
Streak	18	8	30	2	11	4	25	-
Friend	18	7	31	5	11.4	2	26	2
Olonga	6.2	0	18	3	5	1	17	-
Murphy	6	1	22	-	12	4	37	-
Marillier					7	2	16	1

Fall of Wickets
1-6, 2-6, 3-11, 4-13, 5-30, 6-38, 7-49, 8-56, 9-84
1-6, 2-108, 3-120

ZIMBABWE

	First innings	
DD Ebrahim	lbw b Manjural Islam	3
TR Gripper	c Javed Omar b Manjural Islam	0
SV Carlisle	c Khaled Mashud b Mashrafe Mortaza	33
GW Flower	c Al Sahariar b Mashrafe Mortaza	10
*A Flower	b Enamul Haque	28
CB Wishart	run out (Khaled Mashud)	94
DA Marillier	lbw b Enamul Haque	73
HH Streak	c Khaled Mashud b Mashrafe Mortaza	65
TJ Friend	b Enamul Haque	81
BA Murphy (capt)	c Habibul Bashar b Mashrafe Mortaza	25
HK Olonga	not out	2
Extras	b 4, lb 7, w 4, nb 2	17
		431

	First innings			
	O	M	R	W
Manjural Islam	26	5	74	2
Mashrafe Mortaza	32	8	106	4
Khaled Mahmud	15	2	59	-
Enamul Haque	43	13	74	3
Naimur Rahman	18	1	56	-
Mohammad Ashraful	15	3	49	-
Aminul Islam	1	0	2	-

Fall of Wickets
1-3, 2-4, 3-31, 4-60, 5-89, 6-226, 7-259, 8-367, 9-417

Umpires: Mian Mohammad Aslam & AFM Akhtaruddin
Toss: Zimbabwe
Test Debut: Khaled Mahmud, Mashrafe Mortaza
Man of the Match: TJ Friend

Match drawn

SECOND TEST
15–19 November 2001 at Chittagong

Zimbabwe won the second Test by an imposing margin of eight wickets to wrap up the two-match series with 1–0 victory at lunch on the fifth and final day. Bangladesh, forced to follow on after being bowled out for 251 in reply to Zimbabwe's 542 for 7, batted well second time around to avoid the humiliation of an innings defeat. Surprisingly, needing only 11 runs to win, Zimbabwe then lost two wickets before they had scored.

On the first day, Zimbabwe finished on 236 for 6 after being put in. Trevor Gripper batted well to give Zimbabwe a solid start, and the likeable opener went on to make 112, his maiden Test century, before being run out shortly before the close of the day's play. On the second, Andy Flower – on 70 – had a collision with Bangladesh spinner Enamul Haque and had to retire hurt for 90 minutes before coming back to reach his 12th Test century. Another centurion was Craig Wishart who hit 11 fours and two sixes in his innings of 114.

Zimbabwe declared their innings closed at 542 for 7 and the home team was quickly dismissed for 251, despite a fine century by Habibul Bashar. He made 108 with 15 fours in 209 balls, but his team, following on, were 51 for 1 at the close on the third day and still required 276 to avoid an innings defeat. Bashar and Javed Omar added a record 122 for the second wicket against Zimbabwe to offer a ray of hope. To add to his century in the first innings Bashar notched up 76 this time with 12 boundaries, but he lost Omar on the final morning.

Grant Flower did the damage again, taking 4 for 63 – including three after tea in the second innings – to add to his four in the first and won the Man of the Match award.

It was hardly the battle of the giants, but Andy Flower's century at Chittagong helped Zimbabwe to beat Bangladesh in the second Test.

SECOND TEST – BANGLADESH v. ZIMBABWE
15–19 November 2001 at Chittagong

ZIMBABWE

	First innings		Second innings	
DD Ebrahim	b Mashrafe Mortaza	41	b Mashrafe Mortaza	0
TR Gripper	run out (Javed Omar)	112	not out	11
SV Carlisle (capt)	lbw b Enamul Haque	14	c Akram Khan b Mashrafe Mortaza	0
GW Flower	c Naimur Rahman b Enamul Haque	33	not out	0
*A Flower	not out	114		
GB Brent	c Habibul Bashar b Mashrafe Mortaza	25		
CB Wishart	c Mohammad Sharif b Mohammad Ashraful	114		
DA Marillier	c Habibul Bashar b Aminul Islam	52		
HH Streak	not out	16		
TJ Friend				
HK Olonga				
Extras	b 2, lb 5, w 2, nb 12	21		
	(7 wickets dec.)	542	(2 wickets)	11

	First innings				Second innings			
	O	M	R	W	O	M	R	W
Mashrafe Mortaza	28	4	101	2	1.4	1	10	2
Mohammad Sharif	29	7	118					
Enamul Haque	54	12	134	2	1	0	1	–
Naimur Rahman	15	2	54	–				
Mohammad Ashraful	17	0	62	1				
Animul Islam	17	1	66	1				

Fall of Wickets
1-108, 2-145, 3-210, 4-214, 5-280, 6-469, 7-496
1-0, 2-0

BANGLADESH

	First innings		Second innings	
Javed Omar	c A Flower b Streak	8	lbw b Friend	80
Al Sahariar	lbw b Olonga	29	lbw b Olonga	40
Habibul Bashar	b GW Flower	108	c sub (SM Ervine) b GW Flower	76
Aminul Islam	c & b Marillier	21	c Gripper b GW Flower	1
Akram Khan	lbw b Marillier	6	b GW Flower	2
Mohammad Ashraful	c Ebrahim b GW Flower	33	c sub (PA Strang) b Marillier	10
Naimur Rahman (capt)	lbw b Streak	5	lbw b Marillier	28
*Khaled Mashud	b GW Flower	8	c Ebrahim b GW Flower	12
Enamul Haque	not out	12	c & b Marillier	0
Mashrafe Mortaza	lbw b Brent	1	st A Flower b Marillier	0
Mohammad Sharif	c Brent b GW Flower	3	not out	24
Extras	b 3, lb 3, w 2, nb 9	17	b 2, lb 16, w 1, nb 9	28
		251		301

	First innings				Second innings			
	O	M	R	W	O	M	R	W
Friend	16	3	63	–	16	3	63	–
Streak	19	6	32	2	19	6	32	2
Olonga	12	0	40	1	12	0	40	1
Marillier	15	6	39	2	15	6	39	2
Brent	19	9	30	1	17	9	30	1
GW Flower	15.3	3	31	4	15.3	3	41	4
Gripper	1	1	–	–	1	1	–	–

Fall of Wickets
1-15, 2-80, 3-135, 4-146, 5-204, 6-217, 7-226, 8-235, 9-244
1-73, 2-195, 3-201, 4-203, 5-227, 6-264, 7-267, 8-267, 9-267

Umpires: EAR de Silva & Showkatur Rahman
Toss: Bangladesh
Man of the Match: GW Flower

Zimbabwe won by eight wickets

TEST MATCH AVERAGES
Bangladesh v. Zimbabwe

BANGLADESH

Batting	M	Inns	NO	HS	Runs	Av	100	50	c/st
Habibul Bashar	2	4	0	108	249	62.25	1	2	3
Enamul Haque	2	3	2	24*	36	36.00	-	-	-
Javed Omar	2	4	0	80	126	31.50	-	1	1
Al Sahariar	2	4	0	40	78	19.50	-	-	1
Naimur Rahman	2	3	0	28	46	15.33	-	-	1
Mohammad Ashraful	2	4	1	33	43	14.33	-	-	-
Aminul Islam	2	4	1	21	40	13.33	-	-	-
Khaled Mashud	2	3	0	12	26	8.66	-	-	2
Mashrafe Mortaza	2	3	0	8	9	3.00	-	-	-

Also batted in one Test: Akram Khan 6, 2 (1 ct); Khaled Mahmud 6; Manjural Islam 9; Mohammad Sharif 3, 24* (1 ct)

Bowling	Overs	Mds	Runs	Wkts	Av	Best	10m	5/inn
Mashrafe Mortaza	61.4	13	217	8	27.12	4-106	-	-
Enamul Haque	98	25	209	5	41.80	3-74	-	-

Also bowled: Aminul Islam 18-1-68-1; Khaled Mahmud 15-2-59-0; Manjural Islam 26-5-74-2; Mohammad Ashraful 32-3-111-1; Mohammad Sharif 29-7-118-0; Naimur Rahman 33-3-110-0

ZIMBABWE

Batting	M	Inns	NO	HS	Runs	Av	100	50	c/st
A Flower	2	2	1	114*	142	142.00	1	-	3/1
CB Wishart	2	2	0	114	208	104.00	1	1	1
HH Streak	2	2	1	65	81	81.00	-	1	-
DA Marillier	2	2	0	73	125	62.50	-	2	2
TR Gripper	2	3	1	112	123	61.50	1	-	3
GW Flower	2	3	1	33	43	21.50	-	-	1
SV Carlisle	2	3	0	33	47	15.66	-	-	1
DD Ebrahim	2	3	0	41	44	14.66	-	-	2

Also batted in two Tests: BJ Friend 81; HK Olonga 2* (1 ct)
Also batted in one Test: GB Brent 25 (1 ct); BA Murphy 25 (1 ct)

Bowling	Overs	Mds	Runs	Wkts	Av	Best	10m	5/inn
GW Flower	54.1	21	104	8	13.00	4-41	-	-
DA Marillier	41	12	112	7	16.00	4-57	-	-
HK Olonga	38.2	6	106	5	21.20	3-18	-	-
TJ Friend	70.4	19	173	8	21.62	5-31	-	1

Also bowled: GB Brent 42-15-88-1; TR Gripper 5-3-21-0; BA Murphy 18-5-59-0; HH Streak 48-18-87-4

ONE-DAY INTERNATIONALS

Following their 1–0 win in the two-match Test series, Zimbabwe carried their form into the one-day internationals to make a clean sweep of the three-match series. They won the first match at Chittagong by five wickets, the second at Dhaka by 42 runs and, in the third and final match, they breezed past the 215-run target with contributions from the opener Dion Ebrahim (84) and by Stuart Carlisle who made an unbeaten 55. Ebrahim struck 11 fours in his 130-ball 84 and was involved in a solid stand of 107 for the first wicket with Grant Flower. Earlier Bangladesh failed to capitalize on a sound opening stand of 103 between Javed Omar (54) and Al

Although Bangladesh lost the two-match Test series, Habibul Bashar confirmed his potential with a century and two 50s.

Sahariar (59). Wickets tumbled and their middle order perished against some fine bowling by Heath Streak, Douglas Marillier and Grant Flower. The home side's last nine wickets fell for 83 runs as they were all out for 215 in the 49th over.

In the opening match at Chittagong, Craig Wishart scored an unbeaten 79 with 11 fours and two sixes from only 91 balls to gain a five-wicket win for his team. Replying to Bangladesh's paltry 156, Zimbabwe scored 161 for 5 and reached their target in the 43rd over. This ended Zimbabwe's dismal run of 16 successive defeats in one-day matches. They lost three wickets for 20 in the chase, but Stuart Carlisle, 46, and Craig Wishart, with an unbeaten 79, salvaged the innings.

At Dhaka, Ebrahim scored 121 with 11 fours to set up Zimbabwe's 42-run win in a floodlit match. Zimbabwe piled up 309 for 6 and then restricted the home team to 267 for 9, despite 66 by Habibul Bashar, 52 by Sanuar Hossain and another half-century by Khaled Masud.

Match One
23 November 2001 at Chittagong Stadium
Bangladesh 156 (48.4 overs)
Zimbabwe 161 for 5 (42.2 overs) (CB Wishart 79*)
Zimbabwe won by five wickets
Man of the Match: CB Wishart

Match Two

25 November 2001 at Bagabandhu National Stadium,
Dhaka (floodlit)
Zimbabwe 309 for 6 (50 overs) (DD Ebrahim 121,
CB Wishart 68)
Bangladesh 267 for 9 (50 overs) (Habibul Bashar 66,
Sanwar Hossain 52, Khaled Mahmud 50)
Zimbabwe won by 42 runs
Man of the Match: DD Ebrahim

Match Three

26 November 2001 at Bangabandhu National Stadium,
Dhaka (floodlit)
Bangladesh 215 (48.1 overs) (Al Sahariar 59,
Javed Omar 54)
Zimbabwe 219 for 3 (49.1 overs) (DD Ebrahim 84,
SV Carlisle 55*)
Zimbabwe won by seven wickets
Man of the Match: DD Ebrahim
Player of the Series: DD Ebrahim

Danish Kaneria, Pakistan's young leg spinner, routed
Bangladesh in Dhaka, taking 7 for 77 in the second
innings. The home team lasted only 34 overs.

PAKISTAN IN BANGLADESH
By Qamar Ahmed

FIRST TEST
9–11 January 2002 at Dhaka

Pakistan's victory in the first Test by an innings
and 178 runs was achieved on the third day as
Bangladesh, trailing by 330 runs, were bowled
out a second time for 152. The leg spinner Danish
Kaneria took 7 for 77 to have a match haul of 9 for
113. Bangladesh had run into him before – he had
taken 12 wickets for 94 against them in August at
Multan in the Asian Test championship. It might
have been worse: Bangladesh slumped to 90 for 7 in
their second innings before the tail-enders offered
some resistance with Fahim Mantasir being the
highest scorer.

Pakistan won the toss, put them in and shattered
their innings for 160 on the first day. Pakistan's
captain Waqar Younis – bowling at a brisk pace –
accounted for six wickets for 55 runs. It was a
remarkable collapse as Bangladesh were 103 for 3 at
lunch, but then lost their last seven wickets only 15
minutes before tea, of which Waqar Younis had
taken six. Bowling without the help of Wasim
Akram, who had to retire after bowling only 2.4
overs because of a hamstring injury, Waqar
spearheaded the attack and completely destroyed a
rather feeble Bangladesh batting line-up.

Abdur Razzaq, brought in to complete Wasim
Akram's third over, started the rot by nipping out
both openers, Mehrab Hossain and Al Sahariar, for
11 and 18. Mohammad Ashraful, the youngest
centurion in Tests, and Habibul Bashar, made 27
and 53 respectively later on, but the late middle order
and the tail offered little to halt the home side's slide.

Pakistan reached 126 for 3 by the close, having lost
openers Taufiq Umar (53) and Shadab Kabir (55)
after a century stand. Next morning Bangladesh
struck by removing the nightwatchman Saqlain
Mushtaq to left-arm spinner Enamul Haque. But
Yousuf Youhana batted with great assurance,
unleashing his strokes all around the wicket to make
72 before being run out.

Razzaq and Rashid Latif then got into the act,
slaughtering the unimpressive home attack to add
175 for the sixth wicket. Latif was caught off
Mohammad Sharif for 94, made with ten fours and
two sixes. Pakistan continued mercilessly to pile on
the runs – Razzaq reached his third Test hundred,
and his innings ended at 134 made in 341 minutes in
which he hit 17 fours and three sixes.

Finally Pakistan declared their innings at 490 for 9 after Inzamam-ul-Haq was out to Enamul Haque for 43 and Bangladesh's second innings began a mere 330 runs behind. Danish Kaneria captured six wickets in his second spell while conceding only 21 runs, to seal Bangladesh's ninth defeat in their first ten Tests.

Men against boys: Waqar Younis also filled his boots at Bangladesh's expense with 12 wickets in the two-match series.

FIRST TEST – BANGLADESH v. PAKISTAN
9–11 January 2002 at Bangabandhu National Stadium, Dhaka

BANGLADESH

	First innings		Second innings	
Al Sahariar	lbw b Abdur Razzaq	18	(7) lbw b Waqar Younis	21
Mehrab Hossain	c Shadab Kabir		(1) c Inzamam-ul-Haq	
	b Abdur Razzaq	11	b Danish Kaneria	19
Mohammad Ashraful	c Yousuf Youhana		(2) c Younis Khan	
	b Danish Kaneria	27	b Abdur Razzaq	22
Habibul Bashar	c Danish Kaneria		(3) c Waqar Younis	
	b Waqar Younis	53	b Danish Kaneria	0
Aminul Islam	lbw b Danish Kaneria	25	(4) lbw b Abdur Razzaq	11
Sanwar Hossain	c Inzamam-ul-Haq		(5) c Shadab Kabir	
	b Waqar Younis	3	b Danish Kaneria	1
*Khaled Mashud (capt)	lbw b Waqar Younis	0	(6) c Waqar Younis	
			b Danish Kaneria	5
Enamul Haque	c Inzamam-ul-Haq			
	b Waqar Younis	19	b Danish Kaneria	12
Fahim Muntasir	b Waqar Younis	0	c sub (Mohammad Sami)	
			b Danish Kaneria	33
Mohammad Sharif	b Waqar Younis	0	c Waqar Younis b Danish Kaneria	11
Manjural Islam	not out	0	not out	2
Extras	lb 8, w 1, nb 2	11	lb 5, nb 3	8
		160		**152**

	First innings				Second innings			
	O	M	R	W	O	M	R	W
Wasim Akram	2.4	1	5	–				
Waqar Younis	16.2	2	55	6	9	3	27	1
Abdur Razzaq	8.2	2	42	2	10	2	29	2
Danish Kaneria	19	5	36	2	19.4	4	77	7
Saqlain Mushtaq	7	2	14	–	5	1	14	–

Fall of Wickets
1-30, 2-45, 3-77, 4-140, 5-146, 6-146, 7-147, 8-147, 9-151
1-38, 2-38, 3-49, 4-52, 5-64, 6-86, 7-90, 8-112, 9-139

PAKISTAN

	First innings	
Taufeeq Umar	lbw b Mohammad Sharif	53
Shadab Kabir	b Enamul Haque	55
Younis Khan	c Khaled Mashud b Enamul Haque	0
Yousuf Youhana	run out (Mehrab Hossain)	72
Saqlain Mushtaq	lbw b Enamul Haque	9
Abdur Razzaq	c Aminul Islam b Manjural Islam	134
*Rashid Latif	c Al Sahariar	
	b Mohammad Sharif	94
Inzamam-ul-Haq	c Mehrab Hossain	
	b Enamul Haque	43
Waqar Younis (capt)	c Al Sahariar b Manjural Islam	8
Danish Kaneria	not out	3
Wasim Akram		
Extras	lb 13, w 2, nb 4	19
	(9 wickets dec.)	**490**

	First innings			
	O	M	R	W
Manjural Islam	33	4	124	2
Mohammad Sharif	35	9	95	2
Fahim Muntasir	32	6	109	–
Enamul Haque	39.4	9	136	4
Mohammad Ashraful	1	0	13	–

Fall of Wickets
1-100, 2-100, 3-116, 4-162, 5-221, 6-396, 7-463, 8-471, 9-490

Umpires: JH Hampshire and AFM Akhtaruddin
Toss: Pakistan
Test Debut: Fahim Muntasir
Man of the Match: Abdur Razzaq

Pakistan won by an innings & 178 runs

SECOND TEST
16–18 January 2002 at Chittagong

Pakistan's prolific batsman, Yousuf Youhana, made an unbeaten 204 to set up Pakistan's victory in the second Test by an innings and 169 runs with two days to spare. The second Test followed much the same pattern as the first. Pakistan restricted Bangladesh's first innings to only 148, replied with 465 for 9 and then bowled them out again cheaply. Yousuf Youhana hit 34 boundaries and two sixes in his double century. He offered one chance – on 113 he offered a catch to Fahim Muntasir who dropped him off his own bowling.

On the opening day, spinners Saqlain Mushtaq and Danish Kaneria shared nine wickets to demolish the Bangladesh innings. Saqlain took 5 for 35, his 12th haul of five wickets or more in Tests, and Kaneria 4 for 62 as Bangladesh crashed within two sessions having elected to bat. Aminul Islam with 25 and Khaled Masud with 28 were the only significant contributors with the bat.

Pakistan's Younis Khan, 47 overnight, made 119, which was his fourth Test century. He hit 20 fours during his four-hour stay. Younis had partnered

Taufiq Umar to add 87 for the second wicket, and 67 for the third wicket with Inzamam-ul-Haq before he was caught off Fahim Muntasir. Yousuf Youhana then took control and was 174 at close of the second day with Pakistan on 429 for 7 – already taking a huge lead of 281. Waqar waited for Youhana to reach his double

Yousuf Youhana piled on the runs at Chittagong. Younis Khan also scored a century as Pakistan won by an innings and 169 runs.

After Kaneria took the wickets in the first Test, it was now Saqlain Mushtaq's turn. He finished with seven wickets in the second Test.

century before declaring and ushering Bangladesh towards their inevitable defeat. He took 4 for 36 and Shoaib Akhtar 4 for 48 as the pace pair terrorized the home team with their speed and bounce. Shoaib narrowly missed a hat-trick in the 38th over. He first bowled Fahim Muntasir for two with a swinging yorker, then uprooted Mohammad Sharif's stumps with the next delivery. However, Manjurul Islam managed to defend his next ball to avert the hat-trick.

Habibul Bashar, with 51, did show some guts to defy both Waqar and Shoaib in full swing, but it was another one-sided Test series which proved once again that Bangladesh have a great deal of ground to make up if they are to compete at this level.

SECOND TEST – BANGLADESH v. PAKISTAN
16–18 January 2002 at Chittagong

BANGLADESH

	First innings		Second innings	
Javed Omar	c Shadab Kabir b Saqlain Mushtaq	17	c Rashid Latif b Waqar Younis	0
Al Sahariar	c Rashid Latif b Waqar Younis	13	c Rashid Latif b Waqar Younis	8
Mehrab Hossain	b Danish Kaneria	16	c Rashid Latif b Waqar Younis	14
Habibul Bashar	c Shadab Kabir		(5) c Shadab Kabir	
	b Saqlain Mushtaq	2	b Saqlain Mushtaq	51
Aminul Islam	c Yousuf Youhana		(4) b Shoaib Akhtar	2
	b Danish Kaneria	25		
Sanwar Hossain	lbw b Saqlain Mushtaq	11	(6) c Younis Khan	
			b Saqlain Mushtaq	30
Enamul Haque	c Shadab Kabir b Danish Kaneria	0	(8) b Shoaib Akhtar	9
*Khaled Mashud (capt)	c Taufeeq Umar		(7) not out	15
	b Saqlain Mushtaq	28		
Fahim Muntasir	c Inzamam-ul-Haq		b Shoaib Akhtar	2
	b Danish Kaneria	9		
Mohammad Sharif	st Rashid Latif b Saqlain Mushtaq	0	b Shoaib Akhtar	0
Manjural Islam	not out	4	c Shadab Kabir b Waqar Younis	0
Extras	b 5, lb 9, nb 9	23	b 8, lb 1, nb 8	17
		148		**148**

	First innings				Second innings			
	O	M	R	W	O	M	R	W
Waqar Younis	7	2	19	1	8.5	0	36	4
Shoaib Akhtar	6	2	15	-	11	1	48	4
Danish Kaneria	22	6	62	4	6	3	9	-
Abdur Razzaq	5	2	3	-	2	0	12	-
Saqlain Mushtaq	16.4	3	35	5	11	3	34	2

Fall of Wickets
1-21, 2-57, 3-60, 4-65, 5-84, 6-85, 7-112, 8-126, 9-127
1-0, 2-23, 3-24, 4-41, 5-110, 6-128, 7-144, 8-147, 9-147

PAKISTAN

	First innings	
Taufeeq Umar	c Aminul Islam b Mohammad Sharif	47
Shadab Kabir	c Khaled Mashud b Mohammad Sharif	4
Younis Khan	c Mehrab Hossain b Fahim Muntasir	119
Inzamam-ul-Haq	c Aminul Islam b Fahim Muntasir	30
Yousuf Youhana	not out	204
Abdur Razzaq	b Mohammad Sharif	18
*Rashid Latif	lbw b Manjural Islam	15
Waqar Younis (capt)	c Mehrab Hossain b Fahim Muntasir	10
Saqlain Mushtaq	c Aminul Islam b Mohammad Sharif	7
Shoaib Akhtar	c Sanwar Hossain b Manjural Islam	2
Danish Kaneria	not out	4
Extras	w 1, nb 4	5
	(9 wickets dec.)	**465**

	First innings			
	O	M	R	W
Manjural Islam	35	9	95	2
Mohammad Sharif	35.5	10	98	4
Enamul Haque	33	6	114	-
Fahim Muntasir	27	3	131	3
Aminul Islam	4	0	27	-

Fall of Wickets
1-12, 2-99, 3-166, 4-236, 5-274, 6-315, 7-339, 8-438, 9-447

Umpires: RB Tiffin & Mahbubur Rahman
Toss: Bangladesh
Man of the Match: Yousuf Youhana
Player of the Series: Danish Kaneria

Pakistan won by an innings & 169 runs

TEST MATCH AVERAGES
Bangladesh v. Pakistan

BANGLADESH

Batting	M	Inns	NO	HS	Runs	Av	100	50	c/st
Habibul Bashar	2	4	0	53	106	26.50	-	2	-
Khaled Mashud	2	4	1	28	48	16.00	-	-	2
Aminul Islam	2	4	0	25	63	15.75	-	-	4
Al Sahariar	2	4	0	21	60	15.00	-	-	2
Mehrab Hossain	2	4	0	19	60	15.00	-	-	3
Sanwar Hossain	2	4	0	30	45	11.25	-	-	1
Fahim Muntasir	2	4	0	33	44	11.00	-	-	-
Enamul Haque	2	4	0	19	40	10.00	-	-	-
Manjural Islam	2	4	3	4*	6	6.00	-	-	-
Mohammad Sharif	2	4	0	11	11	2.75	-	-	-

Also batted in one Test: Javed Omar 17, 0; Mohammad Ashraful 27, 22

Bowling	Overs	Mds	Runs	Wkts	Av	Best	10m	5/inn
Mohammad Sharif	70.5	19	193	6	32.16	4-98	-	-

Also bowled: Aminul Islam 4-0-27-0; Enamul Haque 72.4-15-250-4; Fahim Muntasir 59-9-240-3; Manjural Islam 68-13-219-4; Mohammad Ashraful 1-0-13-0

PAKISTAN

Batting	M	Inns	NO	HS	Runs	Av	100	50	c/st
Yousuf Youhana	2	2	1	204*	276	276.00	1	1	2
Abdur Razzaq	2	2	0	134	152	76.00	1	-	-
Younis Khan	2	2	0	119	119	59.50	1	-	2
Rashid Latif	2	2	0	94	109	54.50	-	1	4/1
Taufeeq Umar	2	2	0	53	100	50.00	-	1	1
Inzamam-ul-Haq	2	2	0	43	73	36.50	-	-	4
Shadab Kabir	2	2	0	55	59	29.50	-	1	7
Waqar Younis	2	2	0	10	18	9.00	-	-	3
Saqlain Mushtaq	2	2	0	9	16	8.00	-	-	-

Also batted in two Tests: Danish Kaneria 3*, 4* (1 ct)
Also batted in one Test: Shoaib Akhtar 2
Wasim Akram played in one Test but did not bat

Bowling	Overs	Mds	Runs	Wkts	Av	Best	10m	5/inn
Waqar Younis	41.1	7	137	12	11.41	6-55	-	1
Saqlain Mushtaq	39.4	9	97	7	13.85	5-35	-	1
Danish Kaneria	66.4	18	184	13	14.15	7-77	-	1

Also bowled: Abdur Razzaq 25.2-6-86-4; Shoaib Akhtar 17-3-63-4; Wasim Akram 2.4-1-5-0

ONE-DAY INTERNATIONALS

To add to their triumph in the two-match Test series, Pakistan continued in the same vein to gain a whitewash in the three-match one-day international series as well. All-rounders Abdur Razzaq and Shahid Afridi excelled with ball and bat to aid Pakistan's victory in the floodlit third and final match by eight wickets at Dhaka to gain the clean sweep. Razzaq claimed a career best 6 for 35 and Afridi took 2 for 38 to dismiss Bangladesh for 220. Afridi then scored 83 in only 44 balls and Razzaq 25 in 21 as Pakistan raced to their target in the 36th over. Afridi hit seven sixes and six fours in his

belligerent innings which included four sixes in one over off left-arm spinner Enamul Haque which conceded 28 runs.

In the opening match at Chittagong, Pakistan won by 49 runs. Wicketkeeper Rashid Latif smashed a career-best 79 to rescue his team after Pakistan had lost five wickets for 88 runs. Pakistan then bowled well to restrict the home team to 153 in 50 overs. Then, at Dhaka, Yousuf Youhana struck an unbeaten 112 in 108 balls to put Pakistan on the road to their second win of the series. He added 135 for the fifth wicket with Younis Khan (73) and 98 for the unbroken sixth wicket with Razzaq to enable Pakistan to recover from 48 for 4 to 281 for 5. Bangladesh, in reply, could reach 209 for 8. Unfortunately, the floodlit match was held up for nearly half an hour after Shoaib Akhtar was hit on the head by an object thrown from the crowd. He had to be taken carried away on a stretcher, and took no further part in the game.

Match One
22 January 2002 at Chittagong Stadium
Pakistan 202 (49.5 overs) (Rashid Latif 79)
Bangladesh 153 for 7 (50 overs)
(Khaled Mashud 54*)
Pakistan won by 49 runs
Man of the Match: Rashid Latif

Match Two
24 January 2002 at Bangabandhu
National Stadium, Dhaka (floodlit)
Pakistan 281 for 5 (50 overs)
(Yousuf Youhana 112*, Younis Khan 73)
Bangladesh 209 for 8 (50 overs)
(Tushar Imran 65)
Pakistan won by 72 runs
Man of the Match: Yousuf Youhana

Match Three
25 January 2002 at Bangabandhu National Stadium,
Dhaka (floodlit)
Bangladesh 220 (48.5 overs)
(Abdur Razzaq 6 for 35)
Pakistan 221 for 2 (35.3 overs)
(Shahid Afridi 83, Younis Khan 66*)
Pakistan won by eight wickets
Man of the Match: Shahid Afridi
Player of the Series: Abdur Razzaq

Pakistan won the dreadfully one-sided international series with Abdur Razzaq claiming 6 for 35 in the final match to win the Player of the Tournament award.

BANGLADESH DOMESTIC FIRST-CLASS CRICKET
By Qamar Ahmed and Utpal Shuvro

It was once again an action-packed domestic season consisting of both international and domestic games.

Bangladesh's inaugural Test match in November 2000 was a one-off affair. Bangladesh got the first taste of hosting a Test series when Zimbabwe came to Bangladesh to play two Tests and three one-day internationals in November 2001. To make the home season more memorable Pakistan also toured in January.

Bangladesh lost all their international matches except the first Test match against Zimbabwe at Dhaka. That was Bangladesh's first draw in Test cricket after suffering defeat in five consecutive Tests. But the main credit should go to the rain god. Not a single ball was bowled on the fourth and fifth days due to persistent rain and as a result Zimbabwe were robbed off a sure victory.

The domestic first-class tournament, the National Cricket League lost some of its gloss due to the busy international calendar. It started in late December when the Bangladesh national team was in New Zealand. When they returned home, the Pakistan team had already arrived.

As a result of their international commitments, the national players were only able to play three or four matches out of the ten played by each team.

Interestingly, the National Cricket League lost its defending champion even before the start of the tournament. Bangladesh Biman, the 2000–01 champions were unceremoniously dumped, along with Dhaka Metropolis, according to the ICC's instruction to make the competition truly regional.

When the tournament was first introduced in 1999–2000, it was contested by only six divisional teams (Dhaka, Chittagong, Sylhet, Rajshahi, Khulna and Barisal). In the next season, Biman and Dhaka Metropolis were included. As the Dhaka division has more players compared to other divisions, the Dhaka metropolis team was formed, which consisted of the players only from the Dhaka City.

There was also a logical change in the format. In the previous two editions, there was no separate champion for the longer version of the game and the one-day competition, the total points acquired from both forms of the game decided the championship. But this time, though the one-day match followed the four-day match, there were two different competitions. The teams played with each other on a home-and-away basis. For an outright win, teams got six points. In case of a draw, the team with the first-innings lead got four points. Dhaka Division were runaway winners in this third version of the tournament, which was known as Ispahani Mirzapore Tea National cricket league.

Champions of the inaugural event and runners-up in the previous season, Chittagong Division had to be content with second place again. But Chittagong's most experienced batsman Minhazul Abedin was the undisputed star of the tournament. The former national captain, despite missing one match, became the first player to score more than 1,000 runs in the National League. He finished with 1,012 runs at an average of 72.28 with three centuries and four 50s. By scoring a double century and a century in two innings of the same match, the 37-year-old made a strong claim to be in the Test team. But though he was called into the camp, he was discarded on fitness grounds.

Other than Minhazul, Rajshahi Division's two young batsmen Nuruzzaman and Anisur Rahman also scored three centuries. National skipper Khaled Mashud, who led Rajshahi in four matches, scored the only other double century in the tournament. The bowling honour went to Dhaka's left-arm spinner Mohammad Rafique, who captured 42 wickets at a brilliant average of 12.76. Two off spinners, Imran Parvez of Rajshahi and Sabbir Khan of Chittagong, were not far behind with 40 wickets.

BANGLADESH DOMESTIC ONE-DAY CRICKET
By Qamar Ahmed and Utpal Shuvro

Bangladesh's national one-day tournament was run alongside the first-class tournament. The one-day match was staged on the very next day after the conclusion of the four-day fixture.

Like the four-day competition, the one-day tournament was also a home-and-away affair, and it was a much more closely contested one. Barisal Division, who became the whipping boys in Bangladesh, faced the ignominy of losing all their matches. But all the other five teams led the points table at one stage or other.

Sylhet Division emerged as the champions by winning eight matches out of ten. They were followed by Chittagong, who lost three matches and, as was the case in the first-class tournament, had to be content with second place. Rajshahi finished in third place by dint of winning six matches.

Dhaka, the champions of the longer version of the

game, won five and lost five and
finished behind Sylhet, Chittagong
and Rajshahi. Jahangir Alam of
Dhaka Division was the highest
scorer with 354 runs at an average
of 39.33. Only two centuries were
scored in the whole competition –
Jahangir scored one and
Chittagong's Sabbir Khan scored
the other. Sabbir's 140 against
Barisal was the highest score of the
tournament. Leg-spinning all-
rounder Alok Kapali headed the
averages with 50.50.

He scored 202 runs and took
seven wickets. In the first-class
matches he was more successful
with the ball taking 33 wickets and
earning himself a call-up to both
the Test and one-day sides.

On the bowling front, discarded
international pace bowler
Shafiuddin Ahmed of Chittagong
captured the highest number of
wickets (18), his 6 for 39 was the
best bowling performance by any
bowler in the one-day
competition.

Dhaka Premier Cricket League,
which is the most popular cricket
tournament in Bangladesh, saw the
emergence of a new power named
Victoria sporting club. The 99-
year-old club won the league only
for the second time. Their first
success was 26 years before.

The title could not have come at
a better time as the Victoria club is
planning to celebrate its centenary
year in 2003 in grand style. They
dedicated the title to their late
coach Dowlutuzzaman, who died
due to cardiac failure during his
team's third match of the season.
The heat of the match was simply
too much for him.

Mohammad Rafiq was the most
successful bowler in Bangladesh's
domestic season. The Dhaka left–arm
spinner took 42 wickets at only
12 runs each.

FIRST-CLASS AVERAGES
Bangladesh

BATTING

	M	Inns	NO	HS	Runs	Av	100	50
Minhazul Abedin	9	15	1	210	1012	72.28	3	4
Nuruzzaman	10	16	1	161	806	53.73	3	2
Azam Iqbal	8	12	1	71	521	47.36	-	6
Rajin Saleh	10	16	1	130*	671	44.73	2	3
Habibul Bashar	4	8	0	108	355	44.37	1	4
Jahangir Alam	10	16	2	120	594	42.42	2	2
Khaled Mashud	8	13	2	201*	450	40.90	1	2
Nafis Iqbal	4	7	1	77	243	40.50	-	2
Halim Shah	10	14	1	161*	521	40.07	1	3
Sajjad Kadir	9	11	1	72*	399	39.90	-	3
Anisur Rahman	10	15	1	135	520	37.14	3	1
Sanwar Hossain	8	16	1	117*	538	35.86	-	2
Asadullah Khan	9	17	1	108	539	33.68	2	-
Rafiqul Islam	10	16	0	109	513	32.06	1	3
Parvez Ahmed	10	18	0	121	572	31.77	1	3
Mohammad Rafique	6	8	3	76	156	31.20	-	1
Imran Ahmed	8	16	0	141	499	31.18	1	2
Anisul Hakim	10	17	0	112	518	30.47	2	2
Shamimul Haque	9	12	1	59	315	28.63	-	1
Fahim Muntasir	8	12	2	60	281	28.10	-	2
Faisal Khan	7	11	3	55*	220	27.50	-	1
Javed Omar	4	8	0	80	214	26.75	-	2
Imtiaz Hossain	9	15	0	78	384	25.60	-	2
Moinuzzaman	3	6	1	67	125	25.00	-	1
Khaled Mahmud	5	7	0	66	173	24.71	-	2
Faisal Hossain	7	13	0	105	312	24.00	1	-
Enamul Haque	8	12	3	46	214	23.77	-	-
Aminul Islam	7	12	2	61	236	23.60	-	1
Kamal Ahmed	9	18	3	55*	354	23.60	-	1
Raju Parvez	10	19	0	85	442	23.26	-	3
Sajjad Ahmed	10	15	1	68	324	23.14	-	1
Mohammad Mostadir	10	16	4	65*	276	23.00	-	2
Mohammad Ashraful	6	11	1	64	229	22.90	-	1
Mehrab Hossain	5	9	0	60	205	22.77	-	2
Abdur Razzaq (Khulna)	7	11	1	57	222	22.20	-	2
Sohel Islam	4	8	2	43	133	22.16	-	-
Safaiat Islam	9	18	0	70	399	22.16	-	3
Hasanuzzaman (Khulna)	10	18	1	77	376	22.11	-	3
Rashidul Haque	7	12	0	54	263	21.91	-	2
Saleh Ahmed	5	9	2	53	152	21.71	-	1
Jamaluddin Ahmed	10	18	2	82	340	21.25	-	2
Naimur Rahman	5	7	0	55	148	21.14	-	1
Sadid Hossain	3	6	0	54	125	20.83	-	1
Nahidul Haque	6	12	0	55	250	20.83	-	1
Mohammad Salim	10	17	1	44	333	20.81	-	-
Golam Mawla	5	8	0	85	166	20.75	-	1
Nasirul Alam	9	15	1	68	287	20.50	-	2
Najimuddin	5	9	0	110	179	19.88	1	-
Monirul Islam	4	7	0	45	133	19.00	-	-
Hasanuzzaman (Rajshahi)	10	15	1	73	265	18.92	-	1
Ekrimul Hadi	7	12	0	43	212	17.66	-	-
Mafizul Islam	3	6	0	47	105	17.50	-	-
Nayan Kumar	3	6	0	38	105	17.50	-	-
Al Sahariar	4	8	0	40	138	17.25	-	-
Masumud Dowla	5	8	0	38	136	17.00	-	-
Masudur Rahman	5	10	0	59	169	16.90	-	1
Tamim Bashir	6	9	2	30*	118	16.85	-	-
Alok Kapali	10	17	1	69	269	16.81	-	1
Shahin Hossain	7	14	0	54	235	16.78	-	1
Imran Parvez	10	14	2	37*	196	16.33	-	-
Hasibul Hossain	4	7	1	51	95	15.83	-	1
Niamur Rashid	9	12	1	37	171	15.54	-	-
Sajjadul Hasan	6	12	1	61	169	15.36	-	1
Mohammad Sharif	4	8	2	36*	90	15.00	-	-
Suja Irfan	7	10	2	29	120	15.00	-	-
Tapash Baisya	9	14	4	34	146	14.60	-	-
Salahuddin Ahmed	4	8	1	37	102	14.57	-	-
Shabbir Khan	10	17	0	47	243	14.29	-	-
Mahbub Alam	10	16	2	50*	197	14.07	-	1
Anisur Rahman	6	12	0	56	167	13.91	-	1
Golam Mortaza	8	14	2	56	160	13.33	-	1
Akram Khan	4	8	1	37	93	13.28	-	-

FIRST-CLASS AVERAGES
Bangladesh

BATTING

	M	Inns	NO	HS	Runs	Av	100	50
Mashiur Rahman	3	6	1	23*	66	13.20	-	-
Ashfaq Ali	8	15	9	21	76	12.66	-	-
Selim Shahid	4	8	0	31	98	12.25	-	-
Enamul Haque (Sylhet)	3	6	4	18	23	11.50	-	-
Rana Miah	5	8	1	41	80	11.42	-	-
Shamimul Islam	3	6	0	49	68	11.33	-	-
Rezaul Haque	10	17	1	38	177	11.06	-	-
Moniruzzaman	6	12	0	32	120	10.00	-	-

Qualification: 6 innings, average 10.00

BOWLING

	Overs	Mds	Runs	Wkts	Av	Best	10m	5/inn
Mohammad Rafique	298.4	114	536	42	12.76	7-52	1	3
Alok Kapali	223.3	55	537	33	16.27	7-33	1	1
Aminul Islam (Rajshahi)	281.3	64	650	37	17.56	5-52	-	2
Hasibul Hossain	130.2	19	334	18	18.55	6-58	1	1
Sohel Islam	138.3	20	355	19	18.68	5-84	-	1
Rezaul Haque	309.4	94	590	30	19.66	7-73	-	2
Tamin Bashir	144	31	443	22	20.13	6-41	-	1
Imran Parvez	362.1	98	884	40	22.10	5-35	-	1
Naimur Rahman	186.5	42	488	22	22.18	5-76	-	1
Mohammad Mostadir	289.4	73	741	33	22.45	6-95	-	2
Mahbub Alam	219.3	51	631	28	22.53	5-25	-	1
Saiful Islam	118	25	296	13	22.76	4-82	-	-
Shafiuddin Ahmed	345	99	788	34	23.17	8-86	-	2
Ashfaq Ali	197.2	39	560	23	24.34	4-58	-	-
Shabbir Khan	408	106	1020	40	25.50	6-76	-	3
Niamur Rashid	200.5	53	496	19	26.10	4-62	-	-
Imran Rahim	147	48	264	10	26.40	3-27	-	-
Saleh Ahmed	229.3	63	504	19	26.52	4-54	-	-
Enamul Haque	419.4	137	969	36	26.91	6-64	1	2
Jamaluddin Ahmed	369.4	84	913	33	27.66	5-32	-	1
Abdur Razzaq (Khulna)	254.1	67	637	23	27.69	5-67	-	1
Fahim Muntasir	291.4	78	863	30	28.76	5-31	-	2
Faisal Khan	104	24	297	10	29.70	3-42	-	-
Kamal Ahmed	162	40	418	14	29.85	3-27	-	-
Tapash Baisya	244	62	539	18	29.94	5-30	-	1
Parvez Ahmed	148	56	308	10	30.80	3-6	-	-
Hasanuzzaman (Khulna)	109	18	333	10	33.30	3-49	-	-
Suja Irfan	299	120	515	15	34.33	5-69	-	1
Ranjan Das	176	39	535	14	38.21	5-88	-	1
Al Amin	311	79	761	19	40.05	5-27	-	1
Anisur Rahman	149	29	438	10	43.80	3-52	-	-
Masudur Rahman	150	26	446	10	44.60	4-102	-	-

Qualification: 10 wickets in 8 innings

The following bowlers took 10 wickets in fewer than 10 innings:

Waqar Younis	56.1	14	154	14	11.00	6-55	-	1
Danish Kaneria	94.4	28	245	20	12.25	7-53	-	2
Ahsanullah Hasan	71.2	20	178	12	14.83	4-43	-	-
Tareq Aziz	98.1	22	270	14	19.28	5-44	1	2
Sanwar Hossain	99.5	13	295	14	21.07	3-18	-	-
Mosaddek Hossain	69.4	9	228	10	22.80	3-37	-	-
Khaled Mahmud	105.4	34	288	10	28.80	4-44	-	-
Mohammad Sharif	134.1	31	415	10	41.50	4-98	-	-

FIELDING

29 - Sajjad Kadir (28ct, 1st); 24 - Mohammad Salim (19ct, 5st);
21 - Golam Mortaza (17ct, 4st); 20 - Rajin Saleh; 17 - Shamimul Haque (15ct, 2st);
16 - Shahin Hossain (15ct, 1st); 12 - Jahangir Alam, Raju Parvez; 11 - Mahbub Alam;
10 - Asadullah Khan, Moniruzzaman (8ct, 2st), Rafiqul Islam

Qualification: 10 catches or more

OTHER TOURNAMENTS

Asian Test Championship
Sharjah Cup 2002
Sharjah Champions Trophy

ASIAN TEST CHAMPIONSHIP
By Charlie Austin

The pivotal importance of India to the future health of Asia's cricket was laid bare during the Asian Test Championship (ATC). It was a tournament conceived to quell the Asian Cricket Council's (ACC) coffers, spurring on cricket development in the region, as well as signal a seismic eastern shift in world cricket power, but India's non-participation for political reasons left it an irrelevant sideshow in an already congested international cricket calendar. Sponsors, broadcasters and spectators wanted nothing to do with it, and at one stage it looked like it may never be completed.

India were forced to pull out at the last minute; their nationalist government severing sporting ties with Pakistan. The ACC, however, were stubbornly determined to press ahead regardless. Pakistan, winners in 1999, Sri Lanka and Bangladesh were to play each other once before the two top teams progressed to a final.

Predictably, Bangladesh suffered two humiliating defeats, losing to Pakistan by an innings and 264

The Asian Test Championship was ruined because of India's refusal to compete on political grounds. Danish Kaneria returned to haunt Bangladesh again, picking up 12 for 94 in the match at Multan.

Previous page: Marvan Atapattu feasted on the Bangladesh bowling attack (201 retired hurt) when the Sri Lankans met the Test minnows in the Asian Test Championship. The absence of India rendered the competition impotent.

PAKISTAN v. BANGLADESH
29–31 August 2001 at Multan

BANGLADESH

	First innings		Second innings	
Javed Omar	c Shoaib Malik b Waqar Younis	12	c Abdur Razzaq b Waqar Younis	4
Mehrab Hosain	c Faisal Iqbal b Danish Kaneria	19	c Rashid Latif b Waqar Younis	9
Habibul Bashar	c Rashid Latif b Waqar Younis	13	not out	56
Aminul Islam	b Shoaib Malik	10	c sub (Younis Khan) b Danish Kaneria	18
Akram Khan	c Yousuf Youhana b Danish Kaneria	12	c sub (Younis Khan) b Danish Kaneria	8
Naimur Rahman (capt)	c Faisal Iqbal b Danish Kaneria	8	c sub (Younis Khan) b Danish Kaneria	4
*Khaled Mashud	lbw b Danish Kaneria	4	c & b Danish Kaneria	0
Enamul Haque	c Waqar Younis b Danish Kaneria	14	c Yousuf Youhana b Danish Kaneria	7
Hasibul Hossain	c Taufeeq Umar b Danish Kaneria	18	c sub (Younis Khan) b Danish Kaneria	31
Mohammad Sharif	b Shoaib Malik	13	c Rashid Latif b Waqar Younis	3
Manjural Islam	not out	0	b Waqar Younis	2
Extras	lb 5, w 1, nb 5	11	lb 3, nb 3	6
		148		**134**

	First innings				Second innings			
	O	M	R	W	O	M	R	W
Wasim Akram	10	2	17	–	9	1	32	–
Waqar Younis	6	0	25	2	7.1	1	19	4
Abdur Razzaq	8	1	27	–	8	0	34	–
Danish Kaneria	13	3	42	6	15	3	52	6
Shoaib Malik	4.1	0	18	2	2	0	8	–

Fall of Wickets
1–20, 2–50, 3–55, 4–67, 5–76, 6–83, 7–101, 8–107, 9–134
1–5, 2–22, 3–52, 4–72, 5–84, 6–84, 7–96, 8–141, 9–144

PAKISTAN

	First innings	
Saeed Anwar	c Hasibul Hossain b Mohammad Sharif	101
Taufeeq Umar	c Khaled Mashud b Hasibul Hossain	104
Faisal Iqbal	b Mohammad Sharif	9
Inzamam-ul-Haq	retired hurt	105
Yousuf Youhana	not out	102
Abdur Razzaq	not out	110
*Rashid Latif		
Wasim Akram		
Waqar Younis (capt)		
Shoaib Malik		
Danish Kaneria		
Extras	b 1, lb 3, w 3, nb 8	15
	(3 wickets dec.)	**546**

	First innings			
	O	M	R	W
Manjural Islam	19	2	103	–
Mohammad Sharif	24.5	4	110	2
Hasibul Hossain	31	5	145	1
Naimur Rahman	19	1	77	–
Enamul Haque	16	1	78	–
Animul Islam	4	0	17	–
Javed Omar	1	0	12	–

Fall of Wickets
1–168, 2–178, 3–258
Inzamam-ul-Haq retired hurt at 381-3

Umpires: DB Hair & PT Manuel
Toss: Bangladesh
Test Debut: Shoaib Malik, Taufeeq Umar (Pakistan)
Man of the Match: Danish Kaneria

Pakistan won by an innings & 264 runs

Murali was the next spinner to torment Bangladesh. He took ten wickets in the Test at SSC, Colombo.

runs at Multan and to Sri Lanka by an innings and 137 runs the following week – the wide margin of victory highlighting the long and arduous road ahead for the world's newest Test nation.

At Multan, five out of Pakistan's top six cruised past three figures as Pakistan glided nonchalantly to 546 for 3 declared. Promising 21-year-old leg spinner, Danish Kaneria, whose cousin Anil Dalpat was the first Hindu to represent Pakistan in 1983–84, then reeked havoc, claiming 12 for 94 in the match.

And at Colombo, just days after they had completed a series win against India, their first Test success for over 18 months, Sri Lanka's batsmen continued the greedy run fest. Marvan Atapattu (201) waltzed to a fifth Test double century – a feat achieved before by only Sir Donald Bradman (12), Walter Hammond (7) and Javed Miandad (6) – and Mahela Jayawardene cracked 150. Both were eventually retired as Sanath Jayasuriya, ever the egalitarian, tried to share around the fun.

Fortunately, Bangladesh's self-respect, which must have nose-dived dangerously during the two maulings, was salvaged somewhat in the later stages by a young, fresh-cheeked and hitherto little-known teenager called Mohammad Ashraful, who smashed his way into the record books. Although there was the customary Asian confusion over his exact age – it was the day before his 17th birthday according to some sources, and 63 days after it according to others – he had still broken Mushtaq Mohammad's long-standing record (17 years 82 days) for the youngest centurion in Test cricket.

After the first two games, the tournament was to lay dormant, waiting for a rare space in the cricket calendar. Pakistan were scheduled to play Sri Lanka at Colombo on 30 January 2002 to finish the group stages, but administrators appeared to lose interest in the tournament. Finally, after that scheduled game, which was cancelled without any public statement from the ACC, news filtered through that a straight final would be played on 6 March 2002.

There had also been confusion over where the match would be staged. However, Sri Lanka agreed to play in Lahore, a generous gesture considering the financial crisis that had engulfed Pakistan's cricket since the events of 11 September. Scheduled tours by New Zealand and West Indies had been cancelled and Sri Lanka's was the first international visit since that World Trade Centre attack.

But the final was never going to be a gold pot. The Pakistan Cricket Board (PCB) secured sponsorship from Instantphone, but satellite television networks had already filled their schedules with international cricket elsewhere. TransWorld International (TWI) eventually answered the PCB's plea for help, ensuring domestic coverage at least, but Sri Lanka was forced to endure a television and radio blackout, as television stations were unable to generate sufficient advertising in a depressed market to cover the satellite transmission costs.

When the teams arrived in Lahore it was an administrative nightmare. ACC officials were conspicuous by their absence and the rules were changed without proper communication. Sri Lankan team officials were surprised when the previous ACC requirement for two neutral umpires was jettisoned without any prior notice, apparently on the grounds of cost.

At least, after two hopelessly one-sided encounters involving Bangladesh, the final offered hope of a fierce contest, with both Pakistan (six wins) and Sri Lanka (eight wins) clashing after a record run of victories. Unfortunately, the close tussle anticipated never materialized: Sri Lanka had established a position of dominance after the first day and an unassailable lead by sunset on day two.

The first day was pivotal. A well-grassed Gaddafi Stadium surface and the temperate Punjabi weather, looked tailor-made for Pakistan's battery of fast bowlers. But its appearance was deceiving, and when Sri Lanka won the toss and bowled, it soon looked a gamble with both lateral movement and bounce conspicuous by its absence.

Nevertheless, Sri Lanka wheeled out four top-order wickets in the morning. Taufeeq Umar clipped generously into the hands of short leg and Shahid Afridi was left fuming when Younis Khan, perched

SRI LANKA v. BANGLADESH
6-8 September 2001 at Sinhalese Sports Club Ground, Colombo

BANGLADESH

	First innings		Second innings	
Javed Omar	c Jayasuriya b Vaas	7	lbw b Muralitharan	40
Mehrab Hosain	run out (Atapattu)	23	lbw b Muralitharan	4
Habibul Bashar	b Vaas	4	(5) c Jayawardene b Muralitharan	19
Aminul Islam	c Sangakkara b Perera	6	b Jayasuriya	56
Al Sahariar	c Sangakkara b Muralitharan	16	(3) lbw b Samaraweera	7
Naimur Rahman (capt)	b Muralitharan	0	(7) c Atapattu b Perera	48
Mohammad Ashraful	c Jayasuriya b Muralitharan	26	(6) c & b Perera	114
*Khaled Mashud	b Muralitharan	0	lbw b Muralitharan	3
Hasibul Hossain	b Muralitharan	2	c Sangakkara b Perera	0
Mohammad Sharif	c Vandort b Vaas	1	c & b Muralitharan	19
Manjural Islam	not out	3	not out	1
Extras	lb 1, nb 1	2	b 5, lb 5, nb 7	17
		90		**328**

	First innings				Second innings			
	O	M	R	W	O	M	R	W
Vaas	14	2	47	3	16	2	71	-
Pushpakumara	7	4	9	-	8	5	15	-
Perera	5	1	17	1	13	3	40	3
Muralitharan	9.4	4	13	5	35.3	6	98	5
Samaraweera	1	0	3	-	13	2	42	1
Jayasuriya					16	2	52	1

Fall of Wickets
1-10, 2-16, 3-29, 4-57, 5-58, 6-61, 7-61, 8-67, 9-72
1-31, 2-54, 3-54, 4-8172, 5-207, 6-303, 7-308, 8-308, 9-314

SRI LANKA

	First innings	
MS Atapattu	retired out	201
ST Jayasuriya (capt)	lbw b Naimur Rahman	89
*K Sangakkara	c Aminul Islam b Hasibul Hossain	54
DPMD Jayawardene	retired out	150
MG Vandort	c Manjural Islam b Naimur Rahman	36
HP Tillekeratne	not out	10
TT Samaraweera		
M Muralitharan		
KR Pushpakumara		
WPUJC Vaas		
PDRL Perera		
Extras	lb 5, w 2, nb 8	15
	(5 wickets dec.)	**555**

	First innings			
	O	M	R	W
Manjural Islam	18	1	94	-
Mohammad Sharif	17	0	120	-
Hasibul Hossain	23	6	122	1
Naimur Rahman	30.3	8	117	2
Mohammad Ashraful	10	0	63	-
Habibul Bashar	5	0	34	-

Fall of Wickets
1-144, 2-269, 3-440, 4-530, 5-555

Umpires: RE Koertzen & Mian Mohammad Aslam
Toss: Sri Lanka
Test Debut: MG Vandort (Sri Lanka), Mohammad Ashraful (Bangladesh)
Men of the Match: Mohammad Ashraful & M Muralitharan

Sri Lanka won by an innings & 137 runs

comfortably on his bat at the non-striker's end, left him stranded after turning down a request for an easy single (18 for 2).

Sri Lanka's dream start was followed by a sturdy 86-run partnership – the highest of the innings – between Khan and Inzamam. However, just before lunch, Buddika Fernando, a slightly built fast bowler with the ability to surprise unsuspecting batsman with unexpected nip, forced both batsmen into edging his leg cutter.

Thereafter, the visitors chipped their way through the middle order, with Muttiah Muralitharan, brushing aside fresh accusations over the legality of his action from India spinner Bishen Bedi, picking up four wickets with a typically deceptive performance. Pakistan were bowled out for 234, saved from an even worse total by 26 no-balls and some fumbled catches. In the 21 overs remaining in the day, Sri Lanka moved quickly into a formidable position, despite the first-ball loss of Atapattu, caught at long leg off a top-edged pull. Jayasuriya and Sangakkara feasted on some wayward Pakistan pace bowling and a speedy outfield, racing to 91 for 1 at the close.

During the following two days, Sri Lanka glided towards 528 as Sangakkara provided further confirmation that they had unearthed a wicketkeeper- batsman of rare potential. The left-hander, leaving the ball well and ruthlessly dispatching the loose ball, scored 230, just two runs short of Andy Flower's record Test total for a wicketkeeper.

He was well supported by an unusually responsible Jayasuriya (88), a glistening innings from Mahela Jaywardene (68) and useful middle-order contributions from Russel Arnold (44) and Vaas (43). Even though the innings slipped away at the end, with Mohammad Sami snatching a hat-trick, Pakistan's fate appeared sealed. But rain all but washed out day four and Sri Lanka started to fret, their desperation apparent when the players rolled up their trousers to assist the dawdling groundsman with the removal of the covers. Pakistan fans, only a sprinkling of whom watched from the shady stadium, started to contemplate a fortuitous escape.

However, the final day started with clear skies and Sri Lanka, needing five wickets to wrap up victory, quickly broke through with the second new ball. Crucially, Inzamam, who had led the home team's resistance with characteristic authority, was trapped lbw by Vaas. That precipitated a lower-order slide and a short Sri Lankan sprint to victory.

FINAL – PAKISTAN v. SRI LANKA
6–10 March 2002 at Lahore

PAKISTAN

	First innings		Second innings	
Shahid Afridi	run out (Samaraweera/ Sangakkara)	0	st Sangakkara b Muralithan	70
Taufeeq Umar	c Samaraweera b Vaas	6	b Vaas	19
Younis Khan	b Muralitharan	46	c Samaraweera b Zoysa	19
Inzamam-ul-Haq	c Jayasuriya b Fernando	29	lbw b Vaas	99
Yousuf Youhana	c Sangakkara b Fernando	6	c Atapattu b Muralitharan	7
Abdur Razzaq	lbw b Vaas	24	lbw b Muralitharan	5
Shoaib Malik	c Sangakkara b Fernando	13	c Samaraweera b Zoysa	21
*Rashid Latif	c Sangakkara b Muralitharan	36	c Muralitharan b Vaas	2
Waqar Younis (capt)	b Muralitharan	19	c Tillekeratne b Muralitharan	25
Shoaib Akhtar	lbw b Muralitharan	15	not out	4
Mohammad Sami	not out	0	c Sangakkara b Vaas	0
Extras	lb 4, w 1, nb 26	31	b 12, lb 2, w 1, nb 39	54
		234		**325**

	First innings				Second innings			
	O	M	R	W	O	M	R	W
Vaas	17	2	62	2	22.5	3	85	4
Zoysa	9	2	29	-	21	3	54	2
Fernando	16	1	84	3	14	2	68	-
Muralitharan	25	9	55	4	34	8	72	4
Jayasuriya					1	0	7	-
Samaraweera					9	1	25	-

Fall of Wickets
1-18, 2-18, 3-104, 4-108, 5-127, 6-147, 7-176, 8-216, 9-219
1-31, 2-66, 3-150, 4-166, 5-181, 6-281, 7-285, 8-291, 9-321

SRI LANKA

	First innings		Second innings	
MS Atapattu	c Shoaib Akhtar b Waqar Younis	0	c Rashid Latif b Mohammad Sami	1
ST Jayasuriya (capt)	c Rashid Latif b Abdur Razzaq	88	c Yousuf Youhana b Shoaib Akhtar	1
*K Sangakkara	c Younis Khan b Abdur Razzaq	230	not out	14
DPMD Jayawardene	c Inzamam-ul-Haq b Mohammad Sami	68	not out	12
RP Arnold	b Shoaib Akhtar	44		
WPUJC Vaas	c Taufeeq Umar b Abdur Razzaq	43		
HP Tillekeratne	not out	19		
TT Samaraweera	c Rashid Latif b Shoaib Akhtar	8		
TCB Fernando	lbw b Mohammad Sami	7		
DNT Zoysa	lbw b Mohammad Sami	0		
M Muralitharan	b Mohammad Sami	0		
Extras	b 1, lb 7, w 5, nb 8	21	lb 1, w 2, nb 2	5
		528	(2 wickets)	**33**

	First innings				Second innings			
	O	M	R	W	O	M	R	W
Waqar Younis	30	4	123	1				
Shoaib Akhtar	27	4	114	2	3.2	0	17	1
Mohammad Sami	36.5	4	120	4	3	0	15	1
Abdur Razzaq	29	5	82	3				
Shoaib Malik	14	3	55	-				
Shahid Afridi	3	0	26	-				

Fall of Wickets
1-0, 2-203, 3-376, 4-447, 5-447, 6-501, 7-519, 8-528, 9-528
1-1, 2-14

Umpires: DJ Harper & Athar Zaidi
Toss: Sri Lanka
Man of the Match: K Sangakkara

Sri Lanka won by eight wickets

SHARJAH CUP
By Qamar Ahmed

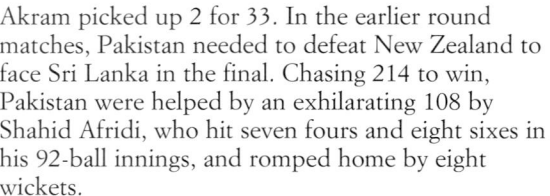

The three-nation Sharjah Cup – competed between Pakistan, New Zealand and Sri Lanka – was won by Pakistan who defeated the tournament leaders Sri Lanka by an emphatic margin of 217 runs in the final. Pakistan owed a great deal to Yousuf Youhana who had a lean start to the competition, but suddenly came into his own. He played an innings of pristine quality to make 129 off 131 balls as Pakistan accumulated an impressive 295 for 6 in 50 overs. Imran Nazir made 63 opening the innings, having hit ten fours and a six in 61 deliveries, but it was the fifth-wicket stand of 155 off 149 balls between Yousuf Youhana and Younis Khan which helped Pakistan reach the highest total in the tri-nation tournament. Younis Khan made 66 in 71 balls and Yousuf Youhana struck eight fours and three sixes in his 100th one-day international. Sri Lanka were handicapped by an injury to their star spinner Muttiah Muralitharan, who damaged his shoulder in the 11th over of the Pakistan innings without having bowled a single ball in the final.

Chasing a huge target, Sri Lanka, who had finished at the top of the table with two victories over Pakistan and one against New Zealand in the preliminary league round, crashed to only 78 runs in 16.5 overs to hand the match to Pakistan on a plate. Only Sanath Jayasuriya, Kumar Sangakkara and Russel Arnold reached double figures as the middle order collapsed.

Waqar Younis and Shoaib Akhtar – backed up by unusually brilliant fielding – captured three wickets each for 33 and 11 respectively, while Wasim

Shahid Afridi was his customary eccentric self in the Sharjah Cup.

Akram picked up 2 for 33. In the earlier round matches, Pakistan needed to defeat New Zealand to face Sri Lanka in the final. Chasing 214 to win, Pakistan were helped by an exhilarating 108 by Shahid Afridi, who hit seven fours and eight sixes in his 92-ball innings, and romped home by eight wickets.

Match One
8 April 2002 at Sharjah Stadium (floodlit)
Sri Lanka 242 for 9 (50 overs)
(ST Jayasuriya 87, RP Arnold 57)
Pakistan 201 (45.5 overs) (Abdur Razzaq 56)
Sri Lanka (4 pts) won by 41 runs
Man of the Match: ST Jayasuriya

Match Two
9 April 2002 at Sharjah CA Stadium (floodlit)
New Zealand 218 for 8 (50 overs) (M Muralitharan 5 for 9)
Sri Lanka 207 (49.1 overs) (MS Atapattu 61)
New Zealand (4pts) won by 11 runs
Man of the Match: JDP Oram

Match Three
11 April 2002 at Sharjah CA Stadium (floodlit)
Pakistan 288 for 6 (50 overs) (Inzamam-ul-Haq 68, Shahid Afridi 56, Younis Khan 56, SB Styris 4 for 30)
New Zealand 237 for 8 (50 overs) (CZ Harris 54, CD McMillan 51)
Pakistan (4pts) won by 51 runs
Man of the Match: Inzamam-ul-Haq

Match Four
12 April 2002 at Sharjah CA Stadium (floodlit)
Sri Lanka 239 for 6 (50 overs) (MS Atapattu 77*, UDU Chandana 64)
Pakistan 230 for 5 (50 overs)
Sri Lanka (4pts) won by 9 runs
Man of the Match: MS Atapattu

Match Five
14 April 2002 at Sharjah CA Stadium (floodlit)
Sri Lanka 243 for 9 (50 overs) (MS Atapattu 82, K Sangakkara 50)
New Zealand 197 for 9 (50 overs)
Sri Lanka (4pts) won by 46 runs
Man of the Match: MS Atapattu

Match Six
15 April 2002 at Sharjah CA Stadium (floodlit)
New Zealand 213 for 9 (50 overs)
Pakistan 217 for 2 (31.3 overs) (Shahid Afridi 108*, Imran Nazir 57)

Pakistan (5pts) won by eight wickets
Man of the Match: Shahid Afridi

Final
17 April 2002 at Sharjah CA Stadium (floodlit)
Pakistan 295 for 6 (50 overs) (Yousuf Youhana 129,
Younis Khan 66, Imran Nazir 63)
Sri Lanka 78 (16.5 overs)
Pakistan won by 217 runs
Man of the Match: Yousuf Youhana
Player of the Series: MS Atapattu

SHARJAH CHAMPIONS TROPHY
By Qamar Ahmed

Pakistan made sure of the US$120,000 purse by beating Sri Lanka in the final of the *Kahleej Times* Champions Trophy by five wickets. For both teams, reaching the final was made easier by

Wasim Akram spearheaded Pakistan's attack which bowled Sri Lanka out for only 173 in the final of the Champions Trophy.

Zimbabwe – the third team in the tournament – failing to win any of its four league matches.

The final seemed destined to be a one-sided affair. Waqar Younis, Shoaib Akhtar and Wasim Akram shared eight wickets between them to make short work of the Sri Lankan innings by bowling them out for 173 in only the 45th over. Naved Latif and Shahid Afridi then put on 45 for the first wicket. Afridi scored 35 off 38 balls before being dismissed by Muttiah Muralitharan, who also claimed Yousuf Youhana for 40 and Younis Khan, taking 3 for 22 in his ten overs. After Inzamam-ul-Haq was removed for 28 by Chaminda Vaas, Pakistan were on 138 in the 37th over and, suddenly, the game was alive once more.

Pakistan, though, were rescued by a sixth-wicket stand of 39 between Rashid Latif and Abdur Razzaq to reach the target in the 44th over. Rashid Latif earlier had caught four victims during the Sri Lankan innings which included Sanath Jayasuriya for 34, Mahela Jayawardene for 43 – the two had added 58 runs for the third wicket. Marvan Atapattu was out without scoring and Kumar Sangakkara for three. Russel Arnold, with 47, was highest scorer of Sri Lankan innings.

In the preliminary matches, Sri Lanka defeated Zimbabwe by 63 runs and Pakistan by seven wickets to record their second win in a row at the start of the tournament. Later Sri Lanka beat Zimbabwe once again by 79 runs to qualify for the finals. Pakistan's first victory in the championship was against Zimbabwe, who were restricted to 173 in the 40th over chasing 280 to win. Off spinner Shoaib Malik, with 3 for 42, was the most successful Pakistan bowler.

In another match against Zimbabwe, Pakistan won by the narrow margin of 29 runs. Having made 261 for 9, with the help of 58 by Shahid Afridi and 59 by Younis Khan, Pakistan bowled Zimbabwe out for 232 in the 47th over, despite the efforts of Andy Flower who was run out for 91 opening the innings.

Immediately prior to their victorious final, Pakistan had another convincing victory against Sri Lanka by seven wickets. Replying to Sri Lanka's 272 for 9, Pakistan reached the target without much fuss losing only three wickets as Naved Latif made 113 with nine fours and a six and Inzamam-ul-Haq hammered 118 with ten fours and two sixes. In Sri Lanka's innings Mahela Jayawardene scored 84 with six fours and a six in 83 balls.

Match One
26 October 2001 at Sharjah CA Stadium (floodlit)

Sri Lanka 256 for 6 (50 overs) (MS Atapattu 92, RP Arnold 76*)
Zimbabwe 193 (50 overs) (TCB Fernando 5 for 67)
Sri Lanka (5 pts) won by 63 runs
Man of the Match: TCB Fernando

Match Two
27 October 2001 at Sharjah CA Stadium (floodlit)
Pakistan 176 (46.2 overs)
Sri Lanka 177 for 3 (38.1 overs) (DA Gunawardene 88)
Sri Lanka (5 pts) won by seven wickets
Man of the Match: DA Gunawardene

Match Three
28 October 2001 at Sharjah CA Stadium (floodlit)
Pakistan 279 for 6 (50 overs) (Shahid Afridi 67, Saeed Anwar 64)
Zimbabwe 173 (39.1 overs) (A Flower 51)
Pakistan (5pts) won by 106 runs
Man of the Match: Shahid Afridi

Match Four
30 October 2001 at Sharjah CA Stadium (floodlit)
Sri Lanka 250 (49.4 overs) (DPMD Jayawardene 63, RP Arnold 55, HH Streak 4 for 59)
Zimbabwe 171 for 8 (50 overs) (DA Marillier 52*)
Sri Lanka (5 pts) won by 79 runs
Man of the Match: DPMD Jayawardene

Match Five
31 October 2001 at Sharjah CA Stadium (floodlit)
Pakistan 261 for 9 (50 overs) (Younis Khan 59, Shahid Afridi 58)
Zimbabwe 232 (46.2 overs) (GW Flower 91)
Pakistan (4 pts) won by 29 runs
Man of the Match: GW Flower

Match Six
2 November 2001 at Sharjah CA Stadium (floodlit)
Sri Lanka 272 for 9 (50 overs) (DPMD Jayawardene 84, DA Gunawardene 57)
Pakistan 276 for 3 (49.2 overs) (Inzamam-ul-Haq 118*, Naved Latif 113)
Pakistan (4pts) won by seven wickets
Man of the Match: Naved Latif

Final
4 November 2001 at Sharjah CA Stadium (floodlit)
Sri Lanka 173 (44.2 overs)
Pakistan 177 for 5 (43.4 overs)
Pakistan won by five wickets
Man of the Match: Waqar Younis
Player of the Series: DPMD Jayawardene

FORM CHARTS

Derbyshire
Durham
Essex
Glamorgan
Gloucestershire
Hampshire
Kent
Lancashire
Leicestershire
Middlesex
Northamptonshire
Nottinghamshire
Somerset
Surrey
Sussex
Warwickshire
Worcestershire
Yorkshire

DERBYSHIRE CCC

FIRST-CLASS MATCHES
BATTING

	SD Stubbings	MJ DiVenuto	AI Gait	DR Hewson	LD Sutton	DG Cork	KM Krikken	JID Kerr	G Welch	KJ Dean	LJ Wharton	SMA Bukhari	CWG Bassano	MP Dowman	JP Pyemont	SA Selwood	T Lungley	P Aldred	NEL Gunter	RM Khan	NRC Dumelow	CJ Warn	Extras	Total	Wickets	Result	Points
v. Glamorgan	4	38	24	0	7	33	20	58	0	7*	1												25	217	10		
(Cardiff) 19–22 April	128	62	80	102*	15	22	25	2*	-	-	-												26	462	6	W	16
v. Durham	19	56	22	0	9	56	0	28		0	3*	53											17	263	10		
(Derby) 24–27 April	4	46	35	7*	8	2	18	18		50	8*	16											17	229	10	W	17
v. Northamptonshire	8	230	53	13	24	60		8	26	11*		11	41										53	538	10		
(Derby) 8–10 May	12*	-	3	17	-	-		-	-	-		-	0*										1	33	2	W	19.75
v. Essex	41	25	0	10			0	23	4	9*	0	38	0										8	158	10		
(Chelmsford) 26–29 May	0	41	8	9			48	6	9	48	0*	16	9										5	199	10	L	3
v. Glamorgan	0	98	37			28	9		63*	21	5	5	35	0									53	354	10		
(Derby) 31 May–1 June	0	1*	4*			-	-		-	-	-	-	-	-									0	5	1	W	18.25
v. Nottinghamshire	45	79	52			31	14		0	16	8*	43	64	9									31	392	10		
(Trent Bridge) 12–15 June	7	17	20			5	12*		0*	-	-	-	79	27									14	181	6	W	19
v. West Indies A	25		13	0	80						1*		17		7	0	19	29	18				29	238	10		
(Derby) 26–28 June	0		9	47	28						0			71	34	7	4	9*	0				24	233	10	W	
v. Gloucestershire	32	3	88	7	67		8		29*	0		8	78			38							40	398	10	D	
(Derby) 3–6 July	-	-	-	-	-		-		-	-		-	-			-							-	-	-		11
v. Durham	0	57	0	4			1		0	8*	13	0	1			2							10	96	10		
(Chester-le-Street) 10–12 July	30	40	0	18			1		44	2	0*	49				20							5	209	10	L	3
v. Nottinghamshire		91	76		1	2			16	10*	6	11	83	9		21							27	353	10		
(Derby) 19–21 July		2	53		19	8			20	4	6*	4	14	40		15							24	209	10	L	7
v. Northamptonshire		30	175		0	0			6	4*	26	57	28	32		8							22	388	10		
(Northampton) 25–27 July		24	5		80	3			2*	0	12	69	41	32		3							11	282	10	W	19
v. Essex	4	9	2	58					17*	0	2		152	6		23	6						22	301	10		
(Derby) 7–10 August	3	22	10	14					7	0	20*		0	15		24	7						29	151	10	L	6
v. Worcestershire		3	0	1					64	2	0*	20	85	0		1	3						11	190	10		
(Derby) 14–16 August		1	21	7					9	54*	16	6	0	1		99	0						29	243	10	L	3
v. Middlesex		192*	3	32					50	23	1	13	26	3		21	14						36	414	10		
(Lord's) 21–24 August		113	8	11					36*				34	33		0	44						22	301	7	W	20
v. Indians	66			66				6*					16	43	9			2	0	91	23	1	35	358	10		
(Derby) 28–30 August	-			-									-	-	-			-	-	-	-	-	-	-	-	D	
v. Gloucestershire		8	24	12	46				11	9	0*	0	4	16		37							20	187	10		
(Bristol) 4–7 September		175*	33	7	6*								51	3		10							34	319	5	D	7
v. Middlesex		4	0	36	0		0		3	0	0	21*	49			13							11	137	10		
(Derby) 11–13 September		71	0	15	1		28		23	0	0*	8	44			14							28	232	10	L	3
v. Worcestershire			58	9	51		54		2	40*	0	0	49			22					1		9	246	10		
(Worcester) 18–21 September			67	14	2		68		27	11	0	39	44			77					56		19	391	10	L	3.75
Matches	11	15	17	11	10	8	9	7	14	16	14	15	14	8	4	10	7	2	2	1	2	1					
Innings	20	28	33	20	19	13	16	12	23	25	23	24	26	14	7	19	13	3	3	1	3	1					
Not Out	1	3	1	1	1	0	1	2	5	8	12	2	1	0	0	0	0	1	0	0	5	0					
Highest Score	128	230	175	102*	80	80	48	68	64	54*	16	53	152	71	34	99	44	29	18	91	80	1					
Runs	428	1538	983	393	400	404	169	299	460	333	83	333	1063	298	121	457	168	40	18	91	80	1					
Average	22.52	61.52	30.71	20.68	22.22	31.07	11.26	29.90	25.55	19.58	7.54	15.13	42.52	21.28	17.28	24.05	12.92	20.00	6.00	26.60	26.60	1.00					
100s	1	4	1	1	-	-	-	-	-	-	-	-	1	-	-	-	-	-	-	-	-	-					
50s	1	7	8	1	3	4	-	3	3	2	-	1	8	1	-	2	-	-	-	1	1	-					
Catches/Stumpings	5	29	14	7	30/1	11	26/-	2	8	6	7	5	13	6	2	1	4	2	3	-	1	3/-					

DERBYSHIRE CCC

FIRST-CLASS MATCHES

BOWLING

Match	DG Cork	KJ Dean	G Welch	JID Kerr	LJ Wharton	SMA Bukhari	MP Dowman	T Lungley	P Aldred	NEL Gunter	Overs	Total	Byes/Leg-Byes	Wickets	Run outs
v. Glamorgan (Cardiff) 19–22 April	17.4-3-51-6	14-4-45-2	10-2-44-0	7-2-33-2	–						48.4	175	2	10	–
	19-3-70-2	11-2-41-1	11-3-35-0	20-5-73-1	29-5-103-6						90	341	18	10	–
v. Durham (Derby) 24–27 April	23.1-7-72-5	26-9-53-2		8-2-34-1	1-0-11-0	22-4-81-2					80.1	258	7	10	–
	14.3-3-54-5	14-2-62-0			1-0-9-0	17-1-69-3					55.3	232	4	10	–
v. Northamptonshire (Derby) 8–10 May	11-3-29-4	10-2-28-3	12-5-29-2	5.5-0-23-1				7-4-14-0			45.5	131	8	10	–
	25-7-61-1	27.1-10-57-2	34-11-107-4	15-2-95-0				21-3-106-3			122.1	439	13	10	–
v. Essex (Chelmsford) 26–29 May		19-9-58-3	8-4-13-1	6.3-0-39-1		1-0-4-1-		9-1-56-1			52.3	168	6	9	–
		10-0-57-2	9-1-36-0	5-0-38-0	–			18-5-48-3			33	193	6	4	1
v. Glamorgan (Derby) 31 May–1 June	16-3-36-2	17.4-7-42-7	12-7-19-0			10-4-35-1					55.4	157	25	10	–
	14.5-3-50-4	14-3-67-3	12-4-35-2		4.3-2-8-0	5.3-1-25-1					50.5	200	10	10	–
v. Nottinghamshire (Trent Bridge) 12–15 June	28-9-89-3	22-3-73-4	21-4-83-1		11-2-60-0	15-3-76-2	2-0-8-0				99	393	4	10	–
	27.2-4-78-6	16-1-50-1	–		–	11-2-37-2					54.2	175	10	10	1
v. West Indies A (Derby) 26–28 June					13-5-52-1		13-6-28-4	18-5-57-1	22.2-8-37-2	13-4-39-2	79.2	220	7	10	–
					3.2-0-9-2		4-2-15-0	8-3-24-2	8-1-30-2	8-4-14-4	31.2	106	14	10	–
v. Gloucestershire (Derby) 3–6 July	25-7-67-5	19-6-51-2	10-6-27-1				1-0-7-0	3.2-1-20-2			58.2	179	7	10	–
	17-7-44-3	18-4-74-2	10-1-50-2				9-0-50-0	–			54	225	7	7	–
v. Durham (Darlington) 10–12 July		19-4-65-4	15-4-40-2			13-1-57-1		9-5-23-2			56	191	6	10	–
		24.2-8-67-4	29-10-71-3	3-1-10-0		9-4-25-1		11-4-21-2			76.2	203	9	10	–
v. Nottinghamshire (Derby) 19–21 July	25-11-55-4	11-0-60-1	21-7-53-0			12.1-1-49-2	9-5-16-3				78.1	240	7	10	–
	31.4-8-68-2	26-7-81-2	18-4-57-2		6-1-19-1	23-4-74-2	–				104.4	323	24	9	–
v. Northamptonshire (Northampton) 25–27 July	15-2-56-3	15-6-33-1			4-0-15-0	8-0-37-2		8-1-43-3			53	210	11	10	1	A
	13-1-71-2	15-4-48-3			11-2-43-2	14-2-72-2		11-3-33-0			64	283	16	10	1
v. Essex (Derby) 7–10 August		15-3-78-0	23-10-34-3			16.1-1-71-3	4-0-28-1	15-5-46-2			75.1	268	3	10	–	A
		16-1-60-1	29-11-66-5			15.4-2-65-2	16-4-53-0	14-3-59-2			91.4	324	12	10	–	A
v. Worcestershire (Derby) 14–16 August		25-7-69-3	23-6-66-2		20-0-69-2	15.5-1-71-3		3-0-19-0			89.5	320	18	10	–	B
		0.2-0-0-0	8-2-35-0		2-0-29-0	3.4-0-34-0		1.2-0-13-1			15.2	115	4	1	–	B
v. Middlesex (Lord's) 21–24 August		26.4-6-73-4	25-8-61-4		24-5-44-2	14-3-64-0		10-1-42-0			104.4	304	8	10	–	B
		13-7-18-0	10.1-2-21-2		31-11-62-6	21-4-73-2		6-1-16-0			84.1	207	4	10	–	B
v. Indians (Derby) 28–30 August				25-9-97-3				12-4-28-1	35-9-109-1	23.1-7-76-2	121.1	445	21	8	–	CD
				3-0-10-0				3-0-11-1	8-1-35-0	7-3-24-0	43.3	182	2	3	–	ABDE
v. Gloucestershire (Bristol) 4–7 September		24-9-63-3	20-7-60-6		–	12.2-3-60-1	1-1-0-0				57.2	192	9	10	–
		21-3-105-1	33-8-147-3		29-9-87-2	35-4-170-3	8-2-36-0				129	577	16	9	–	D
v. Middlesex (Derby) 11–13 September		25.3-8-59-6	34-16-52-2	23-4-84-0	7-2-31-0	18-3-51-2					107.3	292	15	10	–	B
		15.5-3-66-4	9-3-26-2	9-2-32-4	–	3-0-20-0					36.5	150	6	10	–
v. Worcestershire (Worcester) 18–21 September		19.3-4-75-4	23-7-57-2	5-0-43-1	7-0-26-0	14-2-48-3					68.3	265	16	10	–
		28-3-143-5	17-4-85-4	6-1-17-0	1-0-4-0	11.4-0-63-0					69.4	373	26	9	–	C

	DG Cork	KJ Dean	G Welch	JID Kerr	LJ Wharton	SMA Bukhari	MP Dowman	T Lungley	P Aldred	NEL Gunter
Overs	323.1	578	486.1	147.2	208.5	405	72	117.4	73.2	51.1
Maidens	81	145	157	29	45	63	24	32	19	18
Runs	951	1922	1409	652	695	1708	223	416	211	153
Wickets	57	80	55	16	25	47	10	17	5	8
Average	16.68	24.02	25.61	40.75	27.80	36.34	22.30	24.47	42.20	19.12

A   SA Selwood 3-0-15-0; 2-1-8-1, 1-0-9-0; 7-2-35-1
B   JP Pyemont 3-0-8-0; 5-0-12-0, 3-1-13-0; 4.3-1-37-1
C   NRC Dumelow 24-5-110-0; 6-0-35-0
D   DR Hewson 2-1-4-0, 8-3-13-0; 3-0-16-0
E   RM Khan 3-0-15-0

FIELDING

31	LD Sutton (30ct, 1st)
29	MJ DiVenuto
26	KM Krikken
14	AI Gait
13	CWG Bassano
11	DG Cork
8	G Welch
7	DR Hewson, LJ Wharton
6	KJ Dean, MP Dowman
5	SMA Bukhari, SD Stubbings
4	T Lungley
3	NEL Gunter, CJ Warn
2	P Aldred, JID Kerr, JP Pyemont
1	NRC Dumelow, SA Selwood

DURHAM CCC

FIRST-CLASS MATCHES

BATTING

	JJB Lewis	GJ Pratt	JA Daley	PD Collingwood	N Peng	DR law	A Pratt	AM Davies	N Killeen	NC Phillips	SJ Harmison	ML Love	GJ Muchall	SJE Brown	GD Bridge	AM Thorpe	MJ Symington	ID Hunter	P Mustard	NG Hatch	MA Gough	BJ Hodge	I Pattison	Extras	Total	Wickets	Result	Points
v. **Durham UCCE** (Chester-le-Street) 13–15 April	102	13	17	74	82	11	15	13	27*	15*	–													46	415	8		
	2	16	28	1	25	15	18*		–	–	–													33	138	5	D	
v. **Middlesex** (Chester-le-Street) 19–21 April	15		21	7	47		8	4		0*	0	0	48	abs inj										10	160	9		
	11		0	19	6		49	0		abs inj	10	101*	0	abs inj										17	213	8	L	3
v. **Derbyshire** (Derby) 24–27 April	7		5	42	108		18	15*	0		0	43	0		1									19	258	10		
	12		59*	76	9		12	9	7		0	19	14		1									14	232	10	L	5
v. **Sri Lankans** (Chester-le-Street) 7–9 May	9	4		190	17							69		21	29	8	16	75	6*					25	469	10		
	–			–											–									–	–	–	D	
v. **Glamorgan** (Cardiff) 15–18 May	9	16		15	8		7	4	0		71	6		5*			0							21	162	10		
	0	0		99	4		8	15	5*		13	77		2			0							20	243	10	L	3
v. **Gloucestershire** (Chester-le-Street) 24–27 May		66		65	19		93	1*	–		78	52		12*			33			32				15	470	8		
		–		–							–													–	–	–	D	12
v. **Middlesex** (Lord's) 31 May–3 June	71	42					43	4*	–		251	127		22		41*			–	6rh				38	645	6		
	–	–						–	–							–			–	–				–	–	–	D	11
v. **Worcestershire** (Chester-le-Street) 12–15 June	0	20			68		67	0	4		abs inj	46		0		20			1*					17	243	9		
	–						–				abs inj					–								–	–	–	D	8
v. **Worcestershire** (Worcester) 26–28 June	13	34		21	0		12	0	5*			1		6		16			5					7	120	10		
	22	33		0	72*		1	3	16			4		33		4			0					27	215	10	L	2
v. **Northamptonshire** (Northampton) 3–6 July	7	78		29	31		0		13	21*		33		5		42	65							28	352	10		
	–			–					–	–						–	–							–	–	–	L	4
v. **Derbyshire** (Chester-le-Street) 10–12 July	6	1		21			1	33	3*	22	0	29		49		8								18	191	10		
	31	46		57			2	4	0	18*	7	0		6		5								27	203	10	W	15
v. **Nottinghamshire** (Chester-le-Street) 24–26 July	15	17	14		14	5	3	4	5	6*						0				21				12	116	10		
	70	42	34		36	8	25	18	0	3*						7				44				41	328	10	L	3
v. **Glamorgan** (Chester-le-Street) 16–17 August		8		5	6	40	0	4*	3	6					4					30		6		12	124	10		
		35		11	0	10*	0	0	0	0					5					37		0		16	114	10	L	3
v. **Essex** (Colchester) 21–24 August		0		9		14	17*	17	0		27				9	4	32			103				272	59	10		
		65		0		51	5	0	58*		16				61	6	10			34				26	332	10	L	5
v. **Northamptonshire** (Chester-le Street) 27–29 August		18		22		19	14*	11	47	0	10				2	25				35				20	240	10		
		23		8		6	6*	5	0	1	0				0	10				67				10	136	10	L	4
v. **Nottinghamshire** (Trent Bridge) 6–9 September		9				5		5	20*	0	0				8	16	7			0	48			14	132	10		
		65				0*		–	–	–	12				12	12*	–			40	1			11	153	5	D	5.75
v. **Essex** (Chester-le-Street) 11–14 September		20				10		11	12	0	7				14		7			75*	2	7		22	187	10		
		28				8		23	5	19*	0				95		12			46	56	0		22	314	10	L	3
v. **Gloucestershire** Chester-le-Street) 18–20 September		6				25	4*		1		6			17	1		2			33	73	27		21	216	10		
		41				1	5		15		29			4	31		20*			78	39	21		28	312	20	L	4

	JJB Lewis	GJ Pratt	JA Daley	PD Collingwood	N Peng	DR law	A Pratt	AM Davies	N Killeen	NC Phillips	SJ Harmison	ML Love	GJ Muchall	SJE Brown	GD Bridge	AM Thorpe	MJ Symington	ID Hunter	P Mustard	NG Hatch	MA Gough	BJ Hodge	I Pattison
Matches	11	16	3	7	12	6	17	14	15	10	10	6	15	1	10	7	10	8	1	4	8	4	3
Innings	18	27	6	12	21	10	30	24	22	16	17	8	25	–	15	13	16	12	1	4	14	8	6
Not Out	1	0	1	0	0	1	3	7	5	6	3	1	0		2	0	2	1	0	2	2	0	0
Highest Score	102	78	59*	190	108	72*	93	33	27*	58*	17	251	127		49	95	42	65	75	6*	103	73	27
Runs	402	746	130	636	508	253	556	184	178	226	85	576	613		184	271	224	204	75	12	616	275	61
Average	**23.64**	**27.62**	**26.00**	**53.00**	**24.19**	**28.11**	**20.59**	**10.82**	**10.47**	**22.60**	**6.07**	**82.28**	**24.52**		**14.15**	**20.84**	**16.00**	**18.54**	**75.00**	**6.00**	**51.33**	**35.50**	**10.16**
100s	1	–	–	1	1	–	–	–	–	–	–	2	1		–	–	–	–	–	–	1	–	–
50s	2	4	1	4	2	2	3	–	–	1	–	2	3		–	2	–	1	1	–	3	2	–
Ct/St	2	12	1	5	8	2	42/3	3	5	4	4	3	14	–	4	5	6	2	2	2	6	3	2

DURHAM CCC

FIRST–CLASS MATCHES

BOWLING

	N Killeen	SJ Harmison	AM Davies	NC Phillips	DR Law	PD Collingwood	GD Bridge	ID Hunter	NG Hatch	MJ Symington	Overs	Total	Byes/Leg-Byes	Wickets	Run outs	
v .Durham University CCE	14-3-56-0	15.4-6-37-2	16-8-22-3	37-10-82-1	12-3-41-3	6-3-15-0					101.4	268	11	9	-	A
(Chester-le-Street) 13–15 April	11-5-25-2	2-0-8-0	5-3-10-0	4-1-8-0	7-1-17-0	7-4-12-2					36	83	3	4	-	B
v. Middlesex		27-7-72-3	22-4-77-2	27-6-75-2		16-2-49-1					110.4	347	9	10	-	B
(Chester-le-Street) 19–21 April		2-1-9-0	2-0-13-0	-							4	27	5	0	-	
v. Derbyshire	19-4-52-4	13-3-50-0	12-3-51-3			7.4-1-22-1	24-9-79-2				75.4	263	9	10	-	
(Derby) 24–27 April	18-1-55-2	12-1-71-2	20-5-57-2			12-2-31-4					62	229	15	10	-	
v. Sri Lankans							3-0-12-0	15-3-44-3	16.5-4-63-2	12-5-27-4	48.5	167	7	9	-	CDE
(Chester-le-Street) 7–9 May							12-1-40-2	11-2-66-0	11-0-63-1	11-3-38-0	60	282	19	4	-	C
v. Glamorgan	20-6-37-1		15-6-20-2			17-5-36-2	13-5-32-2	24-8-67-2			89	205	13	10	1	
(Cardiff) 15–18 May	11-2-44-0		11-3-29-2			8-1-22-0	11-1-45-2	10-0-62-1			51	204	2	5	-	
v. Gloucestershire	18-7-34-2		14-6-28-2			3-2-4-0	2.2-1-1-2	16-5-62-3			53.2	132	3	10	1	
(Chester-le-Street) 24–27 May	26-12-31-0		24-6-49-0			12-2-37-0	35-14-50-4	23-5-68-3			127	261	11	8	1	F
v. Middlesex	33-10-69-2		33-15-69-3				36-14-66-1		38-9-121-2	21-3-100-1	167	465	10	10	1	DF
(Lord's) 31 May–3 June	12-5-23-2		7-2-28-0				15-2-41-0		8-4-12-0	12-2-44-1	70	194	5	5	1	DF
v. Worcestershire	17-3-69-0		17.5-5-39-3		6-1-28-0		3-2-3-0		22-7-61-4	12-3-43-3	77.5	250	7	10	-	
(Chester-le-Street) 12–15 June	9-1-26-4		-		4-1-17-1		-		5-0-14-0	1.4-0-2-0	19.4	60	1	5	-	
v. Worcestershire	30-10-107-3		28-5-77-1		27-7-104-2		30-3-143-0		23-2-110-0	10-0-88-1	148	643	14	7	-	
(Worcester) 26–28 June	-		-		-		-		-	-	-	-	-	-	-	
v. Northamptonshire	1-1-0-0		-		-		-			-	1	0	0	0	-	
(Northampton) 3–6 July	13-3-41-1			17-1-94-3	11-2-43-0		26.2-3-102-4	13-5-36-1		2-0-15-0	82.2	353	22	9	-	
v. Derbyshire	10-3-27-3	6-2-25-0	6-2-18-2				1-0-6-0			3.5-0-12-2	26.5	96	8	10	3	
(Darlington) 10–12 July	6-0-47-0	17-6-54-3	12-4-34-1	4-4-0-3			10.5-1-35-2			7-1-36-1	56.5	209	3	10	-	
v. Nottinghamshire	17-2-72-1	24.1-2-81-2	19-5-48-2	21-2-81-2	12-2-45-1	8-2-30-0					101.1	362	5	10	2	G
(Chester-le-Street) 24–26 July	5-0-28-1	7-1-22-1	4-1-9-0	-	3-0-13-0	-					20.4	83	3	2	-	
v. Glamorgan	14-2-34-0	24.5-1-75-3	22-7-61-5	4-2-6-1	3-0-22-0						70.5	233	10	10	1	H
(Chester-le-Street) 16–17 August	-	-	-	-							3.3	9	0	0	-	AH
v. Essex	19-7-49-4		15-3-44-0	25-8-66-2				21-2-67-3		12-3-30-1	92	271	15	10	-	
(Colchester) 21–24 August	14-4-53-0		15-2-39-1	27-3-103-4				7-0-40-0		18-4-51-1	87	322	13	6	-	F
v. Northamptonshire	12-4-34-3	22.5-5-83-4	16-6-39-1		12-3-37-2				3-0-21-0		68.5	236	10	10	-	D
(Chester-le-Street) 27–29 August	4-0-30-0	6-0-45-0	-						6.3-3-11-1		24.3	141	3	3	-	D
v. Nottinghamshire	18.1-5-67-1	29-9-79-1		12-3-39-0				24-7-83-2		15-2-72-1	105.1	400	30	6	1	DF
(Trent Bridge) 6–9 September	-			-				-		-	-	-	-	-	-	
v. Essex	20-8-55-1	29-10-74-2		20-4-80-1				28-4-107-2			130.3	463	26	10	1	DFGH
(Chester-le-Street) 11–14 September	-	4-1-11-0		-							8.3	42	4	0	-	H
v. Gloucestershire		22.5-5-65-5	17-3-63-1				21-5-68-0	7-0-35-0			98.5	359	9	10	-	FGH
(Bristol) 18–20 September		11-3-20-0	5-2-18-0				4.2-0-30-0	3-1-17-0			33.2	171	10	0	-	GH

	N Killeen	SJ Harmison	AM Davies	NC Phillips	DR Law	PD Collingwood	GD Bridge	ID Hunter	NG Hatch	MJ Symington
Overs	391.1	275.2	357.5	210	85	96.4	247.5	206	123.5	147
Maidens	108	63	106	47	17	24	61	42	26	29
Runs	1165	881	942	671	330	258	753	775	444	590
Wickets	37	28	36	21	7	10	21	20	9	17
Average	**31.48**	**31.46**	**26.16**	**31.95**	**47.14**	**25.80**	**35.85**	**38.75**	**49.33**	**34.70**

A   GJ Pratt 1-0-4-0; 1.3-0-8-0
B   SJE Brown 18.4-3-65-2
C   AM Thorpe 2-0-14-0, 6-0-18-0
D   GJ Muchall 8-0-36-1; 3-0-13-0, 11-3-28-1; 3-0-12-0, 8-2-52-2; 2-1-8-0; 5-0-19-0; 3-0-26-0
E   N Peng 1-0-2-0
F   MA Gough 7-4-15-0; 3-0-17-0, 5-1-13-0; 6-0-23-0; 5-0-22-0; 4-0-20-0; 11-4-22-2
G   BJ Hodge 1.4-0-8-0; 8-0-41-0; 10-3-28-1, 3-0-25-0
H   I Pattison 3-1-25-0, 2-1-1-0; 16.3-6-41-3, 0.3-0-6-0; 10-1-69-0, 4-0-25-0

FIELDING

45   A Pratt (42ct, 3st)
14   GJ Muchall
12   GJ Pratt
8   N Peng
6   MA Gough, MJ Symington
5   PD Collingwood, N Killeen, AM Thorpe
4   GD Bridge, SJ Harmison, NC Phillips
3   AM Davies, BJ Hodge, ML Love
2   NG Hatch, ID Hunter, DR Law, JJB Lewis, P Mustard, I Pattison
1   JA Daley

ESSEX CCC

FIRST–CLASS MATCHES
BATTING

	DDJ Robinson	AP Grayson	A Flower	Aftab Habib	RC Irani	RS Clinton	JM Dakin	JD Middlebrook	AP Cowan	AC McGarry	JB Grant	N Hussain	JD Stephenson	GR Napier	MC Ilott	WI Jefferson	ZK Sharif	RS Bopara	ML Pettini	TJ Phillips	AJ Clarke	JE Bishop	JS Foster	BJ Hyam	Extras	Total	Wickets	Result	Points
v. Cambridge University CCE (Cambridge) 20–22 April	26 / 100*	105 / –	20 / 1	64 / –	37 / 107	19	34* / 15	2 / 0	10 / 2*	11* / –															42 / 20	370 / 245	8 / 4	/ W	
v. Gloucestershire (Chelmsford) 24–27 April	131 / –	18 / –	91 / –	18 / –	35 / –	24 / –	14 / –	0 / –	7 / –	5* / –	3 / –														33 / –	379 / –	10 / –	/ D	11
v. Nottinghamshire (Cardiff) 8–10 May	7 / 0	19 / 83	4 / 25	20 / 15	37 / 28		6 / 17	11 / 27	9 / 42	0 / 0	1* / 3*	1 / 4													15 / 26	130 / 270	10 / 10	/ L	2.5
v. Worcestershire (Worcester) 15–18 May	71 / 0	15 / 26	45 / 47	117 / 4	48 / 32*	4 / 2	24 / –	4* / –	1 / –		0 / –		0 / 13*												44 / 11	373 / 135	10 / 5	W	19
v. Derbyshire (Chelmsford) 26–29 May	43 / 16	8 / 55*	1 / 5*	28 / 101	10rh / –		7 / –	15 / –	40 / –				0 / 7	2 / 1	0* / –										14 / 8	168 / 193	9 / 4	W	15
v. Northamptonshire (Northampton) 31 May–3 June	68 / 31	103* / 92*	93 / 5	54 / 7			1 / 57	67 / 8					37* / 25*	– / 41	22 / –	– / –	2 / –								50 / 25	497 / 291	7 / 6	W	19
v. Northamptonshire (Ilford) 12–15 June	3 / 16	85 / –	6 / –	207* / –			17 / 9*	0 / –	22 / –				22 / –	43 / –	4* / –	59 / 33*									30 / 10	498 / 68	9 / 1	W	20
v. Gloucestershire (Gloucester) 26–29 June	33 / 175	3 / 13	66 / 82				29 / 6*	4 / 9	60* / 3				57 / 4*	4 / 20	10 / –	2 / 47	42 / –								15 / 22	325 / 381	10 / 7	W	18
v. Glamorgan (Swansea) 3–6 July	72 / 0	16 / 33	61 / 20				32 / 0						10* / 5	1 / 26	43 / 26		19 / 1	2 / 0*	0 / 0	0 / 7					27 / 21	283 / 139	10 / 10	L	5
v. Worcestershire (Ilford) 10–13 July	0 / 15	41 / 17	38 / 13				9 / 0	16 / 53					44 / 1		3 / 0			13 / 58	3 / 24	11* / 31	0 / 23*				19 / 22	197 / 257	10 / 10	L	3
v. Middlesex (Southgate) 18–21 July	73 / 0	0 / –	1 / –	182* / –	27 / –	21 / –	6 / –						31* / –					42 / 20*	– / –	0 / –	36 / –				53 / 2	441 / 53	10 / 1	D	11
v. Glamorgan (Chelmsford) 24–27 July	48 / 119	5 / 172*	0 / 31	34 / 18			42 / –		10 / –				46* / 29*	6 / 109			14 / –	19 / –	4 / –						3 / 36	231 / 514	10 / 4	D	8
v. Derbyshire (Derby) 7–10 August	69 / 115	10 / 75	6 / 18				40 / 3	12 / 22	1* / 1*				28 / 8	11 / 9	59 / 12	11 / 20	0 / –								21 / 38	268 / 324	10 / 10	W	17
v. Indians (Chelmsford) 14–17 August	59 / –	59 / 23rh		20 / –	23 / 53	4 / 6	13 / 24		30 / –				– / –		3* / –	29 / 47*	8 / –						12 / 16*		19 / 17	279 / 186	10 / 3	D	
v. Durham (Colchester) 21–24 August	0 / 48	6 / 27					38 / 12	4 / 3*	15 / –				39 / 100*	54* / –	28 / –	0 / 39	48 / 8	2 / 64							37 / 21	271 / 322	10 / 6	W	17
v. Middlesex (Chelmsford) 4–6 September	20 / 4	5 / –	32 / 43*	65 / 9*	43 / 42		6 / –	33 / –	0 / –				10 / 8	38* / –	14 / 4										12 / 1	278 / 111	10 / 4	W	17
'v. Durham (Chester-le-Street) 11–14 September	33 / 16*	36 / –	123 / –				38* / –	12 / –	0 / –				0 / –	21 / –	46 / 22*							11 / –			26 / 4	463 / 42	10 / 0	W	20
''v. Nottinghamshire (Chelmsford) 18–21 September	41 / 22	2 / –	50 / 57*				1 / –	25 / –	0 / –				65 / 4	0 / –	165* / –							29 / –			20 / 19	282 / 343	10 / 3	W	16.25

ME Waugh played in two matches
'v. **Durham** 11–14 September 117 / –
''v. **Nottinghamshire** 18–21 September 49 / 76
His figures read: 2, 3, 0, 117, 242 , **80.66**, 1, 1, 4

	DDJ Robinson	AP Grayson	A Flower	Aftab Habib	RC Irani	RS Clinton	JM Dakin	JD Middlebrook	AP Cowan	AC McGarry	JB Grant	N Hussain	JD Stephenson	GR Napier	MC Ilott	WI Jefferson	ZK Sharif	RS Bopara	ML Pettini	TJ Phillips	AJ Clarke	JE Bishop	JS Foster	BJ Hyam
Matches	18	7	16	15	12	5	14	18	10	3	11	1	13	9	6	12	2	4	3	5	2	5	4	1
Innings	34	9	29	25	19	8	20	28	15	4	12	2	24	13	5	24	1	7	6	8	4	8	4	2
Not Out	2	0	6	3	3	1	3	4	2	4	0	8	2	3	4	0	1	0	2	1	1	0	1	
Highest Score	175	105	172*	123	207*	107	57	67	60*	11*	30	4	100*	54*	28	165*	42	48	64	42	31	23*	36	16*
Runs	1474	309	1151	964	977	242	359	417	305	16	64	5	562	230	45	783	42	165	157	113	42	52	80	28
Average	46.06	34.33	50.04	43.81	61.06	34.57	21.11	17.37	23.46	8.00	8.00	2.50	35.12	20.90	22.50	39.15	42.00	27.50	26.16	18.83	14.00	7.42	20.00	28.00
100s	5	1	2	2	3	1	–	–	–	–	–	–	1	–	–	2	–	–	–	–	–	–	–	–
50s	6	1	6	8	1	1	1	1	2	–	–	–	2	1	–	2	–	–	2	–	–	–	–	–
Ct/St	17	7	35/1	13	–	2	3	7	6	1	–	2	7	6	4	14	–	6	2	6	1	2	9/1	–/2

ESSEX CCC

FIRST-CLASS MATCHES

BOWLING

	AP Cowan	JB Grant	RC Irani	JM Dakin	JD Middlebrook	AP Grayson	JP Stephenson	MC Ilott	GR Napier	JE Bishop	AJ Clarke	TJ Phillips	Overs	Total	Byes/Leg-Byes	Wickets	Run outs
v. Cambridge University CCE (Cambridge) 20–22 April	11-6-11-1	16.4-5-35-1	7-1-21-3	5-3-5-1	11-5-33-1	-							61.4	139	11	10	1 A
	10-4-15-1	12-1-38-5	-	9-2-41-1									55.5	218	6	10	- A
v. Gloucestershire (Chelmsford) 24–27 April	26-6-96-3	16-3-59-1	23-8-56-2	23.3-4-62-4	2-0-21-0	5-0-12-0							110.3	379	11	10	- A
	5-1-23-0	10-0-68-2	-	7-3-8-2	13-1-48-0	9-3-18-0							48	195	5	4	- A
v. Nottinghamshire (Trent Bridge) 8–10 May	24-5-70-3	3-1-18-1	23.5-10-71-6	9-2-22-0									67.5	213	3	10	- A
	10-0-41-1	9-0-71-1	8-1-29-0	8-3-16-1									41.5	188	11	3	- A
v. Worcestershire (Worcester) 15–18 May	21-4-72-1	14.5-4-66-2	19-4-60-2	16-5-76-2	5-2-9-0	5-1-17-0	19-5-60-3						99.5	367	7	10	-
	7-0-31-0	-	15-5-48-1	-	1-0-4-0	-	14-5-44-7						37	140	13	9	-
v. Derbyshire (Chelmsford) 26–29 May	12-1-41-3		13-6-27-2	3.4-0-13-2	-		8-5-9-2	13-3-64-1					49.4	158	4	10	-
	5-2-21-2		18-5-33-3	10-2-33-3	13-5-19-0		18-5-47-2	11-3-41-0					75	199	5	10	-
v. Northamptonshire (Northampton) 31 May–3 June			19-6-61-2	23-4-108-0	32-4-143-0		25.2-4-116-3	27-3-100-1					146.2	632	6	10	- B
			-	18-6-75-3	6-1-26-2		7.2-2-25-4	13-4-28-1					44.2	155	1	10	-
v. Northamptonshire (Ilford) 12–15 June	18-4-62-4			-	9-1-15-2		19-5-64-2	17-5-43-2	2-0-15-0				65	204	5	10	-
	20-6-57-2			5-0-22-0	42.3-9-122-4		23-4-87-4	13-2-51-0	5-1-18-0				108.3	361	4	10	-
v. Gloucestershire (Gloucester) 26–29 June	20.2-6-68-5			5-0-30-0	20-2-58-0		12-1-58-1	22-6-53-1	11-1-70-3				96.2	383	13	10	- B
	11-0-40-0			-	25-9-57-1		29-5-105-3	12-5-25-2	16-4-46-1				98	322	16	7	- B
v. Glamorgan (Swansea) 3–6 July					9-4-21-0		18-0-74-2		20-3-69-1	11-0-55-1	17.3-1-54-5	9-3-30-1	84.3	311	8	10	-
					13.2-2-28-0		-			3-0-20-0	6-0-25-1	9-0-38-1	31.2	112	1	2	-
v. Worcestershire (Chelmsford) 10–13 July	30.5-13-51-3				28-8-81-1		15-0-84-2			18-3-59-3	13-4-34-1	12-0-51-0	116.5	373	13	10	-
	5-2-9-0				7-1-19-0					4-0-27-1	-	7.4-0-26-1	23.4	82	1	2	-
v. Middlesex (Southgate) 18–21 July	21-5-77-0			31.2-7-103-3	35-7-126-1					29-4-110-2		25-6-102-4	141.2	538	20	10	-
	-			18-4-72-0	29-5-102-0					14-5-37-1		32-5-127-2	108	426	15	4	1 CD
v. Glamorgan (Chelmsford) 24–27 July		18-1-108-2	25-6-67-1		19-0-90-1		20-0-99-1			25-4-103-3		18.3-2-98-2	125.3	575	10	10	-
		-	-		-		-			-		-	-	-	-	-	-
v. Derbyshire (Derby) 7–10 August	14-4-47-2	12-3-34-1	22-6-60-2		20.1-1-67-4				13-5-43-1	9-0-38-0			90.1	301	12	10	-
	5-1-11-0	9-1-45-4	12-5-15-2		20.1-7-28-3				6-0-35-1	-			52.1	151	17	10	-
v. Indians (Chelmsford) 14–17 August		23-10-69-2		23-6-85-0	36-5-164-4			26-4-103-1				15.4-2-70-3	129.4	516	7	10	- E
		20-8-46-0		16-3-54-0	9-1-48-0			17-3-67-4				18-3-62-1	88	327	7	6	- E
v. Durham (Colchester) 21–24 August		19.1-4-75-2		18-4-47-1	11-4-23-1		14-6-20-2	11-3-44-2	13-3-37-1				86.1	259	13	10	1
		13-0-66-1		15-0-73-3	23-8-58-0		13-4-43-2	11.5-4-20-1	16-3-47-3				93.5	332	12	10	- E
v. Middlesex (Chelmsford) 4–6 September		21-4-76-2	11-4-21-1	23-4-60-2	27-8-60-2	7-3-10-1	3-0-17-0		17-3-45-2				109	295	6	10	-
		6.1-1-19-3	12-5-22-2	9-3-17-4	-	7-1-22-0	-		4-2-11-1				38.1	93	2	10	-
v. Durham (Chester-le-Street) 11–14 September		13-2-38-2		12-3-26-1	18.4-6-38-4	9-5-11-1	3-0-12-0		11-2-48-2				66.4	187	14	10	-
		3-0-27-0		15-4-49-1	27-3-94-2	15.1-3-39-3	11-2-31-3		9-1-40-1				84.1	314	20	10	- F
v. Nottinghamshire (Chelmsford) 18–21 September		15-2-62-0		18.5-2-87-3	25-8-69-3	2-0-7-0	11-2-42-2		15-3-65-2				86.5	341	9	10	-
		14-0-66-1		19-3-49-3	11.3-3-37-2	5-1-19-0	13-4-45-3		14-2-50-1				76.3	280	14	10	-

	AP Cowan	JB Grant	RC Irani	JM Dakin	JD Middlebrook	AP Grayson	JP Stephenson	MC Ilott	GR Napier	JE Bishop	AJ Clarke	TJ Phillips
Overs	276.1	267.5	227.5	360.2	555.2	70	295.4	193.5	172	113	36.3	146.5
Maidens	70	50	72	75	121	18	59	45	33	16	5	21
Runs	843	1086	591	1233	1736	176	1082	639	639	449	113	604
Wickets	31	33	29	40	38	8	48	16	20	11	7	15
Average	27.19	32.90	20.37	30.82	45.68	22.00	22.54	39.93	31.95	40.81	16.14	40.26

A AC McGarry 11-1-23-2, 12-1-69-0; 15-3-62-0, 4-0-25-0; 8-2-29-0, 6.5-2-20-0
B ZK Sharif 20-0-98-4; 6-0-33-0, 5-0-33-0
C A Flower 6-0-19-0
D DDJ Robinson 9-1-54-0
E RS Bopara 6-1-18-0, 8-0-43-1; 2-0-13-0
F ME Waugh 4-1-14-0

FIELDING

36 A Flower (35ct, 1st)
17 DDJ Robinson
14 WI Jefferson
13 Aftab Habib
10 JS Foster (9ct, 1st)
7 AP Grayson, JD Middlebrook, JD Stephenson
6 RS Bopara, AP Cowan, GR Napier, TJ Phillips
4 MC Ilott, ME Waugh
3 JM Dakin
2 JE Bishop, RS Clinton, N Hussain, BJ Hyam (2st), ML Pettini
1 AJ Clarke, AC McGarry

GLAMORGAN CCC

FIRST-CLASS MATCHES

BATTING

Match	SP James	DL Hemp	A Dale	MJ Powell	MP Maynard	RDB Croft	MA Wallace	SD Thomas	MS Kasprowicz	DA Cosker	SP Jones	IJ Thomas	J Hughes	AG Wharf	DD Cherry	OT Parkin	AP Davies	DS Harrison	Extras	Total	Wickets	Result	Points
v. Derbyshire (Cardiff) 19–22 April	15	0	56	16	0	46	0	12	8	4*	0								18	175	10		
	78	8	6	33	6	0	106*	6	36	8	18								36	341	10	L	3
v. Worcestershire (Worcester) 8–11 May	1	0	24	53	59	0	0	33		7*		18	74						17	286	10		
	25	64	39	59	39	9	13	8		22*		19	26						25	348	10	W	17
v. Durham (Cardiff) 15–18 May	2	31	5	62*		3	0	0	0		12	39	30						21	205	10		
	121	16	16	1		4*						18	26*						2	204	5	W	16
v. Sri Lankans (Cardiff) 25–26 May																							
																						D	
v. Derbyshire (Derby) 31 May–1 June	11	26	0	17		34	21	0	0		2*	0	5						41	157	10		
	26	7	40	33		15	34	1	11		2*	0	4						27	200	10	L	3
v Middlesex (Lord's) 12–15 June	6	18	19	122	90	18	37	32	10*	0	0								17	369	10		
																						D	11
v. Middlesex (Cardiff) 26–29 June	40	19	8	9	66	6	16	6	17*	0	26								22	235	10		
	118	8	46	18	41	75	59	47	12	10*	9								38	481	10	L	2
v. Essex (Swansea) 3–6 July	1	25		90	16	35	37	11	19*	3	24				26				24	311	10		
	56	23*		13*											11				9	112	2	W	18
v. Nottinghamshire (Trent Bridge) 10–12 July		9	3	7	15	15	20*	0	4		2	76			26				36	213	10		
	25	36	20	55	2	6*	6	27			13				5				16	211	10	L	4
v. Gloucestershire (Cheltenham) 19–22 July	16		25	20	140	21	69	11	25	1	8*				47				32	415	10		
	74		49	3	118*	6	11	11	1		11*				10				26	320	8	W	20
v. Essex (Chelmsford) 24–27 July	249	12	46	76	62	34	24*		37					6	1	0			28	575	10		
																						D	12
v. Gloucestershire (Cardiff) 7–9 August	3	36	135	33	101*	0	9			3					3	7	30		47	407	10		
																						D	12
v. Durham (Chester-le-Street) 16–17 August	47		35	1	15	33	18	11	26*	12	15			0					20	233	10		
	6*										3*								0	9	0	W	16
v. Northamptonshire (Northampton) 21–23 August	20		37	12	43	7	4		8*	0	2	0					4		7	144	10		
	12		52	33	19	14	25		72*	36	17	10					6		16	312	10	L	3
v. Nottinghamshire (Colwyn Bay) 27–30 August	184	4	109		56	9	20	33	35*	1	12	4							27	495	10		
																						D	10
v. Worcestershire (Cardiff) 5–8 September		33	127*	84	37	17	9	2				56	31			16	0		35	447	10		
		69*	60*	31								2							19	181	2	D	12
v. Northamptonshire (Cardiff) 18–21 September		12	29	113	50	59*	12	22		0	26						18	0	7	348	10		
		108	50	92	151	71*	1	17				3							35	527	7	D	10

	SP James	DL Hemp	A Dale	MJ Powell	MP Maynard	RDB Croft	MA Wallace	SD Thomas	MS Kasprowicz	DA Cosker	SP Jones	IJ Thomas	J Hughes	AG Wharf	DD Cherry	OT Parkin	AP Davies	DS Harrison
Matches	14	12	16	16	13	17	17	16	12	10	11	9	7	3	5	3	5	1
Innings	22	20	24	36	20	24	25	22	19	13	17	15	10	2	8	3	6	1
Not Out	1	2	1	3	1	3	4	1	7	2	6	1	1	0	0	0	0	0
Highest Score	249	108	127*	135	151	101*	106*	47	72*	37	26	76	74	6	47	16	30	0
Runs	1111	505	859	1152	1058	747	553	274	352	115	174	273	225	6	129	23	58	0
Average	52.90	28.05	37.34	50.08	55.69	35.57	26.33	13.04	29.33	10.45	15.81	19.50	25.00	3.00	16.12	7.66	9.66	–
100s	4	1	2	3	3	1	1	–	–	–	–	–	–	–	–	–	–	–
50s	3	2	3	7	6	5	2	–	1	–	–	2	1	–	–	–	–	–
Ct/St	7	6	7	7	14	8	58/3	4	7	8	4	2	2	–	4	1	–	–

GLAMORGAN CCC

FIRST–CLASS MATCHES

BOWLING

	MS Kasprowicz	SD Thomas	RDB Croft	SP Jones	A Dale	DA Cosker	AG Wharf	OT Parkin	AP Davies	Overs	Total	Byes/Leg-Byes	Wickets	Run outs
v. Derbyshire (Cardiff) 19–22 April	17-3-67-0	13-1-56-1	6.3-2-17-2	14-4-45-6	7-3-17-1	-				57.3	217	15	10	-
	24-1-104-0	21-2-78-2	38-11-91-1	23-3-65-1	2-0-15-0	20-4-91-1				128	462	18	6	1
v. Worcestershire (Worcester) 8–11 May	24.1-7-77-2	25-5-77-5	23-6-54-1	18-3-59-2	6-2-14-0					96.1	298	17	10	-
	23-3-77-5	15-3-54-3	14-0-41-2	6-0-30-0	3-0-7-0					61	226	17	10	-
v. Durham (Cardiff) 15–18 May	18-4-55-2	15.2-6-33-7	7-4-13-0	8-0-37-1	3-0-15-0					51.2	162	9	10	-
	19-3-61-3	14.1-4-50-3	14-1-33-1	13-1-42-3	7-2-41-0					67.1	243	16	10	-
v. Sri Lankans (Cardiff) 24–27 May		20-1-102-1	27-11-61-1	20-1-79-1	7-3-18-0		25-2-71-4			99	337	6	7	-
		-	-	-	-		-			-	-	-	-	-
v. Derbyshire (Derby) 31 May–1 June	22-4-101-3	22-3-81-2	20-10-40-1	19.3-1-75-3	9-0-44-1					92.3	354	13	10	-
	1-1-0-1	0.5-0-5-0	-	-	-					1.5	5	0	1	-
v. Middlesex (Lord's) 12–15 June	32-6-108-4	27.5-5-97-1	31-6-87-2		8-0-29-1		18-4-76-0			116.5	403	6	9	1
	-	-			-					-	-	-	-	-
v. Middlesex (Cardiff) 26–29 June	28-4-109-0	27-1-108-0	43-5-151-4	26-5-90-1		39.1-2-159-2				163.1	633	16	7	-
	3-0-33-0	-	8-1-26-0	3-1-10-0		3.2-1-16-2				17.2	85	0	2	-
v. Essex (Swansea) 3–6 July	19-7-43-0	21-3-43-3	33-11-71-5	15-3-42-1		35-9-75-1				123	283	9	10	-
	13-4-27-3	12-2-39-0	26-14-28-2	14.4-4-28-5		4-1-6-0				69.4	139	11	10	-
v. Nottinghamshire (Trent Bridge) 10–12 July	33-5-104-5	20-2-67-1	8-1-27-0	25.4-5-72-4	14-3-38-0					100.4	328	20	10	-
	8.4-0-34-2	6-0-31-0	2-0-6-0	8-1-27-1						24.4	100	2	3	-
v. Gloucestershire (Cheltenham) 19–22 July	30-6-120-3	29-3-66-2	26.5-8-73-3	31-9-93-1	4-0-15-0	8-1-45-0				128.5	438	26	9	-
	15.4-3-40-2	17.2-1-66-2	25-2-84-1	14-3-67-4	-	6.3-2-17-1				78.3	293	19	10	-
v. Essex (Chelmsford) 24–27 July		16.1-3-46-2	20-7-23-2		14-5-39-1	12.5-3-19-0	22-2-54-3	18-5-47-2		103	231	3	10	-
		24-4-72-2	54-8-164-1		5-0-13-0	40-7-108-0	21-1-65-0	25-5-58-1		171	514	26	4	- AB
v. Gloucestershire (Cardiff) 7–11 August		21-3-98-2	11-1-57-0			3-0-20-0	21-9-48-2	17.4-3-66-2	25-5-90-3	98.4	396	17	9	-
		-	-			-	-	-		5	7	0	0	- AB
v. Durham (Chester-le-Street) 16–17 August	15.1-3-47-6	13-6-23-4	1-0-3-0		4-2-11-0			9-1-32-0		42.1	124	8	10	-
	13-0-58-5	6-0-17-1	15-3-20-4					4-1-17-0		38	114	2	10	-
v. Northamptonshire (Northampton) 21–23 August	23-2-63-4		19-2-68-1	16-4-58-0	4-0-29-0				13.4-1-53-4	97.4	375	16	10	-
	5-2-16-1		4-1-17-0	4-0-26-0	-				-	17.1	84	0	2	- C
v. Nottinghamshire (Colwyn Bay) 27–30 August	32-10-69-2	23-3-83-2	39.4-1-136-2	1-0-4-0	4-0-23-0	43-4-135-4				142.4	464	14	10	-
	-	5-0-11-0	33-3-106-0	abs inj	5-2-15-1	29-6-101-3				78	274	15	5	- C
v. Worcestershire (Cardiff) 5–8 September		16-0-91-0	32-10-82-2		11-1-47-1			23-6-76-2	23.4-3-79-5	105.4	381	6	10	-
		-	-		-			-		-	-	-	-	-
v. Northamptonshire (Cardiff) 18–21 September		23.3-3-104-5	19-5-63-0		3-0-9-0	18-5-61-1			21-0-95-2	109.3	430	13	10	- AD
		13-2-39-1	19-4-59-2		2-2-0-0	12-3-22-1			20-3-54-1	83	242	10	6	- DE

	MS Kasprowicz	SD Thomas	RDB Croft	SP Jones	A Dale	DA Cosker	AG Wharf	OT Parkin	AP Davies
Overs	418.4	467.1	619	279.5	125	317.5	86	83.4	116.2
Maidens	78	66	138	48	25	60	9	19	14
Runs	1413	1637	1701	949	459	1012	266	247	420
Wickets	53	52	40	34	6	20	7	7	15
Average	26.66	31.48	42.52	27.91	76.50	20.24	38.00	35.28	28.00

A MJ Powell 1-0-8-0; 3-0-7-0; 2-0-6-0
B DD Cherry 1-1-0-0; 2-2-0-0
C IJ Thomas 0.1-0-4-0; 6-0-26-1
D DS Harrison 23-0-79-2, 16-6-53-1
E MP Maynard 1-0-5-0

FIELDING

61 MA Wallace (58ct, 3st)
14 MP Maynard
8   DA Cosker, RDB Croft
7   A Dale, SP James, MS Kasprowicz, MJ Powell
6   DL Hemp
4   DD Cherry, SP Jones, SD Thomas
2   J Hughes, IJ Thomas
1   OT Parkin

GLOUCESTERSHIRE CCC

FIRST–CLASS MATCHES

BATTING

	CM Spearman	THC Hancock	CG Taylor	MGN Windows	IJ Harvey	MW Alleyne	JN Snape	RC Russell	ID Fisher	JMM Averis	J Lewis	KJ Barnett	MA Hardinges	MCJ Ball	RJ Sillence	BW Gannon	AM Smith	APR Gidman	JA Pearson	Extras	Total	Wickets	Result	Points
v. Worcestershire (Worcester) 19–22 April	111	3	1	60	9	7	24	12	1*	0	4									36	268	10		
	14	abs inj	8	12	41	13	11	0	5	17	16*									17	154	9	L	5
v. Essex (Chelmsford) 24–27 April	80		0	13	4	142*	5	6	65	6	26	3								29	379	10		
	0		29	5	-	33*	11	-	-	-	-	100*								17	195	4	D	11
v. Oxford University CCE (Oxford) 8–10 May	2		30	145			16	63*	8				172	0*						47	483	6		
	54		18*	-							55*									5	132	1	W	
v. Nottinghamshire (Bristol) 15–17 May	118	20	53		13	3	16	41	43	1	4			2*						33	347	10		
	0	0	4*	-	6*	-	-	-	-	-	23			-						0	33	3	W	18
v. Durham (Chester-le-Street) 24–27 May	4	37	1		18	28	15	6	0	0*	2					14				7	132	10		
	4	2	73	19	19	78*		0	14	6*	31					-				15	261	8	D	6
v. Worcestershire (Bristol) 31 May–2 June	18	12	25	15	1	32*					5	0		2	4	7				9	130	10		
	55	6	0	5		29	20				17	25	abs inj	0*	4					16	177	9	L	3
v. Essex (Gloucester) 26–29 June	0		5	21	56	87		0	1		11	106		63	0*					33	383	10		
	15		36	12	0	11		107	103*	-		5		5*						28	322	7	L	7
v. Derbyshire (Derby) 3–6 July	12		1	6	1		26	5	17	9				6	0*			67		29	179	10		
	95		15	10	0		2	0	0*	0				-	5*					49	225	7	D	7
v. Middlesex (Southgate) 10–13 July	46	16		11		45	22	7		0		182*		5		14	7			33	388	10		
	1	63*	30*	-	-	-						47		-						11	152	2	L	7
v. Glamorgan (Cheltenham) 19–22 July	13	14	126	10	19rh	84		79*	19		0					0	14			60	438	10		
	180*	6	12	0	18	0		27	0		0	2				8	9			31	293	10	L	8
v. Middlesex (Cheltenham) 24–27 July	12	112	67	55		62		4	18	8	30			33	5*			94		24	494	10		
	35*	28	32	21		23		34	5		30			3			6			13	230	10	D	12
v. Glamorgan (Cardiff) 7–9 August	32	40	74rh	20	123	4		52	0		11					9*	6			25	396	10		
	7*	0*	-	-	-	-		-	-		-					-				0	7	0	D	11
v. Northamptonshire (Bristol) 15–18 August	71		9	83	79		16	22		0		6*				0		28	51	57	422	10		
	15		42	21	41	104*		69										117	0	37	446	7	D	10
v. Nottinghamshire (Trent Bridge) 21–23 August	0		7	5	0	54		57	3	5*					0			10	17	15	173	10		
	20		15	40		15		45*	1	0	0			33				22	9	19	219	10	L	2.25
v. Derbyshire (Bristol) 4–7 September	30	54	22	8		13		26	0		1				0		2*	2		34	192	10		
	26	15	12	144		12		119*	0		57				101		18*	9		64	577	9	D	7
v. Northamptonshire (Northampton) 11–13 September	107	10	16	89	1		5	3	13*					21			21	0		13	299	10		
	64	1	3	52		0		14	8		13			3			0*	66		10	234	10	L	4
v. Durham (Bristol) 18–20 September	89	3		38	0	35		37	13					9	7*			96	19	13	359	10		
	114*	23*																	18rh	16	171	0	W	19

	CM Spearman	THC Hancock	CG Taylor	MGN Windows	IJ Harvey	MW Alleyne	JN Snape	RC Russell	ID Fisher	JMM Averis	J Lewis	KJ Barnett	MA Hardinges	MCJ Ball	RJ Sillence	BW Gannon	AM Smith	APR Gidman	JA Pearson
Matches	17	9	15	17	6	14	5	17	16	5	16	8	1	7	5	7	9	10	3
Innings	34	17	29	31	10	25	8	28	26	8	25	15	1	10	7	8	13	17	6
Not Out	4	3	2	2	1	3	0	6	3	0	6	3	0	3	0	4	6	1	1
Highest Score	180*	112	126	145	123	142*	28	119*	103*	43	57	182	172	63	101	14	21	117	51
Runs	1444	406	664	1062	390	555	117	991	568	83	273	641	172	119	167	31	90	558	114
Average	48.13	29.00	24.59	36.62	43.33	25.22	14.62	45.04	24.69	10.37	14.36	53.41	172.00	17.00	23.85	7.75	12.85	34.87	22.80
100s	5	1	1	2	1	1	-	3	1	-	-	3	1	-	1	-	-	1	-
50s	7	2	2	7	2	2	-	5	4	-	1	1	-	1	-	-	-	4	1
Ct/St	16	1	15	6	6	12	2	39/2	8	3	6	1	-	5	2	1	3	5	2

GLOUCESTERSHIRE CCC

FIRST–CLASS MATCHES

BOWLING

	J Lewis	JMM Averis	IJ Harvey	MW Alleyne	ID Fisher	BW Gannon	RJ Silence	MCJ Ball	AM Smith	APR Gidman	Overs	Total	Byes/Leg-Byes	Wickets	Run outs
v. Worcestershire (Worcester) 19–22 April	29.4-9-77-6	18-4-56-0	29-8-85-4	19-5-44-0	21-5-53-0						118.4	333	8	10	- A
	17-4-54-6	16.1-5-58-2	13-0-49-1	14-6-36-1	17-2-85-0						77.1	295	13	10	-
v. Essex (Chelmsford) 24–27 April	24-11-41-1	23-6-60-1	25.2-6-68-6	17-5-51-1	27-10-95-1						126.2	379	17	10	- A
	-	-	-	-							-				
v. Oxford University CCE (Oxford) 8–10 May					16-3-48-0	15-4-66-3	10-2-41-2	21-9-38-3			99	306	4	10	1 ABC
					19.5-7-34-2	10-2-39-1	5-1-11-0	33-12-54-6			76.5	150	1	10	1 AB
v. Nottinghamshire (Bristol) 15–17 May	17-0-61-1	16-4-51-5		12-4-37-1	12-2-41-3						57	197	7	10	-
	21-8-59-3	15.5-8-34-3		12-6-15-2	9-1-34-0	11-2-33-2					68.5	182	7	10	-
v. Durham (Chester-le-Street) 24–27 May	30-10-62-0	19-3-71-0		24-3-76-3	36-10-118-2	17-3-74-0					140	470	15	8	1 A
	-	-		-	-						-				
v. Worcestershire (Bristol) 31 May–3 June	23.2-9-65-2			19-5-48-1		17-4-50-3		20-7-57-0	23-8-61-4		102.2	287	6	10	-
	12-1-63-0			16-1-59-1		11-0-83-0		abs inj	11-2-51-1		61.4	324	7	3	- C
v. Essex (Gloucester) 26–29 June	34-11-79-3		22.1-5-64-5	7-3-15-0	18-6-45-0	23-7-56-1		23-6-57-0			127.1	325	9	10	1
	16-1-63-0		17.5-1-90-6	15-2-54-0	12-0-58-0	5-1-28-0		12-3-62-1			78.5	381	20	7	- C
v. Derbyshire (Derby) 3–6 July	30-7-94-2			10-2-33-0	14-1-69-2	17-5-67-1			24.2-4-87-4	9-3-24-1	104.2	398	24	10	-
	-			-	-				-		-				
v. Middlesex (Southgate) 10–13 July	22-6-62-0			-	38-12-87-5			39-12-74-3	20-8-48-1	4-1-20-0	123.2	301	6	9	- D
	10-2-36-2			13-2-39-1				10-1-54-2	5-0-30-0		52	241	9	5	-
v. Glamorgan (Cheltenham) 19–22 July	24.4-8-94-3				11-1-35-1			27-2-102-2	29-7-122-3	13-2-48-1	104.4	415	14	10	-
	10-3-36-0				26.2-3-111-3			23-1-93-3	9-0-39-1	4-0-23-0	72.2	320	18	8	1
v. Middlesex (Cheltenham) 24–27 July	24-8-87-2			17-3-58-1	21-6-54-2	16-4-66-0		17-4-60-0			108	363	5	10	2
	7-1-23-0			-	25-2-123-1	8-2-23-1		30-7-68-1		10-2-18-2	80	265	10	5	-
v. Glamorgan (Cardiff) 7–10 August	21-3-94-1		20-5-71-4	11-0-61-1	18-2-57-0				27-5-83-4	3-1-10-0	100	407	31	10	-
	-		-		-				-		-				
v. Northamptonshire (Bristol) 15–18 August	29-7-95-1		25-4-106-2		27-2-129-2			32-2-157-2	31-3-113-1	20-2-121-1	167	746	9	9	- D
	-		-		-				-		-				
v. Nottinghamshire (Trent Bridge) 21–23 August	32-4-100-3	20-3-102-0		16-2-60-2	15.4-2-66-2		17-0-85-0			5-1-42-1	105.4	476	21	10	-
	-	-		-	-		-				-				
v. Derbyshire (Bristol) 4–7 September	20-5-63-4			7-2-19-0	-		6-0-36-1		20.4-6-69-5		53.4	187	0	10	-
	24-5-78-1			5-2-33-0	25.2-7-54-1		13-4-50-3		13-2-44-0	6-1-50-0	86.2	319	10	5	-
v. Northamptonshire (Northampton) 11–13 September	29-9-75-0			12-1-72-0	58.1-9-172-3		18-2-84-1		27-5-96-3	11-0-45-1	165.1	592	12	8	- E
	-			-	-		-		-		-				
v. Durham (Bristol) 18–20 September	15.3-2-59-2			3-1-2-0	23-7-58-1		15-1-63-5		12-2-29-2	-	68.3	216	5	10	-
	14-3-42-1			17-4-64-2	21.4-5-67-4		16-1-79-1		18-3-44-2	1-0-8-0	87.4	312	8	10	-

	J Lewis	JMM Averis	IJ Harvey	MW Alleyne	ID Fisher	BW Gannon	RJ Silence	MCJ Ball	AM Smith	APR Gidman
Overs	536.1	128	152.2	266	514	162	100	287	270	99
Maidens	137	33	29	59	103	36	11	66	55	16
Runs	1662	432	533	876	1725	626	449	876	916	442
Wickets	44	13	28	17	32	15	13	23	31	10
Average	37.77	33.23	19.03	51.52	53.90	41.73	34.53	38.08	29.54	44.20

A JN Snape 2-0-10-0; 10-0-47-0; 17-1-59-0, 7-4-9-0; 14-1-54-2

B MA Hardinges 10-1-43-0; 2-1-2-0

C KJ Barnett 10-5-7-1; 11.4-1-61-1; 1-0-6-0

D MGN Windows 0.2-0-4-0; 3-0-16-0

E CG Taylor 10-1-36-0

FIELDING

41 RC Russell (39ct, 2st)
16 CM Spearman
15 CG Taylor
12 MW Alleyne
8 ID Fisher
6 IJ Harvey, J Lewis, MGN Windows
5 MCJ Ball, APR Gidman
3 JMM Averis, AM Smith
2 JA Pearson, RJ Silence, JN Snape
1 KJ Barnett, BW Gannon, THC Hancock

HAMPSHIRE CCC

FIRST–CLASS MATCHES

BATTING

Match	DA Kenway	WS Kendall	JP Crawley	RA Smith	NC Johnson	N Pothas	SD Udal	AC Morris	CT Tremlett	AD Mullally	AN Aymes	JRC Hamblin	AD Mascarenhas	GW White	LR Prittipaul	JS Laney	JD Francis	JA Tomlinson	JHK Adams	JEK Schofield	Extras	Total	Wickets	Result	Points
v. Kent (Canterbury) 19–22 April	18	21	272	31	117	48	36rh	12	40*	23	abs inj										53	671	8		
	-																				-	-	-	D	11
v. Leicestershire (Southampton) 24–27 April	9	18	80	44	0	6	19	28*	0		46	11									12	273	10		
	10	53*	35	1	0	3	8		2	0	16										16	146	10	L	5
v. Kent (Southampton) 8–10 May	18	10	2	104	0	24	88		4*		50	0	17								28	345	10		
	11	6	50*	-	-	-	-	-	-	-	-	-	27*								17	111	2	D	10
v. Warwickshire (Edgbaston) 15–18 May	1	25	44	79	59	27*		1	5		0		36	1							24	302	10		
	54	21	43	74*	71*	-	-	-	-	-	-	-	0	7							36	306	5	W	18
v. Yorkshire (Headingley) 25–27 May	20	67	79	41	5	8	43*	7	6				2	22							54	354	10		
	30*	4	19*	-	-	-	-	-	-	-	-	-	-	-							9	62	1	D	11
v. Warwickshire (Southampton) 31 May–3 June	14	27	60	5	33	1	23	4	5*				27	21							57	277	10		
	16	14	16	41	3	6	5*	-	-				11	10*							20	142	7	D	9
v. Somerset (Bath) 12–15 June	4	88	-	6	35	22	12	9*	0				28	33	0						15	252	10		
	0	1	-	41*	2	0	3	9	2				31	2	0						7	98	10	D	9
v. Sussex (Southampton) 3–6 July	4	4	-	9	3	10	16	18*	1				49	17							28	163	10		
	29*	17*	-	-	-	-	-	-	-				-	-							10	56	0	D	7
v. Leicestershire (Leicester) 10–13 July		19	60	12	4	63	23	28	1*				22	28		2					49	311	10		
	0	0	104	25	0	1		13	3*				9	19		82					27	283	10	D	10
v. Indians (Southampton) 20–22 July	0	15	6	45			0			2	13	18			0		10	1*			13	123	10		
	7	abs ill	19	0			36*			18	2	5			32		19	23			25	186	9	L	
v. Lancashire (Southampton) 25–27 July		54	12	14	18	2	3	1*	0				1	1			10				16	132	10		
		3	12	28	9	7	2*	0	1				13	1			27				24	127	10	L	3
v. Lancashire (Old Trafford) 8–11 August		1		1	26	24	24	24	22*				7			9	4				4	122	8		
		-		-	-	-	-	-	-				-			-	-				-	-	-	D	7
v. Somerset (Southampton) 24–17 August		46	52	10	5	10		16*	3	8			3		15	53					15	236	10		
		25	34	57	17			1*					27*		46	10					16	233	6	W	16
v. Surrey (Oval) 22–25 August		36	7	15	58	4				10	20			0	5	6	1*				28	190	10		
		36	28	32	24	18				16	94			5	39	0	0*				34	326	10	L	2
v. Yorkshire (Southampton) 27–29 August		36	21	58	37	6	40				23		15			10	0	0*			23	269	10		
		1	26	18	18	2	24				0		32*			10	0	5			25	161	10	L	5
v. Sussex (Hove) 5–8 September		4	60	51	8	11		0					36			89	48	0*	48		46	401	10		
		-	51*	-	-	-		-					-			10	-	-	3*		3	67	1	D	10
v. Surrey (Southampton) 11–14 September		38	82	32	4	8*					30					48	59	1	17	0	8	327	10		
		23	0	86	99	28					67					8	28	2	8	18*	11	390	10	L	6

	DA Kenway	WS Kendall	JP Crawley	RA Smith	NC Johnson	N Pothas	SD Udal	AC Morris	CT Tremlett	AD Mullally	AN Aymes	JRC Hamblin	AD Mascarenhas	GW White	LR Prittipaul	JS Laney	JD Francis	JA Tomlinson	JHK Adams	JEK Schofield
Matches	8	17	10	15	17	16	17	2	11	13	5	5	16	8	3	7	9	5	2	1
Innings	15	31	17	25	29	26	26	2	14	16	7	9	26	14	6	13	16	9	4	2
Not Out	2	2	2	1	2	1	6	0	6	5	2	0	2	2	0	0	0	5	1	1
Highest Score	54	88	272	104	117	99	88	22	40*	23	22*	50	94	36	32	89	82	23	48	18*
Runs	238	705	821	832	857	597	516	36	180	54	52	162	574	234	45	289	358	33	76	18
Average	18.30	24.31	54.73	34.66	31.74	23.88	25.80	18.00	22.50	4.90	10.40	18.00	23.91	19.5	7.50	22.23	22.37	8.25	25.33	18.00
100s	-	-	1	2	1	-	-	-	-	-	-	-	-	-	-	-	-	-	-	-
50s	1	4	6	3	6	5	1	-	-	-	-	1	2	-	-	1	3	-	-	-
Ct/St	15	11	8	6	27	30/4	9	-	4	1	16/1	4	8	6	1	7	5	1	2	

HAMPSHIRE CCC

FIRST–CLASS MATCHES
BOWLING

	AD Mullally	NC Johnson	CT Tremlett	SD Udal	JRC Hamblin	AD Mascarenhas	JA Tomlinson	JEK Schofield	Overs	Total	Byes/Leg-Byes	Wickets	Run outs	
v. Kent	37-9-120-0	10-2-33-1	31-5-129-4	37-6-178-1					144	577	5	7	1	A
(Canterbury) 19-22 April	7-1-27-1	5-0-19-1	10-2-63-2						37	163	1	4	-	BC
v. Leicestershire	34-12-88-3	11-3-41-1	25-7-87-3	24-5-81-1	21-2-104-1	0.4-0-4-0			120	428	15	10	-	B
(Southampton) 24-27 April	-								-	-	-	-	-	
v. Kent	17-5-49-2	3-1-3-2		3-2-2-2	2-0-11-0	14-4-49-4			39	118	4	10	-	
(Southampton) 8-10 May	24-6-62-2	16-5-54-2		31-6-100-1	7-1-26-0	25.4-5-73-4			106.4	337	8	10	1	B
v. Warwickshire	38-14-92-3	12-3-47-1	23-8-69-2	44.1-7-140-0		24.5-11-59-3			163.1	472	6	10	-	BDE
(Edgbaston) 15-18 May	-								-	-	-	-	-	
v. Yorkshire	29-10-74-1	16-4-54-0	29-6-105-2	27-6-87-2		29.5-6-87-5			134.5	423	10	10	-	E
(Headingley) 24-27 May	-								-	-	-	-	-	
v. Warwickshire	27.2-7-56-6	12-2-34-0	23-10-38-2	24-9-62-1		17-2-54-1			111.2	250	4	10	-	B
(Southampton) 31 May – 3 June	34-15-87-3	4-0-17-1	21-5-56-1	13-0-63-1		21-10-60-2			103	329	11	7	-	BE
v. Somerset	27-10-64-4	11-5-22-3	17-7-41-0	3-1-8-0		16-10-23-2			74	161	3	9	-	
(Bath) 12-15 June	19-4-51-2	11.5-5-36-3	16-8-45-3	2-2-0-0		12-6-31-0			60.5	173	10	8	-	
v. Sussex	19-5-44-3	13-1-38-1	14-2-60-0	24.4-7-56-5		15-3-41-0			85.4	246	7	10	1	
(Southampton) 3-6 July	14-4-28-2	1.3-0-3-0	10-2-27-0	9-3-19-2		6-3-11-0			42.3	111	5	4	-	E
v. Leicestershire	27-7-54-3	10-1-39-0	26-4-80-2	29.2-11-78-2		29-17-39-2			121.2	300	10	9	-	
(Leicester) 10-13 July	4-1-7-1	3-1-6-0	5-0-24-0	5-4-4-1		4-1-7-0			29	72	3	4	-	BEF
v. Indians		11-2-45-1		29-5-59-5	13-3-41-1	11-6-26-1	15.1-1-55-2		81.1	236	7	10	-	D
(Southampton) 20-22 July		-		19-5-43-1	7-0-44-2	2-1-5-0	-		41.2	139	3	4	-	BD
v. Lancashire	16-6-28-1	5-2-11-0	22.2-4-68-5	19-9-25-4		14-3-38-0			76.2	183	13	10	-	
(Southampton) 25-27 July	13-3-36-3	6-0-29-0	11-1-36-2	23-3-59-5		7-1-22-0			60	187	5	10	-	
v. Lancashire	17-9-32-1	5-3-14-1	17-2-57-5	13-5-24-2		11-5-25-1			63	163	11	10	-	
(Old Trafford) 8-11 August	4-2-11-0	6-1-20-0	5-2-4-0			5-2-16-0			20	52	1	0	-	
v. Somerset	25-8-58-4	12-3-39-1	14-5-30-0	28-6-89-3		17.5-7-48-2			96.5	278	14	10	-	
(Southampton) 14-17 August	3-1-6-1	7-1-24-1	16.4-3-42-3	35-9-74-3		13-7-23-2			74.4	190	21	10	-	
v. Surrey		10-0-45-0		47-7-213-4	16-2-81-1	21-3-94-1	28-0-91-2		135.3	576	9	10	-	D
(Oval) 22-26 August		-		-	-	-			-	-	-	-	-	
v. Yorkshire		9-1-26-1		29-6-69-5	10-1-44-1	23-7-56-2	17-1-73-1		88	280	12	10	-	
(Southampton) 27-29 August		5-1-21-0		16-3-53-1	5-0-22-0	9-2-18-1	6.4-0-34-1		41.4	152	4	3	-	E
v. Sussex	28-6-82-0	19-3-78-1		34-7-121-1		31-8-114-2		30-5-154-1	156	631	15	6	-	BG
(Hove) 5-8 September	-			-					-	-	-	-	-	
v. Surrey		8-2-16-0		34-6-82-3		29-9-79-1	26.2-3-118-2	30-7-98-3	127.2	418	25	10	1	
(Southampton) 11-14 September		-		25-6-69-0		12-5-39-1	23.2-3-112-2	23-7-94-3	103.2	422	12	8	-	BG

	AD Mullally	NC Johnson	CT Tremlett	SD Udal	JRC Hamblin	AD Mascarenhas	JA Tomlinson	JEK Schofield
Overs	463.2	242.2	336	627.1	81	420.5	146.3	53
Maidens	145	52	83	146	9	144	13	14
Runs	1156	814	1061	1858	373	1141	637	192
Wickets	46	22	36	56	6	37	11	6
Average	**25.13**	**37.00**	**29.47**	**33.17**	**62.16**	**30.83**	**57.90**	**32.00**

A AC Morris 29-5-112-0
B WS Kendall 14-2-45-0; 4.2-1-8-1; 3-0-14-0; 4-0-11-0; 8-6-2-0; 7-1-20-0; 5-1-12-1; 5.2-2-13-0; 11-1-46-1; 2-0-15-0
C DA Kenway 1-0-8-0
D LR Prittipaul 15-4-31-0; 2-0-3-0, 8-2-31-1; 13.3-4-43-2
E GW White 2.1-0-17-1; 4-1-6-0; 3-0-15-0; 2-0-18-0; 1-0-8-0
F JD Francis 2-1-1-1;
G JHK Adams 3-1-21-0; 18-3-81-2

FIELDING

34	N Pothas (30ct, 4st)
27	NC Johnson
17	AN Aymes (16ct, 1st)
15	DA Kenway
12	WS Kendall
9	SD Udal
8	JP Crawley, AD Mascarenhas
7	JS Laney
6	RA Smith, RA White
5	JD Francis
4	JRC Hamblin, CT Tremlett
2	JHK Adams
1	AD Mullally, LR Prittipaul, JA Tomlinson

KENT CCC

FIRST–CLASS MATCHES

BATTING

	DP Fulton	RWT Key	ET Smith	A Symonds	MJ Walker	PA Nixon	MV Fleming	MM Patel	JP Hewitt	DD Masters	Amjad Khan	JB Hockley	GO Jones	JM Golding	MJ Saggers	BJ Trott	MA Ealham	JC Tredwell	SR Waugh	Extras	Total	Wickets	Result	Points
v. Hampshire (Canterbury) 19-22 April	98	160	52	89	0	52	1	50*	48*											27	577	7		
	24	33	44	25*	11	11*														15	163	4	D	10
v. Sri Lankans (Canterbury) 26-28 April	116	7	6		40		102	–			2		76*	18*						52	419	6		
	–	–	–					–												–	–	–	D	
v. Hampshire (Southampton) 8-10 May	6	3	20	39	2	4	25	4		5*			0	0						10	118	10		
	11	29	77	21	2	77*	12	58		26			1	1						22	337	10	L	3
v. Yorkshire (Canterbury) 15-18 May	71	114	22	48	0	28	15	29*		0				9			34			48	418	10		
	13	37	26	0	31*	10	42*			–				–			0			10	169	6	W	20
v. Sussex (Tunbridge Wells) 31 May-3 June	20	39	29	89	14	6	0			8					2	26	83*			27	343	10		
	20	13	82		13*		13*										17			5	195	6	W	18
v. Surrey (Oval) 12-14 June	2	15	20	1	6	54	12	0		0				5*			25			13	153	10		
	48	4	44	14	18	23	2	37		42*				7			21			8	268	10	L	5
v. Lancashire (Liverpool) 26-29 June	27	0	14	12	42	49	20			0			13*		0		24			13	214	10		
	116	78	6	116*	10	19*				–			–				–			15	360	4	W	15.5
v. Warwickshire (Maidstone) 3-6 July	101	62	7	9	43	7	17						2	32	1*		7			18	306	10		
	7	8	0	16	20	34*				–			–				24*			9	118	5	D	10
v. Sussex (Hove) 10-13 July	14	6	141*	32	11	0	28	5			58				0		27			27	349	10		
	1	25	0	6	20	19*				–							5*			9	85	5	D	10
v. Surrey (Canterbury) 19-22 July	62	57	19	118	8		1			1		46	24*	0			18			20	374	10		
	11	68	6	51	1		43*			11		8	26	2			0			33	260	10	L	7
v. Leicestershire (Leicester) 24-27 July		127	10	45	4	41	20			4	18*		6				22			42	339	10		
		18	48*	25	46	–	–	–		–	15*		16				–			25	193	4	W	18
v. Somerset (Canterbury) 7-10 August	89	14	69	13	9	15	3	6		1					0		36*			16	271	10		
	35	55	19	24	1	71*	–	7*		4							60			10	286	7	W	17
v. Warwickshire (Edgbaston) 14-17 August	20	22	0	14		103				13	15	0			16*		25	1		23	252	10		
	44	26	23	0		26				68	7	6			5*		83	17		12	317	10	L	3
v. Leicestershire (Canterbury) 22-25 August	13	87	1	86	82	7	3			40			0*		0				16	44	379	10		
	41*		11*														6			6	58	0	D	11
v. Somerset (Taunton) 4-7 September	35		154	88	6*		28										15*	58	37	16	400	6		
	26		0	51*													26*	22		9	171	4	D	12
v. Lancashire (Canterbury) 11-14 September	177	75	68	1	15		0*			18			1				33	2	5	10	405	10		
	6	37	68	6			–						–				3*	–	20*	4	144	4	W	19
v. Yorkshire (Headingley) 18-20 September	16	1	67	5		52	17			4					2*		6	61	146	22	399	10		
	12	33*	30	14*			–			–					–		–	–	–	14	103	2	W	19

	DP Fulton	RWT Key	ET Smith	A Symonds	MJ Walker	PA Nixon	MV Fleming	MM Patel	JP Hewitt	DD Masters	Amjad Khan	JB Hockley	GO Jones	JM Golding	MJ Saggers	BJ Trott	MA Ealham	JC Tredwell	SR Waugh
Matches	16	14	17	12	12	16	5	16	1	8	16	5	4	4	16	3	14	4	4
Innings	31	27	32	24	23	30	8	20	1	7	19	9	4	5	19	3	24	6	6
Not Out	1	1	2	2	3	7	1	6	1	0	5	1	1	3	6	0	7	0	1
Highest Score	177	160	154	118	46	103	102	82	48*	68	58	46	76*	32	16*	26	83*	61	146
Runs	1282	1097	1239	858	382	865	211	561	48	117	213	82	162	113	73	27	594	161	224
Average	42.73	42.19	41.30	39.00	19.10	37.60	30.14	40.07	–	16.71	15.21	10.25	54.00	56.5	5.61	9.00	34.94	26.83	44.80
100s	4	3	2	2	0	1	1	–	–	–	–	–	1	–	–	–	–	–	1
50s	4	5	8	4	–	6	–	5	–	1	1	–	1	–	–	–	3	1	–
Ct/St	33	10	4	16	3	49/4	–	9	–	3	5	1	5/–	–	6	–	14	6	3

KENT CCC

FIRST-CLASS MATCHES
BOWLING

Match	DD Masters	Amjad Khan	MM Patel	MV Fleming	A Symonds	MJ Saggers	BJ Trott	JM Golding	MA Ealham	JC Tredwell	Overs	Total	Byes/Leg-Byes	Wickets	Run outs	Note
v. Hampshire (Canterbury) 19-22 April	28-7-92-1	37-2-165-3	48-13-130-2	27-3-81-1	26-5-93-0						195	671	12	8	1	AB
	-	-	-	-	-						-	-	-	-	-	
v. Sri Lankans (Canterbury) 26-28 April			3-0-16-0	15-1-41-0		23.3-2-84-4	18-1-109-2	22-4-76-4			90.3	375	8	10	-	B
			-	-		-	-	-			-	-	-	-	-	
v. Hampshire (Southampton) 8-10 May		18-2-80-1	21-3-45-0	14-6-25-1	7-3-19-0	30.1-5-74-5	22-6-83-3				112.1	345	19	10	-	
		5-0-27-0	4-1-10-0	1-0-11-0	3.2-1-8-0	9-0-35-2	4-0-13-0				26.2	111	7	2	-	
v. Yorkshire (Canterbury) 15-18 May		21.2-7-52-6	14-7-11-3		5-1-15-0	19-2-68-0			14-5-36-1		87.2	239	12	10	-	
		32-11-63-1	35-11-82-4	8-2-21-0	9-0-36-0	30.1-8-82-5			14-4-36-0		128.1	346	26	10	-	
v. Sussex (Tunbridge Wells) 31 May -3 June		12-3-34-0	10-5-16-1		9-3-20-0	18-6-39-6	8-1-22-1		11-2-30-2		68	180	19	10	-	
		8.4-0-47-1	33-4-99-2		31-3-105-6	10-2-38-0	6-0-33-1				92.4	354	23	10	-	B
v. Surrey (Oval) 12-14 June		16-2-81-3	11.1-3-31-1	23-5-68-4		22-2-96-1			15-4-68-1		87.1	361	17	10	-	
		6-2-15-0	5-2-8-1	-		4-0-15-0			4-1-7-0		22.3	61	1	1	-	B
v. Lancashire (Liverpool) 26-29 June		18-0-74-5	7-2-14-1		-	19-5-49-1		6.1-1-27-1	11-2-54-2		61.1	226	8	10	-	
		22-3-92-3	8.2-0-22-1		5-1-27-0	25-2-86-3		6-2-52-0	25-7-53-3		102.2	347	10	10	-	B
v. Warwickshire (Maidstone) 3-6 July		16-3-50-1	20-6-56-5			13-2-36-1			11.3-2-22-3		60.3	172	8	10	-	
		-	-		-	-			-		-	-	-	-	-	
v. Sussex (Hove) 10-13 July	7-0-19-2	15-4-56-6	3-0-10-0		-	17-4-44-2			8-3-10-0		50	145	6	10	-	
	29-7-86-2	23-2-111-2	31-8-51-3		31-6-82-0	32.2-6-93-3			4-1-8-0		151.2	450	14	10	-	B
v. Surrey (Canterbury) 19-22 July		16-2-91-4	6-3-21-0		1-1-0-0	13.5-3-66-5	8-2-13-1		6-2-21-0		50.5	225	13	10	-	
		20-3-91-1	20-6-50-0		28-5-85-3	31-6-85-3	8-1-27-0		19.3-7-42-1		126.3	410	30	8	-	
v. Leicestershire (Leicester) 24-27 July	16-6-36-4	6-1-20-0	-		4-0-17-0	17.2-6-44-5			9-7-5-1		52.2	131	9	10	-	
	29-8-86-3	12-4-48-1	44-16-95-1		11-3-31-1	21.4-7-68-4			26-9-62-0		143.4	400	10	10	-	
v. Somerset (Canterbury) 7-10 August	12.5-3-35-1	18-3-76-5	4-2-3-1		5-1-25-1	19-4-48-1			12-5-29-1		70.5	227	11	10	-	
	5-1-23-1	14-1-54-2	8-1-22-0		5-1-10-0	10.3-2-42-5			6-2-21-2		48.3	177	13	10	-	
v. Warwickshire (Edgbaston) 14-17 August	25-6-110-1	24-1-129-2			7-0-29-2	33-6-95-1			22-3-76-0	34-8-103-4	145	565	23	10	-	C
	-	-			-						0.3	8	0	0	-	
v. Leicestershire (Canterbury) 22-25 August	15-2-65-1	16-5-50-0	23-13-30-2			19-4-68-4			18-8-37-3		91	259	9	10	-	
	21-2-116-1	24-0-170-2	52.5-18-99-4			23-5-66-2			15-7-44-1		138.5	530	18	10	-	B
v. Somerset (Taunton) 4-7 September	18-1-68-1	21-2-88-4	16-0-84-0			22.5-6-87-4			20-4-62-1	11-1-42-0	111.5	460	14	10	-	D
	15.4-2-49-3	7-2-17-0	19-1-52-1			16-3-64-2			5-3-13-0	29-4-112-3	91.4	316	9	9	-	
v. Lancashire (Canterbury) 11-15 September		14-0-67-2	14-7-20-0			21-5-34-4			20-7-47-2	2.2-0-9-1	71.2	197	20	10	1	
		17-3-63-3	49-16-73-1			20.4-3-64-4			17-3-57-0	40-15-66-2	143.4	351	28	10	-	
v. Yorkshire (Headingley) 18-20 September	9-1-23-0	11-1-52-2	9.1-2-32-1			13-7-44-4			16-3-55-3	2-1-8-0	60.1	218	4	10	-	
	12.4-1-56-2	15-4-41-3	7-2-24-1			17-3-72-2			22-6-59-1	6-0-18-0	79.4	283	13	10	1	

	DD Masters	Amjad Khan	MM Patel	MV Fleming	A Symonds	MJ Saggers	BJ Trott	JM Golding	MA Ealham	JC Tredwell
Overs	243.1	485	525.3	102	187.2	571	58	60.1	351	124.2
Maidens	47	75	152	19	34	111	8	10	107	29
Runs	864	2004	1206	292	602	1786	260	195	954	358
Wickets	23	63	36	6	13	83	7	6	28	10
Average	37.56	31.80	33.50	48.66	46.30	21.51	37.14	32.50	34.07	35.80

A   JP Hewitt 26-5-92-0
B   MJ Walker 3-2-6-0; 9-0-41-0; 4-1-9-0; 3.3-1-15-0; 1-0-5-0; 1-0-5-0; 3-0-17-0
C   PA Nixon 0.3-0-8-0
D   SR Waugh 3-0-15-0

FIELDING

53	PA Nixon (49ct, 4st)
33	DP Fulton
16	A Symonds
14	MA Ealham
10	RWT Key
9	MM Patel
6	MJ Saggers, JC Tredwell
5	Amjad Khan, GO Jones
4	ET Smith
3	DD Masters, MJ Walker, SR Waugh
1	JB Hockley

LANCASHIRE CCC

FIRST–CLASS MATCHES

BATTING

	MJ Chilton	AJ Swann	D Bysa	SG Law	GD Lloyd	WK Hegg	G Chapple	KW Hogg	PJ Martin	G Keedy	MP Smethurst	A Flintoff	J Wood	CP Schofield	NH Fairbrother	JM Anderson	JJ Haynes	TW Roberts	RC Driver	MR Currie	SI Mahmood	G Yates	TM Rees	Extras	Total	Wickets	Result	Points
v. Leicestershire (Old Trafford) 19-22 April	13	80	0	22	51	8	15	6	21*	3	13													43	275	10		
	53	49	24	69	73	34	38	11	1	7*	0*													29	388	9	W	17
v. Warwickshire (Edgbaston) 24-26 April	45	29	4	30	80	10	9	9	2	4	6*													23	251	10		
	12	27	83*	-	18	34*	-	-	-	-	-													21	197	4	W	17
v. Surrey (Oval) 8-11 May	26	18	31	27	29	9	16	1		0*	137	4												22	320	10		
	35	11	12	39	15	43	1	4		10*	6	0												24	200	10	L	6
v. Sussex (Old Trafford) 15-18 May	0	51	0	218	15	5	11	8	4	25*				4										25	366	10		
	-	-	-	-	-	-	-	-	-	-				-										-	-	-	D	11
v. Surrey (Old Trafford) 31 May-3 June	13	18		18	9	1	51	16	7	3				35	0*									23	194	10		
	23	3		33*	6*	-	-	-	-	-				38	-									9	112	3	D	6
v. Durham University CCE (Durham Racecourse) 12-14 June	107	8	-	-	62				-	-		-	0*			53	0	25*						24	279	5	D	
	-	-			-				-	-		-	-			-	-	-						-	-	-	D	
v. Kent (Liverpool) 26-29 June	4	7		75	8	10	4		11*	7		24		12				56						8	226	10		
	60	85		4	0	11	55		80*	10		14		9				1						18	347	10	L	4
v. Leicestershire (Leicester) 3-6 July	57	20	48			0	0		8			3		3	1*		2	5						33	180	10		
	-	-	-			-	-		-			-		-	-		-	-						-	-	-	D	7
v. West Indies A (Liverpool) 10-13 July		14	11		68			4		2*	13			101	6	6		5	2					47	279	10		
		45	39		77			-		-	-				7*		16*	48rh						33	265	3	D	
v. Yorkshire (Headingley) 19-22 July	3	128	15	51		25	60		47	57		64		0	4*									24	478	10		
	-	-	-	-		-	-		-	-		-		-	-									-	-	-	D	10
v. Hampshire (Southampton) 25-27 July	8	66	29	22		5	0		5			26		0	1*			0						21	183	10		
	22	0	0	38		23	31		16*			3		39	1			5						9	187	10	W	15
v. Hampshire (Old Trafford) 8-11 August	2	84*	1	9		7	3		1			14		5	0					18				19	163	10		
	18*	29*	-	-		-	-		-			-		-	-					-				5	52	0	D	6
v. Yorkshire (Old Trafford) 14-17 August	45	112	4	47	6*	9			4			22		27	5*						3			17	301	9		
	16	12	14	13	abs inj	11			6			11		38	4*						14			9	148	9	L	6
v. Sussex (Hove) 22-25 August	44	23	71	147		36*		14	7			1		16	0	4								62	425	10		
	0	4	24	45*		-		-	-			13*		-	-	-								7	93	3	W	20
v. Somerset (Blackpool) 27-29 August	1	36	6	77		22	1		12	10		40		23	8*									15	251	10		
	3	1	81	24		9	10		39	18*		77		17	2									15	296	10	W	17
v. Warwickshire (Old Trafford) 4-7 September	38	62	101	28		12	65		117*	5		91		7	16									56	598	10		
	-	-	-	-		-	-		-	-		-		-	-									-	-	-	D	12
v. Kent (Canterbury) 11-14 September	23	38	6	13		13	14		25	16*		0		10	5									34	197	10		
	90	8	2	90		43	17		0	3		33		13	2*									50	351	10	L	2
v. Somerset (Taunton) 18-19 September	0	4	15	18		24	36	50	34*			16		3								16		12	228	10		
	0	1	63*	57*		-	-	-	-			-		-								-		3	124	2	W	16
Matches	17	18	15	15	7	16	16	7	12	16	4	1	8	7	12	13	3	2	5	1	1	1	1					
Innings	29	31	25	26	13	23	23	9	16	22	4	2	11	9	19	16	4	2	8	2	1	2	1					
Not Out	1	2	2	3	1	2	1	0	5	8	2	0	1	1	8	1	0	2	1	0	0	0						
Highest Score	107	128	101	218	80	62	65	50	117*	57	13	137	64	91	101	16	53	2	56	48rh	18	14	16					
Runs	761	1073	684	1216	449	416	493	109	422	219	32	143	185	262	406	58	70	2	113	50	18	17	16					
Average	27.17	37.00	29.73	52.86	37.41	19.80	22.40	12.11	38.36	15.64	16.00	71.50	16.81	32.75	22.55	7.25	23.33	1.00	18.83	50.00	18.00	8.50	16.00					
100s	1	2	1	2					1			1		1	1													
50s	4	6	4	6	5	1	4	1	1	1	-	-	1	2	-	-	1	-	1	-	-	-	-					
Ct/St	15	12	15	21	4	44/2	6	5	4	4	1	1	2	4	10	2	4/-	1	5	-	-	-	1					

LANCASHIRE CCC

FIRST–CLASS MATCHES

BOWLING

	PJ Martin	G Chapple	MP Smethurst	KW Hogg	G Keedy	J Wood	CP Schofield	JM Anderson	RC Driver		Overs	Total	Byes/Leg-Byes	Wickets	Run outs
v. Leicestershire	24-8-52-2	23.5-7-61-3	14-2-74-2	16-3-67-1	16-1-79-1						99.5	385	6	10	- A
(Old Trafford) 19-22 April	22-8-69-3	19-5-64-1	18-2-73-0	16-3-48-5	6.5-3-13-1						81.5	277	10	10	-
v. Warwickshire	21-7-77-4	20-7-58-2	13.2-2-68-3	10-1-45-0	12-4-35-1						78.2	297	8	10	- A
(Edgbaston) 24-26 April	20-5-41-4	17.4-4-51-2	8-2-33-1	8-5-16-3	-						53.4	150	9	10	-
v. Surrey		18.3-1-65-5		14-7-26-1	8-0-51-1	11-2-41-0					64.3	216	1	10	1 B
(Oval) 8-11 May		26-4-91-0		10-2-32-1	9.4-0-42-1	14-0-52-3					85.4	309	15	7	- AB
v. Sussex	33-6-97-3	28-3-94-0		19-5-39-3	39.3-8-121-3		10-1-40-0				135.3	423	20	10	- A
(Old Trafford) 15-18 May	21-6-53-4	18-5-55-0		8-2-27-0	30-8-54-2		8-1-27-1				85	221	5	7	-
v. Surrey	30-17-36-1	28-6-72-0		20-4-54-1	45-13-122-5			19-4-65-2			147	382	20	10	1 AC
(Old Trafford) 31 May-3 June	11-4-17-0	15-5-36-1		9-0-46-2	17-0-84-1			9-1-22-2			67	246	16	6	- AD
v. Durham University CCE			20-7-60-1		15-7-28-1	12-7-13-1	23-9-33-2	14-4-48-0	14-3-41-1		99	242	17	7	1 A
(Durham Racecourse) 12-14 June			-		-	-	-	-	-		-	-	-	-	-
v. Kent	22-7-54-5	23-6-58-3			-	17-3-68-0			9-4-29-1		71	214	5	10	1
(Liverpool) 26-29 June	30-4-96-1	25-4-81-1			24-9-58-2	12-3-55-0			11-1-56-0		105	360	8	4	- A
v. Leicestershire	16-6-41-3	15-5-63-1				13-2-41-1		14-4-33-3	8-3-22-2		67	219	17	10	- F
(Leicester) 3-6 July	10-4-21-1	12-2-34-0				5-1-13-2		5-1-12-0	16-5-32-1		63	206	8	4	- ACEF
v. West Indies A			20.4-1-87-1	10-1-73-0	14-2-47-1			20-1-83-3	21-3-70-5		85.4	369	9	10	-
(Liverpool) 10-13 July			16-4-76-1	17-3-82-0	26-6-77-0			17-3-49-1	19-6-63-2		95	361	14	5	1
v. Yorkshire	27-5-73-2	26-6-73-0			16.3-3-77-2	25-3-113-0		24-4-109-1			123.3	515	47	5	- A
(Headingley) 19-22 July	-	12-3-20-3			10-3-31-2	6-1-29-1		11-3-33-1			39	124	11	7	-
v. Hampshire		13-6-21-1			2-0-7-0		17-3-53-3	14-6-23-6	7-3-18-0		53	132	10	10	-
(Southampton) 25-27 July		13-2-39-1			7-1-22-2		4.5-0-17-4	9-2-27-3			33.5	127	22	10	-
v. Hampshire		10-2-33-3			5.1-1-6-1		10-5-16-1	14-3-59-3			41.1	122	2	8	- G
(Old Trafford) 8-11 August		-			-		-	-			-	-	-	-	-
v. Yorkshire		21-6-63-3			31-11-54-1	19-1-56-1		28-8-61-5			115	294	18	10	- H
(Old Trafford)) 14-17 August		15-3-41-1			24-3-63-3	15-3-64-1		15-1-70-2			91.4	305	9	10	2 DH
v. Sussex	22-10-45-3	15-1-61-4			7-0-38-0		13.2-6-21-3	10-2-54-0			74.2	240	10	10	- A
(Hove) 22-25 August	26.2-12-45-1	31-14-66-6			20-5-38-0		12-0-31-1	17-1-58-1			116.2	277	11	10	1 AD
v. Somerset	16-5-43-2	14-9-28-1					4-2-8-1	11.5-2-41-6			51.5	140	2	10	- A
(Blackpool) 27-29 August	11-7-15-1	12.3-1-30-6					-	7-1-16-3			30.3	71	10	10	-
v. Warwickshire	24-8-67-2	17-1-80-2			16-6-50-0		8.2-2-25-3	20-3-70-2			89.2	328	15	10	1 D
(Old Trafford)) 4-7 September	-	-			-		-	-			-	-	-	-	-
v. Kent	25.4-4-69-2	22-5-48-2			28-5-93-2		18-2-59-0	22-3-88-3			133.4	405	10	10	1 ADF
(Canterbury) 11-14 September	7-0-34-1	9-0-27-1			8-3-23-0		5-0-16-2	9.2-0-42-0			38.2	144	2	4	-
v. Somerset	19-3-52-4	10-2-44-0		13-4-52-2			9.4-1-36-1	10 -2-37-2			61.4	221	0	10	1
(Taunton) 18-19 September	14-7-29-4	10-3-37-1		5-1-14-0			11-3-35-4	6.3-2-14-1			46.3	129	0	10	-

	PJ Martin	G Chapple	MP Smethurst	KW Hogg	G Keedy	J Wood	CP Schofield	JM Anderson	RC Driver	
Overs	452	539.3	110	175	437.4	180.5	122.2	326.4	105	
Maidens	143	128	20	41	102	34	27	61	28	
Runs	1126	1594	471	621	1313	631	331	1114	331	
Wickets	53	54	9	19	33	18	18	50	12	
Average	21.24	29.51	52.33	32.68	39.78	35.05	18.38	22.28	27.58	

A MJ Chilton 6-1-46-1; 2-0-6-0; 7-3-10-1; 6-3-12-1; 3-0-10-0, 5-0-14-0; 1-0-2-0; 3-1-6-0; 5-0-28-0; 5-0-23-0; 7-4-11-0, 3-1-14-0; 6-2-18-0; 12-2-26-0
B A Flintoff 13-4-32-2; 19-4-67-1
C AJ Swann 2-1-3-0; 6-0-37-0
D SG Law 1-0-11-0; 9.4-1-24-1; 7-1-14-0; 4-2-21-0; 3-1-2-0
E TW Roberts 2-0-6-0
F NH Fairbrother 1-0-2-0; 2-0-15-0
G SI Mahmood 2-1-6-0
H G Yates 16-5-42-0; 13-2-34-0

FIELDING

46	WK Hegg (44ct, 2st)
21	SG Law
15	D Byas, MJ Chilton
12	AP Swann
10	NH Fairbrother
6	G Chapple
5	RC Driver, KW Hogg
4	JJ Haynes, G Keedy, GD Lloyd, PJ Martin, TM Rees, TW Roberts, CP Schofield
2	JM Anderson, J Wood
1	A Flintoff, MP Smethurst

LEICESTERSHIRE CCC

FIRST-CLASS MATCHES
BATTING

	RJ Cunliffe	IJ Sutcliffe	DL Maddy	MG Bevan	VJ Wells	DI Stevens	ND Burns	PAJ DeFreitas	CD Crowe	CE Dagnall	DE Malcolm	TR Ward	MJA Whiley	GW Flower	JO Grove	Mohammad Kaif	AS Wright	J Srinath	GW Walker	RD Stemp	DG Brandy	Extras	Total	Wickets	Result	Points
v. Lancashire	9	27	6	66	74	74	51	51	7	2	2*											16	385	10		
(Old Trafford) 19-22 April	19	8	66	27	0	28	62	41	6	8	0*											12	277	10	L	6
v. Hampshire		35	0	34	150	82	26	51	3	4*	0	10										33	428	10		
(Southampton) 24-27 April		-	-	-	-	-	-	-	-	-	-	-										-	-	-	W	20
v. Warwickshire		71	12	146	33	125	16	39*	0		14	7	0									60	523	10		
(Leicester) 8-11 May		15	1*	38*	-	13	15	-	-		-	-	-									12	94	3	W	19
v. Somerset		73	22	9	35	73	33	6	8*		4*	7	-									18	288	8		
(Taunton) 15-18 May		-	-	-	-	-	-	-	-		-	-	-									-	-	-	D	4
v. Sussex		12	21	4	86*	50	0	26	4	3	0	48										10	264	10		
(Horsham) 24-27 May		8	31*	28*	-	-	-	-	-	-	-	24										3	94	2	D	9
v. Yorkshire		14	61	142	0	31	5	0	29	16	6*	4										38	346	10		
(Leicester) 31 May-3 June		36	58	76*	0	0*	-	6	-	-	-	8										23	207	5	W	18
v. Warwickshire		31	16		5	38	64	7			11	89	13*	75	6							15	370	10		
(Edgbaston) 12-15 June		6	22		43	20	34	1			2*	18	0	7	0							1	154	10	L	6
v. Lancashire		36	59	4	18	21	2	25	20*		0	0		5								29	219	10		
(Leicester) 3-6 July		38	79*	-	50	15*	0				-	4		-								20	206	4	D	8
v. Hampshire	23	18	12	62		1	101	44	18*		1	0		4*								16	300	10		
(Leicester) 10-13 July	5*	11*	9	-		1	-	15	-		-	18		-								3	72	4	D	9
v. Kent		17	15	0	0	23	40*	2	0		12	1	6									15	131	10		
(Leicester) 24-27 July		103	0	61	8	4	4	114	16*		0	70	0									20	400	10	L	3
v. Surrey	8	48	81			15	29*	8			4	39	0		4	13						41	290	10		
(Leicester) 14-16 August	4	64	94			14	11	0			4*	16	13		3	43						23	289	10	L	5
v. Kent	23	125*	9			8	23	18			9	3					1	15	7			18	259	10		
(Canterbury) 22-25 August	0	21	156			0	24	94			44	66					28	0	37*			60	530	10	D	9
v. Sussex		75	29		36	7	0	16	34		24*	0					0	18				8	247	10		
(Leicester) 27-29 August		30*	23		-	31*	-	-	-		-	26					-	-				1	111	2	W	16
v. Yorkshire		27	44	13		22	59	0			1	11					11	52	8*			31	279	10		
(Scarborough) 4-7 September		26	86	7*	80	-	-				1	-					0*	-	0			31	231	5	D	9
v. Somerset		17	36		8	46	38*	9			0	84					25	3			5	39	310	10		
(Leicester) 12-14 September		-	-		-	-	-	-			-	-					-	-				-	-	-	W	18
v. Surrey	30	72	127*		53	7	4	4			0						22	1			23	18	361	10		
(Oval) 18-21 September	0	24	12		0	68	9	8			0*						7	9			0	5	142	10	L	7

	RJ Cunliffe	IJ Sutcliffe	DL Maddy	MG Bevan	VJ Wells	DI Stevens	ND Burns	PAJ DeFreitas	CD Crowe	CE Dagnall	DE Malcolm	TR Ward	MJA Whiley	GW Flower	JO Grove	Mohammad Kaif	AS Wright	J Srinath	GW Walker	RD Stemp	DG Brandy
Matches	5	16	16	9	11	16	16	16	12	4	16	14	7	1	2	1	5	5	1	1	2
Innings	10	29	29	14	17	28	24	23	16	5	22	24	9	2	4	2	8	7	2	2	3
Not Out	1	3	4	3	2	3	2	2	4	1	8	0	2	0	0	1	1	0	1	1	0
Highest Score	30	125*	156	146	150	125	101	114	34	16	44	89	13*	75	6	43	28	52	37*	8*	23
Runs	121	1088	1187	697	558	847	720	609	172	33	138	554	41	82	13	56	94	98	44	8	28
Average	13.44	41.84	47.48	63.36	37.20	33.88	32.72	29.00	14.33	8.25	9.85	23.08	5.85	41.00	3.25	28.00	13.42	14.00	44.00	8.00	9.33
100s	-	2	2	2	1	1	1	1	-	-	-	-	-	-	-	-	-	-	-	-	-
50s	-	5	8	4	3	6	5	3	-	-	-	4	-	1	-	-	-	1	-	-	-
Catches/Stumpings	1	4	22	4	9	16	61/2	10	4	1	4	7	1	1	-	1	2	1	-	1	

LEICESTERSHIRE CCC

FIRST–CLASS MATCHES
BOWLING

	DE Malcolm	PAJ DeFreitas	CE Dagnall	DL Maddy	VJ Wells	CD Crowe	MJA Whiley	GW Flower	J Srinath	Overs	Total	Byes/Leg-Byes	Wickets	Run outs
v. Lancashire (Old Trafford) 19-22 April	14.3-4-64-1	23-4-101-6	10-3-26-0	13-4-52-2	6-3-21-1	-				66.3	275	11	10	-
	24.3-3-100-2	24-4-67-2	27-10-66-2	8-0-35-0	8-3-30-2	13-2-52-1				106.3	388	27	9	A
v. Hampshire (Southampton) 24-27 April	21-1-77-0	22.4-8-46-2	18-3-55-3	17-4-37-4	8-0-27-0	10-3-20-0				97.4	273	10	10	1 B
	13-4-39-3	10.4-4-18-0	11-4-29-1	17-7-37-5	5-3-9-0	4-2-2-1				60.4	146	12	10	-
v. Warwickshire (Leicester) 8-11 May	15-5-30-1	14-4-43-2		-		3-1-14-1	17-2-64-3			56	177	1	10	- A
	27.1-7-91-2	26-6-83-2		26-6-59-3	3-0-12-0	25-11-26-0	22-3-108-3			138.1	439	22	10	- AC
v. Somerset (Taunton) 15-18 May	26-3-101-1	30-4-101-2		22-4-88-1	20-5-52-1	17.2-3-63-4	23-3-123-1			146.2	565	14	10	- A
	-	-		-	-	-	-			-	-	-	-	-
v. Sussex (Horsham) 24-27 May	19.5-4-76-7	13-2-43-1	5-1-24-1	5-0-15-0	12-3-31-1	14-2-47-0				69.5	247	8	10	- A
	-	-	-		-	-				-	-	-	-	-
v. Yorkshire (Leicester) 31 May-3 June	26.4-5-72-6	19-7-53-0	20-3-70-0	20-5-49-2	7-3-7-2	13-4-43-0				105.4	310	16	10	-
	23-3-76-4	22.4-10-38-5	-	14-1-50-1	12-0-42-0	12-4-22-0				83.4	239	11	10	-
v. Warwickshire (Edgbaston) 12-15 June	12.4-2-55-2	32-8-100-1		23-6-57-1			23-3-94-0	30-11-66-4		142.4	462	15	10	1 D
	21-4-63-2	22-7-53-3		-			8-2-38-0	5-1-32-2		59	206	6	7	- D
v. Lancashire (Leicester) 3-6 July	16-6-52-5-	18.4-9-39-2		4-1-9-1	11-7-18-2		6-0-53-0			55.4	180	9	10	-
	-			-			-			-	-	-	-	-
v. Hampshire (Leiceste) 10-13 July	22-2-72-2	20-8-33-1		17.3-7-45-2		19-6-63-3	18-4-89-2			96.3	311	9	10	-
	17-3-59-1	32-11-79-3		17-4-37-4		17-6-56-1	8.4-2-22-1			98.4	283	11	10	- A
v. Kent (Leicester) 24-27 July	21-2-100-1	21-7-46-1		16-4-52-2	15-3-38-1	5-1-19-2	17-3-60-3			95	339	24	10	- B
	9-1-43-1	11-1-49-0		13-4-38-2	8-2-16-1	-	7.5-2-33-0			49.5	193	9	4	-
v. Surrey (Leicester) 14-16 August	22-3-114-0	34-6-91-2		25.4-4-104-5			22-4-85-2			128.4	540	8	10	- DEF
	3-0-7-2	-		-			3.1-0-34-1			6.1	42	1	3	-
v. Kent (Canterbury) 22-25 August	20.2-0-98-2	32-8-71-3		20-3-83-1					26-8-70-4	109.2	379	17	10	- BG
	-	-		-					-	16	58	0	0	- BCFG
v. Sussex (Leicester) 27-29 August	16.2-6-38-5	16-6-25-1		15-2-50-2	11-2-32-0	3-0-18-0			19-5-47-2	80.2	215	5	10	-
	13.5-5-29-2	19-7-42-4		6-3-17-1	-	-			17-1-48-3	55.5	142	6	10	-
v. Yorkshire (Scarborough) 4-7 September	21-2-95-4	15-6-31-0		6-2-16-0	12-1-47-3				18-7-38-3	82	276	8	10	- H
	19-2-87-0	24-3-84-1		14-6-30-0	17-6-39-5				22-1-70-1	103	347	19	8	- H
v. Somerset (Leicester) 12-14 September	10-1-51-0	10-3-35-3		5.3-0-29-2		3-0-15-1			14-1-60-4	42.3	191	1	10	-
	4-0-26-1	10-3-28-1		4.5-1-20-2		-			11-4-25-5	29.5	101	2	10	1
v. Surrey (Oval) 18-21 September	13-0-70-1	28-3-121-3		5-0-16-0		28-4-100-1			26.2-1-114-5	111.2	494	5	10	- BI
	6-1-41-2	17-1-74-0		-		7-2-33-1			26-1-89-3	105.1	492	6	9	- BCIJ

	DE Malcolm	PAJ DeFreitas	CE Dagnall	DL Maddy	VJ Wells	CD Crowe	MJA Whiley	GW Flower	J Srinath
Overs	477.5	566.4	91	334.3	155	193.2	175.4	35	179.2
Maidens	79	150	24	78	41	51	28	12	29
Runs	1826	1594	270	1025	421	593	803	98	561
Wickets	60	51	7	43	19	16	16	6	30
Average	**30.43**	**31.25**	**38.57**	**23.83**	**22.15**	**37.06**	**50.18**	**16.33**	**18.70**

A   MG Bevan 2-0-11-0; 7-1-25-0; 8-0-37-0; 8-0-23-0; 1-0-3-0; 7-0-19-0
B   DI Stevens 1-0-1-0; 1-0-5-0; 6-1-14-0; 4-1-16-0; 7-0-40-0; 30-1-125-1
C   IJ Sutcliffe 1-0-1-0; 1-0-3-0; 5-0-35-0
D   JO Grove 22-6-75-1; 3-0-14-0; 10-0-63-0
E   Mohammad Kaif 7-0-43-0
F   TR Ward 8-0-32-1; 3-0-15-0
G   GW Walker 5-0-26-0; 8-2-24-0
H   RD Stemp 10-1-41-0; 7-1-18-1
I   DG Brandy 4-0-28-0; 13-0-86-2
J   RJ Cunliffe 1.1-0-3-0

FIELDING

63   ND Burns (61ct, 2st)
22   DL Maddy
16   DI Stevens
10   PAJ DeFreitas
9   VJ Wells
7   TR Ward
4   MG Bevan, CD Crowe, DE Malcolm, IJ Sutcliffe
2   J Srinath
1   DG Brandy, RJ Cunliffe, CE Dagnall, A Flower, GW Walker, MJA Whiley, AS Wright

MIDDLESEX CCC

FIRST–CLASS MATCHES

BATTING

Match	AJ Strauss	SG Koenig	RMS Weston	EC Joyce	BL Hutton	DC Nash	PN Weekes	SJ Cook	CB Keegan	AW Laraman	TA Hunt	OA Shah	AA Noffke	ARC Fraser	PCR Tufnell	D Alleyne	TF Bloomfield	Abdur Razzaq	J Jones	JWM Dalrymple	Extras	Total	Wickets	Result	Points
v. Cambridge University CCE (Cambridge) 13-15 April	121	141*	67*	-	-	-	-														29	358	1		
	-	-	-	8	6	4	100*	43*	-	42	-										37	240	4	W	
v. Durham (Chester-le-Street) 19-21 April	70	100	8	14	-	66*	3	7				34	4	16	8						17	347	10		
	19*	3*	-	-	-	-	-	-				-	-	-	-						5	27	-	W	18
v. Nottinghamshire (Lord's) 24-27 April	62	47	24	119	-	21	50	4				63	1	20	0*						51	462	10		
	-	-	-	-		-	-	-				-	-	-	-									W	20
v. Sri Lankans (Shenley) 11-13 May	27	0	0	93	0	-	3	-	39*	3		65				31	0				13	274	10		
	-	-	-	-	-		-	-	-	-		-				-	-							D	
v. Northamptonshire (Northampton) 15-17 May	2	101	72	29	55	107	29	-	43	-		2	31			31*					39	541	10		
	-	-	-	-	-	-	-		-	-		-	-			-								W	20
v. Durham (Lord's) 31 May-3 June	96	29	44	44	22	1	4	-	-	45*		112		15			15				38	465	10		
	18	4	71	0	29*	-	-	-	-	-		37		-			20*				15	194	5	D	9
v. Glamorgan (Lord's) 12-15 June	38	86	25	73	44*	17	34	5	-	-		23		4*			38				16	403	9		
	-	-	-	-	-	-	-	-	-	-		-		-			-							D	12
v. Glamorgan (Cardiff) 26-29 June	141	30	17	129	1*	17	5	-				62						203*			28	633	7		
	48	27	0*	-	-	-	-	-				4*						-			6	85	2	W	20
v. Worcestershire (Lord's) 3-6 July	19	63	5	70	26	127*	33	-				4		-			28				42	417	8		
	-	-	-	-	-	-	-	-				-		-			-							D	10
v. Gloucestershire (Southgate) 10-13 July	82	59	21	29	2	10	38*	-	0	-		13		4*					29		14	301	9		
	30	38	0	0*	-	10	-	-	-	82*		63		-					-		18	241	5	W	18
v. Essex (Southgate) 18-21 July	1	113	1	65	81*	71	19	-	21	-		60		-	45		11				50	538	10		
	59	5	81	57	-	-	-	-	-	-		148*		-	35*		-				41	426	4	D	12
v. Gloucestershire (Cheltenham) 24-27 July	49	33	5	22	43	102	13	-	2	-		65		0*			0				29	363	10		
	26	53	32*	88	-	37*	-	-	-	-		5		-			14				10	265	5	D	10
v. Northamptonshire (Lord's) 7-10 August	43	8	43	116	-	2*	-	-				172*	-								16	400	4		
	-	-	-	-		-	-	-				-												D	12
v. Nottinghamshire (Trent Bridge) 14-16 August	15	30	3	2	40*	21	0	0	4			7		0							16	138	10		
	110	52	41*	0	5	8	0	0	5			25		0							13	259	10	D	3
v. Derbyshire (Lord's) 21-24 August	1	1	-	129	55	28	-	11	-	36		9	6	0							288	304	10		
	21	0	51	27	0	17	3	6	-	-		20	31*	7							24	207	10	L	6
v. Worcestershire (Worcester) 27-30 August	8	81	-	125	0	100	46	24				0	76			26*		14			31	531	10		
	27	33	46*	-	-	40*	-	-				19	-			-		-			28	193	4	W	19.75
v. Essex (Chelmsford) 4-6 September		26	15	85	26	12	25	5				47	19	2*				17			16	295	10		
		5	3	0	33	0	1	0				25	22	0*				2			2	93	10	L	5
v. Derbyshire (Derby) 11-13 September		72	1	21	4	88	5	7				13		0*	13	13				33	35	282	10		
		11	18	0	17	33	0	4				0*		4	49*					0	14	150	10	W	17

	AJ Strauss	SG Koenig	RMS Weston	EC Joyce	BL Hutton	DC Nash	PN Weekes	SJ Cook	CB Keegan	AW Laraman	TA Hunt	OA Shah	AA Noffke	ARC Fraser	PCR Tufnell	D Alleyne	TF Bloomfield	Abdur Razzaq	J Jones	JWM Dalrymple
Matches	16	18	9	18	11	15	18	15	9	11	2	16	8	2	14	3	3	6	1	3
Innings	25	29	11	27	19	19	25	18	10	13	2	25	10	2	15	3	3	9	1	5
Not Out	1	2	2	3	1	5	6	2	0	3	0	3	1	0	8	1	2	3	0	0
Highest Score	141	141*	72	129	116	100	127*	43*	24	82*	3	172*	76	20	45	49*	31*	203*	29	33
Runs	1133	1251	237	1267	518	646	990	267	58	330	3	1084	203	36	89	93	57	364	29	66
Average	47.20	46.33	26.33	52.79	28.77	46.14	52.10	16.68	5.80	33.00	3.00	49.27	22.55	18.00	12.71	46.50	57.00	60.66	29.00	13.20
100s	3	4	-	4	1	1	4	-	-	-	-	3	-	-	-	-	-	1	-	-
50s	5	7	2	6	4	4	3	-	-	1	-	6	1	-	-	-	-	-	-	-
Catches/Stumpings	16	6	4	17	19	36/1	23	3	3	3	-	5	3	-	3	8/-	-	1	-	1

MIDDLESEX CCC

FIRST–CLASS MATCHES

BOWLING

	CB Keegan	SJ Cook	AW Larama	PN Weekes	ARC Fraser	AA Noffke	PCR Tufnell	TF Bloomfield	BL Hutton	Abdur Razzaq	Overs	Total	Byes/Leg-Byes	Wickets	Run outs
v. Cambridge University CCE	11-1-29-1	11-5-11-5	6-0-18-0	3.4-2-1-1							40.4	111	9	10	– A
(Cambridge) 13-15 April	7-0-20-0	12-1-51-4	11-3-40-3	13.5-6-39-2							52.5	205	15	10	– AB
v. Durham		12-3-37-3		–	14-5-32-0	18-5-51-3	10.3-2-36-2				54.3	160	4	9	1
(Chester-le-Street) 19-21 April		10-2-36-1		3-0-21-0	20-6-65-2	15-4-63-3	8.5-2-19-1				56.5	213	9	8	1
v. Nottinghamshire		10-5-10-2		–	22-9-61-5	16.4-2-57-2	12-5-23-1				60.4	159	8	10	–
(Lord's) 24-27 April		14-1-53-1		12-2-36-0	16-6-32-0	23.2-3-100-7	19-4-40-1				84.2	272	11	9	–
v. Sri Lankans			9-1-32-3	1-0-4-0				11-1-43-0	16-7-37-4		50.4	186	2	10	2 A
(Shenley) 11-13 May			10-2-55-1	11-1-54-0				17-4-45-3	16-4-43-0		66	281	11	4	– AC
v. Northamptonshire		18-3-63-8	8-1-43-0	7-1-19-0		22-5-89-1		15.1-5-57-1			70.1	286	15	10	–
(Northampton) 15-17 May		13-2-42-1	19-5-55-4	7-1-18-0		20.4-4-77-3		16-5-39-2			75.4	253	22	10	–
v. Durham	15-1-87-0	26-1-108-1	23-5-89-2	28-3-109-1			35-1-137-1			26-4-91-1	153	645	24	6	–
(Lord's) 31 May-3 June	–						–				–	–	–	–	–
v. Glamorgan		24.2-5-116-3	19.5-5-55-3	11-1-32-0			19-4-70-1			28-4-91-3	101.2	369	5	10	–
(Lord's) 12-15 June															
v. Glamorgan	12-4-39-1	3-0-23-0		7-1-27-3		25-5-96-6				9-0-42-0	56	235	8	10	–
(Cardiff) 26-29 June	17-2-70-2	20-4-57-1		34-6-106-2		45-7-133-2				24-3-104-3	140	481	11	10	–
v. Worcestershire	29-3-139-1	26-2-126-1		14-2-57-0		18-2-71-0				33-5-86-2	123	502	9	4	– B
(Lord's) 3-6 July	–	7-1-24-0		3-0-14-0		7-1-15-2				7-2-28-3	28	99	6	5	– B
v. Gloucestershire		24-2-88-2	27-5-62-1	26-5-50-3		41-9-83-0		7-0-14-1			141.3	388	19	10	– D
(Southgate) 10-13 July		11-1-42-1	5-0-25-0	6-0-16-0		7-1-30-0		1-0-8-0			36	152	3	2	– D
v. Essex		17-5-39-0	25-5-88-1	27-2-78-1		27-3-96-1				33.4-4-133-7	129.4	441	7	10	–
(Southgate)18-21 July		4-1-7-0	5-2-11-0	7-2-14-0		–				1-0-2-1	23	53	2	1	– B
v. Gloucestershire		17-3-103-2	33-5-99-2	23-3-74-0		28-8-64-1			3-0-16-0	34.2-3-125-5	139.2	494	2	10	– B
(Cheltenham) 24-27 July		–	2-0-10-0	31-4-95-1		39-12-66-8			–	10.3-0-55-1	82.3	230	4	10	–
v. Northamptonshire		18-8-32-2	18-4-48-3	–		16-5-71-0	20.2-6-53-3		4-0-17-2		76.2	231	10	10	–
(Lord's) 7-10 August											–	–	–	–	–
v. Nottinghamshire	29-4-113-4	16-2-76-1	22.4-0-123-3	23-5-49-1			24-2-69-0		4-0-27-0		118.4	470	13	10	1
(Trent Bridge) 14-16 August	–	–	–	–			–		–		–	–	–	–	–
v. Derbyshire	16-3-84-1		20-4-67-1	11-4-20-0		33-0-138-6	36.5-7-91-2				116.5	414	14	10	–
(Lord's) 21-24 August	6-0-28-1		–	33.3-5-104-1		18-2-69-0	38.3-11-80-5				96	301	20	7	–
v. Worcestershire	20.1-8-47-4			9-2-21-0		26-5-84-4		20-4-100-1	12-2-42-1		90.1	319	17	10	– E
(Worcester) 27-30 August	24.4-3-92-4			21-2-65-1		30-6-110-4		14-1-56-0	4-1-18-0		102.4	401	35	10	1 E
v. Essex	10-2-33-0	12-4-27-4		21-1-59-3		20-1-88-0	22-1-58-3		3-0-9-0		88	278	4	10	–
(Chelmsford) 4-6 September	4-1-20-0	10-3-26-3		3-0-16-1		8-2-23-0	8.5-1-25-0		–		33.5	111	1	4	–
v. Derbyshire	7-0-36-0	11-1-44-1				15-6-24-8	–		9-4-24-1		42	137	9	10	–
(Derby) 11-13 September	4-0-18-0	21-6-64-1				23.3-7-84-4	23-10-35-5		4-2-7-0		75.3	232	24	10	–

	CB Keegan	SJ Cook	AW Larama	PN Weekes	ARC Fraser	AA Noffke	PCR Tufnell	TF Bloomfield	BL Hutton	Abdur Razzaq
Overs	211.5	367.2	262.4	397	72	305.1	514.5	93.1	83	206.3
Maidens	32	71	47	61	26	57	104	20	20	25
Runs	855	1305	920	1198	190	1128	1390	340	262	757
Wickets	19	48	27	21	7	45	45	7	9	26
Average	45.00	27.18	34.07	57.04	27.14	25.06	30.88	48.57	29.11	29.11

A   TA Hunt 9-0-43-3; 5-1-20-0; 13.4-1-68-1; 10-1-58-0
B   EC Joyce 4-0-20-1; 3-0-14-0; 4-0-12-0; 6-2-17-0; 1-0-11-0
C   OA Shah 2-0-15-0
D   I Jones 16.3-2-72-3; 6-1-28-1
E   JWM Dalrymple 3-1-8-0; 9-3-25-0

FIELDING

37	DC Nash (36ct, 1st)
23	PN Weekes
19	BL Hutton
17	EC Joyce
16	AJ Strauss
8	D Alleyne
6	SG Koenig
5	OA Shah
4	RMS Weston
3	SJ Cook, CB Keegan, AW Laraman, AA Noffke, PCR Tufnell
1	Abdur Razzaq, JWM Dalrymple

NORTHAMPTONSHIRE CCC

FIRST–CLASS MATCHES

BATTING

	MEK Hussey	MB Loye	AS Rollins	DJG Sales	GP Swann	JW Cook	TMB Bailey	BJ Phillips	JAR Blain	CG Greenidge	DM Cousins	RJ Warren	AL Penberthy	RSG Anderson	JF Brown	DE Paynter	GL Brophy	ME Cassar	MS Panesar	RA White	MWH Inness	MJ Powell	Extras	Total	Wickets	Result	Points
v. Oxford University CCE (Oxford) 18–20 April	11	4	36	51	14	29	50*	17	0	13*	–												18	243	8		
	52	64	35*		38		18*																19	226	3	W	
v. Worcestershire (Northampton) 24–27 April	170	139		16	12	12*						150*	63										52	614	5		
																							–	–	–	D	11
v. Derbyshire (Derby) 8–10 May	13	0		0	44		0		0	46	18*	0	0	0									10	131	10		
	150	109		16	62	21			4	1	4*	20	17	4									31	439	10	L	8
v. Middlesex (Northampton) 15–17 May	84		107	0	10	4	11		1		0*	0	18	8									43	286	10		
	27		28	0	0	84	34		8*		5	2	19	10									36	253	10	L	4
v. Nottinghamshire (Trent Bridge) 24–27 May	10	37	7		0	4	4			1	16	42	106*	26									24	277	10		
	36	1	60		0	11	0			9	2*	0	31	0									9	159	10	L	3.5
v. Essex (Northampton) 31 May–3 June	140	0	89		90	64			17*	4		87	50	51	12								28	632	10		
	41	17	1		9	15			2	1		6	23	31	2*								7	155	10	L	7
v. Essex (Ilford) 12–15 June	67	0	1		23	16				14	6*	28	37	1	0*								11	204	10		
	71	24	34		43	68				8	5	34	25	35	0*								14	361	10	L	3
v. Nottinghamshire (Northampton) 26–29 June	39	105	23	179	12	0	8			7	13	2	3*										29	420	10		
	4	104*	39	1		68							5*										21	242	4	W	20
v. Durham (Northampton) 3–6 July	0*															0*							0	0	0		
	15	19	74	109	29	12				2	2*	47	2*			20							22	353	9	W	15
v. Worcestershire (Worcester) 19–21 July	174	16	0			0				17	23*	41	0	2			30	55					29	387	10		
	6	4	12			0				1	1	1	19	10			14*	1					8	77	10	L	7
v. Derbyshire (Northampton) 25–27 July	13	1	8	15	88	0				0	2	29	0*	18									36	210	10		
	0	34	29	12	21	50*				0	1	62	15	8									51	283	10	L	4
v. Middlesex (Lord's) 7–10 August	9	30	7	23	46	0	7			15		2					58	2*					32	231	10		
																							–	–	–	D	6
v. Gloucestershire (Bristol) 15–18 August	310*	16	70	183	32	26	8			2		61						11	2*				25	746	9		
																							–	–	–	D	12
v. Glamorgan (Northampton) 21–23 August		41	37	5	21	0				4*		99					68	80	0				20	375	10		
		3	8		13*													60*					0	84	2	W	19
v. Durham (Chester-le-Street) 27–29 August			0	44	30	0						3					61*			19	21	28	30	236	10		
				24	14*												0*			45	–	39	19	141	3	W	16
v. Gloucestershire (Northampton) 11–13 September			0		8	2				16		33						101*	0	277	20*	107	28	592	8		
																							–	–	–	W	20
v. Glamorgan (Cardiff) 18–21 September			14		23	4				4			130*		11		110	8		69	25	7	25	430	10		
			5		30	24*							6				5	41		6	–	108*	18	242	6	D	12

	MEK Hussey	MB Loye	AS Rollins	DJG Sales	GP Swann	JW Cook	TMB Bailey	BJ Phillips	JAR Blain	CG Greenidge	DM Cousins	RJ Warren	AL Penberthy	RSG Anderson	JF Brown	DE Paynter	GL Brophy	ME Cassar	MS Panesar	RA White	MWH Inness	MJ Powell
Matches	13	13	6	14	11	15	17	1	7	15	11	6	16	5	8	2	4	7	5	4	4	3
Innings	23	22	12	22	16	24	25	1	9	19	16	11	25	10	11	4	8	9	5	7	4	5
Not Out	2	1	1	0	0	3	4	0	2	2	7	1	3	0	5	2	3	1	2	1	1	1
Highest Score	310*	139	107	179	183	90	68	17	17*	46	23*	150*	130*	51	19	20	110	101*	2*	277	25	108*
Runs	1442	768	460	551	539	746	457	17	47	160	103	369	909	166	64	32	246	343	4	556	66	289
Average	68.66	36.57	41.81	25.04	33.68	35.52	21.76	17.00	6.71	9.41	11.44	36.90	41.31	16.60	10.66	16.00	49.20	42.87	1.33	92.66	22.00	72.25
100s	5	4	1	1	2	–	–	–	–	–	–	1	2	–	–	–	1	1	–	1	–	2
50s	4	1	2	3	1	4	4	–	–	1	–	1	5	1	–	–	1	3	–	3	–	–
Catches/Stumpings	21	7	6	11	5	4	43/6	–	2	7	4	1	9	–	2	2	5	4	3	1	5	6

NORTHAMPTONSHIRE CCC

FIRST–CLASS MATCHES

BOWLING

Match	DM Cousins	CG Greenidge	JAR Blain	JW Cook	GP Swann	AL Penberthy	RSG Anderson	JF Brown	ME Cassar	MS Panesar	MWH Inness	RA White	Overs	Total	Byes/Leg-Byes	Wickets	Run outs
v. Oxford University CCE (Oxford) 18-20 April	14-8-25-1	15-2-44-2	11-4-22-2	5-2-20-1	6.4-2-13-3								61.4	149	12	10	– A
	7-1-11-1	11.5-3-24-2	8-0-26-0	8-5-7-2	12-6-17-2								53.5	113	0	10	– A
v. Worcestershire (Northampton) 24-27 April	17-4-46-0	33-7-124-3	29-5-144-4	15-6-48-0	13-2-72-0	21.1-3-71-1							128.1	524	19	8	–
	-	-	-	-	-	-							-	-	-	-	-
v. Derbyshire (Derby) 8-10 May	27-9-64-2	18.2-0-95-1	20-1-128-1		16-2-69-1	18-3-74-0	20-6-97-4						119.2	538	11	10	1
	-	4-2-6-1	4.4-1-26-1		-	-	-						8.4	33	1	2	-
v. Middlesex (Northampton) 15-17 May	32.3-7-90-2		31-2-129-2	15-3-47-2	20-3-64-1	27-6-67-1	33-4-129-2						158.3	541	15	10	-
	-		-	-	-	-	-						-	-	-	-	-
v. Northamptonshire (Trent Bridge) 24-27 May	23-2-70-2	20-3-66-5	-			8-2-25-1	11-2-38-0						62	207	8	8	-
	18.5-1-88-2	13-1-59-1				9-1-27-0	10-3-37-0						52.5	231	3	3	-
v. Essex (Northampton) 31 May-3 June	30-6-100-0		28-4-127-2	2-0-11-0		10.5-5-31-1	29-8-82-1	51-11-130-3					150.5	497	16	7	-
	11-0-67-1		3-1-20-0			12-0-49-1	7-0-46-0	16.5-2-102-2					49.5	291	7	6	2
v. Essex (Ilford) 12-15 June	29-8-89-0	34-10-86-4		10-2-37-1		33-12-82-2	29-5-102-1	27-3-86-1					162	498	16	9	-
	2-1-3-0	2-0-13-0		1-0-11-0			4-1-19-1	5-0-14-0					14	68	8	1	-
v. Nottinghamshire (Nottingham) 26-29 June	29-3-103-2	24-4-95-2		3-2-3-0		31-5-94-2	20-5-56-0	40.1-16-105-3					147.1	489	33	10	1
	8-4-21-1	9.4-0-27-3		-		20-5-55-3		22-6-59-3					59.4	172	10	10	-
v. Durham (Northampton) 3-6 July	22-7-75-4	20-2-95-0				29-9-81-4	9-2-20-0	29.4-10-59-2					109.4	352	22	10	-
	-					-		-					-	-	-	-	-
v. Worcestershire (Worcester) 19-21 July	20-1-91-3	25-6-90-3				18-3-60-2		18-3-60-0	14-3-59-2				95	383	23	10	-
	4-0-24-0	6-1-28-2				-		3-0-25-0	0.1-0-0-0				13.1	82	5	2	-
v. Derbyshire (Northampton) 25-27 July	12-5-31-1	15-2-69-1		10-2-14-1		27.1-3-126-6	12-3-44-0	26-6-88-1					102.1	388	16	10	-
	5-0-26-0	10-2-37-2		4-0-14-0		26-6-112-4	-	25.1-5-88-4					70.1	282	5	10	-
v. Middlesex (Lord's) 7-10 August		24-3-101-0	26-1-88-1	10-1-38-1	6-3-22-0	22-12-29-1			3-0-19-0	20.5-2-99-1			111.5	400	4	4	-
		-	-	-	-	-			-	-			-	-	-	-	-
v. Gloucestershire (Bristol) 15-18 August		18-2-63-0	13-0-117-1	12-3-53-0	14-3-39-1	12-0-47-0			10.3-4-34-6	18-5-56-2			97.3	422	13	10	-
		18-2-78-0	19-2-82-2	6-1-33-0	26-2-50-1	4-1-5-0			21.5-1-100-4	40-13-80-0			136.5	446	17	7	– B
v. Glamorgan (Northampton) 21-23 August		12-3-44-5				9-2-31-2			8-2-31-1		11.4-3-33-2		40.4	144	5	10	-
		14-3-68-3			24-6-70-3	4-1-9-0			4-2-7-0	30-3-120-3	7-2-32-1		83	312	6	10	-
v. Durham (Chester-le-Street) 27-29 August		13-0-52-1		7-2-12-0		14-7-33-1			13-4-38-2	15.3-7-31-2	22-4-60-4		84.3	240	14	10	-
		15.1-4-40-6		-		10-3-21-3			8-1-28-1	-	12-3-39-0		45.1	136	8	10	-
v. Gloucestershire (Northampton) 11-13 September		16-2-67-2						26-4-106-4	3-0-13-0	28.3-14-42-4	16-5-64-0	-	89.3	299	7	10	-
		7-0-29-1						15-3-47-3		22-6-74-3	8-2-48-1	12.4-3-30-2	64.4	234	6	10	-
v. Glamorgan (Cardiff) 18-21 September		18-3-73-0		10-2-38-1		14-5-30-1		16-5-45-0	12-0-50-0		26-5-90-7	4-0-19-1	100	348	3	10	-
		15-0-108-3		12-0-71-0		5-0-22-0		32-2-124-2	16-1-85-0		14-1-63-0	10-0-42-2	104	528	13	7	-

	DM Cousins	CG Greenidge	JAR Blain	JW Cook	GP Swann	AL Penberthy	RSG Anderson	JF Brown	ME Cassar	MS Panesar	MWH Inness	RA White
Overs	311.2	431	192.4	132	270.5	292	143	352.5	113.3	174.5	116.4	26.4
Maidens	67	67	21	31	60	76	29	76	18	50	25	3
Runs	1024	1681	909	474	884	833	550	1138	464	502	429	91
Wickets	22	53	16	9	31	17	9	28	16	15	15	5
Average	46.54	31.71	56.81	52.66	28.51	49.00	61.11	40.64	29.00	33.46	28.60	18.20

A BJ Phillips 10-3-13-1; 7-2-28-3
B MB Loye 2-1-1-0

FIELDING

49	TMB Bailey (43ct, 6st)
21	MEK Hussey
11	DJG Sales
9	AL Penberthy
7	CG Greenidge, MB Loye
6	MJ Powell, AS Rollins
5	GL Brophy, MWH Inness, GP Swann
4	ME Cassar, JW Cook, DM Cousins
3	MS Panesar
2	JAR Blain, JF Brown, DE Paynter
1	RJ Warren, RA White

NOTTINGHAMSHIRE CCC

FIRST-CLASS MATCHES

BATTING

	DJ Bicknell	JER Gallian	Usman Afzaal	KP Pietersen	GE Welton	BM Shafayat	CMW Read	DS Lucas	RJ Logan	AJ Harris	NM Malik	L Klusener	SJ Randall	GJ Smith	N Boje	P Johnson	PJ Franks	PJ McMahon	V Atri	S Patel	WM Noon	WR Smith	GD Clough	TE Savill	Extras	Total	Wickets	Result	Points
v. Durham University CCE	23	13	5	133	97	2	25	49	0*	1															47	395	9		
(Trent Bridge) 20–22 April	0	68	4	–	–	71	54	–	4*	1*	–														19	221	5	W	
v. Middlesex	48	16	4	1	13		26*		18	9	0	0	0												24	159	10		
(Lord's) 24–27 April	46	0	11	10	51		20		2rh		18	42	8	39*											25	272	10	L	2.5
v. Essex	32	52	4	19			18		1	4	2			35*	25	16									5	213	10		
(Trent Bridge) 8–10 May	39	9	85*	–			18		–	–	–			–	–	25*									25	188	3	W	16
v. Gloucestershire	38		34	29	0		16		3	9	0			9*	36	0									23	197	10		
(Bristol) 15–17 May	0		4	46*	68		9		0	5	0			6	15	18									11	182	10	L	3
v. Northamptonshire	34	12	21	35			8		20	7*				0*	36	16									18	207	8		
(Trent Bridge) 24–27 May	0	111*	88	0												25*									7	231	3	W	16
v. Derbyshire	24	69	35	34			6		9	1	3			3*	84	96									29	393	10		
(Trent Bridge) 12–15 June	24	20	2	14			13		0	11	0*			27	10	34									20	175	10	L	8
v. Northamptonshire		100	13	3	0		127		32	41*						37	12	67	15						42	489	10		
(Northampton) 26–29 June		2	34	0	0		6		13	4*						18	70	15	0						10	172	10	L	8
v. West Indies A			1	43	27				–							0	98	35	15	38*	5	0			25	287	9		
(Trent Bridge) 3–5 July				–	8*	18*			–							–	–	–	–	–	–	–			12	38	0	D	
v. Glamorgan		5	88	31	115		24		7	0				14*	0	9	1								34	328	10		
(Trent Bridge) 10–12 July		55*	11	–	28		–		–	–					2*	0	–								4	100	3	W	18
v. Derbyshire		4	58	103*	27		0		0	23				3	0	6	1								15	240	10		
(Derby) 19–21 July		111*	3	30	4		47		11	0				16*	22	39	0								40	323	9	W	16
v. Durham		75	103	37	27		39		0	0*				10	2		60								9	362	10		
(Chester-le-Street) 24–26 July		11	12*	42*			–		–	–				–	–		11								7	83	2	W	19
v. Worcestershire	13	8	0	13	4		26		0					2		52*	0								21	161	10		
(Kidderminster) 8–11 August	8	27	91	0	76		14*		–					–		56*	–								20	292	5	D	7
v. Middlesex	108	5	4	254*	24		12		15	3				18		9									17	470	10		
(Trent Bridge) 14–16 August	–	–	–	–	–		–		–	–				–		–									–	–	–	W	20
v. Gloucestershire	9	34	61	116	9		80		8*					1		83	26								44	476	10		
(Trent Bridge) 21–23 August	–	–	–	–	–		–		–					–		–	–								–	–	–	W	20
v. Glamorgan	20	171	40		92	44	31*		0				5	5	31		5								20	464	10		
(Colwyn Bay) 27–30 August	16	1	104*		33	31	0*		–				–	–		70	–								19	274	5	D	12
v. Durham	54	7	103		77	48	27*		–								23	15*							46	400	6		
(Trent Bridge) 6–9 September	–	–	–		–	–	–		–								–	–							–	–	–	D	12
v. Worcestershire	112	62	4	16	31	50			8					0		36	57*								19	204	10		
(Trent Bridge) 11–14 September	2	4	4	38	104	4			0*					35		13	21								14	241	10	W	20
v. Essex	53	23	134	1	4		73		16*					4		16	0								17	341	10		
(Chelmsford) 18–21 September	31	12	0	23	70		18		17					16		13	33								38	280	10	L	6

	DJ Bicknell	JER Gallian	Usman Afzaal	KP Pietersen	GE Welton	BM Shafayat	CMW Read	DS Lucas	RJ Logan	AJ Harris	NM Malik	L Klusener	SJ Randall	GJ Smith	N Boje	P Johnson	PJ Franks	PJ McMahon	V Atri	S Patel	WM Noon	WR Smith	GD Clough	TE Savill
Matches	13	16	17	12	16	7	17	1	13	14	7	1	2	15	9	14	10	2	1	1	1	1	1	1
Innings	23	29	31	17	28	13	27	1	19	20	7	2	3	20	16	25	14	3	1	1	1	1	1	1
Not Out	0	3	3	3	2	1	5	0	4	7	1	0	0	7	2	3	2	0	0	0	0	1	0	0
Highest Score	114	171	134	254*	115	104	127	49	32	41*	18	42	8	39*	84	96	67	15	98	35	15	38*	5	0
Runs	734	1087	1164	871	954	450	773	49	143	151	32	42	13	243	409	662	301	15	98	35	15	38	5	0
Average	31.91	41.80	41.57	62.21	36.69	37.50	35.13	49.00	9.53	11.61	5.33	21.00	4.33	18.69	29.21	30.09	25.08	5.00	98.00	35.00	15.00	–	5.00	–
100s	2	4	4	4	1	1	1	–	–	–	–	–	–	–	–	–	–	–	–	–	–	–	–	–
50s	2	6	6	–	6	2	4	–	–	–	–	–	2	5	3	–	1	–	–	–	–	–	–	–
Catches/Stumpings	5	16	11	12	16	5	62/2	–	5	6	1	1	1	4	10	7	2	–	2	–	1/–	–	–	–

NOTTINGHAMSHIRE CCC

FIRST–CLASS MATCHES

BOWLING

	RJ Logan	MN Malik	AJ Harris	KP Pietersen	GJ Smith	N Boje	PJ Franks	SCG MacGill	Overs	Total	Byes/Leg-Byes	Wickets	Run outs	
v. **Durham University** (Trent Bridge) 20–22 April	12-5-36-0	16-2-67-5	9-4-29-1	5-1-20-1					63	210	11	10	1	AB
	5-2-13-0	5-0-22-1	12-5-35-3	27-9-54-2					90	215	24	10	-	AB
v. **Middlesex** (Lord's) 24–27 April	28-7-105-4	24-4-79-1		4-0-29-0	23.2-6-70-4				114.2	462	17	10	-	BCD
	-								-	-	-	-	-	
v. **Essex** (Trent Bridge) 8–10 May	4-0-15-0	17-5-45-3	14.4-4-41-4		10-3-21-3	2-0-3-0			47.4	130	5	10	-	
	10-1-51-1	12-0-57-0	18-2-72-1		23-6-53-8	6-0-26-0			69	270	11	10	-	
v. **Gloucestershire** (Bristol) 15–17 May	25-6-81-2	18-4-55-4	20-5-69-2	2-0-9-0	23-4-69-1		21-4-48-1		109	347	16	10	-	
	2-0-14-0	3.4-1-14-2					2-1-5-1		7.4	33	0	3	-	
v. **Northamptonshire** (Trent Bridge) 24–27 May	14-2-66-1	10-2-44-0	20.4-3-68-4		23-5-56-2		4-0-29-1		71.4	277	14	10	2	
	4-0-24-0	5-1-26-1	11-2-54-7		10.2-1-48-2	-			30.2	159	7	10	-	
v. **Derbyshire** (Trent Bridge) 12–15 June	18-4-66-3	18-7-50-3	23-7-94-2	6-0-25-0	16-4-59-0	31.4-11-83-2			112.4	392	15	10	-	B
	3-0-29-0	5-1-19-0	6-1-19-0	4-0-32-1	6-0-24-2	9-1-28-3			37	181	6	6	-	
v. **Northamptonshire** (Northampton) 26–29 June	16.1-2-64-4		29-4-107-2			31-7-115-3	16-3-77-0		104.1	420	17	10	1	BE
	10-1-45-1		11-4-46-2			18-2-51-0	4-1-32-0		58.3	242	12	4	1	BE
v. **West Indies A** (Trent Bridge) 3–5 July		13-2-84-2							37.5	223	2	8	-	EFGH
		-							-	-	-	-	-	
v. **Glamorgan** (Trent Bridge) 10–12 July	12-1-55-2		20-4-70-4		9-2-28-0	-	15.5-3-46-4		56.5	213	14	10	-	
	16.1-6-29-3		22-3-65-1		14-3-50-1	1-0-4-0	19-3-51-5		72.1	211	12	10	-	
v. **Derbyshire** (Derby) 19–21 July	17-2-85-1		24-2-87-2	3-1-12-0	12.3-3-46-1	25-9-45-4	24-9-67-2		105.3	353	11	10	-	
	6-0-23-0		10-2-38-2	-	11-3-20-0	23.2-5-66-5	17-4-47-3		67.2	209	15	10	-	
v. **Durham** (Chester-le-Street) 24–26 July	9-3-36-3		9-1-33-2		11.5-4-24-4		7-0-21-1		36.5	116	2	10	-	
	20.2-3-73-3		18-7-60-4	3-1-13-0	20-4-81-2	22-11-40-1	9-1-36-0		92.2	328	25	10	-	
v. **Worcestershire** (Kidderminster) 8–11 August			14-4-43-3	-	15-3-45-2		6-0-39-0	18.4-5-63-5	53.4	201	11	10	-	
			13-2-40-1	3-0-27-1	21-2-94-3		13-4-56-0	21-2-108-0	71	336	11	5	-	
v. **Middlesex** (Trent Bridge) 14–16 August	8-3-14-0		6-0-30-2	-	12-1-30-2			12.4-0-54-6	38.4	138	10	10	-	
	13-3-47-1		13-4-42-1	5-1-5-0	5-2-20-0			24.2-1-111-8	67.4	259	9	10	-	B
v. **Gloucestershire** (Trent Bridge) 21–23 August	20.5-3-58-2				18-8-31-1		14-4-33-4	11-2-44-3	63.5	173	7	10	-	
	22-11-63-2				16-4-45-3		-	29-9-92-5	67	219	19	10	-	
v. **Glamorgan** (Colwyn Bay) 27–30 August	24-6-99-2				22-5-73-2	42-6-128-6	16-1-62-0		131	495	21	10	-	BDH
	-				-	-			-	-	-	-	-	
v. **Durham** (Trent Bridge) 6–9 September			13.3-5-40-4		12-3-40-1		10-3-30-3	11-6-14-2	46.3	132	8	10	-	
			4-1-25-0		6-0-39-0		3-1-15-2	10-2-52-3	28	153	7	5	-	B
v. **Worcestershire** (Trent Bridge) 11–14 August			26.5-4-115-5		23-4-65-1		19-3-76-3	30-2-126-1	98.5	397	15	10	-	
			15-2-56-5		9-1-21-2		7-1-21-0	6-2-29-3	37	134	7	10	-	
v. **Essex** (Chelmsford) 18–21 September			20-10-42-3		17-3-60-1		21-7-50-3	28.4-4-116-3	88.4	282	6	10	-	H
			11-2-65-0		11-1-63-0		14-5-54-2	25-1-121-1	68.2	343	9	3	-	HI

	RJ Logan	MN Malik	AJ Harris	KP Pietersen	GJ Smith	N Boje	PJ Franks	SCG MacGill
Overs	319.3	146.4	413.4	62	400	238	234.5	227.4
Maidens	71	29	93	13	85	58	53	37
Runs	1191	562	1475	226	1275	671	813	930
Wickets	35	22	67	5	48	27	32	40
Average	34.02	25.54	22.01	45.20	26.56	24.85	25.40	23.25

A   DS Lucas 13-5-21-1; 16-6-35-1

B   Usman Afzaal 8-3-26-1; 25-15-32-3; 4-0-23-0; 4-0-24-0; 4-0-11-0; 4.3-1-14-0; 7-1-25-0; 2-0-10-0; 5-0-15-0

C   L Klusener 20-4-88-1

D   SJ Randall 11-1-51-0; 22-5-89-0

E   PJ McMahon 8-1-29-0; 11-1-52-0; 3.5-0-22-2

F   TE Savill 5-1-42-2

G   GD Clough 13-1-61-2

H   BM Shafayat 3-0-12-0; 3-0-13-0; 2-0-8-0; 6-0-19-0

I   P Johnson 1.2-0-12-0

FIELDING

64	CMW Read (62ct, 2st)
16	JER Gallian, GE Welton
12	KP Pietersen
11	Usman Afzaal
10	N Boje
7	P Johnson
6	AJ Harris
5	DJ Bicknell, RJ Logan, SCG MacGill, BM Shafayat
4	GJ Smith
2	V Atri, PJ Franks
1	L Klusener, NM Malik, WM Noon, SJ Randall

SOMERSET CCC

FIRST–CLASS MATCHES

BATTING

	J Cox	MJ Wood	M Burns	PD Bowler	KA Parsons	ID Blackwell	RJ Turner	KP Dutch	RL Johnson	MPL Bulbeck	PS Jones	ME Trescothick	AR Caddick	SRG Francis	GD Rose	PCL Holloway	PD Trego	N Edwards	AV Suppiah	WJ Durston	CM Gazzard	Extras	Total	Wickets	Result	Points
v. Sussex	65	54	33	94	29	24	20	23	24	9	1*											25	401	10		
(Hove) 24-27 April	40*	4	38	8*																		4	94	2	D	12
v. Yorkshire	4		32	0	6	114	0	46		1		0	5	13*								11	232	10		
(Taunton) 8-10 May	17		6	79*	13*							134										14	263	3	W	16
v. Leicestershire	176	79	52	60	7	6	44	70	8					0*	20							43	565	10		
(Taunton) 15-18 May																									D	7
v. Surrey	34		13	21	5	98	34	3		4	4*	7	15									15	253	10		
(Oval) 24-27 May	14*		10*									12										9	45	1	D	9
v. Hampshire	8	25	9	4	0	42	33	24	9	0*				0*								7	161	9		
(Bath) 12-15 June	27	0	3	48	22	15	0	15*	20	13*												10	173	8	D	7
v. Warwickshire		4	54	57	31	15	11	0	12*	12	0				0							12	208	10		
(Edgbaston) 26-29 June		32	54	16	16	64	83*	3	38	4	1				28							18	357	10	L	4
v. Surrey		106	99	19	47	34	56*	2	27	23			8		77							56	554	10		
(Taunton) 3-6 July		131	68	6	33*	22	5	6	1*						33							24	329	7	D	7
v. Yorkshire		5	21	84	59	44	63	74	29*					24	65							30	498	9		
(Scarborough) 10-13 July																									D	11
v. Sussex	27	31	26	0	17	18	9	30		53*	6					26						27	270	10		
(Taunton) 19-21 July	0	13	98	20	0	114	31	2	22		37*					4						32	373	10	L	4
v. West Indies A		51			3		6								8	4	12*	31	1	26	24	13	183	10	Tie	
(Taunton) 24-26 July		12			17		12		11*						32	88	140	27	5	55	7	47	453	10	d	
v. Kent	1	55	4	50	11	0	19	0	49*	2			7									29	227	10		
(Canterbury) 7-10 August	3	5	10	6	52	12	35	0	18*	16			7									13	177	10	L	4
v. Hampshire	31	9	31	51	0	57	61	4					1	0*		17						16	278	10		
(Southampton) 14-17 August	5	3	11	6	6	34	26						16	0*		48						29	190	10	L	5
v. Warwickshire	29	0	95	31	25	110	35	18	2	31				8*								24	408	10		
(Taunton) 21-24 August	44	68	80	12	0	81	37	1	10	9				4*								48	394	10	D	12
v. .Lancashire	20	10	18	7	27	8	8	35	3				2	0*								2	140	10		
(Blackpool) 27-29 August	1	16	3	18	0	0	5	0	7*				0	7								14	71	10	L	3
v. Kent	62	196	6	31	68	39	9*	1	5		4			4								35	460	10		
(Taunton) 4-7 September	79	25	21	81	36	13	11	19*	10					6								15	316	9	E	11
v. Leicestershire	4	1	97*	8	0	4	18	22							0	15	15					7	191	10		
(Leicester) 12-14 September	4	2	4	6	0	14*	11	18							17	8	9					8	101	10	L	2.75
v. Lancashire	24	22	32			45	23	2	18*				0	0		47			0			8	221	10		
(Taunton) 18-19 September	5	12	19				7*	1	0				0	0		45	17		21			2	129	10	L	4

	J Cox	MJ Wood	M Burns	PD Bowler	KA Parsons	ID Blackwell	RJ Turner	KP Dutch	RL Johnson	MPL Bulbeck	PS Jones	ME Trescothick	AR Caddick	SRG Francis	GD Rose	PCL Holloway	PD Trego	N Edwards	AV Suppiah	WJ Durston	CM Gazzard
Matches	13	15	16	14	15	14	16	16	9	16	7	2	5	10	3	7	4	1	2	1	1
Innings	25	28	30	25	26	23	27	27	17	27	8	4	8	16	4	13	8	2	4	2	2
Not Out	2	0	2	2	2	0	4	3	4	7	3	0	0	8	0	0	1	0	0	0	0
Highest Score	176	196	99	94	68	114	83*	74	61	53*	37*	134	16	17	32	88	140	31	21	55	24
Runs	724	971	1047	766	581	879	691	432	290	359	76	153	53	67	84	428	270	58	27	81	31
Average	31.47	34.67	37.39	33.30	24.20	38.21	30.04	18.00	22.30	17.95	15.20	38.25	6.62	8.37	21.00	32.92	38.57	29.00	6.75	40.50	15.50
100s	1	3	-	-	-	3	-	-	-	-	-	1	-	-	-	-	1	-	-	-	-
50s	3	5	9	7	4	3	4	2	1	1	-	-	-	-	3	-	-	-	1	-	
Catches/Stumpings	6	5	14	22	16	4	50/1	20	2	3	-	-	2	-	1	4	2	1	1		3/1

SOMERSET CCC

FIRST–CLASS MATCHES

BOWLING

	RL Johnson	MPL Bulbeck	PS Jones	KP Dutch	M Burns	KA Parsons	ID Blackwell	AR Caddick	SRG Francis	PD Trego	Overs	Total	Byes/Leg-Byes	Wickets	Run outs
v. Sussex (Hove) 22-27 April	23-3-92-2	28-3-104-4	14-3-58-1	12-4-20-0	13.2-2-54-3	-					90.2	337	9	10	-
	6-8-87-2	25-5-75-2	-	5-1-26-0	10-0-85-1	18-3-74-2	14-1-38-0				98	396	11	7	-
v. Yorkshire (Taunton) 8-10 May		18-2-90-2		-		3-0-8-1	-	23.3-5-72-5	12-1-37-2		56.3	213	6	10	-
		18-1-71-1		9-1-27-0		6-2-10-1		26.4-6-73-3	10-2-44-2		85.4	280	11	10	-
v. Leicestershire (Taunton) 15-18 May		22-4-69-3		3-3-0-1		11-2-53-2	2.2-0-12-0	1-1-0-0	13-0-102-2		65.2	288	10	8	A
				-		-					-	-	-	-	-
v. Surrey (Oval) 24-27 May		20.1-2-60-4	17-3-69-1	-		4-0-19-0		28-10-66-5			69.1	220	6	10	
		20-3-80-2	15-2-40-0	13-1-52-2		11-1-37-1	15-8-19-3	27-6-94-1			101	332	10	10	1
v. Hampshire (Bath) 12-15 June	19.3-6-32-3	19-2-68-3		4-1-16-0	9-2-29-2	9-2-31-0			16-2-69-2		76.3	252	7	10	-
	14.2-5-43-7	11-2-31-3		4-2-5-0		-			4-0-12-0		36.2	98	1	10	-
v. Warwickshire (Edgbaston) 26-29 June	4.2-0-13-1	17-4-62-1	16.1-4-46-4	8-2-34-1	2-0-13-0	15-3-38-2	6-2-19-1				68.3	230	5	10	-
	-	19-2-106-1	33.3-5-110-6	14-4-42-2		12-2-51-0	42-12-95-1				120.3	423	19	10	-
v. Surrey (Taunton) 3-6 July		28-4-141-0	33.1-6-157-2	12-1-70-0			7-0-37-0	24.5-3-89-1	25.5-2-104-3		130.5	608	10	6	-
		17.4-3-63-1	17-4-59-0	9-3-35-0			17.1-4-91-3	9-0-69-1	-		69.5	324	7	5	-
v. Yorkshire (Scarborough) 10-13 July		34-7-94-4	17-4-46-0	28.2-6-77-2			4-0-20-0	37-13-49-4			131.2	323	15	10	A
		9-4-25-0	5-2-3-0	25-6-73-2			-	25-4-78-2			70	213	14	5	B
v. Sussex (Taunton) 19-21 July		13-1-66-0	37.3-6-147-3	15-1-42-0	17-3-77-1		19-2-67-3	33-9-124-1		17-1-110-2	151.3	644	11	10	-
		-	-	-				-			-	-	-	-	-
v. West Indies 'A' (Taunton) 25-26 July		18-3-47-4		26.1-5-104-3			12-0-59-3			9-1-62-0	86.1	370	18	10	ACD
		12-4-34-1		11-2-54-1			7-1-24-1			12-2-77-0	56	266	6	7	CD
v. Kent (Canterbury) 7-10 August	18-2-62-2	16-3-68-2		-	6-1-21-1		12-3-30-0	4-0-21-0	22-5-65-5		78	271	4	10	-
	24-4-79-2	17-2-50-2		3-1-7-0	2-1-2-0		7-2-29-0	3-0-7-0	29-4-108-3		85	286	4	7	-
v. Hampshire (Southampton) 14-17 August	22-6-53-2	10-1-22-1					3-0-14-0	31-12-49-5	22-5-61-2	8-2-32-0	96	236	5	10	-
	15.1-3-50-1	9-1-40-0					7-2-18-1	23-4-69-2	9-0-20-2	-	73.1	233	8	6	-
v. Warwickshire (Taunton) 21-24 August	20-3-61-1	19.4-4-75-3	-		17.2-3-62-1	7-0-29-0	-		18.1-0-73-5		82.1	304	4	10	-
	33-11-60-4	23-7-60-2		20-7-57-1	7-0-24-0		9-5-14-0		23-7-87-2		117	310	8	9	-
v. Lancashire (Blackpool) 27-29 August	18.1-5-47-6			1-0-1-0		4-0-18-0	12-1-51-1	23.5-8-81-2	9-1-50-1		67.1	251	3	10	-
	19-2-73-2			6-2-18-0	-		4-0-23-0	16-4-40-0	14-0-51-2		82.1	296	7	10	-
v. Kent (Taunton) 4-7 September		24-7-89-2	24-5-73-1	20-3-48-0		8-2-24-0	19-1-70-2		25-4-93-1		120	400	3	6	-
		15-5-40-0	10-1-37-1	11-1-27-0			8-5-11-0		16-3-44-3		61	171	9	4	B
v. Leicestershire (Leicester) 12-14 September	23.4-3-71-3	21-4-69-3		9-2-17-0					11-1-65-1	17-2-65-3	81.4	310	23	10	-
	-	-		-							-	-	-	-	-
v. Lancashire (Taunton) 18-19 September	22-4-68-4	24.3-3-93-6							3-0-32-0	6-0-23-0	55.3	228	12	10	-
	5-1-23-1	6-0-48-1							3.3-1-32-0	2-0-20-0	16.3	124	1	2	-

	RL Johnson	MPL Bulbeck	PS Jones	KP Dutch	M Burns	KA Parsons	ID Blackwell	AR Caddick	SRG Francis	PD Trego
Overs	307.1	534	239.2	268.3	101.4	216.3	312.5	247.2	222.3	63
Maidens	66	93	45	59	15	30	83	53	26	6
Runs	914	1940	845	852	444	830	830	773	947	357
Wickets	43	58	19	15	11	21	22	34	28	5
Average	21.25	33.44	44.47	56.80	40.36	39.52	37.72	22.73	33.82	71.40

A GD Rose 13-5-42-0; 11-5-22-0; 6-0-31-0
B PD Bowler 1-0-3-0
C WJ Durston 10-0-40-0; 4-0-25-1
D AV Suppiah 5-2-9-0; 10-2-46-3

FIELDING

51 RJ Turner (50ct, 1st)
22 PD Bowler
20 KP Dutch
16 KA Parsons
14 M Burns
6 J Cox
5 MJ Wood
4 ID Blackwell, CM Gazzard (3ct,1st), PCL Holloway
3 MPL Bulbeck
2 AR Caddick, RL Johnson, PD Trego
1 WJ Durston, N Edwards, GD Rose, AV Suppiah

SURREY CCC

FIRST-CLASS MATCHES

BATTING

	MA Butcher	IJ Ward	MR Ramprakash	AJ Stewart	AD Brown	N Shahid	Azhar Mahmood	AJ Tudor	DJ Bicknell	IDK Salisbury	J Ormond	GP Thorpe	MA Carberry	R Clarke	JD Ratcliffe	JN Batty	TJ Murtagh	PJ Sampson	RM Amin	ESH Giddins	Saqlain Mushtaq	AJ Hollioake	Mushtaq Ahmed	SA Newman	Extras	Total	Wickets	Result	Points
v. Sussex (Oval) 19–22 April	15	12	56	99	177	150	16	1	28*	-	-														21	575	8		
	68*	43*	-	-	-	-	-	-	-																5	116	0	W	19.5
v. Yorkshire (Headingley) 24–26 April	83	70	65	96	10	45	64*	2	0	27	3														45	510	10		
	-	-	-	-	-	-	-	-	-	-	-														-	-	-	W	20
v. Lancashire (Oval) 8–11 May	12	48	5	0	16		1	61	18	7	35*	0													13	216	10		
	16	37	119*	46	10		15	8	7*	-	-	20													31	309	7	W	15.75
v. Cambridge University CCE (Cambridge) 15–17 May		27	121		65								36	107*	3*	-	-	-							43	402	4		
		24											153*	13	2	6	42	-							58	332	6	D	
v. Somerset (Oval) 24–27 May	4	62	1	7	30		24	9	26	7*	19										21				10	220	10		
	9	67	7	53	48		44	35*	4	0	29										10				26	323	10	D	8
v. Lancashire (Old Trafford) 31 May–3 June		61	71		28	0			5	19	2		10	41	104						19*				22	382	10		
		106	0		30	1			29*	-	-		24	24	12*						-				20	246	6	D	10
v. Kent (Oval) 12–14 June		0	1		188	20			27	13	33			5	24			4*	25						21	361	10		
		15	11*		-	-			-	-	-			-	32*										3	61	1	W	19
v. Somerset (Taunton) 3–6 July		13	218		10	51			46*					153*	0							87			30	608	6		
		75	53		-	8*			2					22	151							-			13	324	5	D	8
v. Warwickshire (Oval) 10–13 July		34	210*		0	2			30	13				79	16					9	0	56			26	475	10		
		7	0		33	15			6	9				5	0					0*	1	52			9	137	10	L	8
v. Kent (Canterbury) 19–22 July	34	7	0	9					2	4				5	8					1	4	122*			29	225	10		
	20	168*	2	0					5	43*				66	0					-	60	8			38	410	8	W	16
v. Yorkshire (Guildford) 24–27 July		12	0		50	45			0	39				56	99					8*	44	5			24	382	10		
		124*	16		5*	7			59	-				-	16					-	-	-			10	237	4	W	10
v. Sussex (Hove) 8–11 August		28	32		49	28	0							17	16	0*				0	9	7			7	193	10		
		76	64		7	5	28							2	46	4				1*	0	47			16	296	10	L	3
v. Leicestershire (Leicester) 14–16 August	116	28	0	104		8		23*			6			95	28							80	12		40	540	10		
	8	6	5*	14*										4											5	42	3	W	20
v. Hampshire (Oval) 22–25 August		87	38	135	22		24	27	1*					89						18	9			99	27	576	10		
		-	-	-	-		-	-	-					-						-	-			-	-	-	-	W	20
v. Warwickshire (Edgbaston) 27–30 August		114	99	57	116		0	8	0				10	8							6	82*			44	544	10		
		-	-	-	-		-	-	-				-	-							-	-			-	-	-	D	12
v. Hampshire (Southampton) 11–14 September		112		60	82		25	7	4	19					0	15*					55*			4	35	418	10		
		156		9	20		28	16	-	143					13	15*					15*			15	16	422	8	W	20
v. Leicestershire (Oval) 18–21 September		118		34	2			0	0	44					74	0*	0					20		183	19	494	10		
		22		107	28			36*	9	0					0	22	1*					208		21	38	492	9	W	20

	MA Butcher	IJ Ward	MR Ramprakash	AJ Stewart	AD Brown	N Shahid	Azhar Mahmood	AJ Tudor	DJ Bicknell	IDK Salisbury	J Ormond	GP Thorpe	MA Carberry	R Clarke	JD Ratcliffe	JN Batty	TJ Murtagh	PJ Sampson	RM Amin	ESH Giddins	Saqlain Mushtaq	AJ Hollioake	Mushtaq Ahmed	SA Newman
Matches	6	17	15	4	16	13	3	6	10	14	15	4	2	10	1	13	4	2	1	7	10	9	2	3
Innings	11	31	25	6	26	20	4	9	14	20	17	8	4	16	2	23	6	3	-	7	13	13	3	5
Not Out	1	3	4	0	2	1	1	0	5	2	4	0	1	2	1	2	3	1	-	4	2	2	0	0
Highest Score	116	168*	218	99	188	150	64*	61	35*	59	43*	143	153*	153*	13	151	22	42	-	9	60	208	47	183
Runs	385	1759	1194	301	1211	712	96	176	258	340	208	274	223	711	16	742	47	43	-	23	278	738	66	322
Average	38.50	62.82	56.85	50.16	50.45	37.47	32.00	19.55	28.66	18.88	16.00	34.25	74.33	50.78	16.00	35.33	15.66	21.50	-	7.66	25.27	67.09	22.00	64.40
100s	1	7	4	0	5	2	-	-	-	-	-	1	1	2	2	-	2	-	-	-	-	2	-	1
50s	2	7	6	3	3	3	1	1	-	1	-	-	4	3	-	3	-	-	-	-	2	5	-	1
Catches/Stumpings	3	10	6	18/2	18	24	3	1	6	11	6	1	2	9	-	41/5	3	-	1	4	10	1		3

SURREY CCC

FIRST–CLASS MATCHES
BOWLING

	MP Bicknell	AJ Tudor	J Ormond	Azhar Mahmood	IDK Salisbury	ESH Giddins	PJ Sampson	TJ Murtagh	R Clarke	Saqlain Mushtaq	AJ Hollioake	Mustaq Ahmed	Overs	Total	Byes/Leg-Byes	Wickets	Run outs
v. Sussex	17-3-48-0	16-1-84-4	16-4-52-2	16-5-59-3	15.2-2-60-1								80.2	308	5	10	-
(Oval) 19-22 April	19-8-60-1	21-2-81-3	13-6-33-1	23-3-95-2	19-0-93-3								95	379	17	10	-
v. Yorkshire	22-7-39-2	19-8-31-4	17-6-31-1	17.5-7-33-3									75.5	140	6	10	-
(Headingley) 24-26 April	14-4-43-3	15-3-72-2	11-2-40-2	13.3-5-18-3									57.3	202	8	10	- A
v. Lancashire	20-4-68-2	14-3-79-2	12-0-56-1	14-2-79-1	10.1-3-30-3								70.1	320	8	10	-
(Oval) 8-11 May	19-4-41-0	14-2-48-0	13.4-1-42-2	25-5-61-8									71.4	200	8	10	-
v. Cambridge University CCE						18-5-33-0	19-5-54-2	15-2-37-3	12-5-25-1				89.4	218	7	10	- BCDE
(Cambridge) 15-17 May						6-3-7-3	4-2-5-0	6-3-9-1	6-3-28-0				39	96	5	5	1 BCD
v. Somerset	22-4-72-4	19-7-64-3	13-2-53-0		13-3-22-1					13.2-3-31-2			80.2	253	11	10	-
(Oval) 24-27 May	-	4-1-22-1	5-1-17-0		-								10	45	5	1	- E
v. Lancashire	17-6-43-1		15-3-47-2		10.1-2-16-2				5-0-34-0	29-10-43-4			76.1	194	11	10	1
(Old Trafford) 31 May-3 June	11-2-52-2		12-2-58-1		-					3-2-1-0			26	112	1	3	-
v. Kent	13-5-42-6		14-2-56-3			9-2-37-1			4-2-6-0	3-0-7-0			43	153	5	10	-
(Oval) 12-14 June	23-7-78-2		11-1-39-0			18-3-80-3			-	15-0-62-2			70.4	268	4	10	1
v. Somerset			33-3-137-3	22-4-85-1		21-5-83-1			20-2-104-3	35.2-8-110-2	3-0-16-0		134.2	554	19	10	-
(Taunton) 3-6 July			13-1-65-0	11-0-79-1		5-0-29-0			-	23.4-3-111-4	4-0-33-1		56.4	329	12	7	1
v. Warwickshire			23-5-116-5	8-0-25-0		8.5-2-32-1			3-0-8-0	29-3-97-4	-		71.5	293	15	10	-
(Oval) 10-13 July			18-2-62-5	26-4-95-2		19-1-63-1			4-0-24-0	43.2-14-90-2	1-0-1-0		111.2	350	15	10	-
v. Kent			14-2-80-0	17-3-59-4		17-5-39-0			8-0-56-0	33.5-8-122-5	2-0-8-0		91.5	374	10	10	1
(Canterbury) 19-22 July			17-3-61-2	18-1-55-2		15-3-40-2			4-0-23-0	19.5-3-60-4	-		73.5	260	21	10	-
v. Yorkshire			13-3-51-2	-		15-3-48-3			8-0-41-3	10-1-21-2	-		46	172	11	10	-
(Guildford) 24-27 July			29-4-106-2	13-2-62-1		35-6-113-4			9.3-2-39-2	29-4-82-0	7-1-27-1		122.3	446	17	10	-
v. Sussex		22-4-66-5				21-4-68-2		10.1-2-22-2	-			13-3-40-0	66.1	203	7	10	1
(Hove) 8-11 August		23-5-80-2				25-7-64-1		13.1-3-47-3	3-0-9-0			29-6-79-0	93.1	288	9	6	-
v. Leicestershire	15-1-76-1	18-6-58-1	21.3-9-46-2								2-0-18-0	30-7-71-5	87.3	290	21	10	1 A
(Leicester) 14-16 August	16-2-41-2	17.1-2-54-4	14-2-44-1								-	33-7-115-3	83.1	289	13	10	- A
v. Hampshire			18-7-41-2	18-4-44-3						34.2-12-59-5	1-0-1-0		85.2	190	16	10	- E
(Oval) 22-25 August			14-1-51-1	27.4-5-104-3						39-9-121-6			90.4	326	34	10	-
v. Warwickshire	24-6-87-2		30.2-5-108-4	14-2-48-0					1-0-5-0	49-16-94-4	-		118.2	345	3	10	-
(Edgbaston) 27-30 August	20-5-71-0		24-2-95-1	25-4-53-1					7-1-49-2	43-15-80-4	4-0-12-0		134	404	16	9	- DFG
v. Hampshire	17-2-92-1		20-1-87-4	10-2-24-2				9-1-52-0		20-1-68-3			76	327	4	10	-
(Southampton) 11-14 September	14-3-56-5		14-2-52-0	25.2-1-116-4				11-1-54-0		16-0-100-0			81.2	390	11	10	- D
v. Leicestershire			13-2-49-0				11-1-53-2	18.5-2-62-3			9-0-39-2		93.5	361	10	10	- F
(Oval) 18-21 September			-	12.5-4-28-2			10-3-49-2	12-2-39-5			4-0-23-1		38.5	142	3	10	1

	MP Bicknell	AJ Tudor	J Ormond	Azhar Mahmood	IDK Salisbury	ESH Giddins	PJ Sampson	TJ Murtagh	R Clarke	Saqlain Mushtaq	AJ Hollioake	Mustaq Ahmed
Overs	326	202.1	485.1	109.2	341.3	232.5	44	95.1	94.3	488.4	37	105
Maidens	78	44	87	27	59	49	11	16	15	112	1	23
Runs	1067	739	1780	345	1192	736	160	322	451	1359	178	305
Wickets	34	31	51	20	37	22	7	17	11	53	5	8
Average	31.38	23.83	34.90	17.25	32.21	33.45	22.85	18.94	41.00	25.64	35.60	38.12

A   MA Butcher 4-0-21-0; 1-1-0-0; 3-1-22-0
B   RM Amin 15-4-40-2; 9-4-15-0
C   JD Ratcliffe 3-3-0-1; 3-1-14-0
D   IJ Ward 1.4-0-1-1; 5-2-13-0; 2-1-4-1; 1-0-1-1
E   MR Ramprakash 6-1-21-0; 1-0-1-0; 1-0-1-0
F   N Shahid 6-0-17-0; 16-1-55-1
G   AD Brown 3-0-7-0

FIELDING

46   JN Batty (41ct, 5st)
24   N Shahid
20   AJ Stewart (18ct, 2st)
18   AD Brown
11   IDK Salisbury
10   AJ Hollioake, IJ Ward
9   R Clarke
6   MP Bicknell, J Ormond, MR Ramprakash
4   Saqlain Mushtaq
3   Azhar Mahmood, MA Butcher, TJ Murtagh, SA Newman
2   MA Carberry
1   ESH Giddins, Mushtaq Ahmed, GP Thorpe, AJ Tudor

SUSSEX CCC

FIRST–CLASS MATCHES

BATTING

	RR Montgomerie	MW Goodwin	CJ Adams	PA Cottey	MH Yardy	RSC Martin-Jenkins	MJ Prior	MJG Davis	RJ Kirtley	JD Lewry	PM Hutchison	KJ Innes	DA Clapp	TR Ambrose	BV Taylor	MA Robinson	B Zuiderent	CD Nash	CD Hopkinson	Extras	Total	Wickets	Result	Points
v. Surrey	27	36	11	2	93	24	35	28	10	0	1*									41	308	10		
(Oval) 19-22 April	0	34	114	114	10	8	2	14	34	21*	1									27	379	10	L	5
v. Somerset	37	162	8	19	5	25	5	3	36*	1	7									29	337	10		
(Hove) 24-27 April	27	29	101	6	73	86	37*	1	5*	-										31	396	7	D	10
v. Lancashire	14	5	217	17	41	44	24	8	9*		11									28	423	10		
(Old Trafford) 15-18 May	80	14	15	29	19	8	14	-	7*			24*								11	221	7	D	12
v. Leicestershire	122*	4		6	8	22	29	34	3	5			6	0						8	247	10		
(Horsham) 24-27 May	-	-		-	-	-	-	-	-	-			-	-						-	-	-	D	8
v. Kent	35	18		17	28	7	10	24*	1	0		13		0						27	180	10		
(Tunbridge Wells) 31 May-3 June	79	76		2	10	19	67	18	14	7*		28		9						25	354	10	L	3
v. Yorkshire	11	18		5	3	30	83	22	4			34		149	18*					58	435	10		
(Headingley) 13-15 June	-	-		-	-	-	-	-	-			-		-	-					-	-	-	W	20
v. Yorkshire	78	35	10		38	35	85	70*				0		19	1	6				15	392	10		
(Arundel) 26-29 June	10	2	23		8	32	70*	5				28		18	2	4*				14	216	10	D	11
v. Hampshire	10	3	27		34	80*	10	8		4		1		49*	7					13	246	10		
(Southampton) 3-6 July	20	5	20		39	1*	-	-						17*						9	111	4	D	8
v. Kent	14	12	18		33	1	0	1		20		17		4	11*					14	145	10		
(Hove) 10-13 July	2	135	10		14	8	53	1		15*		56		124	0					32	450	10	D	7
v. Somerset	25	42		120	36	205*	8	111	0	3		68		1						25	644	10		
(Taunton) 19-21 July	-	-		-	-	-	-	-	-	-				-						-	-	-	W	20
v. Warwickshire	51	16		137	34	47			8			30*		42	9	0	0			3	377	10		
(Edgbaston) 25-27 July	45	0		64	40	16			0			7		7	1	10	0*			2	192	10	L	7
v. Surrey	1	3	21	35	23	0	30	8				41*		25	5					11	203	10		
(Hove) 8-11 August	10	100	62	22	23*	20	-	-				12*		16	-					23	288	6	W	16
v. Lancashire	0	87	36	6	22	7	8	1	1*	0		0		60						12	240	10		
(Hove) 22-25 August	43	1	61	41	55	0	5*	6	0			7		39						19	277	10	L	4
v. Leicestershire	10	5	60	21	62	0	6*	0				0		34	2					15	215	10		
(Leicester) 27-29 August	2	14	0	3	8	4	7	12				49*		30	3					10	142	10	L	4
v. Hampshire	196	119	34	28	64	102*	-	-				17*		32	-					39	631	6		
(Hove) 5-8 September	-	-		-	-	-	-	-				-		-	-					-	-	-	D	12
v. Warwickshire	34	93		5	33	10	4			0		60*		26	10				33	44	352	10		
(Hove) 18-21 September	43	111		0	9	3	66			20*		40		30	0				9	10	341	10	L	7

	RR Montgomerie	MW Goodwin	CJ Adams	PA Cottey	MH Yardy	RSC Martin-Jenkins	MJ Prior	MJG Davis	RJ Kirtley	JD Lewry	PM Hutchison	KJ Innes	DA Clapp	TR Ambrose	BV Taylor	MA Robinson	B Zuiderent	CD Nash	CD Hopkinson
Matches	16	16	10	13	10	16	16	15	10	10	3	13	1	13	10	1	1	1	1
Innings	28	28	19	22	17	28	27	22	15	15	5	22	1	22	14	2	2	2	2
Not Out	1	0	0	0	0	4	3	4	3	5	2	7	0	1	2	1	0	1	0
Highest Score	196	162	217	137	93	205*	102*	111	36*	21*	20*	60*	6	149	18*	18*	6	0*	33
Runs	1026	1179	848	699	492	1008	741	474	146	91	29	478	6	798	70	10	10	0	42
Average	38.00	42.10	44.63	31.77	28.94	42.00	30.87	26.33	12.16	9.10	9.66	31.86	6.00	38.00	5.83	10.00	5.00	-	21.00
100s	2	5	3	3	1	1	1	-	-	-	-	2	-	-	-	-	-	-	-
50s	4	3	3	1	2	5	5	2	-	-	-	2	-	2	-	-	-	-	-
Catches/Stumpings	16	13	2	5	11	1	39/2	7	4	5	-	3	-	9	1	-	-	1	2

SUSSEX CCC

FIRST–CLASS MATCHES

BOWLING

	JD Lewry	RJ Kirtley	PM Hutchison	RSC Martin-Jenkins	MJG Davis	KJ Innes	BV Taylor	MA Robinson	Overs	Total	Byes/Leg-Byes	Wickets	Run outs	
v. Surrey (Oval) 19-22 April	19-4-89-2	32-8-122-3	28-0-146-3	24-4-112-0	12-2-44-0				126	575	15	8	-	AB
	4.2-1-20-0	8-0-43-0	7-0-43-0	-	2-0-9-0				21.2	116	1	0	-	
v. Somerset (Hove) 24-27 April	26-3-89-1	27.5-4-90-5	13-2-56-0	19-2-74-1	20-4-60-2				111.5	401	15	10	-	B
	8-2-27-0	4-1-10-1	-	7-0-19-1	-				32	94	0	2	-	ABC
v. Lancashire (Old Trafford) 15-18 May	27-5-88-5	27-3-117-2		21-0-58-0	30.5-7-71-3	5-0-15-0			110.5	366	17	10	-	
	-	-		-	-	-			-	-	-	-	-	
v. Leicestershire (Horsham) 24-27 May	10-0-51-0	19-4-62-0		16.4-4-51-7	18-2-56-2				70.4	264	8	10	-	B
	4-0-9-0	11-5-26-1		8-3-32-1	6-1-24-0				29	94	3	2	-	
v. Kent (Tunbridge Wells) 31 May-3 June	27-5-90-3	30.4-8-88-4		26-5-84-2	4-1-11-0	15-7-31-1			106.4	343	15	10	-	B
	6-0-36-2	16-5-39-3		13-4-35-0	17.5-4-66-1	3-0-16-0			55.5	195	3	6	-	
v. Yorkshire (Headingley) 12-15 June		27.5-9-49-5		25-13-47-2	2-0-8-0	12-4-35-2	19-8-37-1		92.5	216	11	10	1	B
		16.2-5-41-5		15-3-30-2	-	6-2-20-2	7-0-28-1		44.2	125	6	10	-	
v. Yorkshire (Arundel) 26-29 June				15.5-3-46-3	17-4-45-2	17-4-45-2	20-6-51-2	20-6-57-3	93.5	255	12	10	-	B
				25-4-77-1	31.1-4-111-2	12-0-57-0	28-8-82-3	20-2-81-2	126.1	458	8	8	-	BC
v. Hampshire (Southampton) 3-6 July	16-3-56-1			15-7-37-5	1.3-0-3-1	5-1-13-1	16-6-46-2		53.3	163	8	10	-	
	6-2-26-0			3-1-9-0	3-0-14-0	-	1-0-5-0		13	56	2	0	-	
v. Kent (Hove) 10-13 July	25-4-82-3			31-10-81-2	17-3-40-2	16-4-36-1	27.4-7-86-2		119.4	349	13	10	-	B
	11-2-44-2			5-1-12-2	5-2-3-0	-	6-1-20-1		29	85	5	5	-	D
v. Somerset (Taunton) 19-21 July	16.2-3-84-3			20-2-67-0	4-1-20-2	4-0-28-3	20-8-56-2		68.2	270	5	10	-	B
	22-1-112-4			14-3-43-0	19-0-88-2	13-4-44-0	20.2-3-68-4		88.2	373	18	10	-	
v. Warwickshire (Edgbaston) 24-27 July	38-4-151-4			5.1-0-32-0		28.5-2-106-3	35.3-4-110-2		127.3	493	4	10	-	E
	8-1-32-1			6-2-24-0		10-1-34-1	21-3-83-3		67	284	6	6	-	EF
v. Surrey (Hove) 8-11 August		15-7-49-3		16-6-34-1	2-0-18-0	14.4-5-41-4	11-1-44-1		58.4	193	7	10	-	
		17.2-4-59-3		15-2-53-0	26-2-97-6	13-3-48-1	6-0-29-0		77.2	296	10	10	-	
v. Lancashire (Hove) 22-25 August	24.5-4-118-2	34-6-94-2		26-2-67-3	19-1-66-1	20-6-53-2			123.5	425	27	10	-	
	6-1-23-0	5-3-10-2		8-0-25-1	2-0-17-0	4-1-10-0			25.2	93	4	3	-	F
v. Leicestershire (Leicester) 27-29 August		26-6-89-4		15-4-60-0	25-15-27-2	20-8-36-2	15-4-31-2		101	247	4	10	-	
		13.4-3-47-1		4-0-19-0	6-1-24-0	4-2-15-1	4-1-5-0		31.4	111	1	2	-	
v. Hampshire (Hove) 5-8 September		29.2-7-107-6		27-3-111-2	25-11-45-0	18-5-48-2	22-6-74-0		121.2	401	10	10	-	
		6-2-10-0		6-2-14-0	11-2-26-1	2-0-7-0	-		37	67	3	1	-	CFG
v. Warwickshire (Hove) 18-21 September			12-1-52-2	15.4-3-56-3	13-1-66-0	9-3-27-0	17-2-90-5		66.5	293	2	10	-	
			19-3-92-1	23-7-68-2	8-2-32-1	17-3-69-1	22.2-5-96-1		96.2	405	13	7	-	H

	JD Lewry	RJ Kirtley	PM Hutchison	RSC Martin-Jenkins	MJG Davis	KJ Innes	BV Taylor	MA Robinson
Overs	304.3	366	79	470.2	347.2	268.3	318.5	40
Maidens	45	90	6	100	71	65	73	14
Runs	1227	1152	389	1477	1081	834	1041	138
Wickets	33	50	6	41	28	29	32	5
Average	37.18	23.04	64.83	19.33	36.02	28.75	32.53	27.60

A   CJ Adams 4-0-19-0; 3-1-5-0
B   MH Yardy 7-0-28-0; 6-2-17-1; 8-2-33-0; 7-1-36-1; 4-1-24-0; 7-1-29-0; 4-1-9-0, 8-0-34-0; 3-11-11-0; 4-0-10-0
C   RR Montgomerie 2-2-0-0; 2-0-8-0; 2-0-2-0
D   MW Goodwin 2-1-1-0
E   CD Nash 20-0-90-1; 15-1-81-1
F   PA Cottey 7-0-24-0; 0.2-0-5-0; 9-5-4-0
G   TR Ambrose 1-0-1-0
H   CD Hopkinson 7-0-35-1

FIELDING

41   MJ Prior (39ct, 2st)
16   RR Montgomerie
13   MW Goodwin
11   MH Yardy
9   TR Ambrose
7   MJG Davis
5   PA Cottey, JD Lewry
4   RJ Kirtley
3   KJ Innes
2   CJ Adams, CD Hopkinson
1   RSC Martin-Jenkins, CD Nash, BV Taylor

WARWICKSHIRE CCC

FIRST–CLASS MATCHES

BATTING

	MJ Powell	NV Knight	IR Bell	DP Ostler	DR Brown	JO Troughton	SM Pollock	NMK Smith	KJ Piper	MM Betts	A Richardson	AF Giles	T Frost	NM Carter	IJ Clifford	GG Wagg	JAS Spires	MA Wagh	MA Sheikh	NA Warren	APW Allen	SE Bond	Extras	Total	Wickets	Result	Points
v. Lancashire (Edgbaston) 24-26 April	14	38	11	15	4	2	16	96	13	56	0*												32	297	10		
	6	49	22	2*	0	19	0	5	13	22	1												11	150	10	L	5
v. Leicestershire (Leicester) 8-11 May	0	11	5	33	12	59	24	1	7	5*	1												19	177	10		
	67	130	13	14	66	66	21	0	1	0*	17												44	439	10	L	1
v. Hampshire (Edgbaston) 15-18 May	19	255*	22		15	0	4		19	4	91	20	5										18	472	10		
																										D	10
v. Hampshire (Southampton) 31 May-3 June	92	14	2	1	5	63	16	0		7*	0		28										22	250	10		
	24	31	37	9	23	131*	37	18		2*			0										17	329	8	D	9
v. Leicestershire (Edgbaston) 12-15 June	0	47	72	81	35	130	11	0		21*			18	12									35	462	10		
	2	13	11	25	26*	37	65	7		10*													10	206	7	W	20
v. Somerset (Edgbaston) 26-29 June	28		46	11	10	42	9	13		23					1	42*	0						5	230	10		
	3		42	175	38	52	10	9		15					0	51	9*						19	423	10	W	16
v. Kent (Maidstone) 3-6 July	6		31	21		30*	5	8		22			1	4		18	2						24	172	10		
																										D	7
v. Surrey (Oval) 10-13 July	2		39	22	16	12	50	74	1	3	18		7*					17					33	293	10		
	95	8	13	5	94	24	6	25*	4				2					43					31	350	10	W	17
v. West Indies A (Edgbaston) 20-22 July	0			0	65	5										18*		0	10	2*			23	123	6		
	14			31	35	10					0					1	10	86	16	11	18*		19	251	10	L	
v. Sussex (Edgbaston) 24-27 July	57	245*	12	6	2	45	29		4		28		38					4					23	493	10		
	5	97	30	45	14*	16	19*											39					19	284	6	W	20
v. Yorkshire (Headingley) 7-10 August	0	79	0	35	15	0		6		7*								23	18			7	24	233	10		
	23	109	55*	2		0*												9					18	216	4	D	8
v. Kent (Edgbaston) 14-17 August	1	69	0	80	44	115						68	13*	7				10				8	51	565	10		
	8*	0*																					0	8	0	W	20
v. Somerset (Taunton) 21-24 August	26	98	31	23	24		39					17*	4	4				4				20	14	304	10		
	7	28	77	55	30		17					27*	4	9				11				29*	16	310	9	D	10
v. Surrey (Edgbaston) 27-30 August	36	74	34		6	61	2		47		3	35						3	19*				25	345	10		
	48	133	4		20	63	3		0*		25	13						39	7*				49	404	9	D	9
v. Lancashire (Old Trafford) 4-7 September	21		10	63	68*	43			0		2		70	18				4	10				19	328	10		
																										D	9
v. Yorkshire (Edgbaston) 12-15 September	58		15	225	28		64*		0				103	15		8*	2	33					50	601	9		
	92*		6	9	17								3*					90					15	232	4	W	20
v. Sussex (Hove) 18-21 September	15		5	0	0				0				73	10			37*	8	32				20	293	10		
	103		18	90	79*				15				28	30*				6	43				23	405	7	W	17
Matches	17	10	16	14	16	14	10	8	8	9	10	4	7	9	4	5	6	10	5	1	1	3					
Innings	31	19	28	25	28	24	18	15	12	16	12	6	11	12	6	8	7	18	8	2	1	4					
Not Out	2	3	1	1	4	3	1	0	2	5	4	0	1	5	0	2	3	0	2	1	1	1					
Highest Score	103	255*	77	225	79*	131*	66	96	64*	56	91	68	103	103	7	51	37*	109	43	11	18*	29*					
Runs	872	1520	658	1039	671	1067	425	337	163	259	132	134	308	305	20	161	70	503	178	13	18	64					
Average	30.06	95.00	24.37	43.29	27.95	50.80	25.00	22.46	16.30	23.54	16.50	22.33	30.80	43.57	3.33	26.83	17.50	27.94	29.66	13.00	-	21.33					
100s	1	5	-	2	-	3	-	-	-	-	-	-	1	1	-	-	-	1	-	-	-	-					
50s	6	5	3	5	3	6	4	2	1	1	1	1	1	-	-	1	-	2	-	-	-	-					
Catches/Stumpings	13	10	6	24	9	8	13	7	14/1	2	5	1	6/2	4	15/1	1	3	3	1	-	-	1					

WARWICKSHIRE CCC

FIRST–CLASS MATCHES

BOWLING

	SM Pollock	MM Betts	DR Brown	A Richardsson	AF Giles	NMK Smith	NM Carter	JAS Spires	GG Wagg	MA Wagh	MA Sheikh	SE Bond	Overs	Total	Byes/Leg-Byes	Wickets	Run outs	
v. Lancashire (Edgbaston) 24-26 April	16-6-38-0	17-4-67-1	24.2-4-78-4	21-4-59-5									78.2	251	9	10	-	
	13.4-3-56-1	7-1-28-0	8-1-42-0	11-1-62-3									39.4	197	9	4	-	
v. Leicestershire (Leicester) 8-11 May	24-8-37-1	28-6-87-1	28-6-101-1	31-9-84-1	38.5-7-126-5	2-0-16-0							162.5	523	28	10	-	A
	4-0-27-0	3-0-20-0	-	4-0-29-1	3.3-0-16-0	-							14.3	94	2	3	2	
v. Hampshire (Edgbaston) 15-18 May	18.5-7-31-1	22-5-75-3	12-2-31-1	18-3-61-2	35-9-96-3								105.5	302	8	10	-	
	20-6-47-0	15-2-59-1	15-3-38-1	21-6-41-2	33-4-90-1								108	306	16	5	-	B
v. Hampshire (Southampton) 31 May-3 June	17-3-37-4	24-3-84-2	23-7-44-3	16-2-63-0		5-0-12-0							104	277	15	10	-	A
	11-5-25-0	13.4-3-48-2	12-2-33-3	13-2-36-2		-							49.4	142	0	7	-	
v. Leicestershire (Edgbaston) 12-15 June	22.2-7-36-3	25-3-115-3	19-2-78-1			27-7-56-1	17-3-60-2						115.2	370	5	10	-	C
	16-10-23-3	14-2-58-1	-			23.1-11-42-5	7-2-30-1						60.1	154	1	10	-	
v. Somerset (Edgbaston) 26-29 June	15-7-33-2	13-3-46-2	13-3-57-2			5-0-27-0		1-1-0-0	10-2-43-4				57	208	2	10	-	
	25-5-97-3	13-0-54-1	20-1-58-2			14.4-1-64-2		12-2-50-2	4-0-28-0				88.4	357	6	10	-	
v. Kent (Maidstone) 3-6 July	16.4-7-18-1	13-0-54-1				13-2-62-2	8-0-47-0	28-8-68-3	14-2-38-3				94.4	306	4	10	-	B
	8-1-23-1	-				4-0-10-0	10-3-24-3	9-2-32-1	-				37	118	7	5	-	BCD
v. Surrey (Oval) 10-13 July	22-11-37-1	17-0-106-1	33.5-7-110-7			12-1-49-0	21-1-114-1		4-1-9-0				115.5	475	20	10	-	AC
	12-2-44-4	-	8-1-26-2			0.1-0-1-0	9-1-37-2		-				32.1	137	5	10	1	C
v. West Indies A (Edgbaston) 20-22 July			10-1-61-0	17-7-32-1				9-0-41-1	13-2-66-0	8-1-37-0	8-2-20-1		79	358	26	3	-	BCE
			6-0-29-0	4-1-14-0				2-0-16-1	3-0-18-0	1-0-1-0	-		28	135	4	3	-	BE
v. Sussex (Edgbaston) 24-27 July	19-6-60-2		20.2-3-72-3	21-6-72-0			20-3-77-3			28-4-86-2			110.2	377	3	10	-	C
			10-0-45-0	23.5-10-46-8			9-5-14-0			24-3-85-2			66.5	192	2	10	-	
v. Yorkshire (Headingley) 7-10 August			19-4-61-3	23.3-2-73-3						14-6-26-0	18.3-0-80-1	23.4-8-60-2	98.4	313	13	10	-	
			-	-						-	-	-						
v. Kent (Edgbaston) 14-17 August			22-2-60-1		30.5-6-74-5		9-1-26-0		5-1-11-0			19-4-70-4	85.5	252	11	10	-	
			12-2-54-2		40.3-3-142-		19-7-51-0		6-4-3-1			14-1-59-0	91.3	317	8	10	-	
v. Somerset (Taunton) 21-24 August			29-5-84-2		20-5-73-1		14-2-65-0	17.2-5-62-4				13-3-77-1	106.2	408	5	10	-	B
			20-1-84-0		-		11-0-46-4	16.3-1-72-1	5-3-13-0			26-7-64-5	96.3	394	42	10	-	B
v. Surrey (Edgbaston) 27-30 August	21-7-64-1	24-2-122-1	28.1-1-124-4		34-4-134-4				3-1-16-0	26-7-79-0			136.1	544	5	10	-	
v. Lancashire (Old Trafford) 5-7 September			35-6-117-2	28-4-102-3			34-6-165-2	20.5-2-91-1	5-1-16-0	15-5-27-1			152.5	598	32	10	-	B
			-	-														
v. Yorkshire (Edgbaston) 12-15 September			3-1-18-0	1-0-11-0			7-0-41-1	35.1-5-99-4	36-7-137-5	3-0-13-0			86.1	351	23	10	-	F
			19-3-53-0	8-1-29-3			12-0-55-0	44.4-4-165-5	28-1-97-2	17-3-44-0			128.4	481	38	10	-	
v. Sussex (Hove) 18-21 September			29-4-103-5	23-4-76-4			13.1-1-59-1	3-1-12-0	26-6-56-2	27-5-82-0			95.1	352	20	10	-	
			15-3-55-3	16-2-61-0			8-0-46-0	7-0-39-0	-	31-8-78-4			103	341	6	10	1	

	SM Pollock	MM Betts	DR Brown	A Richardsson	AF Giles	NMK Smith	NM Carter	JAS Spires	GG Wagg	MA Wagh	MA Sheikh	SE Bond
Overs	301.3	248.4	493.4	300.2	215.4	126	228.1	171.4	82.5	203	130.3	95.4
Maidens	101	34	75	64	33	27	35	25	13	43	25	23
Runs	733	1023	1716	951	678	411	957	613	343	604	396	330
Wickets	28	20	52	38	25	12	20	18	12	15	6	12
Average	26.17	51.15	33.00	25.02	27.12	34.25	47.85	34.05	28.58	40.26	66.00	27.50

A   IR Bell 11-2-44-1; 19-6-22-1; 4-0-23-0
B   MJ Powell 4-1-15-0; 2-0-15-0; 1-1-0-0; 3-0-12-0; 1-0-5-0; 8-1-29-2; 23-1-86-0; 15-3-48-1
C   JO Troughton 5-0-20-0; 4-0-9-0; 2-0-7-0; 3-0-25-0; 2-0-21-0; 2-0-7-0
D   DP Ostler 1-0-13-0
E   NA Warren 9-0-42-0; 11-3-48-2
F   T Frost 1-0-9-0

FIELDING

24	DP Ostler
16	IJ Clifford (15ct, 1st)
15	KJ Piper (14ct, 1st)
13	SM Pollock, MJ Powell
10	NV Knight
9	DR Brown
8	T Frost (6ct,2st), JO Troughton
7	NMK Smith
6	IR Bell
5	A Richardsson
4	NM Carter
3	JAS Spires, MA Wagh
2	MM Betts
1	SE Bond, AF Giles, MA Sheikh, GG Wagg

WORCESTERSHIRE CCC

FIRST–CLASS MATCHES

BATTING

	RMS Weston	A Singh	GA Hick	BF Smith	VS Solanki	DA Leatherdale	GJ Batty	SJ Rhodes	Kabir Ali	CG Liptrot	A Sheriyar	SD Peters	AJ Bichel	MJ Rawnsley	AA Donald	MS Mason	DJ Pipe	S Lee	Extras	Total	Wickets	Result	Points
v. Oxford University CCE (Oxford) 13-15 April	0	40	164	137	85	11	18*	4*	-	-	-								64	523	6		
	4	7	-	-	22rh	0	48	5	25*	10	17*								21	159	6	W	
v. Gloucestershire (Worcester) 19-22 April	6	35	2	129		55	11	38*	5		0	34	0						18	333	10		
	15	13	92	4	49*		31	13		2	26	27							23	295	10	W	18
v. Northamptonshire (Northampton) 24-27 April		8	8	24	154	33	34*	51*			-	146	25	4					37	524	8		
		-	-	-	-	-	-	-			-	-	-	-					-	-	-	D	11
v. Glamorgan (Worcester) 8-11 May		81	8	3	25	29	17	20*	10		1	71	8						25	298	10		
		26	4	61	4	24	10	7	19		4*	40	8						19	226	10	L	5
v. Essex (Worcester) 15-18 May		60	30	61	0	0	32	30	40		0*	24	65						25	367	10		
		23	10	14	15	1	4	22	24	4	abs inj	2*							21	140	9	L	6
v. Gloucestershire (Bristol) 31 May-3 June	82	16	79	25	41	2	16	7	9*		2		0						8	287	10		
	54	187	72	4*	-		-				-								7	324	3	W	17
v. Durham (Chester-le-Street) 12-15 June	13	29	6	22	12	63	56	10	0		15			5*					19	250	10		
	1*	16	0	14	17	9	0*	-	-		-			-					3	60	5	D	9
v. Durham (Worcester) 26-28 June	4	88	315*	83	11	5	0	27	-		-		78*						32	643	7		
	-	-	-	-	-	-	-	-	-		-		-						-	-	-	W	20
v. Middlesex (Lord's) 3-6 July	52	7	88	124	153*	59*	-	-	-		-		-						19	502	4		
	0	12	-	6	16	5	10*	42*	-		-		-						8	99	5	D	11
v. Essex (Chelmsford) 10-13 July	39	124	9	20	56		0	56	3		2	30	9*						25	373	10		
	20*	0	34	23*	-		-	-	-		-	-	-						5	82	2	W	10
v. Northamptonshire (Worcester) 19-21 July	7	51	8	108	116	5	3	6	-		5*	31				18			25	383	10		
	18	5	36*	18*	-	-	-	-	-		-	-				-			5	82	2	W	19
v. Indians (Worcester) 31 July-3 August		46	27	5	5	30*		0*	-		50		-				12		25	200	6		
		-	-	-	-	-		-	-		-		-				-		-	-	-	D	
v. Nottinghamshire (Kidderminster) 8-11 August		57	13	32	0		2	34	0		4	5	1*					32	21	201	10		
		13	126	65	5		66*	24*			-	10	0						27	336	5	D	11
v. Derbyshire (Derby) 14-16 August		41	0	49	22		2	83	8		5*		7			11		48	44	320	10		
		14	4*	-	81*		-	-	-		-		-			-			16	115	1	W	18
v. Middlesex (Worcester) 27-30 August		50	101	50	24	39	3	2	0	6	0*	13							31	319	10		
		40	69	60	4	42	33	47	35	16	2*	14							39	401	10	L	6
v. Glamorgan (Cardiff) 5-8 September		20	58	10	94	8	4		3		6*	130				12	26		10	381	10		
		-	-	-	-	-	-		-		-	-				-	-		-	-	-	D	11
v. Nottinghamshire (Trent Bridge) 11-14 September		44	25	14	9	120	3	124	9		4	8			8*				29	397	10		
		4	39	8	8	30*	0	15	4		16	1			0				9	134	10	L	7
v. Derbyshire (Worcester) 18-21 September		5	16	2	81	13	21	4			0*	72				7	14		30	265	10		
		5	10*	27	12	89*	74	9			18	23				50	12		44	373	10	W	17

	RMS Weston	A Singh	GA Hick	BF Smith	VS Solanki	DA Leatherdale	GJ Batty	SJ Rhodes	Kabir Ali	CG Liptrot	A Sheriyar	SD Peters	AJ Bichel	MJ Rawnsley	AA Donald	MS Mason	DJ Pipe	S Lee
Matches	8	18	18	18	16	14	18	15	17	2	18	10	9	4	1	7	3	2
Innings	15	32	30	30	26	23	27	22	21	3	20	16	11	3	1	8	4	2
Not Out	2	0	4	3	4	4	4	4	4	0	9	0	2	1	1	2	0	0
Highest Score	82	187	315*	137	153*	154	74	124	51*	16	18	146	78*	9*	5*	50	26	48
Runs	315	1167	1453	1202	944	823	491	636	271	32	107	667	274	20	5	107	64	80
Average	24.23	36.46	55.88	44.51	42.90	43.31	21.34	39.75	15.94	10.66	9.72	41.68	30.44	10.00	-	17.83	16.00	40.00
100s	-	2	4	4	2	2	-	1	-	-	-	2	-	-	-	-	-	-
50s	3	6	6	6	5	4	3	2	1	-	-	3	2	-	-	1	-	-
Catches/Stumpings	7	11	30	6	18	4	9	37/4	3	-	1	6	7	2	-	1	-	12/1

WORCESTERSHIRE CCC

FIRST–CLASS MATCHES

BOWLING

	A Sheriyar	Kabir Ali	DA Leatherdale	GJ Batty	AJ Bichel	MS Mason	Overs	Total	Byes/Leg-Byes	Wickets	Run outs
v. Oxford University CCE (Oxford) 13-15 April	21-8-46-5	17-5-45-3	6-2-16-0	5.2-1-7-2			57.2	145	13	10	- A
	15-5-35-0	13.2-4-43-7	5-2-17-0	18-7-44-1			68.2	205	7	10	- AB
v. Gloucestershire (Worcester) 19-22 April	15-2-56-0	21-6-60-0	3-0-18-0	11-3-27-1	23.1-4-93-9		73.1	268	14	10	-
	11-3-42-2	11-2-32-2		7.4-1-33-3	16-4-38-1		45.4	154	9	9	1
v. Northamptonshire (Northampton) 24-27 April	29-8-84-0	23-2-102-2	16-2-53-1	38-7-131-2	29-8-81-0		128.1	524	19	8	- BCD
	-	-	-	-	-		-	-	-	-	-
v. Glamorgan (Worcester) 8-11 May	19-3-66-0	23.4-5-80-5	6-0-33-0	19-3-55-1	24-10-39-4		91.4	286	13	10	-
	30-6-86-5	23-6-67-2		21-5-74-2	32-9-93-1		108	348	13	10	- B
v. Essex (Worcester) 15-18 May	42-15-111-5	32-9-75-0	8-1-37-1	41.5-13-109-3	12-6-22-0		135.5	373	19	10	1
	11.4-3-46-3	16-5-52-2	3-0-10-0	4-0-18-0			34.4	135	9	5	-
v. Gloucestershire (Bristol) 31 May – 3 June	18.5-7-44-2	16-6-32-5	1-0-1-0	-	20-4-50-3		55.5	130	3	10	-
	18-4-65-1	13.5-4-34-5	8-2-40-2	13-4-21-0	4-0-13-0		56.5	177	4	9	1
v. Durham (Chester-le-Street) 12-15 June	19-6-46-1	21-6-55-0	3-0-16-0	15.3-4-42-3			82.3	243	7	9	- E
	-	-	-	-			-	-	-	-	-
v. Durham (Worcester) 26-28 June	12-6-23-1	10-2-31-4	-	5-3-7-1	12.5-2-58-4		39.5	120	1	10	-
	14-6-26-2	18-2-77-4	3-1-16-0	5.3-2-11-1	21-4-84-3		62.3	215	1	10	- F
v. Middlesex (Lord's) 3-6 July	24-1-127-0	29-10-82-2		30.2-11-84-3	32-11-102-3		117.2	417	14	8	- F
	-	-		-	-		-	-	-	-	-
v. Essex (Chelmsford) 10-13 July	14-7-28-1	15-4-28-1		34.2-9-71-6	18-6-48-2		87.2	197	7	10	- C
	14-3-30-2	11.1-2-32-3		43-12-71-3	15-4-46-1		116.1	257	12	10	- CF
v. Northamptonshire (Worcester) 19-21 July	28-9-69-3		9-1-48-1	18-3-61-0	29-3-119-3	21-4-59-3	109	387	13	10	- D
	10-4-15-1		7.3-2-23-4	-	9-2-16-2	9-4-15-3	35.3	77	8	10	-
v. Indians (Worcester) 31 July-3 August	25-3-109-4	19-4-99-1		18-2-68-2		20-8-32-0	105	417	22	8	- CD
	-	-		-		-	-	-	-	-	-
v. Nottinghamshire (Kidderminster) 8-11 August	17-6-59-5	7-1-29-0		1.4-0-4-0	16.4-3-50-5		42.4	161	11	10	- G
	11-3-42-2	16-4-64-0		32-9-97-3	16-1-42-0		86	292	18	5	- F
v. Derbyshire (Derby) 14-16 August	15-2-71-6	9.5-2-20-2		6-1-30-0	12-3-37-2		46.5	190	5	10	- CF
	12.3-4-36-2	23-6-80-2		34-14-74-5	-		84.3	243	17	10	- CF
v. Middlesex (Worcester) 27-30 August	31.3-8-119-1	33-9-100-5	24-4-61-2	34-10-126-1			145.3	531	15	10	- AF
	13-0-54-1	17.4-2-54-1	9-1-31-1	-			45.4	193	18	4	- A
v. Glamorgan (Cardiff) 5-8 September	30.5-9-81-4	24-6-70-3	11-2-33-0	32-7-104-2	28-6-119-0		130.5	447	21	10	1 B
	8-0-34-1	5-0-15-1	1-0-5-0	17-3-39-0	8-0-17-0		56	181	7	2	- BF
v. Nottinghamshire (Trent Bridge) 11-14 September	28-7-79-1	28.4-7-117-4	-	28-8-94-3	32-6-94-2		118.4	404	13	10	- F
	20-4-70-3	15-1-65-0	2-1-8-0	22-6-53-2	17.3-5-37-4		76.3	241	8	10	1
v. Derbyshire (Worcester) 18-21 September	14-3-43-0	19-3-72-4	4-0-19-0	30-10-60-5	21-7-49-1		88	246	3	10	-
	25-5-63-2	16-4-69-1	11-1-50-4	28-4-118-1	23.3-8-62-2		107.3	391	13	10	- F

	A Sheriyar	Kabir Ali	DA Leatherdale	GJ Batty	AJ Bichel	MS Mason
Overs	616.2	547.1	140.3	613.1	297	224.4
Maidens	160	129	22	162	77	55
Runs	1905	1781	535	1733	902	613
Wickets	66	71	16	56	36	22
Average	**28.86**	**25.08**	**33.43**	**30.94**	**25.05**	**27.86**

A   CG Liptrot 8-4-18-0; 14-1-51-2; 21-0-105-1; 6-0-36-1
B   GA Hick 3-2-8-0; 7-2-16-0; 2-0-15-0; 5-0-19-0; 7-3-21-0
C   MJ Rawnsley 29-10-108-0; 6-1-15-0; 31-12-61-1; 13-1-42-0; 3-0-22-0; 11-4-26-1
D   BF Smith 3-0-14-0; 4-0-18-0; 10-2-45-1
E   AA Donald 24-3-77-5
F   VS Solanki 1-1-0-0; 2-0-8-0; 2-0-5-0; 11-1-29-0; 1-0-5-0; 4-0-10-0; 2-1-5-0; 10-2-43-0; 2-0-7-0; 4-1-16-0
G   S Lee 0.2-0-8-0

FIELDING

41   SJ Rhodes (37ct, 4st)
30   GA Hick
18   VS Solanki
13   DJ Pipe (12ct, 1st)
11   A Singh
9   GJ Batty
7   AJ Bichel, WPC Weston
6   SD Peters, BF Smith
4   DA Leatherdale
3   Kabir Ali
2   MJ Rawnsley
1   MS Mason, A Sheriyar

YORKSHIRE CCC

FIRST–CLASS MATCHES
BATTING

Match	MJ Wood	SA Richardson	MJ Lumb	DS Lehmann	CR Taylor	GM Fellows	GM Hamilton	RJ Blakey	CEW Silverwood	RJ Sidebottom	SP Kirby	C White	MP Vaughan	A McGrath	RKJ Dawson	MJ Hoggard	VJ Craven	SM Katich	ADK Gray	CJ Elstub	D Gough	DH Wigley	MTG Elliott	ND Thornicroft	Extras	Total	Wickets	Result	Points
v. Surrey (Headingley) 24-26 April	0	16	30	16	8	15	0	16	3	15*	7														14	140	10		
	0	0	15	1	52*	24	7	31	38	14	2														18	202	10	L	3
v. Somerset (Taunton) 8-10 May			66	12	13			7	44*	3	16	3	13	23	5										8	213	10		
			62	43	9			4	4	6	69	19	48*	3	2										11	280	10	L	4
v. Kent (Canterbury) 15-18 May	12		17	31	42		13	0	1*	1	104		0	4											14	239	10		
	7		0	72	0		90	10	6*	1	9		24	87											40	346	10	L	4
v. Hampshire (Headingley) 24-27 May	0	25	21				83	18		57	67	54	10	15	21*										52	423	10		
	-	-	-				-	-		-	-	-	-	-	-										-	-	-	D	12
v. Leicestershire (Leicester) 31 May-3 June	23	21	51				48*	33	0	0	62		25	8	13										26	310	10		
	1	46	119*				10	6	12	0	18		18	0	0										19	239	10	L	6
v. Sussex (Headingley) 12-15 June	20	0				11	52	6	0	2*	12		71			6	21								15	216	10		
	18	1				5	28	11	0*	9	7		18			2	16								10	125	10	L	4
v. Sussex (Arundel) 26-29 June	15	0	17				14		0		7		7	33		37		40	0*						31	255	10		
	9	92	216				28*		0		0		33	7		1		40	18*						14	458	8	D	9
v. Somerset (Scarborough) 10-13 July	18	57	64				26		0*		19		16	42		51		1							21	323	10		
	30	15	75				20*				40		5			12*									16	213	5	D	9
v. Lancashire (Headingley) 19-22 July	5	43	187				4*				11		165	-		36*			-						64	515	5		
	0	24	14				18*				1		1	7		14			-						15	124	7	D	11
v. Surrey (Guildford) 24-27 July	0	16	7		16		23	2	6*				26	15		21					15				25	172	10		
	43	124	61		33		50	6	1				13	20		56					4*				35	446	10	L	3
v. Warwickshire (Headingley) 7-10 August		2	75	50	24		20	38					34	14		4		13	4*						35	313	10		
		-	-		-		-	-					-	-		-		-	-						-	-	-	D	10
v. Lancashire (Old Trafford) 14-17 August		15	0	0			77	14	16				17	14		36						83	4*		18	294	10		
		14	0	109			13	9	10				86	27*		6						8	0		23	305	10	W	17
v. Hampshire (Southampton) 27-29 August		18	16	35			34*	3	5	2			31	19		6						92			19	280	10		
		13*	7				-	-	-	-			4	-		72						52*			4	152	3	W	17
v. Leicestershire (Scarborough) 4-7 September		17	6	9			0		4*	22	161			3		2		25				2			25	276	10		
		24	11	17			63*		10	-	36			2		40		74*				31			39	347	8	D	9
v. Warwickshire (Edgbaston) 12-15 September		1		11			70	12	0		53		46			5						74	0*		29	351	10		
		11		88			103	2	3*	2			66	9		19						127	1		50	481	10	L	6
v. Kent (Headingley) 18-20 September	0	8			34		2	28	4		62		17	47								8	0*		8	218	10		
	29	0			14		94	10	5*		48		9	47								10	4		13	283	10	L	2.25

	MJ Wood	SA Richardson	MJ Lumb	DS Lehmann	CR Taylor	GM Fellows	GM Hamilton	RJ Blakey	CEW Silverwood	RJ Sidebottom	SP Kirby	C White	MP Vaughan	A McGrath	RKJ Dawson	MJ Hoggard	VJ Craven	SM Katich	ADK Gray	CJ Elstub	D Gough	DH Wigley	MTG Elliott	ND Thornicroft
Matches	9	2	16	10	5	10	2	16	12	13	10	11	2	14	14	2	11	1	4	2	1	1	5	3
Innings	17	4	30	18	9	18	4	29	19	21	17	21	3	26	23	3	21	2	6	3	-	2	10	6
Not Out	0	0	1	1	0	1	0	7	2	7	3	0	0	1	1	2	0	1	3	1		1	1	3
Highest Score	43	29	124	216	52*	109	-	103	44*	28	57	161	54	165	87	21*	72	21	74*	18*	-	15	127	4*
Runs	201	45	777	1136	150	493	23	1041	283	135	141	794	76	803	496	28	439	37	193	22	-	19	487	9
Average	11.82	11.25	26.79	36.82	18.75	27.38	5.75	37.31	16.64	9.64	10.07	37.80	25.33	32.12	22.54	4.00	23.10	8.50	38.60	-	-	9.00	54.11	3.00
100s	-	-	1	3	-	1	-	1	-	-	-	2	-	1	-	-	-	-	-	-	-	-	1	-
50s	-	-	4	7	2	1	-	8	-	-	1	5	1	3	2	-	3	-	1	-	-	-	4	-
Ct/St	12	2	8	5	4	9	-	29/1	3	4	-	5	-	7	1	-	8	1	-	1	-	-	7	-

YORKSHIRE CCC

FIRST–CLASS MATCHES

BOWLING

	CEW Silverwood	SP Kirby	RJ Sidebottom	GM Fellows	DS Lehmann	MJ Hoggard	C White	RKJ Dawson	A McGrath	AKD Gray	Overs	Total	Byes/Leg-Byes	Wickets	Run outs
v. Surrey (Headingley) 24-26 April	23-2-124-1	27-2-129-5	28-6-71-0	27.5-5-90-3	11-1-35-0						127.5	510	13	10	– A
	-	-	-	-	-						-	-	-	-	-
v. Somerset (Taunton) 8-10 May	10.1-4-28-4		14-4-37-2	5-0-25-1	-	24-5-104-3	6-2-25-0	2-1-10-0			61.1	232	3	10	-
	12-0-42-1		7-1-17-0	6-2-23-0	2-0-6-0	14-3-51-1	4-1-25-0	16-4-64-1			64.2	263	14	3	– B
v. Kent (Canterbury) 15-18 May	21-4-82-4	17-3-87-1	20.3-2-82-3	7-1-24-0	14-3-35-0		14-1-39-0	12-0-53-2	-		105.3	418	16	10	-
	16-4-38-2	8-2-28-1	-	3-0-13-0	18-5-40-3		3-0-9-0	10-1-27-0	0.2-0-8-0		58.2	169	6	6	-
v. Hampshire (Headingley) 24-27 May	20-9-50-2	23.3-4-93-3				2-2-0-0	11-2-30-0	17-3-52-1	9-3-20-0		109.3	354	16	10	-
	-	4-2-18-1				-	6-1-20-0	-	5-3-3-0		18	62	5	1	– C
v. Leicestershire (Leicester) 31 May-3 June	18-3-52-0	21-3-86-3	19-5-60-2		2-0-16-0		9.4-0-53-2	14-3-37-0	12-1-33-3		95.4	346	9	10	-
	14-4-30-2	11-3-35-2	10-3-47-0		8-3-16-0		8-2-26-0	7-1-19-1	4-1-23-0		62	207	11	5	-
v. Sussex (Headingley) 12-15 June	26-2-87-2	35-9-113-3	29-8-78-3				20.1-4-44-2		16-2-55-0		129.1	435	16	10	– AD
	-	-	-				-		-		-	-	-	-	-
v. Sussex (Arundel) 26-29 June			19-2-87-2		10-1-26-1		17.2-5-49-4	24-3-86-2		25-5-65-1	111.2	392	13	10	– E
			11-1-33-1		11-3-24-1		5-0-16-0	24-7-55-2		20-2-62-3	79	216	10	9	1 E
v. Somerset (Scarborough) 10-13 July	26-5-75-1		30-8-59-3		21-4-53-1		23-6-55-0	40.1-7-154-4	7-0-14-0	18-3-70-0	165.1	498	18	9	-
	-		-		-		-	-	-	-	-	-	-	-	-
v. Lancashire (Headingley) 19-22 July	20-5-67-1		27-6-81-3		12-6-18-0		24-3-85-2	39-10-118-0	4.3-1-8-2		145.3	478	16	10	– F
	-		-		-		-	-	-		-	-	-	-	-
v. Surrey (Guildford) 24-27 July	21-5-71-3		22-7-57-3	-	9.3-1-43-1			12-0-68-0	15-3-55-1		94.4	382	12	10	– G
	17-7-45-1		13-2-39-1	5-1-21-2	9-3-27-0			16-3-57-1	3-1-2-0		68.3	237	6	4	– G
v. Warwickshire (Headingley) 7-10 August	17-3-49-3			4-0-17-0	3.5-0-7-2			22-5-65-2	9-3-24-2	11-3-16-1	73.5	301	15	9	– IJ
	8-2-21-0			5-0-23-2	-			23-6-50-2	13-4-28-0	11-3-27-0	72	216	8	4	– EH
v. Lancashire (Old Trafford) 14-17 August	19-2-66-2	15-2-52-2						32.4-9-97-2	6-1-13-1		87.4	301	15	9	– IJ
	13-5-44-1	12-4-27-2						14.3-5-42-5	6-1-18-1		49.3	148	3	9	– I
v. Hampshire (Southampton) 27-29 August	5-2-14-0	19.2-3-80-2	20-4-48-3	1-0-13-0				22-6-52-1	16-3-49-4		83.2	269	13	10	-
	-	18-6-45-2	10-2-39-1	-				22-4-49-5	5.4-1-7-2		55.4	161	21	10	-
v. Leicestershire (Scarborough) 4-7 September		23.2-4-71-3	21-8-60-5	1-0-9-0				20-3-67-1		6-0-34-0	79.2	279	13	10	– H
		21-6-56-3	17-6-48-1	3-0-29-0				13-4-43-1		6-1-23-0	63	231	15	5	– H
v. Warwickshire (Edgbaston) 12-15 September		30-2-161-1	26-3-129-2	6-0-28-0				42-10-121-2	17-6-33-1		145	601	12	9	1 HIJ
		9-4-35-0	4-0-23-0	-				17-0-85-3	4-0-14-0		48	232	11	4	– J
v. Kent (Headingley) 18-20 September		29-9-109-3	25.2-7-61-4					18-5-62-1	24-6-85-1		116.2	399	16	10	1 I
		8-0-37-0	8-0-34-2					-	3-1-9-0		21.1	103	10	2	– I

	CEW Silverwood	SP Kirby	RJ Sidebottom	GM Fellows	DS Lehmann	MJ Hoggard	C White	RKJ Dawson	A McGrath	AKD Gray
Overs	306.1	331.1	380.5	73.5	133.2	71	145.1	484.2	174.3	97
Maidens	68	68	85	9	32	14	26	103	38	17
Runs	985	1262	1190	315	346	268	456	1536	498	297
Wickets	30	37	41	8	9	8	10	39	18	5
Average	32.83	34.10	29.02	39.07	38.44	33.50	45.60	39.38	27.66	59.40

A GM Hamilton 11-2-48-1; 1-0-17-0
B MP Vaughan 3.2-0-21-0
C MJ Lumb 3-0-16-0
D SM Katich 2-0-25-0
E CJ Elstub 16-3-66-0; 8-3-16-1; 7-0-47-0; 10-1-52-0
F D Gough 19-3-85-2
G DH Wigley 10.4-0-71-1; 10-2-45-0
H VJ Craven 2-0-7-0; 8-3-25-1; 3-0-17-0; 2-0-7-0
I ND Thornicroft 14-4-51-2; 4-0-14-0; 21-5-104-2; 20-4-66-0; 2.1-1-13-0
J MTG Elliott 1-0-7-0; 1-0-6-0; 14-1-64-1

FIELDING

30 RJ Blakey (29ct, 1st)
12 MJ Wood
9 GM Fellows
8 VJ Craven, MJ Lumb
7 MTG Elliott, A McGrath
5 DS Lehmann, C White
4 RJ Sidebottom, CR Taylor
3 CEW Silverwood
2 SA Richardson
1 RKJ Dawson, CJ Elstub, SM Katich